Lecture Notes in Computer Scie
Edited by G. Goos, J. Hartmanis, and J. van

Springer
Berlin
Heidelberg
New York
Hong Kong
London
Milan
Paris
Tokyo

Vijay A. Saraswat (Ed.)

Advances in Computing Science – ASIAN 2003

Progamming Languages and Distributed Computation

8th Asian Computing Science Conference
Mumbai, India, December 10-12, 2003
Proceedings

Springer

Volume Editor

Vijay A. Saraswat
The Pennsylvania State University and
IBM TJ Watson Research Center
P.O. Box 704, Yorktown Heights, NY 10598, USA
E-mail: saraswat@cse.psu.edu

Cataloging-in-Publication Data applied for

A catalog record for this book is available from the Library of Congress.

Bibliographic information published by Die Deutsche Bibliothek
Die Deutsche Bibliothek lists this publication in the Deutsche Nationalbibliografie; detailed bibliographic data is available in the Internet at <http://dnb.ddb.de>.

CR Subject Classification (1998): D.2, D.3, D.4, F.3, F.4, C.2

ISSN 0302-9743
ISBN 3-540-20632-9 Springer-Verlag Berlin Heidelberg New York

Springer-Verlag is a part of Springer Science+Business Media

springeronline.com

Printed in Germany

Typesetting: Camera-ready by author, data conversion by Olgun Computergrafik
Printed on acid-free paper SPIN: 10973981 06/3142 5 4 3 2 1 0

Preface

This volume contains 18 papers that were presented at the Eighth Asian Computing Science Conference (ASIAN 2003) in Mumbai in December 2003. The theme of the conference this year was programming languages and distributed computation. Papers were invited on all aspects of theory, practice and applications related to this theme.

The Program Committee invited Greg Morrisett to give the keynote talk (in a joint session with the International Conference on Logic Programming). Andrew Birrell and Mark S. Miller were also invited to give talks. The Program Committee selected 16 papers out of the 53 submitted. Together, these papers were authored by 48 people from 11 countries.

I thank the Program Committee for doing an outstanding job under severe time pressure, and the Executive Committee for inviting me to chair the Program Committee.

I also thank the sponsoring institutions for this conference:

Asian Institute of Technology
Institut National de Recherche en Informatique et en Automatique
United Nations University/International Institute for Software Technology
National University of Singapore
Waseda University
Tata Institute of Fundamental Research
The Pennsylvania State University
IBM TJ Watson Research Lab

Mountain Lakes, NJ
September 2003

Vijay Saraswat

Organization

ASIAN 2003 was organized under the auspicies of the Executive Committee.

Executive Committee

Shigeki Goto, Waseda University, Japan
Stephane Grumbach, INRIA, France
Joxan Jaffar, National University of Singapore, Singapore
R.K. Shyamasundar, Tata Institute of Fundamental Research, India
Gilles Kahn, INRIA, France
Kazunori Ueda, Waseda University, Japan
Kanchana Kanchansut, Asian Institute of Technology, Thailand

Program Committee

Gul Agha (University of Illinois at Urbana-Champaign, USA)
Guruduth Banavar (IBM Research, USA)
Gilad Bracha (Sun Microsystems, USA)
Luca Cardelli (Microsoft Research, UK)
Georges Gonthier (INRIA, France)
Seif Haridi (SICS, Sweden and National University of Singapore, Singapore)
Nevin Heintze (Agere Research, USA)
Radha Jagadeesan (DePaul University, USA)
Naoki Kobayashi (Tokyo Institute of Technology, Japan)
Doug Lea (State University of New York at Oswego, USA)
Sanjiva Prasad (Indian Institute of Technology, Delhi, India)
Padma Raghavan (The Pennsylvania State University, USA)
Vijay Saraswat, CHAIR
(The Pennsylvania State University, and IBM Research, USA)
R.K. Shyamasundar (Tata Institute of Fundamental Research, India)
Anand Sivasubramaniam (The Pennsylvania State University, USA)
Kazunori Ueda (Waseda University, Japan)
Sanjiva Weerawarana
(IBM Research, USA, and University of Moratuwa, Sri Lanka)
Feng Zhao (Palo Alto Research Center, USA)

Referees

Bharat Adsul
V.S. Borkar
Krishnendu Chatterjee
Deepak D'Souza
Vineet Gupta
Martin Hofmann
Soham Mazumdar
Dino Oliva
Paritosh Pandya
N. Raja
Uday Reddy
Daby M. Sow
Prasanna Thati
Daniel C. Wang
Reza Ziaei

Table of Contents

Achieving Type Safety for Low-Level Code

Greg Morrisett

Cornell University, Ithaca NY 14853, USA

Abstract. Type-safe, high-level languages such as Java ensure that a wide class of failures, including buffer overruns and format string attacks, simply cannot happen. Unfortunately, our computing infrastructure is built with type-unsafe low-level languages such as C, and it is economically impossible to throw away our existing operating systems, databases, routers, etc. and re-code them all in Java.
Fortunately, a number of recent advances in static analysis, language design, compilation, and run-time systems have given us a set of tools for achieving type safety for legacy C code. In this talk, I will survey some of the progress that has been made in the last few years, and focus on the issues that remain if we are to achieve type safety, and more generally, security for our computing infrastructure.

1 Overview

In November of 1988, Robert Morris, Jr. released a worm into the Internet. One of the ways the worm propagated was by overflowing an input buffer for the `gets` routine of the finger daemon. The worm also took advantage of a flaw in the configuration of the sendmail program, where remote debugging was enabled by default, as well as a password cracking program. Based on infection rates at MIT, some have concluded that roughly 10% of the supposedly 60,000 machines connected to the Internet were infected by the worm over a period of a few days. During those few days, heroic engineers disassembled the worm, figured out what it was doing, and took steps to block its propagation by pushing out changes to various sites [1].

Not much has changed in 15 years, except that there are many more hosts on the Internet, we are more dependent on these hosts, and the worms are a lot faster. For instance, in January 2003, someone released the so-called "Sapphire" worm (also known as the SQL-Slammer worm) which took advantage of a buffer overrun in Microsoft's SQL servers. This worm doubled in size every 8.5 seconds and managed to traverse and infect about 90% of the 100,000 susceptible hosts on the Internet in about 10 minutes [2]. There simply wasn't time to determine what the worm was doing, construct a patch, and get the patch in place before the whole Internet had been hit. In fact, a patch to prevent the flaw Sapphire took advantage of had been out for a number of months, but many users had failed to apply the patch, perhaps in fear that the cure was worse than the poison, or perhaps out of simple laziness.

In the case of the Blaster worm, released in August of 2003 and which took advantage of a buffer overrun in Windows 2000 and XP, a counter-worm was

V.A. Saraswat (Ed.): ASIAN 2003, LNCS 2896, pp. 1–2, 2003.

released in a vain attempt to patch machines. Unfortunately, it managed to clog networks in the same way that Blaster did. At Cornell University, about 1,000 out of a roughly 30,000 Windows machines were infected by Blaster and even though the infection rate was so low, we estimate that it has cost about $133,000 in IT time so far to contain and deal with the damage. Other universities have reported as much as $800,000 in IT costs [3].

Security and reliability are hard issues. Misconfiguration, social issues, and many other problems will not be solved by technology alone. But surely after 15 years, we should be able to prevent buffer overruns and other "simple" errors in a proactive fashion before we ship code. In this talk, I will survey some of the approaches that people have used or are proposing for addressing buffer overruns and related problems in legacy C and C++ code.

References

1. Spafford, E. The Internet Worm Program: An Analysis. Purdue Technical Report CSD-TR-823, 1988.
2. Moore, D., Paxson, V., Savage, S., Shannon, C., Staniford, S., Weaver, N. The Spread of the Sapphire/Slammer Worm. http://www.cs.berkeley.edu/ nweaver/sapphire/.
3. http://whodunit.uchicago.edu/misc/infection-costs.html.

Kernel Mode Linux: Toward an Operating System Protected by a Type Theory

Toshiyuki Maeda and Akinori Yonezawa

University of Tokyo, 7-3-1 Hongo, Bunkyo-ku, Tokyo 113-0033 Japan
{tosh,yonezawa}@yl.is.s.u-tokyo.ac.jp

Abstract. Traditional operating systems protect themselves from user programs with a privilege level facility of CPUs. One problem of the protection-by-hardware approach is that system calls become very slow because heavy operations are required to safely switch the privilege levels of user programs. To solve the problem, we design an operating system that protects itself with a type theory. In our approach, user programs are written in a typed assembly language and the kernel performs type-checking before executing the programs. Then, the user programs can be executed in the kernel mode, because the kernel knows that the type-checked programs do not violate safety of the kernel. Thus, system calls become mere function calls and can be invoked very quickly. We implemented Kernel Mode Linux (KML) that realizes our approach. Several benchmarks show effectiveness of KML.

1 Introduction

One problem of traditional operating systems is that system calls are very slow. This is because they protect themselves from user programs by using hardware facilities of CPUs. For example, the Linux kernel [8] for the IA-32 CPUs [7] protects itself by using a memory protection facility integrated with a privilege-level facility of the CPUs. The kernel runs in the kernel mode, the most privileged level, and user programs run in the user mode, the least privileged level. System calls are implemented by using a software interruption mechanism of the CPUs that can raise a privilege level in a safe and restricted way. This software interruption and associated context switches require heavy and complex operations. For example, on the recent Pentium 4 CPU of the IA-32, the software interruption and the context switches are about 132 times slower than an ordinary function call. Recent Linux kernels for the IA-32 CPUs, in fact, use a pair of special instructions, *sysenter* and *sysexit*, for fast invocation of system calls. But this is still 36 times slower than an ordinary function call.

The obvious way to accelerate system calls is to execute user programs in the kernel mode. Then system calls can be handled very quickly because no software interruptions and context switches are needed because user programs can access the kernel directly. However, if we naively execute user programs in the kernel mode, safety of the kernel is totally lost, because the user programs can perform any privileged action in the kernel mode.

V.A. Saraswat (Ed.): ASIAN 2003, LNCS 2896, pp. 3–17, 2003.

In this paper, we propose an approach for protecting an operating system kernel from user programs not with the traditional hardware protection facilities, but with static type-checking. In our approach, user programs are written in a typed assembly language (TAL) [12], which is an ordinary assembly language (except for being typed) that can ensure type safety of programs at the level of machine instructions. Then, the kernel performs type-checking before executing them. If the programs are successfully type-checked, the kernel can safely execute them because the kernel knows that the programs never perform an illegal access to its memory. Moreover, in this paper, we show that the type-checking can ensure safety of the kernel at the same level as the traditional protection-by-hardware approach.

Based on our approach, we implemented an operating system, called Kernel Mode Linux (KML), that can execute user programs in the kernel mode. The notable feature of KML is that user programs are executed as ordinary processes of the original Linux kernel (of course, except for their privilege levels). That is, the memory paging and the scheduling of processes are performed as usual. Therefore, user programs that consume very large memory or enter an infinite loop can be safely executed in the kernel mode. We also conducted several benchmarks on KML and the result shows that system calls are invoked very fast on KML

The rest of this paper is organized as follows. Sect. 2 formally describes that the hardware protection can be replaced with a type-based static program analysis without losing safety. Sect. 3 describes the implementation of Kernel Mode Linux. Sect. 4 presents the result of some performance benchmarks. Sect. 5 mentions related work. Sect. 6 concludes this paper.

2 Formal Arguments

To show that the protection-by-hardware approach can be replaced with static type-checking, we first define an idealized abstract machine that has a notion of privilege levels of CPUs and system calls. Then, we show that the protection-by-hardware approach of traditional operating systems actually ensures safety of the kernel. Next, we define our typed assembly language for the abstract machine and show that its static type-checking ensures safety of the kernel. The following argument is almost the same line of the arguments of TAL [12, 11], FTAL [5], TALT [3] etc. The fundamental difference between the previous approaches and ours is that our abstract machine has an explicit notion of privilege levels and an operating system kernel.

2.1 Abstract Machine

Figure 1 defines the syntax of states of the abstract machine. The machine state S is defined as a tuple of code memory, data memory, a register file, a program counter, a privilege level and a kernel. The code memory C represents execute-only memory for instructions. The data memory D represents mutable memory for data. The register file R is defined as a map from registers to word values. The program counter pc is a word value that points to an instruction that is about to be executed. The privilege level p consists of two values: $user$ and $kernel$. The

(*Register*)	$r ::= r_0 \mid r_1 \mid \ldots \mid r_{31}$
(*Word*)	$w ::= 0 \mid 1 \mid \ldots \mid 2^{32}-1$
(*Program counter*)	$pc ::= 0 \mid 1 \mid \ldots \mid 2^{32}-1$
(*Privilege level*)	$p ::= user \mid kernel$
(*Code memory*)	$C ::= \{0 \mapsto \iota_0,\ \ldots,\ 2^{30}-1 \mapsto \iota_{2^{30}-1}\}$ $(Dom(C) = \{n \mid 0 \leq n \leq 2^{30}-1\})$
(*Data memory*)	$D ::= \{2^{30} \mapsto w_{2^{30}},\ \ldots,\ 2^{31}-1 \mapsto w_{2^{31}-1}\}$ $(Dom(D) = \{n \mid 2^{30} \leq n \leq 2^{31}-1\})$
(*Register file*)	$R ::= \{r_0 \mapsto w_0,\ \ldots,\ r_{31} \mapsto w_{31}\}$
(*Kernel*)	$K ::= \{w_0 \mapsto MetaFunc_0,\ \ldots\}$ $(Dom(K) \subseteq \{n \mid 2^{31} \leq n \leq 2^{32}-1\})$
(*Instruction*)	$\iota ::=$ `add` r_{s_1}, r_{s_2}, r_d | `movi` w, r_d | `mov` r_s, r_d | `jmp` r_s | `blt` $r_{s_1}, r_{s_2}, r_{s_3}$ | `ld` $w[r_s], r_d$ | `st` $r_s, w[r_d]$ | `illegal`
(*State*)	$S ::= (C, D, R, pc, p, K)$ | `user_error` | `kernel_error`

Fig. 1. Syntax of the abstract machine states

value *user* represents that the abstract machine runs in the user mode and the value *kernel* represents that it runs in the kernel mode. The kernel K represents an operating system kernel. It is defined as a map from addresses represented as word values to meta functions ($MetaFunc$) that translate a machine state to another. The meta functions can be viewed as inner functions of the kernel that implement system calls. In a real machine, the meta functions are only sequences of instructions. In this paper, however, we do not care the real representation because they are regarded as a trusted computing base in practice and there are not significant points in the representation. In addition, there are two special machine states that represent an error state: `user_error` and `kernel_error`. `user_error` represents an error only for user programs that does not affect safety or integrity of the whole system. On the other hand, `kernel_error` represents a fatal error that may crash the whole system.

Figure 2 defines the operational semantics of the abstract machine. They are defined as a conventional small-step function that translates a machine state S to another S'. If the program counter pc points into the domain of the code memory C, then an instruction, $C(pc)$, is executed as usual. The branch instruction `jmp` and `blt` can be viewed as special instructions for invocation of system calls if their target addresses are in the domain of the kernel. If the memory access instructions (`ld` and `st`) access the illegal memory, that is, the code memory or the kernel, then a machine state evaluates to `user_error` (if $p = user$) or `kernel_error` (if $p = kernel$). If the program counter pc points into the domain of the kernel K, a system call is executed, that is, S' becomes a machine state that is obtained by applying S to a meta function which is pointed by pc.

2.2 Safety of the Traditional Protection-by-Hardware Approach

The traditional protection-by-hardware approach can be expressed simply in the abstract machine. It only sets the privilege levels of the machine states to *user* to prevent `kernel_error` from occurring.

$$(C, D, R, pc, p, K) \mapsto S'$$

If $pc \notin Dom(K) \cup Dom(C)$	$S' = error(p)$
If $pc \in Dom(K)$	$S' = K(pc)(S)$
If $pc \in Dom(C)$:	

if $C(pc) =$	then $S' =$	
`add` r_{s_1}, r_{s_2}, r_d	$(D, R', pc+1)$	$R' = R\{r_d \mapsto R(r_{s_1}) + R(r_{s_2})\}$
`movi` w, r_d	$(D, R', pc+1)$	$R' = R\{r_d \mapsto w\}$
`mov` r_s, r_d	$(D, R', pc+1)$	$R' = R\{r_d \mapsto R(r_s)\}$
`jmp` r_s	$(D, R, R(r_s))$	
`blt` $r_{s_1}, r_{s_2}, r_{s_3}$	$(D, R, R(r_{s_3}))$	when $R(r_{s_1}) < R(r_{s_2})$
	$(D, R, pc+1)$	when $R(r_{s_1}) \geq R(r_{s_2})$
`ld` $w[r_s], r_d$	$(D, R', pc+1)$	$R' = R\{r_d \mapsto D(R(r_s) + w)\}$ when $R(r_s) + w \in Dom(D)$
	$error(p)$	when $R(r_s) + w \notin Dom(D)$
`st` $r_s, w[r_d]$	$(D', R, pc+1)$	$D' = D\{R(r_d) + w \mapsto R(r_s)\}$ when $R(r_d) + w \in Dom(D)$
	$error(p)$	when $R(r_d) + w \notin Dom(D)$
`illegal`	`user_error`	

where $error(p) =$ `kernel_error` when $p = kernel$
`user_error` when $p = user$

C, p and K are omitted in the above table because they never change.

Fig. 2. Operational semantics of the abstract machine

Theorem 1 (Safety of the Traditional Protection-by-Hardware). *If meta functions of K never alter privilege levels and never translate machine states to* `kernel_error`*, then any machine state of the form $(C, D, R, pc, user, K)$ never evaluates to* `kernel_error`.

Proof. Straightforward from the operational semantics of the abstract machine. □

2.3 Typed Assembly Language

Now, we define a TAL that prevents `kernel_error` from occurring. Figure 3 shows the syntax of the typed assembly language for the abstract machine. (It only shows the difference from the syntax of the abstract machine.)

Our TAL has 6 kinds of basic types: α (type variable), int (word value), $\langle\tau_1, \ldots, \tau_n\rangle$ (tuple), $\forall[\Delta].\Gamma$, $sizeof(\alpha)$, and $sizeof(\langle\tau_1, \ldots, \tau_n\rangle)$. $\forall[\Delta].\Gamma$ is a type of instruction sequences. For example, if an instruction sequence I has a type $\forall[\Delta]\Gamma$, then the register file of the abstract machine must have a register file type (explained below) represented by Γ, to jump to and execute the instruction sequence. $sizeof(\langle\tau_1, \ldots, \tau_n\rangle)$ is a type of a word value that represents a size of a tuple of the type $\langle\tau_1, \ldots, \tau_n\rangle$. For example, if a word value w has a type $sizeof(\langle int, int, int\rangle)$, then we know that $w = 3$. $sizeof(\alpha)$ is a type of a word value that represents a size of a tuple of the type α. Our TAL also has 4 kinds of types for the components of the abstract machine. Ψ_C is a type of code memory, Ψ_D is a type of data memory, Γ is a type of a register file, and Ψ_K is

(type)	$\tau ::= \alpha \mid int \mid \forall[\Delta].\Gamma \mid \langle\tau_1,\ldots,\tau_n\rangle$
	$\mid sizeof(\langle\tau_1,\ldots,\tau_n\rangle) \mid sizeof(\alpha)$
(type variables)	$\Delta ::= \alpha_1,\ldots,\alpha_n$
(code memory type)	$\Psi_C ::= \{w_0 : \forall[\Delta_0].\Gamma_0,\ldots,w_n : \forall[\Delta_n].\Gamma_n\}$
(data memory type)	$\Psi_D ::= \{w_0 : \langle\tau_0,\ldots\rangle,\ldots,w_n : \langle\tau_n,\ldots\rangle\}$
(kernel type)	$\Psi_K ::= \{w_0 : \forall[\Delta_0].\Gamma_0,\ldots,w_n : \forall[\Delta_n].\Gamma_n\}$
(register file type)	$\Gamma ::= \{r_0 : \tau_0,\ldots,r_{31} : \tau_{31}\}$
(tuple)	$T ::= \langle w_1,\ldots,w_n\rangle$
(instruction sequence)	$I ::= \iota_1;\ldots;\iota_n$

Fig. 3. Syntax of the typed assembly language for the abstract machine. Only the difference from the syntax of the abstract machine is shown

Judgment	Meaning
$\Delta \vdash \tau$	τ is a well-formed type
$\vdash \Psi_C$	Ψ_C is a well-formed code memory type
$\vdash \Psi_D$	Ψ_D is a well-formed data memory type
$\vdash \Psi_K$	Ψ_K is a well-formed kernel type
$\Delta \vdash \Gamma$	Γ is a well-formed register file type
$\vdash (C,D) : \Psi$	C is well-formed code memory of type Ψ_C
	D is well-formed data memory of type Ψ_D
$\Psi \vdash R : \Gamma$	R is a well-formed register file of type Γ
$\Psi,\Delta \vdash w : \tau$	w is a well-formed word value of type τ
$\Psi \vdash T : \tau$	T is a well-formed tuple of type τ
$\Psi,\Delta,\Gamma \vdash I$	I is a well-formed instruction sequence
$\Psi_K \vdash K$	K is a well-formed kernel
$\Psi_K \vdash S$	S is a well-formed machine state

where $\Psi = (\Psi_c, \Psi_d, \Psi_k)$

Fig. 4. Static judgments of the typed assembly language

a type of a kernel and corresponds to the interface of system calls of the kernel. Although our TAL does not have rich types, we can extend it with them, such as existential types [12], recursive types [5], array types [10] and stack types [11], in theory.

The dynamic semantics of our TAL are unchanged from the abstract machine. This indicates that we can erase type information of programs and no type-checking is required at runtime.

Figure 4 presents static judgments of our TAL that assert the well-formedness of the components of the TAL. To have a well-formed machine state, the code memory, the data memory, the kernel, the register file and the instruction sequence that starts from the address of the program counter must be well-formed. The static semantics for the well-formedness are presented in Appendix A. Because of space limitations, the rules for word values, tuples and instructions are omitted. They are basically the same line of the rules of FTAL [5] etc.

The well-formedness of the kernel is defined as follows. The basic idea is that system calls never break the well-formedness of machine states.

Definition 1 (The Well-formedness of the Kernel). *The kernel K is well-formed, denoted as $\Psi_K \vdash K$, if:*

1. *Ψ_K is well-formed, that is, $\vdash \Psi_K$.*
2. *The domain of K is equal to the domain of Ψ_K.*
3. *For all w in the domain of K, if $\Psi_K \vdash S$ where $S = (C, D, R, w, p, K)$, then $K(w)(S) \neq$ `user_error` or `kernel_error` and $\Psi_K \vdash K(w)(S)$.*

2.4 Safety of the Typed Assembly Language

Now, we show that, if a machine state S and a kernel K are well-formed, then S never evaluates to `kernel_error`. For that purpose, we first show that our typed assembly language satisfies the following usual Preservation and Progress lemmas.

Lemma 1 (Preservation). *If $\Psi_K \vdash K$, $\Psi_K \vdash S$ and $S \mapsto S'$, then $\Psi_K \vdash S'$.*

Lemma 2 (Progress). *If $\Psi_K \vdash K$ and $\Psi_K \vdash S$, then there exists S' such that $S \mapsto S'$.*

Proof. By case analysis on $C(pc)$ (if $pc \in Dom(C)$) and $K(pc)$ (if $pc \in Dom(K)$), and induction on the typing derivations. Here, we only show the proof for the case that $pc \in Dom(K)$.

If $pc \in K$, there exists $S' = K(pc)(S)$ such that $S \mapsto S'$. Thus, the progress lemma is satisfied. In addition, from the well-formedness of the kernel $\Psi_K \vdash K$, we have $\Psi_K \vdash S'$. Thus, the preservation lemma is also satisfied. □

From these two lemmas, we can prove that, if a user program can be type-checked, that is, if a machine state that represents the user program is well-formed, then the program never violates safety of the kernel from the fact that the machine state never evaluates to `kernel_error`, as long as the kernel is correctly implemented. Thus, we can safely replace the hardware protection facilities (the privilege levels) with the static type-checking of our TAL.

Theorem 2 (Safety of the Typed Assembly Language). *If $\Psi_K \vdash K$ and $\Psi_K \vdash S$, then S never evaluates to `kernel_error`.*

Proof. Straightforward from Lemma 1 and Lemma 2.

2.5 Dynamic Memory Allocation

In our framework, a dynamic memory allocation mechanism can be realized by having the kernel include it as a system call, instead of having a special macro instruction as Morrisett's TAL [12]. For example, we can use the following kernel.

Example 1 (The Kernel with the Malloc System Call).

$$\Psi_K = \{\ w_{malloc} : \forall[\alpha].\{r_0 : sizeof(\alpha), r_1 : \alpha, r_{31} : \forall[\beta].\{r_0 : \alpha, r_1 : \alpha, r_{31} : \beta\}\}\}$$
$$K = \{\ w_{malloc} \mapsto Malloc\ \}$$

(Registers other than r_0, r_1 and r_{31} are omitted here for the sake of brevity.)

The meta function *Malloc* allocates unused memory of the size specified by r_0 from the data memory D. Then, it initializes the allocated memory with the contents of the memory specified by r_1 and sets the register r_0 to the address of the allocated memory. Finally, it jumps to the return address specified in the register r_{31}.

3 Kernel Mode Linux

Based on the argument of the previous section, we implemented Kernel Mode Linux (KML), a modified Linux kernel for IA-32 CPUs which can execute user programs in the kernel mode. In this section, we describe the implementation of Kernel Mode Linux (KML).

3.1 How to Execute User Processes in the Kernel Mode

In IA-32 CPUs, the privilege level of a running program is determined by the privilege level of the code segment in which the program is executed. A program counter of IA-32 CPUs consists of the CS segment register, which specifies a code segment, and the EIP register, which specifies an offset into the code segment.

To execute a user process in the kernel mode, the only thing KML does is to set the CS register of the process to the kernel code segment, the most-privileged segment, instead of the user code segment, the least-privileged segment. Then the process is executed in the kernel mode. We call such processes as "kernel-mode user processes".

Because of this simple approach of KML, a kernel-mode user process can be an ordinary user process (except for its privilege level). Therefore, even if a kernel-mode user process consumes huge amount of memory and/or enters an infinite loop, the kernel can reclaim the memory through its paging facility and suspend the process through its process-scheduling facility, because KML does not modify any code or data of the facilities.

3.2 How to Invoke System Calls from Kernel-Mode User Processes

To ensure safety of the kernel, user programs that will be executed in the kernel mode must be written in TALx86 [10], a notable typed assembly language implementation for IA-32 CPUs, or Popcorn [10], a safe dialect of the C programming language which can be translated to TALx86.

In the current KML, the interface of the system calls (that is, a kernel type Ψ_K mentioned in Sect. 2) is exported as TAL's interface file. The interface file contains pairs of a name of a system call and its TAL type. The actual address of a system call is looked up from the name of the system call at link time, as usual. Then, programmers write their programs in TALx86 or Popcorn according to the interface file. Invocations of system calls are written as usual function calls, as expected. Though almost all system calls can be exported to user programs safely, there are a few exceptions that cannot be exported directly because they may violate the well-formedness of the kernel (e.g., `mmap`/`munmap` system calls).

Actually, KML must type-check user programs just before executing them for ensuring safety. However, the current KML itself does not perform type-checking, because the current TALx86 implementation cannot type-check executable binaries (though intermediate relocatable binary objects can be checked). Thus, the current KML needs to trust the external TALx86 assembler. We plan to develop our own TAL type-checker for checking the executable binaries to solve this problem.

3.3 Executing Existing Applications in the Kernel Mode

The current KML has a loophole mechanism to execute existing applications in the kernel mode and eliminate the overhead of system calls without modifying them. Though safety is not ensured, the mechanism is useful for measuring the performance improvement of applications due to the elimination of the overhead of system calls.

To implement the loophole mechanism, we exploit the facility of the recent original Linux kernel for multiplexing a system call invocation into a traditional software interruption (*int* 0x80) or *sysenter*/*sysexit* instructions depending on a kind of CPU. We implemented a third branch for the multiplexer that invokes system calls with direct function calls. Because the multiplexer executes additional instructions to invoke system calls, a system call invocation with this mechanism is not optimal. However, it is sufficiently fast compared to the software interruptions and the *sysenter*/*sysexit* instructions.

3.4 The Stack Starvation Problem

As described in Section 3.1, the basic approach of KML is quite simple. However, there is one problem we call *stack starvation.* In the original Linux kernel, interrupts are handled by interrupt handling routines specified in the Interrupt Descriptor Table (IDT). When an interrupt occurs, an IA-32 CPU stops execution of the running program, saves its execution context and executes the interrupt handling routine.

How the IA-32 CPU saves the execution context of the running program at interrupts depends on the privilege level of the program. If the program is executed in the user mode, the IA-32 CPU automatically switches its memory stack to a kernel stack. Then, it saves the execution context (EIP, CS, EFLAGS, ESP and SS registers) to the kernel stack. On the other hand, if the program is executed in the kernel mode, the IA-32 CPU does not switch its memory stack and saves the context (EIP, CS and EFLAGS registers) to the memory stack of the running program.

What happens if a user process that is executed in the kernel mode on KML accesses its memory stack, which is not mapped by page tables of a CPU? First, a page fault occurs, and the CPU tries to interrupt the user process and jump to a page fault handler specified in the IDT. However, the CPU cannot accomplish this work, because there is no stack for saving the execution context. Because the process is executed in the kernel mode, the CPU never switches the memory stack to the kernel stack. To signal this fatal situation, the CPU tries to generate a special exception, a double fault. However, again, the CPU cannot generate the double fault because there is no stack for saving the execution context of the running process. Finally, the CPU gives up and resets itself. We call this problem *stack starvation.*

To solve the *stack starvation* problem, KML exploits the task management facility of IA-32 CPUs. The IA-32 task management facility is provided to support process management for kernels. Using this facility, a kernel can switch processes with only one instruction. However, today's kernels do not use this facility because it is slower than software-only approaches. Thus the facility is almost forgotten by all.

The strength of this task management facility is that it can be used to handle exceptions and interrupts. Tasks managed by an IA-32 CPU can be set to the IDT. If an interrupt occurs and a task is assigned to handle the interrupt, the CPU first saves the execution context of the interrupted program to a special memory region (called a task state segment, or TSS) of the running task, instead of to the memory stacks. Then, the CPU switches to the task specified in the IDT to handle the interrupt. The most important point is that there is no need to switch a memory stack if the task management facility is used to handle interrupts. That is, if we handle page fault exceptions with the facility, a user process executed in the kernel mode can access its memory stack safely.

However, if we handle all page faults with the task management facility, the performance of the whole system degrades because the task-based interrupt handling is slower than the ordinary interrupt handling. Therefore, in KML, only double fault exceptions are handled with the task management facility. That is, only page faults caused by memory stack absence are handled by the facility. Thus, the performance degradation is very small and negligible because memory stacks rarely cause page faults.

4 Benchmarks

To measure the degree of performance improvement by executing user programs in the kernel mode, we conducted two benchmarks that compared performance of the original Linux kernel with that of KML. In each benchmark, we executed exactly the same benchmark program both on the original Linux kernel and KML with the system call multiplexing mechanism described in the previous section. We also compared KML with the *sysenter/sysexit* mechanism. The experimental environment is shown in Table 1.

4.1 First Benchmark: Latencies of System Calls

The first benchmark measured latencies of 5 system calls by using LMbench [9] (version 2.0). `getpid` is the simplest system call that only obtains a process ID.

Table 1. Experimental environment

CPU	Pentium 4 3.000GHz (L2 cache 512KB)
Memory	1GB (PC3200 DDR SDRAM)
Hard disk	120GB
OS	Linux kernel 2.5.72 (KML_2.5.72_001)

Table 2. Latencies of system calls. "Original" means the original Linux kernel and "sysenter" means the original Linux kernel using *sysenter/sysexit*

	`getpid`	`read`	`write`	`stat`	`fstat`
Original	371.3	439.3	402.3	1157.3	608.7
sysenter	135.1	201.1	164.9	896.5	383.5
KML	16.9	91.0	53.4	756.2	204.1

(Unit: nanoseconds)

Therefore, the overhead of system calls becomes very large in it. `read` and `write` are basic I/O system calls. In the benchmark, `read` and `write` were performed on the null device (i.e., /dev/null). `stat` and `fstat` are system calls for obtaining file statistics. The result is presented in Table 2.

The result shows that the `getpid` system call was about 22 times faster in KML than in the original Linux kernel. It also shows that it was about 8 times faster in KML than using *sysenter/sysexit*. The latencies of the other system calls were also improved in KML.

4.2 Second Benchmark: Throughputs of File I/O Operations

The second benchmark examined how performance of file I/O is improved in KML by using IOzone [13] (version 3.172). In the benchmark, we measured throughputs of 4 I/O operations in 4 tests: `Write`, `Re-write`, `Read` and `Re-read`. The `Write` test measures the throughput of writing a new file. The `Re-write` test measures the throughput of writing a file that already exists. The `Read` test measures the throughput of reading an existing file. The `Re-read` test measures the performance of reading a file that is recently read. In all of the 4 tests, we measured the throughput of the I/O operations on files whose size is from 16 Kbytes to 512 Kbytes. We fixed the buffer size to 16 Kbytes. The benchmark was performed on a file system of Ext3fs. The result is shown in Figure 5.

The result indicates that KML can improve various I/O operations for files of small size. The result shows that, compared to the original Linux kernel, the throughputs of `Write`, `Re-write`, `Read` and `Re-read` were improved up to 8 %, 15.9 %, 25.9 % and 14.7 % respectively. Compared to the *sysenter/sysexit* mechanism, the throughputs of `Write`, `Re-write`, `Read` and `Re-read` were improved up to 2 %, 13.3 %, 12.6 % and 15.3 % respectively. There is performance degradation in some cases (especially, in the `Write` test). This is mainly due to CPU cache effects.

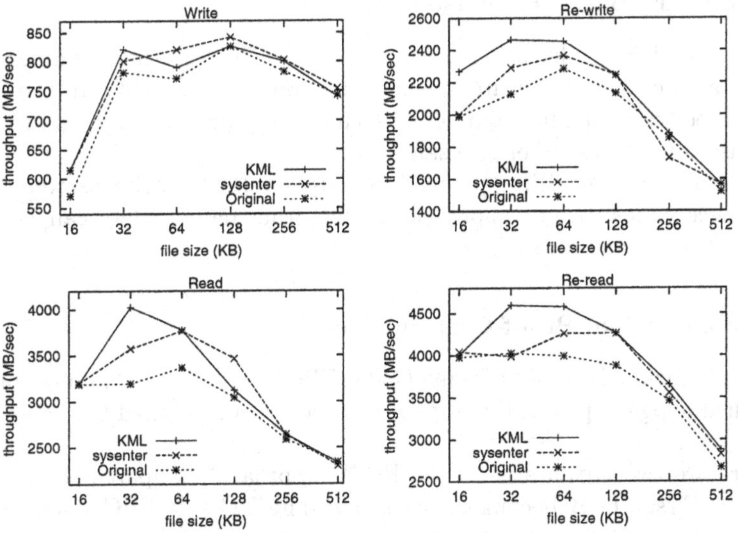

Fig. 5. Throughputs of I/O operations. "Original" means the original Linux kernel and "sysenter" means the original Linux kernel using *sysenter/sysexit*

5 Related Work

In the field of operating system and programming language research, there are several works related to safe execution of user programs in a kernel. An interesting difference between our research and the previous work lies in their objective. Our objective is to execute ordinary user programs in the kernel mode safely while the work below is concentrated on how to extend a kernel safely.

5.1 SPIN Operating System

SPIN [2] is an extensible kernel that ensures safety by a language-based protection. In SPIN, kernel extensions are written in the Modula-3 programming language [6]. Safety of SPIN is ensured by the fact that Modula-3 is a type-safe language. That is, programmers cannot write malicious kernel extensions.

This approach of SPIN has two problems. The first problem is that its trusted computing base (TCB) becomes large because the kernel must trust external compilers of Modula-3. In SPIN, the kernel cannot check safety of binary codes. In our approach, on the other hand, TCB is smaller than SPIN because safety is checked at the machine language level and we need not trust external compilers. The second problem is that the kernel extensions must be written in Modula-3. In our approach, we can write user programs in various programming languages, if there exist compilers that translate the languages to TALs.

5.2 Software-Based Fault Isolation

Software-based Fault Isolation (SFI) [16] is a technique that modifies binary codes of applications to ensure memory and control flow safety. In the SFI approach, check codes are inserted before each memory access and jump instruction of untrusted programs to ensure safety.

The problem of the SFI approach is its large overhead of the inserted runtime safety check codes. In our approach, on the other hand, safety can be mostly ensured at load time through type-checking.

5.3 Foundational Proof-Carrying Code

In the Foundational Proof-Carrying Code (FPCC) [1] approach, a user program is attached a logical proof of its safety, and the proof is verified before executing the program.

There are two advantages in the FPCC approach, compared to the simple TAL [12]. First, TCB becomes very small. The TCB of FPCC consists of a proof-checker, a machine specification that represents a behavior of a CPU and memory, and a safety policy. On the other hand, the TCB of the simple TAL system becomes larger because it includes a TAL type-checker. To solve this problem, we can take the approach of Hamid et al [5]. They showed that their TAL that is carefully defined so that well-formed TAL programs are mapped to valid machine states of FPCC can be syntactically translated to a FPCC program that does not violate memory safety and control flow safety. In their approach, the TCB can be as small as the FPCC approach.

Second, a safety policy can be flexible. In the FPCC approach, a safety policy is specified in logics of a proof-checker. Therefore, we can specify a safety policy that cannot be expressed in a simple TAL type system. For example, a limitation of memory or CPU usage can be ensured by the FPCC approach. However, there is a drawback of this flexibility of a safety policy: Proof generation may become very hard. In TALs, on the other hand, type-checking is simple and easy. In addition, to replace the hardware protection mechanisms, type safety suffices because they ensure only memory safety and control flow safety.

6 Conclusion

In this paper, we showed that the hardware protection mechanisms that traditional operating systems exploit can be safely replaced with static program analysis, mainly type-checking. By discarding the hardware protection mechanisms, the overhead of switching a privilege level of a CPU can be eliminated and efficiency of applications can be improved. Based on this approach, we developed KML, an operating system in which user programs can be executed in the kernel mode of a CPU (available at http://www.taplas.org/~tosh/kml). The result of several benchmarks shows effectiveness of KML.

7 Future Work

Although the current KML is effective for improving performance of programs, there should be a limitation because it only eliminates the overhead of system calls. To improve the performance further, we should modify the kernel and its interface and exploit the TAL type system more aggressively. For example, we think that a kernel can be modified to export network communication hardware to user programs as user-level communication technologies (e.g., [14, 15, 4]). The problem of the user-level communication is a tradeoff between performance and safety. To achieve high performance, the kernel must export network hardware to user programs directly and give up its safety because the user programs can access the kernel directly. To achieve safety, on the other hand, the kernel must encapsulate network hardware by system calls and give up high-performance communication. By using our approach, we can achieve both high-performance communication and safety because the overhead of system calls can be eliminated without losing safety.

As other directions, our approach can be applied to microkernels. Traditional microkernels have a problem of the overhead of communication between a kernel and user servers. By applying our approach, the overhead can be reduced largely. In addition, we think that the large part of a kernel itself can be written in a strongly typed low-level language as TALs. Of course, it is difficult to ensure total safety of the kernel. We think, however, that the simple memory and control flow safety is still valuable. For example, consider synchronization primitives such as mutex locks and semaphores. It is difficult to ensure that these primitives are properly used for preventing deadlocks. However, it is very easy to ensure memory safety, because they only make a decent memory access.

References

1. A. W. Appel. Foundational proof-carrying code. In *In proc. of 16th Annual IEEE Symposium on Logic in Computer Science*, pages 247–258, June 2001.
2. B. N. Bershad, C. Chambers, S. J. Eggers, C. Maeda, D. McNamee, P. Pardyak, S. Savage, and E. G. Sirer. SPIN - an extensible microkernel for application-specific operating system services. In *In proc. of ACM SIGOPS European Workshop*, pages 68–71, September 1994.
3. K. Crary. Toward a foundational typed assembly language. In *Proc. of Symposium on Principles of Programming Languages*, pages 198–212, January 2003.
4. C. Dubnicki, A. Bilas, Y. Chen, S. Damianakis, and K. Li. VMMC-2: efficient support for reliable, connection-oriented communication. In *Proc. of Hot Interconnects*, pages 37–46, August 1997.
5. N. Hamid, Z. Shao, V. Trifonov, S. Monnier, and Z. Ni. A syntactic approach to foundational proof-carrying code. Technical Report YALEU/DCS/TR-1224, Dept. of Computer Science, Yale University, 2002.
6. S. P. Harbison. *Modula-3.* Prentice Hall, 1992.
7. Intel Corporation. *IA-32 Intel Architecture Software Developer's Manual.*
8. The Linux kernel. http://www.kernel.org.

9. L. W. McVoy and C. Staelin. lmbench: Portable tools for performance analysis. In *Proc. of USENIX Annual Technical Conference*, pages 279–294, 1996.
10. G. Morrisett, K. Crary, N. Glew, D. Grossman, R. Samuels, F. Smith, D. Walker, S. Weirich, and S. Zdancewic. TALx86: A realistic typed assembly language. In *Proc. of ACM SIGPLAN Workshop on Compiler Support for System Software*, pages 25–35, 1999.
11. G. Morrisett, K. Crary, N. Glew, and D. Walker. Stack-based typed assembly language. In *In proc. of Types in Compilation*, pages 28–52, 1998.
12. G. Morrisett, D. Walker, K. Crary, and N. Glew. From System F to typed assembly language. *ACM Transactions on Programming Languages and Systems*, 21(3):527–568, 1999.
13. W. D. Norcott. The IOzone file system benchmark. http://www.iozone.org.
14. L. Prylli and B. Tourancheau. BIP: a new protocol designed for high performance networking on Myrinet, March 1998.
15. H. Tezuka, A. Hori, and Y. Ishikawa. PM : a high-performance communication library for multi-user parallel environments. Technical Report TR-96015, Real World Computing Partnership, 1996.
16. R. Wahbe, S. Lucco, T. E. Anderson, and S. L. Graham. Efficient software-based fault isolation. *ACM SIGOPS Operating Systems Review*, 27(5):203–216, December 1993.

A The Static Semantics of Our Typed Assembly Language (Rules for Types and Machine States Only)

$$\frac{FTV(\tau) \subseteq \Delta}{\Delta \vdash \tau} \quad \text{(TYPE)}$$

$$\frac{\begin{array}{c}\forall w_i \in Dom(\Psi_C).\ w_i \in [0, 2^{30} - 1] \\ \text{and } \Psi_C(w_i) = \forall[\Delta].\Gamma \text{ and } \Delta \vdash \Gamma\end{array}}{\vdash \Psi_C} \quad \text{(CODE MEMORY TYPE)}$$

$$\frac{\begin{array}{c}\forall w_i \in Dom(\Psi_K).\ w_i \in [2^{31}, 2^{32} - 1] \\ \text{and } \Psi_K(w_i) = \forall[\Delta].\Gamma \text{ and } \Delta \vdash \Gamma\end{array}}{\vdash \Psi_K} \quad \text{(KERNEL TYPE)}$$

$$\frac{\begin{array}{c}\forall w_i \in Dom(\Psi_D).\ TupleRange(\Psi_D, w) \subseteq [2^{30}, 2^{31} - 1] \\ \text{and } \Psi_D(w_i) = \langle \tau_1, \ldots, \tau_n \rangle \text{ and } \cdot \vdash \Psi_D(w_i) \\ \text{and } \forall w_j \in Dom(\Psi_D)\ s.t.\ w_j \neq w_i. \\ TupleRange(\Psi_D, w_i) \text{ and } TupleRange(\Psi_D, w_j) \text{ do not overlap}\end{array}}{\vdash \Psi_D} \quad \text{(DATA MEMORY TYPE)}$$

$$\frac{\forall r_i \in Dom(\Gamma).\Delta \vdash \Gamma(r_i)}{\Delta \vdash \Gamma} \quad \text{(REGISTER FILE TYPE)}$$

where
$TupleRange(\Psi_D, w) = [w, w + n - 1]$ where $\Psi_D(w) = \langle \tau_1, \ldots, \tau_n \rangle$

Fig. 6. The static semantics of the typed assembly language: types

$$\frac{\begin{array}{c}\vdash (C,D):\Psi \qquad \Psi \vdash R:\Gamma \\ \text{(1) If } pc \in C, \quad \Psi,\cdot,\Gamma \vdash \mathit{InstrDec}(C,pc) \\ \mathit{or} \\ \text{(2) If } pc \in K, \quad \Psi_K(pc) = \forall[\Delta'].\Gamma' \qquad \cdot \vdash \tau_i \qquad [\tau_1,\ldots,\tau_n/\Delta']\Gamma' = \Gamma\end{array}}{\Psi_K \vdash (C,D,R,pc,p,K)} \text{ (STATE)}$$

$$\frac{\begin{array}{c}\vdash \Psi_C \qquad \vdash \Psi_D \\ \forall w_i \in \mathit{Dom}(\Psi_C).\Psi,\Delta_i,\Gamma_i \vdash \mathit{InstrDec}(C,w_i) \text{ where } \Psi_C(w_i) = \forall[\Delta_i].\Gamma_i \\ \forall w_i \in \mathit{Dom}(\Psi_D).\Psi \vdash \mathit{TupleDec}(D,w_i,n) : \Psi_D(w_i) \text{ where } \Psi_D(w_i) = \langle \tau_1,\ldots,\tau_n \rangle\end{array}}{\vdash (C,D):\Psi} \text{ (MEMORY)}$$

$$\frac{\forall r_i \in \mathit{Dom}(\Gamma).\Psi,\cdot,\cdot \vdash R(r_i) : \Gamma(r_i)}{\Psi \vdash R:\Gamma} \text{ (REGISTER FILE)}$$

where

$\mathit{InstrDec}(C,w) \quad = \iota_w,\ldots,\iota_{2^{30}-1}$ where $\iota_i = C(i)$

$\mathit{TupleDec}(D,w,n) = \langle w_0,\ldots,w_{n-1} \rangle$ where $w_i = D(w+i)$

Fig. 7. The static semantics of the typed assembly language: state, memory and register file

Self-configurable Mirror Servers for Automatic Adaptation to Service Demand Fluctuation

Masakuni Agetsuma[1], Kenji Kono[2], Hideya Iwasaki[2], and Takashi Masuda[2]

[1] Course in Computer Science and Information Mathematics,
Graduate School of Electro-Communications,
The University of Electro-Communications, Japan
[2] Department of Computer Science,
The University of Electro-Communications, Japan

Abstract. Various network services are becoming more and more important serving roles in the social infrastructure in the Internet. The more clients a service has, the more load the server has, which obviously lowers the quality of service. To balance load and maintain quality, multiple servers (mirror servers) are commonly provided that are able to provide access to the same service. However, it is difficult to estimate the required number of mirror servers in advance. To overcome this, we propose a new concept called *self-configurable server groups* and discuss its basic mechanism where all server nodes communicate with one another in a peer-to-peer style to adjust to the expected number of servers. We also demonstrate the effectiveness of the proposed mechanism via some simulations.

1 Introduction

The Internet is becoming more and more important as a basic infrastructure for many organizations and companies providing various kinds of services other than electronic mail or Web pages. Since server and network resources are limited, increasing requests from clients may inflict excess loads on servers or occupy excess network bandwidth, creating serious problems such as delays or cessation (in the worst case) of services. One approach to avoid these is to prepare *mirror servers* that offer, as the name suggests, exactly the same services. Mirror servers are quite helpful in balancing both the service request load and occupation of network bandwidth.

However, this approach has the following problems from the administrative point of view. First, it is difficult to estimate a reasonable number of mirror servers. If too many servers are set up against the expected peak for requests, parts (and possibly most) of their resources will not be used most of the time except for the peak period. Second, it is difficult to predict the peak time and area for the service requests. If mirror servers are placed at inappropriate locations, their effect is negated because of communication delays or network bottlenecks.

These problems result from the fact that the demands for services are ever-changing[1], i.e., they fluctuate every moment both temporally and spatially. A

V.A. Saraswat (Ed.): ASIAN 2003, LNCS 2896, pp. 18–32, 2003.

naive way of coping with these fluctuations is to keep a constant watch over the service requests from the clients and incrementally adjust (increase or decrease) the mirror servers manually at appropriate times and locations. However, this needs experienced administrators who are capable of making suitable decisions about these adjustment based on accurate estimates. In addition, setting up or stopping mirror servers is very time-consuming. Thus, this naive approach is difficult to implement in practice.

This paper proposes a new system called *self-configurable server groups* to solve these problems. In this system, all server nodes communicate with one another in a peer-to-peer (P2P) style to automatically adjust the number of mirror servers according to the fluctuations in demand for services. Administrators do not need to statically determine the number or location of mirror servers in advance, or dynamically (or manually) set up or stop the mirror servers according to fluctuations in service requests. The targets of the self-configurable server groups are the services with static contents such as static Web pages, FTP service and so on.

The proposed system has the following features.

- It clearly distinguishes the *policy* of adjusting mirror servers from the *mechanism* that implements the adjustment. The policy determines *when* and *where* mirror servers will be increased (or decreased), and the mechanism determines *how* mirror servers will be increased (or decreased). This design principle enables administrators to set their own policies to control the adjustment behavior.
- Because the system has no global states such as the total number of mirror servers or the total number of requests from clients, it thus needs no centralized servers. Although each server acts according to a given policy to only use local information such as the number of requests to individual servers, the whole system can attain an almost optimal number of servers. This design enables the services based on the system to be scalable.
- The system can be used by servers that offer multiple services at the same time. These services are able to share the same server resources, (possibly) with some priority policies. Thus, the resources are appropriately and flexibly assigned to high-priority services or frequent requests.

This paper is organized as follows. Section 2 discusses basic structure and mechanism of self-configurable server groups through some concrete examples, and demonstrates how the proposed system is able to adapt the configuration of mirror servers to fluctuations in service requests. Section 3 describes details on policies that can be customized by the designer or the service administrator. Section 4 provides details on the design of the system. To demonstrate just how effective the proposed system is, by setting the appropriate policies, we provide some simulation results under different policies and reveal that it can configure mirror servers as expected in Section 5. Section 6 describes related work and Section 7 concludes the paper.

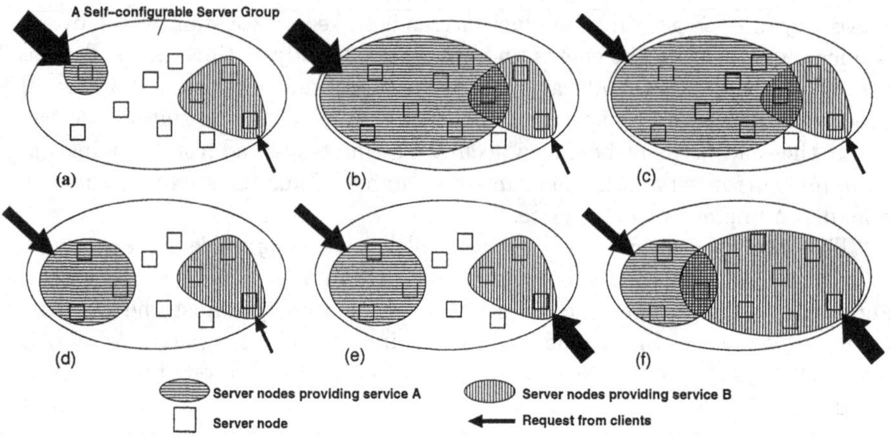

Fig. 1. Dynamically adjusting number of mirror servers.

2 Self-configurable Server Group

2.1 Basic Behavior

The goal of a *self-configurable server group* is to make it easier to adjust the number of mirror servers and by doing this we can constrain the maximum service delay under some constant. A self-configurable server group consists of a large number of *server nodes*, each of which donates its computing resources to the group. A server node can provide multiple services at the same time and thus enables the group to flexibly apportion the computing resources among these services. A self-configurable server group responds to dynamic fluctuations in service demands, i.e., it increases/decreases the number of mirror servers, depending on the increased/decreased demands for a specific service. The server nodes communicate with one another in a peer-to-peer fashion (i.e., no centralized nodes) to adjust the number of mirror servers. Each server node *autonomously* starts and stops a certain service.

Figure 1 illustrates a self-configurable server group that consists of 10 server nodes, and provides two services (A and B). Demand for service A increases in Fig. 1 (a). In response to this increase, several server nodes start to run the mirror servers for service A (Fig. 1 (b)). After that, demand for service A decreases (Fig. 1 (c)). Therefore, as we can see from Fig. 1 (d), some server nodes spontaneously stop service A. Likewise, the server node starts to run service B's mirror server, when demand for it increases (Figs.1 (e) and (f)).

A self-configurable server group promotes effective utilization of shared resources in the group because it allows resource sharing among several services. A single server node may provide more than one service at the same time. We can see a server node that provides both services A and B in Figs. 1 (b),(c) and (f).

Because the server nodes in a self-configurable server group are distributed all over the Internet, it is quite difficult to share global states such as the load information for every server node. If we establish a centralized server that provides such global information, this obviously becomes a hot spot as well as a single failure point. To avoid this, we employ a peer-to-peer model for execution; i.e., all server nodes are equivalent in the group. Each server node communicate with some "neighbor" nodes, and autonomously determine whether to start or stop a specific service. We proved that satisfactory performance could be obtained even though global information was not shared.

2.2 Mechanism

In what follows, we will briefly describe the protocol used to dynamically adjust the number of mirror servers. The protocol consists of two stages: (1) a service-starting phase and (2) a service-stopping phase.

Service-Starting Phase:
A server node acquires a *service package*, in the service-starting phase, registers its intention to provide that service, and starts the service if the demand for the service increases. A service package consists of all files necessary to provide the service. For example, a service package for the web includes an Apache web server, HTML files, and the server's configuration files.

Figure 2 illustrates how a self-configurable server group adjusts the number of mirror servers. Here, the group consists of 10 (A to J) server nodes. As can be seen in Fig. 2 (a), two server nodes A and B are providing a service. These server nodes are called *running* nodes. The other nodes (C to J), called *idle* nodes, do not provide any services. Server node A in Fig. 2 (a), is a *well-known* node, which is the original source for the service provided.

(1) Acquisition of Service Package: First of all, an idle node accesses a well-known node to obtain node information (e.g. IP address and so on) on running nodes. If the idle node does not have a service package, it requests one of the running nodes to send one. In Fig. 2 (b), idle nodes D and E request the package from A, while nodes H and I request these from B. Well-known node A informs these idle nodes that B is also running the service. The running node sends the package to the idle node after receiving the request. Note that the running node can delay sending the package, e.g., until the load is reduced.

(2) Registration: After receiving a service package, an idle node announces its intention of helping a running node by registering itself as a *helper node.* A helper node is a candidate for the mirror server, and waits for a request from the running node to start the service. Idle nodes D and E in Fig. 2 (c) register themselves on running node A, and wait for A to request them to start the service.

(3) Starting Service: To request a helper node to start a service, a running node monitors its own CPU load and the number of accesses from clients. If the running node determines that this is too heavy to manage all accesses from the client, it requests the helper nodes to start the service. As running nodes A and B

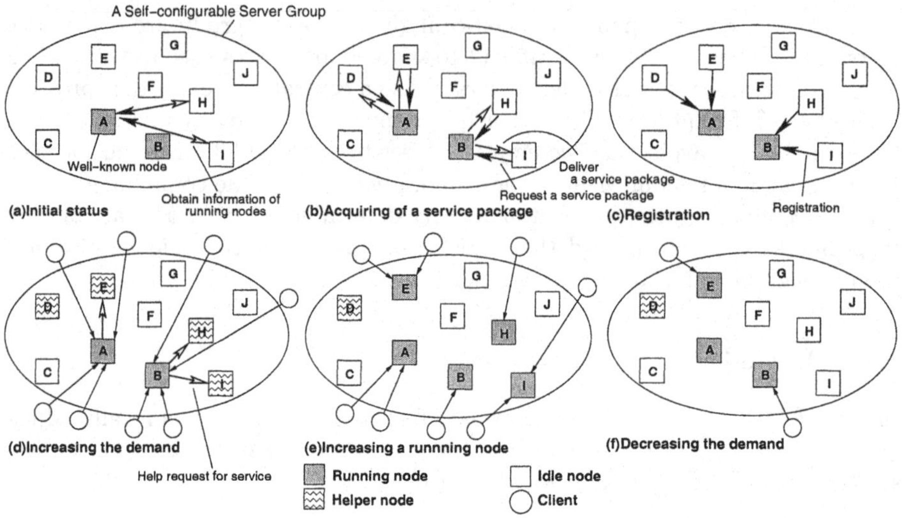

Fig. 2. Basic operation of self-configurable server groups.

in Fig. 2 (d) have become heavily loaded, this results in increased demand for the service. Thus, running node A requests helper node E to start the service. In the same way, helper nodes H and I start the service at B's request. Consequently, there are five running nodes (A, B, E, H, I) in Fig. 2 (e). The load can be shared between these running nodes because there are more mirror servers.

Service-Stopping Phase:
A running node, other than a well-known node, can cease providing a service independently of the other server nodes. It typically stops the service when demand for the service decreases significantly. Because a running node monitors its own CPU load and the number of accesses from clients, it can decide when to stop the service. To prevent all server nodes from stopping a specific service, a well-known node must continue services even if no accesses from clients are attempted. Server nodes H and I in Fig. 2 (f) cease the service in response to the decreased demand. Section 3 discusses the policy used to determine when to stop a service in more detail. To restart the service, the server node that stopped the service must register itself again and be requested to start the service. The protocol used to implement a self-configurable server group is listed in Tables 1.

3 Customizable Policies

The mechanism described in Section 2.2 is controlled by a set of policies that determines when and where to start or stop mirror servers. The system designer or administrator can define tailor-made policies to meet various service user needs. For example, we can discriminate between the quality of two services; one is prioritized higher so that its overall delay has to be reduced more than the

Table 1. List of messages.

(Explanatory Note)

<table>
<tr><td>Message name</td><td>argument</td></tr>
<tr><td colspan="2">Description of this message</td></tr>
</table>

<table>
<tr><td>INFO</td><td>service-name !C*</td></tr>
<tr><td colspan="2">This message is used to obtain information on the service specified by service-name. The server node that received this message sends back the name and file size of the service package, and the IP addresses of the mirror servers. If the receiver does not know the specified service, an error message is returned. If the letter "*" is specified as a service-name, the receiver returns information on all services it knows.</td></tr>
<tr><td>REGISTER</td><td>service-name</td></tr>
<tr><td colspan="2">This message is used by an idle node to announce its intention of helping a running node. The running node that receives this message registers the sending idle node as a helper node, if it is running the service specified by service-name. Otherwise, an error message is returned.</td></tr>
<tr><td>UNREGISTER</td><td>service-name</td></tr>
<tr><td colspan="2">A helper node uses this message to cancel its intention of helping a running node. The service-name specifies the service that the helper node was going to help. If the sending node is not registered as the helper node of the service-name, an error message is returned.</td></tr>
<tr><td>GET</td><td>service-name</td></tr>
<tr><td colspan="2">This message is used to obtain a service-name service package. If the received node has this, it sends it at the time determined by the service-acquisition policy.</td></tr>
<tr><td>START</td><td>service-name</td></tr>
<tr><td colspan="2">This message is sent by a running node to request a helper node to start the service specified by service-name. After receiving this message, a helper node starts the service and becomes a running node of the service.</td></tr>
<tr><td>STOP</td><td>service-name</td></tr>
<tr><td colspan="2">In case of emergencies, e.g., when a critical security hole is found, this message is used to stop the service specified by service-name.</td></tr>
<tr><td>ADVERTISE</td><td>service-name</td></tr>
<tr><td colspan="2">When a helper node starts the service specified by service-name, this message is sent to some "neighbor" nodes (obtained by INFO message) to advertise the fact that the helper node is now running the service.</td></tr>
<tr><td>UNADVERTISE</td><td>service-name</td></tr>
<tr><td colspan="2">When a running node stops the service specified by service-name, this message is sent to all the helper nodes registered on the running node to inform them that they can no longer help this running node.</td></tr>
</table>

other. In a self-configurable server group, we can define the following policies. Note that no policy can utilize global information because our mechanism does not allow global states to be shared. Rather, each policy must be designed to only utilize local information — such as the CPU load of the node on which the policy is evaluated.

Policies Used by Idle Nodes

- **Policy for Requesting Service Package:** This policy is used to select the node from which a service package is obtained. Before starting a service, an idle node obtains a list of the running nodes for the service, evaluates the policy, and selects the node from which it will request a service package. For example, we can select a node based proximity within the network.
- **Policy for Registration:** This policy determines to *which* and *how many* running nodes the intention to provide a service should be sent. For example, an idle node can register itself as a helper all over the network. Conversely, it can be registered on just a few neighbor nodes.

Policies Used by Running Nodes

- **Policy for Distributing a Service Package:** This policy determines when a service package is to be distributed. As mentioned earlier, a running node need not send a service package immediately it is requested to. For example, a running node may send the package when its own load is sufficiently low not to affect the performance of the service. Conversely, it can send the package immediately on request so that the helper node is ready as soon as possible.
- **Policy for Starting Helper Nodes:** This policy determines 1) when to request a helper node to start a service, and 2) which and how many helper nodes are requested. For example, a running node requests helper nodes to start a service when its own CPU load exceeds a pre-defined threshold. The running node may select the helper nodes from the "busy" area from which many clients are accessing to the node so that the mirror servers can be effectively deployed. In another example, if the peak time has been statistically established, a running node can request helper nodes to start a service before this peak occurs.
- **Policy for Stopping a Service:** This policy determines when to stop a service. Typically, a running node ceases a service when the number of access attempts from clients drops to a pre-defined threshold.

4 Design of Self-configurable Server Groups

This section provides details on the design of the implementation for the proposed system. Section 4.1 describes the implementation of the mechanism while Section 4.2 describes customizable policies.

4.1 Modules

The mechanism for self-configurable server groups is composed of three modules: the protocol processing module, the monitoring module and the dispatcher module (Fig. 3). These modules form the daemon process for the proposed mechanism which is on each server node. The details on each module are as follows.

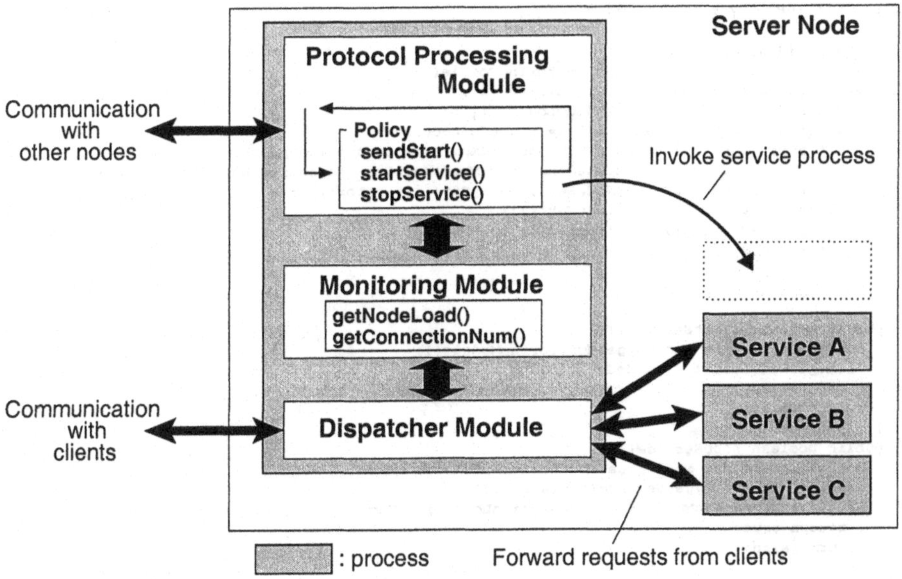

Fig. 3. Basic design of self-configurable server groups.

- **Protocol Processing Module:** This module has three main roles. First, it communicates with daemon processes on other server nodes by exchanging messages that obey the protocol defined by the proposed system. Whether or not to send INFO, REGISTER and START messages and the destination nodes of these messages are determined based on the given policies. Second, this module manages service packages that have been received from other mirror servers. Third, this module starts the service by creating a new server process in response to requests from other mirror servers. After creating a server process, it informs the monitoring module of various information (e.g., process ID) on the server process.
- **Monitoring Module:** This module continuously collects the statistical information of the node by monitoring the CPU load and the number of service requests for each service and so on. The protocol processing module refers this information to determine the current state of the node.
- **Dispatcher Module:** This module forwards each network connection from a client to the corresponding server process on the node. This forwarding makes it easy to update the service to a new version, while its old version is still running.

4.2 Description of a Policy

The system we propose is implemented in Java, and its policies are supplied by a class of Java. To customize the policies for a service, programmers have to extend, i.e., make a subclass of, the predefined abstract class `Policy`. There is a simple example in Fig. 4 that shows a definition of a subclass named `SamplePolicy`.

```
class SamplePolicy extends Policy {
  ...
  public void sendService(){
    MonitorModule m = Module.getMonitoringModule();
    ServiceInfo s = m.getServiceInfo(serv_id);
    if(getNodeMaxLoad() <= m.getNodeLoad() ||
      getConnectionUpperLimitNum() <= s.getConnectionNum()){
      int start_num = (int)((s.getConnectionNum()/getConnectionUpperLimitNum()+
                             s.getConnectionNum()/getConnectionLowerLimitNum()-1)/2);
      Iterator i = s.getHelperNodeSet().entrySet().iterator();
      while(start_num > 0 && i.hasNext()){
        s.getStartQueue().add(i.next());
        start_num--;
      }
    }
  }
  public boolean startService(){
    MonitorModule m = Module.getMonitoringModule();
    if(m.getNodeLoad() < getNodeMaxLoad())
      return true;
    return false;
  }
  public boolean stopService(){
    MonitorModule m = Module.getMonitoringModule();
    ServiceInfo s = m.getServiceInfo(serv_id);
    if(s.getConnectionNum() < getConnectionLowerLimitNum())
      return true;
    return false;
  }
  ...
}
```

Fig. 4. SamplePolicy class.

Each policy that can be customized corresponds to an instance method in Policy, and designers and administrators who want to customize these have to define a new subclass of Policy and override the instance method by a method defined in the subclass. For example, the method startService() decides the policy for starting helper nodes, and the method stopService() decides the policy for stopping a service.

Instance methods that describe policies are able to refer to the statistical information collected by the monitoring module using methods in the Monitor Module class. For example, in Fig. 4, startService() method calls getNode Load() method to obtain the current CPU load of the node, and stopService() method uses getConnectionNum() method to obtain the number of connections for the service.

As we can see from Fig. 3, policies defined in a subclass of Policy are referred by the protocol processing module.

5 Simulations

This section discusses the results we obtained from simulating the basic mechanism of self-configurable server groups. The purpose of these simulations was to insure that the proposed system was really effective in adjusting the number of mirror servers autonomously according to given policies.

5.1 Simulation Environment

Physical Network and Nodes: The physical network is a mesh topology with a size of 10 × 10 nodes. The network latency NL between two nodes in the mesh is proportional to their Manhattan distance D and the number of packets p. Thus,

$$NL = k \cdot p \cdot s \cdot D, \tag{1}$$

where k is a constant.

We define the packet size s as 1.5 KB because the MTU size of the Ethernet is 1.5 KB. A message of the self-configurable server groups protocol, a request from a client, and a reply message from a server node consists of one packet. Each service package is the same size as 500 packets (750 KB). We set the proportionality constant of network latency at $k = 4$, which means that the communication speed between the nearest two nodes is 2 Mbps and that of the farthest two nodes is 0.111 Mbps. All server nodes were assumed to have the same computing power.

Clients and Mirror Servers: The locations of clients were randomly selected from nodes in the physical network. Each client also randomly selected a mirror server from running ones, to which the client had sent a service request.

Service Processing and Latency Times: We assumed that service processing time ST_i for service i by a mirror server depended on total load l of the server; when the load was small (i.e., less than some threshold L^{bound}), ST_i took constant time c_i. When the load becomes heavier, ST_i increases because of the race to access the resources. Thus, service processing time ST_i is defined as follows:

$$ST_i = \begin{cases} c_i & l \leq L^{bound} \\ c_i + k'_i(l - L^{bound}) & \text{otherwise} \end{cases} \tag{2}$$

where k'_i is the proportionality constant of service processing time. Since all server nodes have the same power, ST_i is independent of each node.

For a client, service latency SL_i for service i is the sum of twice the network latency NL and service processing time ST_i on the server.

$$SL_i = 2 \cdot NL + ST_i \tag{3}$$

We assumed that c_i, k'_i and ST_i (and thus SL_i) were independent of i, so we omit the subscript and simply describe them as c, k', ST and SL. We set the constant of service processing time c to 5 milliseconds and the proportionality constant of service processing time k' to 2.0.

5.2 Policies

To determine the policies for simulations, we adopted the following conditions concerning the load of each mirror server.

- The total load l of all services must not be larger than the maximum limit L^{max}.

– The load of the i-th service l_i has to be between the lower limit l_i^{lower} and the upper limit l_i^{upper}.

The former is a condition that keeps the service time within an acceptable latency. The latter means that a node's load for service i must be within an appropriate range, i.e., with not too few or too many access attempts.

These conditions can be expressed as:

$$\begin{cases} l \leq L^{max} \\ l_i^{lower} \leq l_i \leq l_i^{upper}. \end{cases} \tag{4}$$

Note that $l = \sum_i l_i$. Additionally, l_i^{lower} and l_i^{upper} have to satisfy the following equations.

$$\begin{cases} \sum_i l_i^{lower} \leq L^{max} \\ l_i^{lower} \leq l_i^{upper} \leq L^{max} \end{cases} \tag{5}$$

We defined the policies we used in simulations based on the above conditions.

Policy for Starting Helper Nodes: If the load of a node increases so that it does not satisfy condition (4), i.e., $L^{max} < l$ or $l_i^{upper} < l_i$, the node requests some of the helper nodes to start the service. Customizable policy is used here to decide the appropriate number of helper nodes to which requests are sent.

If a server issues a_i requests to helper nodes, the number of server nodes around it becomes $1 + a_i$, so the server load is expected to be $l_i/(1 + a_i)$. Thus, a_i has to be determined to satisfy $l_i^{lower} \leq l_i/(1+a_i) \leq l_i^{upper}$. Notice that a_i can be set to any value that satisfies this inequality. We selected a_i so that $l_i/(1+a_i)$ was close to $(l_i^{lower} + l_i^{upper})/2$.

Policy for Stopping Service: If the load of service i of a node become $l_i < l_i^{min}$, the server stops service, except where the server is well-known for the service.

Other Policies: We did not use information on the distance between nodes for policies, because we mostly found that self-configurable server groups have the ability to resolve temporal fluctuations. The following discusses the customizable policies in Section 3.

The package request policy is where a node randomly sends requests to some of the currently running mirror servers. The registration policy is where a node randomly send registration messages to mirror server nodes. The package distribution policy when a node receives a package request, it immediately replies with a service package.

5.3 Results

We assume that one time unit in the simulations corresponded to 1 millisecond. Each simulation was executed in 180 million time units (30 minutes). The total number of service requests from clients periodically fluctuated between 0 and 3000. As there were 100 or fewer server nodes, the number of accesses per node was expected to be less than 100. We thus set L^{max}, the maximum load for each server node, to 100, which was a larger value than the average number of accesses. We also set L^{bound} to 35. We conducted two types of simulations where each measured the latency in a service.

In simulation (1), we established the same priority for both services A and B by giving them the same policy ($l_A^{upper} = l_B^{upper} = 60$ and $l_A^{lower} = l_B^{lower} = 15$). The purpose of this was to insure that the system we propose can restrict service latency within an appropriate range even if client accesses increase.

The results for this simulation are in Fig. 5 (1). Service B starts after 56,250 time units have elapsed. This clearly shows that this system can quickly adapt to dynamic fluctuations in access from clients.

When the average number of accesses to each node comes close to upper limit $l_i^{upper}(= 60)$, the running nodes increase and the load is shared among many mirror servers. In the meanwhile, when the average number of accesses to each node comes close to lower limit $l_i^{lower}(= 15)$, some of the running nodes spontaneously stop the service to conserve resources.

This also means that the increased demand on one service does not seriously affect the other service's latency. The average time of latency is approximately between 100 and 180 milliseconds for both services. This demonstrates that the new system can effectively provide many services.

We applied different policies for services A and B. Since $l_B^{upper}(= 45)$ was set lower than $l_A^{upper}(= 75)$, service B had a higher priority than service A and thus the mirror servers for B were expected to increase more rapidly (Fig. 5 (2)). Compared to the results for simulation (1), the latency for service B with a higher priority is shorter by 9.0%, sacrificing the increase in latency for service A. This is also supported by the number of running nodes (Fig. 5), where service B has more than service A. Therefore, we can control the QoS by applying different policies to different services.

6 Related Work

Bernardo et al. [2] proposed a dynamic content distribution system in response to changes in the Internet environment. Its main purpose was to automatically achieve scalable services. It deployed server agents to use location servers to provide lookup services and manage server agent information. Their mechanism was different from the one we proposed in this paper in that it needed location servers to be hierarchized while our mechanism allows nodes to communicate with one another in a peer-to-peer manner without hierarchy.

Hadas [3] and FarGo [4–6] can effectively adapt a network service by deploying application components and their layouts of components in response to changes in a node's load and the effective bandwidth between components. Since their aim was to automatically layout components, they could not autonomously adjust the number of mirror servers according to fluctuations in service requests.

Akamai's [7] purpose was to decrease the download time from web servers. A client is able to download cached contents automatically from the closest

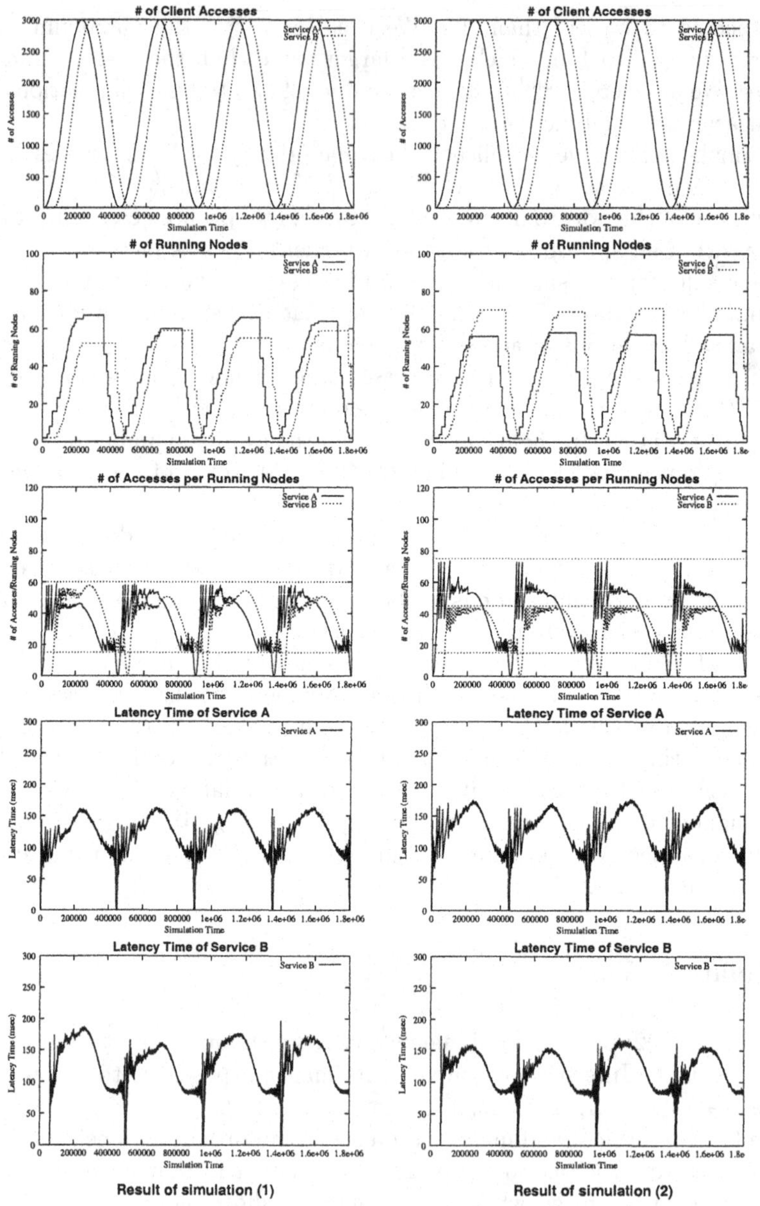

Fig. 5. Results of simulations.

Akamai server, which can reduce latency time and effectively conserve network bandwidth. This mechanism is the automatic distribution of service requests to the server nearest the client without adjusting the number of server nodes.

There are many related works [8–12] that are designed for data centers, hosting centers or clusters, but do not target an Internet-wide collection of servers.

HotRod [8] can adjust the number of servers on the basis of long-term or short-term predictions. This system resembles ours in that it can dynamically change the number of servers. However, the exploited mechanisms are totally different. Each node in our mechanism autonomously behaves in response to local information such as CPU load, while HotRod changes the number of servers according to a plan established by monitoring all server nodes in a cluster.

The N1 Provisioning Server [9] is a management system for many server machines inside a data center, and the Oceano project [10] is a scalable infrastructure that are easy to administer for utility computing. Like our system, the server program is automatically distributed in these systems. The purpose of this automatic distribution is to configure a recently added machine in N1, or to control the number of server nodes in Oceano, but they do not target the server machines all over the Internet.

Muse [11] is an operating system for hosting centers that can manage energy and server resources. Pinheiro et al. [12] also focus on the resource and energy used by a cluster. They dynamically control the number of nodes offering services based on load, but unlike our system, they are mainly interested in energy management.

7 Conclusion

This paper proposed a new system called self-configurable server groups as the basis for network servers to autonomously adjust the numbers and locations of mirror servers according to fluctuations in service demand. Since the system allows individual policies to be decided to cope with these fluctuations, the administrators are able customize the way they offer services. Simulation results revealed that the system we propose is very effective in automatically adjusting the number of mirror servers according to two kinds of policies.

References

1. Iyengar, A., Squillante, M., Zhang, L.: Analysis and Characterization of Large-scale Web Server Access Patterns and Performance. In World Wide Web Journal (Baltzer) (1999)
2. Bernardo, L., Pinto, P.: Scalable Service Deployment using Mobile Agents. In: 2nd Int'l Workshop on Mobile Agents (MA'98), Lecture Notes in Computer Science 1477 (1998) 261–272
3. Ben-Shaul, I., Holder, O., Lavva, B.: Dynamic Adaptation and Deployment of Distributed Components In Hadas. IEEE Transactions on Software Engineering **27** (2001) 769–787
4. Holder, O., Ben-Shaul, I., Gazit, H.: Dynamic Layout of Distributed Applications in FarGo. In: Int'l Conf. on Software Engineering. (1999) 163–173
5. Holder, O., Ben-Shaul, I., Gazit, H.: System Support for Dynamic Layout of Distributed Applications. In: Proc. 19th Int'l Conf. Distributed Computing Systems (ICDCS'99). (1999) 403–411

6. Ben-Shaul, I., Gazit, H., Holder, O., Lavva, B.: Dynamic Self Adaptation in Distributed Systems. In: 1st Int'l Workshop on Self-Adaptive Software (IWSAS 2000). Lecture Notes in Computer Science 1936 (2001) 134–142
7. Akamai. (http://www.akamai.com)
8. IBM: HotRod. (http://www-6.ibm.com/jp/autonomic/casestudies/hotrod_eg. html)
9. Sun Microsystems: N1 Provisioning Server. (http://wwws.sun.com/software/ products/provisioning_server/)
10. IBM Research: The Oceano Project. (http://www.research.ibm.com/oceano project/)
11. Chase, J.S., Anderson, D.C., Thakar, P.N., Vahdat, A., Doyle, R.P.: Managing Energy and Server Resources in Hosting Centres. In: Symposium on Operating Systems Principles (SOSP'01). (2001) 103–116
12. Pinheiro, E., Bianchini, R., Carrera, E.V., Heath, T.: Dynamic Cluster Reconfiguration for Power and Performance. In: Compilers and Operating Systems for Low Power, Kluwer Academic Publishers (2002)

Information Flow Security for XML Transformations

Véronique Benzaken[1], Marwan Burelle[1], and Giuseppe Castagna[2]

[1] LRI (CNRS), Université Paris-Sud, Orsay, France
[2] CNRS, Département d'Informatique, École Normale Supérieure, Paris, France

Abstract. We provide a formal definition of information flows in XML transformations and, more generally, in the presence of type driven computations and describe a sound technique to detect transformations that may leak private or confidential information. We also outline a general framework to check middleware-located information flows.

1 Introduction

XML is becoming the *de facto* standard document format for data on the Web. Its diffusion however is characterized by two correlated paradoxes:

1. Despite the increasing success of XML for exchanging and manipulating information on the Web, little attention has been paid to characterize and analyze information flows of XML transformations and, specifically, their security implications.
2. As shown by the standardization process, XML documents are intrinsically typed (cf. the notions of well-formedness and validity). Nevertheless, the "standard" programming languages used to manipulate them are essentially untyped, in the sense that even when they are equipped with a type system the latter does not use the type information of XML documents.

If we consider the self-descriptive nature of XML documents, these paradoxes are less surprising than it may seem: XML documents use tags to delimit some content, and these tags can be considered as type information about the content they delimit. Therefore, XML documents—even those that do not contain a DTD—are in some sense "self-typed" constructions and this makes the definition of a type system for XML transformers difficult. As long as a type system often constitutes a first basic step toward the definition of security analyses of transformations, this may partially explain the absence of formal tools to characterize insecure information flows.

Goal. The aim of this article is to define and characterize information flows in XML transformations in order to single out potentially insecure transformations, that is transformations that may leak confidential or private information. To that end we study transformations defined in a typed programming language for XML documents. There are several candidates for such a language, since several attempts have been made in the literature to overcome the second of the XML paradoxes (e.g., HaXML [21], JWIG [3], Xtatic [11], XDuce [13], XQuery [8], and YATL [4]).

In this work we characterize and analyze information flows for transformations defined in ℂDuce [2]. There are several reasons to choose ℂDuce as target language for our study. First and foremost, unlike other XML-oriented languages, ℂDuce is general

V.A. Saraswat (Ed.): ASIAN 2003, LNCS 2896, pp. 33–53, 2003.

purpose, in that it provides besides XML types several other datatypes, enabling to program general (even XML unrelated) applications. Second, among the known languages for XML, it possesses the richest type algebra. Finally, its semantic and set theoretic foundations make it a good candidate for defining or hosting a declarative query language (see [2]) and, as such, it nicely fits our scenario of global queries on the Web.

Problems. We said that the difficulty of defining type systems for XML transformations resides in the self-typing nature of the documents. More precisely, this self-typing characteristic induces "type based" (or "type driven") computations: matching on document tags roughly corresponds to matching documents' types; similarly, producing elements with different tags corresponds to outputting results of different types. In some sense, typed XML transformations are akin to the application of **typecase** constructions where the different cases may return differently typed results (this is accounted for in ℂDuce by the use of *dynamically bound* overloaded functions). The presence of type driven computations makes the task of capturing information flows much harder and constitutes the main novelty and challenge of this study. In fact we cannot resort to classical data flow analyses since they are usually applied to computational frameworks whose dynamic semantics does not strictly depend on run-time types. A second challenge is that information flows (more precisely, their absence) are usually characterized in terms of the so-called *non-interference* property [12]. Our study demonstrates that in the presence of type driven computations this notion must be modified so as to include static type knowledge, otherwise we end up with very trivial analyses. Finally, the last challenge is to define flow analysis for a pattern-matching based language—as ℂDuce is—since this stands at least two obstacles: (*i*) pattern matching is a dynamic type-case, therefore we have to propagate type information in the subsequent matches; (*ii*) the use of a matching policy (first-match as in ℂDuce or best match as in XSLT) induces dependencies among the different components of an alternative pattern as well as among different cases of a pattern-matching expression and this must be taken into account when characterizing information flows (the sole fact of knowing that a pattern did *not* match may produce a flow of information).

Contributions. The contributions of this article are essentially three:

1. it provides a formal definition and study of information flows in the context of XML transformations and, more generally, in the presence of type driven computations;
2. it describes a sound technique to detect XML document transformations that cause insecure information flows, and formally proves its correctness;
3. by defining security annotations and by relating various kind of analyses (static/dynamic, sound/complete) to different query scenarios, it proposes a general framework for checking security of middleware-located information flows.

Example. The development of our presentation can be illustrated by an example. Consider the following XML document which stores names and salaries of the workers of a fictive company. We imagine that while generic users are allowed to perform queries on this document, the information about salaries must only be accessible to authorized users. Therefore we need a way to detect queries that may reveal information about salaries, in order to reject them when they are performed by unauthorized users. A first naive technique to obtain it would be to mark the salary elements and dynamically reject all queries that contain marks in their result. Unfortunately, this approach is clearly inadequate since the information about salaries can be deduced as follows: perform a query that returns the list of all workers whose salary is greater than n and then iterate the query by varying n until we obtain as many different results as workers.

```xml
<?xml version="1.0"?>
<company>
  <worker>
    <surname>Durand</surname>
    <name>Paul</name>
    <salary>6500</salary>
  </worker>
  <worker>
    <surname>Dupond</surname>
    <name>Jean</name>
    <salary>1800</salary>
  </worker>
  <worker>
    <surname>Martin</surname>
    <name>Jules</name>
    <salary>1200</salary>
  </worker>
</company>
```

A more effective solution is to reject all the queries whose result *accesses* the value of the salary elements. For example consider the following two queries:

[Q1] Get the list of all workers

[Q2] Get the list of all workers whose salary is greater than € 1600

The first query can be always safely executed while the second one must be forbidden to unauthorized users. This can be obtained by enforcing an access control policy. For instance this is done in [7, 6] by executing a query on a *view* (in the database sense) obtained by pruning from the XML documents all data the owner of the query has not the right to access.

While enforcing access control is enough for simple policies like the above, it soon becomes inadequate with slightly more complicated policies. For instance imagine that instead of forbidding access to salaries we want to allow queries owned by generic users to access salaries (e.g. for statistical purposes) but in a way that prevents these queries from associating a specific worker with her/his salary. This corresponds to rejecting all queries whose result *depends* both on the value of salary elements and on that of name or surname elements (but queries like Q1 or a query that returns all salaries are acceptable). To enforce this constraint we have to switch from an *access* analysis to a *dependency* (or information flow) analysis[1].

Causal security policies, such as above, can be formalized by the notion of *non-interference*, that can be restated for XML documents as follows: a set of elements does not interfere with the result of a given query if for all possible contents of the elements the query always returns the same result. In our example, consider the set of all documents obtained from our XML document by replacing the content of salary elements by arbitrary numeric values. Query Q1 is interference-free since when it is applied to all these documents it always returns the same result. Query Q2 instead is not interference-free since its results may differ.

A precise definition of non-interference constitutes the first step of our approach since it defines the set of queries that are safe. The following step is to devise one or more techniques to determine the safety/unsafety of queries. To that end we first classify components that store confidential information by annotating data elements by labels of the form ℓ_t. The ℓ intuitively represents a security classification of the information stored in the element (e.g., public or private, but it could be any label from a possibly unordered set) while t is a type that describes the static information publicly available about the data's content (e.g. for salaries it records that the element stores an integer

[1] While for this specific example it is still possible to resort to access control techniques (execute the query on two different views obtained by stripping in one all salaries and in the other all names and surnames) these sole techniques soon become insufficient, as shown by the example in Section 6.

in a given range)[2]. Next we recast the notion of non-interference in terms of labeled elements, namely, we say that a transformation is free of interference from all elements labeled by ℓ, if its result does not change when the content of the ℓ-labeled elements vary over the type indicated in the label. Our research plan consists of the definition of three different analyses to be used as in the scenario of Figure 1 in the next page. According to it an interactive query (that is, a query that was written to be executed just once) will first pass through a complete static analysis (that rejects transformations that are manifestly unsafe) and then through a sound dynamic analysis. Instead, programs that are expected to be used several times will pass through a cycle of sound static analysis (possibly preceded by a complete analysis) before being executed without any further dynamic check. In this paper we concentrate on the sound dynamic analysis for $\mathbb{C}$Duce programs, that is, the grayed part of the figure.

Outline. We start in Section 2 by a brief overview of the functional core of $\mathbb{C}$Duce. In Section 3 we formally define the non-interference property for $\mathbb{C}$Duce programs and introduce $\mathbb{C}\text{Duce}_{\mathscr{L}}$ a conservative extension[3] of $\mathbb{C}$Duce in which expressions occurring in a program may appear labeled by security labels. Section 4 is the core of our work. It defines the dynamic analysis that detects interference free programs. The idea is to define an operational semantics for $\mathbb{C}\text{Duce}_{\mathscr{L}}$ such that (i) it preserves the semantics of unlabeled programs and (ii) it ensures that whenever a label ℓ is absent from the final result of a program, then the program is free of interference from all expressions labeled by ℓ. Thanks to these properties the analyzer has simply to label and run a transformation and to refuse to return the (unlabeled) result when this contains unauthorized labels. Of course the heart of the problem is label propagation in pattern matching, whose definition is made difficult by the type driven semantics, the presence of subtyping, and the use of a first-match policy. In Section 5 we prove that our analysis satisfies the aforementioned properties; this goes through proving that $\mathbb{C}\text{Duce}_{\mathscr{L}}$ satisfies the subject-reduction property, that it preserves the semantics of $\mathbb{C}$Duce, and that it constitutes a sound analysis for the non-interference property. The last two points present some technical difficulties (without any practical impact) due to the type system of $\mathbb{C}$Duce that does not satisfy the minimum typing property and induces in $\mathbb{C}\text{Duce}_{\mathscr{L}}$ a non-deterministic seman-

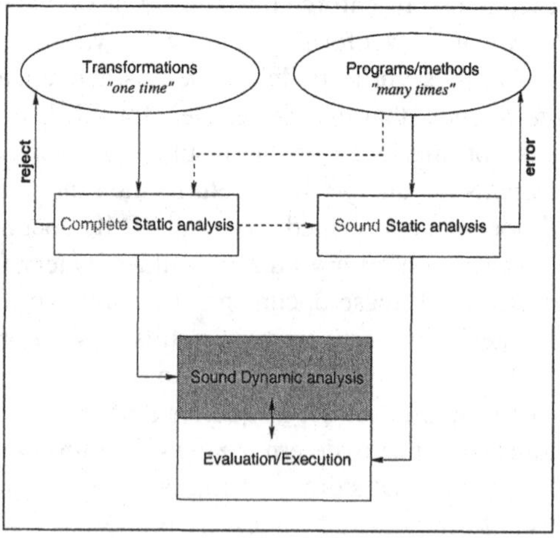

Fig. 1. Analysis scenarios

[2] We do not require the existence of any order on such labels (in our framework security policies will be expressed in terms of presence/absence rather than relative order of label), therefore our labels must not to be confounded with the security labels used in multilevel security systems.

[3] The extension is conservative with respect to both the type theory and the equational (reduction) theory.

tics: thus the two properties must be proved to hold for *all* possible reductions of a program. In Section 6 we comment a more significant example that illustrates some security policies that cannot be expressed in terms of access control. We conclude our presentation by sketching in Section 7 some research perspectives.

Related Work. Security issues for XML have been addressed by several works but none of them tackles the problem of information flows. They either focus on access control (e.g., [10, 7, 6]) or on lower level security features such as encryption and digital signatures for which commercial products are becoming available (e.g [14]). For instance, Damiani et al. [7, 6] detect accesses to confidential data by applying a static marking of the documents and by dynamically stripping off marked elements. In other words, they deal with access control (confidential *data* is *accessed* for computing the result) whereas our approach accounts for implicit flows (confidential *information* can be *inferred* from the result) like the detection of covert channels. The same holds true for the work of Gabillon and Bruno [10] where access control is performed by running queries on *views* of the XML documents dynamically generated by stripping off unauthorized data. Other works devise flow analyses for programming languages for XML (e.g., [3]) but these analyses are not developed to verify security properties.

The study presented here draws ideas from several sources. The dynamic propagation of labels was first introduced in Abadi et al. [1], where a dependency analysis for call-by-name λ-calculus is defined by extending the reduction semantics to labeled λ-terms. Although their work was not motivated by security reasons (they address optimization issues) what we describe here essentially adapts their technique to type driven reductions. Label propagation was successively used for security purposes in later works, for instance [5, 15–17]. In particular, in [15] Myers and Liskov use labels for the same purposes as we do; however their security model is defined for and relies on languages that explicitly manipulate labels, while in our or in Abadi's et al. approach, properties are stated for an unlabeled language and labels are introduced on the top of it as a technique to identify (unlabeled) programs satisfying these properties. Finally, all the cited label-based approaches fundamentally differ from the study presented here in that they do not account for type driven semantics (nor for pattern matching) distinctive of XML transformations.

The presence of type driven computations preclude us the use of classical definitions and detection techniques of non-interference (e.g. those of [19, 20]), since in this case ignoring static type information would yield a far too weak definition of non-interference. Actually, our notion of non-interference differs from the classical one in that the latter usually relies on a hierarchical structuring of security levels (high-level inputs do not interfere with low-level outputs) while here we spot non-interference of single pieces of code (the value of some data does not interfere with the result of a query). This difference must be understood as the fact that we want to characterize the flows in a single transformation while classical non-interference rather applies to system-wide flows.

2 The CDuce Language

```
<company>[
  <worker>[
    <surname>"Durand"
    <name>"Paul"
    <salary>[6500] ]
  <worker>[
    <surname>"Dupond"
    <name>"Jean"
    <salary>[1800] ]
  <worker>[
    <surname>"Martin"
    <name>"Jules"
    <salary>[1200] ]
]

type Company = <company>[Worker*]
type Worker  = <worker>[Sname Name Salary]
type Sname   = <surname>String
type Name    = <name>String
type Salary  = <salary>[Int]
```

ℂDuce is a functional programming language tailored to the manipulation of XML documents, for which it uses its own notation. The XML document in the previous section becomes in ℂDuce the expression on the right. The syntax is mostly self describing: tags are denoted by angle brackets and are followed by sequences. Sequences are delimited by square brackets and in this case are formed by other elements, but in general they may contain expressions of any type (note that some tags are followed by strings as the latter are encoded in ℂDuce as sequences of characters). This expression has the type Company defined right below it. The types of sequences are defined by regular expressions on types. For example, the first type declaration states that a company is a sequence tagged by <company> and composed of zero or more worker elements. Had we defined the type of workers as follows:

```
Worker2 = <worker ceo=?Bool>[ Sname Name Salary (Email | Tel)? ]
```

then workers elements would have an optional (as indicated by =?) boolean attribute and list a last optional element that is either of type Tel or of type Email. Note also that Worker is a subtype of Worker2 since every value of the former type is also a value of the latter type. The queries defined in the previous section can be expressed as:

```
[Q1:] let <company>x = mycompany in transform x with <worker>[ y z _ ] → [ <worker>[ y z ] ]

[Q2:] type MoreThanMe = <salary>[1600--*]
        let <company>x = mycompany in transform x with <worker>[ y z MoreThanMe ] → [ <worker>[ y z ] ]
```

where mycompany is a variable that denotes our previous <company> XML document.

In the first query the let expression matches mycompany against a pattern that binds the variable x to the sequence of worker elements of mycompany. The transform expression applies to each element of a sequence a pattern that returns a sequence and then concatenates all the results (non matching elements are simply discarded). In this case it transforms the sequence of Worker elements into a sequence of <worker>-tagged elements containing just surname and name elements (y and z respectively capture the surname and name elements, while the _ pattern matches every value). Had we defined the type Company as <company>[(Worker|Client)*], that is a heterogeneous sequence of workers and clients, then Q1 would still have returned the same result as transform would discard client elements. The query Q2 is similar, with the only difference that the transform pattern matches only if the salary element has type MoreThanMe, that is, if its content is an integer greater than or equal to 1600[4].

A detailed presentation of ℂDuce is out of the scope of this paper. The interested reader can refer to [2] and try the interactive prototype at www.cduce.org. For the purpose

[4] The results the two queries are the central and right expressions in Figure 4 from which we erase all the label annotations of the form ℓ_t:, m_t:, or n_t:.

of this work it will suffice to say that all ℂDuce constructions are encoded in the following core language defined in [9]:

$$t ::= \alpha \mid C \mid \mu\alpha.C \quad C ::= A \mid \neg C \mid C \vee C \mid C \wedge C \quad A ::= t \rightarrow t \mid t \times t \mid b \mid \mathbf{0} \mid \mathbf{1}$$

We use t to range over types, C over boolean combinations, A over atoms, and b over basic types (Int, Char, ...); **0** and **1** denote respectively the empty and top type, and together with arrows and products they form the atoms of arbitrary boolean combinations (negation, union, and intersection types) and recursive types $\mu\alpha.C$ [5]. The expressions of the language are:

$$e ::= c \mid x \mid \mathsf{fun}\ f^{(t_1 \rightarrow s_1;\ldots;t_n \rightarrow s_n)}(x).e \mid e_1 e_2 \mid (e_1,e_2) \mid \mathsf{match}\ e\ \mathsf{with}\ p_1 \Rightarrow e_1 \mid p_2 \Rightarrow e_2$$

The syntax is essentially that of a higher-order functional language with constants, pairs and pattern-matching. What distinguishes it from similar languages is the definition of patterns (given later) and of functions. In the latter note that the name of a function (which may appear in its body as functions can be recursive) is annotated by a non empty list of arrow types (this list is called the *interface* of the function). The presence of more than one arrow type declares the overloaded nature of the function, which has all these types, thus their intersection as well (see the typing rule for functions later on).

The operational semantics is defined in terms of the set $\mathscr{V}$ of *values*, ranged over by v and formed by all *closed* and *well-typed* ℂDuce expressions of the form

$$v \quad ::= \quad c \mid \mathsf{fun}\ f^{(t_1 \rightarrow s_1;\ldots;t_n \rightarrow s_n)}(x).e \mid (v_1,v_2)$$

The semantics is given by the reduction relation $\leadsto$, which is defined as follows:

$$\begin{array}{rcll} (v_1 v_2) & \leadsto & e[v_1/f; v_2/x] & (v_1 = \mathsf{fun} f^{(\ldots)}(x).e) \\ (\mathsf{match}\ v\ \mathsf{with}\ p_1 \Rightarrow e_1 \mid p_2 \Rightarrow e_2) & \leadsto & e_1[v/p_1] & (v/p_1 \neq \Omega) \\ (\mathsf{match}\ v\ \mathsf{with}\ p_1 \Rightarrow e_1 \mid p_2 \Rightarrow e_2) & \leadsto & e_2[v/p_2] & (v/p_1 = \Omega, v/p_2 \neq \Omega) \end{array}$$

where Ω denotes the matching failure and $e[v/p]$ is the expression obtained by applying the substitution v/p to e. The first rule is standard β-reduction for recursive functions. The second rule states that if the first pattern matches, then the expression of the first branch is executed after having applied to it the substitution v/p_1 of the variables captured by p_1 when matching v. The second rule states that the same happens for the second branch when the first pattern fails and the second matches (the static type system of ℂDuce ensures that the patterns cannot both fail).

Reductions can take place in any *evaluation context*. A *context*, denoted by $\mathscr{C}$ is an expression with a hole substituted for a sub-expression. An *evaluation context*, denoted by $\mathscr{E}$, is a context whose hole is not in the scope of an abstraction or of a pattern and which induces a (leftmost) evaluation order on applications and pairs. Formally, $e \leadsto e'$ implies $\mathscr{E}[e] \leadsto \mathscr{E}[e']$, where $\mathscr{E}$ is defined as

$$\mathscr{E} ::= [\,] \mid (\mathscr{E},e) \mid (v,\mathscr{E}) \mid \mathscr{E}e \mid v\mathscr{E} \mid \mathsf{match}\ \mathscr{E}\ \mathsf{with}\ p_1 \Rightarrow e_1 \mid p_2 \Rightarrow e_2$$

As anticipated, key definitions for ℂDuce are those of pattern and pattern matching. A regular tree built from the following grammar

$$p ::= x \mid t \mid p_1 \& p_2 \mid p_1 | p_2 \mid (p_1,p_2) \mid (x := c)$$

[5] The distinction between atoms and combinations is introduced in order to avoid meaningless recursive types such as $\mu\alpha.\alpha \vee \alpha$.

is a pattern if (*i*) on every infinite branch of it there are infinite occurrences of the pair constructor[6], (*ii*) patterns in an alternative capture the same variables, and (*iii*) patterns in a conjunction capture pairwise distinct variables. The semantics of patterns is defined by the matching operation: the matching of value v against a pattern p is denoted by v/p and returns either Ω (matching failure) or a substitution from the variables of p into $\mathscr{V}$:

$$
\begin{array}{llll}
v/t = \{\} & \text{if } v : t & v/t = \Omega & \text{if } v : \neg t \\
v/x = \{x \mapsto v\} & & v/(x := c) = \{x \mapsto c\} & \\
v/p_1|p_2 = v/p_1 & \text{if } v/p_1 \neq \Omega & v/p_1|p_2 = v/p_2 & \text{if } v/p_1 = \Omega \\
v/p_1 \& p_2 = v/p_1 \otimes v/p_2 & & v/(p_1,p_2) = \Omega & \text{if } v \text{ is not a pair} \\
(v_1,v_2)/(p_1,p_2) = v_1/p_1 \otimes v_2/p_2 & & &
\end{array}
$$

where $\gamma_1 \otimes \gamma_2$ is Ω when $\gamma_1 = \Omega$ or $\gamma_2 = \Omega$ and otherwise is the substitution $\gamma \in \mathscr{V}^{Dom(\gamma_1) \cup Dom(\gamma_2)}$ defined as $\gamma(x) = \gamma_1(x)$ when $x \in Dom(\gamma_1) \backslash Dom(\gamma_2)$, as $\gamma(x) = \gamma_2(x)$ when $x \in Dom(\gamma_2) \backslash Dom(\gamma_1)$, and as $\gamma(x) = (\gamma_1(x), \gamma_2(x))$ when $x \in Dom(\gamma_1) \cap Dom(\gamma_2)$.

The semantics of patterns is rather intuitive. There are two possible causes of failure for a pattern matching: a type constraint which is not satisfied by the matched value, or a pair pattern applied to a value that is not a pair. The alternative pattern $p_1|p_2$ has a first-match policy: the object is matched against p_2 if and only if the matching against p_1 fails. When a variable x appears on both sides of a pair pattern, the two captured elements are paired together as expressed by the third case of the definition of $\otimes$. The default-value pattern $(x := c)$ usually appears in the right-hand side of an alternative pattern to return a default value when the left-hand side fails. The combination of multiply-occurring variables and default-value patterns within recursive patterns allow very expressive captures: for instance, the recursive pattern $p = (x\&\mathsf{Int},p)|(\_,p)|(x{:=}\mathsf{nil})$ binds x to the sublist of all integers occurring in a heterogeneous list (encoded *à la* lisp) when this is matched against it. On the whole, all a pattern does is to decompose values in subcomponents that are bound to variables and/or matched against types, whence the type driven computation.

Values are also at the basis of the definition of subtyping. Indeed, the key characteristic of $\mathbb{C}$Duce (from which all others derive) is that the subtyping relation is defined semantically via a set theoretic interpretation of the types. This interpretation is very easy to define: a type is interpreted as the set of all values that have that type. So for example $t_1 \times t_2$ is the set of all expressions (v_1,v_2) where v_i is a value of type t_i; $t_1 \rightarrow t_2$ is the set of all closed functional expressions $\mathsf{fun}\, f^{(s_1;\ldots;s_n)}(x)e$ that when applied to a value of type t_1 return a result in t_2; union, intersection, and negation of types have the usual set theoretic meaning. This (semantic) interpretation is used to define the (syntactic) subtyping relation: a type s is a subtype of t if the interpretation of s is contained in the interpretation of t.

Typing rules for $\mathbb{C}$Duce are summarized in Figure 2. For a more detailed explanation the reader can refer to [9]. Rules (*var*), (*pair*), and (*subsum*) are standard. The rule (*appl*) is less common, since one usually expects t_1 to be of the form $s_1 \rightarrow s_2$ and the rule to infer for the application the type s_2 provided that $t_2 \leq s_1$. However because of the

[6] Infinite trees represent recursive patterns while the condition on infinite branches endows the set of patterns with a well-founded order that ensures termination for the algorithms of typing and matching.

$$\frac{}{\Gamma \vdash x : \Gamma(x)}\ (var) \qquad \frac{\Gamma \vdash e_1 : t_1 \quad \Gamma \vdash e_2 : t_2}{\Gamma \vdash (e_1,e_2) : t_1 \times t_2}\ (pair) \qquad \frac{\Gamma \vdash e_1 : t_1 \quad \Gamma \vdash e_2 : t_2}{\Gamma \vdash e_1 e_2 : t_1 \bullet t_2}\ (appl)$$

$$\frac{\begin{array}{c}(\text{for } s_1 \equiv s \wedge \wr p_1 \int,\ s_2 \equiv s \wedge \neg \wr p_1 \int)\\ \Gamma \vdash e : s \leq \wr p_1 \int \vee \wr p_2 \int \quad \Gamma, (s_i/p_i) \vdash e_i : t_i\end{array}}{\Gamma \vdash \mathsf{match}\ e\ \mathsf{with}\ p_1 \rightarrow e_1 \mid p_2 \rightarrow e_2 : \bigvee_{\{i \mid s_i \not\simeq \mathbf{0}\}} t_i}\ (match)$$

$$\frac{(\forall i) \quad \Gamma, (x : t_i), (f : \bigwedge_{i=1..n} t_i \rightarrow s_i) \vdash e : s_i}{\Gamma \vdash \mathsf{fun}\ f^{(t_1 \rightarrow s_1; \ldots; t_n \rightarrow s_n)}(x).e : \bigwedge_{i=1..n} t_i \rightarrow s_i}\ (abstr) \qquad \frac{\Gamma \vdash e : s \leq t}{\Gamma \vdash e : t}\ (subsum)$$

Fig. 2. Typing rules

presence of boolean combinations t could be for example of the form $((s_1 \rightarrow u_1) \wedge (s_2 \rightarrow u_2))$. To that end we introduce a partial binary operator on types $\bullet$. Intuitively $t \bullet s$ denotes the least type (if it exists) such that $t \leq s \rightarrow (t \bullet s)$ and the rule (*appl*) does not fail only if the operator is defined (in practice, we subsume t_1 to the least arrow type with domain t_2). So, for example, if our function of type $((s_1 \rightarrow u_1) \wedge (s_2 \rightarrow u_2))$ is applied to an expression of type $(s_1 \vee s_2)$, then the type system will infer that the result of the application has type $((s_1 \rightarrow u_1) \wedge (s_2 \rightarrow u_2)) \bullet (s_1 \vee s_2) = (u_1 \vee u_2)$. Similarly we introduce two projections operators π_1 and π_2 such that $\pi_1(t)$ (respectively $\pi_2(t)$) is the least type that makes $t \leq \pi_1(t) \times \mathbf{1}$ (respectively $\mathbf{1} \times \pi_2(t)$) hold. It is important to note that $\bullet$, π_1, and π_2 are all computable (once more see [9]).

Rule (*abstr*) is not very standard, either. It states that a (possibly overloaded) function is typed by the intersection of all the types declared in its interface: we repeat the check for each type in the interface and handle the typing of recursive calls by recording for f the expected type. Actually the rule in Figure 2, is a simplification of the ℂDuce rule in [9], the latter is very technical and makes the minimum typing property fail (so that there does not exist a canonical type representing the set of all types of a given expression). However, we will see that this does not affect our analysis and, therefore, that the rule defined in Figure 2 is enough.

Finally the rule (*match*) states that the type of a matching operation is the union of the types of the branches[7], and for that it uses several auxiliary notations: $\equiv$ denotes syntactic equivalence of types whereas $\simeq$ denotes the semantic one ($s \simeq t$ only if s and t denote the same set of values); s/p denotes the type environment that assigns types to the capture variables of p when this is matched against a value of type s; $\wr p \int$ denotes the *type* accepted by p, that is, the type whose interpretation is the set of all values for which p does not fail: $\wr p \int = \{v \mid v/p \neq \Omega\}$. Again, $\wr\ \int$ is computable. The type system is sound since it satisfies the subject reduction property: if $\Gamma \vdash e : t$ and $e \leadsto^* e'$, then $\Gamma \vdash e' : t$ (where $\leadsto^*$ means "reduces in zero or more steps").

3 Non-interference and Labels

The first step toward the definition of our security analysis is the characterization of information flows. In general, these are difficult to define and therefore it is customary to

[7] Precisely, of the branches that have a chance to match, that is those for which $s_i \not\simeq \mathbf{0}$. This distinction matters when typing overloaded functions: see [9].

rather characterize their absence via the *non-interference* property: given an expression e, a sub-expression e' occurring in e does not interfere with e if and only if whenever e returns some result, then also every expression obtained from e by replacing e' by a different expression yields the same result. Note that this (informal) definition does not involve types and because of that it is unsuitable to describe non-interference for type driven semantics. A definition of non-interference for ℂDuce transformations must take types into account.

Types have been widely used in previous work on language-based information-flow security (see [18] for a very broad review) and non-interference definitions have been given for typed languages. What is new in our framework is that the essence of the definition of non-interference relies on types. In particular, changing the type of an expression occurrence in a program can change the non-interference properties of that expression occurrence. Therefore our definition of non-interference is stated *with respect to* a type t:

Definition 1 (Occurrence). *Let e be a ℂDuce expression. An* occurrence Δ *of e is a (root starting) path of the abstract syntax tree of e. If Δ is an occurrence of e, we use e_Δ to denote the sub-expression of e occurring at Δ, and $\mathscr{C}^e_\Delta[]$ to denote the context obtained from e by inserting a hole at Δ. Thus $e = \mathscr{C}^e_\Delta[e_\Delta]$.*

Definition 2 (Non-interference w.r.t. t). *Let e be a ℂDuce expression, Δ an occurrence of e, and t a type. The occurrence Δ* does not interfere in e with respect to t *if and only if for all ℂDuce values v and v', if $\varnothing \vdash v' : t$ and $e \rightsquigarrow^* v$ then $\mathscr{C}^e_\Delta[v'] \rightsquigarrow^* v$.*

Let e be the application of a query to an XML document that stores some information of type t in an element located at Δ. We want to define when the query allows one to infer information about Δ more precise than its type. The definition above states that the information stored in Δ is not disclosed if the fact of storing any value v' of type t in Δ does not change the result of the query.

The definition is reasonable as it simply encompasses the static knowledge about the type of an occurrence. For instance, on our example it states that a query is safe (i.e. interference free) if and only if it cannot distinguish two documents that contain two different *integers* in corresponding salary elements. Similarly, a query that distinguishes documents with integer salaries from documents in which salaries elements contain boolean values is safe, too[8]: this is reasonable to the extent that such a test cannot in practice be performed as it would contradict the static knowledge we (or an attacker) have of the document. This new definition induces also a very nice interpretation of security, according to which *a transformation is safe if it does not reveal (about confidential data) any information that is not already statically known.*

A last more technical point. In Definition 2 we tested non-interferent occurrences against values rather than against generic expressions. This simplifies the definition inasmuch as we do not have to take into account the typing and the possible capture of variables that are free in the expressions inserted in the context. However, this does not undermine the generality of our definition as shown by Proposition 1:

[8] More interestingly, had we defined salaries to be of type `<salary>[1600--*]`, then also the query `Q2` would result safe (i.e. interference free).

Definition 3 **((Γ/Θ)-contexts).** *Let Γ and Θ be type environments, t and t' types, and $\mathscr{C}[\,]$ a context. $\mathscr{C}[\,]$ is a $(\Gamma/\Theta, t/t')$-context if $\Gamma \vdash \mathscr{C}[\,] : t$ is provable under the hypothesis that $\Theta' \vdash [\,]{:}t'$ holds for every extension Θ' of Θ.*

Proposition 1 **(Generality).** *Let e be a $\mathbb{C}$Duce expression such that $\Gamma \vdash e : t$. Let Δ be an occurrence that does not interfere in e w.r.t. t'. Then for all Γ', Γ'', and e', if $\Gamma', \Gamma, \Gamma'' \vdash e'{:}t'$, $e \rightsquigarrow^* v$, and $\mathscr{C}^e_\Delta[\,]$ is a $((\Gamma',\Gamma)/\Gamma'', t/t')$-context, then $\mathscr{C}^e_\Delta[e'] \rightsquigarrow^* v$.*

Our next step consists in defining a way to identify occurrences. This can be easily obtained by marking $\mathbb{C}$Duce expressions by security labels. Thus we define $\mathbb{C}\text{Duce}_{\mathscr{L}}$ obtained from $\mathbb{C}$Duce by adding expressions of the form "$\ell_t : e$", where t is a type and ℓ is a metavariable ranging over a set $\mathscr{L}$ of labels. As anticipated labels are indexed by types that record the static knowledge of the expression at issue. The type is used to verify non-interference of the expression. This is considered not to interfere with a given computation if the fact of making the labeled occurrence vary over the values of the type specified by the label does not affect the final result of the computation.

Of course, this is sensible only if the fact of making the occurrence vary over such a type yields well-typed expressions. In other terms, as suggested by Proposition 1, the type indexing a label must be a viable type for the expression marked by the label. In order to formalize this property we endow $\mathbb{C}\text{Duce}_{\mathscr{L}}$ with a type system formed by all the typing rules of $\mathbb{C}$Duce, summarized in Figure 2, plus the one on right.

$$\frac{\Gamma \vdash e : s \qquad s \leq t}{\Gamma \vdash (\ell_t{:}e) : t}$$

By definition a $\mathbb{C}\text{Duce}_{\mathscr{L}}$ expression is a $\mathbb{C}$Duce expression where some subexpressions are marked by a list of labels. We call *strip* the function that transforms the former into the latter by erasing all the lists of labels and we denote if by $\lfloor\ \rfloor$.

Technically, we consider the syntax of $\mathbb{C}\text{Duce}_{\mathscr{L}}$ as a description of a decoration of the syntax tree of e in the sense that the (lists of) labels are not nodes of the syntax trees but tags marking these nodes.[9] The reason for this choice is that in this way the same path Δ denotes an occurrence of a $\mathbb{C}\text{Duce}_{\mathscr{L}}$ expression and the corresponding occurrence in the stripped expression. In this way we avoid to define complex mappings between occurrences of expressions in $\mathbb{C}\text{Duce}_{\mathscr{L}}$ and the corresponding ones in the stripped version. In particular this makes the following property hold

Proposition 2. *Let e be a $\mathbb{C}\text{Duce}_{\mathscr{L}}$ term with an occurrence Δ, then (i) $\lfloor e_\Delta \rfloor = \lfloor e \rfloor_\Delta$ and (ii) $\lfloor \mathscr{C}^e_\Delta[e_\Delta] \rfloor = \mathscr{C}^{\lfloor e \rfloor}_\Delta[\lfloor e \rfloor_\Delta]$*

which yields a simpler statement of the non-interference theorem (Theorem 2).

4 Security Analysis

Our analysis is defined by endowing $\mathbb{C}\text{Duce}_{\mathscr{L}}$ with an operational semantics defined so that (i) it preserves $\mathbb{C}$Duce semantics on stripped terms ($e \rightsquigarrow^* v \Rightarrow \lfloor e \rfloor \rightsquigarrow^* \lfloor v \rfloor$) and (ii) label propagation provides a sound non-interference analysis for $\mathbb{C}$Duce expression

[9] More formally we consider that a $\mathbb{C}\text{Duce}_{\mathscr{L}}$ term denotes a pair formed by a $\mathbb{C}$Duce term and a map from the (root starting) paths of the abstract syntax tree of the term to possibly empty lists of labels.

(i.e., if a label is not propagated, then the labeled expression does not interfere with the result). It is not difficult to define a trivially sound analysis (just propagate all labels)[10]. The hard task is to define a fine-grained analysis that propagates as few labels as possible. Needless to say that the core of the definition is label propagation in pattern matching, where several kinds of information flows are possible:

- Direct (or "explicit") information flows, due to the binding of labeled expressions to variables, such as in: `match e with <worker>[ x y <salary>[z] ] → ...z... | ...` where the value of the salary is bound to **z** and flows through it into the first branch expression.
- Indirect (or "implicit") information flows due to patterns: the information flows by the deconstruction of the matched value and/or the satisfaction of type constraints, such as in: `match e with <worker>[ x y <salary>[1--900] ] → e1 | ...` where the information of the range of the salary flows into $\mathbf{e_1}$.
- Indirect information flows due to use of a first match policy: information can be acquired from the failure of the previous branch: `match e with <worker>[ x y <salary>[1--900] ] →e1 | _ →e2` where the information that the salary value is *not* in (1--900) flows into $\mathbf{e_2}$.

The last example also shows that non-interference is undecidable as the non- interference of the value of the salary element is equivalent to deciding the equivalence of e_1 and e_2 (ℂDuce is Turing-complete).

Once we have established whether a label must be propagated or not, here comes the problem to decide with which type we have to decorate it so as not to infringe subject-reduction. Consider the example of the application of a labeled function value to another value: $(\ell_{s\to t}{:}v_1)v_2$. Surely the function, seen as a piece of data, interferes with the computation. Therefore its label must be propagated. A sound solution is to reduce the application to $\ell_u{:}(v_1 v_2)$, for a suitable choice of u. Here the choice for u is easy: the type system ensures that v_2 is of type s therefore it suffices to take $u = t$. When the type of the label is not an arrow but a generic type t', then we resort to the $\bullet$ operator and set u equal to $t' \bullet s'$ for some s' such that $v_2 : s'$.

Formally, we start by (i) defining ℂDuce$_{\mathscr{L}}$ values, which are obtained by adding to the definition of ℂDuce values the production $v ::= \ell_t : v$; (ii) defining the semantics of v/t for the new values in the following case: $(\ell_t : (v_1, v_2))/(p_1, p_2) = v_1/p_1 \otimes v_2/p_2$; and (iii) adding to evaluation contexts the production $\mathscr{E} ::= \ell_t : \mathscr{E}$. Note however that we do not define a pattern for labels, as we want labels to describe information flow, rather than to affect it.

Next we define the operator "$/\!\!/$" that calculates the set of labels that must be propagated at pattern matching. More precisely, $e /\!\!/ p$ denotes the list of all labels that must be propagated when matching expression e against pattern p, and is defined in Figure 3 (where "@" and "::" are the "append" and "cons" list operators, respectively). This definition forms the core of our analysis, therefore it is worth explaining it in some details. Let $\mathscr{L}(e)$ denote the set of labels occurring in e, then all the labels in $v /\!\!/ p$ are contained in $\mathscr{L}(v)$. The idea is to collect in $v /\!\!/ p$ all the labels that mark expressions whose value *may* affect the result of the matching. Intuitively, the definition of "$/\!\!/$" must ensure that if a label ℓ in $\mathscr{L}(v)$ is not in $v /\!\!/ p$, then for all v' obtained by substituting in v some

[10] The analogous trivially complete analysis is the one that does not propagate any label.

$$
\begin{array}{ll}
v /\!\!/ x = \varnothing_{\mathbf{ok}} & \\
v /\!\!/ (x := c) = \varnothing_{\mathbf{ok}} & \\
c /\!\!/ p = \varnothing_{\mathbf{ok}} & \text{if } c \in \llparenthesis p \rrparenthesis \\
c /\!\!/ p = \varnothing_{\mathbf{fail}} & \text{if } c \notin \llparenthesis p \rrparenthesis \\
(\ell_t : v) /\!\!/ p = \varnothing_{\mathbf{fail}} & \text{if } t \wedge \llparenthesis p \rrparenthesis \simeq \mathbf{0} \\
(\ell_{t'} : v) /\!\!/ t = \varnothing_{\mathbf{ok}} & \text{if } (t' \leq t) \\
(\ell_{t'} : v) /\!\!/ t = \ell :: (v /\!\!/ t) & \text{if } (t \wedge t' \not\simeq \mathbf{0}) \wedge (t' \not\leq t) \\
(v_1, v_2) /\!\!/ t = (v_1 /\!\!/ \pi_1(t)) @ (v_2 /\!\!/ \pi_2(t)) & \text{if } \pi_i(t) \text{ are defined and } v_i /\!\!/ \pi_i(t) \neq \varnothing_{\mathbf{fail}} \\
(v_1, v_2) /\!\!/ t = \varnothing_{\mathbf{fail}} & \text{otherwise} \\
(\mathsf{fun}\ f^{(t_1;\dots;t_n)}(x).e) /\!\!/ t = \varnothing_{\mathbf{ok}} & \text{if } \mathsf{fun}\ f^{(t_1;\dots;t_n)}(x).e/t \neq \Omega \\
(\mathsf{fun}\ f^{(t_1;\dots;t_n)}(x).e) /\!\!/ t = \varnothing_{\mathbf{fail}} & \text{if } \mathsf{fun}\ f^{(t_1;\dots;t_n)}(x).e/t = \Omega \\
v /\!\!/ p_1 \& p_2 = \varnothing_{\mathbf{fail}} & \text{if } (v_1 /\!\!/ p_1) = \varnothing_{\mathbf{fail}} \text{ or } (v_2 /\!\!/ p_2) = \varnothing_{\mathbf{fail}} \\
v /\!\!/ p_1 \& p_2 = (v /\!\!/ p_1) @ (v /\!\!/ p_2) & \text{otherwise} \\
(\ell_t : v) /\!\!/ (p_1, p_2) = \ell :: (v /\!\!/ (p_1, p_2)) & \text{if } (t \wedge \llparenthesis (p_1, p_2) \rrparenthesis \not\simeq \mathbf{0}) \\
(v_1, v_2) /\!\!/ (p_1, p_2) = \varnothing_{\mathbf{fail}} & \text{if } (v_1 /\!\!/ p_1) = \varnothing_{\mathbf{fail}} \text{ or } (v_2 /\!\!/ p_2) = \varnothing_{\mathbf{fail}} \\
(v_1, v_2) /\!\!/ (p_1, p_2) = (v_1 /\!\!/ p_1) @ (v_2 /\!\!/ p_2) & \text{otherwise} \\
(\mathsf{fun}\ f^{(t_1;\dots;t_n)}(x).e) /\!\!/ (p_1, p_2) = \varnothing_{\mathbf{fail}} & \\
(\ell_t : v) /\!\!/ p_1 | p_2 = ((\ell_t : v) /\!\!/ p_1) & \text{if } t \leq \llparenthesis p_1 \rrparenthesis \\
(\ell_t : v) /\!\!/ p_1 | p_2 = ((\ell_t : v) /\!\!/ p_2) & \text{if } t \wedge \llparenthesis p_1 \rrparenthesis \simeq \mathbf{0} \\
(\ell_t : v) /\!\!/ p_1 | p_2 = \ell :: (v /\!\!/ p_1 | p_2) & \text{otherwise} \\
v /\!\!/ p_1 | p_2 = \varnothing_{\mathbf{ok}} & \text{if } v /\!\!/ p_1 = \varnothing_{\mathbf{ok}} \\
v /\!\!/ p_1 | p_2 = \varnothing_{\mathbf{fail}} & \text{if } v \neq c,\ v \neq \ell_t{:}v' \text{ and} (v_1 /\!\!/ p_1) = (v_2 /\!\!/ p_2) = \varnothing_{\mathbf{fail}} \\
v /\!\!/ p_1 | p_2 = (v /\!\!/ p_1) @ (v /\!\!/ p_2) & \text{if } v \neq c,\ v \neq \ell_t{:}v',\ v /\!\!/ p_1 \neq \varnothing_{\mathbf{ok}}, \text{ and} \\
 & \quad (v /\!\!/ p_1) \text{ and } (v /\!\!/ p_2) \text{ are not both equal to } \varnothing_{\mathbf{fail}}
\end{array}
$$

Fig. 3. Propagating labels with patterns

ℓ-labeled occurrences by "admissible" (i.e. that respect the type constraints indexing ℓ) values, the match v'/p either always succeeds or always fails[11].

The first two cases in Figure 3 are the easiest ones insofar as variables and default-value patterns always succeed; therefore no label needs to be propagated.

Matching a constant is also simple as there is no label to propagate. Note, however, that we use an index to distinguish two different cases of non-propagation: the case in which labels are not propagated because the pattern always fails ($\varnothing_{\mathbf{fail}}$) and the case in which they are not propagated because the pattern always succeed ($\varnothing_{\mathbf{ok}}$). When we match a labeled value against a pattern p and the type of the label does not intersect the type accepted by p, then we know that making v varying over t always fails.

The case for a type constraint pattern is the key one, as ℂDuce's pattern matching is nothing but a highly sophisticated type-case with capture variables: if $t' \wedge t \simeq \mathbf{0}$, then we are in the previous case so v/t always fails; if $t' \leq t$, then for every v of type t', v/t always succeeds so no label is propagated; otherwise, for all v' in the intersection of t and t' v'/t succeeds, while for v' in their difference it fails, thus we propagate ℓ and check for other labels.

[11] However, this is not enough to ensure non-interference: for instance consider $(\ell_{\mathsf{Bool}} : v) /\!\!/ (\mathsf{true}\&(x{:=}1)) | (\mathsf{false}\&(x{:=}0))$ which always succeeds.

When the matched value is a pair then we propagate the union of the labels propagated by matching each sub-value against the corresponding projection of t provided that: (i) the projections are defined, because otherwise we are matching a pair against a type with no product among its super-types (e.g., $s \to t$) and the pattern always fails, and (ii) none of the two sub-matching fails, because the whole pattern would then fail and therefore it would be silly to propagate the labels of the other component. Note that this case uses the distinction between $\varnothing_{\mathbf{ok}}$ and $\varnothing_{\mathbf{fail}}$, the other cases being in conjunction and pair patterns—which fail if any sub-check fails—and in disjunction patterns—which fail if both sub-checks fail—. Since there is no pattern that deconstructs functions, these can be soundly matched only against types (or captured). Note however that the type of a function value is fixed by its interface. Therefore even if we make labeled expressions occurring in the function vary, this does not affect the type of the function, ergo the result of pattern matching. For this reason $(\mathsf{fun}\ f^{(t_1,\ldots,t_n)}(x).e) \mathbin{/\!\!/} t$ is dealt in the same way as constant values. The cases of conjunction patterns as well as those for pair patterns need no particular insight. It may be worth just noticing that in the first case of pair patterns ℓ is propagated also when the pattern always succeeds (i.e. $t \leq \llparenthesis (p_1,p_2) \rrparenthesis$) as the simple fact of deconstructing the pair may yield interference[12].

The cases for alternative patterns are more interesting as they take into account the use of the first match policy. In particular in the first two equations for match, propagation is calculated only on p_1 or p_2 according to whether the first match always succeeds or always fails. If instead the result cannot be determined with certainty, then the label is propagated and the search for other labels is continued on v. All remaining rules are straightforward.

Now that we have determined the labels to propagate we have to choose the type constraints to decorate them with. Let L be a list $[\ell^1\ell^2\ldots\ell^n]$ of labels, t a type, and e an expression, we use the notation $(L)_t{:}e$ to denote the expression $\ell^1_t : \ell^2_t : \ldots \ell^n_t : e$ obtained by prefixing e by the t-indexed labels in L. This notation is used to index the labels deduced by "$/\!\!/$" and define the operational semantics of $\mathbb{C}\mathrm{Duce}_{\mathscr{L}}$ as follows (a better definition can be found in the on-line extended version available atwww.cduce.org):

$$
\begin{array}{rr}
v_1 v_2 \leadsto e[v_1/f; v_2/x] & \text{if } v_1 = \mathsf{fun}\, f^{(\ldots)}(x).e \\
(\ell_t : v_1)v_2 \leadsto \ell_{t\bullet s} : (v_1 v_2) & \text{if } \varnothing \vdash v_2 : s \text{ and } t \bullet s \text{ is defined} \\
\mathsf{match}\ v\ \mathsf{with}\ p_1 \to e_1 \mid p_2 \to e_2 \leadsto (v \mathbin{/\!\!/} p_1)_t : e_1[v/p_1] & \text{if } v/p_1 \neq \Omega \text{ and } \varnothing \vdash e_1[v/p_1] : t \\
\mathsf{match}\ v\ \mathsf{with}\ p_1 \to e_1 \mid p_2 \to e_2 \leadsto (v \mathbin{/\!\!/} \llparenthesis p_1 \rrparenthesis)_t : (v \mathbin{/\!\!/} p_2)_t : e_2[v/p_2] & \text{if } v/p_1 = \Omega, v/p_2 \neq \Omega \\
 & \text{and } \varnothing \vdash e_2[v/p_2] : t
\end{array}
$$

The rule for "unlabeled" applications does not change, while the one for applications of a labeled function changes as we explained early in this section. Matching clearly is the key rule. Branch selection is performed as in $\mathbb{C}$Duce but the labels determined by $/\!\!/$ and indexed by the type of the reductum are prepended to the result. In particular if the first branch is selected, then we just propagate the labels in $v \mathbin{/\!\!/} p_1$, as the second pattern is not even checked. But if the second branch is selected then the result is prepended by both $v \mathbin{/\!\!/} p_2$ *and* $v \mathbin{/\!\!/} \llparenthesis p_1 \rrparenthesis$: while the first set of labels highlights the first of the two kinds of indirect flows present in $\mathbb{C}$Duce, namely, those due to pattern matching, the second

12 For example , consider $(\ell_{\mathsf{Bool} \times t} : v) \mathbin{/\!\!/} (\ (\mathsf{true} \& (x := 1)) | (\mathsf{false} \& (x := 0))\ ,\ \_\ )$.

```
<company>[
  <worker>[
    <surname>m_String:"Durand"
    <name>n_String:"Paul"
    <salary>[ ℓ_Int:6500 ]
  ]
  <worker>[
    <surname>m_String:"Dupond"
    <name>n_String:"Jean"
    <salary>[ℓ_Int:1800]
  ]
  <worker>[
    <surname>m_String:"Martin"
    <name>n_String:"Jules"
    <salary>[ℓ_Int:1200]
  ]
]
```

```
<company>[
  <worker>[
    <surname>m_String:"Durand"
    <name>n_String:"Paul"
  ]
  <worker>[
    <surname>m_String:"Dupond"
    <name>n_String:"Jean"
  ]
  <worker>[
    <surname>m_String:"Martin"
    <name>n_String:"Jules"
  ]
]
```

```
<company>[
  (ℓ_<worker>[Surname Name]:
  <worker>[
    <surname>m_String:"Durand"
    <name>n_String:"Paul"
  ])
  (ℓ_<worker>[Surname Name]:
  <worker>[
    <surname>m_String:"Dupond"
    <name>n_String:"Jean"
  ])
]
```

Fig. 4. Labeled XML document and the results of queries Q1 and Q2

set of labels fingers the other kind of flows possible in ℂDuce, that is those generated by branch dependency induced by first match policy. Since we selected the second branch e_2 knows that p_1 failed and, therefore, that the matched value v does not belong to (the semantic interpretation of) the type $\llparenthesis p \rrparenthesis$. Therefore, we must also propagate all those labels in v whose content can be (even partially) deduced from the failure of p_1. By definition these are the labels of $v /\!\!/ (\neg \llparenthesis p_1 \rrparenthesis)$ or equivalently (see Lemma 2) of $v /\!\!/ \llparenthesis p_1 \rrparenthesis$.

The reduction semantics we obtain is non deterministic since in case of reduction of a pattern matching or of a labeled function we resort to the type system for determining the type decoration of the reductum's labels (and we know that ℂDuce type system does not enjoy the minimum typing property). As a matter of facts, we have not described a single analysis but a whole family of analyses. This is slightly annoying from a theoretical viewpoint since we have to prove that *all* of them are sound so that, in practice, we can use any of them. However this has no consequence under the practical aspect: first, since we deal with a finite number of labels and types it is always possible to find the best analysis; second, since this problem already resides in the ℂDuce type system a choice was already made by the implementation. So we follow the implementation of ℂDuce and use in Figures 3 and in the operational semantics of $\mathbb{C}\mathrm{Duce}_{\mathscr{L}}$ the types inferred by the ℂDuce's type-checker: we end up with the best analysis (in the family described above) that is sound with the current implementation of ℂDuce.

Let us finally apply the analysis to the queries of Section 1. In order to trace how information of each data flows in the queries, we label the content of each sub-element of <worker> elements by a different label as shown on the left expression of Figure 4. The results of the analysis of Q1 and Q2 respectively are the central and right expressions in Figure 4[13]. Note that Q1 propagates only the labels of name and surname (the propagation is a consequence of an explicit flow), thus the analysis has correctly indicated that it is safe. The analysis of Q2 instead propagates also the salary label and therefore is rejected as insecure. The propagation of $\ell_{\texttt{<worker>[Surname Name]}}$ is caused by

[13] Sequences are encoded by right associative nested pairs ended by 'nil, XML elements <tag *attributes*>*s* become triples ('tag,(*attributes*, *s*)), while transform is obtained by iterating matching expressions on the elements, and encapsulating the results into a sequence.

the "//" in the first match rule in $\mathbb{C}$Duce$_{\mathscr{L}}$'s operational semantics. In particular when matching the pattern of transform against an element, the third rule for pairs in Figure 3 decomposes the test over each projection, one of which calculates, say in the first loop, (ℓ_{Int}:6500) // MoreThanMe which by the second rule for types in Figure 3 is equal to ℓ. Note also how the position of the label denotes different kinds of properties: for example we specified <salary>[ℓ :1200] since we wanted to capture only transformations that depended on the content of the salary element, while if we rather had specified ℓ :<salary>[1200] we would have captured also transformations that test the presence of this element (in the case it were optional).

We want to stress that our analysis can check very complex security entailments. As explained in the introduction, the independence of the result from salary can also be ensured by access control techniques or by stripping salary values from the source document. However, our technique allows one to check that even if a query can access both salaries and names it cannot correlate them. To that end it just suffices to verify that the presence of a m or of a n label in the result implies the absence of the ℓ label, and vice-versa. According to this policy query Q1 would be accepted since ℓ does not occur in the result while query Q2 would be rejected since all the three labels are in the result. A query that plainly returned the list of all salaries (without any name or surname) or some statistic about them, would be considered safe, too. More generally, by using label propagation and some logic (e.g. propositional one) on labels we can define complex security policies whose verification, trivial in our technique, would be very hard (if not impossible at all) by standard access control techniques, as we show in Section 6.

Finally, we can recast the analysis scenarios we outlined in the introduction (Figure 1) to the present setting. A sound static analysis for our system is an analysis that computes labels that will be surely absent from result of the dynamic analysis, while a complete static analysis will determine labels that will be surely present in the same result. Therefore, here completeness is stated with respect to the dynamic analysis rather than with respect to the non-interference property. With that respect the work presented here constitutes the cornerstone of the outlined architecture.

5 Properties

In this section we briefly enumerate the various properties of our approach. For space reasons proofs and less important lemmas are omitted or just sketched. They are all reported in extended version of the article available on-line.

In what follows, when we state that e is a $\mathbb{C}$Duce or $\mathbb{C}$Duce$_{\mathscr{L}}$ expression we implicitly mean that e is a *well-typed* ($\mathbb{C}$Duce or $\mathbb{C}$Duce$_{\mathscr{L}}$) expression.

Lemma 1 (Strip). *Let e be a* $\mathbb{C}$*Duce*$_{\mathscr{L}}$ *expression. If* $e \leadsto^* e'$, *then* $\lfloor e \rfloor \leadsto^* \lfloor e' \rfloor$.

This lemma has two important consequences, namely (i) that $\mathbb{C}$Duce$_{\mathscr{L}}$ is a conservative extension of $\mathbb{C}$Duce with respect to the reduction theory, and (ii) that despite being non-deterministic the reduction of $\mathbb{C}$Duce$_{\mathscr{L}}$ preserves the semantics of $\mathbb{C}$Duce programs:

Corollary 1. *Let e be a* $\mathbb{C}$*Duce*$_{\mathscr{L}}$ *expression. If* $e \leadsto e'$, *and* $e \leadsto e''$, *then* $\lfloor e' \rfloor = \lfloor e'' \rfloor$.

The soundness of $\mathbb{C}$Duce$_{\mathscr{L}}$ type system is proved by subject reduction and is instrumental to the soundness of the analysis.

Theorem 1 (Subject reduction). *Let e be a* $\mathbb{C}Duce_{\mathscr{L}}$ *expression. If* $\Gamma \vdash e : t$ *and* $e \leadsto^* e'$, *then* $\Gamma \vdash e' : t$.

The next lemma is useful to understand the match reduction rules of $\mathbb{C}\mathrm{Duce}_{\mathscr{L}}$.

Lemma 2. *For every value v and type t,* $(v /\!\!/ t) = (v /\!\!/ \neg t)$ *(modulo the indexes of* $\varnothing$*)*

In order to prove non-interference we need two lemmas, one that characterizes $/\!\!/$ and a second that is the non-interference counterpart of the standard substitution lemma in typed λ-calculi:

Lemma 3. *Let p be a pattern, v a* $\mathbb{C}Duce_{\mathscr{L}}$ *value with an occurrence* Δ *such that* $v_\Delta = \ell_t{:}v_1$. *If* $\ell \notin v /\!\!/ p$, *then for all* v' *such that* $\varnothing \vdash v'{:}t$, $\left(v/p \neq \Omega \Leftrightarrow \mathscr{C}^v_\Delta[v']/p \neq \Omega\right)$ *holds true.*

Lemma 4 (Substitution). *Let p be a pattern, v a* $\mathbb{C}Duce_{\mathscr{L}}$ *value whose occurrence* Δ *is such that* $v_\Delta = \ell_t : v'$. *If* ℓ *does not occur in the image of* v/p *and* $\ell \notin v /\!\!/ p$, *then for all* v'' *such that* $\varnothing \vdash v''{:}t$, *we have that* $\mathscr{C}^v_\Delta[v'']/p$ *is pointwise equal to* v/p.

We can state the non-interference theorem: note that the non-determinism of $\mathbb{C}\mathrm{Duce}_{\mathscr{L}}$'s reduction is accounted for by the quantifying on all results v of the expression e.

Theorem 2 (Non-interference). *Let e be a* $\mathbb{C}Duce_{\mathscr{L}}$ *expression, with an occurrence* Δ *such that* $e_\Delta = \ell_t : e_1$. *For every value v such that* $e \leadsto^* v$, *if* $\ell \notin \mathscr{L}(v)$, *then* Δ *is non interfering in* $\lfloor e \rfloor$ *with respect to t, i.e.,* $\forall v' \in \mathbb{C}Duce$ *s.t.* $\varnothing \vdash v' : t$, *we have* $\lfloor \mathscr{C}^e_\Delta[v'] \rfloor \leadsto^* \lfloor v \rfloor$

By using Proposition 2 it is easy to see that the conclusion of the theorem implies the Definition 2 of non-interference, justifying in this way the "i.e." we used in the statement of the theorem.

6 A Last Example

We end our presentation by commenting a more articulated example to illustrate the use of our technique to define and verify complex security policies that cannot be expressed in terms of access control. We suppose to store in XML-documents information about persons that have to pass some examination. The form of the documents is described by the type declarations on the right.

```
type ExamBase = <exam_base>[Person*]
type Person = <person gender="M"|"F">
                         [Name Birth Grade?]
type Name = <name>String
type Birth = <birth>[Year Month Day]
type Year = <year>[Int]
type Month = <month>MName
type MName= "Jan"|"Feb"|"Mar"|"Apr"| ···
type Day = <day>[1--31]
type Grade = <grade>[Int]
```

As we see every document records a list of names, with personal information, and with an *optional* <grade> element that stores the numerical result of the examination. The absence of such an element denotes that the person has not passed (that is, either not taken or taken and failed) the examination, yet. An XML document that verifies this schema is shown in the left column of Figure 5, while the central column reports the result of importing the same document in $\mathbb{C}$Duce.

Imagine that examination documents can be accessed by three different categories of users, academic staff, administrative staff, and normal users. We want academic staff to have unconstrained access to the information stored in the examination documents while we may wish to constrain the accesses for administration and normal users. As an example of security requirements we may wish to enforce we have:

```
<?xml version="1.0"?>
<exam_base>
  <person gender="M">
    <name>Durand</name>
    <birth>
      <year>1970</year>
      <month>Aug</month>
      <day>10</day>
    </birth>
    <grade>110</grade>
  </person>
  <person gender="M">
    <name>Dupond</name>
    <birth>
      <year>1953</year>
      <month>Apr</month>
      <day>22</day>
    </birth>
  </person>
  <person gender="F">
    <name>Dubois</name>
    <birth>
      <year>1965</year>
      <month>Sep</month>
      <day>2</day>
    </birth>
    <grade>120</grade>
  </person>
</exam_base>
```

```
let eb : ExamBase =
<exam_base>[
  <person gender="M">[
    <name>"Durand"
    <birth>[
      <year>[1970]
      <month>"Aug"
      <day>[10]
    ]
    <grade>[110]
  ]
  <person gender="M">[
    <name>"Dupond"
    <birth>[
      <year>[1953]
      <month>"Apr"
      <day>[22]
    ]
  ]
  <person gender="F">[
    <name>"Dubois"
    <birth>[
      <year>[1965]
      <month>"Sep"
      <day>[2]
    ]
    <grade>[120]
  ]
]
```

```
let eb : ExamBase =
<exam_base>[
  <person gender= stat_{"M"|"F"} : "M">[
    <name> name_{String} : "Durand"
    <birth>[
      <year>[ stat_{Int} : 1970]
      <month> private_{MName} : "Aug"
      <day>[ private_{(1--31)} : 10]
    ]
    passed_{Grade} : <grade>[ result_{Int} : 110]
  ]
  <person gender= stat_{"M"|"F"} : "M">[
    <name> name_{String} : "Dupond"
    <birth>[
      <year>[ stat_{Int} : 1953]
      <month> private_{MName} : "Apr"
      <day>[ private_{(1--31)} : 22]
    ]
  ]
  <person gender= stat_{"M"|"F"} : "F">[
    <name> name_{String} : "Dubois"
    <birth>[
      <year>[ stat_{Int} : 1965]
      <month> private_{MName} : "Sep"
      <day>[ private_{(1--31)} : 2]
    ]
    passed_{Grade} : <grade>[ result_{Int} : 120]
  ]
]
```

Fig. 5. A database of examinations: in XML, in ℂDuce, and in ℂDuce$_{\mathcal{L}}$

1. Only academic users can have information both on names and grades or on names and birthdays simultaneously.
2. The administrative users can check whether a person passed the examination (that is, they can check for the presence of a<grade> element) but cannot access the result.
3. Every user can ask for statistical results on grades upon criteria limited to year of birth and gender (so that they cannot select sufficiently restrictive sets to infer personal data).

To dynamically verify these constraints we introduce five labels that we use to classify the information stored in documents: *private* (that classifies the month and the day of birth), *stat* (that classifies the year of birth and the gender attribute), *name* (that classifies names), *passed* (that classifies grade elements), and *result* (that classifies the *content* of grade elements). Rather than document-wise, this classification is described directly on types as shown by the definitions on the right. Note that in these definitions labels have no indexes (in documents they will be indexed by the types they are labeling). Before executing a query the system uses this specification to generate a labeled version of the document as shown in the last column of Figure 5. The query is then executed

```
type Person = <person gender= stat:("M"|"F")>
                      [ Name Birth ( passed:Grade)? ]
type Name = <name>( name:String)
type Year = <year>[ stat:Int]
type Month = <month>( private:MName)
type Day = <day>[ private:(1--31)]
type Grade = <grade>[ result:Int]
```

on the labeled document (according to the semantics of $\mathbb{C}\text{Duce}_{\mathscr{L}}$) and the following constraints[14] are checked in the result:

If the owner of the query is a normal user, then the result must satisfy:

$$name \Rightarrow \neg(private \vee stat \vee result \vee passed) \wedge private \Rightarrow \neg(stat \vee result)$$

if the owner of the query is an administrative user, then the result must satisfy:

$$name \Rightarrow \neg(private \vee stat \vee result) \wedge private \Rightarrow \neg(stat \vee result)$$

where a propositional label is satisfied if and only if the label is present in the result. Thus, for instance, the second constraint must be read: if the label *name* occurs in the result then *private*, *stat*, and *result* cannot occur in it, and if *private* occurs in the result then *stat*, and *result* do not. The difference with respect to the constraint for normal users is that the second constraint allows *name* and *passed* to occur simultaneously in the same result. Therefore a query that just tested the presence of a <grade> element without checking its content would satisfy this second constraint.

If the result of a query satisfies the corresponding constraint, then its stripped version is returned to the owner of the query.

7 Perspectives

This paper contains exploratory work toward the definition of information flows security in XML transformations. As such it opens several perspectives both for the practical and the theoretical aspects.

First and foremost the cost of the dynamic analysis must be checked against an implementation (we are currently working on it). We expect this cost to be reasonably low: ℂDuce's pattern matching fully relies on dynamic type checking, therefore if we embed the dynamic generation of typed security labels in ℂDuce's runtime the resulting overhead should be small. Also, to fill the gap with practice we must devise expressive and user-friendly ways to describe the labeling of XML documents in the meta-data (that is, XML Schemas and DTDs) and to express the associated security policies (for instance, in Section 6 we expressed them in propositional logic). These security properties should be defined by sets of constraints (i.e., formulæ of an appropriate logic) that are automatically generated from a specification expressed in an "ad hoc" language (e.g., like the authorizations defined in [6]).

The precision of the dynamic analysis must be enhanced by program rewriting techniques. To exemplify, an obvious "optimization" consists in rewriting all closed (i.e., without capture variables) patterns into an equivalent type constraint pattern, by replacing $\wedge$ for **&**, $\vee$ for **|**, and $\times$ for (,), so as to transform the pattern $(s\,|\,t,u\&v)$ into the type $(s \vee t) \times (u \wedge v)$. Indeed, the analysis on types is more precise than that on equivalent patterns as the latter is recursively applied to subcomponents forgetting, in doing so, many interdependencies. But other subtler rewritings could improve our analysis: for instance $p_1 = (x\&\mathsf{true})|(x\&\mathsf{false})$ is equivalent to $p_2 = x\&(\mathsf{true} \vee \mathsf{false})$ but $(\ell_{\mathsf{Bool}}{:}e) /\!\!/ p_1 = \ell_{\mathsf{Bool}}{::}(e /\!\!/ p_1)$ while $(\ell_{\mathsf{Bool}}{:}e) /\!\!/ p_2 = \varnothing_{\mathbf{ok}}$. This discrepancy can be identified

[14] For the sake of the example we expressed these constraints in a propositional logic where the labels are atoms, but different languages are possible. The definition of such languages is out of the scope of the paper and matter of future research: see Section 7.

with the fact that the analyses of pair, intersections, and union patterns are performed independently on the two subpatterns. Thus a possible way to tackle this problem is by transferring some information from one pattern to the other, for example by mimicking the automaton-based technique used by ℂDuce for the just-in-time compilation of patterns.

Finally note that one of the main technical novelties of this work is to endow security labels with constraints. The constraints at issue are quite simple, since they just express the static knowledge of the type of the labeled expression. It is then natural to think of much more expressive constraints. For example we can think of endowing labels with integrity constraints and define non-interference just in terms of consistent databases. In this perspective a program that checked the integrity of a base would be always interference-free even if it accessed private information. Of course checking non-interference in this case would be even more challenging but it could pave the way to (security) proof carrying code for XML.

Acknowledgments

We are very grateful to Nicole Bidoit and Nevin Heintze for their careful reading and invaluable suggestions, and to Dario Colazzo, Alain Frisch, Alban Gabillon, and Massimo Marchiori for their feedback.

References

1. M. Abadi, B. Lampson, and J.-J. Levy. Analysis and caching of dependencies. In *ICFP '96, 1st ACM Conference on Functional Programming*, pages 83–91, 1996.
2. V. Benzaken, G. Castagna, and A. Frisch. CDuce: An XML-Centric General Purpose Language. In *ICFP '03, 8th ACM Conference on Functional Programming*, pages 51–63, 2003.
3. A. Christensen, A. Møller, and M. Schwartzbach. Extending Java for high-level web service construction. *ACM TOPLAS*, 2003. To appear.
4. S. Cluet and J. Siméon. Yatl: a functional and declarative language for XML, 2000. Draft manuscript.
5. S. Conchon. Modular information flow analysis for process calculi. In *FCS 2002, Proceedings of the Foundations of Computer Security Workshop*, Copenhagen, Denmark, 2002.
6. E. Damiani, S. De Capitani di Vimercati, S. Paraboschi, and P. Samarati. A fine-grained access control system for XML documents. *ACM TOISS*, 5(2):169–202, 2002.
7. E. Damiani, S. De Capitani di Vimercati, S. Paraboschi, and P. Samarati. Design and implementation of an access control processor for XML documents. *Computer Networks*, 33(1–6):59–75, 2000.
8. M. Fernández, J. Siméon, and P. Wadler. An algebra for XML query. In *FST&TCS*, number 1974 in LNCS, pages 11–45, 2000.
9. A. Frisch, G. Castagna, and V. Benzaken. Semantic Subtyping. In *LICS '02, Seventeenth Annual IEEE Symposium on Logic in Computer Science*, pages 137–146, 2002.
10. A. Gabillon and E. Bruno. Regulating access to XML documents. In *15th Annual IFIP WG 11.3 Working Conference on Database Security.*, July 15-18 2001.
11. V. Gapayev and B. Pierce. Regular object types. In *Proc. of ECOOP '03*, Lecture Notes in Computer Science. Springer, 2003.

12. J.A. Goguen and J. Meseguer. Security policy and security models. In *Proceedings of Symposium on Secrecy and Privacy*, pages 11–20. IEEE Computer Society, april 1982.
13. H. Hosoya and B. Pierce. XDuce: A typed XML processing language. *ACM TOIT*, 2003. To appear.
14. IBM AlphaWorks. *XML Security Suite*. http://www.alphaworks.ibm.com/tech/xmlsecuritysuite.
15. A. Myers and B. Liskov. A decentralized model for information flow control. In *Proceedings of the 16th ACM Symposium on Operating Systems Principles (SOSP)*, pages 129–142, 1997.
16. F. Pottier and S. Conchon. Information flow inference for free. In *ICFP '00, 5th ACM Conference on Functional Programming*, pages 46–57, September 2000.
17. F. Pottier and V. Simonet. Information flow inference for ML. *ACM SIGPLAN Notices*, 31(1):319–330, January 2002.
18. A. Sabelfeld and A. Myers. Language-based information-flow security. *IEEE Journal on Selected Areas in Communications*, 21(1):5–19, 2003.
19. D. Volpano and G. Smith. A type-based approach to program security. In *TAPSOFT '97*, number 1214 in Lecture Notes in Computer Science, pages 607–621. Springer, 1997.
20. D. Volpano, G. Smith, and C. Irvine. A sound type system for secure flow analysis. *Journal of Computer Security*, 4(3):167–187, 1996.
21. C. Wallace and C. Runciman. Haskell and XML: Generic combinators or type based translation? In *ICFP '99, 4th ACM Conference on Functional Programming*, pages 148–159, 1999.

Unreliable Failure Detectors via Operational Semantics*

Uwe Nestmann and Rachele Fuzzati

School of Computer and Communication Sciences
EPFL-I&C, 1015 Lausanne, Switzerland

Abstract. The concept of *unreliable failure detectors for reliable distributed systems* was introduced by Chandra and Toueg as a fine-grained means to add weak forms of synchrony into asynchronous systems. Various kinds of such failure detectors have been identified as each being the weakest to solve some specific distributed programming problem. In this paper, we provide a fresh look at failure detectors from the point of view of programming languages, more precisely using the formal tool of operational semantics. Inspired by this, we propose a new failure detector model that we consider easier to understand, easier to work with and more natural. Using operational semantics, we prove formally that representations of failure detectors in the new model are equivalent to their original representations within the model used by Chandra and Toueg.

1 Executive Summary

Background. In the field of Distributed Algorithms, a widely-used computation model is based on *asynchronous* communication between a fixed number n of connected processes, where *no timing assumptions* can be made. Moreover, processes are subject to *crash-failure*: once crashed, they do not recover. The concept of *unreliable failure detectors* was introduced by Chandra and Toueg [CT96] as a fine-grained means to add weak forms of synchrony into asynchronous systems. Various kinds of such failure detectors have been identified as each being the weakest to solve some specific distributed programming problem [CHT96].

The two communities of Distributed Algorithms and Programming Languages do not always speak the same "language". In fact, it is often not easy to understand each other's terminology, concepts, and hidden assumptions. Thus, in this paper, we provide a fresh look at the concept of failure detectors from the point of view of programming languages, using the formal tool of operational semantics. This paper complements previous work [NFM03] in which we used an operational semantics for a distributed process calculus to formally prove that a particular algorithm (also presented in [CT96]) solves the Distributed Consensus problem. Readers who are interested in proofs about algorithms *within* our new model (rather than proofs *about* it) are thus referred to our previous paper.

* Supported by the Swiss National Science Foundation, grant No. 21-67715.02, the Hasler Foundation, grant No. DICS 1825, an EPFL start-up grant, and the EU FET-GC project PEPITO.

V.A. Saraswat (Ed.): ASIAN 2003, LNCS 2896, pp. 54–71, 2003.

Table 1. Uniform "Abstract" Operational Semantics Scheme

$$(\textsc{env})\ \frac{\text{`` failure detection events happens in the environment ''}}{\Gamma \longrightarrow \Gamma'}$$

$$(\textsc{tau})\ \frac{\Gamma \longrightarrow \Gamma' \qquad N \xrightarrow{\tau@i} N' \qquad \text{`` } i \text{ not crashed in } \Gamma \text{ ''}}{\Gamma \vdash N \longrightarrow \Gamma' \vdash N'}$$

$$(\textsc{suspect})\ \frac{\Gamma \longrightarrow \Gamma' \qquad N \xrightarrow{\mathsf{suspect}_j@i} N' \qquad \text{`` } i \text{ not crashed in } \Gamma \text{ ''} \qquad \boxed{\text{`` } j \text{ may be suspected by } i \text{ in } \Gamma \text{ ''}}}{\Gamma \vdash N \longrightarrow \Gamma' \vdash N'}$$

The work of Chandra and Toueg emphasized the axiomatic treatment of qualitative properties rather than quantitative ones. Like them, also our current focus is on issues of correctness, not of performance. Moreover, Chandra and Toueg did not primarily aim at providing concrete design support for an implementation of failure detectors. Like them, also we rather seek mathematically useful and convincing semantic abstractions of failure detectors.

Vehicle of Discussion. In Table 1, we propose a *uniform scheme* to describe the operational semantics of process networks in the context of failure detectors. For convenience, we abstract from the way how the steps $N \longrightarrow N'$ of process networks are generated (from the code that implements the respective algorithm), so we do not provide rules for this. It is sufficient for our purposes to observe that a process i in a network carries out essentially two kinds of transitions $N \longrightarrow N'$, distinguished by whether it requires the suspicion of some process j by process i, or not. Formally, we use labels $\mathsf{suspect}_j@i$ and $\tau@i$ to indicate these two kinds.

In summary, Table 1 presents a two-layered operational semantics scheme. One layer, in addition to the transitions $N \longrightarrow N'$ of process networks, also describes the transitions $\Gamma \longrightarrow \Gamma'$ of the network's environment, keeping track of crashes and providing failure detection, as indicated by rule (ENV). Another layer, with the rules (TAU) and (SUSPECT), deals with the compatibility of network and environment transitions, conveniently focusing on the environment conditions for the two kinds of transitions of process networks. For example, the boxed condition exploits the failure detector information that in our scheme is to be provided via the environment component Γ.

A *system run* in this uniform scheme is an infinite sequence of transitions

$$\Gamma_0 \vdash N_0 \longrightarrow \Gamma_1 \vdash N_1 \cdots \longrightarrow \Gamma_t \vdash N_t \longrightarrow \cdots$$

that we often simply abbreviate as $(\Gamma_t \vdash N_t)_{t\in\mathbb{N}_0}$. We also use the projections onto the respective *environment runs* $(\Gamma_t)_{t\in\mathbb{N}_0}$ and *network runs* $(N_t)_{t\in\mathbb{N}_0}$, which exist by definition of the rules (TAU) and (SUSPECT) of Table 1.

Overview. We start the main part of the paper by an introduction (§2) to the various kinds of failure detectors proposed by Chandra and Toueg, including Ω which appeared in [CHT96]. Already in this introduction, we rephrase their previous work using the scheme of Table 1. In addition, we use this exercise to come up with a well-motivated proposal for a new model and way to represent failure detectors (§3). We formalize our proposal according to the scheme of Table 1 and redefine all previously introduced FDs within the new model (§4). Exploiting the common scheme and the formality of the framework of operational semantics, we formally prove that our redefinitions are "equivalent" to the original definitions by a mutual simulation of all possible system runs that are derivable in either case (§5) and draw some conclusions from having done so (§6).

Contribution. In summary, this paper contains an original presentation, using operational semantics, of existing work by Chandra and Toueg, which is targeted at an audience in process calculi and programming language semantics. The paper also provides, as its main contribution, a new model to represent failure detectors that tries to eliminate a number of drawbacks of the original model used by Chandra and Toueg. Many other failure detectors have been studied in the literature; for the current paper, we restrict our attention to the ones introduced in [CT96,CHT96]. The technical contribution is a formal comparison of the representations of these classical failure detectors in the new model with their representations on the old model, which was greatly simplified by having both models fit the scheme of Table 1. To conclude, we argue that our new model for FDs is easier to understand, easier to work with, and more natural than the one used by Chandra and Toueg (see the justification in §6).

Related Work. We are not aware of any related or competing approaches.

Acknowledgments. We very much thank André Schiper and Sam Toueg for enlightening discussions about failure detectors and, more generally, distributed algorithms, but they may not necessarily agree with all conclusions that we drew from our work. Many thanks also to Pawel Wojciechowski and the anonymous referees for their comments on a draft of this paper.

2 A Fresh Look at the Model of Chandra and Toueg

Recall that we are addressing asynchronous message-passing distributed system with no bounds on message delays and a fixed number n of processes. Let $\mathbb{P} := \{1 \ldots, n\}$ denote the set of process names. All processes are supposed to run the very same algorithm. Processes may crash; when they do so, they do not recover. Systems evolve in time. $\mathbb{T}$ denotes some discrete time domain; for simplicity, we may just assume that $\mathbb{T} = \mathbb{N}_0$. At any time, the *state* of a system is fully determined by the states of the individual processes while running the algorithm, together with the messages currently present in the global message buffer. We do not formalize global states, but treat them abstractly throughout the paper.

2.1 Schedules

A *schedule*, of the form $(\mathbb{T}, I, S)$, is essentially a sequence S of global steps in time $\mathbb{T}$, while running some algorithm starting within the initial global state I, where the message buffer is empty. Sometimes, we refer to just S as being the schedule. A *step* is usually produced by any one of the n processes according to the algorithms' instructions: in atomic fashion, a process receives some messages (possibly none) from the message buffer, *possibly* checks whether it is allowed to suspect another process, and sends out new messages (possibly none) to the message buffer, while changing its state. Often, it is left rather informal and imprecise how steps are actually defined, and there are a number of variations for this. In both papers [CT96,CHT96], it is assumed that *schedules are infinite.*

A Simple Operational Semantics View. To avoid the details of generating global steps from an algorithm, and to abstract away from the details of message-passing, we model schedules simply as infinite sequences of *labeled transitions*

$$N \xrightarrow{\mu @ i} N'$$

that denote steps between abstract global states (ranged over by N) by performing an action μ due to the activity of some process i. The label μ depends on whether i needs to (be able to) suspect another process j, or not. If it does so, we indicate this by a transition arrow labeled with $\mu := \text{suspect}_j$, otherwise we simply use the label $\mu := \tau$, which is commonly used to indicate that "some" not further specified activity takes place by process i.

In this paper, we are not at all interested in how schedules themselves are generated. An example of this can be found in our earlier paper [NFM03], where we used a reasonably standard process calculus to do this.

2.2 Unreliable Failure Detectors

According to Chandra and Toueg [CT96], a failure detector (FD) is a separate module attached locally to a process; each process i has its own private FD_i. At any moment in time, each FD outputs a list of (names of) processes that it currently suspects to have crashed. FDs are unreliable: they may

- make mistakes,
- disagree among them, and
- change their mind indefinitely often.

Process i interacts with *its* FD_i explicitly by only being allowed to suspect another process j at any given time t, if FD_i's output list contains j at this time.

Example 1 ("Application"). When a process needs to go on by the help of another process — e.g., via reception of a message — it may typically specify to "either wait for this process, or suspect it and continue otherwise". However, it is only allowed to choose the second option if its FD permits it at the very moment that the process looks at the FDs output, which it may have to do infinitely often if the FD insists on not permitting the required suspicion.

More formally, the concept of process crashes is modeled by means of *failure patterns* $F : \mathbb{T} \rightarrow 2^{\mathbb{P}}$ that describe monotonically when in a run crashes happen. For example, $F(42) = \{3, 7\}$ means that processes 3 and 7 have crashed during the time interval $[0, 42]$. Similarly, the concept of failure detection is modeled by so-called *failure detector histories* $H : \mathbb{T}\times\mathbb{P} \rightarrow 2^{\mathbb{P}}$. For example, $H(42, 5) = \{6, 7\}$ means that at time 42 processes 6 and 7 are suspected by the FD of process 5. Given the previous example F, this means that process 7 is correctly suspected, while process 6 is erroneously suspected. Mathematically, a FD is a function[1]

$$\mathcal{D} : (\mathbb{T} \rightarrow 2^{\mathbb{P}}) \rightarrow 2^{(\mathbb{T}\times\mathbb{P}\rightarrow 2^{\mathbb{P}})}$$

that maps failure patterns F to sets of failure detector histories. Such sets may be specified by additional properties, as exemplified in Section 2.3. From now on, whenever we mention some F and H in the same context, then $H \in \mathcal{D}(F)$ is silently assumed; we may write $H_{\mathcal{D}}$ to indicate the referred FD.

Finally, *system runs* R are quintuples $(F, H, \mathbb{T}, I, S)$. Subject to the shared time domain $\mathbb{T}$, the schedule S of a run is required to be "compatible" with the failure pattern F and detector history H: (1) a process cannot take a step after it has crashed (according to F); (2) when a process takes a step and queries its failure detector module, it gets the current value output by its local failure detector module (according to H).

A process is *correct in a given run*, if it does not crash in this run. It may, though, crash in other runs. Let $\text{crashed}(R) := \text{crashed}(F) := \bigcup_{t\in\mathbb{T}} F(t)$ denote the processes that *have crashed* in run R according to its failure pattern F. Consequently, $\text{correct}(R) := \text{correct}(F) := \mathbb{P}\setminus\text{crashed}(F)$. Usually, one considers only runs in which $\text{correct}(F) \neq \emptyset$, i.e., in every run at least one process survives. Sometimes, as for the Consensus algorithm that we studied in [NFM03], it is even required that less than $n/2$ processes may crash. Abstractly, we use $\text{maxfail}(n)$ to denote the maximal number of crashes permitted in a run.

A Simple Operational Semantics View. To make the model fit our universal scheme of Table 1, we need to recast the information contained in failure patterns F and failure detector histories H in an evolutionary manner as environment transitions. Both F and H are totally defined over the whole time domain $\mathbb{T}$. Thus, we may simply use transitions $(t, F, H) \longrightarrow (t{+}1, F, H)$, in which time t just passes, while we leave F and H unchanged. Rule ($\mathbb{T}$-ENV) of Table 2 serves us to generate such transitions formally.

System configurations are of the form $\Gamma \vdash N$, where Γ is an element of the domain $\mathbb{T} \times (\mathbb{T} \rightarrow 2^{\mathbb{P}}) \times (\mathbb{T} \times \mathbb{P} \rightarrow 2^{\mathbb{P}})$, and N represents some state of the algorithm. The rules ($\mathbb{T}$-TAU) and ($\mathbb{T}$-SUSPECT) in Table 2 formally describe the conditions for a transition of an algorithm in state N to produce system transitions depending on the current information about crashes and failure detectors

[1] The term *failure detector* is overloaded to denote the single devices that are attached to processes, as well as the mathematical object that governs the output that any of these single devices may yield during runs.

Table 2. Operational Semantics for the Failure Detectors of [CT96]

$$(\mathbb{T}\text{-ENV})\ \frac{\Box}{(t,F,H) \longrightarrow (t{+}1,F,H)}$$

$$(\mathbb{T}\text{-TAU})\ \frac{(t,F,H) = \Gamma \longrightarrow \Gamma' \qquad N \xrightarrow{\tau @ i} N' \qquad i \notin F(t)}{\Gamma \vdash N \ \longrightarrow\ \Gamma' \vdash N'}$$

$$(\mathbb{T}\text{-SUSPECT})\ \frac{(t,F,H) = \Gamma \longrightarrow \Gamma' \qquad N \xrightarrow{\mathsf{suspect}_j @ i} N' \qquad i \notin F(t) \qquad \boxed{j \in H(i,t)}}{\Gamma \vdash N \ \longrightarrow\ \Gamma' \vdash N'}$$

at any time $t \in \mathbb{T}$. Note that in both cases the process i who is responsible for the transition must not (yet) have crashed at the time t when the transition is supposed to happen: $i \notin F(t)$. Note further that if it is required to suspect some process j to perform the transition, then the respective failure detector of process i must *currently permit* to do so: $j \in H(i,t)$. It is easily possible to generalize this representation to the case where, to carry out a single transition, process i would need to suspect more than one other process; for simplicity, we only consider a single suspicion.

System runs can now be fit together dynamically as infinite sequences of system transitions that are derivable by operational semantics rules.

Definition 1. *A $\mathbb{T}(\mathcal{D})$-run is an infinite sequence $((t,F,H) \vdash N_t)_{t \in \mathbb{T}}$ generated by* ($\mathbb{T}$-ENV), ($\mathbb{T}$-TAU), *and* ($\mathbb{T}$-SUSPECT), *for some F, H with $H \in \mathcal{D}(F)$.*

2.3 "Sufficiently Reliable" Failure Detectors

Probably the main novelty of Chandra and Toueg's paper [CT96] was the definition and study of a number of FDs $\mathcal{D}$ that only differ in their degree of reliability, as expressed by a combination of safety and liveness properties. These are formulated in terms of permitted and enforced suspicions according to the respective failures reported in F and the failure detection recorded in $H \in \mathcal{D}(F)$:

completeness addresses *crashed processes that must be suspected*
by (the FDs of) "complete" processes.

accuracy addresses *correct processes that must not be suspected*
by (the FDs of) "accurate" processes.

Note that these definitions refer to suspicions allowed by the output of the individual FDs at *any* time (according to H). By "complete" and "accurate" processes, we indicate that there is some flexibility in the definition of the set of processes that the property shall be imposed on. Note that H is, in principle, a total function. Therefore, at any moment, it provides FD output for every process — crashed or not — so there are at least three obvious possibilities to define the meaning of "complete" and "accurate" processes:

1. *all* processes ($\in \mathbb{P}$)
2. only processes that are still *alive* at time t ($\in \mathbb{P} \setminus F(t)$)
3. only *correct* processes ($\in \text{correct}(F) = \mathbb{P} \setminus \text{crashed}(F)$)

Obviously, it does not make much sense to speculate, as in solution 1, about the output of FDs of crashed processes, because the respective process would never ever again contact its FD[2]. It seems much more natural to select solution 2, because it precisely considers just those processes that are alive. If completeness or accuracy shall hold only eventually, then solution 3 becomes interesting: since every incorrect process that is still alive at some moment will crash later on, the property would just hold at a later time. In infinite runs, and for properties with an eventual character, solutions 2 and 3 become "equivalent" [CT96].

Eight Candidates. Various instantiations of completeness and accuracy have been proposed. We recall the eight FDs of Chandra and Toueg, defined by all possible combinations of the following variations of completeness and accuracy. Note that their defining properties are quantified over *all possible runs.* For every given run, the components F and $H \in \mathcal{D}(F)$ are fixed, as well as the derived notions of which processes are considered to be correct in this run.

strong completeness. *Eventually,* every process that crashes is permanently suspected by *every* correct process.

$$\forall F, H : \exists \hat{t} : \forall p \in \text{crashed}(F) : \forall q \in \text{correct}(F) : \forall t \geq \hat{t} : p \in H(q,t)$$

weak completeness. *Eventually,* every process that crashes is permanently suspected by *some* correct process.

$$\forall F, H : \exists \hat{t} : \forall p \in \text{crashed}(F) : \exists q \in \text{correct}(F) : \forall t \geq \hat{t} : p \in H(q,t)$$

Combined with the strong/weak versions of completeness, the following notions of accuracy induce eight variants of FDs, with their denotations listed in brackets.

strong accuracy. ($\mathcal{P}/\mathcal{Q}$) No process is suspected before it crashes.

$$\forall F, H : \forall t : \forall p, q \in \mathbb{P} \setminus F(t) : p \notin H(q,t)$$

Note that the "accuracy set" is the alive processes.

weak accuracy. ($\mathcal{S}/\mathcal{W}$) Some correct process is never suspected.

$$\forall F, H : \exists p \in \text{correct}(F) : \forall t : \forall q \in \mathbb{P} \setminus F(t) : p \notin H(q,t)$$

Note that also here the "accuracy set" is the alive processes.

---

[2] It might be more appropriate to define H as partial function where $H(i,t)$ is only defined if $i \notin F(t)$. One might also conclude that the (F, H)-based model is too rich.

eventual strong accuracy. ($\Diamond\mathcal{P}/\Diamond\mathcal{Q}$) There is a time after which *correct* processes are *not suspected* by any correct process.

$$\forall F, H : \exists \hat{t} : \forall t \geq \hat{t} : \forall p \in \text{correct}(F) : \forall q \in \text{correct}(F) : p \notin H(q,t)$$

eventual weak accuracy. ($\Diamond\mathcal{S}/\Diamond\mathcal{W}$) There is a time after which *some correct* processes is *never suspected* by any correct process.

$$\forall F, H : \exists \hat{t} : \exists p \in \text{correct}(F) : \forall t \geq \hat{t} : \forall q \in \text{correct}(F) : p \notin H(q,t)$$

Note that, except under strong and weak accuracy, (the FDs of) processes that crash (in a given run) may behave completely unconstrained (in this run) before they have crashed. Although the formulation of the above FDs might appear a bit ad-hoc (see Gärtner [Gär01] for a gentle and systematic overview), some of them are known to provide the weakest FDs required to solve certain well-known distributed programming problems: $\Diamond\mathcal{W}$ solves Consensus, where less than $n/2$ processes may crash; $\mathcal{S}$ solves Consensus, where less than n processes may crash; $\mathcal{P}$ solves the Byzantine General's Problem [CT96].

Another important contribution found in [CT96] is the concept of reducibility between FDs. Essentially, it studies reduction algorithms $T_{\mathcal{D}\to\mathcal{D}'}$ that transform the outputs of $\mathcal{D}$ into outputs of $\mathcal{D}'$. As a consequence, any problem that can be solved using $\mathcal{D}'$ can also be solved using $\mathcal{D}$, written $\mathcal{D} \succeq \mathcal{D}'$. If such a relation holds in both directions, then we write $\mathcal{D} \cong \mathcal{D}'$. Interestingly, FDs with either strong or weak completeness are not that much different with respect to their ability to solve problems: $\mathcal{P} \cong \mathcal{Q}$, $\mathcal{S} \cong \mathcal{W}$, $\Diamond\mathcal{P} \cong \Diamond\mathcal{Q}$, $\Diamond\mathcal{S} \cong \Diamond\mathcal{W}$.

2.4 Another Prominent Candidate: Ω

In this subsection, we try to explain that completeness is required in the (F, H)-based model used by Chandra and Toueg only because this model is unrealistically rich, which we might regard as a deficiency of the model.

Without the completeness property, the (F, H)-based model allows a FD to be *incomplete*, i.e., to indefinitely not suspect a crashed process. We may conceive this as unrealistic if we, for instance, assume that FDs work with time-outs. Given that any crashed process can only have sent a finite number of messages before having crashed, any FD will be reporting suspicion of a crashed process at the latest after "timeout" times "number of sent messages" units of time.

It is instructive to replay the argument in the dual model of "presence detectors", where the outputs of FDs are inversed, i.e., where H tells which processes are currently "trusted" by the FD. Intuitively, this dual model feels more direct since the trust in a process to be alive is often based on "feeling its heartbeat". Of course, since it is just a mathematically dual, also this model is too rich: an incomplete FD may be expressed by always listing a crashed process as being trusted[3]. However, it is easy to constrain this model as to avoid incomplete FDs.

[3] In this model, completeness more intuitively specifies the natural requirement that "you cannot feel the heartbeat of a crashed process infinitely long". Strong completeness makes sense in precisely this respect. The intuition of weak completeness is less clear: why should the heartbeat argument apply to only one process?

Table 3. Operational Semantics for the "Presence" Detector Ω of [CHT96]

$$(\Omega\text{-ENV}) = (\mathbb{T}\text{-ENV}) \qquad\qquad (\Omega\text{-TAU}) = (\mathbb{T}\text{-TAU})$$

$$(\Omega\text{-SUSPECT})\ \frac{(t,F,H) = \Gamma \longrightarrow \Gamma' \qquad N \xrightarrow{\mathsf{suspect}_j @ i} N' \qquad i \notin F(t) \qquad \boxed{j \neq H(i,t)}}{\Gamma \vdash N \ \longrightarrow\ \Gamma' \vdash N'}$$

Interestingly, the detector Ω, as introduced in another paper by Chandra and Toueg, jointly with Hadzilacos [CHT96], represents one particular model variant of presence detectors that is "sufficiently poor" to render incomplete FDs impossible. With Ω, every FD at any moment in time outputs *only a single process* that is believed to be "correct"[4] or trusted; $H : \mathbb{P} \times \mathbb{T} \to \mathbb{P}$.

(Ω) Eventually, all correct processes always trust the same correct process.

$$\exists \hat{t} \in \mathbb{T} : \exists q \in \text{correct}(F) : \forall p \in \text{correct}(F) : \forall t > \hat{t} : H(p,t) = q$$

Observe why it is no longer possible to indefinitely enforce trust on crashed processes: since the output of H contains only a single process, the associated process *can* always suspect any of the $n-1$ other processes. The property above eventually stabilizes to a single correct process, then permanently allowing the suspicion of the remaining other processes.

It is straightforward to provide an operational semantics view for Ω by adapting the previous configurations to the new type of H. The rule (Ω-SUSPECT) in Table 3 shows the duality of presence detectors versus failure detectors: the condition on a suspected j is inversed.

Definition 2. *A $\mathbb{T}(\Omega)$-run is an infinite sequence $((t,F,H) \vdash N_t)_{t \in \mathbb{T}}$ generated by (Ω-ENV), (Ω-TAU), and (Ω-SUSPECT), for some F, H with $H \in \Omega(F)$.*

The FD Ω was introduced only as an auxiliary concept in the proof that $\Diamond\mathcal{W}$ is the weakest FD solving Consensus, which works because $\Omega \cong \Diamond\mathcal{W}$.

3 Proposal of a New Model of FDs

There are a number of observations on the (F,H)-based specification of FDs that motivate us to do it differently.

From Static to Dynamic. The use of (F,H) as "predicting" the failures of processes and their detection by others in a run appears to be counter-intuitive from the point of view of programming language semantics where events of a computation are to happen dynamically and possibly non-deterministically.

[4] Original called this way in [CHT96], but it is different from the notion of a correct process which is precisely about a full run, and not just one moment in it.

From Failure Detection to Presence Detection. In Subsection 2.4, we mentioned the problem of completeness, which is inherent in the (F, H)-model, and how Ω does a good job in avoiding the problem in a poorer dual model. We propose to use similar ideas also for FDs that are not equivalent to Ω.

Intuition Mismatch. The use of a *total* function H to model outputs of FD modules counters the intuition that a process crash should imply the crash of its attached FD at the same time. This could be repaired by making H a partial function that is only defined when the respective process has not yet crashed. Below, we go even further and replace the H completely.

We do not see the need to record in H an abundance of unreliable information. The quest to model a minimal amount of information has two consequences.

From Unstable to Stable. The use of unreliable FD-outputs listed in H very carefully models a lot of unstable (and therefore questionable!) information, namely information that changes nondeterministically over time. However, in order to characterize the above six FD properties, only (eventually) stable information is used. We therefore propose to model only this kind of stable information — once it has become stable — and to freely allow any suspicions for which there is no stable information yet, as in the "poor" output of Ω.

From Local to Global. Chandra and Toueg intended to give an abstract model of FDs, but we feel that by attaching individual modules to every process it is still too concrete, i.e., close to implementation aspects. Furthermore, the above completeness and accuracy properties are all defined globally on the set of all FD modules, not on individual ones. Thus, we rather propose to model FDs as a single global entity and have all processes share access to it. As a side-effect, the freedom (="imprecision") in the formulation of FD properties with respect to the proper choice of the "accuracy set" disappears.

Summing up, we seek to model the environment of process networks dynamically as a global device that exclusively stores stable information. But, apart from crashes that occur irrevocably, which information should this precisely be?

Looking again at the previous (F, H)-based FDs, the principle behind the more complicated notions of accuracy seems to be that of "justified trust". Correct processes — those that, according to F, were *immortal* in the given run — are *trusted forever* (according to H) in the given run, either eventually or already from the very beginning. If, in some dynamic operational semantics scenario, we want to model the moment when such a process becomes trusted, we must ensure this process not to crash afterwards — it must become immortal at this very moment. Then, we call such a process *trusted-immortal*.

4 An Operational Semantics View of the New Model

As motivated in the previous section, we propose a new model — defined by its operational semantics — that can be used to represent all of the FDs of

Table 4. Operational Semantics Scheme with Reliable Information

$$(\mathbb{D}\text{-ENV})\ \frac{(\mathsf{TI} \cup \mathit{TI}) \cap \mathit{C} = \emptyset \qquad (\mathsf{C} \cup \mathit{C}) \cap \mathit{TI} = \emptyset \qquad |\mathsf{C} \cup \mathit{C}| \leq \text{maxfail}(n)}{(\mathsf{TI}, \mathsf{C}) \ \rightarrow \ (\mathsf{TI} \uplus \mathit{TI}, \mathsf{C} \uplus \mathit{C})}$$

$$(\mathbb{D}\text{-TAU})\ \frac{(\mathsf{TI}, \mathsf{C}) = \Gamma \ \rightarrow \Gamma' \qquad N \xrightarrow{\tau @ i} N' \qquad i \notin \mathsf{C}}{\Gamma \vdash N \rightarrow \Gamma' \vdash N'}$$

$$(\mathcal{X}\text{-SUSPECT})\ \frac{(\mathsf{TI}, \mathsf{C}) = \Gamma \ \rightarrow \Gamma' \qquad N \xrightarrow{\mathsf{suspect}_j @ i} N' \qquad i \notin \mathsf{C} \qquad \boxed{\text{condition}_{\mathcal{X}}(\Gamma, j)}}{\Gamma \vdash N \ \rightarrow \Gamma' \vdash N'}$$

[CT96] solely based on stable/reliable information that is not fixed before a run starts, but is dynamically appearing along its way. It turns out that two kinds of information suffice: (1) which processes have crashed, and (2) which processes have become *trusted-immortal*. Both kinds of information may occur at any moment in time, and they remain irrevocable in any continuation of the current run.

We use the symbol $\mathbb{D}$ to recall the softer more *d*ynamic character as opposed to time $\mathbb{T}$ just passing for some predefined crash and detection schedule.

Modeling Stable Reliable Information. Rule ($\mathbb{D}$-ENV) in Table 4 precisely models the nondeterministic appearance of crashed and trusted-immortal processes in full generality. Environments $\Gamma = (\mathsf{TI}, \mathsf{C}) \in 2^{\mathbb{P}} \times 2^{\mathbb{P}}$ record sets TI of trusted-immortal processes and sets C of crashed processes. In a single step, an environment may be increased by further trusted-immortal processes ($\in \mathit{TI}$) and further crashed processes ($\in \mathit{C}$). The two empty-intersection conditions on TI and C assure a simple sanity property: processes shall not be crashed and trusted-immortal at the same time. Note that we also assume the operator $\uplus$ to imply the empty intersection of its operands: processes may crash or become trusted-immortal only once. The condition concerning maxfail(n) is obvious: we should not have more processes crash than permitted. The sets TI and C may both be empty, which implies that the environment may also do idle steps; this is necessary for runs whose number of steps is greater than the number of processes, like in the infinite runs that we are looking at.

Rule ($\mathbb{D}$-TAU) straightforwardly permits actions $\tau@i$ if $i \notin \mathsf{C}$. Rule ($\mathcal{X}$-SUSPECT) requires in addition that the suspected process j is permitted to be suspected by Γ, depends on the FD accuracy that we intend to model.

Failure Detection. In our model, trusted-immortal processes are intended to be never again suspected by *any* other process. In Table 5, we specify different incarnations for the rule ($\mathcal{X}$-SUSPECT) that are targeted at the the various notions of accuracy that our FDs are intended to satisfy.

Table 5. Operational Semantics with Reliable Detectors

$$(\mathcal{P}/\mathcal{Q}\text{-SUSPECT})\ \frac{(\mathsf{TI},\mathsf{C}) = \Gamma \to \Gamma' \qquad N \xrightarrow{\text{suspect}_j @ i} N' \qquad i \notin \mathsf{C} \qquad \boxed{j \in \mathsf{C}}}{\Gamma \vdash N \to \Gamma' \vdash N'}$$

$$(\mathcal{S}/\mathcal{W}\text{-SUSPECT})\ \frac{(\mathsf{TI},\mathsf{C}) = \Gamma \to \Gamma' \qquad N \xrightarrow{\text{suspect}_j @ i} N' \qquad i \notin \mathsf{C} \qquad \boxed{j \notin \mathsf{TI} \neq \emptyset}}{\Gamma \vdash N \to \Gamma' \vdash N'}$$

$$(\Diamond\text{-SUSPECT})\ \frac{(\mathsf{TI},\mathsf{C}) = \Gamma \to \Gamma' \qquad N \xrightarrow{\text{suspect}_j @ i} N' \qquad i \notin \mathsf{C} \qquad \boxed{j \notin \mathsf{TI}}}{\Gamma \vdash N \to \Gamma' \vdash N'}$$

Strong Accuracy (as in $\mathcal{P}/\mathcal{Q}$) can be expressed very simply and directly in our environment model, because it does not explicitly talk about *correct* processes. Rule ($\mathcal{P}/\mathcal{Q}$-SUSPECT) says precisely that "no site is suspected before it has crashed" by requiring that any suspected process j must be part of the set C. Note that the component TI is not used at all; if we were interested in just strong accuracy, it would suffice to record information about crashed processes.

Definition 3. *A $\mathbb{D}(\mathcal{P}/\mathcal{Q})$-run is an infinite sequence $(\Gamma_t \vdash N_t)_{t\in\mathbb{T}}$ generated by* ($\mathbb{D}$-ENV), ($\mathbb{D}$-TAU), *and* ($\mathcal{P}/\mathcal{Q}$-SUSPECT).

Weak Accuracy (as in $\mathcal{S}/\mathcal{W}$) builds on rule ($\mathcal{S}/\mathcal{W}$-SUSPECT). In order to get that "some correct process is never suspected", the idea is that some process must become trusted-immortal before *any* suspicion in the system may take place. A process i may always suspect process j unless the failure detector tells otherwise, i.e., unless it imposes to trust j by $j \notin \mathsf{TI}$. Note that if we allowed suspicions before the "election" of at least one trusted-immortal, then even a process becoming trusted-immortal later on might have been suspected before.

Definition 4. *A $\mathbb{D}(\mathcal{S}/\mathcal{W})$-run is an infinite sequence $(\Gamma_t \vdash N_t)_{t\in\mathbb{T}}$ generated by* ($\mathbb{D}$-ENV), ($\mathbb{D}$-TAU), *and* ($\mathcal{S}/\mathcal{W}$-SUSPECT).

The other versions of "eventual accuracy" cannot be expressed solely by operational semantics rules; additional liveness properties are required.

Eventual Weak Accuracy (as in $\Diamond\mathcal{S}/\Diamond\mathcal{W}$) builds on rule ($\Diamond$-SUSPECT), which is a slightly more liberal variant of ($\mathcal{S}/\mathcal{W}$-SUSPECT): suspicions may take place without some process having become trusted-immortal. However, we need to add to the condition on runs that *eventually* at least one process indeed turns out to be trusted-immortal such it cannot be suspected *afterwards*. The detector Ω of [CHT96] is very close to this very intuition, as well (confirming $\Omega \cong \Diamond\mathcal{W}$).

Definition 5. *A $\mathbb{D}(\Diamond\mathcal{S}/\Diamond\mathcal{W})$-run is an infinite sequence $(\Gamma_t \vdash N_t)_{t\in\mathbb{T}}$ generated by* ($\mathbb{D}$-ENV), ($\mathbb{D}$-TAU), *and* ($\Diamond$-SUSPECT), *where there is a reachable state* $(\mathsf{TI}_{\hat{t}}, \mathsf{C}_{\hat{t}}) \vdash N_{\hat{t}}$ *with* $\mathsf{TI}_{\hat{t}} \neq \emptyset$.

Eventual Strong Accuracy (as in $\Diamond\mathcal{P}/\Diamond\mathcal{Q}$) is a nuance trickier: like its weak counterpart, it builds directly on rule ($\Diamond$-SUSPECT) and adds to it a condition on runs, but now a more restrictive one: in any run, there must be a state $\Gamma = (\mathsf{TI}, \mathsf{C})$ with $\mathsf{TI} \cup \mathsf{C} = \mathbb{P}$. In such a state, all decisions about correctness and crashes have been taken. This witnesses that $\Diamond\mathcal{P}$ is called *eventually perfect* [CT96]: in fact, the condition $j \notin \mathsf{TI}$ becomes equivalent to the perfect condition $j \in \mathsf{C}$ of $\mathcal{P}/\mathcal{Q}$.

Definition 6. *A* $\mathbb{D}(\Diamond\mathcal{P}/\Diamond\mathcal{Q})$*-run is an infinite sequence* $(\Gamma_t \vdash N_t)_{t\in\mathbb{T}}$ *generated by* ($\mathbb{D}$-ENV), ($\mathbb{D}$-TAU), *and* ($\Diamond$-SUSPECT), *where there is a reachable state* $(\mathsf{TI}_{\hat{t}}, \mathsf{C}_{\hat{t}}) \vdash N_{\hat{t}}$ *with* $\mathsf{TI}_{\hat{t}} \cup \mathsf{C}_{\hat{t}} = \mathbb{P}$.

Note that we did not explicitly mention completeness properties in our redefinitions. In fact, as inspired by Ω (see Subsection 2.4), they are built-in implicitly. With the rules ($\mathcal{S}/\mathcal{W}$-SUSPECT) and ($\Diamond$-SUSPECT), the suspicion of a crashed process is *always* allowed. With rule ($\mathcal{P}/\mathcal{Q}$-SUSPECT), the suspicion of a crashed process is allowed *immediately after it crashed.* Note that completeness is thus provided in the strongest possible manner, strictly implying strong completeness. It does not only hold eventually, but "as soon as possible", subject only to accuracy constraints. This built-in strength is a consequence of the principle of our model to store only stable information to govern the possibility of suspicions, leaving complete freedom to suspect in all those cases where the fate of the suspected process has not yet been decided on in the current run.

Having *re*defined runs that are allowed for particular FDs, we must of course also argue that they correspond to the original counterparts of Chandra and Toueg. This we do formally in the following section.

5 Validation of the New Model

We compare our $\mathbb{D}$-representations of FDs with the $\mathbb{T}$-representations proposed in [CT96] extensionally through mutual "inclusion" of their sets of runs. Essentially, we are looking for a mutual simulation of $\mathbb{T}$-runs and $\mathbb{D}$-runs sharing the same network run (by projecting onto the N-component). To this aim, it will be crucial to formally relate the respective notions of environment.

Definition 7. $(\mathsf{TI}, \mathsf{C})$ corresponds to (t, F, H), *written* $(\mathsf{TI}, \mathsf{C}) \sim (t, F, H)$, *if*

1. $\mathsf{C} = F(t)$, *and*
2. $j \in \mathsf{TI}$ *implies that* $\forall i \in \mathbb{A}_t : \forall t' \geq t : j \notin H(i, t')$.

where $\mathbb{A}_t := F(t)$ *or* $\mathbb{A}_t := \mathrm{correct}(F)$ *depending on the respective "accuracy set" (see Section 2) of the version of accuracy that we are considering.*

It is also convenient to use case 2 in the opposite direction for the case of $t' = t$: If $(\mathsf{TI}, \mathsf{C}) \sim (t, F, H)$, then $\forall i \in \mathbb{A}_t : \forall j : j \in H(i, t)$ implies that $j \notin \mathsf{TI}$.

Example 2. For all F, H: $(\emptyset, F(0)) \sim (0, F, H)$. This correspondence holds, because $\mathsf{C} = F(0)$ is defined to satisfy case 1, and $\mathsf{TI} = \emptyset$ trivially implies case 2.

We present the main theorems in a generic manner. Let $\mathcal{D}^{s} \in \{\mathcal{P}, \mathcal{S}, \Diamond\mathcal{P}, \Diamond\mathcal{S}\}$ and $\mathcal{D}^{w} \in \{\mathcal{Q}, \mathcal{W}, \Diamond\mathcal{Q}, \Diamond\mathcal{W}\}$ denote the FDs with respect to strong and weak completeness. We use $\mathcal{D}^{s}/\mathcal{D}^{w}$ to conveniently denote the respective variants.

First, we offer a rather obvious observation.

Lemma 1. *Let* $\mathcal{D}^{s}/\mathcal{D}^{w} \in \{\mathcal{P}/\mathcal{Q},\ \mathcal{S}/\mathcal{W},\ \Diamond\mathcal{P}/\Diamond\mathcal{Q},\ \Diamond\mathcal{S}/\Diamond\mathcal{W}\}$.
Every $\mathbb{T}(\mathcal{D}^{s})$*-run is also a* $\mathbb{T}(\mathcal{D}^{w})$*-run.*

Proof. Trivial, because strong completeness implies weak completeness. □

Now, we show the main mutual simulation theorem. It also underlines the fact that the kind of completeness does not really matter much, which confirms the respective result of [CHT96], that the eight FDs collapse into just four.

Theorem 1. *Let* $\mathcal{D}^{s}/\mathcal{D}^{w} \in \{\mathcal{P}/\mathcal{Q},\ \mathcal{S}/\mathcal{W},\ \Diamond\mathcal{P}/\Diamond\mathcal{Q},\ \Diamond\mathcal{S}/\Diamond\mathcal{W}\}$.

1. *If* $((t, F, H) \vdash N_t)_{t\in\mathbb{T}}$ *is a* $\mathbb{T}(\mathcal{D}^{w})$*-run,*
then there is $(\Gamma_t)_{t\in\mathbb{T}}$ *such that* $(\Gamma_t \vdash N_t)_{t\in\mathbb{T}}$ *is a* $\mathbb{D}(\mathcal{D}^{s}/\mathcal{D}^{w})$*-run.*
2. *If* $(\Gamma_t \vdash N_t)_{t\in\mathbb{T}}$ *is a* $\mathbb{D}(\mathcal{D}^{s}/\mathcal{D}^{w})$*-run,*
then there are F, H *such that* $((t, F, H) \vdash N_t)_{t\in\mathbb{T}}$ *is a* $\mathbb{T}(\mathcal{D}^{s})$*-run.*

Note that part 1 requires only a $\mathbb{T}(\mathcal{D}^{w})$-run, while part 2 provides a $\mathbb{T}(\mathcal{D}^{s})$-run, which is due to the strength of the built-in completeness of the $\mathbb{D}$-model.

Proof. See Appendix A.

We also show that Ω is "equivalent" to $\Diamond\mathcal{S}/\Diamond\mathcal{W}$.

Theorem 2.

1. *If* $((t, F, H) \vdash N_t)_{t\in\mathbb{T}}$ *is a* $\mathbb{T}(\Omega)$*-run,*
then there is $(\Gamma_t)_{t\in\mathbb{T}}$ *such that* $(\Gamma_t \vdash N_t)_{t\in\mathbb{T}}$ *is a* $\mathbb{D}(\Diamond\mathcal{S}/\Diamond\mathcal{W})$*-run.*
2. *If* $(\Gamma_t \vdash N_t)_{t\in\mathbb{T}}$ *is a* $\mathbb{D}(\Diamond\mathcal{S}/\Diamond\mathcal{W})$*-run,*
then there are F, H *such that* $((t, F, H) \vdash N_t)_{t\in\mathbb{T}}$ *is a* $\mathbb{T}(\Omega)$*-run.*

This theorem allows us to denote $\mathbb{D}(\Diamond\mathcal{S}/\Diamond\mathcal{W})$-runs as $\mathbb{D}(\Omega)$-runs, and justifies the model that we used when proving a Consensus algorithm correct in [NFM03].

We could prove Theorem 2 "directly" just like we did in the proof of Theorem 1. However, we can also profit from the work of Chandra and Toueg, whose results translate into our setting as in Proposition 1 below.

There are algorithmic FD-transformations $T_{\Omega\to\Diamond\mathcal{W}}$ and $T_{\Diamond\mathcal{S}\to\Omega}$ such that

- for all F, H : $H \in \Omega(F)$ implies $T_{\Omega\to\Diamond\mathcal{W}}(H) \in \Diamond\mathcal{W}(F)$, and
- for all F, H : $H \in \Diamond\mathcal{S}(F)$ implies $T_{\Diamond\mathcal{S}\to\Omega}(H) \in \Omega(F)$.

Proposition 1 ([CHT96]). *Let* R *denote* $((t, F, H) \vdash N_t)_{t\in\mathbb{T}}$.

1. *If* R *is a* $\mathbb{T}(\Omega)$*-run, then* $((t, F, T_{\Omega\to\Diamond\mathcal{W}}(H)) \vdash N_t)_{t\in\mathbb{T}}$ *is a* $\mathbb{T}(\Diamond\mathcal{W})$*-run.*
2. *If* R *is a* $\mathbb{T}(\Diamond\mathcal{S})$*-run, then* $((t, F, T_{\Diamond\mathcal{S}\to\Omega}(H)) \vdash N_t)_{t\in\mathbb{T}}$ *is a* $\mathbb{T}(\Omega)$*-run.*

Proof (of Theorem 2).

1. By Proposition 1(1) and Theorem 1(1).
2. By Theorem 1(2) and Proposition 1(2).

□

6 Conclusions

We propose a new model of FDs that we consider easier to understand, easier to work with, and more natural than the model used by Chandra and Toueg.

- It is arguably easier to understand, because the environment information that it provides to check the conditions of the rules of Table 5 is designed to be minimal — shared, global, and reliably stable — and to support just those moments when suspicions are effectively needed with a maximal flexibility. This is in contrast to the (F, H)-based model with individual FD modules that at any moment in time produce unreliable output (sets of currently suspected processes) that their master process may not be interested in for a long time; they might even have crashed already.

  It is certainly easier to understand from the computational point of view due to the dynamic modeling of events concerning crashes and their detection.
- It is easier to work with, because it is generally more light-weight in that only stable information is considered. Moreover, our model is simpler since the strongest possible completeness property is built-in, so we do not have to explicitly care about it when, e.g., looking for the weakest FD solving a distributed computing problem in our model. Also, to exploit any of the accuracy properties in proofs, it suffices to check rather simple syntactic conditions in states of a given run. Starting in the initial state, a finite search suffices, profiting from the built-in monotonicity of the stable information.
- It is more natural, for two reasons: (1) It avoids the need to impose additional completeness properties by allowing dynamic nondeterminism on suspicions until they possibly become forbidden forever. (2) It avoids the problem of selecting the "accuracy set" of eventually reliable individual FDs, where the (F, H)-based model leaves the choice to FDs of correct, alive, or all processes. In our model, FD modules are not modeled individually as belonging each to individual processes, but failure detection is modeled by using a global shared entity. In a dynamic operational scenario as ours, the only reasonable choice for the counterpart of the "accuracy set" is the alive processes.

In this paper, we concentrated on the FDs presented in [CT96,CHT96], but we see no obstacle in applying our principles of Section 3 to other (F, H)-based FDs.

References

[CHT96] T.D. Chandra, V. Hadzilacos, and S. Toueg. The weakest failure detector for solving consensus. *Journal of the ACM*, 43(4):685–722, 1996.

[CT96] T.D. Chandra and S. Toueg. Unreliable failure detectors for reliable distributed systems. *Journal of the ACM*, 43(2):225–267, 1996.

[Gär01] F.C. Gärtner. A gentle introduction to failure detectors and related problems. Technical Report TUD-BS-2001-01, TU Darmstadt, April 2001.

[NFM03] U. Nestmann, R. Fuzzati, and M. Merro. Modeling consensus in a process calculus. In Roberto Amadio and Denis Lugiez, editors, *Proceedings of CONCUR 2003*, volume 2761 of *LNCS*, pages 399–414. Springer, August 2003.

A Proofs of Theorem 1

Proof. For each case of $\mathcal{D}^{s}/\mathcal{D}^{w}$, the proof follows the same pattern.

1. Let $((t,F,H) \vdash N_t)_{t\in\mathbb{T}}$ be a $\mathbb{T}(\mathcal{D}^{w})$-run. Any step

$$(t,F,H) \vdash N_t \longrightarrow (t{+}1,F,H) \vdash N_{t+1} \tag{1}$$

must now be simulated by a *derivable* step

$$\Gamma_t \vdash N_t \longrightarrow \Gamma_{t+1} \vdash N_{t+1} \tag{2}$$

for some $(\Gamma_t)_{t\in\mathbb{T}}$. In order to *verify* the derivability of transition (2), the semantics tells us to check the two possibilities of action $\tau@i$ and $\mathsf{suspect}_j@i$ carried out by N_t. Naturally, knowing the derivability of transition (1), we can deduce some knowledge about the output of F and H at time t.
We construct Γ_t using this knowledge; formally, we establish $\Gamma_t \sim (t,F,H)$. To this aim, we prove that the correspondence is preserved under appropriately defined environment transitions, indicated by $\Gamma_t :\longrightarrow \Gamma_{t+1}$.

Lemma 2. *If* $\Gamma_t \sim (t,F,H)$ *and* $\boxed{\Gamma_t :\longrightarrow \Gamma_{t+1}}$, *then* $\Gamma_{t+1} \sim (t{+}1,F,H)$.

Proof (of Lemma 2 by construction of $\Gamma_t :\longrightarrow \Gamma_{t+1}$*).*
In fact, it is never a problem to have $\Gamma_{t+1} \sim (t{+}1,F,H)$ satisfy its first condition $\mathsf{C}(t{+}1) = F(t{+}1)$ by simply setting $\mathsf{C}(t{+}1) := F(t{+}1)$. Note that since F is steadily increasing, then the condition $\mathsf{C}\uplus C$ of ($\mathbb{D}$-ENV) is satisfied. In order to have $\Gamma_{t+1} \sim (t{+}1,F,H)$ satisfy its second condition, we must be very cautious *when* we add elements to TI_t to become TI_{t+1}.

case $\mathcal{D}^{w}{=}\mathcal{Q}$ **:** Never add elements to TI_{t+1}. Then any transition $\Gamma_t \longrightarrow \Gamma_{t+1}$ is derivable, and Lemma 2 holds immediately.

case $\mathcal{D}^{w}{=}\mathcal{W}$ **:** Here, we may assume *weak accuracy*: some correct process p is never suspected. We simply set $\mathsf{TI}_0 := \{p\}$ to get the desired effect, and afterwards never again change the TI_t component.
Note that with $\Gamma_0 := (\{p\},F(0))$, we have $\Gamma_0 \sim (0,F,H)$ precisely due to the weak accuracy assumption of the $\mathbb{T}(\mathcal{W})$-run.
Note that then, as a consequence, Lemma 2 immediately holds for all transitions (of all $t>0$). Of course, it is also needed in these transition to check that p will not accidentally be chosen to crash; this is guaranteed, because of weak accuracy requiring a *correct* process, which is thus $\notin$ $\mathsf{crashed}(F)$ and will therefore never enter any C_t.

case $\mathcal{D}^{w}{=}\Diamond\mathcal{W}$ **:** Here, we may assume *eventual weak accuracy*: eventually, after time $\hat{t}$, some correct process p will never again be suspected, so we set $\mathsf{TI}_0 = \cdots = \mathsf{TI}_{\hat{t}-1} = \emptyset$ and $\mathsf{TI}_{\hat{t}} := \{p\}$.
The critical transition for Lemma 2 to hold is $\Gamma_{\hat{t}-1} \longrightarrow \Gamma_{\hat{t}}$. Here, the eventual weak accuracy property makes $\Gamma_{\hat{t}} \sim (\hat{t},F,H)$ satisfy condition 2.

case $\mathcal{D}^{w}{=}\Diamond\mathcal{Q}$ **:** Here, we may assume *eventual strong accuracy*: eventually, after time $\hat{t}$, no correct process p will ever again be suspected, so we set $\mathsf{TI}_0 = \cdots = \mathsf{TI}_{\hat{t}-1} = \emptyset$ and $\mathsf{TI}_{\hat{t}} := \mathsf{correct}(F)$.
The argument for Lemma 2 to hold is a replay of the previous case. □

The "constructive preservation" property of Lemma 2 provides us with the required assumptions to simulate subsequent steps and, thus, allows us to iteratively simulate the whole infinite run, starting in all cases but one at $\Gamma_0 = (\emptyset, F(0))$. Let us first look at individual simulation steps.

Lemma 3. *If* $\Gamma_t \sim (t, F, H)$ *and transition* (1), *then transition* (2).

Proof (of Lemma 3). Check the conditions to derive transitions (1), either due to ($\mathbb{T}$-TAU) or due to ($\mathbb{T}$-SUSPECT), and then observe that the correspondence of environments also enables to derive the respective transition (2). If transition (1) required $i \notin F(t)$, which it does in both ($\mathbb{T}$-TAU) and ($\mathbb{T}$-SUSPECT), then the first condition on $\sim$ provides us with the required $i \notin \mathsf{C}_{\Gamma_t}$ in ($\mathbb{D}$-TAU) and in any of the ($\mathcal{X}$-SUSPECT). We may then focus on the more interesting boxed condition of the rules ($\mathcal{X}$-SUSPECT).

case $\mathcal{D}^{\mathrm{w}}{=}\mathcal{Q}$ **:** The enabling conditions for ($\mathcal{P}/\mathcal{Q}$-SUSPECT) only depend on the respective C and hold trivially.

case $\mathcal{D}^{\mathrm{w}}{=}\mathcal{W}$ **:** Recall that the second condition on $\sim$ tells us that $j \in H(i,t)$ implies $j \notin \mathsf{TI}_t$. Since, by definition of $\Gamma_t :\longrightarrow \Gamma_{t+1}$ for the case $\mathcal{W}$, also $\mathsf{TI}_t \neq \emptyset$ holds for all $t > 0$. Together, this ($j \notin \mathsf{TI}_t \neq \emptyset$) implies that suspicion steps can always be simulated using ($\mathcal{S}/\mathcal{W}$-SUSPECT).

cases $\mathcal{D}^{\mathrm{w}}{=}\Diamond\mathcal{W}$ **and** $\mathcal{D}^{\mathrm{w}}{=}\Diamond\mathcal{Q}$ **:** Again, $j \in H(i,t)$ implies $j \notin \mathsf{TI}_t$. This is already sufficient to simulate suspicion steps using ($\Diamond$-SUSPECT). □

The basic requirement on $\mathbb{D}(\mathcal{D}^{\mathrm{s}}/\mathcal{D}^{\mathrm{w}})$-runs (matching the Definitions 3–6) is to consist of sequences of derivable transitions. This holds in all cases by the infinite iteration of Lemma 3. However, the $\Diamond$-runs (i.e., the $\mathbb{D}(\Diamond\mathcal{S}/\Diamond\mathcal{W})$-runs and $\mathbb{D}(\Diamond\mathcal{P}/\Diamond\mathcal{Q})$-runs) require an additional condition.

case $\mathcal{D}^{\mathrm{w}}{=}\Diamond\mathcal{W}$ **:** The resulting run is a $\mathbb{D}(\Diamond\mathcal{S}/\Diamond\mathcal{W})$-run, because there is $\hat{t}$ in which we set $\mathsf{TI}_{\hat{t}} := \{p\}$.

case $\mathcal{D}^{\mathrm{w}}{=}\Diamond\mathcal{Q}$ **:** The resulting run is a $\mathbb{D}(\Diamond\mathcal{P}/\Diamond\mathcal{Q})$-run, because there is $\hat{t}$ in which we set $\mathsf{TI}_{\hat{t}} := \mathrm{correct}(F)$. However, this is not necessarily yet the moment needed to establish a $\mathbb{D}(\Diamond\mathcal{P}/\Diamond\mathcal{Q})$-run. In order to find this moment $\hat{t}'$, we only have to wait until all the processes in crashed(F) have actually crashed. By our definition of C_t, the required property of Definition 5 that $\mathsf{TI}_{\hat{t}'} \cup \mathsf{C}_{\hat{t}'} = \mathbb{P}$ becomes valid.

2. The structure of this proof is similar to the previous one. Let $R := (\Gamma_t \vdash N_t)_{t\in\mathbb{T}}$ be a $\mathbb{D}(\mathcal{D}^{\mathrm{s}}/\mathcal{D}^{\mathrm{w}})$-run with $\Gamma_t = (\mathsf{TI}_t, \mathsf{C}_t)$ for $t \in \mathbb{T}$. Before, we constructed a sequence of Γ_t for some fixed F, H such that $\Gamma_t \sim (t, F, H)$ for all $t \geq 0$. Here, we construct the functions F_R, H_R with $H_R \in \mathcal{D}^{\mathrm{s}}(F_R)$ by means of the information found in the various Γ_t. While it is obvious that F_R should very closely follow the information recorded in C, there is a lot of freedom in the choice of H_R — allowing suspicions or not — because it is supposed to contain a lot of information that is never checked in the projection $(N_t)_{t\in\mathbb{T}}$ of R. We are going to choose H_R to permit the maximum amount of suspicions. As a consequence, this choice gives us the strongest possible completeness property essentially for free.

Independent of the FD, we may transform any given $\mathbb{D}$-run into a $\mathbb{T}$-run by constructing F_R in a uniform manner:

$$\forall t \in \mathbb{T} : F_R(t) \stackrel{\text{def}}{=} \mathsf{C}_t$$

For the construction of H_R, we need to distinguish among the cases of $\mathcal{D}^{\mathsf{s}}$ between the perfect FD ($\mathcal{P}$) and the imperfect FDs ($\mathcal{S}, \Diamond\mathcal{P}, \Diamond\mathcal{S}$).
For the perfect FD, we set:

$$\forall t \in \mathbb{T} : \forall i \in \mathbb{P} : H_R(i,t) \stackrel{\text{def}}{=} \mathsf{C}_t$$

For the imperfect FDs, we need some auxiliary functions.
Let R denote the run $(\Gamma_t \vdash N_t)_{t\in\mathbb{T}}$.
Let $\text{ti}(R) := \bigcup_{t\in\mathbb{T}} \mathsf{TI}_t$ denote the set of trusted-immortal processes of R.
If $j \in \text{ti}(R)$, then let t_j be (uniquely!) defined by $j \notin \mathsf{TI}_{t_j-1}$ and $j \notin \mathsf{TI}_{t_j}$, thus denoting the moment in which j becomes trusted-immortal.
To define H_R, we start by allowing suspicions of every process by every other process at any time. (We may, of course, leave out useless permissions to self-suspect, but this does not matter for the result.)

$$\forall t \in \mathbb{T} : \forall i \in \mathbb{P} : H_R(i,t) \stackrel{\text{def}}{=} \mathbb{P}$$

From these sets, we subtract (in imperative programming style, with $\forall$ denoting `forall` loops) a number of processes, depending on the time at which trusted-immortal processes have become so.

$$\forall j \in \text{ti}(R) : \forall i \in \mathbb{P} : \forall t \geq t_j : H_R(i,t) \stackrel{\text{def}}{=} H_R(i,t) \setminus \{j\}$$

By construction, we immediately get that $\Gamma_t \sim (t, F_R, H_R)$.
The correspondence is also preserved by the Γ-transitions of R.

Lemma 4. *If* $\Gamma_t \sim (t, F_R, H_R)$ *and* $\Gamma_t \;\longrightarrow \Gamma_{t+1}$, *then* $\Gamma_{t+1} \sim (t{+}1, F_R, H_R)$.

As before, we need a simulation lemma; now, it addresses the other direction.

Lemma 5. *If* $\Gamma_t \sim (t, F_R, H_R)$ *and transition* (2), *then transition* (1).

It holds for symmetric reasons, because it is also exploiting the same correspondence properties of the constructed pair F_R, H_R.
The only difference (in fact, a simplification) in the final iteration of the simulation is in the case of the $\mathbb{D}(\Diamond\mathcal{P}/\Diamond\mathcal{Q})$-run. Here, the moment $\hat{t}$ that according to Definition 6 shows $\mathsf{TI}_{\hat{t}} \cup \mathsf{C}_{\hat{t}} = \mathbb{P}$ is *precisely* the earliest moment that provides weak accuracy for the $\mathbb{T}(\Diamond\mathcal{P})$-run.
Now, the remaining argument is to show that the components (F_R, H_R) of a $\mathbb{T}(\mathcal{D}^{\mathsf{s}})$-run also satisfy *strong completeness.* In fact, by construction, we have the following completeness property for the case of imperfect FDs:

in every run,
every crashed process is always suspected by every process.

This obviously strictly implies strong completeness. The case of perfect FDs is similar, just replacing the words *always suspected* by the words *suspected right after it crashed*, which also strictly implies strong completeness. □

Bankable Postage for Network Services

Martín Abadi[1], Andrew Birrell[2], Mike Burrows[3], Frank Dabek[4], and Ted Wobber[2]

[1] University of California, Santa Cruz, CA
[2] Microsoft Research, Silicon Valley, CA
[3] Google, Mountain View, CA
[4] MIT Laboratory for Computer Science, Cambridge, MA

Abstract. We describe a new network service, the "ticket server". This service provides "tickets" that a client can attach to a request for a network service (such as sending email or asking for a stock quote). The recipient of such a request (such as the email recipient or the stockbroker) can use the ticker server to verify that the ticket is valid and that the ticket hasn't been used before. Clients can acquire tickets ahead of time, independently of the particular network service request. Clients can maintain their stock of tickets either on their own storage, or as a balance recorded by the ticket server. Recipients of a request can tell the ticket server to refund the attached ticket to the original client, thus incrementing the client's balance at the ticket server. For example, an email recipient might do this if the email wasn't spam. This paper describes the functions of the ticket server, defines a cryptographic protocol for the ticket server's operations, and outlines an efficient implementation for the ticket server.

1 Motivation

Several popular network services today have the characteristic that the person using the service doesn't pay for it, even though the provider of the service incurs real costs. In a variety of cases this largesse has led to abuse of the services. The primary example is email, where the result is the spam business. Other examples include submitting URL's to a web indexing service, or creating accounts at a free service such as Yahoo or Hotmail, or even in some cases reading a web site (which can be abused, for example, by parsing out the web site's contents and presenting them as part of another site, without permission).

To appreciate the scale and difficulty of the spam problem, consider some statistics. In February 2003 AOL reported that their spam prevention system was detecting, and suppressing, 780 million incoming spam emails per day for their 27 million users [5]. On August 4th 2003 Hotmail, with 158 million active user accounts, received 2.6 billion emails (plus 39 million from within Hotmail). 2.1 billion (78%) of the emails were mechanically classified as spam, roughly 24,000 per second. That same day Hotmail also had more than 1 million new accounts created—most likely those were not all for normal users. Today, spam is extremely cheap for the sender. If you search at Google for "bulk email" you will find organizations willing to deliver your email

V.A. Saraswat (Ed.): ASIAN 2003, LNCS 2896, pp. 72–90, 2003.

to one million addresses (provided by them) for a total cost of $190 (i.e., 0.019 cents per message). Accordingly, there is a lot of current work on techniques for deterring spam [4, 9, 12, 13, 15, 20].

This paper is about one technology for preventing such abuse, which we call the "ticket server". For ease of exposition in this paper, and because spam was our primary motivation, we will mostly describe the application of this technology to email, though in general it applies equally well to other network services. To read what we say in a more general form, replace "email" with "network service"; replace "sender" with "client requesting the service"; replace "recipient" or "recipient's ISP" with "service provider"; and replace "email message" with "service request".

As was originally pointed out by Dwork & Naor [11], and subsequently used in several systems such as HashCash [6] and Camram [8], we can potentially reduce the abuse of email by forcing senders to attach to the email proof that the sender has performed a lengthy computation as part of the process of sending the email.

Straightforward computation is not the only plausible cost that we might impose on a sender. We might use a function that's designed to incur delays based on the latency of memory systems [2, 10] — this is more egalitarian towards people with low-powered computers. We might hope to force the sender to consult a human for each message by using a Turing test [3]. We might also rely on real money, and use a proof-of-purchase receipt as the proof. In all these cases, after the cost has been incurred the sender can assemble proof that it has been incurred. In this paper we call any such proof a "ticket". Our design is essentially independent of the particular form of cost that the ticket represents.

In all these schemes, it is critical that the sender can't use the same ticket for lots of messages. The way that this has been achieved in the past is by making the email message itself be involved in the creation of the proof. For example, you could require that the computation be parameterized by the message date, recipient, and some abstract or digest of the message body.

Unfortunately, this means that the sender must incur the cost after composing the message and before committing the message to the email delivery system. The sending human must wait for the cost to be incurred before knowing that the message has been sent. For example, the sender could not disconnect from the network until after the computation completes. In addition to causing an unfortunate delay, this synchronization limits how long a computation we can require, and thus limits the economic impact of the computational cost on spammers.

The ticket server design was created to avoid this problem. By introducing a stateful server, we allow the sender to acquire tickets independently of a particular email message. Instead, the ticket server maintains a database of tickets issued. When a recipient receives the email, he calls the ticket server to verify that the ticket is not being reused, and to update the ticket server's database to prevent subsequent reuse. The operation of the ticket server is reminiscent of how postage stamps work.

Introduction of a stateful server allow us to provide three key benefits:

(1) *Asynchrony:* senders can incur the cost (for example, perform the computation) well before composing or sending the email (perhaps overnight). This makes the whole mechanism much less intrusive on users' normal workflows, and therefore

more likely to be acceptable to the non-spamming user community. It also makes it reasonable to demand much higher computational costs, since a non-spam sender can incur the cost at a convenient time.

(2) *Stockpiles:* since the tickets are now independent of what they'll be applied to, users can maintain a stockpile of tickets for future use. They could also acquire such a stockpile from elsewhere (for example, bundled with their purchase of email software or bundled with signing a contract to use a certain ISP, or presented to them by recipients who would welcome their email).

(3) *Refunds:* having a stateful server allows us to introduce the notion of an "account" for a user. This provides a small convenience for the sender, as a way for managing the user's stockpile of tickets. But it also enables a new feature: if a recipient receives a ticket with an email from a sender, and the recipient decides that the email didn't need to be paid for, then the recipient can refund the ticket to the sender, by telling the ticket server to do so.

Refunds are potentially a powerful tool. If we can arrange that most tickets on non-spam email will be refunded, then most non-spamming users will end up having most of their tickets refunded, and have little need to acquire new ones. In that case it would be reasonable to make tickets even more expensive, and thereby make it even more likely that we can price the tickets in a way that will increase the sender's cost for sending spam to a level comparable to (or even exceeding) that of physical junk mail. We will consider the feasibility of this level of refunding in section 3.

The remainder of the paper is as follows. We provide an overview of our design in section 2. In section 3 we show how the ticket server can be applied to the particular case of spam reduction. Section 4 outlines a secure protocol for the ticker server operations. Section 5 describes an efficient implementation of the ticket server. Section 6 discusses the issues that would arise from trying to deploy the ticket server and apply it to spam reduction. Finally, section 7 discusses some related work, and we summarize our conclusions in section 8.

2 Overview

In its simplest form, the ticket server provides two operations to its customers: "Request Ticket" and "Cancel Ticket". A third operation, "Refund Ticket", is also useful.

The "Request Ticket" operation has no arguments. It returns a "ticket kit" (assuming the requestor has no account balance, see below). The ticket kit specifies one or more "challenges". The challenges can take a variety of forms, such as computing a hard function (paying for the ticket by CPU or memory cycles), or passing a Turing test, or paying for the ticket by credit card (in some separate transaction not described here). The requestor decides which challenge to accept and does whatever it takes to respond to the challenge. The requestor can then take the response, and the rest of the ticket kit, and assemble them into a new, valid ticket. (Details of how this is achieved are described below).

The requestor can use this ticket, once, in any manner he chooses (for example, he can transmit it as a header line in an email message). Someone receiving a ticket (for example, the recipient of the email) can take the ticket and invoke the ticket server's "Cancel Ticket" operation. This operation verifies that the ticket is valid, and that it hasn't been cancelled before. It then records in the ticket server's database that the ticket has been cancelled, and returns to the caller (for example, the recipient of the email) indicating that the operation succeeded. Of course, the "Cancel Ticket" operation will return a failure response if the ticket is invalid or has previously been cancelled.

Finally, whoever received the ticket and successfully performed the "Cancel Ticket" operation can choose to refund the ticket to the originator by invoking the "Refund Ticket" operation at the ticket server. This causes the ticket server to credit the ticket to the original requestor's account, by incrementing the requestor's account balance. The ticket server also records in its database the fact that this ticket has been refunded. Of course, the ticket server rejects a "Refund Ticket" request for a previously refunded ticket.

When a requestor whose account has a positive balance calls the "Request Ticket" operation, instead of a ticket kit (with a challenge) he receives a new, valid, unused ticket, and his account balance is decremented.

The ticket server is designed to guarantee that tickets cannot be forged; that a ticket can be cancelled only if it's valid and hasn't previously been cancelled; and that a ticket can be refunded only after it has been cancelled, and only if authorized by the principal who cancelled the ticket, and at most once. We describe later a cryptographically protected protocol to achieve these guarantees.

As will be seen in the detailed protocol description, the use of tickets provides some additional benefits. The ticket identifies the requestor by an anonymous account identifier created by the ticket server. In addition to the ticket itself, the requestor is given a ticket-specific encryption key; the requestor is free to use this key to protect material that is shipped with the ticket, since the same key is returned to the caller of the "Cancel Ticket" operation.

3 Application to Spam Reduction

To use the ticket server for spam reduction, an email recipient (or his ISP) arranges that he will see only messages that either have a valid ticket attached, or are from a "trusted sender". This restriction can be implemented in the receiving ISP's mail servers, or by the recipient's email viewing program. There is a wide range of options for the notion of "trusted sender", which we'll discuss later in this section.

3.1 Basic Scenario

The figure below shows the basic scenario for using tickets for spam prevention, in the absence of trusted senders. We describe later what happens if the ticket is omitted, and/or the sender is trusted.

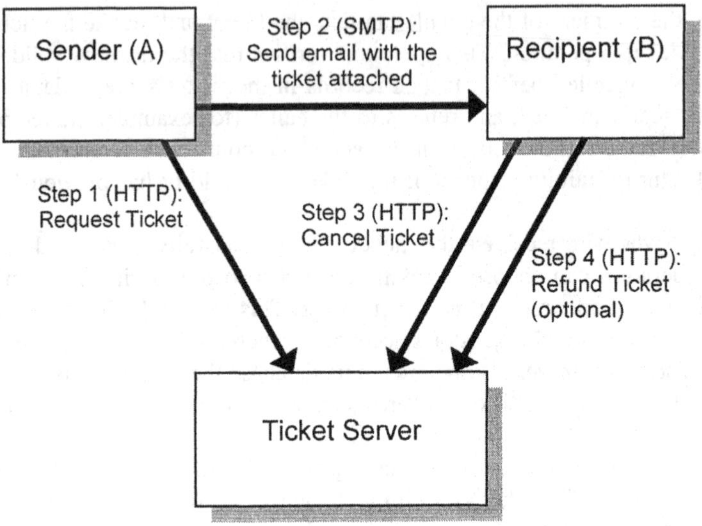

Fig. 1. The basic scenario for using tickets for spam prevention.

The prospective sender acquires a ticket kit by interacting with the ticket server by HTTP, constructs a ticket from the kit by responding to its challenge, and sends the ticket to the recipient with the email message by SMTP. The recipient (or the recipient's ISP) validates and cancels the ticket with the assistance of the ticket server by HTTP, and optionally uses HTTP once more to refund the ticket. It is of course possible for a frequent sender to acquire many ticket kits in a single HTTP request, and for a busy ISP to verify, cancel, and optionally refund many tickets in a single HTTP request.

3.2 Who Is a Trusted Sender?

We envisage several different ways of categorizing a sender as "trusted". Some senders should probably be trusted on a per-recipient basis. A user might reasonably decide to trust everyone in his address book. He might additionally trust everyone to whom he has previously sent email. There might also be a mechanism for a user to add recipients to a "safe list" exempted from spam prevention. (The safe list would be stored by the ISP if the ISP was responsible for checking tickets, or by the user's email viewing program otherwise.) More broadly a user or his ISP might decide that some groups of senders are to be trusted. For example, if the ISP has a strong (and enforced!) policy of canceling spammers' accounts, then email from within the same ISP should be trusted. It might also be wise to trust senders from other ISP's with similarly acceptable anti-spam policies.

There is of course an issue about trusting senders, given the fact that most SMTP transactions do not authenticate the asserted sender name. The ISP can no doubt assure itself that asserted senders within the ISP's own domain name space occur only on messages originating within the ISP, and that those are authentic. However, there is always some suspicion about unauthenticated sender names arriving from outside. There are reasonable part-way measures available, though. For example, an ISP could accept as authentic a sender in "aol.com" if and only if the SMTP server transmitting the message is owned by AOL, as proved by reverse IP address lookup in DNS (and similarly for Hotmail, Yahoo, and numerous others). Overall we believe that with care it is possible to have a reasonable degree of confidence in the authenticity of a very large proportion of sender names. There are other groups currently exploring ideas for stronger authentication of sender names in email (see section 7.3).

3.3 Variations of the Basic Scenario

We can now explain what happens in all the variations of the basic scenario: messages with or without tickets, from trusted or untrusted senders. In the following, the actions described as being performed by the recipient's ISP could equally well be performed by the recipient's email program — either form of deployment would work.

Variation 1: Trusted Sender, but No Ticket
When a message arrives with no ticket attached, but from a trusted sender, the message appears in the recipient's inbox in the usual way. The ticker server is not involved at all.

Variation 2: Trusted Sender with a Ticket Attached
When a message arrives with a ticket attached from a trusted sender, it appears in the recipient's inbox in the usual way. Additionally, the ticket server is told that it should refund the ticket, crediting the sender's account. This step can be taken automatically by the ISP, and requires no explicit action from the recipient. In this case the "Cancel Ticket" and "Refund Ticket" operations at the ticket server can be combined for efficiency.

Variation 3: Untrusted Sender with a Ticket Attached
When a message arrives with a ticket attached from an untrusted sender, the recipient's ISP calls the ticket server's "Cancel Ticket" operation, to verify and cancel the ticket. If the ticket is invalid or previously cancelled, the message is silently discarded. Otherwise, it appears in the recipient's inbox. When the recipient sees the message, if the recipient decides that the sender should indeed pay for the message, he need do nothing more. However, if the recipient decides that this message wasn't spam, the recipient can choose to call the ticket server's "Refund Ticket" operation, to refund the ticket's value to the sender. (Note that there is an interesting human-factors decision to be made here: should "Refund Ticket" require an explicit action from the user, or should it be the default, which can be overridden by the user classifying the message as spam?)

Variation 4: Untrusted Sender and No Ticket

When a message arrives without a ticket attached and from an untrusted sender, the ISP might choose to respond in one of two ways. First, the ISP might treat the message as suspicious, and flag it but nevertheless deliver it to the recipient.

Alternatively, the ISP could hold the message (but invisibly to the recipient) and send a bounce email to the sender. The bounce email would offer the sender two choices: he can provide some previously acquired ticket, or he can acquire a new ticket by interacting with the ticket server.

In the case where the sender chooses to use a previously acquired ticket, he simply provides it to the ISP by passing it over HTTP to the ISP (perhaps through an HTML form provided as part of the bounce message). On receipt of this, the ISP calls the "Cancel Ticket" operation to verify and cancel the ticket, and provided this succeeds, makes the message available to the recipient's inbox.

Alternatively, if the sender wants to acquire a new ticket at this time, he must call the ticket server. To simplify doing so, the bounce email contains a link (URL) to the ticket server. Clicking on the link performs a "Request Ticket" operation at the ticket server. The result appears to the sender as a web page describing the available challenges. For example, for the computational challenge the web page will contain a link that would cause the sender to perform the computation (via an ActiveX control or a Java applet, perhaps). As another example, the web page resulting from the "Request Ticket" operation could include a Turing test such as those used by the Captcha system [3]. In either case, the result of the challenge is combined with the ticket kit data (also on the web page), and the resulting ticket is passed via HTTP to the recipient's ISP. The ISP now proceeds as if the message had originally arrived with the ticket attached, verifying and canceling the ticket and delivering the message to the recipient.

If a message remains in the "held" state too long without the sender responding to the bounce message, it is silently discarded by the ISP. The same happens if the sender failed to provide an appropriate return address, or if the sender responds to the bounce message with an invalid ticket.

4 Protocol

This section describes a specific protocol for the ticket server's operations. The description is fairly abstract, and deliberately leaves a lot of flexibility: in how the data is represented and transported (for example, through HTML pages and HTTP in the spam scenario described above), in how the cryptography is implemented, and in some semantic choices (such as whether to encrypt data in transit or just protect it with a message authentication code or MAC [17]). While these are all important design decisions for an actual implementation, they are largely irrelevant to the overall ticket server concept. We do describe how to achieve appropriately transactional semantics in the presence of communication failures and retransmissions.

The following datatypes and messages implement the ticket server's three operations. "Request Ticket" is message (1) and its response (2); "Cancel Ticket" is message (4) and its response (5); "Refund Ticket" is message (6) and its response (7).

The participants in the protocol are the ticket server itself, client "A" who requests a ticket, and client "B" who receives the ticket from A and uses it in messages (4) through (7). In the case of email spam prevention, A is the sender (or perhaps the sender's ISP) and B is the recipient's ISP (or perhaps the recipient mail user-agent software).

The functions and values involved are as follows. See section 5.3 for further discussion of how the items related to the challenge (P, X, F, and C) are represented.

- S is a unique identifier for a ticket (in practice, a sequence number issued by the ticket server).
- K_T, K_A, K_B, and K_S are secret keys (for ticket T, for A, for B, and for the ticket server).
- I_A identifies A (and K_A) to the ticket server.
- I_B identifies B (and K_B) to the ticket server.
- $TransID_A$ is an identifier chosen by A to identify a "Request Ticket" transaction.
- $TransID_B$ is an identifier chosen by B to identify a "Use Ticket" transaction.
- H(D) is a secure hash of some data D (such as might be obtained by applying the SHA1 algorithm); H(K, D) is a keyed secure hash of D using a key K.
- K(D) uses key K to protect some data D in transit. This might provide a secure MAC for D, and/or it might encrypt D using K, and/or it might prove the timeliness of D by including a secured real-time clock value.
- P is a Boolean predicate. It occurs in a ticket kit (see "TK", below), where it specifies a particular, ticket-specific, challenge. It will be represented by an integer or a URL.
- X is the answer to a challenge. It will be represented by an integer or short string. If a particular ticket kit contains predicate P, and if P(X), then X is an appropriate value for constructing a valid ticket from the ticket kit. In other words, the challenge for A is to find an X such that P(X) is true.
- F is a function that the ticket server will use in verifying that a ticket has a correct value of X. It will be represented by an integer. Note that F is visible to the ticket requestor.
- C is a secret that assists the ticket server in verifying a ticket's X value. It will be represented by an integer or short string. For any valid ticket, F(X) = C.
- M is a message, or other request for a service that might require a ticket.

The ticket server maintains the following state, in stable storage:

- Its own secret key, K_s.
- The largest value of S that it has ever issued.
- State(S) = "Issued" or "Cancelled", for each ticket S that has been issued (subject to a maximum ticket lifetime, not specified in this paper).
- Balance(I_A) = an integer, the account balance for A's account.
- Result($TransID_A$) = result of the most recent "Request Ticket" operation that contained $TransID_A$ (maintained by the ticket server only for recently requested tickets, then discarded).

- Canceller(S) = $TransID_B$, the identifier used by B in a recent "Use Ticket" request for ticket S (maintained by the ticket server only for recently used tickets, then discarded).
- Refunded(S) = a Boolean indicating whether the ticket S has been refunded to an account (subject to a maximum ticket lifetime, not specified in this paper).

The following are trivially derived from other values:

- TK = (S, P, F, I_A, H(K_s, ("Hash for T", S, F, C, I_A))), a ticket kit.
- T = (S, X, F, I_A, H(K_s, ("Hash for T", S, F, C, I_A))), a ticket issued to A.
- T.S is the S used in forming T; similarly for the other components of T, and for components of TK.
- K_T = H(K_S, ("Hash for KT", T.S)), the requestor's secret key for T.
- K_T' = H(K_S, ("Hash for KT prime", T.S)), the canceller's secret key for T.
- K_A = H(K_S, ("Hash for KA", I_A)), the secret key identified by I_A.
- K_B = H(K_S, ("Hash for KB", I_B)), the secret key identified by I_B.

A ticket T is "valid" if and only if T.S has been issued by the ticket server, and H(K_S, (T.S, T.F, Y, T.I_A)) = H_T, where H_T is the keyed hash in T and Y = T.F(T.X). Note that this definition includes valid but cancelled tickets (for ease of exposition).

The ticket server creates each ticket kit TK in such a way that the ticket constructed by replacing TK.P with X, for any X for which TK.P(X) is true, will be a valid ticket. Thus, A should find an X such that P(X) is true. This arrangement turns out to be highly flexible, and usable for a wide variety of challenges. Moreover, this arrangement has the property that the ticket server does not need to compute X — it only verifies it. This property is important in the case where computing X is hard, for example when doing so is expensive in CPU time or memory cycles. See the commentary section for discussion and some examples.

When client A wishes to acquire a new ticket, it chooses a new $TransID_A$, and calls the ticket server:

(1) A → ticket server: I_A, K_A("Request", $TransID_A$)

The ticket server uses I_A to compute K_A, and verifies the integrity and timeliness of the message (or else it discards the request with no further action). Now, there are three possibilities:

- If Result($TransID_A$) is already defined, then it is left unaltered.
- If Balance(I_A) > 0, then it is decremented and Result($TransID_A$) is set to a new valid ticket T such that State(T.S) = "Issued". Note that in this case the sender does not need to deal with a challenge.
- If Balance(I_A) = 0, then Result($TransID_A$) is set to a ticket kit TK for a new valid ticket, such that State(TK.S) = "Issued". Note that the ticket server does not compute the response to the challenge implicit in TK: it's up to A to do that.

The ticket server computes K_T from TK.S or T.S, and sends it and Result($TransID_A$) to A:

(2) ticket server → A: K_A("OK", Result($TransID_A$), K_T, $TransID_A$)

A verifies the integrity of this message (or else discards it). Note that if message (2) is lost or corrupted, A can retransmit (1), causing the ticket server to retransmit an identical copy of (2). If the result is a ticket kit TK, not a complete ticket, then A can take TK, solve the challenge by determining some X such that P(X), and assemble the complete ticket T from the elements of TK.

When A wants to use T to send B the message M (or other request for service), A sends:

(3) A → B: T, K_T(M)

Note that B does not yet know K_T. B now asks the ticket server to change the state of T.S to "Cancelled". B chooses a new $TransID_B$, and sends:

(4) B → ticket server: I_B, K_B("Cancel", T, $TransID_B$).

The ticket server verifies the integrity of this message (or discards it). If T is not "valid" (as defined above), or if State(T.S) = "Cancelled" and Canceller(T.S) is not $TransID_B$, then the result of this call is "Error". Otherwise, the ticket server sets the state of T.S to "Cancelled", sets Canceller(T.S) to $TransID_B$, computes K_T, and sends it back to B:

(5) Ticket server → B: K_B(("Error" | ("OK", K_T, K_T')), $TransID_B$).

B verifies the integrity of this message (or else discards it). Note that if message (5) is lost or corrupted, B can retransmit (4), causing the ticket server to retransmit an identical copy of (5). B can now use K_T to verify the integrity of (3), and to extract M from it if it was in fact encrypted with K_T. The key K_T' will be used to authenticate B if B decides to refund the ticket.

In the spam-prevention application, when B is the recipient's ISP, the ISP will now proceed to make the email visible to the recipient. If the recipient decides that M should be accepted without payment, then the recipient (or the recipient's ISP) tells the ticket server to recycle this ticket:

(6) B → ticket server: T.S, K_T'("Refund", T).

The ticket server verifies the integrity of this message (or discards it). Note that in doing so it computes K_T' from T.S, so the verification will succeed only if B truly knew K_T'. If Refunded(T.S) is false, the ticket server sets Refunded(T.S) and increments Balance(T.I_A). Regardless of the previous value of Refunded(T.S), the ticket server then reports completion of the operation:

(7) Ticket server → B: T.S, K_T'("OK").

Some aspects of the protocol call for further explanation:

- The transaction ID in step (1) allows for the error case where the response (2) is lost. Because the ticket server retains Result($TransID_A$), A can retransmit the request and get the ticket that he's paid for (in the case where A's account was decremented) without needing to pay again. The key K_A authenticates A, so that nobody else can acquire tickets charged to A's account.

- Since I_A is embedded in T and in the secure hash inside T, it authenticates the ticket as having been issued to A (or more precisely, to a principal that knows I_A and K_A).
- The key K_T returned to A in step (1) allows A to construct $K_T(M)$; in other words, it authorizes A to use T for a message of A's choosing.
- When B receives (3), B does not know K_T so B cannot reuse T for its own purposes. B acquires K_T only after canceling the ticket.
- The transaction ID used in request (4) allows B to retransmit this request if the response is lost. Because the ticket server has recorded Canceller(T.S), it can detect the retransmission and return a successful outcome even though the ticket has already been cancelled in this case.
- If the result (7) is lost, B can retransmit the request. Because of the ticket server's "Refunded" data structure, this will not cause any extra increment of A's account balance.
- The use of K_T' in messages (6) and (7) authenticate the principal authorized to re-use T. Only the principal that cancelled T can credit A's account. It's fine for A to do this himself, but if he does so he can't use T for any other purpose – it's been cancelled.

5 Implementation

We have implemented the ticket server, and applied it in a prototype spam-prevention system. In this section we outline the techniques that we used, which provides a simple, robust, and highly efficient server. At the end of this section we discuss the performance of this design.

5.1 Ticket State

The ticket server uses sequential serial numbers when creating the field S for a new ticket. The ticket server maintains in stable storage an integer which indicates the largest serial number that it has used in any ticket. It's easy to implement this efficiently, if you're willing to lose a few serial numbers when the ticket server crashes. The ticket server maintains in volatile memory the largest serial number that has actually been used (S_{used}), and in stable storage a number always larger than this (S_{bound}). When enough serial numbers have been used that S_{used} is approaching S_{bound}, the ticket server rewrites S_{bound} with the new value S_{used}+K, where K is chosen to make the number of stable storage writes for this process insignificant (K = 1,000,000 would suffice). If the ticket server crashes, up to K serial numbers might be lost. In no case will serial numbers be reused.

The ticket server maintains 2 bits of state for each ticket S (with $S \leq S_{used}$). One bit is set iff the ticket has been cancelled, and the other is set iff the ticket has been refunded. The "truth" for these bits necessarily resides on disk, and the server must read it from there after any cold restart. However, during normal running the ticket server can maintain this in volatile memory with an array indexed by ticket serial number.

When a ticket changes state (from "issued" to "cancelled" or from "cancelled" to "refunded") the ticket server updates this array, and synchronously with the operation records the transition in stable storage. All it needs to record is the ticket serial number, and the new state.

5.2 Ticket Request and Cancellation Logs

It is possible that the ticket server will crash in the vicinity of responding to a "Request Ticket" operation. However, the worst that this does to A is to cause him to lose a single ticket, which we believe is acceptable. We saw no need, in this application, to keep a log in stable storage that would allow A to replay his request after the server restarts.

The ticket server does need to maintain a volatile data structure containing Result($TransID_A$). However, this is only relevant for as long as it might receive a transmission of the corresponding "Request Ticket" operation. The ticket server can apply a relatively short limit to this time interval, to keep the data structure small.

5.3 Representing the Challenge

The protocol values P, X, F, and C are used to represent the challenge and the proof that A has responded appropriately, and to assist the ticket server in verifying this response. It's a somewhat complex mechanism, because it's designed to deal with a variety of challenge styles (computational, Turing test, perhaps others). Here are some examples of how these values can be used.

In all cases F is represented by a small integer, indicating to the ticket server what it should do to verify that a ticket has an appropriate value of X, i.e., that F(X) = C.

For a computational test, P describes the test. It can be represented by a small integer P_i and a parameter P_n. The small integer selects a function P_f to be computed, from a list known to the participants in the protocol. The challenge for A is to find a value X such that $P_f(P_n, X) = 0$. For this case, C is always 0 and the ticket server implements F(X) by computing $P_f(P_n, X)$.

For a Turing test that requires recognizing a word from a distorted image, P specifies the image. We have not implemented this case, but it seems straightforward. We could use the image itself as P, but more likely we would use a URL at which the image resides. The challenge for A is to find a string X such that X is embedded in the image. For this case C is the correct string, and the ticket server implements F(X) by comparing the strings X and C.

5.4 Performance

Although we have not fully tuned our implementation, we believe that this ticket server design, implemented on a single inexpensive PC, could handle as many ticket operations as could be accommodated on a 100 Mb/sec network connection.

- In terms of memory usage, this implementation uses approximately 2 bits of main memory for each outstanding uncancelled ticket. So each GByte of DRAM suffices to keep the state for 4 billion tickets, roughly one week's email traffic at Hotmail (after we ignore the messages that Hotmail already categorizes as spam, and before allowing for the fact that email messages from trusted senders don't need tickets).
- In terms of disk performance, each operation (Request, Cancel, and Refund) requires a disk write. However, this doesn't need to overload the disk channel. We use a simple "group commit" design to keep the delays caused by the disk transfers negligible. To commit one of the operations we need to write only 16 bytes to disk: 8 bytes for S and 8 bytes for either $\mathrm{ID_A}$ (for Request or Refund) or $\mathrm{TransID_B}$ (for Cancel). If the operation waits until any previous disk request has completed, and meanwhile we accumulate the transaction records for multiple operations into a 4 KByte buffer, we can record 256 operations with a single 4 KByte disk write. Writing 4 KBytes takes about 16 milliseconds even on an ATA disk, allowing us to record about 16,000 ticket transactions per second on a single disk. So while each individual operation incurs the latency of a 4 KByte disk request, the overall throughput of the ticket server is not limited by the disk.
- In terms of CPU performance, our current implementation is still unsatisfactorily slow. Most of the time is spent in the overheads of communicating through our TCP stack, which has not yet been optimized for this application. At the moment, the protocol and its cryptography are not significant in limiting the server's performance.

Of course, full deployment of this design would require multiple ticket servers, and arranging cooperation between them is a significant design problem. We discuss this, briefly, in the next section.

6 Deployment Issues

If everyone's email system used the ticket server, it seems highly likely that we would have solved the spam problem. We can tune the effective cost of sending email so as to increase it, in real dollar terms, to a level comparable to physical mail: a few cents per message instead of 0.019 cents. This would clearly cause the demise of the more absurd sorts of spam, since the economic model would no longer support mailings with extremely low response rates. As with physical mail, a small level of junk traffic would necessarily remain. However, there are several problems with the ticket server idea, and any of them might prevent it succeeding. We address them next.

6.1 User Acceptance

Certainly any scheme based on making the sender incur costs will make email marginally less pleasant for normal users. The question here is how large that margin is. We believe it's small. Two aspects of the design encourage us in this belief. First, most senders will fall into the category of trusted senders for almost all of their recipients: in general we send email to people who know us. We'll be in their address book, in the same organization as them, or they'll accept our email as being non-spam and they'll refund our ticket. The net effect is that most users will actually consume very few tickets. If we start everyone out with a moderate stockpile (for example, 1000 tickets bundled with a software purchase), they most likely will never be inconvenienced by needing to perform a lengthy computation.

There is a separate issue about users of low-powered devices: PDA's, phones, and old computers. One possibility we have already mentioned is use of memory-bound functions instead of CPU-bound computations. Since memory speed is relatively uniform across devices, there is not a lot of disparity in the cost of tickets. Additionally, email access from PDA's and phones is always through an intermediary with whom the user has a service contract. It would be perfectly reasonable for that intermediary to provide a moderate number of tickets to each user as part of that contract.

The most intrusive part of the scheme occurs in a transition period, where some recipients are requiring use of the scheme and some senders have not yet adopted it. This will produce irritating bounce messages demanding tickets. This is a problem of "you can't get there from here", and might well be a fatal flaw (although it's one shared by virtually all other anti-spam technologies apart from ever-smarter filtering rules). The most plausible way to avoid the flaw would be to get the scheme distributed, but disabled, in a wide range of email software, and once it's widely deployed then starting to actually use it. We don't know if this is feasible.

6.2 Trust

The scheme depends on everyone having some level of trust in the ticket server. While it's easy to see that, for example, a Hotmail user would be willing to trust a ticket server run by Microsoft, it's much less clear why anyone else should. So while an organization such as Hotmail could unilaterally start requiring tickets, it is less likely that any one organization could provide a universal ticket service (nor would they want to).

Equally, if several organizations (Hotmail, AOL, Yahoo, etc.) independently started using ticket servers, senders would be distressed at the complexity of acquiring all the appropriate forms of ticket. It would be like the postal system without the international agreements on mutual acceptance of foreign postage stamps.

So it is more likely that a set of ticket servers would be run cooperatively several organizations, with contractual agreements about accepting each other's tickets. This is less unlikely than it might seem: there are some extremely large, but highly competitive, players in the email business (AOL, Hotmail, Yahoo, and MSN). A system run jointly by them would have a reasonably appearance of neutrality (at least within the U.S.), good credibility, and would automatically be trusted by a very large community of users. There would be many technical (and business) issues in how such a federation would work, and we do not explore them in this paper.

6.3 Reliability

Introduction of the ticket server adds a new failure mode to the email system. No doubt we could build a ticket server that had negligibly few programming bugs, but of course that isn't enough. Certainly we would need multiple servers, for tolerance of physical and environmental failures, and to handle the total load. Some such replication would come from a federation created to handle the trust issues, but probably more would be needed.

A more worrisome problem is that the ticket server would be an appealing target for a denial-of-service attack. But the large email services are already that appealing. It's not terribly hard to engineer the ticket server to be able to handle anything that its network connection can handle, and if we assume that the servers are co-resident with existing large data centers such as those of Hotmail and AOL, then the problem reduces to the (admittedly unsolved) one of protecting those data centers.

Finally, note that the ticket server need not be essential, and the consequences of a successful attack need not be dire. If a sender cannot contact the ticket server, and his local stockpile of tickets is empty, he can send the email anyway and just hope that he doesn't get a "ticket needed" bounce message. If a recipient cannot contact the ticket server, he can just read the email regardless.

6.4 Cheating

The ticket server protocol is designed to prevent obvious attacks, like forging or reusing tickets. There is one behavior pattern that might be considered at least "misuse": ticket farming. A spammer might, for example, acquire tickets by running a popular web site (such as a gamer site or a porn site) and requiring that customers perform the challenge part of ticket construction before being rewarded by the web site (for example, being allowed to play or to see a picture). This isn't really a violation of the protocol. We make the sender incur a cost, but fundamentally there's no way we can prevent the sender delegating the required work. A similar criticism applies to using Turing tests: there are, unfortunately, parts of the world where labor is so cheap as to make the cost of the tests exceedingly small.

7 Related Work

There are several other systems aimed at causing bulk emailers to incur costs when sending their email. The earliest proposal we know is that of Dwork and Naor [11], which we used as one of the starting points for the current work. Actual deployed systems of this sort include Back's HashCash system [6]. The Camram system [8] adds mechanisms that in effect automate the accumulation of a safe list. None of these systems provide the benefits of the ticket server that we outlined in section 1 of this paper.

The ticket server is reminiscent of several other classes of system, although in aggregate it has distinctly different properties than any of them. There are authentication systems that work by issuing "tickets"; there are numerous systems aimed at offering and enforcing small-scale payments ("micro-payments"); there are other systems for incurring cost when sending email; and there are other systems intended to reduce spam. We consider here a few examples from those classes of system.

7.1 Authentication & Authorization Systems

Systems such as Kerberos [16] produce "tickets" as the result of an authentication. These tickets, like those from the ticket server, enable the clients to perform some operations (such as accessing a file system or a network service). However, the functionality of the tickets is quite different: there is no notion of tickets being consumed or cancelled, nor being refunded. The only way in which tickets become invalid is by expiry after a timeout (or conceivably through a revocation mechanism).

Note that the clients of the ticket server, despite being identified by an ID, can be anonymous. We verify that a client is the same client as one who made a previous request, but we have no knowledge whatsoever of the client's identity. Clients can casually acquire or discard identities.

Our tickets are also reminiscent of capability systems such as Amoeba [19], except that they are explicitly single-use and the ticket server enforces this. We are unaware of any capability system that provides such a feature. Note that the enforcement of single-use necessarily produces a protocol structure involving more communication with the ticket server (just as a revocation mechanism does in capability systems).

It is conceivable that one could extend Kerberos or Amoeba to make them into tools for preventing spam and similar abuses, much like the ticket server, but the extensions would be quite substantial, and it seems preferable to start from scratch rather than attempt to build a more complex system on the prior substrates.

7.2 Micro-payment Systems

Micro-payment systems come closest in functionality to the ticket server. They achieve very similar goals: the purchaser incurs a cost. It might conceivably be feasible to take an existing micro-payment system and rework it to use some form of virtual currency instead of real cash. But again, we believe that we will produce a more satisfactory system by building it from scratch with the present applications in mind. The differences are substantial, as we show next.

One such system was Millicent [14], which is a convenient example (partly because the authors are familiar with it, but primarily because it was developed into a real, deployed system with transactions involving real cash). In Millicent, as in the ticket server, there is protection against double spending. However, to avoid excessive interactions with an online authority, that's done by making currency ("scrip" in Millicent terminology) vendor-specific. For an application such as spam prevention, this would correspond to having scrip specific to the recipient's ISP. The ticket server, by providing a recipient-independent online verification system, avoids this. Also, the simplicity of the ticket server protocols and data structures (and the fact that an ISP can batch its requests to the ticket server) makes using the ticket server as an online authority acceptably efficient for our applications.

There are numerous other issues that spring to mind when considering the use of a straight micro-commerce system. For example, sending email from your email account at your employer to your personal account at home would in effect steal money from your employer.

7.3 Email Systems with Stronger Semantics

There are many email enhancements that provide stronger semantics than basic RFC822 and SMTP email. For example, one can use PGP, S/MIME, and many other elaborate systems to provide features such as certified, authenticated, or secure email. In particular, properly authenticated email would most likely be a powerful tool for reducing spam, since recipients would at least be able to filter out email from repeat offenders or groups. But authentication is not by itself a solution: knowing the author of an email message isn't sufficient to classify the message as being spam or not. Authentication does not address the basic problem, namely that the sender incurs too small a cost when sending email, with the result that vast quantities of worthless email flood our inboxes. (See [1, 7, 21, 22] for some design possibilities in this area, and for numerous further references.)

8 Conclusion

The ticket server is a new tool that we can use to control or limit the use of otherwise free and open services, such as email. By adding a shared, stateful server to the earlier proposals, we get significant benefits. In particular, the cost to be incurred for a service can be independent and prior to any particular requests. Moreover, clients may have account balances and may receive refunds. Therefore, we can escalate the cost of the service to a level where we can be certain that it will deter excessive use.

We have designed a protocol that will allow the ticket server to guarantee the correct functioning of the tickets, and prevent or make impractical any attempts to cheat by forging, stealing, or otherwise maltreating tickets. We have also designed and implemented a concrete mechanism to invoke this protocol with a combination of email messages and HTTP requests. Furthermore, we have outlined how the ticket server can be implemented simply and cheaply.

There remain numerous questions about the ticket server. As discussed earlier, deployment of the service raises several tricky issues. Many of the same issues arise with other schemes for email payment: in all cases, deployment is difficult, involving fundamental and disruptive changes to the way that Internet email works. It's not at all clear that we can achieve such changes. On the other hand, removing spam would be a significant financial benefit to the major email service providers, and a convenience for all of us.

Acknowledgements

The work described here arose from discussions with Cynthia Dwork and Mark Manasse about computational techniques for spam prevention. Most of Martín Abadi's and Mike Burrows's work was done at Microsoft Research, Silicon Valley (where the techniques described in this paper were invented), with Microsoft's support. Martín Abadi's work is also partly supported by the National Science Foundation under Grant CCR-0208800.

References

1. Abadi, M., Glew, N., Horne, B. and Pinkas, B., Certified Email with a Light On-Line Trusted Third Party: Design and Implementation. In *Proceedings of the Eleventh International World Wide Web Conference* (May 2002), 387-395.
2. Abadi, M., Burrows, M., Manasse, M. and Wobber, E., Moderately Hard, Memory-bound Functions. In *Proceedings of the 10th Annual Network and Distributed System Security Symposium* (February 2003), 25-39.
3. Von Ahn, L., Blum, M., Hopper, N. and Langford, A, Captcha. At http://www.captcha.net.
4. Androutsopoloulos, A. *et al.* An experimental comparison of naïve Bayesian and keyword-based anti-spam filtering with personal e-mail messages. In *Proceedings of SIGIR-00, 23rd ACM International Conference on Research and Development in Information Retrieval.* ACM Press (2000), 160-167.
5. AOL press release on Business Wire, as reported by the Washington Post http://sites.stockpoint.com/wpost/newspaperbw.asp?dispnav=&Story=20030220/051b175 3.xml (Feb. 2003)
6. Back, A., *HashCash.* http://www.cyberspace.org/~adam/hashcash (1997).
7. Bahreman, A. and Tygar, J.D., Certified electronic mail. In *Proceedings of the Internet Society Symposium on Network and Distributed System Security* (February 1994), 3-19.
8. *Camram.* At http://www.camram.org.
9. Cranor, L. and LaMacchia, B., Spam!. *Commun. ACM 41,* 8 (August 1998), 74-83.
10. Dwork, C., Goldberg, A. and Naor, M., On memory-bound functions for fighting spam. In *Proceedings of CRYPTO 2003* (to appear).
11. Dwork, C. and Naor, M., Pricing via processing or combating junk mail. In *Advances in Cryptology – CRYPTO '92*. Springer (1992), 139-147.
12. Fahlman, S., Selling interrupt rights: a way to control unwanted e-mail and telephone calls. *IBM Systems Journal 41,* 4 (2002), 759-766.
13. Gabber, E. *et al*, Curbing junk e-mail via secure classification. In *Financial Cryptography,* (1998), 198-213.

14. Glassman, S., Manasse, M., Abadi, M., Gauthier, P. and Sobalvarro, P., The Millicent protocol for inexpensive electronic commerce. In *Proceedings of the Fourth International World Wide Web Conference*. O'Reilly and Associates (1995), 603-618.
15. Ioannidis, J., Fighting spam by encapsulating policy in email addresses. In *Proceedings Symposium on Network and Distributed Systems Security 2003* (February 2003) 17-24.
16. Kohl, J. and Neuman, C., The Kerberos network authentication service. At http://www.rfc-editor.org/rfc/rfc1510.txt.
17. Menezes, A., Van Oorschot, P. and Vanstone, S. *Handbook of applied cryptography*. CRC Press (1996).
18. McCurley, K., Deterrence measures for spam, slides presented at the RSA conference. http://www.almaden.ibm.com/cs/k53/pmail/ (January 1998).
19. Mullender, S. and Tannenbaum, A., The design of a capability-based operating system. *Computer Journal 29*, 4 (August 1986), 289-299.
20. Templeton, B., *E-stamps*. http://www.templetons.com/brad/spume/estamps.html (undated)
21. Tygar, J.D., Yee, B. and Heintze, N., Cryptographic Postage Indicia. In *ASIAN 1996, Lecture notes in computer science 1179* (1996), 378-391.
22. Zhou, J. and Gollmann, D., Certified electronic mail. In *Computer Security–ESORICS '96 proceedings*. Springer-Verlag (1996), 160-171.

Global Predicate Detection under Fine-Grained Modalities

Punit Chandra and Ajay D. Kshemkalyani

Computer Science Department,
Univ. of Illinois at Chicago, Chicago, IL 60607, USA
{pchandra,ajayk}@cs.uic.edu

Abstract. Predicate detection is an important problem in distributed systems. Based on the temporal interactions of intervals, there exists a rich class of modalities under which global predicates can be specified. For a conjunctive predicate ϕ, we show how to detect the traditional $Possibly(\phi)$ and $Definitely(\phi)$ modalities along with the added information of the exact interaction type between each pair of intervals (one interval at each process). The polynomial time, space, and message complexities of the proposed on-line detection algorithms to detect *Possibly* and *Definitely* in terms of the fine-grained interaction types per pair of processes, are the *same as* those of the earlier on-line algorithms that can detect *only* whether the *Possibly* and *Definitely* modalities hold.

1 Introduction

Predicate detection in a distributed system is useful in many contexts such as monitoring, synchronization and coordination, debugging, and industrial process control [2, 4, 6–8, 14, 16, 17]. Marzullo et al. defined two modalities under which predicates can hold for a distributed execution [4, 14].

- $Possibly(\phi)$: There exists a consistent observation of the execution such that ϕ holds in a global state of the observation.
- $Definitely(\phi)$: For every consistent observation of the execution, there exists a global state of it in which ϕ holds.

The formalism and axiom system given in [9] identified an orthogonal set $\Re$ of 40 fine-grained temporal interactions between a pair of intervals in a distributed execution. It was shown in [10] that this formalism provides much more expressive power than the *Possibly* and *Definitely* modalities, and a mapping from $\Re$ to the *Possibly* and *Definitely* modalities was given. A *conjunctive* predicate is of the form $\bigwedge_i \phi_i$, where ϕ_i is any predicate defined on variables local to process P_i. We show that for a conjunctive predicate ϕ (e.g., $x_i = 2 \wedge y_j > 8$), $Possibly(\phi)$ and $Definitely(\phi)$ can be detected along with the added information of the exact interaction type between each pair of intervals, one interval at each process. This provides flexibility and power to monitor, synchronize, and control distributed executions. The time, space, and message complexities of the

V.A. Saraswat (Ed.): ASIAN 2003, LNCS 2896, pp. 91–109, 2003.

Table 1. Comparison of space, message and time complexities. n = number of processes, M = maximum queue length at P_0, p = maximum number of intervals occurring at any process, m_s = total number of messages exchanged between all the processes. Note: $p \geq M$, as all the intervals may not be sent to P_0.

	Avg. time complexity at P_0	Total number of messages	Space at P_0 (= total msg. space)	Avg. space at P_i, $i \in [1, n]$
GW94 [6] (Possibly)	$O(n^2M)$ or $O(nm_s)$	$O(m_s)$	$O(n^2M)$ or $O(nm_s)$	$O(n)$
GW96 [7] (Definitely)	$O(n^2M)$ or $O(nm_s)$	$O(m_s)$	$O(n^2M)$ or $O(nm_s)$	$O(n)$
Fine_Poss, *Fine_Def*, *Fine_Rel*	$O(n^2M)$ or $O(n[min(4m_s, np)])$	$O(min(4m_s, np))$	$O(min[(4n-2)np, 10nm_s])$	$O(n)$

proposed on-line, centralized detection algorithms (Algorithms *Fine_Poss* and *Fine_Def* - the main results) to detect *Possibly* and *Definitely* in terms of the fine-grained modalities per pair of processes, are the *same as* those of the earlier on-line, centralized algorithms [6, 7] that can detect *only* whether the *Possibly* and *Definitely* modalities hold. Table 1 compares the complexities. *Fine_Rel*, which is an intermediate problem we need solve, is introduced later.

The power of our approach stems from the use of intervals as opposed to individual events in the distributed execution. The intervals at each process are identified to be the durations during which the local predicate is true [10, 12]. We now state Problems *Fine_Poss* and *Fine_Def*.

Problem *Fine_Poss* Statement. For a conjunctive predicate ϕ, determine on-line if *Possibly*(ϕ) is true. If true, identify the fine-grained pairwise interaction between each pair of processes when *Possibly*(ϕ) first becomes true.

Problem *Fine_Def* Statement. For a conjunctive predicate ϕ, determine on-line if *Definitely*(ϕ) is true. If true, identify the fine-grained pairwise interaction between each pair of processes when *Definitely*(ϕ) first becomes true.

Section 2 gives the background and objectives. Section 3 presents the framework and data structures. Section 4 and Section 5 present the on-line algorithms. Section 6 gives the conclusions.

2 System Model, Background, and Objectives

2.1 System Model

We assume an asynchronous distributed system in which n processes communicate only by reliable message passing. We do not assume FIFO channels. To model the system execution, let $\prec$ be an irreflexive partial ordering representing the causality relation on the event set E. E is partitioned into local executions at each process. Let N denote the set of all processes. Each E_i is a linearly ordered set of events executed by process P_i. An event e at P_i is denoted e_i. The causality

Table 2. Dependent relations for interactions between intervals are given in the first two columns [9]. Tests for the relations are given in the third column [10].

Relation r	Expression for $r(X,Y)$	Test for $r(X,Y)$
R1	$\forall x \in X \forall y \in Y, x \prec y$	$V_y^-[x] > V_x^+[x]$
R2	$\forall x \in X \exists y \in Y, x \prec y$	$V_y^+[x] > V_x^+[x]$
R3	$\exists x \in X \forall y \in Y, x \prec y$	$V_y^-[x] > V_x^-[x]$
R4	$\exists x \in X \exists y \in Y, x \prec y$	$V_y^+[x] > V_x^-[x]$
S1	$\exists x \in X \forall y \in Y, x \not\preceq y \bigwedge y \not\preceq x$	**if** $V_y^-[y] \not< V_x^-[y] \bigwedge V_y^+[x] \not> V_x^+[x]$ **then** $(\exists x^0 \in X\colon V_y^-[y] \not\leq V_x^{x^0}[y] \wedge V_x^{x^0}[x] \not\leq V_y^+[x])$ **else** $false$
S2	$\exists x_1, x_2 \in X \exists y \in Y, x_1 \prec y \prec x_2$	**if** $V_y^+[x] > V_x^-[x] \bigwedge V_y^-[y] < V_x^+[y]$ **then** $(\exists y^0 \in Y : V_x^+[y] \not< V_y^{y^0}[y] \wedge V_y^{y^0}[x] \not< V_x^-[x])$ **else** $false$

relation on E is the transitive closure of the local ordering relation on each E_i and the ordering imposed by message send events and message receive events [13]. A *cut* C is a subset of E such that if $e_i \in C$ then $(\forall e_i')e_i' \prec e_i \Longrightarrow e_i' \in C$. A *consistent cut* is a downward-closed subset of E in $(E, \prec)$ and denotes an execution prefix. For event e, there are two special consistent cuts $\downarrow e$ and $e \uparrow$. $\downarrow e$ is the maximal set of events that happen before e. $e \uparrow$ is the set of all events up to and including the earliest events at each process for which e happens before the events.

Definition 1. *Cut* $\downarrow e$ *is defined to be* $\{e' \mid e' \prec e\}$ *and cut* $e \uparrow$ *is defined to be* $\{e' \mid e' \not\succeq e\} \bigcup \{e_i, i = 1, \ldots, |N| \mid e_i \succeq e \bigwedge (\forall e_i' \prec e_i, e_i' \not\succeq e)\}$.

The system state after the events in a cut is a global state; if the cut is consistent, the corresponding system state is a consistent global state. We assume that the popular vector clocks are available [5, 15] – the vector clock V has the property that $e \prec f \iff V(e) < V(f)$.

A conjunctive predicate is of the form $\bigwedge_i \phi_i$, where ϕ_i is a predicate defined on variables local to process P_i. The intervals of interest at each process are the durations in which the local predicate is true. Such an interval at process P_i is identified by the (totally ordered) subset of adjacent events of E_i for which the local predicate is true.

2.2 Pairwise Interactions

There are 29 or 40 possible mutually orthogonal ways in which any two durations can be related to each other, depending on whether the dense or the nondense time model is assumed [9]. Informally speaking, with dense time, $\forall x, y$ in interval A, $x \prec y \Longrightarrow \exists z \in A \mid x \prec z \prec y$. These orthogonal interaction types were identified by first using the six relations given in the first two columns of Table 2. Relations R1 (strong precedence), R2 (partially strong precedence), R3 (partially weak precedence), R4 (weak precedence) define *causality conditions*

Table 3. The 40 independent relations in $\Re$ [9]. X and Y are intervals. The upper part of the table gives the 29 relations assuming dense time. The lower part of the table gives 11 additional relations if nondense time is assumed.

Interaction Type	Relation $r(X,Y)$						Relation $r(Y,X)$					
	R1	R2	R3	R4	S1	S2	R1	R2	R3	R4	S1	S2
$IA(=IQ^{-1})$	1	1	1	1	0	0	0	0	0	0	0	0
$IB(=IR^{-1})$	0	1	1	1	0	0	0	0	0	0	0	0
$IC(=IV^{-1})$	0	0	1	1	1	0	0	0	0	0	0	0
$ID(=IX^{-1})$	0	0	1	1	1	1	0	1	0	1	0	0
$ID'(=IU^{-1})$	0	0	1	1	0	1	0	1	0	1	0	1
$IE(=IW^{-1})$	0	0	1	1	1	1	0	0	0	1	0	0
$IE'(=IT^{-1})$	0	0	1	1	0	1	0	0	0	1	0	1
$IF(=IS^{-1})$	0	1	1	1	0	1	0	0	0	1	0	1
$IG(=IG^{-1})$	0	0	0	0	1	0	0	0	0	0	1	0
$IH(=IK^{-1})$	0	0	0	1	1	0	0	0	0	0	1	0
$II(=IJ^{-1})$	0	1	0	1	0	0	0	0	0	0	1	0
$IL(=IO^{-1})$	0	0	0	1	1	1	0	1	0	1	0	0
$IL'(=IP^{-1})$	0	0	0	1	0	1	0	1	0	1	0	1
$IM(=IM^{-1})$	0	0	0	1	1	0	0	0	0	1	1	0
$IN(=IM'^{-1})$	0	0	0	1	1	1	0	0	0	1	0	0
$IN'(=IN'^{-1})$	0	0	0	1	0	1	0	0	0	1	0	1
$ID''(=(IUX)^{-1})$	0	0	1	1	0	1	0	1	0	1	0	0
$IE''(=(ITW)^{-1})$	0	0	1	1	0	1	0	0	0	1	0	0
$IL''(=(IOP)^{-1})$	0	0	0	1	0	1	0	1	0	1	0	0
$IM''(=(IMN)^{-1})$	0	0	0	1	0	0	0	0	0	1	1	0
$IN''(=(IMN')^{-1})$	0	0	0	1	0	1	0	0	0	1	0	0
$IMN''(=(IMN'')^{-1})$	0	0	0	1	0	0	0	0	0	1	0	0

whereas S1 and S2 define *coupling conditions*. Assuming that time is dense, it was shown in [9] that there are 29 possible interaction types between a pair of intervals, as given in the upper part of Table 3. Of the 29 interactions, there are 13 pairs of inverses, while three are inverses of themselves. The twenty-nine interaction types are specified using boolean vectors. The six relations R1-R4 and S1-S2 form a boolean vector of length 12, (six bits for $r(X,Y)$ and six bits for $r(Y,X)$). The interaction types are illustrated in [9]. The nondense time model, whose importance is given in [9], permits 11 interaction types between a pair of intervals, defined in the lower part of Table 3, besides the 29 identified before. Of these, there are five pairs of inverses, while one is its own inverse. These interaction types are illustrated in [9]. The set of 40 relations is denoted as $\Re$.

2.3 Modalities for Global Predicates

Observe that for any predicate ϕ, three orthogonal relational possibilities hold under the *Possibly*/ *Definitely* classification: (i) $Definitely(\phi)$, (ii) $\neg Definitely(\phi) \wedge Possibly(\phi)$, (iii) $\neg Possibly(\phi)$.

Table 4. Refinement mapping [10]. The upper part shows the 29 mappings when the dense time model is assumed. With the nondense time model, the 11 additional mappings in the lower part also apply.

$Definitely(\phi)$	$Possibly(\phi) \wedge \neg Definitely(\phi)$	$\neg Possibly(\phi)$
ID and IX	IB and IR	IA and IQ
ID′ and IU	IC and IV	
IE and IW	IG	
IE′ and IT	IH and IK	
IF and IS	II and IJ	
IO and IL		
IP and IL′		
IM		
IM′ and IN		
IN′		
ID″ and IUX	IM″ and IMN	
IE″ and ITW	IMN″	
IL″ and IOP		
IN″ and IMN′		

Conjunctive predicates form an important class of predicates and have been studied extensively [2, 6–8]. Based on the definitions of the orthogonal temporal interactions [9], the 3 orthogonal relational possibilities based on the *Possibly/Definitely* definitions were refined into the exhaustive set of 40 possibilities [10]. Table 4 shows this refinement mapping, assuming that the conjunctive predicate is defined on two processes. When conjunctive predicate ϕ is defined over variables that are local to $n > 2$ processes, one can still express the three possibilities (i) $Definitely(\phi)$, (ii) $\neg Definitely(\phi) \wedge Possibly(\phi)$, and (iii) $\neg Possibly(\phi)$, in terms of the fine-grained 40 independent relations between C_2^n pairs of intervals. Note that not all $40^{C_2^n}$ combinations will be valid – the combinations have to satisfy the axiom system given in [9].

For $n > 2$ processes, the refinement mappings of the *Possibly* and *Definitely* modalities are given by Theorem 1 [10].

Theorem 1. *[10] Consider a conjunctive predicate $\phi = \wedge_i \phi_i$. The following results are implicitly qualified over a set of intervals, containing one interval per process.*

- *$Definitely(\phi)$ holds if and only if $\bigwedge_{(\forall i \in N)(\forall j \in N)} [Definitely(\phi_i \wedge \phi_j)]$*
- *$\neg Definitely(\phi) \wedge Possibly(\phi)$ holds if and only if*
  - *$(\exists i \in N)(\exists j \in N) \neg Definitely(\phi_i \wedge \phi_j) \bigwedge (\bigwedge_{(\forall i \in N)(\forall j \in N)} [Possibly(\phi_i \wedge \phi_j)])$*
- *$\neg Possibly(\phi)$ holds if and only if $(\exists i \in N)(\exists j \in N) \neg Possibly(\phi_i \wedge \phi_j)$*

Consider the following example (from [10]) of the extra information provided by the fine-grained modalities. Let ϕ be $a_i = 2 \wedge b_j = 3 \wedge c_k = 5$. Let a_i, b_j, and c_k be 2, 3, 5 respectively, in intervals X_i, Y_j, and Z_k, respectively, and

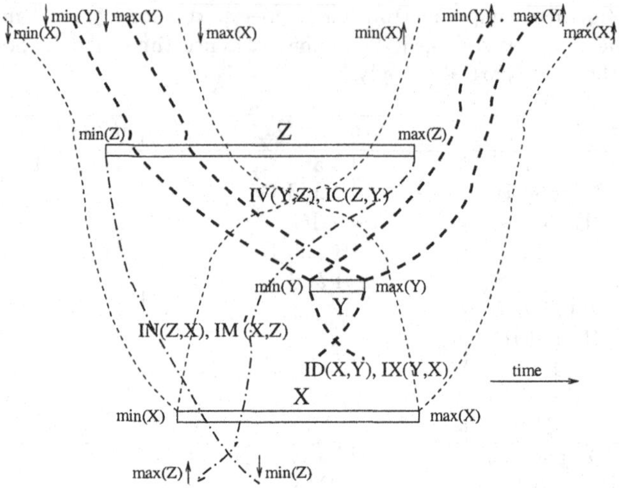

Fig. 1. Example [10] to show fine-grained relations across $n > 2$ processes.

let $ID(X_i, Y_j)$, $IV(Y_j, Z_k)$, and $IN(Z_k, X_i)$ be true. This is shown in Figure 1. Then by Theorem 1, we have (i) $Definitely(a_i = 2 \wedge b_j = 3)$, (ii) $Possibly(b_j = 3 \wedge c_k = 5)$ and $\neg Definitely(b_j = 3 \wedge c_k = 5)$, and (iii) $Definitely(a_i = 2 \wedge c_k = 5)$. By Theorem 1, we have the modality $Possibly(\phi) \wedge \neg Definitely(\phi)$. Conversely, if $Possibly(\phi) \wedge \neg Definitely(\phi)$ is known in the classical course-grained classification, the fine-grained classification gives the added information: $ID(X_i, Y_j)$, $IV(Y_j, Z_k)$, and $IN(Z_k, X_i)$.

2.4 Objective

Our objective is to solve *Fine_Poss* and *Fine_Def*, i.e., to detect $Possibly(\phi)$ and $Definitely(\phi)$, for conjunctive predicates, with the added information of the exact interaction type between each pair of intervals (one at each process) when $Possibly(\phi)$ and $Definitely(\phi)$ are true. The extra information about the pairwise interaction type is useful, as shown in [10] by considering various applications. Another use of the extra information is in multi-player distributed games. The overheads of our algorithms are the same as those of the earlier algorithms, [GW94] [6] for $Possibly(\phi)$ and [GW96] [7] for $Definitely(\phi)$, that can detect **only** whether $Possibly(\phi)$ is true and whether $Definitely(\phi)$ is true. Tables 1 compares all the performance metrics.

3 Detecting Predicates: Framework and Data Structures

Given a conjunctive predicate, for each pair of intervals belonging to different processes, each of the 29 (40) possible independent relations in the dense (non-dense) model of time can be tested for using the bit-patterns for the dependent

1. When an internal event or send event occurs at process P_i, $V_i[i] = V_i[i] + 1$.
2. Every message contains the vector clock and *Interval Clock* of its send event.
3. When process P_i receives a message msg, then $\forall\ j$ do,

   if $(j == i)$ **then** $V_i[i] = V_i[i] + 1$,
   else $V_i[j] = \max(V_i[j], msg.V[j])$.

4. When an interval starts at P_i (local predicate ϕ_i becomes true), $I_i[i] = V_i[i]$.
5. When process P_i receives a message msg, then $\forall\ j$ do,
   $I_i[j] = \max(I_i[j], msg.I[j])$.

Fig. 2. The vector clock and *Interval Clock*.

relations, as given in Table 3. The tests for the relations $R1$, $R2$, $R3$, $R4$, $S1$, and $S2$ are given in the third column of Table 2 using vector timestamps. Recall that the interval at a process is used to identify the period when some local property (using which the predicate ϕ is defined) holds. V_i^- and V_i^+ denote the vector timestamps at process P_i at the start of an interval and the end of an interval, respectively. V_i^x denotes the vector timestamp of event x_i at P_i.

The tests in Table 2 can be run by a central server along the lines of the algorithms in [4, 6–8, 14]. Processes P_1, P_2, ..., P_n send the timestamps of their intervals and certain other local information to the server P_0, which maintains queues Q_1, Q_2, ... ,Q_n for each of the processes. We require that the central server P_0 receive the updates from each P_i, $1 \leq i \leq n$, in FIFO order. For each of the problems to be solved, the server runs different algorithms to process the interval information in the queues. We assume that interval X occurs at P_i and interval Y occurs at P_j. For any two intervals X and X' that occur at the same process, if $R1(X, X')$, then we say that X is a *predecessor* of X' and X' is a *successor* of X. Also, there are a maximum of p intervals at any process.

The operations and data structures required by the algorithms to solve Problems *Fine_Poss* and *Fine_Def* can be divided into two parts. The first, common to all the algorithms, runs on each of the n processes P_1 to P_n, and is given in this section. The second part of each algorithm runs on the central process P_0 and is presented in later sections.

3.1 Log Operations

Each process P_i, where $1 \leq i \leq n$, maintains the following data structures. (1) V_i : array[1..n] of integer. This is the *Vector Clock*. (2) I_i : array[1..n] of integer. This is a *Interval Clock* which tracks the latest intervals at processes. $I_i[j]$ is the timestamp $V_j[j]$ when ϕ_j last became true. (3) Log_i: Contains the information to be sent to the central process. Figure 2 shows how to maintain the vector clock and *Interval Clock*.

To maintain Log_i, the required data structures and operations are defined in Figure 3. Log_i is constructed and sent to the central process using the protocol shown. The central process uses the Log to determine the relationship between two intervals.

```
type Event_Interval = record
    interval_id : integer;
    local_event: integer;
end

type Process_Log = record
    event_interval_queue: queue of Event_Interval;
end

type Log = record
    start: array[1..n] of integer;
    end: array[1..n] of integer;
    p_log: array[1..n] of Process_Log;
end
```

Start of an interval:
    $Log_i.start = V_i^-$.   //Store the timestamp V_i^- of the starting of the interval.
On receiving a message during an interval:
    if (change in I_i) **then**   //Store local component of vector clock and *interval_id*
        for each k such that $I_i[k]$ was changed   //which caused the change in I_i
            insert $(I_i[k], V_i[i])$ in $Log_i.p\_log[k].event\_interval\_queue$.
End of interval:
    $Log_i.end = V_i^+$ //Store the timestamp V_i^+ of the end of the interval.
    if (a receive or send event occurs between start of previous interval and end of current interval) **then**
        Send Log_i to central process.

Fig. 3. Data structures and operations to construct *Log* at P_i $(1 \le i \le n)$.

3.2 Complexity Analysis at P_i $(1 \le i \le n)$

Space complexity of *Log*. Each *Log* stores the start (V^-) and the end (V^+) of an interval, which requires a maximum of $2np$ integers per process. Consider the construction algorithm for *Log*. Besides the start and the end of each interval, an *Event_Interval* is added to the *Log* for every component of *Interval Clock* which is modified due to the receive of a message. As a change in a component of *Interval Clock* implies the start of a new interval on another process, the total number of times the component of *Interval Clock* can change is equal to the number of intervals on all the processes. Thus the total number of *Event_Interval* which can be added to the *Log* of a single process is $(n-1)p$. This takes $2(n-1)p$ integers per process. The total space needed for *Log*s corresponding to all p intervals on a single process is $2(n-1)p+2np$. This gives an average of $4n-2$ integers per *Log*. As only one *Log* exists at a time, the average space requirement at a process P_i $(1 \le i \le n)$ at any time is the sum of space required by vector clock, *Interval Clock*, and *Log*, which is $6n-2$ integers.

Message complexity of control messages sent to the central process P_0 by processes P_1 to P_n. This can be determined in two ways. As one message is sent per interval, the number of messages is $O(p)$ for each P_i $(i \ne 0)$. This gives a total message complexity of $O(np)$. On the average, the size of each message is $4n-2$ as each message contains the *Log*. The total message space overhead for a particular process is the sum of all the *Log*s for that process, which was shown to be $4np-2p$. Hence the total message space complexity is $4n^2p-2np = O(n^2p)$.

An optimization of message size. The *Log* corresponding to an interval is sent to the central process only if the relationship between the interval and all other intervals (at other processes) is different from the relationship which its predecessor interval had with all the other intervals (at other processes). Two successive intervals Y and Y' on process P_j will have the same relationship if no message is sent or received by P_j between the start of Y and the end of Y'. For each message exchanged between processes, a maximum of four interval *Logs* need to be sent to the central process, because two successive intervals (Y and Y') will have different relationships if a receive or a send occurs between the start of Y and end of Y'. This makes it necessary to send two interval *Logs* for a send event and two for a receive event. Hence if there are m_s number of messages exchanged between all processes, then a total of $4m_s$ intervals need to be sent to the central process in $4m_s$ control messages, while the total message space overhead is $2m_s.n + 4m_s.2n = 10m_sn$. The term $2m_s.n$ arises because for every message sent, each other process eventually (due to transitive propagation of *Interval Clock*) may need to insert a *Event_Interval* tuple in its *Log*. This can generate $2nm_s$ overhead in *Logs* across the n processes. The term $4m_s.2n$ arises because the vector clock at the start and end of each interval is sent with each message.

Hence, the total number of control messages sent to the central process and the total message space overhead is the lesser of when either four intervals are sent for each message exchanged or when all the intervals are sent. Thus the total number of messages sent is $O(min(4m_s, np))$ and the total message space overhead is $O(min(4n^2p - 2np, 10m_sn))$.

4 Algorithm *Fine_Rel*: Detecting Fine-Grained Relations

To solve Problems *Fine_Poss* and *Fine_Def*, we first state and solve an intermediate problem.

Problem *Fine_Rel* **Statement:** *Given a relation $r_{i,j}$ from $\Re$ for each pair of processes P_i and P_j, determine on-line the intervals (if they exist), one from each process, such that each relation $r_{i,j}$ is satisfied by the (P_i, P_j) pair.*

Note that the given relations $\{r_{i,j}, \forall i, j\}$ need to satisfy the axioms on $\Re$ [9] for a solution to potentially exist. A distributed and more complex method to solve *Fine_Rel*, using the data structures of Figure 3 and Theorem 2 below, without proofs or a complexity analysis, is presented in [3].

Algorithm Overview: The algorithm detects a set of intervals, one on each process, such that each pair of intervals satisfies the relationship specified for that pair of processes. If no such set of intervals exists, the algorithm does not return any interval set. The central process P_0 maintains n queues, one for *Logs* from each process and determines which orthogonal relation holds between pairs of intervals. The queues are processed using "pruning", described later. If there exists an interval at the head of each queue and these intervals cannot be pruned, then these intervals satisfy $r_{i,j}$ $\forall$ i, j, where $i \neq j$ and $1 \leq i, j \leq n$, and hence these intervals form a solution set.

For $S2(X, Y)$

1. // Eliminate from *Log* of interval Y (on P_j), all receives of messages //which were sent by P_i before the start of interval X (on P_i).

   (1a) **for** each $event\_interval \in Log_j.p\_log[i].event\_interval\_queue$
   (1b) **if** $(event\_interval.interval\_id < Log_i.start[i])$ **then**
   (1c) delete $event\_interval$.

2. // Select from the pruned *Log*, the earliest message sent from interval X to Y.

   (2a) $temp = \infty$
   (2b) **if** $(Log_j.start[i] \geq Log_i.start[i])$ **then** $temp = Log_j.start[j]$
   (2c) **else**
   (2d) **for** each $event\_interval \in Log_j.p\_log[i].event\_interval\_queue$
   (2e) $temp = min(temp, event\_interval.local\_event)$.

3. **if** $(Log_i.end[j] \geq temp)$ **then** $S2(X, Y)$ is true.

For $S1(Y, X)$

1. Same as step 1 of the algorithm to determine $S2(X, Y)$.
2. Same as step 2 of the algorithm to determine $S2(X, Y)$.
3. **if** $(Log_i.end[j] < temp)$ and $(temp > Log_j.start[j])$ **then** $S1(Y, X)$ is true.

Fig. 4. Tests for coupling relations $S1(X, Y)$ and $S2(Y, X)$ at P_0.

We first define the function $S(r_{i,j})$ and the relation $\vdash$. Recall that X and Y are intervals on P_i and P_j, respectively, and Y' is any interval that succeeds Y.

Definition 2. *Function* $S : \Re \rightarrow 2^{\Re}$ *is defined to be* $S(r_{i,j}) = \{R \in \Re \mid R \neq r_{i,j} \wedge$ *if* $R(X, Y)$ *is true then* $r_{i,j}(X, Y')$ *is false for all* Y' *that succeed* Y $\}$.

Intuitively, for each $r_{i,j} \in \Re$, we define a *prohibition function* $S(r_{i,j})$ as the set of all relations R such that if $R(X, Y)$ is *true*, then $r_{i,j}(X, Y')$ can never be *true* for some successor Y' of Y. $S(r_{i,j})$ is the set of relations that prohibit $r_{i,j}$ from being *true* in the future.

Two relations R' and R'' in $\Re$ are related by the *allows* relation $\vdash$ if the occurrence of $R'(X, Y)$ does not prohibit $R''(X, Y')$ for some successor Y' of Y.

Definition 3. $\vdash$ *is a relation on* $\Re \times \Re$ *such that* $R' \vdash R''$ *if (1)* $R' \neq R''$, *and (2) if* $R'(X, Y)$ *is true then* $R''(X, Y')$ *can be true for some* Y' *that succeeds* Y.

For example, $IC \vdash IB$ because (1) $IC \neq IB$ and, (2) if $IC(X, Y)$ is true, then there is a possibility that $IB(X, Y')$ is also true, where Y' succeeds Y.

Lemma 1. *If* $R \in S(r_{i,j})$ *then* $R \not\vdash r_{i,j}$ *else if* $R \notin S(r_{i,j})$ *then* $R \vdash r_{i,j}$.

Proof. If $R \in S(r_{i,j})$, using Definition 2, it can be inferred that $r_{i,j}$ is false for all Y' that succeed Y. This does not satisfy the second part of Definition 3.

Table 5. $S(r_{i,j})$ for the 40 independent relations in $\Re$. The upper part of the table gives the function S on 29 relations assuming dense time. The lower part of the table gives function S for the 11 additional relations assuming non-dense time.

Interaction Type $r_{i,j}$	$S(r_{i,j})$	$S(r_{j,i})$
$IA\ (= IQ^{-1})$	ϕ	$\Re - \{IQ\}$
$IB\ (= IR^{-1})$	$\{IA, IF, II, IP, IO, IU, IX, IUX, IOP\}$	$\Re - \{IQ, IR\}$
$IC\ (= IV^{-1})$	$\{IA, IB, IF, II, IP, IO, IU, IX, IUX, IOP\}$	$\Re - \{IQ, IV\}$
$ID\ (= IX^{-1})$	$\Re - \{IQ, IS, IR, IJ, IL, IL', IL'', ID, ID', ID''\}$	$\Re - \{IQ, IX\}$
$ID'\ (= IU^{-1})$	$\Re - \{IQ, IS, IR, IJ, IL, IL', IL'', ID, ID', ID''\}$	$\Re - \{IQ, IU\}$
$IE\ (= IW^{-1})$	$\Re - \{IQ, IS, IR, IJ, IL, IL', IL'', ID, ID', ID'', IE\}$	$\Re - \{IQ, IW\}$
$IE'\ (= IT^{-1})$	$\Re - \{IQ, IS, IR, IJ, IL, IL', IL'', ID, ID', ID'', IE'\}$	$\Re - \{IQ, IT\}$
$IF\ (= IS^{-1})$	$\Re - \{IQ, IS, IR, IJ, IL, IL', IL'', ID, ID', ID'', IF\}$	$\Re - \{IQ, IS\}$
$IG\ (= IG^{-1})$	$\Re - \{IQ, IR, IJ, IV, IK, IG\}$	$\Re - \{IQ, IR, IJ, IV, IK, IG\}$
$IH\ (= IK^{-1})$	$\Re - \{IQ, IR, IJ, IV, IK, IG, IH\}$	$\Re - \{IQ, IR, IJ, IK\}$
$II\ (= IJ^{-1})$	$\Re - \{IQ, IR, IJ, IV, IK, IG, II\}$	$\Re - \{IQ, IR, IJ\}$
$IL\ (= IO^{-1})$	$\Re - \{IQ, IR, IJ, IL\}$	$\Re - \{IQ, IR, IJ, IO\}$
$IL'\ (= IP^{-1})$	$\Re - \{IQ, IR, IJ, IL'\}$	$\Re - \{IQ, IR, IJ, IP\}$
$IM\ (= IM^{-1})$	$\Re - \{IQ, IR, IJ, IM\}$	$\Re - \{IQ, IR, IJ, IM\}$
$IN\ (= IM'^{-1})$	$\Re - \{IQ, IR, IJ, IN\}$	$\Re - \{IQ, IR, IJ, IM'\}$
$IN'\ (= IN'^{-1})$	$\Re - \{IQ, IR, IJ, IN'\}$	$\Re - \{IQ, IR, IJ, IN'\}$
$ID''\ (= (IUX)^{-1})$	$\Re - \{IQ, IS, IR, IJ, IL, IL', IL'', ID, ID', ID''\}$	$\Re - \{IQ, IUX\}$
$IE''\ (= (ITW)^{-1})$	$\Re - \{IQ, IS, IR, IJ, IL, IL', IL'', ID, ID', ID'', IE''\}$	$\Re - \{IQ, ITW\}$
$IL''\ (= (IOP)^{-1})$	$\Re - \{IQ, IR, IJ, IL''\}$	$\Re - \{IQ, IR, IJ, IOP\}$
$IM''\ (= (IMN)^{-1})$	$\Re - \{IQ, IR, IJ, IM''\}$	$\Re - \{IQ, IR, IJ, IMN\}$
$IN''\ (= (IMN')^{-1})$	$\Re - \{IQ, IR, IJ, IN''\}$	$\Re - \{IQ, IR, IJ, IMN'\}$
$IMN''\ (= (IMN'')^{-1})$	$\Re - \{IQ, IR, IJ, IMN''\}$	$\Re - \{IQ, IR, IJ, IMN''\}$

Hence $R \not\vdash r_{i,j}$. If $R \notin S(r_{i,j})$ and $R \neq r_{i,j}$, it follows that $r_{i,j}$ can be true for some Y' that succeeds Y. This satisfies Definition 3 and hence $R \vdash r_{i,j}$. □

Table 5 gives $S(r_{i,j})$ for each of the 40 interaction types in $\Re$. The table is constructed by analyzing each interaction pair in $\Re$. We now state an important result between any two relations in $\Re$ that satisfy the "allows" relation, and the existence of the "allows" relation between their respective inverses. Specifically, if R' allows R'', then Theorem 2 states that R'^{-1} necessarily does not allow relation R''^{-1}. The theorem can be observed to be true from Lemma 1 and Table 5 by a case-by-case analysis.

Theorem 2. *For $R', R'' \in \Re$, if $R' \vdash R''$ then $R'^{-1} \not\vdash R''^{-1}$.*

Taking the same example, $IC \vdash IB \Rightarrow IV(= IC^{-1}) \not\vdash IR(= IB^{-1})$, which is indeed true. Note that $R' \neq R''$ in the definition of relation $\vdash$ is necessary; otherwise $R' \vdash R'$ will become true and from Theorem 2, we get $R'^{-1} \not\vdash R'^{-1}$ which leads to a contradiction.

Lemma 2. *If the relationship $R(X, Y)$ between intervals X and Y (belonging to process P_i and P_j, resp.) is contained in the set $S(r_{i,j})$, then interval X can be removed from the queue Q_i.*

Proof. From the definition of $S(r_{i,j})$, we get that $r_{i,j}(X, Y')$ cannot exist, where Y' is any successor interval of Y. Hence interval X can never be a part of the solution and can be deleted from the queue. □

Lemma 3. *If the relationship between a pair of intervals X and Y (belonging to processes P_i and P_j resp.) is not equal to $r_{i,j}$, then either interval X or interval Y is removed from the queue.*

Proof. We use contradiction. Assume relation $R(X,Y)$ ($\neq r_{i,j}(X,Y)$) is true for intervals X and Y. From Lemma 2, the only time neither X nor Y will be deleted is when $R \notin S(r_{i,j})$ and $R^{-1} \notin S(r_{j,i})$. From Lemma 1, it can be inferred that $R \vdash r_{i,j}$ and $R^{-1} \vdash r_{j,i}$. As $r_{i,j}^{-1} = r_{j,i}$, we get $R \vdash r_{i,j}$ and $R^{-1} \vdash r_{i,j}^{-1}$. This is a contradiction as by Theorem 2, $R \vdash r_{i,j} \Rightarrow R^{-1} \not\vdash r_{i,j}^{-1}$. Hence $R \in S(r_{i,j})$ or $R^{-1} \in S(r_{j,i})$ or both, and thus at least one of the intervals can be deleted. □

Theorem 3. *Algorithm Fine_Rel run by P_0 in Figure 5 solves Problem Fine_Rel.*

Proof. Lemma 2 which allows queues to be pruned correctly is implemented in the algorithm at P_0. The algorithm deletes interval X as soon as $R(X,Y) \in S(r_{i,j})$ (lines 13-17). Similarly, Y is deleted if $R(Y,X) \in S(r_{j,i})$ (lines 15-17). Thus, an interval gets deleted only if it cannot be part of the solution. Also clearly, each interval gets processed unless a solution is found using a predecessor interval from the same process. Lemma 3 gives the unique property that if $R(X,Y) \neq r_{i,j}$, then either interval X or interval Y is deleted. A consequence of this property is that if *every* queue is non-empty and their heads cannot be pruned, then a solution exists and the set of intervals at the head of each queue forms a solution.

The set *updatedQueues* stores the indices of all the queues whose heads got updated. In each iteration of the **while** loop, the indices of all the queues whose head satisfy Lemma 2 are stored in set *newUpdatedQueues* (lines (13)-(16)). In lines (17) and (18), the heads of all these queues are deleted and indices of the updated queues are stored in the set *updatedQueues*. Observe that only interval pairs which were not compared earlier are compared in subsequent iterations of the **while** loop. The loop runs until no more queues can be updated. If at this stage *all* the queues are non-empty, then a solution is found (follows from Lemma 3). If a solution is found, then for the intervals X (at P_i) and Y (at P_j) stored at the heads of these queues, we have $R(X,Y) = r_{i,j}$. □

For processes P_1 to P_n, the space complexity was shown in Section 3.2 to be on average $O(n)$ at each process. Using the optimization in Section 3.2, the total number of messages sent is equal to $O(min(4m_s, pn))$ and the total message space complexity is $O(min((4n-2)np, 10nm_s))$.

Theorem 4. *Algorithm Fine_Rel has the following complexities.*

- *The total message space complexity is $O(min((4n-2)np, 10nm_s))$.*
- *The total space complexity at process P_0 is $O(min((4n-2)np, 10nm_s))$.*
- *The average time complexity at P_0 is $O((n-1)min(4m_s, pn))$. This is equivalent to $O(n^2M)$, where M is maximum number of entries in a queue.*

Proof. For the central process P_0, the total space required is $O(min((4n-2)np,$-$10nm_s))$ because the total space overhead at P_0 is equal to the total message space complexity, which was computed in Section 3.2.

The time complexity is the product of the number of steps required to determine a relationship and the number of relations determined.

Consider the first part of the product.

queue of *Log*: $Q_1, Q_2, \ldots Q_n = \perp$
set of int: *updatedQueues, newUpdatedQueues* = {}
On receiving interval from process P_z at P_0

(1) Enqueue the interval onto queue Q_z
(2) **if** (number of intervals on Q_z is 1) **then**
(3)   *updatedQueues* = $\{z\}$
(4)   **while** (*updatedQueues* is not empty)
(5)   *newUpdatedQueues*={}
(6)   **for each** $i \in$ *updatedQueues*
(7)   **if** (Q_i is non-empty) **then**
(8) X = head of Q_i
(9)   **for** $j = 1$ to n
(10)   **if** (Q_j is non-empty) **then**
(11) Y = head of Q_j
(12)   Test for $R(X, Y)$ using the tests in Fig. 4 and Tab. 2
(13)   **if** $(R(X, Y) \in S(r_{i,j}))$ **then**
(14)   *newUpdatedQueues* = $\{i\} \cup$ *newUpdatedQueues*
(15)   **if** $(R(Y, X) \in S(r_{j,i}))$ **then**
(16)   *newUpdatedQueues* = $\{j\} \cup$ *newUpdatedQueues*
(17)   Delete heads of all Q_k where $k \in$ *newUpdatedQueues*
(18)   *updatedQueues* = *newUpdatedQueues*
(19)   **if** (all queues are non-empty) **then**
(20)   solution found. Heads of queues identify intervals that form the solution.

Fig. 5. On-line algorithm *Fine_Rel* at P_0.

- The total number of interval pairs between any two processes P_i and P_j is p^2. To determine $R1(X, Y)$ to $R4(X, Y)$ and $R1(Y, X)$ to $R4(Y, X)$, as eight comparisons are needed for each interval pair, a total of $8p^2$ comparisons are necessary for any pair of processes.
- To determine the number of comparisons required by $S1$ and $S2$, consider the maximum number of *Event_Intervals* stored in $Log_j.p\_log[i]$ that are sent over the execution lifetime to the central process as part of the *Logs*. This is the maximum number of *Event_Intervals* corresponding to P_i stored in Q_j over P_j's execution lifetime. An *Event_Interval* is added to $Log_j.p\_log[i]$ only when there is a change in the ith component of *Interval Clock* at the receive of a message. As the ith component of *Interval Clock* changes only when a new interval starts, the total number of times the ith component of *Interval Clock* changes is at most equal to p, the maximum number of intervals occurring on the other process P_i. From Figure 4, it can be observed that for each *Event_Interval*, there is one comparison. Thus, to determine the relationship between an interval on P_i and all other intervals on P_j, the number of comparisons is equal to p. As there are p intervals on P_i, a total of p^2 comparisons are required to determine $S1$ or $S2$. Hence the total number of comparisons to determine $S1(X, Y)$, $S2(X, Y)$, $S1(Y, X)$, and $S2(Y, X)$ is $4p^2$.

This gives a total of $8p^2 + 4p^2 = O(p^2)$ comparisons to determine the relation between each pair of intervals on a pair of processes. As there are a total of p^2 intervals pairs between two processes, the average number of comparisons required to determine a relationship is $O(1)$.

To analyse the second part of the product, consider Figure 5. For each interval considered from one of the queues in *updatedQueues* (lines (6)-(12)), the number of relations determined is $n-1$. Thus the number of relations determined for each iteration of the **while** loop is $(n-1)|updatedQueues|$, where $|updatedQueues|$ denotes the number of entries in *updatedQueues*. The cumulative $\sum |updatedQueues|$ over all iterations of the **while** loop is less than the total number of intervals over all the queues. Thus, the total number of relations determined is less than $(n-1)min(4m_s, pn)$, where $min(4m_s, np)$ is the upper bound on the total number of intervals over all the queues. As the average time required to determine a relationship is $O(1)$, the average time complexity of the algorithm is equal to $O((n-1)min(4m_s, pn))$.

The average time complexity can be equivalently expressed using M, the maximum number of entries in a queue, as follows. The total number of intervals over all the queues is $O(nM)$. As the total number of relations determined is $(n-1)\sum |updatedQueues|$ over all the iterations of the **while** loop, this is equivalent to $(n-1).nM = O(n^2M)$. This is also the average time complexity because it takes $O(1)$ time on the average to determine a relationship. □

Table 1 compares the complexities of *Fine_Rel* with those of GW94 [6] and GW96 [7]. GW94 and GW96 computed their time complexity at P_0 as only $O(n^2M)$, not in terms of m_s or p. They did not give the space complexity at P_0. As each control message in GW94 and GW96 carries a fixed size $O(n)$ message overhead and a control message is sent to P_0 for every message send/receive event, we have computed their total space complexity and average time complexity at P_0 as $O(nm_s)$. This enables a direct comparison with the complexities of our algorithm. Further, we have also computed our average time complexity using M, as $O(n^2M)$. In our algorithm, note that $M \leq p$; $M = p$ if the message overhead optimization is not used. We do not express the total space at P_0 in terms of M because the queue entries are of variable size, with an average size of $(4n-2)$ integers.

5 Algorithms *Fine_Poss* and *Fine_Def*

By leveraging Theorem 1 and the mapping of fine-grained modalities to *Possibly* and *Definitely* modalities, as given in Table 4, we address the problems of determining whether $Possibly(\phi)$ and $Definitely(\phi)$ hold. If either of these two coarse-grained modalities holds, we can also determine the exact fine-grained orthogonal relation/modality between each pair of processes, unlike any previous algorithm. Further, the time, space, and message complexities of the proposed on-line (centralized) detection algorithms (Algorithms *Fine_Poss* and *Fine_Def*) to detect *Possibly* and *Definitely* in terms of the fine-grained modalities per pair of processes, are the *same as* those of the earlier on-line (centralized) algorithms [6, 7] that can detect only whether the *Possibly* and *Definitely* modalities hold.

Recall that $\Re$ is a set of orthogonal relations and hence one and only one relation from $\Re$ must hold between any pair of intervals. Consider the case where, for each pair of processes (P_i, P_j), we are given a set $r^*_{i,j} \subseteq \Re$ such that we are satisfied if some relation in $r^*_{i,j}$ holds. Now consider the objective where we need to identify one interval per process such that for each process pair (P_i, P_j), some relation in $r^*_{i,j}$ holds for that (P_i, P_j). Such an objective would be useful if we can leverage the coarse-to-fine mapping of modalities, given in Table 4. We formalize such an objective by generalizing the detection problem *Fine_Rel* to problem *Fine_Rel'*, as follows.

Problem *Fine_Rel'* **Statement:** *Given a set of relations $r^*_{i,j} \subseteq \Re$ for each pair of processes P_i and P_j, determine on-line the intervals, if they exist, one from each process, such that any one of the relations in $r^*_{i,j}$ is satisfied (by the intervals) for each (P_i, P_j) pair. If a solution exists, identify the fine-grained interaction from $\Re$ for each pair of processes in the first solution.*

To solve *Fine_Rel'*, given an *arbitrary* $r^*_{i,j}$, a solution based on algorithm *Fine_Rel* (Figure 5) will not work because in the crucial tests in lines (13)-(14), neither interval may be removable, and yet none of the relations from $r^*_{i,j}$ might hold between the two intervals. This leads to deadlock! To see this further, let $r1, r2 \in r^*_{i,j}$ and let $R(X,Y)$ hold, where $R \notin r^*_{i,j}$. Now let $R \in S(r1)$, $R^{-1} \notin S(r1^{-1})$, $R \notin S(r2)$, $R^{-1} \in S(r2^{-1})$. Interval X cannot be deleted because $r2(X,Y')$ may be true for a successor Y'. Interval Y cannot be deleted because $r1^{-1}(Y,X')$ may be true for a successor X'. Therefore, a solution based on Algorithm *Fine_Rel* will deadlock, and a more elaborate (and presumably expensive) solution will be needed.

We now identify and define a special property, termed $\mathcal{CONVEXITY}$, on $r^*_{i,j}$ such that the deadlock is prevented. Informally, this property says that there is no relation R outside $r^*_{i,j}$ such that for any $r1, r2 \in r^*_{i,j}$, $R \vdash r1$ and $R^{-1} \vdash r2^{-1}$. This property guarantees that when intervals X and Y are compared for $r^*_{i,j}$ and $R(X,Y)$ holds, either X or Y or both get deleted, and hence there is progress. The sets $r^*_{i,j}$, derived from Table 4, that need to be detected to solve Problems *Fine_Poss* and *Fine_Def* satisfy this property. We therefore observe that problems *Fine_Poss* and *Fine_Def* are special cases of Problem *Fine_Rel'* in which the property $\mathcal{CONVEXITY}$ on $r^*_{i,j}$ is necessarily satisfied. To solve Problems *Fine_Poss* and *Fine_Def*, we then use the generalizations of Lemmas 2 and 3, as given in Lemmas 4 and 5, respectively, to first solve *Fine_Rel'*.

Definition 4.

$$\mathcal{CONVEXITY}: \forall R \notin r^*_{i,j} : (\forall r_{i,j} \in r^*_{i,j}, R \in S(r_{i,j}) \bigvee \forall r_{j,i} \in r^*_{j,i}, R^{-1} \in S(r_{j,i}))$$

Lemma 4. *If the relationship $R(X,Y)$ between intervals X and Y (belonging to processes P_i and P_j, respectively) is contained in the set $\bigcap_{r_{i,j} \in r^*_{i,j}} S(r_{i,j})$, then interval X can be removed from the queue Q_i.*

(13) **if** $(R(X,Y) \in \bigcap_{r_{i,j} \in r^*_{i,j}} S(r_{i,j}))$ **then**
(14) $newUpdatedQueues = \{i\} \cup newUpdatedQueues$
(15) **if** $(R(Y,X) \in \bigcap_{r_{j,i} \in r^*_{j,i}} S(r_{j,i}))$ **then**
(16) $newUpdatedQueues = \{j\} \cup newUpdatedQueues$

Fig. 6. Algorithm *Fine_Rel'*: Changes to algorithm *Fine_Rel* are listed, assuming $r^*_{i,j}$ satisfies property $\mathcal{CONVEXITY}$.

Proof. From the definition of $S(r_{i,j})$, we infer that no relation $r_{i,j}(X, Y')$, where $r_{i,j} \in r^*_{i,j}$ and Y' is any successor interval of Y on P_j, can be true. Hence interval X can never be a part of the solution and can be deleted from the queue. □

Lemma 5. *If the relationship $R(X,Y)$ between a pair of intervals X and Y (belonging to processes P_i and P_j, respectively) does not belong to the set $r^*_{i,j}$, where $r^*_{i,j}$ satisfies property $\mathcal{CONVEXITY}$, then either interval X or interval Y is removed from the queue.*

Proof. We use contradiction. Assume relation $R(X,Y)$ $(\notin r^*_{i,j}(X,Y))$ is true for intervals X and Y. From Lemma 4, the only time neither X nor Y will be deleted is when both $R \notin \bigcap_{r_{i,j} \in r^*_{i,j}} S(r_{i,j})$, and $R^{-1} \notin \bigcap_{r_{j,i} \in r^*_{j,i}} S(r_{j,i})$. However, as $r^*_{i,j}$ satisfies property $\mathcal{CONVEXITY}$, we have that $R \in \bigcap_{r_{i,j} \in r^*_{i,j}} S(r_{i,j})$ or $R^{-1} \in \bigcap_{r_{j,i} \in r^*_{j,i}} S(r_{j,i})$ must be true. Thus at least one of the intervals can be deleted by an application of Lemma 4. □

The proof of the following theorem is similar to the proof of Theorem 3.

Theorem 5. *If the set $r^*_{i,j}$ satisfies property $\mathcal{CONVEXITY}$, then Problem Fine_Rel' is solved by replacing lines (13) and (15) in algorithm Fine_Rel in Figure 5 by the lines (13) and (15) in Figure 6.*

Proof. Analogous to the proof of Theorem 3. Use Lemmas 4 and 5 instead of Lemmas 2 and 3, respectively, and reason with $r^*_{i,j}$ instead of with $r_{i,j}$. □

Corollary 1. *The time, space, and message complexities of Algorithm Fine_Rel' are the same as those of Algorithm Fine_Rel, which were stated in Theorem 4.*

Proof. The only changes to Algorithm *Fine_Rel* are in lines (13) and (15). In Algorithm *Fine_Rel'*, instead of checking $R(X,Y)$ for membership in $S(r_{i,j})$ in line (13), $R(X,Y)$ is checked for membership in $\bigcap_{r_{i,j} \in r^*_{i,j}} S(r_{i,j})$. Both $S(r_{i,j})$ and $\bigcap_{r_{i,j} \in r^*_{i,j}} S(r_{i,j})$ are sets of size between 0 and 40. An analogous observation holds for the change on line (15). Hence, the time, space, and message complexities of *Fine_Rel* are unaffected in *Fine_Rel'*. □

To detect *Possibly*(ϕ), $r^*_{i,j}$ is set to the union of the orthogonal interactions in the first two columns of Table 4. We can verify (by case-by-case enumeration) that $r^*_{i,j}$ does satisfy property $\mathcal{CONVEXITY}$. Similarly, to detect

$Definitely(\phi)$, $r^*_{i,j}$ is set to the union of the orthogonal interactions in the first column of Table 4. We can verify (by case-by-case enumeration) that $r^*_{i,j}$ does satisfy property $\mathcal{CONVEXITY}$.

The following two theorems about using algorithm *Fine_Rel′* (Figure 6) to solve Problems *Fine_Poss* and *Fine_Def* can be readily proved by using Theorem 1, the refinement mapping of Table 4, and Theorem 5. The two resulting algorithms are named *Fine_Poss* and *Fine_Def*, respectively.

Theorem 6. *Algorithm Fine_Rel modified to algorithm Fine_Rel′ (Figure 6) solves Problem Fine_Poss (about Possibly(ϕ)) when $r^*_{i,j}$ is set to the union of the relations in the first and second columns of Table 4.*

Proof. From Theorem 1, $Possibly(\phi)$ is true if and only if $(\forall i \in N)(\forall j \in N)Possibly(\phi_i \wedge \phi_j)$. For any i and j, $Possibly(\phi_i \wedge \phi_j)$ is true if and only if $R(X_i, Y_j)$ is any of the temporal relations given in the first two columns of Table 4. When $r^*_{i,j}$ is set to the union of the relations in these two columns, we can verify (by case-by-case enumeration) that $r^*_{i,j}$ satisfies $\mathcal{CONVEXITY}$. As Algorithm *Fine_Rel′* is correct (by Theorem 6), when its $r^*_{i,j}$ is instantiated with the set above to get Algorithm *Fine_Poss*, we have that *Fine_Poss* is also correct. □

Theorem 7. *Algorithm Fine_Rel modified to algorithm Fine_Rel′ (Figure 6) solves Problem Fine_Def (about Definitely(ϕ)) when $r^*_{i,j}$ is set to the union of the relations in the first column of Table 4.*

Proof. From Theorem 1, $Definitely(\phi)$ is true if and only if $(\forall i \in N)(\forall j \in N)Definitely(\phi_i \wedge \phi_j)$. For any i and j, $Definitely(\phi_i \wedge \phi_j)$ is true if and only if $R(X_i, Y_j)$ is any of the temporal relations given in the first column of Table 4. When $r^*_{i,j}$ is set to the relations in this column, we can verify (by case-by-case enumeration) that $r^*_{i,j}$ satisfies $\mathcal{CONVEXITY}$. As Algorithm *Fine_Rel′* is correct (by Theorem 6), when its $r^*_{i,j}$ is instantiated with the set above to get Algorithm *Fine_Def*, we have that *Fine_Def* is also correct. □

In algorithm *Fine_Rel′*, when $r^*_{i,j}$ is set to the values as specified in Theorems 6 and 7 to detect *Possibly* and *Definitely*, respectively, set $\bigcap_{r_{i,j} \in r^*_{i,j}} S(r_{i,j})$ used in line (13) of the algorithm becomes $\{IA\}$ and $\{IA, IB, IC, IG, IH, II\}$, respectively. An identical change occurs to the set $\bigcap_{r_{j,i} \in r^*_{j,i}} S(r_{j,i})$ on line (15).

Corollary 2. *The time, space, and message complexities of Algorithms Fine_Poss and Fine_Def are the same as those of Algorithm Fine_Rel (stated in Theorem 4) and of Algorithm Fine_Rel′ (stated in Corollary 1).*

Proof. Follows from Corollary 1 and the fact that $r^*_{i,j}$ for *Fine_Poss* and *Fine_Def* satisfy $\mathcal{CONVEXITY}$ and are instantiations of $r^*_{i,j}$ in *Fine_Rel′*. □

6 Discussion & Conclusions

This paper presented algorithms to detect conjunctive predicates under fine-grained modalities. Algorithms *Fine_Poss* and *Fine_Def* not only detect *Possibly(ϕ)* and *Definitely(ϕ)*, respectively, *but also (unlike previous algorithms)* return the pairwise fine-grained relations which exist between all the intervals in the solution set. The space, message, and computational complexities of the previous works for conjunctive predicate detection, GW94 [6] and GW96 [7], for detection of only $Possibly(\phi)$ and $Definitely(\phi)$, respectively, is compared with our algorithms in Table 1. All the complexity measures for algorithms *Fine_Poss* and *Fine_Def* are the same as those for GW94 [6] and GW96 [7]. Thus with the same overhead, Algorithms *Fine_Poss* and *Fine_Def* do the *extra work* of finding the fine-grained relations which exist between the intervals contained in the solution set for *Possibly* and *Definitely*.

A detailed version of these results appears in [1]. Distributed algorithms can be devised for *Fine_Poss* and *Fine_Def* based on the distributed algorithm given in [3] to solve *Fine_Rel*. A discussion of how intervals might be identified when trying to use the fine-grained modalities on nonconjunctive predicates, i.e., general relational predicates, is given in [11].

Acknowledgements

This material is based upon work supported by the National Science Foundation under Grant No. CCR-9875617.

References

1. Chandra, P., Kshemkalyani, A.D.: Algorithms for Detecting Global Predicates under Fine-grained Modalities, Technical Report UIC-ECE-02-05, University of Illinois at Chicago, April 2002.
2. Chandra, P., Kshemkalyani, A.D.: Distributed Algorithm to Detect Strong Conjunctive Predicates, Information Processing Letters, 87(5): 243-249, September 2003.
3. Chandra, P., Kshemkalyani, A.D.: Detection of Orthogonal Interval Relations, Proc. High-Performance Computing Conference, 323-333, LNCS 2552, Springer, 2002.
4. Cooper, R., Marzullo, K.: Consistent Detection of Global Predicates, Proc. ACM/ONR Workshop on Parallel & Distributed Debugging, 163-173, May 1991.
5. Coulouris, G., Dollimore, J., Kindberg, T.: Distributed Systems Concepts and Design, Addison-Wesley, 3rd edition, 2001.
6. Garg, V.K., Waldecker, B.: Detection of Weak Unstable Predicates in Distributed Programs, IEEE Trans. Parallel & Distributed Systems, 5(3), 299-307, Mar. 1994.
7. Garg, V.K., Waldecker, B.: Detection of Strong Unstable Predicates in Distributed Programs, IEEE Trans. Parallel & Distributed Systems, 7(12):1323-1333, Dec. 1996.
8. Hurfin, M., Mizuno, M., Raynal, M., Singhal, M.: Efficient Distributed Detection of Conjunctions of Local Predicates, IEEE Trans. Software Engg., 24(8): 664-677, 1998.
9. Kshemkalyani, A.D.: Temporal Interactions of Intervals in Distributed Systems, Journal of Computer and System Sciences, 52(2): 287-298, April 1996.
10. Kshemkalyani, A.D.: A Fine-Grained Modality Classification for Global Predicates, IEEE Trans. Parallel & Distributed Systems, 14(8): 807-816, August 2003.

11. Kshemkalyani, A.D.: A Note on Fine-grained Modalities for Nonconjunctive Predicates, 5th Workshop on Distributed Computing, LNCS, Springer, Dec. 2003.
12. Kshemkalyani, A.D.: A Framework for Viewing Atomic Events in Distributed Computations, Theoretical Computer Science, 196(1-2), 45-70, April 1998.
13. Lamport, L.: Time, Clocks, and the Ordering of Events in a Distributed System, Communications of the ACM, 558-565, 21(7), July 1978.
14. Marzullo, K., Neiger, G.: Detection of Global State Predicates, Proc. 5th Workshop on Distributed Algorithms, LNCS 579, Springer-Verlag, 254-272, October 1991.
15. Mullender, S.: Distributed Systems, 2nd Edition, ACM Press, 1994.
16. Stoller, S., Schneider, F.: Faster Possibility Detection by Combining Two Approaches, Proc. 9th Workshop on Distributed Algorithms, 318-332, LNCS 972, Springer-Verlag, 1995.
17. Venkatesan, S., Dathan, B.: Testing and Debugging Distributed Programs Using Global Predicates, IEEE Trans. Software Engg., 21(2), 163-177, Feb. 1995.

Combining Hierarchical Specification with Hierarchical Implementation

Naijun Zhan

Lehrstuhl für Praktische Informatik II
Fakultät für Mathematik und Informatik
Mannheim Universität
D7,27, 68163 Mannheim, Deutschland
zhan@pi2.informatik.uni-mannheim.de

Abstract. Action refinement is a practical hierarchical method to ease the design of large reactive systems. Relating hierarchical specification to hierarchical implementation is an effective method to decrease the complexity of the verification of these systems. In our previous work [15], this issue has been investigated in the simple case of the refinement of an action by a finite process.

In this paper, on the one hand, we extend our previous results by considering the issue in general, i.e., refining an abstract action by an arbitrary process; on the other hand, we exploit different techniques such that our method is easier to be followed and applied in practice.

Keywords: Action refinement, modal logic, specification, verification, reactive system.

1 Introduction

Generally speaking, it is not easy, even impossible to capture a complex system at the beginning. *The hierarchical development method* is one of the practical and effective methods for designing large systems by specifying and implementing a system at different levels of abstraction. In process algebraic settings, *action refinement* [8] is such a kind of methods. We are here interested in the question how verification can be incorporated in the hierarchical development. In particular, we investigate how action refinement can be incorporated into a specification logic in such a way that it mimics the refinement in the process algebra. In the literature, some first attempts to solve this problem are given, for example in [10, 13, 14].

The main results obtained in [10, 13, 14] are as follows: Given an abstract specification ϕ in some logic, say the modal μ-calculus, and a model P of a complex system, and a refinement Q for a primitive a in P, where Q is a finite process, build $P[a \rightsquigarrow Q]$ and $\phi[a \rightsquigarrow Q]$ as the refinements of the model P and the specification ϕ respectively. [10] and [13, 14] deal with $P[a \rightsquigarrow Q]$ in different way, but all define $\phi[a \rightsquigarrow Q]$ by replacing $\langle a \rangle$ and $[a]$ in ϕ by some formulae of the forms $\langle a_1 \rangle \langle a_2 \rangle \dots \langle a_n \rangle$ and $[a_1][a_2]\dots[a_n]$ respectively, where $a_1 a_2 \dots a_n$ is

V.A. Saraswat (Ed.): ASIAN 2003, LNCS 2896, pp. 110–124, 2003.

a run of Q. Then they prove that $P \models \phi$ iff $P[a \rightsquigarrow Q] \models \phi[a \rightsquigarrow Q]$ under some syntactical conditions.

In the above approaches, the refinements of the specification and the model are explicitly built on the structure of Q. This restricts the refinement step in two ways: firstly, there are some desired properties of the refined system that cannot be deduced in the setting of [10, 13, 14]. For example, let $P = a; b + a; c$, $\phi = \langle a \rangle$, $Q = a'; (c'; b'; d' + c'; b')$. It's obvious that $P \models \phi$ and $Q \models \langle a' \rangle [c'] \langle b' \rangle$. It is expected that $P[a \rightsquigarrow Q] \models \langle a' \rangle [c'] \langle b' \rangle$. But it cannot be derived using the approaches of [10, 13, 14]; secondly, the refinement step is restricted to one choice of Q for refining an action a, which appears both in the refined process and the refined specification explicitly.

In contrast to this, in [15] we proposed a general approach on how to construct a low-level specification by refining the higher-level specification. But as in [10, 13, 14], we also only considered the simple case to refine an abstract action by a finite process. The basic idea is to define a refinement mapping Ω which maps the high-level specification ϕ and the property ψ of the refinement Q of an abstract action a to a lower-level specification by substituting ψ for $\langle a \rangle$ and $[a]$ in ϕ. Since ψ can be any property that holds in Q, we can get the expected specification if ϕ and ψ are appropriate. For example, in the above example, we can get $\Omega(\phi, \langle a' \rangle [c'] \langle b' \rangle, a) = \langle a' \rangle [c'] \langle b' \rangle$ which is exactly what we expect. However, Q can only be any finite process, which implies that ψ is essentially equivalent to a formula without fixpoint operators.

But, in many applications, an action has to be refined by a process with potentially infinite behaviour. For example, in the programming, we can look the interface of a procedure as an abstract action and its body as its refinement. In an abstract level, we only need to use the interface instead of the procedure, but it is necessary to substitute the body for the interface when the procedure is considered in a lower level. In many cases, we need to implement a procedure with possibly infinite behaviour in order to meet the given requirements. For instance, in the example of a salesman [15] (It can be found in Section 4), if we know that the job of the salesman in London every day is repeatedly to meet some of his customers in his office or contact some of them by phone, the action "work" in the top-most specification should be refined by the above concrete procedure in the lower-level specification. However, it is obvious that such a job can not be done using our previous approach.

So, in order to have more applications, we extend our previous work by refining an abstract action by an arbitrary process in this paper. To this end, we adopt FLC as specification language.

FLC is due to Müller-Olm [16], and is an extension of the μ-calculus by introducing the chop operator ";". FLC is strictly more expressive than the μ-calculus because the former can define non-regular properties [16], whereas the latter can only express regular properties [7, 9]. The model-checking of FLC was addressed in [11, 12]. For technical reasons, here we augment FLC by introducing a special propositional constant $\surd$ to indicate if a process is terminated and re-interpret $[a]$ appropriately.

As discussed in [15], a sound refinement mapping should keep the type of properties to be refined, i.e. an existential property should be refined to an existential property and similarly for the other properties. In order to define a refinement mapping that can preserves the type of the property to be refined, as in [15], the property for the refinement Q will be partitioned into two subformulae: an *universal formula* and an *existential formula*. The former will be used to substitute for $[a]$ and the latter for $\langle a\rangle$ in ϕ. Such partition is justified by the result proved in [4] that every property can be represented as the conjunction of a safety property and a liveness property in branching models. Besides, we require that ψ is only relevant to full executions of Q. If so, a refinement mapping that keeps the type of the property to be refined can be defined like in [15]. Furthermore, we can prove the following theorem:

Theorem. (Refinement Theorem) *If some syntactical conditions hold, $P \models \phi$ and $Q \models \psi; \surd$ then $P[a \rightsquigarrow Q] \models \Omega(\phi, \psi, a)$.*

The above theorem supports 'a priori' verification in the following sense: In the development process we start with $P \models \phi$ and either refine P and obtain automatically a (relevant) formula that is satisfied by $P[a \rightsquigarrow Q]$; or, we refine ϕ using $\Omega(\phi, \psi, a)$ and obtain automatically a refined process $P[a \rightsquigarrow Q]$ that satisfies the refined specification. Of course such refinement steps may be iterated.

To achieve the intended result, we need to assume that action refinement for models is atomic. Our main aim in this work is to establish a correspondence between hierarchical implementation and hierarchical specification of a complex system. But if we allow that the refining process can be interleaved with others problems will arise. E.g. $(a \parallel_{\{\}} b)[a \rightsquigarrow a_1; a_2]$ means the parallel executions of a and b in which a is refined by $a_1; a_2$. It's obvious that $a \parallel_{\{\}} b$ satisfies $\langle a\rangle$, and $a_1; a_2$ satisfies $\langle a_1\rangle; (\langle a_2\rangle \wedge [b]; false)$ which means that $a_1; a_2$ first performs a_1, then a_2 but cannot perform b. We expect that $a \parallel_{\{\}} b$ meets $\langle a_1\rangle; (\langle a_2\rangle \wedge [b]; false)$ after refining a by $a_1; a_2$. This is not true in the case of non-atomic action refinement since b can be performed between the execution of a_1 and a_2. But it is valid if we assume that action refinement is atomic [5, 6]. So, in the sequel, we discuss action refinement for models under the assumption of atomicity.

Besides, we will exploit different techniques such that all the results proved in this paper are represented in a simpler way and easier to be used in practice.

The remainder of this paper is organized as follows: A modeling language is defined in Section 2; Section 3 briefly reviews FLC; A refinement mapping for specifications is given in Section 4; The correspondence between the hierarchical specification and the hierarchical implementation of a complex system is shown in Section 5; Finally, a brief conclusion is provided in Section 6.

2 Modeling Language – A TCSP-like Process Algebra

2.1 Syntax

As in [14], we use a TCSP-like process algebra in combination with an action refinement operator as modeling language. Let *Act* be an infinite set of (atomic) actions, ranged over by $a, b, c, \ldots$, and A be a subset of *Act*. Let $\mathcal{X}$ be a set of process variables, ranged over by $x, y, z, \ldots$. The language of processes, denoted by $\mathcal{P}$ and ranged over $P, Q, \ldots$, is generated by the following grammar:

Definition 1.

$$P ::= \delta \mid nil \mid a \mid x \mid P;Q \mid P+Q \mid P \parallel_A Q \mid rec\, x.P \mid P[a \rightsquigarrow Q]$$

where $a \in Act, x \in \mathcal{X}$, *and* $P, Q \in \mathcal{P}$.

An occurrence of a process variable $x \in \mathcal{X}$ is called *bound* in a process term P iff it does occur within a sub-term of the form $rec\, x.P'$, otherwise called *free*. A process expression P is called *closed* iff all occurrences of each variable occurring in it are bound, otherwise it is called *open*. We will use $fn(P)$ to stand for the variables that have some free occurrence in P, $bn(P)$ for the variables that have some bound occurrence in P. When we say a process P is *terminated*, it means that P does nothing except for terminating (see Definition 2). A variable $x \in \mathcal{X}$ is called *guarded* within a term P iff every occurrence of x is within a sub-term Q where Q lies in a subexpression $Q^*; Q$ such that Q^* is not terminated. A term P is called *guarded* iff all variables occurring in it are guarded. Sometimes, we abuse $Act(P)$ to stand for the set of actions which occur in P.

For technical reasons, as in [8], we require the following well-formedness conditions on $\mathcal{P}$:

- **(i)** None of operands of $+$ is a terminated process;
- **(ii)** All process terms are guarded;
- **(iii)** The refinement of an action can not be a terminated process. As discussed, e.g. in [17], refining an action by a terminated process is not only counter-intuitive but also technically difficult.

Intuitively, $P[a \rightsquigarrow Q]$ means that the system replaces the execution of an action a by the execution of the subsystem Q every time when the subsystem P performs a. This operator provides a mechanism to hierarchically design reactive systems. The other expressions of $\mathcal{P}$ can be conceived as usual ones. The formal interpretation of $\mathcal{P}$ will be provided in the next section.

2.2 Operational Semantics

Here we define an operational semantics for $\mathcal{P}$ employing transition systems. The meaning of the constructs of the language can be interpreted in the standard way except for the refinement operator. In order to guarantee the atomicity of the refinement, the basic idea is to define a transition system for the process that may be refined, then replace all transitions labelled with the action to be refined by the transition system for the refinement.

Similar to [8], the above idea can be implemented by introducing an auxiliary operator $*$ to indicate that a process prefixed with it is the remainder of some process, which has the highest precedence and must be performed completely. The state language, denoted by $\mathcal{P}^*$, ranged over by $s, \ldots$, is given by:

$$s ::= nil \mid \delta \mid a \mid x \mid *s \mid s;s \mid P+Q \mid s \parallel_A s \mid s[a \rightsquigarrow Q] \mid rec\, x.P$$

where $a \in Act, x \in \mathcal{X}, P, Q \in \mathcal{P}$.

According to the above definition, it is clear that $\mathcal{P}$ is a proper subset of $\mathcal{P}^*$, i.e. $\mathcal{P} \subset \mathcal{P}^*$.

In order to define the semantics of $\mathcal{P}^*$, we need the following definition.

Definition 2. *Let* $\surd$ *and* **ab** *be the minimal relations on* $\mathcal{P}^*$ *which satisfy the following rules, respectively:*

$$\frac{}{\surd(nil)} \qquad \frac{\surd(s)}{\begin{array}{c}\surd(*s)\\ \surd(rec\,x.s)\\ \surd(s[a \rightsquigarrow Q])\end{array}} \qquad \frac{\surd(s_1) \wedge \surd(s_2)}{\begin{array}{c}\surd(s_1 \parallel_A s_2)\\ \surd(s_1; s_2)\\ \textit{where } Q \in \mathcal{P}\end{array}}$$

Definition of $\surd$

$$\frac{\surd(s)}{\mathbf{ab}(s)} \qquad \frac{}{\begin{array}{c}\mathbf{ab}(a)\\ \mathbf{ab}(x)\end{array}} \qquad \frac{\mathbf{ab}(s_1) \wedge \mathbf{ab}(s_2)}{\begin{array}{c}\mathbf{ab}(s_1; s_2)\\ \mathbf{ab}(s_1 + s_2)\\ \mathbf{ab}(s_1 \parallel_A s_2)\end{array}} \qquad \frac{\mathbf{ab}(s)}{\begin{array}{c}\mathbf{ab}(rec\,x.s)\\ \mathbf{ab}(s[a \rightsquigarrow Q])\\ \textit{where } Q \in \mathcal{P}\end{array}}$$

Definition of **ab**

Note that in the above definition, $\surd(s)$ means that s is terminated, whereas $ab(s)$ means that s is either in $\mathcal{P}$, or terminated. A state s is called *abstract* if $\mathbf{ab}(s)$, otherwise, called *concrete.*

Besides complying with the three well-formedness conditions for $\mathcal{P}$, $\mathcal{P}^*$ also follows the below well-formedness condition:

(iv) At least one of the operands of $\parallel_A$ is abstract.

An operational semantics of $\mathcal{P}^*$ is given by the following transition rules:

$$\text{Act} \quad a \xrightarrow{a} nil \qquad\qquad \text{Nd} \quad \frac{P \xrightarrow{a} s}{P + Q \xrightarrow{a} s \text{ and } Q + P \xrightarrow{a} s}$$

$$\text{Seq-1} \quad \frac{s_1 \xrightarrow{a} s_1'}{s_1; s_2 \xrightarrow{a} s_1'; s_2} \qquad\qquad \text{Seq-2} \quad \frac{\surd(s_1) \text{ and } s_2 \xrightarrow{a} s_2'}{s_1; s_2 \xrightarrow{a} s_2'}$$

$$\text{Ref-1} \quad \frac{s \xrightarrow{b} s'}{s[a \rightsquigarrow Q] \xrightarrow{b} s'[a \rightsquigarrow Q]} \quad a \neq b \qquad \text{Ref-2} \quad \frac{s \xrightarrow{a} s' \text{ and } Q \xrightarrow{a'} s_1}{s[a \rightsquigarrow Q] \xrightarrow{a'} (*s_1); s'[a \rightsquigarrow Q]}$$

$$\text{Rec} \quad \frac{P[rec\,x.P/x] \xrightarrow{a} s}{rec\,x.P \xrightarrow{a} s} \qquad\qquad \text{Star} \quad \frac{s \xrightarrow{a} s'}{*s \xrightarrow{a} *s'}$$

$$\text{A-Syn} \quad \frac{s_1 \xrightarrow{a} s_1'}{s_1 \parallel_A s_2 \xrightarrow{a} s_1' \parallel_A s_2 \text{ and } s_2 \parallel_A s_1 \xrightarrow{a} s_2 \parallel_A s_1'} \quad a \notin A \wedge \mathbf{ab}(s_2)$$

$$\text{Syn} \quad \frac{s_1 \xrightarrow{a} s_1' \text{ and } s_2 \xrightarrow{a} s_2'}{s_1 \parallel_A s_2 \xrightarrow{a} s_1' \parallel_A s_2' \text{ and } s_2 \parallel_A s_1 \xrightarrow{a} s_2' \parallel_A s_1'} \quad a \in A \wedge \mathbf{ab}(s_1) \wedge \mathbf{ab}(s_2)$$

We'd like to comment on some special rules as follows: The rule Nd says that only two processes in $\mathcal{P}$ can be performed nondeterministically, the other cases are impossible by the definition of $\mathcal{P}^*$. The rule Ref-2 states that the residual s_1 of Q is non-interruptible. The rule Star says that $*s$ behaves like s, but the reached state is still concrete (if not properly terminated). The rule A-Syn gives priority to the concrete component. At any time, if a concrete process is in parallel with an abstract process, the latter has to remain idle till the former finishes the executing. Observe that there is no way to reach a state where both components are concrete, starting from an initial abstract state (in fact, such a state would not be well-formed). Moreover, if both components are abstract, the rule allows any of them to proceed first. The rule Syn states that only two abstract processes can communicate each other. The communication between a concrete process and another process may destroy the atomicity of the refinement. In fact, it is impossible to reach a state where a concrete process synchronizes with another process from an initial abstract state. The other rules can be conceived as usual. The above rules guarantee that the execution of the refinement Q is not only to be non-interruptible, but also to be either executed completely, or not at all.

In the following, we investigate the notion of strong bisimulation on $\mathcal{P}^*$.

Definition 3. – *A binary symmetric relation R over the closed terms of $\mathcal{P}^*$ is a strong bisimulation if for any $(s_1, s_2) \in R$*
  - $\surd(s_1)$ *iff* $\surd(s_2)$; *and*
  - *for any $a \in Act$, $s_1 \xrightarrow{a} s_1'$, there exists s_2' s.t. $s_2 \xrightarrow{a} s_2'$ and $(s_1', s_2') \in R$.*

– *s_1 and s_2 are strong bisimilar, denoted by $s_1 \sim s_2$, if and only if there exists a strong bisimulation R such that $(s_1, s_2) \in R$.*

– *Let $E, F \in \mathcal{P}^*$ and $fn(E) \cup fn(F) \subseteq \{x_1, \ldots, x_n\}$. Then $E \sim F$ iff for any closed terms $s_1, \ldots, s_n$, $E\{s_1/x_1, \ldots, s_n/x_n\} \sim F\{s_1/x_1, \ldots, s_n/x_n\}$.*

According to the above semantics, it is easy to show that

Lemma 1. *For any closed term $s \in \mathcal{P}^*$, $s \sim *s$.*

Because a concrete process has a priority in parallel with an abstract process, $\sim$ is not preserved by $\|_A$. For example, $a_1; a_2 \sim a[a \rightsquigarrow a_1; a_2]$, but $(a_1; a_2) \|_{\{\}} b \not\sim a[a \rightsquigarrow a_1; a_2] \|_{\{\}} b$. However, once we strengthen Definition 3 by adding the following condition:

- $\mathsf{ab}(s_1)$ iff $\mathsf{ab}(s_2)$,

then the resulting largest bisimulation, denoted by $\sim_{\mathbf{ab}}$, is a congruence relation over $\mathcal{P}^*$. Besides, obviously, $\sim_{\mathbf{ab}}$ is a proper subset of $\sim$. That is,

Theorem 1. *$\sim_{\mathbf{ab}}$ is a congruence over $\mathcal{P}^*$ and $\sim_{\mathbf{ab}} \subset \sim$.*

Convention: From now on, we use $P, Q, \ldots$ to stand for processes in $\mathcal{P}^*$.

3 Fixpoint Logic with Chop (FLC)

FLC is an extension of the modal μ-calculus by introducing the chop operator ";", which can express non-regular properties [16]. It is therefore strictly more powerful than the μ-calculus, since [7, 9] proved that only regular properties can be defined in the μ-calculus. For our purpose, we modify FLC [16] slightly.

Let $X, Y, Z, \ldots$ range over an infinite set *Var* of *variables*, *true* and *false* be two propositional constants as usual, and $\surd$ be another one that is used to indicate if a process is terminated.

The formulae of FLC are generated according to the following grammar:

$$\phi ::= true \mid false \mid \surd \mid \tau \mid X \mid [a] \mid \langle a \rangle \mid \phi_1 \wedge \phi_2 \mid \phi_1 \vee \phi_2 \mid \phi_1; \phi_2 \\ \mid \mu X.\phi \mid \nu X.\phi$$

where $X \in Var$ and $a \in Act$[1].

[1] In [16], τ is called *term*.

In the sequel, we use $\boxed{a}$ to stand for $\langle a \rangle$ or $[a]$, p for *true*, *false* or $\surd$, and σ for ν or μ, $Act(\phi)$ for all actions that occur in ϕ.

As in the modal μ-calculus, the two *fixpoint operators* μX and νX bind the respective variable X and we will apply the usual terminology of *free* and *bound occurrences* of a variable in a formula, *closed* and *open* formulae etc. $fn(\phi)$ denotes the variables that have some free occurrence in ϕ and $bf(\phi)$ stands for the variables that have some bound occurrence in ϕ. X is said *guarded* in ϕ if each occurrence of X is in a sub-formula ϕ preceded with $\boxed{a}$ or p. If all variables in ϕ are guarded, then ϕ is called *guarded.*

FLC is interpreted over a given labelled transition system $T = (\mathcal{S}, A, \rightarrow)$, where $\mathcal{S} \subseteq \mathcal{P}^*$, $A \subseteq Act$, and $\rightarrow \subseteq \mathcal{S} \times A \times \mathcal{S}$. A formula is interpreted as a *monotonic predicate transformer*, which is simply a mapping $f : 2^{\mathcal{S}} \rightarrow 2^{\mathcal{S}}$ that is monotonic w.r.t. the inclusion ordering on $2^{\mathcal{S}}$. We use $\mathrm{MPT_T}$ to represent all these monotonic predicate transformers over $\mathcal{S}$. $\mathrm{MPT_T}$, together with the inclusion ordering defined by

$$f \subseteq f' \text{ iff } f(\mathcal{A}) \subseteq f'(\mathcal{A}) \text{ for all } \mathcal{A} \subseteq \mathcal{S},$$

forms a complete lattice. We denote the join and meet operators by $\sqcup$ and $\sqcap$. By Tarski-Knaster Theorem, the least and greatest fixed points of monotonic functions: $(2^{\mathcal{S}} \rightarrow 2^{\mathcal{S}}) \rightarrow (2^{\mathcal{S}} \rightarrow 2^{\mathcal{S}})$ exist. They are used to interpret fixed point formulae of FLC.

The meaning of $true$ and $false$ are interpreted in the standard way, i.e. by $\mathcal{S}$ and $\emptyset$ respectively. The meaning of $\surd$ is to map any subset of $\mathcal{S}$ to the subset of $\mathcal{S}$ which consists of all terminated processes in $\mathcal{S}$. Therefore, a process P meets $\surd$ iff $\surd(P)$. τ is interpreted as an identity. Because *nil* and δ have different behaviour in the presence of ;, they should be distinguished by FLC. To this end, $[a]$ is interpreted as a function that maps a set of processes $\mathcal{A}$ to the set in which each process is not terminated and any of the a-successors of the process must be in $\mathcal{A}$. This is different from its original interpretation in [16]. Therefore, according to our interpretation, $P \models [a]$ only if $\neg\surd(P)$. Whereas in [16], it is always valid that $P \models [a]$ for any $P \in \mathcal{P}^*$. So, it is easy to show that $nil \not\models \bigwedge_{a\in Act}[a]; false$, while $\bigwedge_{a\in Act}[a]; false$ is the characteristic formula of δ. The meaning of variables is given by an *environment* $\rho : var \rightarrow (2^{\mathcal{S}} \rightarrow 2^{\mathcal{S}})$ that assigns variables to monotonic functions of sets to sets. $\rho[X \rightsquigarrow f]$ agrees with ρ except for associating f with X.

Definition 4. *Formally, given a labelled transition system $T = (\mathcal{S}, A, \rightarrow)$, the meaning of a formula ϕ, denoted by $\mathcal{C}_T^\rho(\phi)$, is inductively defined as follows:*

$$\begin{aligned}
\mathcal{C}_T^\rho(true)(\mathcal{A}) &= \mathcal{S} \\
\mathcal{C}_T^\rho(false)(\mathcal{A}) &= \emptyset \\
\mathcal{C}_T^\rho(\surd)(\mathcal{A}) &= \{P \mid P \in \mathcal{S} \wedge \surd(P)\} \\
\mathcal{C}_T^\rho(\tau)(\mathcal{A}) &= \mathcal{A} \\
\mathcal{C}_T^\rho(X) &= \rho(X) \\
\mathcal{C}_T^\rho([a])(\mathcal{A}) &= \{P \mid \neg\surd(P) \wedge \forall P' : P \xrightarrow{a} P' \Rightarrow P' \in \mathcal{A}\}
\end{aligned}$$

$$\begin{array}{rcl}
\mathcal{C}_T^\rho(\langle a\rangle)(\mathcal{A}) & = & \{P \mid \exists P' : P \xrightarrow{a} P' \wedge P' \in \mathcal{A}\} \\
\mathcal{C}_T^\rho(\phi_1 \wedge \phi_2)(\mathcal{A}) & = & \mathcal{C}_T^\rho(\phi_1)(\mathcal{A}) \cap \mathcal{C}_T^\rho(\phi_2)(\mathcal{A}) \\
\mathcal{C}_T^\rho(\phi_1 \vee \phi_2)(\mathcal{A}) & = & \mathcal{C}_T^\rho(\phi_1)(\mathcal{A}) \cup \mathcal{C}_T^\rho(\phi_2)(\mathcal{A}) \\
\mathcal{C}_T^\rho(\phi_1;\phi_2) & = & \mathcal{C}_T^\rho(\phi_1) \cdot \mathcal{C}_T^\rho(\phi_2) \\
\mathcal{C}_T^\rho(\mu X.\phi) & = & \sqcap\{f \in \mathrm{MPT_T} \mid \mathcal{C}_T^{\rho[X\rightsquigarrow f]}(\phi) \subseteq f\} \\
\mathcal{C}_T^\rho(\nu X.\phi) & = & \sqcup\{f \in \mathrm{MPT_T} \mid \mathcal{C}_T^{\rho[X\rightsquigarrow f]}(\phi) \supseteq f\}
\end{array}$$

where $\mathcal{A} \subseteq \mathcal{S}$, and $\cdot$ stands for the composition operator over functions.

A process P is said to satisfy ϕ iff $P \in \mathcal{C}_T^\rho(\phi)(\mathcal{S})$ for some environment ρ, denoted by $P \models \phi$. $\phi \Rightarrow \psi$ means that $\mathcal{C}_T^\rho(\phi)(\mathcal{A}) \subseteq \mathcal{C}_T^\rho(\psi)(\mathcal{A})$ for any T and $\mathcal{A} \subset \mathcal{S}$ and any ρ. $\phi \Leftrightarrow \psi$ means $(\phi \Rightarrow \psi) \wedge (\psi \Rightarrow \phi)$. The other notations can be defined in a standard way.

Convention: In the sequel, we assume the binding precedence among the operators of the logic as follows: "$;$" > "$\vee$" = "$\wedge$" > "$\nu X.$" = "$\mu X.$" > "$\Rightarrow$" = "$\Leftrightarrow$".

Many properties of FLC have been shown in [16], e.g., FLC is strictly more expressive than the μ-calculus since context-free processes can be characterized by it; FLC is decidable for finite-state processes, undecidable for context-free processes; the satisfiability and validity of FLC are undecidable; FLC does not enjoy the finite-model property and so on.

[11] proved that FLC has the tree model property[2], i.e.,

Theorem 2. *Given $P, Q \in \mathcal{P}^*$, and $P \sim Q$, then for any closed ϕ, $P \models \phi$ iff $Q \models \phi$.*

Given a formula ϕ, we define its beginning atomic sub-formulae, denoted by $\mathrm{FSub}(\phi)$, as:

$$\mathrm{FSub}(\phi) \mathrel{\hat=} \begin{cases}
\{\phi\} & \text{if } \phi = p, X, \boxed{a} \text{ or } \tau \\
\mathrm{FSub}(\phi_1) \cup \mathrm{FSub}(\phi_2) & \text{if } \phi = \phi_1 \wedge \phi_2 \text{ or } \phi = \phi_1 \vee \phi_2 \\
\mathrm{FSub}(\phi_1) & \text{if } \phi = \phi_1;\phi_2 \text{ and } \phi_1 \not\Leftrightarrow \tau \\
\mathrm{FSub}(\phi_2) & \text{if } \phi = \phi_1;\phi_2 \text{ and } \phi_1 \Leftrightarrow \tau \\
\mathrm{FSub}(\phi_1) & \text{if } \phi = \sigma X.\phi_1
\end{cases}$$

Symmetrically, we define its ending atomic sub-formulae, denoted by $\mathrm{ESub}(\phi)$, as:

$$\mathrm{ESub}(\phi) \mathrel{\hat=} \begin{cases}
\{\phi\} & \text{if } \phi = p, X, \boxed{a} \text{ or } \tau \\
\mathrm{ESub}(\phi_1) \cup \mathrm{ESub}(\phi_2) & \text{if } \phi = \phi_1 \wedge \phi_2 \text{ or } \phi = \phi_1 \vee \phi_2 \\
\mathrm{ESub}(\phi_1) & \text{if } \phi = \phi_1;\phi_2 \text{ and } \phi_2 \Leftrightarrow \tau \\
\mathrm{ESub}(\phi_2) & \text{if } \phi = \phi_1;\phi_2 \text{ and } \phi_2 \not\Leftrightarrow \tau \\
\mathrm{ESub}(\phi_1) & \text{if } \phi = \sigma X.\phi_1
\end{cases}$$

Example 1. $\mathrm{FSub}(\langle a\rangle;\langle b\rangle \wedge [c];\langle e\rangle;[f]) = \{\langle a\rangle, [c]\}$, whereas $\mathrm{ESub}(\langle a\rangle;\langle b\rangle \wedge [c];\langle e\rangle;[f]) = \{\langle b\rangle, [f]\}$. ⊣

2 The proof for the tree model property of FLC in [11] still works in our case.

When we say that $\surd$ only occurs at the end of ϕ it means that $\surd$ can only be in $\mathrm{ESub}(\phi)$ as a sub-formula of ϕ and can not appear elsewhere in the formula.

Definition 5. *A formula ϕ is called* existential formula *if for any $a \in Act$, $[a] \notin \mathrm{FSub}(\phi)$. We use $\mathcal{EF}$ to stand for the set of existential formulae. Dually, a formula ϕ is called* universal formula *if for any $a \in Act$, $\langle a\rangle \notin \mathrm{FSub}(\phi)$. We use $\mathcal{UF}$ to stand for the set of universal formulae. For technical reasons, we stipulate that $\tau \notin \mathcal{UF}$. A formula ϕ is called a property formula if $\phi \Leftrightarrow \phi_1 \wedge \phi_2$, where $\phi_1 \in \mathcal{EF}$ and $\phi_2 \in \mathcal{UF}$. The set of property formulae is denoted by $\mathcal{PF}$.*

For $\mathcal{EF}$ and $\mathcal{UF}$, we have

Theorem 3. *$\mathcal{EF}$ and $\mathcal{UF}$ are closed under all operators of the logic. I.e., $\phi \, op \, \varphi \in \mathcal{EF}(\mathcal{UF})$ and $\sigma X.\phi \in \mathcal{EF}(\mathcal{UF})$ if $\phi, \varphi \in \mathcal{EF}(\mathcal{UF})$, for any ϕ and φ, where $op \in \{\vee, \wedge, ;\}$.*

4 Towards Hierarchical Specification

As the complexity of reactive system designs becomes overwhelming very quickly, methods which allow to develop designs in a hierarchical fashion must be supported by the design formalisms employed. Such methods allow to develop a design at different levels of abstraction thereby making the development procedure more transparent and thus tractable: Most likely, a developer first divides the intended (complex) design into various "sub-designs" to capture the abstract overall structure of the complete design. Subsequently, the sub-designs will be developed by enriching them step by step with details. This is the design technique usually encountered in practice, see e.g. in [18]. In process algebraic settings, action refinement as introduced in Section 2 supports the hierarchical design.

In [15], we investigated the issue how to provide such a technique in a logical framework. To this end, a refinement mapping is defined by substituting the property of the refinement of an abstract action a for the modalities $\langle a\rangle$ and $[a]$ in a high-level specification and producing a lower-level specification. However, in [15], we only consider the case when all specifications are represented by some formulae in the subset $\mathcal{NF}$ of FLC called normal form formulae, which essentially correspond to the μ-calculus with τ, and the properties of refinements by some formulae without fixpoint operator in the subset. This is because in [15] we concentrated on the simple case to refine an abstract action by a finite process. Here, we consider the issue in general, i.e., refining an abstract action by any process. To this end, we adopt FLC itself as specification language, instead of $\mathcal{NF}$. This is because after refining a formula in $\mathcal{NF}$ with a property for a recursive process, the resulting formula may not be in $\mathcal{NF}$ any more. For example, suppose that $\langle a\rangle\phi \in \mathcal{NF}$ and a is refined by a process with the property $\nu X.\langle a'\rangle X \wedge \langle c'\rangle$. By our definition, the refined specification is $(\nu X.\langle a'\rangle X \wedge \langle c'\rangle)\phi$. It is easy to prove that there exists no $\varphi \in \mathcal{NF}$ such that φ is equivalent to the specification.

In a logical framework, actions are addressed as modalities and descriptions of systems are represented by formulae. In most of modal logics, there are two kinds of modalities, i.e. $\langle a \rangle$ and $[a]$ which are used to express existential and universal properties respectively. As discussed in [15], a refinement mapping should be property-preserving, i.e. an existential property should be refined to an existential property and similarly for the other properties. Otherwise, the mapping is meaningless since it's impossible to establish a correspondence between action refinement for models and action refinement for specifications. For example, $P \widehat{=} a;b + a;c \models \langle a \rangle;\langle b \rangle$, $a_1;a_2 \models [a_1];\langle a_2 \rangle$, but $P[a \rightsquigarrow a_1;a_2] \not\models ([a_1];\langle a_2 \rangle);\langle b \rangle$, since in the high-level specification, $\langle a \rangle;\langle b \rangle$ is an existential property, however its refinement becomes a universal property.

To ensure that the mapping is property-preserving, we partition the property ψ of the refinement of a into two parts: an existential property ψ_1 and an universal property ψ_2 i.e. $\psi \in \mathcal{PF}$. $[a]$ will be replaced by ψ_2, and $\langle a \rangle$ will be replaced by ψ_1. This is justified by the result shown in [4] that any property can be presented as the intersection of a liveness property and a safety property in branching temporal logics. So, $\mathcal{PF}$ is powerful enough to define the properties of reactive systems.

Therefore, we define the refinement mapping as follows:

Definition 6. *Suppose ϕ is a high-level specification, a is an abstract action to be refined, and $\psi \widehat{=} \psi_1 \wedge \psi_2 \in \mathcal{PF}$ is the description of the refinement of a, where $\psi_1 \in \mathcal{EF}$ and $\psi_2 \in \mathcal{UF}$. We define the refinement mapping, denoted by $\Omega(\phi, \psi, a)$, as follows:*

$$\Omega(\phi, \psi, a) \widehat{=} \phi\{\psi_1\{\tau/\surd\}/\langle a \rangle, \psi_2\{\tau/\surd\}/[a]\},$$

where $\phi\{\psi/\chi\}$ means to substitute ψ for each occurrence of χ in ϕ, with $\chi \in \{X, \surd, \langle a \rangle, [a]\}$.

According to the above definition, it is easy to get the following results.

Lemma 2. *Suppose X does not occur in ψ. Then*

$$\Omega(\phi_1\{\phi_2/X\}, \psi, a) \Leftrightarrow \Omega(\phi_1, \psi, a)\{\Omega(\phi_2, \psi, a)/X\}.$$

Lemma 3. (1) *If $\phi \Leftrightarrow \phi'$ then $\Omega(\phi, \psi, a) \Leftrightarrow \Omega(\phi', \psi, a)$;*
(2) *If $\psi \Leftrightarrow \psi'$ and $\surd$ only occurs at the ends of ψ and ψ', then $\Omega(\phi, \psi, a) \Leftrightarrow \Omega(\phi, \psi', a)$.*

Theorem 4 (Applicability). *If $\phi \in FLC$ and $\psi \in \mathcal{PF}$, then $\Omega(\phi, \psi, a) \in FLC$; If $\phi, \psi \in \mathcal{PF}$, then $\Omega(\phi, \psi, a) \in \mathcal{PF}$.*

Here, we further study the example of a salesman that is firstly presented in [6] and has been investigated in [15] to demonstrate how to employ our approach to hierarchically specify a complex systems.

Example 2. Suppose that a salesman has to go by car from his office in Paris to another office in London and work there for some time, and then has to go back to Paris repeatedly. He takes a hovercraft to cross the Channel.

So, the top-most specification of the system can be represented as follows:

$$\phi \mathrel{\widehat{=}} \nu X. \left(\begin{array}{c} \langle \text{leave\_Paris} \rangle; [\text{fr\_thr\_Channel}]; \langle \text{arrive\_in\_London} \rangle; \langle \text{work} \rangle; \\ \langle \text{leave\_London} \rangle; [\text{gb\_thr\_Channel}]; \langle \text{arrive\_in\_Paris} \rangle; X \end{array} \right),$$

where the actions "work" and "x_thr_Channel" will be refined subsequently.

The job of the salesman in London is to contact repeatedly some of his customers by phone, or to meet some of them in his office to discuss something. Therefore, we can refine the action "work" by a process that meets the following property:

$$\psi_1 \mathrel{\widehat{=}} \nu X.((\langle \text{contact\_Customers} \rangle \vee \langle \text{meet\_Customers} \rangle); X \wedge \langle \text{finish\_Work} \rangle.$$

Meanwhile, we can describe "x_thr_Channel" in more detail. There are two platforms lying on the two sides of the Channel respectively that take charge of the hovercraft. At the beginning, one of them loads the salesman's car, then arranges the hovercraft to depart. Then the hovercraft crosses through the Channel. After the hovercraft arrives at the opposite side, the other platform unloads the car. Hence, "x_thr_Channel" can be enriched as follows:

$$\psi_x \mathrel{\widehat{=}} [\text{x\_load}]; [\text{x\_departure}]; \langle \text{cross\_Channel} \rangle; \langle \overline{\text{x}}\text{\_arrival} \rangle; \langle \overline{\text{x}}\text{\_unload} \rangle \wedge \mathit{true}.$$

Furthermore, we can refine "x_departure" by a process with the property

$$\psi_2 \mathrel{\widehat{=}} [\text{finish\_loading}]; \langle \text{engine\_on} \rangle; \langle \text{bye\_bye} \rangle \wedge \text{true},$$

where finish_loading signals the end of loading, and cross_Channel by a process with the property

$$\begin{array}{l} \psi_3 \mathrel{\widehat{=}} \mathit{true} \wedge \langle \text{sit\_down} \rangle; \\ \qquad (\nu \text{X}.((\langle \text{newspaper} \rangle \vee \langle \text{tea} \rangle \vee \langle \text{coffee} \rangle); \text{X} \wedge \langle \text{keep\_idle} \rangle); \langle \text{stand\_up} \rangle. \end{array}$$

So, the specification for the final system can be represented by

$$\Omega(\Omega(\phi, \Omega(\Omega(\psi_x, \psi_2, \text{x\_departure}), \psi_3, \text{cross\_Channel}), \text{x\_thr\_Channel}), \psi_1, \text{work}),$$

where $x \in \{fr, gb\}$, and if $x = fr$ then $\overline{x} = gb$ else $\overline{x} = fr$.

It is obvious that we can not refine "work" and "cross_Channel" by some processes that satisfy ψ_1 and ψ_3 respectively in [15] because on the one hand, the resulting specification is no longer in $\mathcal{NF}$; on the other hand, "work" and "cross_Channel" both are needed to be refined by some processes with possibly infinite behaviour. ⊣

5 Relating Hierarchical Specification to Hierarchical Implementation of a Large System

In this section, we establish a correspondence presented by the Refinement Theorem below between hierarchical specification and hierarchical implementation of a complex system. It states that if $Q \models \psi; \surd$, $P \models \phi$ and some syntactical conditions hold, then $P[a \rightsquigarrow Q] \models \Omega(\phi, \psi, a)$. This result supports 'a priori' verification. In the development process we start with $P \models \phi$ and either refine P and obtain automatically a (relevant) formula that is satisfied by $P[a \rightsquigarrow Q]$. Or, we refine ϕ using $\Omega(\phi, \psi, a)$ and obtain automatically a refined process $P[a \rightsquigarrow Q]$ that satisfies the refined specification. Of course such refinement steps may be iterated.

In order to ensure the Refinement Theorem is valid, the following syntactical conditions are necessary:

Above of all, it is required that $(Act(P) \cup Act(\phi)) \cap (Act(Q) \cup Act(\psi)) = \emptyset$, because of the following considerations:

(i) As far as action refinement for models is concerned, no deadlock will be introduced or destroyed;

(ii) no unsatisfaction between $P[a \rightsquigarrow Q]$ and $\Omega(\phi, \psi, a)$ will be caused because ϕ involves Q. For instance, let $P \widehat{=} a; b$, $\phi \widehat{=} [a]; \langle b \rangle \wedge [c]; \langle d \rangle$, $Q \widehat{=} c; e$ and $\psi \widehat{=} [c]; \langle e \rangle$. It is obvious that $P \models \phi$ and $Q \models \psi; \surd$, but $P[a \rightsquigarrow Q] \not\models \Omega(\phi, \psi, a)$;

(iii) Symmetrically, no unsatisfaction between $P[a \rightsquigarrow Q]$ and $\Omega(\phi, \psi, a)$ will be caused because ψ involves P. For example, let $P \widehat{=} a; b + b; a$, $\phi \widehat{=} [a]; \langle b \rangle$, $Q \widehat{=} c; e$ and $\psi \widehat{=} [c]; \langle e \rangle \wedge [b]; \langle d \rangle$. It is obvious that $P \models \phi$ and $Q \models \psi; \surd$, but $P[a \rightsquigarrow Q] \not\models \Omega(\phi, \psi, a)$.

It is clear that this condition can guarantee the above three requirements.

Besides, it's possible that ψ only describes partial executions of Q, so the refined specification may not be satisfied by the refined system. For example, it's obvious that $a; b + a; c \models \langle a \rangle; \langle b \rangle$ and $a_1; a_2 \models \langle a_1 \rangle$, but $(a; b + a; c)[a \rightsquigarrow a_1; a_2] \not\models \langle a_1 \rangle; \langle b \rangle$. In order to solve such a problem, we require that ψ describes full executions of Q, i.e., $Q \models \psi; \surd$. Normally, we only consider to refine an abstract action a by a normed process Q, i.e., for any derivative Q' of Q, Q' may terminate in finite steps. If so, for any given Q and $\psi \in \mathcal{PF}$ with $Q \models \psi$, the above requirement can be satisfied by constructing φ as $\psi; (\mu X.(\bigvee_{a \in Act} \langle a \rangle); X \vee \tau)$ instead of ψ. It is clear that $\varphi \in \mathcal{PF}$, $P \models \psi$ iff $P \models \varphi$ for each $P \in \mathcal{P}^*$, and $Q \models \varphi; \surd$. Therefore, in most cases, the above constraint does not give rise to any restriction to the applications of the theorem.

Finally, it is possible that $\surd$ as a sub-formula of ψ makes the sub-formulae following it with ; no sense during calculating the meaning of ψ, but the sub-formulae play a nontrivial role during interpreting $\Omega(\phi, \psi, a)$. E.g. $a'; nil \models \langle a' \rangle; \surd; [a']; \langle b' \rangle$ and $a; a; c \models \langle a \rangle; \langle a \rangle; \langle c \rangle$, but

$$(a; a; c)[a \rightsquigarrow a'; nil] \not\models (\langle a' \rangle; \tau; [a']; \langle b' \rangle); (\langle a' \rangle; \tau; [a']; \langle b' \rangle); \langle c \rangle.$$

So, we require that $\surd$ only can appear at the end of ψ as a sub-formula. In fact, such a requirement is reasonable because all formulae can be transformed to such kind of forms equivalently because $p; \phi \Leftrightarrow p$.

Now, we can represent our Refinement Theorem as follows:

Theorem 5 (Refinement Theorem).
If $(Act(P) \cup Act(\phi)) \cap (Act(\psi) \cup Act(Q)) = \emptyset$, $Q \models \psi;\surd$ *and* $P \models \phi$, *then* $P[a \rightsquigarrow Q] \models \Omega(\phi, \psi, a)$, *where* $\psi \in \mathcal{PF}$ *and* $\surd$ *only occurs at the end of* ψ.

In order to demonstrate how to apply the Refinement Theorem to verify a complex system hierarchically, we continue Example 2.

Example 3. As explained in Example 2, at the top level, we can implement the system as:

$$\mathrm{Sys} \mathrel{\widehat{=}} \mathrm{fr\_Channel} \parallel_{\{\mathrm{fr\_thr\_Channel}\}} \mathrm{Salesman} \parallel_{\{\mathrm{gb\_thr\_Channel}\}} \mathrm{gb\_Channel}.$$

Where x_Channel$\widehat{=}$$rec\, y$.x_thr_Channel; y, and

$$\begin{aligned}\mathrm{Salesman} \mathrel{\widehat{=}} rec\, x.&\mathrm{leave\_Paris; fr\_thr\_Channel; arrive\_in\_London;}\\ &\mathrm{work; leave\_London; gb\_thr\_Channel; arrive\_in\_Paris;}\ x.\end{aligned}$$

It's obvious that Sys $\models \phi$.
Then, we can refine "work" by Subsys_1 which is defined by

$$\mathrm{Subsys}_1 \mathrel{\widehat{=}} rec\ x.((\mathrm{contact\_Customers} + \mathrm{meet\_Customers}); x + \mathrm{finish\_Work}).$$

It's obvious that $\mathrm{Subsys}_1 \models \psi_1;\surd$.
Then, "x_thr_Channel" can be implemented by
$\mathrm{Subsys_x} \widehat{=} \mathrm{x\_load} \parallel_{\{\mathrm{x\_load}\}} \mathrm{Channel}$,

$$\begin{aligned}\text{where Channel} \mathrel{\widehat{=}} \mathrm{fr\_Platform} &\parallel_{\{\mathrm{fr\_arrival,fr\_departure}\}} \mathrm{Hovercraft}\\ &\parallel_{\{\mathrm{gb\_arrival,gb\_departure}\}} \mathrm{gb\_Platform},\end{aligned}$$

where $\mathrm{Hovercraft} \mathrel{\widehat{=}} \mathrm{fr\_departure;cross\_Channel;\ gb\_arrival} +$
$\mathrm{gb\_departure;cross\_Channel;\ fr\_arrival}$,
$\mathrm{x\_Platform} \mathrel{\widehat{=}} \mathrm{x\_load;x\_departure} + \mathrm{x\_arrival;x\_unload}$.
It's easy to show that $\mathrm{Subsys_x} \models \psi_x;\surd$.
Furthermore, we can refine "x_departure" by Subsys_2 and "cross_Channel" by Subsys_3, where,

$$\mathrm{Subsys}_2 \mathrel{\widehat{=}} \mathrm{finish\_loading;\ engine\_on;\ bye\_bye},$$
$$\mathrm{Subsys}_3 \mathrel{\widehat{=}} \mathrm{sit\_down}; rec\, x.([(\mathrm{coffee} + \mathrm{tea}) \parallel_{\{\}} \mathrm{newspaper}]; x + \mathrm{keep\_idle}); \mathrm{stand\_up}.$$

Certainly, $\mathrm{Subsys}_2 \models \psi_2;\surd$ and $\mathrm{Subsys}_3 \models \psi_3;\surd$.
The final system is obtained as:

$$\mathrm{Sys}\ [\mathrm{work} \rightsquigarrow \mathrm{Subsys}_1,\quad \mathrm{x\_thr\_Channel} \rightsquigarrow \mathrm{Subsys_x}[\begin{matrix}\mathrm{x\_departure} \rightsquigarrow \mathrm{Subsys}_2,\\ \mathrm{cross\_Channel} \rightsquigarrow \mathrm{Subsys}_3\end{matrix}]],$$

where $\mathrm{x} \in \{\mathrm{fr}, \mathrm{gb}\}$.
According to the Refinement Theorem, the final system satisfies the final specification. ⊣

6 Concluding Remarks

In this paper, we extend our previous work on combining hierarchical specification with hierarchical implementation of a complex system by allowing to refine an abstract action by an arbitrary process. Technically, we also greatly simplify our previous work such that our method can be more easily applied in practice. Furthermore, we also establish a correspondence between hierarchical specification and hierarchical implementation that supports 'a priori' verification in system design.

Similar results are shown in [10, 14], but in their approaches, a refined specification is obtained from the original specification and the refinement Q, where Q is a finite process. Therefore, besides sharing the restriction of our previous work [15], certain interesting expected properties of the refined system cannot be derived using their approaches. What's more, we can show that their approaches can be seen as a special case of our method from a specification-constructing point of view. [2] discussed composing, refining specifications of reactive systems as some sound rules of a logic. [1] considered the problem given a low-level specification and a higher-level specification, how to construct a mapping from the former to the latter in order to guarantee the former implements the latter. Our refinement mapping Ω maps the abstract specification to the lower-level specification, i.e. we go the converse direction.

In our framework, composing specifications also can be dealt with, for example, supposing $P \models \phi; \surd$, and $\surd$ only occurs at the end of ϕ and $Q \models \psi$, we can get a composite specification like $\phi\{\tau/\surd\}; \psi$ for the combined system $P; Q$.

In this paper, we use the standard interleaving setting, so we only consider the case of atomic action refinement for models because the standard bisimulation notion is not preserved by non-atomic action refinement in this setting. In fact, we believe our approach may be applied to the case of non-atomic action refinement, too, if an appropriate logic which is interpreted over some true concurrent settings such as event-structures is available. But it is still an open question how to establish such kind of logics.

Acknowledgements

The author wants to thank Prof. Mila Majster-Cederbaum and Harald Fecher, who joined the previous work for many fruitful discussions related to the topic. In particular, the author thanks Prof. Mila Majster-Cederbaum for going through the whole paper and for some critical comments on it which improve the presentation of this paper too much. The author also thanks Dr. Wu Jinzhao and some anonymous referees for their useful comments on this paper.

References

1. M. Abadi and L. Lamport. The existence of refinement mappings. *Theoretical Computer Science*, 82:253-284, 1991.

2. M. Abadi and G. Plotkin. A logical view of composition and refinement. *Theoretical Computer Science*, 114:3-30, 1993.
3. L. Aceto and M. Hennessy. Termination, deadlock, and divergence. *Journal of ACM,* Vol. 39, No.1:147-187. January, 1992.
4. A. Bouajjani, J.C. Fernandez, S. Graf, C. Rodriguez, and J. Sifakis. Safety for branching time semantics. ICALP'91, LNCS 510, pp. 76-92.
5. G. Boudol. Atomic actions. *Bull. European Assoc. The. Comp. Sci.* 38:136-144.
6. P. Degano and R. Gorrieri, Atomic Refinement in Process Description Languages. TR 17-91 HP Pisa Center, 1991.
7. E.A. Emerson and C.S. Jutla. Tree automata, μ-calculus, and determinacy. In proc. of 33rd IEEE Symp. on Found. of Comp. Sci., pp.368-377, 1991.
8. R. Gorrieri and A. Rensink. Action refinement. *Handbook of Process Algebra*, Elsevier Science, 1047-1147. 2001.
9. D. Janin and I. Walukiewicz. On the expressive completeness of the propositional μ-calculus with respect to monadic second order logic. CONCUR'96, LNCS 1119, pp.263-277.
10. M. Huhn. Action refinement and properties inheritance in systems of sequential agents. CONCUR'96, LNCS 1119, pp. 639-654.
11. M. Lange and C. Stirling. Model checking fixed point logic with chop. FOSSACS'02, LNCS 2303, pp. 250-263.
12. M. Lange. Local model checking games for fixed point logic with chop. CONCUR'02, LNCS 2421, pp. 240-254.
13. M. Majster-Cederbaum and F. Salger. Correctness by construction: towards verification in hierarchical system development. SPIN'00, LNCS 1885, pp. 163-180.
14. M. Majster-Cederbaum and F. Salger. Towards the hierarchical verification of reactive systems. To appear in *Theoretical Computer Science.*
15. M. Majster-Cederbaum, N. Zhan and H. Fecher. Action refinement from a logical point view. VMCAI'03, LNCS 2575, pp.253-267.
16. M. Müller-Olm. A Modal Fixpoint Logic with Chop. STACS'99, LNCS 1563, pp. 510-520.
17. A. Rensink. *Models and Methods for Action Refinement.* PhD thesis, University of Twente, Enschede, Netherlands, Aug. 1993.
18. J. Sifakis. Research directions for concurrency. *ACM Computing Surveys,* 28(4):55. 1996.

Automatic Generation of Simple Lemmas from Recursive Definitions Using Decision Procedures* – Preliminary Report –

Deepak Kapur[1] and M. Subramaniam[2]

[1] Department of Computer Science, University of New Mexico, Albuquerque, NM
kapur@cs.unm.edu
[2] Department of Computer Science, University of Nebraska, Omaha, NE
msubramaniam@mail.uomaha.edu

Abstract. Using recent results on integrating induction schemes into decidable theories, a method for generating lemmas useful for reasoning about $\mathcal{T}$-based function definitions is proposed. The method relies on terms in a decidable theory admitting a (finite set of) canonical form scheme(s) and ability to solve parametric equations relating two canonical form schemes with parameters. Using nontrivial examples, it is shown how the method can be used to automatically generate many simple lemmas; these lemmas are likely to be found useful in automatically proving other nontrivial properties of $\mathcal{T}$-based functions, thus unburdening the user of having to provide many simple intermediate lemmas. During the formalization of a problem, after a user inputs $\mathcal{T}$-based definitions, the method can be employed in the background to explore a search space of possible conjectures which can be attempted, thus building a library of lemmas as well as false conjectures. This investigation was motivated by our attempts to automatically generate lemmas arising in proofs of generic, arbitrary data-width parameterized arithmetic circuits. The scope of applicability of the proposed method is broader, however, including generating proofs for proof-carrying codes, certification of proof-carrying code as well as in reasoning about distributed computation algorithms.

1 Introduction

A major challenge in automating proofs of inductive properties is the need to generate intermediate lemmas typically needed in such proofs [2,3,15]. Often, many lemmas needed in such proofs are simple properties of functions appearing in an original conjecture and they can be easily proved once they can be properly formulated. Inability to speculate intermediate lemmas is one of the reasons, we suspect, for induction theorem provers not being used by domain experts in their applications including verification of hardware circuits and distributed algorithms, certification of proof-carrying codes, analysis of design specifications,

* This research was partially supported by an NSF ITR award CCR-0113611.

V.A. Saraswat (Ed.): ASIAN 2003, LNCS 2896, pp. 125–145, 2003.

etc. For a novice user of an induction theorem prover, such intermediate lemmas are hard to formulate, since failed proof attempts of the original application specific conjecture have to be analyzed manually. In order to do this successfully, the application expert has to become an expert in understanding the internal representation of proofs, how proofs are generated by theorem provers, and various heuristics employed to generate such proofs. And, this can be tedious and time consuming. This demand can become an added burden on the application user since most such properties are a result of a particular formalization being attempted, and may have little to do directly with the application.

The use of theorem provers can be made more effective if simple and seemingly obvious properties of functions employed in the formalization of application specific properties can be automatically attempted. This can provide immediate feedback to the user about the functions used in the formalization thus either leading to fixes in the formalization or enhancing confidence in the formalization.

In this paper, a method is proposed using decision procedures for speculating and proving "simple" properties of functions likely to be found useful soon after the function definitions are introduced. The proposed approach relies on the structure of $\mathcal{T}$-based function definitions introduced in [11] and properties of decision procedures for decidable theories $\mathcal{T}$. Below, we briefly discuss the main ideas underlying the proposed approach.

This line of research was motivated by our attempts to automatically generate lemmas arising in proofs of generic, arbitrary parameterized arithmetic circuits. The scope of applicability of the proposed method is broader, however, including generating proofs for proof-carrying codes, certification of proof-carrying code as well as in reasoning about distributed computation algorithms.

1.1 Overview

Given a definition of f, the main idea is to hypothesize a conjecture of the form $f(x_1, \cdots, x_k) = r$, where r is a unknown (parameterized) term in a decidable theory $\mathcal{T}$ possibly involving $x_1, \cdots, x_k$ as well as parameters p_i's whose values need to be determined for all possible values of x_j's. In fact, r is one of the many possible canonical forms of a term in $\mathcal{T}$. As shown in [11], such a conjecture can be decided if f is $\mathcal{T}$-based. A proof is attempted of this conjecture, possibly leading to instantiation of various parameters. If all the parameters can be consistently instantiated, then the right hand side r of the conjecture can be determined, thus implying that f is expressible in $\mathcal{T}$.

For example, consider the function *cost* denoting a recurrence relation for a divide and conquer algorithm.

1. $cost(0) \rightarrow 0$,
2. $cost(1) \rightarrow 2$,
3. $cost(s(x)+s(x)) \rightarrow cost(x)+cost(x)+4$.
4. $cost(s(s(x)+s(x))) \rightarrow cost(x)+cost(x)+6$.

As discussed later (also see [11]) in section 2, the above definition can be shown to be based in the quantifier-free theory of Presburger arithmetic, denoted by PA[1].

[1] The theory PA includes $0, s, +, =$; the symbols $1, 2, 3$, etc., stand for $s(0)$, $s(s(0))$, $s(s(s(0)))$, respectively.

It may be speculated that $cost(m)$ is expressible in PA and is thus equivalent to a term in PA, say $k_1\ m + k_2$ with k_1, k_2 as its parameters (without any loss of generality); $k_1\ m$ stands for m repeated k_1 times. So we generate a parametric conjecture $P1 : cost(m) = k_1\ m + k_2$ with the goal of finding k_1, k_2.

An induction proof using the cover set method [16] using the definition of *cost* is attempted. The first subgoal generated by unifying the left side of rule 1 with the left side of *P1* with substitution $\{m \rightarrow 0\}$ is $cost(0) = k_1\ 0 + k_2$, which simplifies using rule 1 to the constraint $s1 : k_2 = 0$. The second subgoal generated by unifying the left side of rule 2 with the left side of *P1* with substitution $\{m \rightarrow 1\}$ is $cost(1) = k_1 + k_2$, which simplifies using rule 2 to the constraint $s2 : k_1 + k_2 = 2$. In the third subgoal, the conclusion generated by unifying the left side of rule 3 with the left side of *P1* with substitution $\{m \rightarrow s(x) + s(x)\}$ is $cost(s(x) + s(x)) = k_1\ x + k_1 + k_1\ x + k_1 + k_2$, which simplifies using rule 3 to $cost(x) + cost(x) + 4 = k_1\ x + k_1 + k_1\ x + k_1 + k_2$, Replacing $cost(x)$ by $k_1\ x + k_2$, one gets $k_1\ x + k_2 + k_1\ x + k_2 + 4 = k_1\ x + k_1 + k_1\ x + k_1 + k_2$ which further simplifies to $s3 : k_2 + 4 = k_1 + k_1$. Similarly, from the fourth subgoal generated using rule 4, we get $s4 : k_2 + 6 = k_1 + k_1 + k_1$.

Solving for the constraints $s1$, $s2$, $s3$, $s4$ (using a decision procedure for PA) gives $k_1 = 2, k_2 = 0$; thus, $cost(m) = 2\ m$, implying that *cost* is expressible in PA[2].

Typically, it will be not be possible to express a recursively defined function in $\mathcal{T}$ since new recursive definitions are often introduced because the functions being defined cannot be expressed in $\mathcal{T}$. (If a defined function can be expressed in $\mathcal{T}$, that is more likely to be an error in the definition than the user's improper grasp of the expressive power of the theory.) What is more likely is that in general, parameters cannot be consistently instantiated; instead, for some specific values of x_i's, parameter values can be obtained, thus implying that for those values of x_i's, the instantiated conjecture equals some term in $\mathcal{T}$.

For example, consider the following definition of *e2plus*:

1. $e2plus(0, 0) \rightarrow 1$,
2. $e2plus(0, s(y)) \rightarrow e2plus(0, y) + 1$,
3. $e2plus(s(x), 0) \rightarrow e2plus(x, 0) + e2plus(x, 0)$,
4. $e2plus(s(x), s(y)) \rightarrow s(e2plus(s(x), y))$.

Similar to the previous example, it may be speculated that *e2plus* can be expressed in PA and a conjecture $P2 : e2plus(x, y) = k_1\ x + k_2\ y + k_3$ may be hypothesized with the goal of finding k_1, k_2, k_3.

To solve for the parameters, constraints are generated from the rules 1-4. The first constraint $s1 : k_3 = 1$ comes from rule 1. The second constraint is generated from rule 2 by replacing the left side and the recursive call with $k_1\ 0 + k_2\ s(y) + k_3$ and $k_1\ 0 + k_2\ y + k_3$. It simplifies to $s2 : k_2 = 1$. The third and fourth constraints are generated in a similar fashion from rules 3 and 4, and they simplify to $s3 : k_1 = k_1\ x + k_3$ and $s4 : k_2 = 1$. These constraints are not satisfiable for all values of x and y, primarily because of $s3$ which restricts $k_1 = 0$ and hence $k_3 = 0$, whereas the constraint $s1$ gives $k_3 = 1$. So, there is no

[2] In almost all cases, it is possible to use the right side of the conjecture in the parametric form to substitute in each of the rules in the definitions and directly get a constraint. The cover set induction method is being used just as a general purpose mechanism to do the same.

solution for all values of x, and hence $e2plus$ cannot be expressed in PA. As the reader would notice, there are two kinds of constraints: (i) constraints purely in terms of parameters, and (ii) constraints involving both parameters and variables (e.g. $s3$).

Now conjectures with proper instances of $e2plus(x, y)$ as their left sides can be speculated. In order to attempt to generate most general conjectures, maximal consistent subsets of the set of inconsistent constraints $\{s1, s2, s3, s4\}$ are identified (see subsection 3.2 for details). One such maximal consistent subset of constraints is $\{s1, s2, s4\}$ giving $k_2 = 1, k_3 = 1$ with k_1 being unconstrained. For these values of parameters, constraint $s3$ can be solved for specific values of variables. Particularly, if $x = 0$, then $s3$ reduces to $s3.1$: $k_1 = k_3$, which can be consistently added to $\{s1, s2, s4\}$[3]. The rules associated with the instances are computing by splitting the rule using the variable substitution (see subsection 2.3 for details), e.g:, rule 3 is split by $\{x \to 0\}$ into two rules,

3.1 $e2plus(s(0), 0) \to 2$,
3.2 $e2plus(s(s(x)), 0) \to e2plus(x, 0) + e2plus(x, 0) + e2plus(x, 0) + e2plus(x, 0)$.

The constraints for rule 3.1 is $s3.1' : k_1 + k_3 = 2$ and rule 3.2 is $s3.2 : 2k_1 = 3k_1\ x + 3k_3$.

The rules to be considered for speculating a conjecture are $\{1, 2, 3.1, 4\}$. From the left side of these rules, a possible conjecture with $e2plus(0, y)$ as the left side is generated (since the left sides of rules 1 and 2 are $e2plus(0, 0), e2plus(0, s(y))$) (see subsection 2.4 for details).

The rules $\{1, 2, 3.1, 3.2, 4\}$ are analyzed to pick their instances which are likely to be used to compute $e2plus(0, x)$. Rules 1 and 2 constitute such a complete set since any ground instance of $e2plus(0, x)$ can be normalized to a PA-term using them (see subsection 3.3 for details). The constraints generated from rules 1 and 2 have the solution $\{k_2 = 1, k_3 = 1\}$, which generates the lemma $e2plus(0, x) = s(x)$. We make it rule 5 and add it to the definition of $e2plus$.

$$5. \quad e2plus(0, y) \to s(y).$$

This lemma can replace rules 1 and 2, and can be used to speculate additional lemmas from rules 3, 4 and 5 which completely define $e2plus$.

Rules associated with the maximal set $\{1, 2, 3.1, 4\}$ may also be expanded to generate additional rules for generating left sides for conjectures (see subsection 3.3 for details). The expansion is done by choosing a rule whose right side is a PA-term, e.g: rule 3.1, and splitting by unifying the recursive calls in other rules with the left side of rule 3.1. The unification of the recursive call $e2plus(s(x), y)$ in rule 4 with $e2plus(s(0), 0)$ of rule 3.1 produces four equivalent rules two of which are:

4.1 $e2plus(s(0), s(0)) \to 3$, 4.2 $e2plus(s(0), s(s(y))) \to s(s(e2plus(s(0), y)))$.

The conjecture with the left side $e2plus(s(0), y)$ can now be hypothesized by abstracting from the left sides of rules 3.1, 4.1, and 4.2, which completely define

[3] Other values of x produce instances with $k_3 = 0$, which contradicts $s1$ and hence cannot be added to $\{s1, s2, s4\}$.

$e2plus(s(0), y)$. The associated constraints, $s3.1 : k_1+k_3 = 2$, $s4.1 : k_1+k_2+k_3 = 3$ and $s4.2 : k_2 = 1$, are solved and give $e2plus(s(0), y) \rightarrow y+2$ as the new lemma.

In order for the approach to be successful, a decidable theory $\mathcal{T}$ needs to have the following properties:

1. The no-theory condition introduced in [6] for $\mathcal{T}$ must be decidable, i.e., whether a term involving defined function symbols with $\mathcal{T}$-based definitions is equivalent to a $\mathcal{T}$-term (with any defined symbols) is decidable.
2. Given a finite set of equations relating parameterized terms in canonical form of $\mathcal{T}$, their solvability can be decided and furthermore, if solvable, find all possible most general solutions for parameters for all values of variables. This problem is related to the unification problem over $\mathcal{T}$. For example, in the case of the quantifier-free theory of Presburger arithmetic, given two parametric expressions, say $k_1\, x_1 + k_2\, x_2 + k_2\, x_2 + k_0 = k_3\, x_1 + k_3\, x_1 + k_2\, x_2 + k_4\, x_2$, where k_0, k_1, k_2, k_3, k_4 are parameters, the most general solution is $k_1 = k_3 + k_3, k_4 = k_2, k_0 = 0$.
3. Terms in $\mathcal{T}$ have a small finite set of canonical forms (to keep the branching factor of the search space low); e.g., the quantifier-free theory of Presburger arithmetic has such a form $\Sigma k_i x_i + k_0$, where x_i are the variables and k_i are the parameters; similarly, the quantifier-free theory of free constructors admit also such canonical forms: a term in this theory is either a variable or one of $c_i(t_1, t_2)$, where c_i is a free constructor in the theory and t_1, t_2 are parametric terms.

The rest of the paper is organized as follows. Section 2 provides background and reviews the definition of a $\mathcal{T}$-based recursive definition, inductive validity, the cover set method, etc; more details can be found in [5, 6]. Section 3 introduces the procedure for generating simple lemmas. There are four major building blocks:

1. Given a conjecture of the form $f(s_1, \cdots, s_k) = r$, where r is a parametric term over $\mathcal{T}$, decide whether such an r can be found; if so, compute r. This operation is decidable for quantifier-free theories of free constructors and Presburger Arithmetic (PA); that is why the focus in this paper is on recursive function definitions over these two theories.
2. Given a finite set of parametric equations over $\mathcal{T}$, generate a finite representation of all assignment of parameters which make the equation true for all values of variables; further, if an assignment of parameters cannot be found for which the equation is true for all values of variables, then generate a finite representation of values of variables and the corresponding assignment of parameters for which the equation is true.
3. Given a set of inconsistent parametric constraints associated with a given rule set, generate maximal consistent subsets of constraints and the associated rule sets.
4. Given a finite set of k-tuples of terms from a decidable theory $\mathcal{T}$, generate a preferably, more general and smaller set of k-tuples of terms that has the same set of ground instances as the input. This construction is needed to generate the left sides of conjectures. For a given $lhs = f(s_1, \cdots, s_k)$,

where f has a $\mathcal{T}$-based definition and each s_i is a $\mathcal{T}$-term, compute from the definition of f, a complete rule set for normalizing all ground instances of lhs to a $\mathcal{T}$-term.

Section 4 is a brief discussion of how the procedure of Section 3 works for a quantifier-free theory of free constructors that may admit multiple canonical forms. Section 5 gives an overview of the notion of compatibility among recursive function definitions and shows how the proposed method can be used to generate lemmas with multiple defined symbols on their left side. This is illustrated using examples of lemmas needed in proofs of verification of generic arbitrary data-width and parametric arithmetic circuits; more details about these experiments can be found in [9, 10, 12].

2 Background

A brief overview of the relevant definitions and results from [11, 5] is given first; see also [6] where some of the results from [11] have been tightened. The example theories considered in this paper are the quantifier-free theory of Presburger arithmetic and the quantifier-free theory of free constructors (natural numbers which are generated by $0, s$ and finite lists which are generated by $nil, cons$ are two examples of this generic theory).

The framework of many-sorted first-order logic where "=" is the only predicate symbol is used below. For a set of function symbols $\mathcal{F}$ and an infinite set of variables $\mathcal{V}$, we denote the set of (well-typed) terms over $\mathcal{F}$ by $Terms(\mathcal{F}, \mathcal{V})$ and the set of ground terms by $Terms(\mathcal{F})$. Terms are represented as trees. Let $root(t)$ stand for the function symbol at the root of a term t and $\mathcal{V}(t)$ denote the variables of t. Given a theory $\mathcal{T}$, "$\models$" is the usual (semantic) first-order consequence relation; $\mathcal{F}_{\mathcal{T}}$ is the set of function symbols of $\mathcal{T}$; $Terms(\mathcal{F}_{\mathcal{T}}, \mathcal{V})$ denotes the terms of $\mathcal{T}$. Terms in $Terms(\mathcal{F}_{\mathcal{T}}, \mathcal{V})$ are called $\mathcal{T}$-terms. Below x^* stands for a k-tuple $\langle x_1, \cdots, x_k\rangle$.

Definition 1 ($\mathcal{T}$-based Function [11]). *A function $f \in \mathcal{F}$ is* $\mathcal{T}$-based *iff all rules $l \to r \in \mathcal{R}$ with $root(l) = f$ have the form $f(s^*) \to C[f(t_1^*), \ldots, f(t_n^*)]$, where $s^*, t_1^*, \ldots, t_n^*$ are k-tuples of $\mathcal{T}$-terms and C is a context over $\mathcal{F}_{\mathcal{T}}$. Moreover, we assume that all terms $f(t_i^*)$ are in normal form.*

Let D_f be the subset of rules $l \to r \in \mathcal{R}$ whose $root(l) = f$. D_f is called a $\mathcal{T}$-based definition of a $\mathcal{T}$-based function f. Henceforth, any $\mathcal{T}$-based definition is assumed to be terminating, sufficiently complete and ground confluent modulo $=_{\mathcal{T}}$, i.e., for every k-tuple of ground $\mathcal{T}$-terms g^*, $f(g^*)$ normalizes in finitely many steps to a unique ground term (equivalent modulo $=_{\mathcal{T}}$) in the range sort of f using D_f.

Definition 2 (Cover Set). *Given a $\mathcal{T}$-based function definition D_f of f, its* cover set *is $C_f = \{\langle s^*, \{t_1^*, \ldots, t_n^*\}\rangle \mid f(s^*) \to C[f(t_1^*), \ldots, f(t_n^*)] \in \mathcal{D}_f\}$.*

Using the cover set method, an induction proof of a conjecture $q = r$ in which f appears, leads to the following subgoals for every $\langle s^*, \{t_1^*, \ldots, t_n^*\}\rangle \in C_f$, the cover set of f:

$$[\sigma_1(q = r) \wedge \ldots \wedge \sigma_n(q = r)] \Rightarrow \theta(q = r), \qquad (1)$$

where $\theta = \{x^* \to s^*\}$, and each $\sigma_i = \{x^* \to t_i^*\}$. If all formulas (1) are inductively valid, then by Noetherian induction, $q = r$ is also inductively valid.

Definition 3 (Simple Conjecture). *A conjecture $f(x_1, \cdots, x_k) = r$, where f is $\mathcal{T}$-based and $\langle x_1, \cdots, x_k \rangle$ are distinct variables, and r is a $\mathcal{T}$-term, is called simple.*

For example, the function *cost* above is based in Presburger arithmetic; the parameterized conjecture $P1$ about *cost* is a simple conjecture.

In [11], it is shown:

Theorem 1. *The inductive validity of a simple conjecture $f(x_1, \cdots, x_k) = r$ where f is a $\mathcal{T}$-based, can be decided based on its cover set.*

2.1 Quantifier-Free Theory of Presburger Arithmetic (PA)

Following [6], we use the following definition for the *theory PA of Presburger Arithmetic*: $\mathcal{F}_{PA} = \{0, 1, +\}$ and AX_{PA} consists of the following formulas:

$$\begin{array}{rr} (x+y)+z = x+(y+z) & \neg\,(1+x=0) \\ x+y=y+x & x+y=x+z \Rightarrow y=z \\ 0+y=y & x=0 \,\vee\, \exists y.\ x=y+1 \end{array}$$

For PA-term t with $\mathcal{V}(t) = \{x_1, \ldots, x_m\}$, there exist $a_i \in \mathbb{N}$ such that $t =_{PA} a_0 + a_1 \cdot x_1 + \ldots + a_m \cdot x_m$. Here, "$a \cdot x$" denotes the term $x + \ldots + x$ (a times) and "a_0" denotes $1 + \ldots + 1$ (a_0 times). For $s =_{PA} b_0 + b_1 \cdot x_1 + \ldots + b_m \cdot x_m$ and t as above, $s =_{PA} t$ iff $a_0 = b_0, \ldots, a_m = b_m$.

When we conjecture a term t involving symbols outside PA to be expressible in PA, i.e., equivalent to some term in PA but we do not know precisely which term, we have to use a *parametric* term of the form $\Sigma k_i x_i + k_0$, where $k_0, \cdots, k_n$ are unknown (hence, *parameters*). Let $\mathcal{K}$ be a finite set of parameters, distinct and disjoint from the variables $\mathcal{V}$. For t to be expressible in PA, there must exist values of $k_0, \cdots, k_n$ such that $t =_{PA} \Sigma k_i x_i + k_0$; otherwise, if t is not expressible in PA, then there cannot exist such values of $k_0, \cdots, k_n$.

There are thus two kinds of terms: (i) a PA-term consisting of variables and functions in PA, whose canonical form is $\Sigma a_i x_i + a_0$, where $x_i \in \mathcal{V}$ and $a_0, \cdots, a_m$ are nonnegative numbers, and (ii) a parametric term consisting of variables, parameters, and functions in PA, whose canonical form is $\Sigma a_i x_i + a_0$, where $x_i \in \mathcal{V}$ and $a_i, \cdots, a_m$ are linear polynomials in parameters in $\mathcal{K}$. Since the second kind of terms subsume the first kind, by a term in PA below, we mean the second kind of term and call it a *parametric* term, in contrast to the first kind of terms, which we will refer to as a *pure* term.

An (pure) equation in PA is $\Sigma a_i x_i + a_0 = \Sigma b_i x_i + b_0$, where $a_0, \cdots, a_m, b_0, \cdots, b_m$ are nonnegative numbers. Using cancellativity, we can simplify the equation so that every variable appears only on one side. A canonical form of the equation is $\Sigma c_i x_i + c_0 = 0$, where $c_0, \cdots, c_m$ are integers (including negative numbers);

this is an abbreviation for the equation where variables with positive coefficients are on one side of the equation and variables with the negative coefficients are on the other side. For example, $2x - 3y - 1 = 0$ stands for $2x = 3y + 1$.

Since it is necessary to consider equations involving parametric terms as well, by a *parametric* equation, we mean $\Sigma p_i x_i + p_0 = 0$, where $x_i \in \mathcal{V}$ and each of $p_0, \cdots, p_m$ is a linear polynomial in parameters in $\mathcal{K}$ with integer coefficients. Again, since a parametric equation subsumes a pure equation, below we only refer to parametric equations.

A parametric equation is *valid* if and only if it is true for all values of its variables and parameters. As an example, the parametric equation $k_1\ x_1 + k_2\ x_2 = k_1\ x_1 + k_2\ x_2$ is valid.

A parametric equation is *strongly satisfiable* if and only if for all values of the variables, there exists parameter values that make equation true. As an example, the parametric equation $(k_1 + k_2)\ x_1 + k_2\ x_2 + k_3 - 1 = 0$ is strongly satisfiable with parameter values $k_1 = k_2 = 0$ and $k_3 = 1$. Similarly, $(k_1 - k_2)\ x = 0$ is strongly satisfiable with parameter values $k_1 = k_2$. A parametric equation $\Sigma p_i x_i + p_0 = 0$ is strongly satisfiable if and only if there exist parameter values for which the conjunction of the equations $p_0 = 0, \cdots, p_m = 0$ is true.

A parametric equation is *weakly satisfiable* if and only if there exist variables and parameter values that make the equation true. As an example, the parametric equation $(k_1 + k_2)\ x_1 + k_2\ x_2 + k_1 - 1 = 0$ is weakly satisfiable for variable values $x_1 = x_2 = 0$ and parameter values $k_1 = 1$ (k_2 is indeterminate and can be any value). This equation is not strongly satisfiable since the conjunction of equations $k_1 + k_2 = 0$, $k_2 = 0$ and $k_1 - 1 = 0$ cannot be satisfied for any parameter values k_1 and k_2.

A parametric equation is *unsatisfiable* if there do not exist any values of parameters and variables which make the equation true. As an example, the equation $2k_1\ x - 1 = 0$ is unsatisfiable.

Every strongly satisfiable parametric equation is also weakly satisfiable. However, an equation may be weakly satisfiable under different sets of parameter values than the parameter values under which the equation is strongly satisfiable. As an example, consider the equation, $k_1 = k_1\ x + k_3$. The equation is strongly satisfiable when $k_1 = k_3 = 0$. However the equation is also weakly satisfiable for $x = 0$ and $k_1 = k_3 = 1$ (in fact any value insofar as $k_1 = k_3$).

A parametric equation that is weakly satisfiable but not strongly satisfiable is called *weak* parametric equation. Whether a given parametric equation $\Sigma p_i x_i + p_0 = 0$ is weak or not, can be easily checked by simplifying it to $p_0 = 0, \cdots, p_m = 0$ and finding a solution for parameters. If there is a solution, then the equation is not weak; otherwise it is weak.

A set S of parametric equations is *consistent* if and only if for all values of variables, there exist parameter values which make each equation in S true i.e., for all x_i there exists k_i such that the conjunction of the equations in the set is true. If S includes a weak parametric equation, it cannot be consistent. So a consistent S must only include strongly satisfiable parametric equations.

A *parametric constraint* is defined to be a linear equation over parameters. If a set S of parametric equations is consistent, then there exists a set of parametric constraints equivalent to it obtained by projecting (elimination of variables).

2.2 Quantifier-Free Theory of Free Constructors

For the *theory* $\mathcal{T}_C$ *of free constructors*, $AX_{\mathcal{T}_C}$ consists of the following formulas.

$\neg c(x^*) = c'(y^*)$	for all $c, c' \in \mathcal{F}_{\mathcal{T}_C}$ where $c \neq c'$
$c(x_1, \ldots x_n) = c(y_1, \ldots y_n) \Rightarrow x_1 = y_1 \wedge \ldots \wedge x_n = y_n$	for all $c \in \mathcal{F}_{\mathcal{T}_C}$
$\bigvee_{c \in \mathcal{F}_{\mathcal{T}_C}} \exists y^*.\ x = c(y^*)$	
$\neg\ (c_1(\ldots c_2(\ldots c_n(\ldots x \ldots) \ldots) \ldots) = x)$	for all sequences $c_1, \ldots, c_n$, $c_i \in \mathcal{F}_{\mathcal{T}_C}$

Note that the last type of axioms usually results in infinitely many formulas. Here, "..." in the arguments of c_i stands for pairwise different variables.

A term in $\mathcal{T}_C$ can be either a variable or of the form $c_i(t_1, \cdots, t_k)$, where c_i is a constructor and t_i's are terms in $\mathcal{T}_C$. As in PA, to check whether a term s involving symbols outside $\mathcal{T}_C$ is expressible in $\mathcal{T}_C$, we hypothesize s to be equivalent to some term in $\mathcal{T}_C$ without knowing exactly which one, i.e., s is equivalent to x, where $x \in s$ or $c_i(t_1, \cdots, t_k)$, where each t_i is a parameter standing for some term in $\mathcal{T}_C$ (expressed using variables in s).

A parametric term over $\mathcal{T}_C$ is thus a parameter, a variable, or $c_i(t_1, \cdots, t_k)$, where each t_i is a parametric term. Using the above axioms of $\mathcal{T}_C$, an equation over parametric terms can be checked for unsatisfiability. If an equation is satisfiable, then values of parameters making it true can be determined.

2.3 Splitting a Rule

In the procedure in Section 3, it becomes necessary to replace a rule in a definition by a finite set of *equivalent* rules. This splitting of a rule is guided by a substitution of variables in the rule. For a substitution σ assigning a variable x the term $\sigma(x)$, a finite set of terms including $\sigma(x)$ must be computed such that their ground instance cover all the ground terms in the sort of x.

Given a linear $\mathcal{T}$-term s in which variables appear at most once, let $cover(s)$ be a finite (preferably, minimal) set of terms in canonical forms including s such that every ground term of $sort(s)$ is equivalent in $\mathcal{T}$ to $\theta(t)$ for some ground substitution θ and $t \in cover(s)$. For examples, in the theory of free constructors, $cover(x) = \{x\}$ and $cover(c_i(x, y)) = \{c_0(\cdots), c_1(\cdots) \cdots c_i(x, y), \cdots, c_m(\cdots)\}$, where $c_0, \cdots, c_m$ are all the constructors of $sort(x)$. For PA, $cover(x) = \{x\}$; $cover(x + y) = \{x + y\}$, $cover(0) = \{0, x+1\}$, $cover(n) = \{0, \cdots, n, x+n+1\}$, etc.

Given a substitution $\sigma = \{x_1 \to s_1, \cdots, x_n \to s_n\}$, where s_i's are linear pairwise disjoint (in variables) $\mathcal{T}$-terms in canonical form, the set of substitutions *complement* to σ, denoted as $compl(\sigma)$, is $\{\theta = \{x_1 \to t_1, \cdots, x_n \to t_n\} \mid \langle t_1, \cdots, t_n \rangle \in cover(s_1) \times cover(s_2) \times \cdots \times cover(s_n) \setminus \langle s_1, \cdots, s_n \rangle\}$[4].

[4] Test sets used for checking the sufficient completeness property of a function definition can be used for this purpose; see, e.g., [7].

Guided by a substitution σ, a rule $l \to r$ can be split into a finite equivalent set of rules $\{\theta(l) \to \theta(r) \mid \theta \in compl(\sigma) \cup \{\sigma\}\}$, denoted by $split(\{l \to r\}, \sigma)$. It is useful to normalize the right side of the rules (using the rule set under consideration).

Consider a substitution $\sigma = \{x \to 0, y \to 0\}$ over the theory of naturals generated by $0, s(x)$. Then $compl(\sigma) = \{\{x \to 0, y \to s(y')\}, \{x \to s(x'), y \to 0\}, \{x \to s(x'), y \to s(y')\}\}$ has three substitutions obtained by deleting the element $\{0, 0\}$ from the cross product $cover(0) \times cover(0)$. A rule such as $4 : e2plus(s(x), s(y)) \to s(e2plus(s(x), y))$ in section 1, can be split into four equivalent rules–one for each substitution in $\{\sigma\} \cup compl(\sigma)$. The rule $4.1 : e2plus(s(0), s(0)) \to s(e2plus(s(0), 0))$ is generated using σ; $4.2 : e2plus(s(0), s(s(y'))) \to s(e2plus(s(0), s(y')))$ comes from the first substitution in $compl(\sigma)$; two more rules are similarly generated from the other two substitutions in $compl(\sigma)$.

2.4 Abstracting Terms

In the procedure in Section 3, it will be necessary to generate a term from the left sides of a finite set of rules in a $\mathcal{T}$-based definition, in order to speculate an equational conjecture with that term as one of its sides. To perform this *abstraction* operation, we define from a given finite set L of k-tuples of variable-disjoint $\mathcal{T}$-terms, preferably a smaller set N of k-tuple of terms such that the ground instances of N and L are identical. (In the worst case, this operation will return L itself.)

The abstraction operation ABS on a finite set of tuples is defined recursively by first defining abs on a finite set of terms. For the theory of free constructors,

1. $abs(\{t\}) = \{t\}$ for any t;
2. $abs(\{x\} \cup L) = \{x\}$;
3. $abs(\{t_1, t_2\} \cup L) = abs(\{t_1\} \cup L)$ if t_2 is an instance of t_1;
4. $abs(\{c_1(x^*), c_2(y^*), \cdots, c_l(z^*)\} \cup L) = abs(\{x\} \cup L)$ where c_i's are all the l constructors of $\mathcal{T}_C$ and x does not appear in L;
5. $abs(\{c_i(s^*), \cdots, c_i(t^*)\} \cup L) = abs(\{c_i(u^*) \mid u^* \in ABS(\{s^*, \cdots, t^*\})\} \cup L)$ where L does not have any term with c_i as its outermost symbol.
6. otherwise, abs returns the input itself.

The function ABS on k-tuples is defined as: $ABS(\{s^*\}) = \{s^*\}$; $ABS(\{s_1^*, \cdots, s_m^*\} \cup L) = ABS(M \cup L)$, where $s_1^*, \cdots, s_m^*$ differ only in their i-th component, $1 \leq i \leq k$, and L does not include any k-tuple that is the same as s_1^* except for its i-th component, $M = \{t^* | t^* = s_1^*$ except for the i-th component and $t_i \in abs(\{s_{1i}, \cdots, s_{mi}\})\}$.

For PA, every ground term can be represented as 0 or $s^k(0), k > 0$, where s is a free constructor; every term with unique occurrences of variables can be represented as $x + y + \cdots + u$ or $s^k(x + y + \cdots + u)$. The function abs is defined as:

1. $abs(\{x + y + \cdots + u\} \cup L) = \{x\}$;
2. $abs(\{s^k(x + y + \cdots + u)\} \cup L) = \{s^k(x)\} \cup L$;

3. $abs(\{t_1, t_2\} \cup L) = abs(\{t_1\} \cup L)$ if t_2 is an instance of t_1;
4. $abs(\{0, s(x)\} \cup L) = abs(\{x\} \cup L)$, where x does not appear in L;
5. $abs(\{s(t_1), \cdots, s(t_m)\} \cup L) = abs(\{s(u) \mid u \in abs(\{t_1, \cdots, t_m\})\} \cup L)$ where L does not have any term with s as its outermost symbol;
6. otherwise, *abs* returns the input itself.

For instance, the three left sides $e2plus(s(0),0)$, $e2plus(s(0),s(0))$ and $e2plus(s(0), s(s(x)))$ of rules 3.1, 4.1 and 4.2 in our running example can be used to formulate the left side of a new conjecture. To compute $ABS(\{\langle s(0), 0\rangle, \langle s(0), s(0)\rangle, \langle s(0), s(s(x))\rangle\})$, apply *abs* on the second component $\{0, s(0), s(s(x))\}$, which gives $abs(\{s(0), s(s(x))\} \cup \{0\}) = abs(\{s(x'), 0\}) = y$. The result of ABS is thus $ABS(\{\langle s(0), y\rangle\}) = \langle s(0), y\rangle$. The abstracted term is $e2plus(s(0), y)$, leading to the lemma $e2plus(s(0), y)) \rightarrow s(s(y)))$.

3 Generating Simple Lemmas

Before discussing the main procedure for generating simple lemma, the four main building blocks in the procedure are presented. The procedure can generate lemmas of the form $f(s_1, \cdots, s_k)$, where the subset of rules from D_f which can be used to normalize every ground instance of $f(s_1, \cdots, s_k)$ to a $\mathcal{T}$-term have left sides which match $f(s_1, \cdots, s_k)$; this condition is necessary to generate parametric constraints from the rules defining $f(s_1, \cdots, s_k)$ as shown below. Even though the presentation below is given using $\mathcal{T} = PA$, the procedure works for any decidable theory satisfying the properties discussed in the introduction. In the next section, the procedure is illustrated for $\mathcal{T}$ whose terms can have one of many canonical forms; in contrast, here terms of PA can be represented using a single canonical form.

3.1 Generating Right Side of a Conjecture

In the procedure, conjectures are speculated by constructing terms of the form $lhs = f(s_1, \cdots, s_k)$, where each s_i is a $\mathcal{T}$-term, and determining whether $f(s_1, \cdots, s_k)$ is equivalent to some $\mathcal{T}$-term, say rhs such that $lhs = rhs$ is an inductive consequence of D_f. For this, every possible candidate for rhs, i.e., every canonical form of a $\mathcal{T}$-term, is attempted. If no such rhs exists, then instances of lhs may be candidates to serve as the left side of other conjectures; this will be discussed in the next subsection. In subsection 3.3, a method for generating such lhs's is given; furthermore, a method for generating from the definition D_f of f, the rule set D_{lhs} consisting of rules necessary to normalize every ground instance of lhs to a $\mathcal{T}$-term is also presented.

For PA, $rhs = \Sigma k_i\ x_i + k_0$ and a solution to the parameters is attempted. The variables x_i's are all the variables in $\mathcal{V}(lhs)$. For each rule $l_i \rightarrow r_i$ in D_{lhs}, a parametric equation is generated by replacing each term of the form $f(t_1, \cdots, t_k)$ in the rule by $\sigma(\Sigma k_i x_i + k_0)$, where $\sigma(f(s_1, \cdots, s_k)) = f(t_1, \cdots, t_k)$[5]. To ensure

[5] Since nested recursive calls are not allowed in the right sides of rules in a PA-based function definition, a constraint so obtained is a parametric equation in PA.

that a parametric equations can be generated corresponding to a rule $l_i \rightarrow r_i$, l_i must match with lhs and each recursive call t to f in r_i must either match with lhs or $\sigma(t)$ must simplify to a $\mathcal{T}$-term.

Let S be the finite set of all the parametric equations so generated. A parametric equation generated from a rule may simplify using PA to a parametric constraint, which is a linear polynomial in parameters. If S includes an unsatisfiable parametric equation or a weak parametric equation, then S is not consistent. Values of parameters constrained by different parametric constraints may clash as well. If S is consistent, i.e., for all values of variables, parameter values can be found making each equation in S valid, then the conjecture $lhs = \delta(\Sigma k_i x_i + k_0)$, where δ is the most general solution of the set of parametric constraints generated from S, is a lemma. And, this implies that lhs is expressible in PA. The lemma generated is added to D_f to simplify other rules and lemmas.

In case S is inconsistent, parametric constraints in S are used to compute maximal consistent subsets from which instances of lhs that can serve as the left sides of new conjectures are generated as discussed in the next subsection.

3.2 Generating Maximal Consistent Subsets

In the previous step, if the set S of parametric equations generated form a given $lhs = f(s_1, \cdots, s_k)$ is inconsistent, S is used to generate instances of lhs possibly serving as the left sides of new conjectures about f. Toward this goal, every maximal consistent subset of S and the associated rule set are computed from S and the associated rule set D_{lhs}.

First, every unsatisfiable parametric equation is deleted from S. The remaining equations are partitioned into the subsets S_{cn}, S_{st}, S_{wk}, standing for parametric constraints, strongly satisfiable parametric equations (which involve both variables and parameters) and weak parametric equations (which also involve both variables and parameters).

A strongly satisfiable parametric equation $st : \Sigma p_i x_i + p_0 = 0$ in S_{st} can either be viewed as a conjunction of parametric constraints $c : p_0 = 0, \cdots, p_m = 0$ which can be included in S_{cn}, or it can be viewed as a weak parametric equation and be included in S_{wk}. For each $st \in S_{st}$, there are two cases leading to an exponentially many possibilities, each consisting of $\langle PC, WPE \rangle$, where PC is the set of parametric constraints and WPE is the set of weak parametric equations. For each maximal consistent subset MCS of PC, a most general solution for parameters δ is computed; let $R(MCS)$ stand for the associated rule set taken from D_{lhs}. The solution δ is then applied on each weak parametric equation in WPE to compute the values of variables, if any, such that the instantiated weak parametric equation is consistent with MCS. For any such substitution of variables of the weak parametric equation, the corresponding rule is split (see subsection 2.3) and $R(MCS)$ is extended to include the instance of the rule. The result is a rule set RF corresponding to MCS and instances of rules corresponding to weak parametric equations in WPE which are consistent with MCS. For each such possibility, the rule set RF is then used in the next subsection to speculate the left sides of the conjectures which are instances of lhs.

For example, consider the inconsistent set of parametric equations $S = \{s1 : k_3 = 1,\ s2 : k_2 = 1,\ s3 : k_1\ x + k_3 = k_1,\ s4 : k_2 = 1\}$ generated from D_{e2plus} in section 1. $S_{cn} = \{s1 : k_3 = 1;\ s2 : k_2 = 1;\ s4 : k_1 = 1\}$, $S_{st} = \{k_1\ x + k_3 = k_1\}$, and $S_{wk} = \{\}$. There are two possibilities based on $\{k_1\ x + k_3 = k_1\}$: $\{\langle PC : \{s1 : k_3 = 1;\ s2 : k_2 = 1;\ s3 : k_1 = 0, k_3 = 0;\ s4 : k_2 = 1\}, WPE : \{\}\rangle, \langle PC : \{s1 : k_3 = 1;\ s2 : k_2 = 1;\ s4 : k_2 = 1\}, WPE : \{s3 : k_1\ x + k_3 = k_1\}\rangle\}$. There are two maximal consistent subsets $MCS_1 = \{k_1 = 0, k_3 = 0, k_2 = 1\}$ and $MCS_2 = \{k_3 = 1, k_2 = 1\}$[6]. Corresponding to MCS_1, the rule set is $\{2, 3, 4\}$. For MCS_2, an instance of rule 3 generated from $s3$ is computed giving x to be 0; the resulting rule set is $\{1, 2, 3.1, 4\}$.

3.3 Identifying Left Sides and Their Complete Definitions

Given a subset R of rules of D_f which possibly generate a consistent set of parametric equations, left sides of conjectures need to be speculated. The rule set R is first preprocessed to ensure that most left sides of conjectures can be generated. After preprocessing, for every speculated left side $lhs = f(s_1, \cdots, s_k)$ of a conjecture, it must be ensured that every ground instance of lhs can be normalized to a ground $\mathcal{T}$-term using the rules in R; if not, additional rules from D_f needs to be added to R to ensure this property (hopefully without violating the consistency condition).

Preprocessing. Rules in R are refined by splitting based on unifying recursive calls with the left sides of nonrecursive rules in R. Let $l_i \to r_i$ be a non-recursive rule in R (i.e. r_i is a PA-term). For every recursive rule $l_j \to r_j$ in R, replace it by $split(\{l_j \to r_j\}, \sigma)$ if a recursive call in r_j unifies with l_i with the mgu σ. The expansion is performed for all possible pairs of non-recursive rules $l_i \to r_i$ and recursive rules $l_j \to r_j$ in R. The output of the preprocessing step is a rule set equivalent to the input rule set which may include instances of rules in the input rule set. We will abuse the notation and let R stand for the output of the preprocessing step.

Speculating Left Sides. The left sides of the rules in R are abstracted using ABS discussed in subsection 2.4 to generate k-tuples of terms to construct the left sides of new conjectures to be speculated. Let LHS be the finite set of possible left sides of the form $f(s_1, \cdots, s_k)$.

Generating a Complete Definition for a Left Side. For each new left side $lhs = f(s_1, \cdots, s_k)$, its complete definition D_{lhs} as a set of rules is computed from R using the function *complete* which is initially invoked with $\{lhs\}$, R, $\{\}$ and a boolean flag set to $false$. The following invariant holds for each recursive call $complete(t, S_1, S_2, b)$; t is always of the form $f(s'_1, \cdots, s'_k)$, where each s'_i is a $\mathcal{T}$-term; every ground instance of t can be normalized to a $\mathcal{T}$-term using rules in $S_1 \cup S_2$.

[6] The reader might have noticed some duplication in computing maximal consistent subsets; better algorithms need to be investigated to avoid it.

1. $complete(\{t\} \cup L, R, D, b) = complete(L, R, D, b)$ if t rewrites using a rule in D.
2. $complete(\{t\} \cup L, R, D) = complete(\{\theta_j(t) \mid \theta_j \in compl(\sigma)\} \cup L, R, D, b)$ if t does not rewrite using a rule in D but there is a rule $l_i \rightarrow r_i$ in D such that $\sigma = mgu(t, l_i)$.
3. $complete(\{t\} \cup L,\ R,\ D, b) = complete(\{\theta_i(t) \mid \theta_i \in compl(\sigma)\} \cup L,\ R',\ D', false)$ where $l_i \rightarrow r_i$ is a rule in R such that $\sigma = mgu(t, l_i)$, $D' = D \cup \{\sigma(l_i) \rightarrow \sigma(r_i)\}$, and $R' = R$ - $\{l_i \rightarrow r_i\} \cup \{\theta_i(l_i) \rightarrow \theta_i(r_i) \mid \theta_i \in compl(\sigma)\}$.
4. $complete(\{\}, R, D, false) = complete(T, R, D, true)$, where $T = \{t_j \mid t_j$ appears as a recursive call to f in the right side of a rule in $D\}$.
5. $complete(\{\}, R, D, true) = D$.

For example, consider computing the complete definition of $lhs = f(0, s(y))$ with R being

1. $f(0,0) \rightarrow 0$,
2. $f(s(x),0) \rightarrow s(f(0,x))$,
3. $f(0,s(x)) \rightarrow s(f(x,0))$,
4. $f(s(x),s(y)) \rightarrow s(s(f(x,y)))$.

The initial call is $complete(\{f(0,s(y))\},\ \{1,2,3,4\},\ \{\}, false)$. The left side of rule 3 unifies with $f(0, s(y))$ by the substitution $x \rightarrow y$ for which the set of complement substitutions is empty; we thus have $complete(\{\},\ \{1,2,4\},\ \{3\}, false)$. By step 4, we get $complete(\{f(y,0)\},\ \{1,2,4\},\ \{3\},\ true)$ based on the recursive call in rule 3. Since $f(y, 0)$ unifies with rules 1, we get $complete(\{f(s(y),0)\}, \{2,4\}, \{1,3\}, false)$; again using step 3 with rule 2, we get $complete(\{\}, \{4\}, \{1,2, 3\}, false)$. From step 4, we get $complete(\{f(0,y),\ f(y,0)\},\ \{4\},\ \{1,2,3\},\ true)$. Using step 2, this reduces to
$complete(\{f(0,s(y)), f(y,0)\}, \{4\}, \{1,2,3\}, true)$; using step 1, this reduces to: $complete(\{f(y,0)\}, \{4\}, \{1,2,3\}, true)$. Again applying steps 2 and 1, respectively, we get
$complete(\{\}, \{4\}, \{1,2,3\}, true)$, which terminates with $\{1,2,3\}$ as the rule set.

3.4 Procedure

The procedure for generating lemmas for PA given below is invoked with the most general $lhs = f(x_1, \cdots, x_m)$ and D_f, where $x_i's$ are distinct variables. If a right side for this lhs can be found (implying that constraints generated from D_{lhs} are consistent), then lhs is expressible in PA and the procedure halts. Otherwise, rule sets associated with maximal consistent subsets of constraints are identified; for each such set, instances of lhs are speculated; for each such instance, say $\theta(lhs)$, a complete definition $D_{\theta(lhs)}$, sufficient to normalize every ground instance of $\theta(lhs)$ to a $\mathcal{T}$-term, is computed, and then the above steps are repeated. Lemmas thus generated are added to D_f to help speculate further conjectures.

For a given lhs, to ensure that parametric equations can be generated from each rule in D_{lhs}, the left side of each rule in D_{lhs} must match lhs using σ (i.e., $\sigma(lhs) = l$) and each recursive call t in r must either match lhs or $\sigma(t)$ must simplify to a $\mathcal{T}$-term using D_{lhs}.

Input: A PA-based, terminating, sufficiently-complete and ground-confluent definition D_f of f.
Output: $\{f(s_1, \cdots, s_k) = r\}$ where each s_i and r are PA terms such that $D_f \models_{\text{ind}} f(s_1, \cdots, s_k) = r$.
Method: Initially, $C_{lhs} = \{\langle f(x_1, \cdots, x_m), D_f \rangle\}$.
While there is an unmarked pair $\langle lhs, D_{lhs} \rangle \in C_{lhs}$ do

1. *Find right side:* Let rhs be a parametric term in PA expressed using variables in lhs. Generate a set of parametric equations S using D_{lhs} and the conjecture $lhs = rhs$.
   1.1 *Success:* If S is consistent then let δ be the most general solution of S. Output lemma $\mathcal{L}$: $lhs = \delta(rhs)$. Mark $\langle lhs, D_{lhs} \rangle$ in C_{lhs}. Add $\mathcal{L}$ to D_f and simplify. Go to step *3* for generating new candidate left sides based on the simplified D_f.
   1.2 *Fail:* $lhs = rhs$ is not expressible in PA; mark $\langle lhs, D_{lhs} \rangle$ in C_{lhs}. Go to step *2*.
2. *Generate maximal consistent subsets of S:* Generate from S, the set of pairs $\{\langle MCS, R(MCS) \rangle \mid MCS$ is a maximal consistent subset of S extended after instantiating weak parametric equations in $S\rangle\}$,where $R(MCS)$ is the rule set associated with MCS.
3. *Identify left sides and definitions:* From each pair $\langle MCS, R(MCS) \rangle$, identify new candidates for the left side of conjectures using ABS. For each new candidate lhs, generate a complete definition D_{lhs} using the procedure *complete*. Add the unmarked pair $\langle lhs, D_{lhs} \rangle$ to C_{lhs}. Repeat the above procedure.

4 Theories Admitting Multiple Canonical Forms

The above procedure is an instance of a general procedure which works for decidable theories admitting multiple canonical form schemes. In the case of PA, a term in PA can be represented using a single parametric form. That is not true in general. A recursive data structure such as finite lists, has more than one canonical forms. In the theory of finite lists, a term can be a variable or *nil* representing an empty list, or $cons(x, l)$, where x is an element and l is a list. Unlike PA, these canonical forms cannot be represented using a single scheme. The theory of finite lists is an instance of the generic theory of free constructors with m distinct constructors, say $c_1, c_2, \cdots, c_m, m > 1$.

Simple lemmas can be generated from recursive function definitions based in such theories by considering each canonical form scheme as the possible right side for the speculated left side of a conjecture. It is shown in [6] that as in the case of PA, no-theory condition for the quantifier-free theory of free constructors is decidable (i.e., whether a term $f(s_1, \cdots, s_k)$ is equivalent to a constructor term is decidable, where f is $\mathcal{T}$-based and each s_i is a constructor term). Furthermore, equations relating parametric terms in this theory can be solved for parameters as in PA. Below, we illustrate the general procedure with *append*:

$$1.\ append(nil, y) \rightarrow y, \qquad 2.\ append(cons(x_1, x), y) \rightarrow cons(x_1, append(x, y)).$$

Since finite lists admit as canonical form schemes, a variable, $nil, cons(t_1, t_2)$, where t_1, t_2 are themselves canonical form schemes, four conjectures with *append* (x, y) as their left side are speculated with the right side being each of the canonical forms: *nil*, x, y, and $cons(t_1, t_2)$.

To check whether $append(x, y)$ can be equivalent to some constructor term s, nonrecursive rules are first used to generate constraints and perhaps rule out most of the candidate canonical forms. From the first rule in the definition, since there is a substitution σ such that $\sigma(append(x, y)) = append(nil, y)$, it must be the case that $\sigma(s) = y$. That is, when *nil* is substituted for x in s, it should be equivalent to y; since in the theory of free constructors, constructor terms cannot be simplified, $s = y$. It is easy to see that assuming $append(x, y) = y$, the constraint from the second rule, $y = cons(x_1, y)$, is unsatisfiable for any value of x_1, y. This implies that there is no constructor-term s such that $append(x, y) = s$. Speculating the right side to be nil, y, or $cons(t_1, t_2)$ can be shown not to lead to any lemmas being speculated either.

Conjecturing $append(x, y) = x$, however, results in the nonrecursive rule generating a constraint $nil = y$ which is weakly satisfiable only if $y = nil$. The second rule generates the constraint $cons(x_1, x) = cons(x_1, x)$, a valid formula. Combining the two constraints, a possible conjecture $append(x, nil) = x$ is speculated, which is valid and thus a lemma.

5 Generating Complex Lemmas

So far, the focus has been on generating *simple* lemmas of the form $f(s_1, \cdots, s_k) = r$, where r and each s_i are $\mathcal{T}$-terms. Using results from [11] (see also [6]), lemmas whose left sides include multiple occurrences of $\mathcal{T}$-based functions can also be generated. With this extension, it is possible to generate many nontrivial lemmas used in the verification of arithmetic circuits [9, 10, 12]. This is illustrated using an example in the next subsection.

To consider conjectures in which many $\mathcal{T}$-based function symbols can occur, it is first necessary to ensure that the definitions of function symbols appearing in such conjectures are *compatible* in the sense of [11, 6]. Compatibility ensure that when a term built from a compatible sequence of function symbols is instantiated and normalized, the result is a term in $\mathcal{T}$. Informally, g is compatible with f if for every rule of f, the *context* created by the rule on its right side can be simplified by the definition of g.

Definition 4 (Compatibility [6]). *Let g, f be $\mathcal{T}$-based, $f \notin \mathcal{F}_\mathcal{T}$, and $1 \leq j \leq m = arity(g)$. The definition of g* is compatible with the definition of f *on argument j iff for all rules $\alpha : f(s^*, y^*) \rightarrow C[f(t_1^*, y^*), \ldots, f(t_n^*, y^*)]$, either $n = 0$ and $\alpha \in Exc_{g,f}$, or $g(x_1, \ldots, x_{j-1}, C[z_1, \ldots, z_n], x_{j+1}, \ldots, x_m) \rightarrow^*_{\mathcal{R}/\mathcal{T}} D[g(x_1, \ldots, x_{j-1}, z_{i_1}, x_{j+1}, \ldots, x_m), \ldots, g(x_1, \ldots, x_{j-1}, z_{i_k}, x_{j+1}, \ldots, x_m)]$ for a context D over $\mathcal{F}_\mathcal{T}$, $i_1, \ldots, i_k \in \{1, \ldots, n\}$, $z_i \notin \mathcal{V}(D)$ for all i.*

$Exc_{g,f}$ stands for the non-recursive rules in the definition of f whose right sides cannot be simplified by the definition of g [6]. Relaxing the requirement that g does not have to be compatible with the nonrecursive rules in the definition of f allows more function definitions to be compatible.

For example, *mod*2 and *half* compute, respectively, the remainder and quotient on division by 2. These definitions are based in the theory of free constructors $0, s$ (and also PA).

1. $mod2(0) \rightarrow 0$,	2. $mod2(1) \rightarrow 1$,	3. $mod2(s(s(x))) \rightarrow mod2(x)$.
4. $half(0) \rightarrow 0$,	5. $half(1) \rightarrow 0$,	6. $half(s(s(x))) \rightarrow s(half(x))$.

It is easy to check that *half* is compatible with *mod*2. However, *mod*2 is not compatible with *half* since $mod2(half(s(s(x))))$ generated from rule 6 reduces to

$mod2(s(half(x)))$ using the rule and cannot be simplified any further. However, $mod2$ is compatible with $mod2$, but $half$ is not compatible with $half$.

The compatibility property can be easily checked from the definitions of function symbols, and compatible sequence of function symbols can be easily generated[7].

Using the procedure discussed in Section 3, it is easy to see that neither $mod2(x)$ nor $half(x)$ are expressible in PA. Furthermore, the procedure will not generate any simple lemma about $mod2$ and $half$.

Given PA-based function symbols g and f such that g is compatible with f, a conjecture $g(y_1, \cdots, f(x_1, \cdots, x_n), \cdots, y_k) = \Sigma k_i x_i + \Sigma k_j y_j + k_0$ can be speculated where $x_i's$ and $y_j's$ are distinct variables and f appears only in the inductive argument positions of g (on which the definition of g recurses). The rest is the same as in Section 3. We illustrate the procedure using the example $half(mod2(x))$.

Given $half(mod2(x)) = k_1\ x + k_2$, where parameters k_1, k_2 are unknown, parametric equations are generated using the rules defining $mod2$. From rule 1, x is instantiated to 0, giving $half(mod2(0)) = k_1\ 0 + k_2$, which simplifies using rules 1 and 4 to the constraint $k_2 = 0$. From rule 2, x is instantiated to 1, giving $half(mod2(1)) = k_1\ 1 + k_2$, which simplifies using rules 2 and 5 to the constraint $k_1 + k_2 = 0$. From rule 3, x is instantiated to $s(s(u))$ giving the conclusion subgoal $half(mod2(s(s(u)))) = k_1\ u + k_1 + k_1 + k_2$ assuming the induction hypothesis $half(mod2(u)) = k_1\ u + k_2$, obtained by instantiating x to be u. After simplifying using rules 3 and 6, and using the induction hypothesis, we get $k_1\ u + k_2 = k_1\ u + k_1 + k_1 + k_2$, which simplifies to $k_1 + k_1 = 0$. These three constraints are consistent, giving $k_1 = k_2 = 0$ as the solution. And, lemma $half(mod2(x)) = 0$ is generated.

The notion of compatibility can be extended to that of a *compatible sequence* involving function symbols $[f_1, \cdots, f_m]$ where each f_i is compatible with f_{i+1}, $1 \leq i \leq m-1$. Given a sequence $[g, f_1, f_2]$, for example, we can generate the left side of conjectures of the form $g(y_1, \cdots, f_1(x_1, \cdots, f_2(z_1, \cdots, z_m), \cdots, x_n) \cdots, y_k)$ such that the variables $x_i's$, $y_j's$ and $z_k's$ are distinct and the variables $z_k's$ the inductive positions of f_2[8] do not appear in $x_i's$ and $y_j's$. The left side of a conjecture thus generated can be checked for the no-theory condition.

If a conjecture generated from a compatible sequence of function definitions cannot be expressed in $\mathcal{T}$, then appropriate instances of the conjecture are found similar to Section 3. Some of the lemmas generated by the proposed approach based on the theories of PA and finite lists are given in Figure 1. Automatic generation of one such lemma is illustrated in the next subsection, where some of the function appearing in Figure 1 are also defined.

---

[7] Note that besides the rules in the definition of f and g, other applicable rules may be used to simplify terms to check compatibility of functions f and g. Properties of function symbols such as associative-commutative(AC) may also be used.

[8] Positions of f_2 involved in recursion in the definition of f_2.

Lemma	Theory	Remarks
$bton(radder(ntob(x), ntob(x), ntob(x))) = x + x + x$	Finite lists, PA	Correctness of ripple carry
$bton(cadder(ntob(x), ntob(x), ntob(x))) = x + x + x$	Finite lists, PA	Correctness of carry save
$bton(leftshift(ntob(x))) = x + x$	Finite lists	Correctness of left-shift
$bton(pad0(ntob(x))) = x$	Finite lists, PA	Correctness of Padding
$compl(compl(x)) = x$	Finite lists	Complement's idempotence
$half(mod2(x)) = 0$	PA	Multiple functions
$mod2(mod2(x)) = 0$	PA	Multiple functions
$ack(1, n) = n + 2$	PA	Nested recursive calls
$ack(2, n) = 2n$ - 3	PA	Nested recursive calls
$rev(rev(x)) = x$	Finite lists	Multiple canonical forms
$append(x, nil) = x$	Finite lists	Multiple canonical forms

Fig. 1. Some Examples of Generated Lemmas

5.1 Generating Lemmas for Arithmetic Circuits

Consider the following definitions of *bton*, *ntob* and *pad0*. The functions *bton* and *ntob* convert binary to decimal representations and vice versa, respectively. The function *pad0* adds a leading binary zero to a bit list. Bits increase in significance in the list with the first element of the list being the least significant. These functions are used to reason about number-theoretic properties of parameterized arithmetic circuits [8, 10].

1. $bton(nil) \to 0$,
2. $bton(cons(b0, y_1)) \to bton(y_1) + bton(y_1)$,
3. $bton(cons(b1, y_1)) \to s(bton(y_1) + bton(y_1))$.
4. $ntob(0) \to cons(b0, nil)$,
5. $ntob(s(0)) \to cons(b1, nil)$,
6. $ntob(s(s(x_2 + x_2))) \to cons(b0, ntob(s(x_2)))$,
7. $ntob(s(s(s((x_2 + x_2))))) \to cons(b1, ntob(s(x_2)))$
8. $pad0(nil) \to cons(b0, nil)$,
9. $pad0(cons(b0, y)) \to cons(b0, pad0(y))$,
10. $pad0(cons(b1, y)) \to cons(b1, pad0(y))$.

The underlying decidable theory $\mathcal{T}$ is the combination of the quantifier-free theories of finite lists of bits and PA; $b0$, $b1$ stand for binary 0 and 1. Definitions of *bton*, *ntob*, and *pad0* are $\mathcal{T}$-based. The function *pad0* is compatible with *ntob*; *bton* is compatible with *pad0*. Hence $[bton, pad0, ntob]$ form a compatible sequence.

Padding of output bit vectors of one stage with leading zeros before using them as input to the next stage is common in multiplier circuits realized using a tree of carry-save adders. An important lemma needed to establish the correctness of such circuits is that the padding does not affect the number output by the circuit. We illustrate how this lemma can be automatically generated.

A conjecture with $bton(pad0(ntob(x)))$ as the left side is attempted. Since the sort of *bton* is natural numbers, the right side of the conjecture is $k_1\ x + k_0$. As before, parametric equations are generated corresponding to the instantiations of x for each of the four rules defining the innermost function *ntob*.

- From rule 4, x gets instantiated to 0, giving $bton(pad0(ntob(0))) = k_1\ 0 + k_2$. This simplifies using the rules 1, 9, 8, 2, and 1 and PA to the constraint $s1$: $0 = k_2$.

- From rule 5, x gets instantiated to 1, giving $bton(pad0(ntob(1))) = k_1\ 1 + k_2$. This simplifies using the rules 5, 10, 8, 2, and 1 and PA to the constraint $s2$: $1 = k_1 + k_2$.
- From rule 6, x is instantiated as $s(s(x_2 + x_2))$ for the conclusion subgoal with x instantiated as $s(x_2)$ for the induction hypothesis. This gives $bton(pad0(ntob(s(s(x_2{+}x_2))))) = k_1\ s(s(x_2{+}x_2)) + k_2$ as the conclusion with $bton(pad0(ntob(s(x_2)))) = k_1 s(x_2) + k_2$ as the hypothesis. The conclusion simplifies using rules 6, 9, 2 to $bton(pad0(ntob(s(x_2)))) + bton(pad0(ntob(s(x_2)))) = k_1\ s(s(x_2 + x_2)) + k_2$. Applying the hypothesis gives $k_1\ s(x_2) + k_2 + k_1\ s(x_2) + k_2 = k_1\ s(s(x_2 + x_2)) + k_2$, which gives the constraint $s3$: $k_2 = 0$.
- Parametric equation from rule 7 is similarly generated and gives constraint $s4{:}k_2 = 0$.

Taking the conjunction of all the constraints gives $\{k_1 = 1, k_2 = 0\}$, implying that it is a consistent set. This gives the lemma

$$bton(pad0(ntob(x))) = x,$$

which states that $pad0$ does not change the numeric representation of a bit list as required in the verification of properties of multiplier circuits. in [8, 12].

6 Conclusion and Further Research

A procedure for automatically generating lemmas from recursive function definition is given using decision procedures. It is expected that after a user has written recursive definitions of functions on theories such as PA and on constructors, the procedure will automatically start generating lemmas whose one side has terms from the underlying decidable theory. In this way, a library of useful lemmas can be automatically built with the hope that these lemmas will be found useful in the proofs of other nontrivial lemmas. This is demonstrated using examples about commonly used function definitions on numbers and finite lists, as well as from our experiments in automatically verifying number-theoretic properties of arithmetic hardware circuits.

Conjectures considered in this paper have one side to be a term from a decidable theory. In [5], the approach proposed in [11] has been extended to decide quantifier-free formulas which are boolean combinations of such equations. Recently in [6], a decision procedure for a class of equations in which function symbols with $\mathcal{T}$-based definitions can appear on both sides of equations has been developed. The proposed procedure needs to be extended so that a wider class of lemmas can be automatically generated from $\mathcal{T}$-based function definitions.

We have discussed two well-known quantifier-free decidable theories on numbers–the theory of free constructors $0, s$, and the quantifier-free theory of Presburger arithmetic. Most of the examples in the paper are done in the framework of the quantifier-free theory of Presburger arithmetic and the theory of finite lists. There exists even a more expressive and decidable theory of numbers involving $0, 1, s, +, 2^y, \geq$; we will call it the theory of *2exp*. These three theories define a strict hierarchy in their expressive power about properties of numbers. Given a function definition on numbers based in a theory $\mathcal{T}$, it is possible to speculate conjectures using the most expressive theory (e.g., the theory of $2exp$). If a given conjecture cannot be expressed in the most expressive theory in the hierarchy, then it cannot be expressed in any theory in the hierarchy. However, the most expressive the theory, solving parametric equations in it can be more complex. There is thus a trade-off. An alternate method is to start with the least expressive power (e.g., $\mathcal{T}$, the theory in which the definition is based), and then move to more expressive theories for conjectures which cannot be expressed in $\mathcal{T}$. The proposed approach will work with either of the two heuristics for trying theories in different orders. In fact, some of the examples in the paper, e.g. *e2plus* could have been attempted using the theory of exponentiation. The function *e2plus*, for instance, can be shown to be expressible in this theory. Similarly, instances of Ackermann's function including $ack(0, y), ack(1, y), ack(2, y), ack(3, y)$ can all be expressed in the theory of exponentiation. The expanded version, available from `http://faculty.ist.unomaha.edu/msubramaniam/subuweb.htm`, includes an Appendix in which derivation of lemmas about Ackermann's function is discussed. Ackermann's function is not even PA-based, because of nested recursive calls in it; however, the proposed approach still works on it provided parametric equations in PA are extended to include nonlinear polynomials over parameters as coefficients of variables as well as limited reasoning about exponentiation and multiplication are available to simplify parametric constraints.

Acknowledgment

We thank Jürgen Giesl for collaborative work which triggered some of the ideas in this paper.

References

1. F. Baader & T. Nipkow. *Term Rewriting and All That.* Cambridge Univ. Pr., 1998.
2. R. S. Boyer and J Moore. *A Computational Logic.* Academic Press, 1979.
3. A. Bundy, A. Stevens, F. van Harmelen, A. Ireland, & A. Smaill. Rippling: A Heuristic for Guiding Inductive Proofs. *Artificial Intelligence*, 62:185-253, 1993.
4. H. B. Enderton. *A Mathematical Introduction to Logic.* 2nd edition, Harcourt/ Academic Press, 2001.
5. J. Giesl & D. Kapur. Decidable Classes of Inductive Theorems. *Proc. IJCAR '01*, LNAI 2083, 469-484, 2001.
6. J. Giesl & D. Kapur. Deciding Inductive Validity of Equations. *Proc. CADE '03*, LNAI 2741, Miami, 2003. An expanded version appeared as Technical Report AIB-2003-03, 2003 is available from `http://aib.informatik.rwth-aachen.de`.
7. D. Kapur, P. Narendran and H. Zhang. Automating Inductionless Induction using Test Sets. *Journal of Symbolic Computation,* 11 (1-2), 81-111, 1991.
8. D. Kapur & M. Subramaniam. New Uses of Linear Arithmetic in Automated Theorem Proving by Induction. *Journal of Automated Reasoning*, 16:39–78, 1996.

9. D. Kapur and M. Subramaniam. Mechanically verifying a family of multiplier circuits. *Proc. Computer Aided Verification (CAV)*, Springer LNCS 1102, 135-146, August 1996.
10. D. Kapur and M. Subramaniam. Mechanical verification of adder circuits using powerlists. *Journal of Formal Methods in System Design*, 13 (2), page 127-158, Sep. 1998.
11. D. Kapur & M. Subramaniam. Extending Decision Procedures with Induction Schemes. *Proc. CADE-17*, LNAI 1831, 324-345, 2000.
12. D. Kapur and M. Subramaniam. Using an induction prover for verifying arithmetic circuits. *Int. Journal of Software Tools for Technology Transfer*, Springer Verlag, 3(1), 32-65, Sep. 2000.
13. D. Kapur & H. Zhang. An Overview of Rewrite Rule Laboratory (*RRL*). *Journal of Computer and Mathematics with Applications*, 29:91–114, 1995.
14. R. E. Shostak. Deciding combinations of theories. *Journal of the ACM*, 31(1):1-12, 1984.
15. C. Walther. Mathematical Induction. Gabbay, Hogger, & Robinson (eds.), *Handbook of Logic in Artificial Intelligence and Logic Programming, Vol. 2*, Oxford University Press, 1994.
16. H. Zhang, D. Kapur, & M. S. Krishnamoorthy. A Mechanizable Induction Principle for Equational Specifications. *Proc. CADE-9*, LNCS 310, 1988.

Deaccumulation – Improving Provability

Jürgen Giesl[1], Armin Kühnemann[2], and Janis Voigtländer[2,*]

[1] LuFG Informatik II, RWTH Aachen, Ahornstr. 55, D–52074 Aachen, Germany
giesl@informatik.rwth-aachen.de
[2] Institute for Theoretical Computer Science, Department of Computer Science, Dresden University of Technology, D–01062 Dresden, Germany
{kuehne,voigt}@tcs.inf.tu-dresden.de

Abstract. Several induction theorem provers were developed to verify functional programs mechanically. Unfortunately, automated verification usually fails for functions with accumulating arguments. In particular, this holds for tail-recursive functions that correspond to imperative programs, but also for programs with nested recursion.
Based on results from the theory of tree transducers, we develop an automatic transformation technique. It transforms accumulative functional programs into non-accumulative ones, which are much better suited for automated verification by induction theorem provers. Hence, in contrast to classical program transformations aiming at improving the efficiency, the goal of our deaccumulation technique is to improve the provability.

1 Introduction

In safety-critical applications, a formal verification of programs is required. However, since mathematical correctness proofs are very expensive and time-consuming, one tries to automate this task as much as possible. Since *induction* is an important proof technique required for program verification, several *induction theorem provers* have been developed, which can be used for mechanized reasoning about program properties (e.g., *NQTHM* [4], *ACL-2* [17], *RRL* [16], *CLAM* [5], *INKA* [1, 26], and *SPIKE* [3]). However, while such provers are successfully applied for *functional* programs, they often have severe problems in dealing with *imperative* programs.

As running example, we consider the calculation of a decreasing list containing the first x_1 even numbers (i.e., $[2x_1 - 2, \ldots, 4, 2, 0]$). This problem can be solved by the following part p_{even} of an imperative program (in C-like syntax):

```
[int] even (int x1)
{ int y1 = 0;  [int] y2 = [];
  while (x1!=0)  { y2 = y1:y2;  y1 = y1+2;  x1--; }
  return y2;                                        }
```

Here, [int] denotes the type of integer lists, [] denotes the empty list, and : denotes list insertion, i.e., $y_1 : y_2$ inserts the element y_1 in front of the list y_2.

* Research of this author supported by the DFG under grants KU 1290/2-1 and 2-4.

V.A. Saraswat (Ed.): ASIAN 2003, LNCS 2896, pp. 146–160, 2003.

Classical techniques for verifying imperative programs are based on inventing suitable *loop invariants* [13]. However, while there are heuristics for finding loop invariants [15, 23], in general this task is hard to mechanize [7].

Instead, our aim is to use the existing powerful induction theorem provers also for the verification of imperative programs. To this end, imperative programs are translated into the functional input language of induction provers. In the absence of pointers, such an automatic translation is easily possible [20] by transforming every while-loop into a separate function whose parameters record the changes during a run through the while-loop. For our program p_{even} we obtain the following tail-recursive program p_{acc} (in Haskell-like syntax) together with an initial call $r_{acc} = (f\ x_1\ 0\ [])$. It uses pattern matching on x_1 (called *recursion argument*) and represents natural numbers with the constructors 0 and S for the successor function:

$$p_{acc}: \quad \begin{array}{lll} f\ (S\ x_1)\ y_1\ y_2 & = & f\ x_1\ (S\ (S\ y_1))\ (y_1 : y_2) \\ f\ 0 \quad\ \ y_1\ y_2 & = & y_2 \end{array}$$

The above translation of imperative into functional programs always yields tail-recursive functions that compute their result using accumulators. Indeed, f accumulates values in its *context arguments* (arguments different from the recursion argument, i.e., f's second and third argument). A function is called *accumulative* if its context arguments are modified in its recursive calls. For instance, f is accumulative, because both the second and the third argument do not remain unchanged in the recursive call. A program like p_{acc} is called *accumulative* if it contains an accumulative function.

Assume that our aim is to verify the equivalence of r_{acc} and $r_q = (q\ x_1)$ for all natural numbers x_1, where p_q is the following functional specification of our problem. Here, $(q\ x_1)$ calculates the desired list and $(q'\ x_1)$ computes $2 \cdot x_1$:

$$\begin{array}{lll} q\ (S\ x_1) & = & (q'\ x_1) : (q\ x_1) \\ q\ 0 & = & [] \end{array} \qquad \begin{array}{lll} q'\ (S\ x_1) & = & S\ (S\ (q'\ x_1)) \\ q'\ 0 & = & 0 \end{array}$$

Note that even if there exists a "natural" non-accumulative recursive specification of a problem, imperative programs are typically written using loops, which translate into accumulative programs. The accumulative version may also be more efficient than a non-accumulative implementation (see e.g., App. B).

But unfortunately, accumulative programs are not suitable for mechanized verification. For example, an automatic proof of

$$(f\ x_1\ 0\ []) = (q\ x_1)$$

by induction (using this equation for fixed x_1 as induction hypothesis) fails, because in the induction step ($x_1 \mapsto (S\ x_1)$) the induction hypothesis cannot be successfully applied to prove $(f\ (S\ x_1)\ 0\ []) = (q\ (S\ x_1))$. For instance, for this conjecture the *ACL-2* prover performs a series of generalizations that do not increase verifiability, and it ends up with consuming all memory available. The reason for the verification problems is that f uses accumulators: the context arguments of the term $(f\ x_1\ \underline{(S\ (S\ 0))}\ \underline{(0 : [\,])})$, which originates from rule application to $(f\ (S\ x_1)\ 0\ [\,])$, do not fit to the context arguments of the term $(f\ x_1\ \underline{0}\ \underline{[\,]})$ in the induction hypothesis! So the problem is that accumulating parameters are typically initialized with some fixed values (like 0 and $[\,]$), which then appear also in the conjecture to be proved and hence in the induction hypothesis. But since accumulators are changed in recursive calls, after rule application we have different values like $(S\ (S\ 0))$ and $(0 : [\,])$ in the induction conclusion of the step case.

In induction theorem proving, this problem is usually solved by transforming the conjecture to be proved. In other words, the aim is to invent a suitable *generalization* (see, e.g., [4, 14, 15, 26]). So, instead of the original conjecture $(f\ x_1\ 0\ [\,]) = (q\ x_1)$, one tries to find a *stronger* conjecture that however is *easier* to prove. In our example, the original conjecture may be generalized to

$$(f\ x_1\ y_1\ y_2) = (\bar{q}\ x_1\ y_1) +\!\!+\ y_2\,,$$

where $+\!\!+$ denotes list concatenation and where $\bar{q}$ and $\bar{q}'$ are defined as follows:

$$\begin{aligned} \bar{q}\ (S\ x_1)\ y_1 &= (\bar{q}'\ x_1\ y_1) : (\bar{q}\ x_1\ y_1) \qquad & \bar{q}'\ (S\ x_1)\ y_1 &= S\ (S\ (\bar{q}'\ x_1\ y_1)) \\ \bar{q}\ 0\ \ \ \ \ \ \ \ y_1 &= [\,] & \bar{q}'\ 0\ \ \ \ \ \ \ \ y_1 &= y_1 \end{aligned}$$

However, finding such generalizations automatically is again very hard. In fact, it is as difficult as discovering loop invariants for the original imperative program. Therefore, developing techniques to verify accumulative functions is one of the most important research topics in the area of inductive theorem proving [14].

In contrast to the classical approach of generalizing conjectures, we suggest an automated program transformation, which transforms functions that are hard to verify into functions that are much more suitable for mechanized verification. The advantage of this approach is that it works fully automatically and that by transforming a function definition, the verification problems with this function are solved once and for all (i.e., for all conjectures one would like to prove about this function). In contrast, when using the generalization approach, one has to find a new generalization for every new conjecture to be proved. In particular, finding generalizations automatically is difficult for conjectures with *several* occurrences of an accumulative function (see e.g., [12] and App. A and B).

The semantics-preserving transformation to be presented in this paper transforms the original program p_{acc} into the following program p_{non}:

$$p_{non}: \qquad \begin{aligned} f'\ (S\ x_1) &= sub\ (f'\ x_1)\ (S\ (S\ 0))\ (0 : [\,]) \\ f'\ 0 &= [\,] \end{aligned}$$

$$\begin{aligned} sub\ (x_1 : x_2)\ y_1\ y_2 &= (sub\ x_1\ y_1\ y_2) : (sub\ x_2\ y_1\ y_2) \qquad & sub\ 0\ y_1\ y_2 &= y_1 \\ sub\ (S\ x_1)\ \ \ \ y_1\ y_2 &= S\ (sub\ x_1\ y_1\ y_2) & sub\ [\,]\ y_1\ y_2 &= y_2 \end{aligned}$$

together with an initial call $r_{non} = (f'\ x_1)$. Since p_{non} contains a function f' without context arguments, and a function *sub* with unchanged context arguments in recursive calls, p_{non} is a *non-accumulative* program and our transformation technique is called *deaccumulation*. An application of the *substitution function*[1] *sub* of the form $(sub\ t\ s_1\ s_2)$ replaces all occurrences of 0 in the term t by the term s_1 and all occurrences of $[\,]$ by s_2. For instance, the decreasing list of the first three even numbers is computed by p_{non} as follows:

$$
\begin{aligned}
f'\ (S^3\ 0) &\Rightarrow^4_{p_{non}} sub\ (sub\ (sub\ [\,]\ (S^2\ 0)\ (0:[\,]))\ (S^2\ 0)\ (0:[\,]))\ (S^2\ 0)\ (0:[\,])\\
&\Rightarrow_{p_{non}} sub\ (sub\ (0:[\,])\ (S^2\ 0)\ (0:[\,]))\ (S^2\ 0)\ (0:[\,])\\
&\Rightarrow^3_{p_{non}} sub\ ((S^2\ 0):(0:[\,]))\ (S^2\ 0)\ (0:[\,])\\
&\Rightarrow^7_{p_{non}} (S^4\ 0):((S^2\ 0):(0:[\,]))
\end{aligned}
$$

This computation shows that the constructors 0 and $[\,]$ in p_{non} are used as "placeholders", which are repeatedly substituted by $(S^2\ 0)$ and $(0:[\,])$, respectively.

Now, the statement $(f'\ x_1) = (q\ x_1)$ (taken as induction hypothesis $IH1$) can be proved automatically by three nested inductions as follows. During the proof, the new subgoals

$$
\begin{aligned}
IH2: &\quad (sub\ (q\ x_1)\ (S^2\ 0)\ (0:[\,])) = ((q'\ x_1):(q\ x_1)) \quad \text{and}\\
IH3: &\quad (sub\ (q'\ x_1)\ (S^2\ 0)\ (0:[\,])) = (S^2\ (q'\ x_1))
\end{aligned}
$$

are generated. Note that there is no need to invent these subgoals manually here, as these proof obligations show up automatically during the course of the proof. We only give the induction steps $(x_1 \mapsto (S\ x_1))$ of the first two inductions and omit the base cases $(x_1 = 0)$. A similar proof can also be generated by existing induction theorem provers like *ACL-2*.

$$
\begin{aligned}
& f'\ (S\ x_1)\\
=\ & sub\ (f'\ x_1)\ (S^2\ 0)\ (0:[\,])\\
=\ & sub\ (q\ x_1)\ (S^2\ 0)\ (0:[\,]) && (IH1)\\
=\ & (q'\ x_1):(q\ x_1) && (IH2)\\
=\ & q\ (S\ x_1)
\end{aligned}
$$

$$
\begin{aligned}
& sub\ (q\ (S\ x_1))\ (S^2\ 0)\ (0:[\,])\\
=\ & sub\ ((q'\ x_1):(q\ x_1))\ (S^2\ 0)\ (0:[\,])\\
=\ & (sub\ (q'\ x_1)\ (S^2\ 0)\ (0:[\,])):(sub\ (q\ x_1)\ (S^2\ 0)\ (0:[\,]))\\
=\ & (sub\ (q'\ x_1)\ (S^2\ 0)\ (0:[\,])):((q'\ x_1):(q\ x_1)) && (IH2)\\
=\ & (S^2\ (q'\ x_1)):((q'\ x_1):(q\ x_1)) && (IH3)\\
=\ & (q'\ (S\ x_1)):(q\ (S\ x_1))
\end{aligned}
$$

In this paper we consider the definition of f in p_{acc} as a *macro tree transducer* (for short *mtt*) [8, 9, 11] with one function: in general, such an f is defined by case analysis on the root symbol of the recursion argument t. The right-hand side of an equation for f may only contain (*extended*) *primitive-recursive function calls*, i.e., the recursion argument of f has to be a variable that refers to a subtree of t. The functions f' and *sub* together are viewed as a *2-modular tree transducer* (for short *modtt*) [10], where it is allowed that a function in module 1 (here f') calls a function in module 2 (here *sub*) non-primitive-recursively.

[1] For simplicity, we regard an untyped language. When introducing types, one would generate several substitution functions for the different types of arguments.

We slightly modify a *decomposition* technique from [19] that is based on results in [8–10] and transforms mtts like f into modtts like f' and *sub* without accumulators. Unfortunately, it turns out that the new programs are still not suitable for automatic verification. Since their verification problems are caused only by the form of the new initial calls, we suggest another transformation step, called *constructor replacement*, which yields initial calls of the innocuous form $(f'\ x_1)$ without initial values like 0 and [ ].

Since the class of mtts contains not only tail-recursive programs, but also programs with nested recursion, we will demonstrate by examples that our transformation can not only be useful for functions resulting from the translation of imperative programs, but for accumulative functional programs in general!

Besides this introduction, the paper contains four further sections and two appendices. In Sect. 2 we fix the required notions and notations and introduce our functional language and tree transducers. Sect. 3 presents the deaccumulation technique. Sect. 4 compares our technique to related work. Finally, Sect. 5 contains future research topics. Two additional examples demonstrating the application of our approach can be found in the appendices.

2 Preliminaries and Language

For every natural number $m \in \mathbb{N}$, $[m]$ denotes the set $\{1, \ldots, m\}$. We use the sets $X = \{x_1, x_2, x_3, \ldots\}$ and $Y = \{y_1, y_2, y_3, \ldots\}$ of *variables*. For every $n \in \mathbb{N}$, let $X_n = \{x_1, \ldots, x_n\}$ and $Y_n = \{y_1, \ldots, y_n\}$. In particular, $X_0 = Y_0 = \emptyset$.

A *ranked alphabet* (C, rank) consists of a finite set C and a mapping $\mathit{rank} : C \to \mathbb{N}$ where $\mathit{rank}(c)$ is the *arity* of c. We define $C^{(n)} = \{c \in C \mid \mathit{rank}(c) = n\}$. The set of *trees* (or ground *terms*) *over* C, denoted by T_C, is the smallest subset $T \subseteq (C \cup \{(\} \cup \{)\})^*$ with $C^{(0)} \subseteq T$ and for every $c \in C^{(n)}$ with $n \in \mathbb{N} - \{0\}$ and $t_1, \ldots, t_n \in T$: $(c\ t_1 \ldots t_n) \in T$. For a term t, pairwise distinct variables $x_1, \ldots, x_n$, and terms $t_1, \ldots, t_n$, we denote by $t[x_1/t_1, \ldots, x_n/t_n]$ the term that is obtained from t by substituting every occurrence of x_j in t by t_j. We abbreviate $[x_1/t_1, \ldots, x_n/t_n]$ by $[x_j/t_j]$, if the involved variables and terms are clear.

We consider a simple first-order, constructor-based functional programming language P as source and target language for the transformations. Every program $p \in P$ consists of several modules. In every module a function is defined by complete case analysis on the first argument (*recursion argument*) via pattern matching, where only flat patterns of the form $(c\ x_1 \ldots x_k)$ for constructors c and variables x_i are allowed. The other arguments are called *context arguments*. If, in a right-hand side of a function definition, there is a call of the same function, then the first argument of this function call has to be a subtree x_i of the first argument in the corresponding left-hand side. To ease readability, we choose an untyped ranked alphabet C_p of constructors, which is used to build up input and output trees of every function in p. In example programs and program transformations we relax the completeness of function definitions on T_{C_p} by leaving out those equations which are not intended to be used in evaluations.

Definition 1 Let C and F be ranked alphabets of *constructors* and *defined function symbols*, respectively, such that $F^{(0)} = \emptyset$, and X, Y, C, F are pairwise disjoint. We define the sets P, M, R of *programs*, *modules*, and *right-hand sides* as follows. Here, p, m, r, c, f range over the sets P, M, R, C, F, respectively.

$$\begin{array}{lll} p & ::= m_1 \ldots m_l & \text{(program)} \\ m & ::= f\ (c_1\ x_1 \ldots x_{k_1})\ y_1 \ldots y_n = r_1 & \text{(module)} \\ & \qquad \ldots & \\ & \quad\ \ f\ (c_q\ x_1 \ldots x_{k_q})\ y_1 \ldots y_n = r_q & \\ r & ::= x_i \mid y_j \mid c\, r_1 \ldots r_k \mid f\ r_0\ r_1 \ldots r_n & \text{(right-hand side)} \end{array}$$

The sets of constructors, defined functions, and modules that occur in $p \in P$ are denoted by C_p, F_p, and M_p, respectively. For every $f \in F_p$, there is exactly one $m \in M_p$ such that f is defined in m. Then, f is also denoted by f_m. For every $f \in F_p^{(n+1)}$ and $c \in C_p^{(k)}$, there is exactly one equation of the form

$$f\ (c\, x_1 \ldots x_k)\ y_1 \ldots y_n = rhs_{p,f,c}$$

with $rhs_{p,f,c} \in RHS(f, C_p \cup F_p - \{f\}, X_k, Y_n)$, where for every $f \in F$, $C' \subseteq C \cup F$, and $k, n \in \mathbb{N}$, $RHS(f, C', X_k, Y_n)$ is the smallest set RHS satisfying:

- For every $i \in [k]$ and $r_1, \ldots, r_n \in RHS$: $(f\ x_i\ r_1 \ldots r_n) \in RHS$.
- For every $c \in C'^{(a)}$ and $r_1, \ldots, r_a \in RHS$: $(c\, r_1 \ldots r_a) \in RHS$.
- For every $j \in [n]$: $y_j \in RHS$. □

Note that, in addition to constructors, defined function symbols may also be contained in the second argument C' of RHS in the previous definition. The functions in C' may then be called with arbitrary arguments in right-hand sides, whereas in recursive calls of f, the recursion argument must be an x_i.

Example 2 Consider the programs p_{acc} and p_{non} from the introduction:

- $p_{acc} \in P$, where $M_{p_{acc}}$ contains one module $m_{acc,f}$ with the definition of f.
- $p_{non} \in P$, $M_{p_{non}}$ contains modules $m_{non,f'}, m_{non,sub}$ defining f' and sub. □

Now, we introduce the classes of tree transducers relevant for this paper. Since in our language every module defines exactly one function, to simplify the presentation we also project this restriction on tree transducers. In the literature, more general classes of *macro tree transducers* [8, 9] and *modular tree transducers* [10] are studied, which allow mutual recursion. Our transformation could also handle these classes. In contrast to the literature, we include an *initial call* r in the definition of tree transducers, which has the form of a right-hand side.

Definition 3 Let $p \in P$.

- A pair (m, r) with $m \in M_p$ and $r \in RHS(f_m, C_p, X_1, Y_0)$ is called a *one-state macro tree transducer of p* (for short *1-mtt* of p), if for every $c \in C_p^{(k)}$ we have $rhs_{p,f_m,c} \in RHS(f_m, C_p, X_k, Y_n)$, where $f_m \in F_p^{(n+1)}$.
  Thus, the function f_m from module m may call itself in a primitive-recursive way, but it does not call any functions from other modules. Moreover, the initial call r is a term built from f_m, constructors, and the variable x_1 as first argument of all subterms rooted with f_m.

- A triple (m_1, m_2, r) with $m_1, m_2 \in M_p$ is called *homomorphism-substitution modular tree transducer of p* (for short *hsmodtt* of p), if there are $n \in \mathbb{N}$ and pairwise distinct *substitution constructors* $\pi_1, \ldots, \pi_n \in C_p^{(0)}$, such that:
  1. $f_{m_1} \in F_p^{(1)}$ and $f_{m_2} = sub \in F_p^{(n+1)}$,
  2. for every $c \in C_p^{(k)}$ we have $rhs_{p,f_{m_1},c} \in RHS(f_{m_1}, C_p \cup \{sub\}, X_k, Y_0)$,
  3. m_2 contains the equations
     $$\begin{array}{lll} sub\ \pi_j & y_1 \ldots y_n = y_j\,, & \text{for every } j \in [n] \\ sub\ (c\ x_1 \ldots x_k) & y_1 \ldots y_n = c\ (sub\ x_1\ y_1 \ldots y_n) \ldots (sub\ x_k\ y_1 \ldots y_n)\,, & \\ & & \text{for every } c \in (C_p - \{\pi_1, \ldots, \pi_n\})^{(k)} \end{array}$$
  4. $r \in RHS(f_{m_1}, (C_p - \{\pi_1, \ldots, \pi_n\}) \cup \{sub\}, X_1, Y_0)$.

  Thus, the function from the module m_1 is unary. In its right-hand sides, it may call itself primitive-recursively and it may call the function *sub* from the module m_2 with arbitrary arguments. The function *sub* has the special form of a *substitution function*, where $(sub\ t\ s_1 \ldots s_n)$ replaces all occurrences of the substitution constructors $\pi_1, \ldots, \pi_n$ in t by $s_1, \ldots, s_n$, respectively. The initial call r is as for 1-mtts, but it may also contain *sub*, whereas the substitution constructors $\pi_1, \ldots, \pi_n$ may not appear in it.
- A 1-mtt (m, r) of p is called *nullary constructor disjoint* (for short *ncd*), if there are pairwise different nullary constructors $c_1, \ldots, c_n \in C_p^{(0)}$, such that $r = (f_m\ x_1\ c_1 \ldots c_n)$ and $c_1, \ldots, c_n$ do not occur in right-hand sides of m. An hsmodtt (m_1, m_2, r) of p is called *ncd*, if $r = (sub\ (f_{m_1}\ x_1)\ c_1 \ldots c_n)$ with pairwise different $c_1, \ldots, c_n \in C_p^{(0)} - \{\pi_1, \ldots, \pi_n\}$ that do not occur in right-hand sides of m_1.
- An hsmodtt (m_1, m_2, r) of p is *initial value free* (*ivf*), if $r = (f_{m_1}\ x_1)$. □

Example 4 (Ex. 2 continued)

- $(m_{acc,f}, r_{acc})$ with initial call $r_{acc} = (f\ x_1\ 0\ [\,])$ is a 1-mtt of p_{acc} that is ncd.
- Our transformation consists of the two steps "decomposition" and "constructor replacement". Decomposition transforms p_{acc} into the following program $p_{dec} \in P$, which contains the modules $m_{dec,f'}$ and $m_{dec,sub}$:

$$\begin{array}{lcl} f'\ (S\ x_1) & = & sub\ (f'\ x_1)\ (S\ (S\ \pi_1))\ (\pi_1 : \pi_2) \\ f'\ 0 & = & \pi_2 \end{array}$$

$$\begin{array}{llll} sub\ (x_1 : x_2)\ y_1\ y_2 = (sub\ x_1\ y_1\ y_2) : (sub\ x_2\ y_1\ y_2) & & sub\ [\,]\ y_1\ y_2 & = [\,] \\ sub\ (S\ x_1)\quad y_1\ y_2 = S\ (sub\ x_1\ y_1\ y_2) & & sub\ \pi_1\ y_1\ y_2 & = y_1 \\ sub\ 0 \qquad\quad y_1\ y_2 = 0 & & sub\ \pi_2\ y_1\ y_2 & = y_2 \end{array}$$

  Here, $(m_{dec,f'}, m_{dec,sub}, r_{dec})$ with the initial call $r_{dec} = (sub\ (f'\ x_1)\ 0\ [\,])$ is an hsmodtt of p_{dec} that is ncd, but not ivf.
- $(m_{non,f'}, m_{non,sub}, r_{non})$ with $r_{non} = (f'\ x_1)$ and the modules from the introduction is an hsmodtt of p_{non} that is ivf ($n = 2$, $\pi_1 = 0$, $\pi_2 = [\,]$). □

For every program $p \in P$, its evaluation is described by a (nondeterministic) reduction relation $\Rightarrow_p$ on $T_{C_p \cup F_p}$. As usual, $\Rightarrow_p^n$ and $\Rightarrow_p^*$ denote the n-fold composition and the transitive, reflexive closure of $\Rightarrow_p$, respectively. If $t \Rightarrow_p^* t'$ and there is no t'' such that $t' \Rightarrow_p t''$, then t' is called a *normal form of* t, which is denoted by $nf_p(t)$, if it exists and is unique. It can be proved in analogy to [10] that for every program $p \in P$, hsmodtt (m_1, m_2, r) of p (and 1-mtt (m, r) of p), and $t \in T_{\{f_{m_1}, f_{m_2}\} \cup C_p}$ (and $t \in T_{\{f_m\} \cup C_p}$, respectively), there exists a unique normal form $nf_p(t)$. In particular, for every $t \in T_{C_p}$ the normal form $nf_p(r[x_1/t])$ exists. The proof is based on the result that for every modtt and mtt the corresponding reduction relation is terminating and confluent. The normal form $nf_p(r[x_1/t])$ is called the *output tree* computed for the *input tree* t.

3 Deaccumulation

To improve verifiability we transform accumulative programs into non-accumulative programs by translating 1-mtts into hsmodtts. The defined functions of the resulting programs have no context arguments at all or they have context arguments that are not accumulating. Moreover, the resulting initial calls have no initial values in context argument positions. The transformation proceeds in two steps: "decomposition" (Sect. 3.1) and "constructor replacement" (Sect. 3.2).

3.1 Decomposition

In [8–10] it was shown that every mtt (with possibly several functions of arbitrary arity) can be decomposed into a *top-down tree transducer* (an mtt with unary functions only) plus a substitution device. In this paper, we use a modification of this result, integrating the constructions of Lemmata 21 and 23 of [19]. The key idea is to simulate an $(n+1)$-ary function f by a new unary function f'. To this end, all context arguments are deleted and only the recursion argument is maintained. Since f' does not know the current values of its context arguments, it uses a new constructor π_j, whenever f uses its j-th context argument. For this purpose, every occurrence of y_j in the right-hand sides of equations for f is replaced by π_j. The current context arguments themselves are integrated into the calculation by replacing every occurrence of the form $(f\ x_i \ldots)$ in a right-hand side or in the initial call by $(sub\ (f'\ x_i) \ldots)$. Here, the new function sub is a substitution function. As explained before, $(sub\ t\ s_1 \ldots s_n)$ replaces every π_j in the first argument t of sub by the j-th context argument s_j.

Lemma 5 For every $p \in P$ and 1-mtt (m, r) of p, there are $p' \in P$ and an hsmodtt (m_1, m_2, r') of p' such that for every $t \in T_{C_p}$: $nf_p(r[x_1/t]) = nf_{p'}(r'[x_1/t])$. Additionally, if (m, r) is ncd, then (m_1, m_2, r') is ncd, too.

Proof. We construct $p' \in P$ by adding modules m_1 and m_2 to p, and we construct r' from r. Let $n \in \mathbb{N}$, $f = f_m \in F_p^{(n+1)}$, $f' \in (F - F_p)^{(1)}$, $sub \in (F - F_p)^{(n+1)}$ with $sub \neq f'$, and pairwise distinct $\pi_1, \ldots, \pi_n \in (C - C_p)^{(0)}$.

1. For every $c \in C_p^{(k)}$ and for every equation $f\ (c\ x_1 \ldots x_k)\ y_1 \ldots y_n = rhs_{p,f,c}$ in m, the module m_1 contains $f'\ (c\ x_1 \ldots x_k) = \underline{dec}(rhs_{p,f,c})$, where $\underline{dec}$: $RHS(f, C_p, X_k, Y_n) \longrightarrow RHS(f', C_p \cup \{sub\} \cup \{\pi_1, \ldots, \pi_n\}, X_k, Y_0)$ with:

$$\begin{array}{ll} \underline{dec}(f\ x_i\ r_1 \ldots r_n) = sub\ (f'\ x_i)\ \underline{dec}(r_1) \ldots \underline{dec}(r_n)\,, & \\ \qquad \text{for all } i \in [k], r_1, \ldots, r_n \in RHS(f, C_p, X_k, Y_n) & \\ \underline{dec}(c'\ r_1 \ldots r_a) \quad = c'\ \underline{dec}(r_1) \ldots \underline{dec}(r_a)\,, & \\ \qquad \text{for all } c' \in C_p^{(a)}, r_1, \ldots, r_a \in RHS(f, C_p, X_k, Y_n) & \\ \underline{dec}(y_j) \qquad = \pi_j\,, \quad \text{for all } j \in [n] & \end{array}$$

For every $j \in [n]$, m_1 contains a dummy-equation $f'\ \pi_j = \pi_j$.

2. m_2 contains the equations

$$\begin{array}{lll} sub\ (c\ x_1 ... x_k)\ y_1 ... y_n = c\ (sub\ x_1\ y_1 ... y_n) ... (sub\ x_k\ y_1 ... y_n)\,, & \text{for all } c \in C_p^{(k)} \\ sub\ \pi_j \qquad y_1 ... y_n = y_j\,, & \text{for all } j \in [n] \end{array}$$

3. $r' = \underline{dec}(r)$.

Note that (m_1, m_2, r') is an hsmodtt of p'. Moreover, for every $t \in T_{C_p}$, we have $nf_p(r[x_1/t]) = nf_{p'}(r'[x_1/t])$. For the proof of this statement, the following statements $(*)$ and $(**)$ are proved by simultaneous induction (cf., e.g., [9, 11, 25]). For space reasons we omit this proof.
$(*)$ For every $t \in T_{C_p}$ and $s_1, \ldots, s_n \in T_{C_p \cup \{\pi_1, \ldots, \pi_n\}}$:
$nf_p(f\ t\ s_1 \ldots s_n) = nf_{p'}(sub\ (f'\ t)\ s_1 \ldots s_n)$.
$(**)$ For every $k \in \mathbb{N}$, $t_1, \ldots, t_k \in T_{C_p}$, $\bar{r} \in RHS(f, C_p, X_k, Y_n)$, and $s_1, \ldots, s_n \in T_{C_p \cup \{\pi_1, \ldots, \pi_n\}}$: $nf_p(\bar{r}[x_j/t_j][y_j/s_j]) = nf_{p'}(sub\ (\underline{dec}(\bar{r})[x_j/t_j])\ s_1 \ldots s_n)$.

Moreover, if (m, r) is ncd, then there are pairwise different $c_1, \ldots, c_n \in C_p^{(0)}$ such that $r = (f\ x_1\ c_1 \ldots c_n)$ and $c_1, \ldots, c_n$ do not occur in right-hand sides of m. Thus, $r' = (sub\ (f'\ x_1)\ c_1 \ldots c_n)$ and by the definition of $\underline{dec}$, $c_1, \ldots, c_n$ are not introduced into right-hand sides of m_1. Hence, (m_1, m_2, r') is ncd, too. □

Example 6 Decomposition translates the 1-mtt $(m_{acc,f}, r_{acc})$ of p_{acc} into the hsmodtt $(m_{dec,f'}, m_{dec,sub}, r_{dec})$ of p_{dec}, which are both ncd, cf. Ex. 4. □

However, we have not yet improved the automatic verifiability of programs:

Example 7 Let $(m_{dec,f'}, m_{dec,sub}, r_{dec})$ be the hsmodtt of p_{dec} created by decomposition and resume the proof attempt from the introduction. Since the initial call has changed from $(f\ x_1\ 0\ [\,])$ to $(sub\ (f'\ x_1)\ 0\ [\,])$, we have to prove $(sub\ (f'\ x_1)\ 0\ [\,]) = (q\ x_1)$ by induction. Again, the automatic proof fails, because in the induction step $(x_1 \mapsto (S\ x_1))$ the induction hypothesis cannot be successfully applied to prove $(sub\ (f'\ (S\ x_1))\ 0\ [\,]) = (q\ (S\ x_1))$. The problem is that the context arguments of $(sub\ (f'\ x_1)\ \underline{(S\ (S\ \pi_1))}\ \underline{(\pi_1 : \pi_2)})$, which originates as subterm from rule application to $(sub\ (f'\ (S\ x_1))\ 0\ [\,])$, do not fit to the context arguments of the term $(sub\ (f'\ x_1)\ \underline{0}\ \underline{[\,]})$ in the induction hypothesis. □

3.2 Constructor Replacement

We solve the above problem by avoiding applications of substitution functions (with specific context arguments like 0 and [] in Ex. 7) in initial calls. Since then an initial call consists only of a unary function, induction hypotheses can be applied without paying attention to context arguments. The idea, illustrated on Ex. 7, is to replace the substitution constructors π_1 and π_2 by 0 and [] from the initial call. Thus, the initial values of *sub*'s context arguments are encoded into the program and the substitution in the initial call becomes superfluous.

We restrict ourselves to 1-mtts that are ncd. Then, after decomposition, the initial calls have the form $(sub\ (f\ x_1)\ c_1 \ldots c_n)$, where $c_1, \ldots, c_n$ are pairwise different. Thus, when replacing each π_j by c_j, there is a unique correspondence between the nullary constructors $c_1, \ldots, c_n$ and the substitution constructors $\pi_1, \ldots, \pi_n$. In Ex. 10 we will demonstrate the problems with identical $c_1, \ldots, c_n$.

When replacing π_j by c_j, the constructors $c_1, \ldots, c_n$ now have two roles: If c_j occurs within a first argument of *sub*, then it acts like the former substitution constructor π_j, i.e., it will be substituted by the j-th context argument of *sub*. Thus, *sub* now has the defining equation $sub\ c_j\ y_1 \ldots y_n = y_j$. Only occurrences of c_j outside of *sub*'s first argument are left unchanged, i.e., here the constructor c_j stands for its original value. To make sure that there is no conflict between these two roles of c_j, we again need the ncd-condition. It ensures that originally, c_j did not occur in right-hand sides of f's definition. Then the only occurrence of c_j, which does not stand for the substitution constructor π_j, is as context argument of *sub* in the initial call. This substitution, however, can be omitted, because the call $(sub\ (f\ x_1)\ c_1 \ldots c_n)$ would now just mean to replace every c_j in $(f\ x_1)$ by c_j. In this way, the resulting hsmodtt is initial value free (ivf).

Lemma 8 Let $p \in P$ and (m_1, m_2, r) be an hsmodtt of p as constructed in the transformation of Lemma 5. Moreover, let (m_1, m_2, r) be ncd and $\pi_1, \ldots, \pi_n$ be its substitution constructors. Then, there are $p' \in P$ and an hsmodtt (m_1', m_2', r') of p' that is ivf, such that for all $t \in T_{C_p - \{\pi_1, \ldots, \pi_n\}}$: $nf_p(r[x_1/t]) = nf_{p'}(r'[x_1/t])$.

Proof. We construct $p' \in P$ by replacing m_1 and m_2 in p by modules m_1' and m_2', and we define r'. Let $f = f_{m_1} \in F_p^{(1)}$, $sub = f_{m_2} \in F_p^{(n+1)}$, and $c_1, \ldots, c_n \in C_p^{(0)} - \{\pi_1, \ldots, \pi_n\}$ be pairwise distinct, such that $r = (sub\ (f\ x_1)\ c_1 \ldots c_n)$ and $c_1, \ldots, c_n$ do not occur in right-hand sides of m_1. Let $C_{p'} = C_p - \{\pi_1, \ldots, \pi_n\}$.

1. For every $c \in C_{p'}^{(k)}$ and for every equation $f\ (c\ x_1 \ldots x_k) = rhs_{p,f,c}$ in m_1, the module m_1' contains $f\ (c\ x_1 \ldots x_k) = \underline{repl}(rhs_{p,f,c})$, where $\underline{repl}$: $RHS(f, (C_p - \{c_1, \ldots, c_n\}) \cup \{sub\}, X_k, Y_0) \to RHS(f, C_{p'} \cup \{sub\}, X_k, Y_0)$ replaces every occurrence of π_j by c_j, for all $j \in [n]$.
2. m_2' contains the equations

$$\begin{array}{lll} sub\ (c\, x_1 \ldots x_k)\ y_1 \ldots y_n = c\ (sub\ x_1\ y_1 \ldots y_n) \ldots (sub\ x_k\ y_1 \ldots y_n)\,, & & \\ & & \text{for all } c \in C_{p'}^{(k)} - \{c_1, \ldots, c_n\} \\ sub\ c_j \qquad\qquad y_1 \ldots y_n = y_j\,, & & \text{for all } j \in [n] \end{array}$$

3. $r' = f\ x_1$.

Note that (m_1', m_2', r') is an hsmodtt of p' that is ivf. For every $t \in T_{C_{p'}}$, we have $nf_p(r[x_1/t]) = nf_{p'}(r'[x_1/t])$. For the proof of this statement, the following statements $(*)$ and $(**)$ are proved by simultaneous induction. For space reasons we omit this proof.

(∗) For every $t \in T_{C_{p'}}$ and $s_1, \ldots, s_n \in T_{C_{p'}}$:
$nf_p(sub\ (f\ t)\ s_1 \ldots s_n) = nf_{p'}(sub\ (f\ t)\ s_1 \ldots s_n)$.
(∗∗) For every $k \in \mathbb{N}$, $t_1, \ldots, t_k \in T_{C_{p'}}$,
$\bar{r} \in RHS(f, (C_p - \{c_1, \ldots, c_n\}) \cup \{sub\}, X_k, Y_0)$, and $s_1, \ldots, s_n \in T_{C_{p'}}$:
$nf_p(sub\ (\bar{r}[x_j/t_j])\ s_1 \ldots s_n) = nf_{p'}(sub\ (\underline{repl}(\bar{r})[x_j/t_j])\ s_1 \ldots s_n)$. □

Example 9 Constructor replacement translates the ncd hsmodtt $(m_{dec,f'}, m_{dec,sub}, r_{dec})$ of p_{dec} into the ivf hsmodtt $(m_{non,f'}, m_{non,sub}, r_{non})$ of p_{non}. Essentially, all occurrences of π_1 and π_2 are replaced by 0 and [ ]. □

Now we demonstrate the problems with hsmodtts violating the condition ncd:

Example 10 Assume that p_{acc} and r_{acc} are changed into the following program:

$$\begin{aligned} f\ (S\ x_1)\ y_1\ y_2 &= f\ x_1\ (S\ (S\ y_1))\ (y_1 + y_2) \\ f\ 0\quad\ y_1\ y_2 &= y_2 \end{aligned}$$

and the initial call $(f\ x_1\ 0\ 0)$, computing the sum of the first x_1 even numbers. Now the same constructor 0 occurs in the initial values for both context arguments. Decomposition delivers the program[2]:

$$\begin{aligned} f'\ (S\ x_1) &= sub\ (f'\ x_1)\ (S\ (S\ \pi_1))\ (\pi_1 + \pi_2) \\ f'\ 0 &= \pi_2 \end{aligned}$$

$$\begin{aligned} sub\ (x_1 + x_2)\ y_1\ y_2 &= (sub\ x_1\ y_1\ y_2) + (sub\ x_2\ y_1\ y_2) & sub\ \pi_1\ y_1\ y_2 &= y_1 \\ sub\ (S\ x_1)\quad y_1\ y_2 &= S\ (sub\ x_1\ y_1\ y_2) & sub\ \pi_2\ y_1\ y_2 &= y_2 \\ sub\ 0\quad y_1\ y_2 &= 0 \end{aligned}$$

and initial call $(sub\ (f'\ x_1)\ 0\ 0)$. Constructor replacement would replace π_1 and π_2 by 0, which leads to different rules $sub\ 0\ y_1\ y_2 = y_1$ and $sub\ 0\ y_1\ y_2 = y_2$ with same left-hand side. In Sect. 5 we give an idea how to overcome this problem. □

We conclude this section with some statements about substitution functions which are often helpful for the verification of transformed programs (cf. the examples in Sect. 4 and App. A and B). Instead of proving these statements during verification, they should be generated during program transformation. This is possible because the substitution functions only depend on the set of constructors but not on the transformed function.

Lemma 11 Let $p \in P$ and (m_1, m_2, r) be an hsmodtt of p with substitution constructors $c_1, \ldots, c_n$ and substitution function *sub*.

1. A_{sub} (Associativity of *sub*). For every $t_0, t_1, ..., t_n, s_1, ..., s_n \in T_{C_p}$ we have $nf_p(sub\ (sub\ t_0\ t_1...t_n)\ s_1...s_n) = nf_p(sub\ t_0\ (sub\ t_1\ s_1...s_n)...(sub\ t_n\ s_1...s_n))$.
2. U_{sub} (Right Units of *sub*). For every $t \in T_{C_p}$ we have $nf_p(sub\ t\ c_1 \ldots c_n) = t$.
3. $+_{sub}$ (Addition by *sub*). If $n = 1$, $C_p = \{S, 0\}$, and $nf_p((S^{z_1}\ 0) + (S^{z_2}\ 0)) = S^{z_1+z_2}\ 0$ for all $z_1, z_2 \in \mathbb{N}$, then $nf_p(sub\ s\ t) = nf_p(s + t)$ for all $s, t \in T_{C_p}$.

Proof. The proofs are straightforward inductions on T_{C_p} and $\mathbb{N}$, respectively. □

[2] During the transformation, + is treated as an ordinary binary constructor.

4 Related Work

Program transformations are a well-established field in software engineering and compiler construction (see, e.g., [2, 6, 21, 22]). However, we suggested a novel application area for program transformations by applying them in order to increase *verifiability*. This goal is often in contrast to the classical aim of increasing efficiency, since a more efficient program is usually harder to verify. In particular, while *composition results* from the theory of tree transducers are usually applied in order to improve the efficiency of functional programs (cf., e.g., [18, 19, 24, 25]), we have demonstrated that also the corresponding *decomposition results* are not only of theoretical interest.

Program transformations that improve verifiability have rarely been investigated before. A first step into this direction was taken in [12]. There, two transformations were presented that can remove accumulators. They are based on the associativity and commutativity of auxiliary functions like + occurring in accumulator arguments. The advantage of the approach in [12] is that it does not require the strict syntactic restrictions of 1-mtts that are ncd. Moreover, [12] does not require that functions from other modules may not be called in right-hand sides. Because of that restriction, in the present paper, we have to treat all auxiliary functions like + as constructors and exclude the use of any information about these functions during the transformation.

On the other hand, the technique of [12] can essentially only remove *one* accumulator argument (e.g., in contrast to our method, it cannot eliminate both accumulators of p_{acc}). Moreover, the approach in [12] relies on knowledge about auxiliary functions like +. Hence, it is not applicable if the context of accumulator arguments on the right-hand side is not associative or commutative. Thus, it fails on examples like the following program p_{exp}. In particular, this demonstrates that in contrast to [12], our technique can also handle nested recursion. Indeed, deaccumulation is useful for functional programs in general — not just for functions resulting from translating imperative programs.

$$\begin{aligned} exp\ (S\ x_1)\ y_1 &= exp\ x_1\ (exp\ x_1\ y_1) \\ exp\ 0\ \quad\ \ y_1 &= S\ y_1 \end{aligned}$$

The initial call is $(exp\ x_1\ 0)$. We want to prove $(exp\ x_1\ 0) = (e\ x_1)$, where $(e\ (S^n\ 0))$ computes $(S^{2^n}\ 0)$, see below. Here, $(S^{z_1}\ 0) + (S^{z_2}\ 0)$ computes $S^{z_1+z_2}\ 0$.

$$\begin{aligned} e\ (S\ x_1) &= (e\ x_1)\ +\ (e\ x_1) \\ e\ 0 &= S\ 0 \end{aligned}$$

Since *exp* is a 1-mtt that is ncd, deaccumulation delivers the program:

$$\begin{aligned} exp'\ (S\ x_1) &= sub\ (exp'\ x_1)\ (sub\ (exp'\ x_1)\ 0) \qquad & sub\ (S\ x_1)\ y_1 &= S\ (sub\ x_1\ y_1) \\ exp'\ 0 &= S\ 0 & sub\ 0\ \quad\ y_1 &= y_1 \end{aligned}$$

and the initial call $(exp'\ x_1)$, which are better suited for induction provers, because there are no accumulating arguments anymore. For instance, instead of proving $(exp\ x_1\ 0) = (e\ x_1)$ for the original program (which requires a generalization), now the statement $(exp'\ x_1) = (e\ x_1)$ (taken as induction hypothesis IH) can be proved automatically. We only show the induction step $(x_1 \mapsto (S\ x_1))$.

$$\begin{array}{rcll} exp'\ (S\ x_1) & = & sub\ (exp'\ x_1)\ (sub\ (exp'\ x_1)\ 0) & \\ & = & sub\ (e\ x_1)\ (sub\ (e\ x_1)\ 0) & (2 * IH) \\ & = & sub\ (e\ x_1)\ (e\ x_1) & (U_{sub}) \\ & = & (e\ x_1)\ +\ (e\ x_1) & (+_{sub}) \\ & = & e\ (S\ x_1) & \end{array}$$

While in many examples generalizations can be avoided by our technique, it does not render generalization techniques superfluous. There exist accumulative functions where our transformation is not applicable, cf. Ex. 10[3], and even if it is applicable, there may still be conjectures that can only be proved via a suitable generalization. However, even then our transformation is advantageous, because the generalizations for the transformed functions are usually much easier than the ones required for the original accumulative functions (cf. App. A).

5 Conclusion and Future Work

Imperative programs and accumulative functional programs resulting from their translation are hard to verify with induction provers. Therefore, we introduced an automatic technique that transforms accumulative functions into non-accumulative functions, whose verification is often significantly easier with existing proof tools. However, it remains to characterize (at least informally) the class of verification problems, for which there is a real improvement.

To increase the applicability of our approach, we plan to extend it to more general forms of algorithms. For example, the requirement ncd should be weakened, such that examples with equal constructors in initial calls can be handled as well. The idea is to use different substitution functions such that at every node of a tree it can be read from the substitution function, how a nullary constructor has to be substituted. To this end, one must analyze the decomposed program prior to constructor replacement to find out which substitution constructors can occur in which contexts. For instance, in Ex. 10 it can be shown that π_1 can only occur in a left subtree of a $+$, whereas π_2 cannot occur in such positions. Thus, in the program after constructor replacement every occurrence of a 0 in a left subtree of a $+$ must be substituted by y_1, whereas all other occurrences must be substituted by y_2.

An extension beyond mtts seems to be possible as well. For example, the requirement of flat patterns on left-hand sides may be relaxed. Moreover, one could consider different constructor *terms* instead of nullary constructors in initial calls. Further extensions include a decomposition that only removes those context arguments from a function that are modified in recursive calls. Finally, we also investigate how to incorporate the transformations of [12] into our approach.

[3] Note that for this example, however, one can construct an equivalent non-accumulative program, cf. Sect. 5.

References

1. S. Autexier, D. Hutter, H. Mantel, and A. Schairer. Inka 5.0 - A logical voyager. In *Proc. CADE-16*, LNAI 1632, pages 207–211, 1999.
2. F. L. Bauer and H. Wössner. *Algorithmic Language and Program Development.* Springer-Verlag, 1982.
3. A. Bouhoula and M. Rusinowitch. Implicit induction in conditional theories. *Journal of Automated Reasoning*, 14:189–235, 1995.
4. R. S. Boyer and J S. Moore. *A Computational Logic.* Academic Press, 1979.
5. A. Bundy, A. Stevens, F. van Harmelen, A. Ireland, and A. Smaill. Rippling: A heuristic for guiding inductive proofs. *Artificial Intelligence*, 63:185–253, 1993.
6. R. M. Burstall and J. Darlington. A transformation system for developing recursive programs. *Journal of the ACM*, 24:44–67, 1977.
7. E. W. Dijkstra. Invariance and non-determinacy. In *Mathematical Logic and Programming Languages*, chapter 9, pages 157–165. Prentice-Hall, 1985.
8. J. Engelfriet. Some open questions and recent results on tree transducers and tree languages. In R. V. Book (ed.), *Formal language theory; perspectives and open problems*, pages 241–286. Academic Press, 1980.
9. J. Engelfriet and H. Vogler. Macro tree transducers. *JCSS*, 31:71–145, 1985.
10. J. Engelfriet and H. Vogler. Modular tree transducers. *TCS*, 78:267–304, 1991.
11. Z. Fülöp and H. Vogler. *Syntax-directed semantics — Formal models based on tree transducers.* Monographs in Theoretical Comp. Science, EATCS. Springer, 1998.
12. J. Giesl. Context-moving transformations for function verification. In *Proc. LOPSTR'99*, LNCS 1817, pages 293–312, 2000.
13. C. A. R. Hoare. An axiomatic basis for computer programming. *Communications of the ACM*, 12:576–583, 1969.
14. A. Ireland and A. Bundy. Automatic verification of functions with accumulating parameters. *Journal of Functional Programming*, 9:225–245, 1999.
15. A. Ireland and J. Stark. On the automatic discovery of loop invariants. In *4th NASA Langley Formal Methods Workshop*. NASA Conf. Publication 3356, 1997.
16. D. Kapur and H. Zhang. An overview of rewrite rule laboratory (RRL). *Journal of Computer and Mathematics with Applications*, 29:91–114, 1995.
17. M. Kaufmann, P. Manolios, and J. S. Moore. *Computer-Aided Reasoning: An Approach.* Kluwer, 2000.
18. A. Kühnemann. Benefits of tree transducers for optimizing functional programs. In *Proc. FST & TCS'98*, LNCS 1530, pages 146–157, 1998.
19. A. Kühnemann, R. Glück, K. Kakehi. Relating accumulative and non-accumulative functional programs. In *Proc. RTA'01*, LNCS 2051, pages 154–168, 2001.
20. J. McCarthy. Recursive functions of symbolic expressions and their computation by machine. *Communications of the ACM*, 3:184–195, 1960.
21. H. Partsch. *Specification and Transformation of Programs.* Springer-Verlag, 1990.
22. A. Pettorossi and M. Proietti. Rules and strategies for transforming functional and logic programs. *ACM Computing Surveys*, 28:360–414, 1996.
23. J. Stark and A. Ireland. Invariant discovery via failed proof attempts. In *Proc. LOPSTR'98*, LNCS 1559, pages 271–288, 1998.
24. J. Voigtländer. Conditions for efficiency improvement by tree transducer composition. In *Proc. RTA'02*, LNCS 2378, pages 222–236, 2002.
25. J. Voigtländer and A. Kühnemann. Composition of functions with accumulating parameters. To appear in *Journal of Functional Programming*, 2004.
26. C. Walther. Mathematical induction. In Gabbay, Hogger, Robinson (eds.), *Handbook of Logic in AI & Logic Prog., Vol. 2,* 127-228. Oxford University Press, 1994.

A Example: Splitting Monadic Trees

The program
$$\begin{aligned} split\ (A\ x_1)\ y_1 &= A\ (split\ x_1\ y_1)\\ split\ (B\ x_1)\ y_1 &= split\ x_1\ (B\ y_1)\\ split\ N\ \ \ \ \ \ y_1 &= y_1 \end{aligned}$$
with initial call $(split\ x_1\ N)$ translates monadic trees with n_1 and n_2 occurrences of the unary constructors A and B, respectively, into the tree $A^{n_1}(B^{n_2}N)$ by accumulating the B's in the context argument of *split*. It is transformed into:

$$\begin{aligned} split'\ (A\ x_1) &= A\ (sub\ (split'\ x_1)\ N) & sub\ (A\ x_1)\ y_1 &= A\ (sub\ x_1\ y_1)\\ split'\ (B\ x_1) &= sub\ (split'\ x_1)\ (B\ N) & sub\ (B\ x_1)\ y_1 &= B\ (sub\ x_1\ y_1)\\ split'\ N &= N & sub\ N\ \ \ \ \ \ y_1 &= y_1 \end{aligned}$$

with initial call $(split'\ x_1)$. If we want to prove the idempotence of the splitting operation, then the proof for the original program requires a generalization from $(split\ (split\ x_1\ N)\ N) = (split\ x_1\ N)$ to $(split\ (split\ x_1\ (b\ x_2))\ (b\ x_3)) = (split\ x_1\ (b\ (x_2 + x_3)))$, where $(b\ n)$ computes $(B^n\ N)$. Such a generalization is difficult to find. On the other hand, $(split'\ (split'\ x_1)) = (split'\ x_1)$ can be proved automatically. In the step case $(x_1 \mapsto (A\ x_1))$, U_{sub} from Lemma 11 is used to infer $(sub\ (split'\ x_1)\ N) = (split'\ x_1)$. In the step case $(x_1 \mapsto (B\ x_1))$, a straightforward generalization step is required by identifying two common subexpressions in a proof subgoal. More precisely, by applying the induction hypothesis, the induction conclusion is transformed into $(split'\ (sub\ \underline{(split'\ x_1)}\ (B\ N))) = (sub\ (split'\ \underline{(split'\ x_1)})\ (B\ N))$. Now, the two underlined occurrences of $(split'\ x_1)$ are generalized to a fresh variable x, and then the proof works by induction on x.

B Example: Reversing Monadic Trees

The program
$$\begin{aligned} rev\ (A\ x_1)\ y_1 &= rev\ x_1\ (A\ y_1)\\ rev\ (B\ x_1)\ y_1 &= rev\ x_1\ (B\ y_1)\\ rev\ N\ \ \ \ \ \ y_1 &= y_1 \end{aligned}$$
with initial call $(rev\ x_1\ N)$ is transformed into the program

$$\begin{aligned} rev'\ (A\ x_1) &= sub\ (rev'\ x_1)\ (A\ N) & sub\ (A\ x_1)\ y_1 &= A\ (sub\ x_1\ y_1)\\ rev'\ (B\ x_1) &= sub\ (rev'\ x_1)\ (B\ N) & sub\ (B\ x_1)\ y_1 &= B\ (sub\ x_1\ y_1)\\ rev'\ N &= N & sub\ N\ \ \ \ \ \ y_1 &= y_1 \end{aligned}$$

with initial call $(rev'\ x_1)$. Taking into account that *sub* is just the concatenation function on monadic trees, the above programs correspond to the efficient and the inefficient reverse function, which have linear and quadratic time-complexity in the size of the input tree, respectively. Thus, this example shows that the aim of our technique contrasts with the aim of classical program transformations, i.e., the efficiency is decreased, but the suitability for verification is improved: If we want to show that the reverse of two concatenated lists is the concatenation of the reversed lists in exchanged order, then the proof of $(rev\ (sub\ x_1\ x_2)\ N) = (sub\ (rev\ x_2\ N)\ (rev\ x_1\ N))$ again requires considerable generalization effort, whereas $(rev'\ (sub\ x_1\ x_2)) = (sub\ (rev'\ x_2)\ (rev'\ x_1))$ can be proved by a straightforward induction on x_1, exploiting U_{sub} and A_{sub} from Lemma 11.

Incentive Compatible Mechanism Based on Linear Pricing Scheme for Single-Minded Auction*

Ning Chen and Hong Zhu

Department of Computer Science, Fudan University, P. R. China
{nchen,hzhu}@fudan.edu.cn

Abstract. In this paper, we study incentive compatible mechanism based on linear pricing scheme for single-minded auction, a restricted case of combinatorial auction, in which each buyer desires a unique fixed bundle of various commodities, improving the previous works [1, 11, 13] on pricing bundles (*i.e.*, payments of buyers).

1 Introduction

With the rapid growth of electronic commerce, the interplay of several important economic concepts, such as Game Theory [16], General Equilibrium [6, 7], Mechanism Design [12, 16] and Auction Theory [10], and Computer Science [5, 15, 17] have become more and more intensive, extensive, and fruitful. The practice of electronic markets allows businesses, merchants and consumers of all types to conduct over the Internet at lightening fast speed across the globe. The extraordinary power of on-line trading systems in aggregating information of sellers and buyers makes it possible to conduct business in varieties of trading models that were only theoretical possibilities before the age of the Internet.

Model of Combinatorial Auction

Combinatorial auction [14, 4] is one such model that has been examined with increasing intensity in the recent years. Buyers entering combinatorial auction are usually assumed to have a function each over all subsets of the traded commodities, rating the different values of different subsets of different commodities to them. Two schemes for pricing the commodities are often used: one gives a price to each subset of commodities (*i.e.*, payment per buyer), and another to each type of commodities where the price of a subset is derived by the sum of prices of commodities in the subset (*i.e.*, price per commodity). In the former case, the pricing function is often required to be subadditive: $p(B \cup C) \leq p(B) + p(C)$. The latter is often referred to as the linear pricing model since $p(B \cup C) = p(B) + p(C)$ if B and C are disjoint.

* This work was supported by grants from China National Natural Science Fund [60273045], and the Ministry of Science and Technology [2001CCA03000].

V.A. Saraswat (Ed.): ASIAN 2003, LNCS 2896, pp. 161–172, 2003.

Even though the latter can be viewed as a special case of the former, in practice, it is more widely applicable. Combinatorial auction involves in sells of different types of commodities at one business transaction. In reality, it is rare that they would all be available with one owner. Normally, each commodity has its own independent market and linear pricing scheme for commodities will be a natural model under such circumstance. This will be the focus of our study.

One may argue that, by its very nature, combinatorial auction requires a pricing mechanism for a bundle of commodities. Non-linearity pricing is thus an inherent nature of the problem. We acknowledge that indeed such cases do exist. However, the linear pricing model for commodities is also a practically useful model. Very often commodities of a bundle cannot be purchased at once with one merchant and each has to be acquired at a market of its own. Though we may not rule out such possibilities in all cases, there are cases one may have a problem with anti-trust law as in the recent case of US vs. Microsoft involving in software packages. As another example, one may observe that travel packages including air-ticket, rooms and cars often get a discount from individual product providers (airlines, hotels, car-rental companies). Those products can be viewed as traded through a separate market (and are indeed so in that many airlines/hotels/car-rental companies set aside a block of their products for such deals). Therefore, the linear pricing model is at least as important as non-linear pricing model in combinatorial auction.

Single-Minded Auction

As a restricted case of combinatorial auction, *single-minded auction*, which specifies that each buyer only desires a fixed bundle of commodities, rather than all the possible combinations, has received more and more attentions recently. Lehmann et al. [11] first introduced the notion of single-minded auction. Mu'alem and Nisan [13] studied a set of techniques that allow designing efficiently computable incentive compatible mechanisms for single-minded auction. Further, Archer et al. [1] showed an incentive compatible mechanism by randomized rounding that achieves $(1+\varepsilon)$ approximation ratio to the value of optimal allocation. Note that in general, the optimal allocation problem (maximizing total valuations) is NP-hard [11]. In addition, Chen et al. [2] studied the complexity of the existence of Walrasian equilibrium in single-minded auction.

Note that all incentive compatible mechanisms previously designed are based on the payment per buyer, rather than the price per commodity. Therefore, in this paper, we follow their basic model of single-minded auction but focus on the linear pricing scheme.

First, we consider the problem that how to interpret the payments of buyers as the linear prices of commodities. Specifically, for the general optimal allocation algorithm and greedy allocation algorithms [13], we discuss the criteria that such interpretation exists or not. Secondly, We propose a mechanism that ensures incentive compatibility and sets price for each individual commodity. The price of a bundle thus follows as the sum of prices of commodities in the bundle. In addition, We compare the revenue generated by our mechanism to that generated by GPS (Greedy Payment Scheme) [11] and VCG mechanism [18, 3, 8], all are incentive compatible. And observe that the revenue generated by our mechanism is higher than or equal to the other two in all the cases originally discussed in [11]. Moreover, we demonstrate the problem of maximizing the revenue of the auctioneer for the case of regular price is NP-hard.

Outline of the Paper

In section 2, we briefly view the definitions of single-minded auction and the characterization of incentive compatible mechanisms proposed in [13]. Next, we discuss some criteria of the interpretation of buyers' payments as the linear price vector. In section 4, an incentive compatible mechanism based on linear pricing scheme is studied and revenue problem is considered. We conclude our work in section 5 with remarks and future directions.

2 Preliminaries

2.1 Single-Minded Auction

We consider the model that an auctioneer sells m heterogeneous commodities $\Omega = \{\omega_1, \ldots, \omega_m\}$, with unit quantity each, to n potential buyers $\mathcal{O} = \{\mathcal{O}_1, \ldots, \mathcal{O}_n\}$. Each buyer $\mathcal{O}_i$ has a privately known *valuation function* $v_i : 2^\Omega \to \mathbb{R}^+ \cup \{0\}$ that describes his true values over the various subsets of commodities. That is, for any $B \subseteq \Omega$, $v_i(B)$ is the maximal amount of money that $\mathcal{O}_i$ is willing to pay in order to win B. We say $\mathcal{O}_i$ is a *single-minded buyer* if there exists a *basic bundle* $\Omega_i = \{\omega_1^i, \ldots, \omega_{q_i}^i\} \subseteq \Omega$, where q_i is the number of various commodities in Ω_i, and a real $v_i^* > 0$ such that for each $B \subseteq \Omega$, $v_i(B) = v_i^*$ if $\Omega_i \subseteq B$ and $v_i(B) = 0$ otherwise. That is, basic bundle Ω_i is the core that $\mathcal{O}_i$ desires. In this paper, we assume that all buyers are restricted to be single-minded, and the auctioneer knows all the basic bundles Ω_i in advance (this assumption is just for the simplicity of our statements). We denote $\mathcal{A} = (\Omega; \Omega_1, v_1; \ldots; \Omega_n, v_n)$ as the *single-minded auction* [11].

We consider *direct revelation* auction mechanisms. That is, each buyer $\mathcal{O}_i$ submits a bid b_i to the auctioneer. Note that in single-minded auction, each buyer only needs to submit the value $b_i(\Omega_i)$ to the auctioneer. Unless stated otherwise, we denote v_i as the value $v_i(\Omega_i) = v_i^*$, and b_i as the value $b_i(\Omega_i)$ in the following discussions.

When receiving the bids $b = (b_1, \ldots, b_n)$ from all buyers, the auctioneer specifies the tuple $(X(b), P_X(b))$, in which

- $X(b) = (X_1, \ldots, X_n)$ is an *allocation* of Ω to all buyers, where X_i represents the collection of commodities allocated to $\mathcal{O}_i$, and $X_i \cap X_j = \emptyset$ for all $i \neq j$. Assume without loss of generality that $X_i = \emptyset$ or Ω_i.
- $P_X(b) = (P_1, \ldots, P_n)$ is the *payment* vector of all buyers, where P_i represents the payment that buyer $\mathcal{O}_i$ pays to the auctioneer.

Note that the payment vector P_X is also a function of the allocation X, which is changed in terms of different allocation algorithms. In this paper, we assume that P_X satisfies the following *voluntary participation* condition, given the allocation $X(b) = (X_1, \ldots, X_n)$,

- $P_i \leq b_i$, for all $X_i = \Omega_i$. (In this case, the *utility* of O_i is defined by $u_i(X_i, P_i) = v_i(X_i) - P_i$).
- $P_i = 0$, for all $X_i = \emptyset$. (In this case, the *utility* of O_i is zero).

Note that to maximize the utilities, buyers may not submit their valuations truthfully. The strategy is determined in terms of various mechanisms. We say an auction mechanism is *incentive compatible* (or *truthful*) if any buyer's utility is maximized by submitting his true valuation, *i.e.*, $b_i = v_i$, for $1 \leq i \leq n$.

2.2 Characterization of Incentive Compatible Mechanisms

Let b_{-i} denote the tuple $(b_1, \ldots, b_{i-1}, b_{i+1}, \ldots, b_n)$, and (b_{-i}, b_i) as $(b_1, \ldots, b_n)$. Given b_{-i}, if O_i wins his basic bundle Ω_i when bidding b_i, we say b_i is a *winning declaration* for O_i. Otherwise, we say b_i is a *losing declaration.*

Definition 1 *An allocation algorithm X is* monotone *if for any given bids b_{-i} and a winning declaration b_i, any higher declaration $b_i' > b_i$ still wins.*

Lemma 1 [13] *Let X be a monotone allocation algorithm. Then for any b_{-i}, there exists a single critical value $c_i(X, b_{-i}) \in \mathbb{R}^+$ such that for $\forall\ b_i > c_i(X, b_{-i})$, b_i is a winning declaration, and for $\forall\ b_i < c_i(X, b_{-i})$, b_i is a losing declaration.*

Definition 2 *The* critical payment *$P_X(b)$ associated with the monotone allocation algorithm X is defined by $P_i = c_i(X, b_{-i})$ if $X_i = \Omega_i$; and $P_i = 0$ otherwise.*

Lemma 2 *Critical payment $P_X(b)$ satisfies the volunteer participation condition.*

Proof. The case of $X_i = \emptyset$ follows from the definition of critical payment directly. As to the other part, $X_i = \Omega_i$, notice that buyer O_i wins his basic bundle, due to Lemma 1, we know that $b_i \geq c_i(X, b_{-i}) = P_i$. □

The most important property of monotone allocation algorithm and critical payment is the following theorem showed by Mu'alem and Nisan [13].

Theorem 1 [13] *A mechanism is incentive compatible if and only if its allocation algorithm is monotone and its payment is critical payment.*

In the rest of the paper, all our discussions are referred to monotone allocation algorithm associated with the critical payment. Therefore, all buyers bid their valuations truthfully, *i.e.*, $b_i = v_i$. Thus, for simplicity, the submitted bid of each buyer is also denoted by v_i, $i = 1, \ldots, n$.

3 Interpretation of Payments as Prices

Mu'alem and Nisan [13] studied a set of techniques on the basis of Theorem 1 to design efficiently computable incentive compatible mechanisms for single-minded auction. Their mechanisms, however, are all based on the payment per buyer, rather than the price per commodity. The following example demonstrates this point clearly.

Example 1 Three buyers bid for two commodities with basic bundles $\{\omega_1\}$, $\{\omega_1, \omega_2\}$, $\{\omega_2\}$ at valuations $8, 10, 8$ respectively. According to the Greedy Allocation Algorithm based on the value ranking [13] (which we will discuss in detail following), buyer $\mathcal{O}_2$ wins at critical value 8. Unfortunately, in this setting, there do not exist the prices of commodities to support the above allocation. That is, no price vector $(p(\omega_1), p(\omega_2))$ satisfies inequalities $p(\omega_1) \geq 8$, $p(\omega_1)+p(\omega_2) \leq 10$, and $p(\omega_2) \geq 8$ simultaneously.

Therefore, we are interested in how to interpret the payments of buyers as the prices of commodities. Specifically, the interpreted price vector $p = (p(\omega_1), \ldots, p(\omega_m))$ should satisfy the following *linear pricing scheme*, given the allocation $X(b) = (X_1, \ldots, X_n)$ and payment $P_X(b) = (P_1, \ldots, P_n)$,

- $p(BC) = p(B) + p(C)$, for any $B, C \subseteq \Omega$, $B \cap C = \emptyset$, *i.e.*, the price of commodity is linear.
- $p(\Omega_i) = P_i$, for all $X_i = \Omega_i$.
- $p(\Omega_i) \geq b_i$ (*i.e.*, v_i), for all $X_i = \emptyset$.

Note that the first condition above implies that $p(\emptyset) = 0$. Essentially, linear pricing scheme specifies that for any winner, his payment is equal to the corresponding bundle's price. Whereas for all losers, the reason that they do not win their basic bundles is due to the high prices.

Definition 3 *Given allocation $X(b) = (X_1, \ldots, X_n)$ and payment $P_X(b) = (P_1, \ldots, P_n)$, we say $P_X(b)$ can be* interpreted *as the prices of commodities if there exists vector $p = (p(\omega_1), \ldots, p(\omega_m))$ that satisfies the above linear pricing scheme.*

Example 1 shows that not all payments can be interpreted as the price, even it's critical payment. In addition, as we will see following, the property of the interpretation of payments is also determined in terms of different allocation algorithms.

3.1 Optimal Allocation

In this subsection, we consider the *optimal allocation* algorithm OPT, that is, the algorithm outputs an allocation X^* with maximal total valuations. Note that there may be several various allocations achieve the same maximal value. Following we consider the fixed one that OPT outputs, *i.e.*,

$$X^* \in \arg\max_X \sum_{i=1}^{n} v_i(X_i) .$$

It's easy to see that OPT is a monotone allocation algorithm. Let $X_0^* = \Omega - \bigcup_{i=1}^n X_i^*$ be the collection of commodities that are not allocated to buyers. Let $\mathcal{O}' = \{\mathcal{O}_i \mid X_i = \Omega_i\}$ be the collection of winners, and $\mathcal{O}'' = \{\mathcal{O}_i \mid X_i = \emptyset\}$ be the collection of losers.

Lemma 3 *If for any $\mathcal{O}_i \in \mathcal{O}''$, $\Omega_i \cap X_0^* \neq \emptyset$, then the critical payment $P_{OPT} = (P_1, \ldots, P_n)$ can be interpreted as the price $p = (p(\omega_1), \ldots, p(\omega_m))$.*

Proof. Note that for any $\mathcal{O}_i, \mathcal{O}_{i'} \in \mathcal{O}'$, we must have $\Omega_i \cap \Omega_{i'} = \emptyset$. Therefore, for all $\mathcal{O}_i \in \mathcal{O}'$, we may define $p(\omega_1^i) = P_i$, and $p(\omega_j^i) = 0$, $j = 2, \ldots, q_i$. For any $\mathcal{O}_i \in \mathcal{O}''$, we know that there exists a commodity $\omega_j \in \Omega_i \cap X_0^*$ that has not been set price yet. Therefore we may define a sufficiently large price to ω_j such that $p(\omega_j) \geq v_i$. Note that if there exists another buyer $\mathcal{O}_{i'} \in \mathcal{O}''$ such that $\omega_j \in \Omega_{i'} \cap X_0^*$, then the defined price of ω_j should satisfy $p(\omega_j) \geq \max\{v_i, v_{i'}\}$. Other commodities' prices are determined arbitrarily. It's easy to see that the prices defined above satisfy all the requirements of the linear pricing scheme. Hence the lemma follows. □

Following, we consider the problem of interpretation from the point of the view of Walrasian equilibrium. Intuitively, Walrasian equilibrium specifies the allocation and price vector such that any remained commodity is priced at zero and all buyers are satisfied with their corresponding allocations under the fixed price vector. Formally,

Definition 4 (Walrasian Equilibrium) *A* Walrasian equilibrium *of single-minded auction $\mathcal{A}$ is a tuple (X, p), where X is an allocation, $p \geq 0$ is a linear price vector of all commodities, such that (i) $p(\Omega \backslash (\bigcup_{i=1}^n X_i)) = 0$, (ii) for any $\mathcal{O}_i$, $u_i(X_i, p(X_i)) \geq u_i(B, p(B))$ for all bundle $B \subseteq \Omega$.*

From the conclusion of [9], we know that the allocation X in Walrasian equilibrium must be an optimal allocation.

Lemma 4 *For any single-minded auction $A = (\Omega; \Omega_1, v_1; \ldots; \Omega_n, v_n)$, if the Walrasian equilibrium (X^*, p) exists and $v_i = c_i(X^*, v_{-i})$ for all $\mathcal{O}_i \in \mathcal{O}'$, then the critical payment can be interpreted as the price.*

Proof. For any $\mathcal{O}_i \in \mathcal{O}''$, from the definition of Walrasian equilibrium, we know that $p(\Omega_i) \geq v_i$. Otherwise, $\mathcal{O}_i$ should be allocated with Ω_i to get more utilities. For any winner $\mathcal{O}_i \in \mathcal{O}'$, we have $p(\Omega_i) \leq v_i = c_i(X^*, v_{-i}) = P_i$. Hence we may increase the price of any commodity in Ω_i such that $p(\Omega_i) = P_i$, which complies with the requirements of linear pricing scheme. In addition, note that $\Omega_i \cap \Omega_{i'} = \emptyset$ for any $\mathcal{O}_i, \mathcal{O}_{i'} \in \mathcal{O}'$, therefore such increased price vector always exists. Hence the lemma follows. □

We stress that in the above lemma, both conditions (*i.e.*, the existence of Walrasian equilibrium and $v_i = c_i(X^*, v_{-i})$) are necessary to maintain the property of interpretation. For example, if we remove the second condition, as shown in Example 1, there exists Walrasian equilibrium (X^*, p), where $X^* = (\{\omega_1\}, \emptyset, \{\omega_2\})$ and $p = (5, 5)$, but we can not interpret the critical payment $P_1 = P_2 = 2$, which is associated with the optimal allocation X^*, as the price. Removing the first condition is similar, let's look at the following example.

Example 2 There are six buyers bid for three commodities. Buyer $\mathcal{O}_1, \mathcal{O}_2, \mathcal{O}_3$ are interested in $\{\omega_1, \omega_2\}$, $\{\omega_2, \omega_3\}$, $\{\omega_3, \omega_1\}$ respectively at valuation 3 each. The other three buyers desire for $\{\omega_1\}$, $\{\omega_2\}$, $\{\omega_3\}$ respectively at valuation 1 each.

In this example, the Walrasian equilibrium does not exist, and all buyers indeed bid their critical payments. However, we can not interpret the critical payment 3, 1 of winners as the prices of commodities.

3.2 Greedy Allocation Algorithms

In the greedy allocation algorithms, the bids of buyers are first reordered according to some monotone ranking criteria, then the commodities are allocated greedily.

Definition 5 *A* ranking r *is a collection of* n *real valued continuous functions* $(r_1, \ldots, r_n)$*, where* $r_i = r_i(v_i, \Omega_i)$ *satisfies* $r_i(0, \Omega_i) = 0$ *and* $r_i(\infty, \Omega_i) = \infty$*. A ranking is* monotone *if each* r_i *is non-decreasing in* v_i*.*

There are a number of ways to define the monotone ranking function r, for example [11, 13], the value ranking $r_i(v_i, \Omega_i) = v_i$, and the density ranking $r_i(v_i, \Omega_i) = \frac{v_i}{|\Omega_i|}$.

Greedy Allocation Algorithm based on monotone ranking r [13]

1. $Winners \leftarrow \emptyset$, $AvailComm \leftarrow \Omega$.
2. Reorder the bids by non-increasing value of $r_i(v_i, \Omega_i)$.
3. For $i = 1, \ldots, n$ (in the new order, ties are broken arbitrarily) if $\Omega_i \subseteq AvailComm$, then
   (i). $Winners \leftarrow Winners \cup \{\mathcal{O}_i\}$.
   (ii). $AvailComm \leftarrow AvailComm - \Omega_i$.
4. Return $Winners$.

Lemma 5 [13] *Any Greedy Allocation Algorithm based on monotone ranking* r *is monotone.*

Theorem 2 *For any Greedy Allocation Algorithm based on monotone ranking* r*, the critical payment can not be interpreted as the price.*

Proof. Our proof is constructive, that is, we show an instance of auction that such interpretation does not exist. Consider a fixed buyer $\mathcal{O}_0$ with basic bundle Ω_0, $|\Omega_0| > 1$, and sufficiently large valuation v_0. Let $k = |\Omega_0|$ and $\Omega_0 = \{\omega_{0_1}, \ldots, \omega_{0_k}\}$. We add another $2k$ buyers $\mathcal{O}_1, \ldots, \mathcal{O}_k, \mathcal{O}_{1'}, \ldots, \mathcal{O}_{k'}$ and k commodities $\omega_1, \ldots, \omega_k$. That is,

$$\mathcal{O} = \{\mathcal{O}_0, \mathcal{O}_1, \ldots, \mathcal{O}_k, \mathcal{O}_{1'}, \ldots, \mathcal{O}_{k'}\} ,$$
$$\Omega = \{\omega_{0_1}, \ldots, \omega_{0_k}, \omega_1, \ldots, \omega_k\} .$$

Let $\widetilde{\mathcal{O}} = \{\mathcal{O}_1, \ldots, \mathcal{O}_k\}$. For any $\mathcal{O}_i \in \widetilde{\mathcal{O}}$, define the basic bundle $\Omega_i = \{\omega_{0_i}, \omega_i\}$, and the valuation $v_i = \frac{v_0}{k} + 1$. For buyer $\mathcal{O}_{i'}$, $1 \le i \le k$, define $\Omega_{i'} = \{\omega_i\}$, and $v_{i'} = \varepsilon$, where $0 < \varepsilon < 1$ is a sufficiently small real, such that $r_{i'}(\varepsilon, \Omega_{i'}) < r_i(v_i, \Omega_i)$ for all $1 \le i \le k$. Due to Definition 5, note that such real ε always exists.

Assume to the contrary, that in the above constructed instance, there exists price vector $p = (p(\omega_{0_1}), \ldots, p(\omega_{0_k}), p(\omega_1), \ldots, p(\omega_k))$ that can be interpreted from the critical payment $P = (P_0, P_1, \ldots, P_k, P_{1'}, \ldots, P_{k'})$. Following we consider the relations of rankings $r_0, r_1, \ldots, r_k$ of buyers $\mathcal{O}_0, \mathcal{O}_1, \ldots, \mathcal{O}_k$ respectively.

Case 1. $\mathcal{O}_0$ wins, *i.e.*, $r_0 \geq r_i$ for all $i = 1, \ldots, k$. In this setting, according to the greedy allocation algorithm, $\mathcal{O}_0, \mathcal{O}_{1'}, \ldots, \mathcal{O}_{k'}$ get their basic bundles. From the requirements of the linear pricing scheme, we must have $p(\Omega_i) \geq v_i$ for all $1 \leq i \leq k$. Note that $\Omega = \bigcup_{i=1}^k \Omega_i$, therefore,

$$p(\Omega) = \sum_{i=1}^{k} p(\Omega_i) \geq \sum_{i=1}^{k} v_i = k \cdot (\frac{v_0}{k} + 1) = v_0 + k \ . \tag{1}$$

On the other hand, since all commodities are sold to buyers $\mathcal{O}_0, \mathcal{O}_{1'}, \ldots, \mathcal{O}_{k'}$, we have

$$p(\Omega) = p(\Omega_0) + \sum_{i=1}^{k} p(\Omega_{i'}) = P_0 + \sum_{i=1}^{k} P_{i'} \leq v_0 + k\varepsilon \ , \tag{2}$$

which contradicts to (1).

Case 2. At least one of $\mathcal{O}_1, \ldots, \mathcal{O}_k$ wins, *i.e.*, there exists l, $1 \leq l \leq k$, such that $r_l \geq r_0$. Hence, $\mathcal{O}_1, \ldots, \mathcal{O}_k$ win, and $\mathcal{O}_0$ does not get his basic bundle Ω_0. Therefore, we have

$$p(\Omega_0) \geq v_0 \ . \tag{3}$$

For any $\mathcal{O}_i \in \widetilde{\mathcal{O}}$, $i \neq l$, due to the property of the monotone ranking function r, we know that there exists sufficiently small real $\varepsilon_i > 0$ such that $r_i(\varepsilon_i, \Omega_i) = r_{i'}(\varepsilon, \Omega_{i'})$, which implies that ε_i is the critical payment of $\mathcal{O}_i$, *i.e.*, $P_i = \varepsilon_i$. Let $\delta = \max\{\varepsilon_1, \ldots, \varepsilon_{l-1}, \varepsilon_{l+1}, \ldots, \varepsilon_k\}$. Trivially, δ is still a sufficiently small real. Therefore, we have

$$p(\Omega_0) \leq p(\Omega) = P_l + \sum_{i \neq l} P_i \leq \frac{v_0}{k} + 1 + (k-1)\delta < v_0 \ , \tag{4}$$

where the last inequality is due to the sufficiently large value of v_0. A contradiction. □

4 Incentive Compatible Mechanism Based on Prices

In this section, we propose an incentive compatible mechanism whose critical payment can be interpreted as the price.

4.1 Greedy Allocation Algorithm Based on Cost Ranking

First, we assume that for each commodity ω_j, there is a positive real $d(\omega_j)$, the *cost* of ω_j to the auctioneer. Let $d(\omega_j) = e \cdot d_j$, $j = 1, \ldots, m$, where e is the greatest common divisor of $d(\omega_1), \ldots, d(\omega_m)$. Similar as the price vector, here we assume the cost of commodity is linear, *i.e.*, $d(BC) = d(B) + d(C)$, for any $B, C \subseteq \Omega$, $B \cap C = \emptyset$.

For each buyer $\mathcal{O}_i$, we *divide* his submitted bid v_i according to the proportion of the costs of commodities $\omega_1^i, \ldots \omega_{q_i}^i$. That is, the "bid" of ω_j^i is calculated in terms of:

$$v_i(\omega_j^i) = v_i \cdot \frac{d(\omega_j^i)}{d(\omega_1^i) + \cdots + d(\omega_{q_i}^i)}, \; j = 1, \ldots, q_i \; . \tag{5}$$

It's easy to see that $v_i = v_i(\omega_1^i) + \cdots + v_i(\omega_{q_i}^i)$. The following example shows this process clearly.

Example 3 In the following figure, there are three buyers bid for three commodities with basic bundle $\{\omega_3\}, \{\omega_1, \omega_2\}, \{\omega_2\}$ at value 15, 24, 14 respectively. For instance, the bid of buyer $\mathcal{O}_2$ is divided as follows: since $d(\omega_1)/d(\omega_2) = 2/4$, one third of the bid 24 is divided to ω_1, and others are divided to ω_2, *i.e.*, $b_2(\omega_1) = 8$, $b_2(\omega_2) = 16$, which is demonstrated in the middle table of the figure. The bids of other buyers are divided similarly.

	w_1	w_2	w_3	Submitted Bid
Cost	2e	4e	3e	
Buyer 1			+	15
Buyer 2	+	+		24
Buyer 3		+		14

→

	w_1	w_2	w_3
Cost	2e	4e	3e
Buyer 1			15
Buyer 2	8	16	
Buyer 3		14	

→

	Ranking
Cost	1e
Buyer 1	5
Buyer 2	4
Buyer 3	3.5

Fig. 1. Dividing Process & Cost Ranking

After dividing the submitted bids for all buyers, the auctioneer adds another virtual commodity ω_0 with cost 1e, and computes the "bid" $v_i(\omega_0)$ in terms of

$$v_i(\omega_0) = v_i \cdot \frac{e}{d(\omega_1^i) + \cdots + d(\omega_{q_i}^i)}, \; i = 1, \ldots, n \; . \tag{6}$$

Let *cost ranking* function $r_i = r_i(v_i, \Omega_i) = v_i(\omega_0)$. In Example 3, the cost rankings of buyers are showed in the right table of Figure 1.

The basic idea of the mechanism is from Vickrey auction [18], following we describe it in detail.

Greedy Allocation Algorithm based on cost ranking:

1. $Winners \leftarrow \emptyset$, $AvailComm \leftarrow \Omega$.
2. For $i = 1, \ldots, n$
   divide bid v_i, and compute the cost ranking r_i.
3. Sorting all rankings (wlog., assume $r_1 \geq \cdots \geq r_n \geq 1$).
4. For $i = 1, \ldots, n$
   if $\Omega_i \subseteq AvailComm$, then
   (i). $Winners \leftarrow Winners \cup \{\mathcal{O}_i\}$.
   (ii). $AvailComm \leftarrow AvailComm - \Omega_i$.
   else, stop and goto to the next step.
5. Return $Winners$.

According to the mechanism above, in Example 3, $\mathcal{O}_1, \mathcal{O}_2$ get their basic bundles with critical payment $P_1 = 10.5, P_2 = 21, P_3 = 0$, which can be interpreted as the price $p(\omega_1) = 7$, $p(\omega_2) = 14$, and $p(\omega_3) = 10.5$.

Lemma 6 *The above Greedy Allocation Algorithm based on cost ranking is monotone.*

Proof. Note that the costs of all commodities are fixed, and according to (6), we know that $r_i(v'_i, \Omega_i) > r_i(v_i, \Omega_i)$ for any $v'_i > v_i$. That is, the cost ranking is monotone. Therefore, if v_i is a winning declaration, given other buyers' bids v_{-i}, v'_i is also a winning declaration for $\mathcal{O}_i$. □

Lemma 7 *The critical payment associated with the Greedy Allocation Algorithm based on cost ranking can be interpreted as the price.*

Proof. Note that according to the algorithm, we have

$$r_1(v_1, \Omega_1) \geq r_2(v_2, \Omega_2) \geq \cdots \geq r_n(v_n, \Omega_n) \geq 1 .$$

First, we consider the case that buyers $\mathcal{O}_1, \ldots, \mathcal{O}_l$ win their basic bundles, where $1 \leq l < n$. For each $\omega_j \in \Omega$, define $p(\omega_j) = r_{l+1} \cdot d_j$.

Due to the critical payment scheme and the mechanism, for each $1 \leq i \leq l$, we know that $r_i(v_i, \Omega_i) \geq r_i(P_i, \Omega_i) = r_{l+1}$, where P_i is the critical payment of buyer $\mathcal{O}_i$, which implies that

$$r_{l+1} = P_i \cdot \frac{e}{d(\omega_1^i) + \cdots + d(\omega_{q_i}^i)} .$$

Therefore,

$$P_i = r_{l+1} \cdot \left(\frac{d(\omega_1^i)}{e} + \cdots + \frac{d(\omega_{q_i}^i)}{e} \right) = p(\omega_1^i) + \cdots + p(\omega_{q_i}^i) = p(\Omega_i) .$$

For any loser $\mathcal{O}_i$, $l < i \leq n$, we know that $r_i(v_i, \Omega_i) \leq r_{l+1}$, *i.e.*,

$$r_{l+1} \geq v_i \cdot \frac{e}{d(\omega_1^i) + \cdots + d(\omega_{q_i}^i)} .$$

Therefore,

$$v_i \leq r_{l+1} \cdot \left(\frac{d(\omega_1^i)}{e} + \cdots + \frac{d(\omega_{q_i}^i)}{e} \right) = p(\omega_1^i) + \cdots + p(\omega_{q_i}^i) = p(\Omega_i) .$$

That is, the linear pricing scheme holds.

As to the case $l = n$, *i.e.*, all buyers win the basic bundles, we may define the price of each commodity to be its cost, *i.e.*, $p(\omega_j) = d(\omega_j)$. Hence, the critical payment of each buyer is the cost of the corresponding basic bundle.

From the above arguments, we know that such price vector, complying with the linear pricing scheme, that can be interpreted from the critical payment indeed exists. □

From the above two lemmas and Theorem 1, we have the following conclusion.

Theorem 3 *The Greedy Allocation Algorithm based on cost ranking associated with the critical payment is incentive compatible mechanism, and the payment can be interpreted as the price.*

4.2 Revenue Consideration

In the following we consider the *revenue*, $r = \sum_{i=1}^{n} P_i$, that the auctioneer receives. Note that for our mechanism showed in the above subsection, $r = \sum_{i=1}^{n} P_i = \sum_{i=1}^{n} p(X_i)$. In Example 3, $r = 31.5$, according to our mechanism. Greedy Payment Scheme (GPS) [11] will allocate $\{\omega_2\}$ to $\mathcal{O}_3$ at payment 12 and $\{\omega_3\}$ to $\mathcal{O}_1$ at payment zero, hence $r = 12$. In addition, in VCG mechanism [18, 3, 8], $\mathcal{O}_1$ pays zero for $\{\omega_3\}$ and $\mathcal{O}_2$ pays 14 for bundle $\{\omega_1, \omega_2\}$, thus $r = 14$. Let's look at another example following.

Example 4 Assume there are three buyers and four commodities $\{\omega_1, \omega_2, \omega_3, \omega_4\}$. $\mathcal{O}_1$ desires bundle $\{\omega_1, \omega_2\}$ at 20, $\mathcal{O}_2$ is interested in $\{\omega_3\}$ at 8, and $\mathcal{O}_3$ desires $\{\omega_1, \omega_4\}$ at 12. Assume the cost of each commodity is constant one. Our mechanism allocates $\{\omega_1, \omega_2\}$ to $\mathcal{O}_1$ and $\{\omega_3\}$ to $\mathcal{O}_2$ at price 6 for each commodity, hence $r = 18$. The allocation under GPS and VCG is same as above, with the revenue $r = 12$ and $r = 4$ respectively.

Note that the price generated by our mechanism has the *regular* property $p(\omega_1) : \cdots : p(\omega_n) = d(\omega_1) : \cdots : d(\omega_n)$. As we will see following, if we do not consider the utilities of buyers, even under this restriction, the problem of maximizing the revenue of the auctioneer in single-minded auction is NP-hard.

Definition 6 (Maximal Revenue Problem) *Given constant $k > 0$ and single-minded auction, does there exist regular price vector and trading buyers such that the revenue of the auctioneer is at least k.*

Theorem 4 *Maximal Revenue Problem is NP-hard.*

Proof. We reduce from EXACT COVER problem: Given a finite set $N = \{1, \ldots, m\}$ and a family of subsets $S = \{s_1, \ldots, s_n\}$ of N, we are asked that whether there exists a subset $S' \subseteq S$, such that every element of N lies in exactly one element of S'?

We construct the following instance of single-minded auction, in which there are m commodities and n buyers. Let $j \in N$ corresponds to commodity ω_j with unit cost each. For any $s_i \subseteq S$, we denote s_i as the basic bundle of buyer $\mathcal{O}_i$, with valuation $v_i(s_i) = \frac{k}{n} \cdot |s_i|$, where $k > 0$ is any constant. Therefore it's easy to see that there exists a subset $S' \subseteq S$ such that every element of N lies in exactly one element of S' if and only if there exist a subset of buyers $\mathcal{O}' \subseteq \mathcal{O}$ such that every commodity is sold to exactly one buyer in $\mathcal{O}'$ and all commodities are sold out, and equivalently, the auctioneer has revenue $r = \frac{k}{n} \cdot \sum_{\mathcal{O}_i \in W'} |s_i| = k$. □

5 Conclusion and Further Research

In this paper, We study incentive compatible mechanism for the model of single-minded auction, a restricted case of combinatorial auction. Our work is focused on the interpretation of payments of buyers as the prices of commodities, and the design of incentive compatible mechanism based on linear pricing scheme. We believe that our work is an important step in the quest for incentive compatible mechanisms based on linear pricing scheme in the general combinatorial auctions.

Acknowledgements

We thank Xiaotie Deng for helpful discussions for this paper. We also thank the anonymous reviewers for their suggestions for improving this paper.

References

1. A. Archer, C. H. Papadimitriou, K. Talwar, Eva Tardos, *An Approximate Truthful Mechanism for Combinatorial Auctions with Single Parameter Agents*, SODA 2003, 205-214.
2. Ning Chen, Xiaotie Deng, Hong Zhu, *Combinatorial Auction across Independent Markets*, ACM Conference on E-Commerce (EC), 206-207, 2003.
3. E. H. Clarke, *Multipart Pricing of Public Goods*, Public Choice, 11:17-33, 1971.
4. Sven de Vries, R. Vohra, *Combinatorial Auctions: A Survry*, INFORMS Journal on Computing, forthcoming.
5. Xiaotie Deng, T. Ibaraki, H. Nagamochi, *Combinatorial Optimization Games*, SODA 1997, 720-729.
6. Xiaotie Deng, C. H. Papadimitriou, S. Safra, *On the Complexity of Equilibria*, STOC 2002, 67-71.
7. N. Devanur, C. H. Papadimitriou, A. Saberi, V. Vazirani, *Market Equilibrium via a Primal-Dual-Type Algorithm*, FOCS, 2002, 389-395.
8. T. Groves, *Incentives in Teams*, Econometrica, 41:617-631, 1973.
9. F. Gul, E. Stacchetti, *Walrasian Equilibrium with Gross Substitutes*, Journal of Economic Theory, 87:95-124, 1999.
10. P. Klemperer, *Auction Theory: A guide to the Literature*, Journal of economics Surveys, 13(3):227-286, 1999.
11. D. Lehmann, L. I. O'Callaghan, Y. Shoham, *Truth Revelation in Approximately Efficient Combinatorial Auctions*, ACM Conference on E-Commerce (EC), 96-102, 1999. Full version appeared in JACM, 49(5):577-602, 2002.
12. A. Mas-Collel, W. Whinston, J. Green, *Microeconomic Theory*, Oxford University Press, 1995.
13. A. Mu'alem, N. Nisan, *Truthful Approximation Mechanisms for Restricted Combinatorial Auctions*, AAAI 2002, 379-384.
14. N. Nisan, *Bidding and Allocation in Combinatorial Auctions*, ACM Conference on E-Commerce (EC), 1-12, 2000.
15. N. Nisan, A. Ronen, *Algorithmic Mechanism Design (Extended Abstract)*, STOC 1999, 129-140. Full version appeared in Games and Economic Behavior, 35:166-196, 2001.
16. M. J. Osborne, A. Rubistein, *A Course in Game Theory*, MIT Press, 1994.
17. C. H. Papadimitriou, *Algorithms, Games, and the Internet*, STOC 2001, 749-753.
18. W. Vickrey, *Counterspeculation, Auctions and Competitive Sealed Tenders*, Journal of Finance, 16:8-37, 1961.

Hierarchical Structure of 1-Safe Petri Nets

Kamal Lodaya[1,*], D. Ranganayakulu[2], and K. Rangarajan[3]

[1] Institute of Mathematical Sciences, CIT Campus, Chennai 600 113
http://www.imsc.res.in/~kamal
[2] SIVET College, Gowrivakkam, Chennai 601 302
nayakulu@imsc.res.in
[3] Madras Christian College, Tambaram, Chennai 600 059
rraguram@md5.vsnl.net.in

Abstract. The hierarchical process structure of Petri nets can be modelled by languages of series-parallel posets. We show how to extract this structure from a 1-safe Petri net. The technique also applies to represent 1-safe S-systems [11] and communication-free systems [5] in terms of structured programs with `cobegin-coend`. We also define *SR-systems*, a class of 1-safe Petri nets which exactly represents programs of this kind.

Let A be a finite nonempty alphabet. A finite-state automaton over A is an abstract version of flowcharts — think of the letters of the alphabet as representing assignments and tests. Rational (or regular) expressions are an abstract version of the control mechanisms of a "structured" programming language. Kleene's theorem thus ties together flowchart and program construct representations of a sequential programming language. (By using the power of assignments, the Böhm-Jacopini theorem shows that one loop is sufficient.)

1-safe Petri nets [16] can be thought of as representing the flowchart structure of a concurrent program. The state of the program is distributed into a set of places and the transitions can be *forking* (with more than one target place) or *joining* (with more than one source place) or both. These can be used to model the hierarchical structure of processes as well as their interaction with each other. One can seek therefore a Kleene theorem which represents a Petri net as a program in an abstract concurrent programming language.

Earlier Work. Several authors have defined expressions for nets. The earliest work we know of is by Grabowski [10] who defined expressions for poset languages of 1-safe net systems. (In this paper, we only deal with posets which are finite and labelled—these are also known as pomsets [17].) Garg and Ragunath [6] defined "concurrent regular expressions" to describe word languages of Petri nets. The Petri Box Calculus (PBC) [1] is a rich formalism for describing concurrent and branching behaviour of Petri nets, following much work in process algebra [9, 8, 20, 3, 15].

* The first author acknowledges partial support from the Indo-French project IFCPAR/CEFIPRA 2102-1 for presenting a first version of the ideas in this paper in the Workshop on Logic and Algebra in Concurrency, Dresden, 2000.

V.A. Saraswat (Ed.): ASIAN 2003, LNCS 2896, pp. 173–187, 2003.

A disadvantage of Grabowski's "Kleene-like" theorem (as also that of Garg and Ragunath) is that the "expressions" allow renaming and hiding operations. Hiding is renaming to an empty poset, and can be represented as manipulation of a local variable in a programming language. For example, the process algebra community usually models the sequential composition of two programs E1;E2 by using a shared variable (called tick below) and synchronization so that the poset corresponding to a run of E1 precedes that corresponding the run of E2.

```
new shared var tick in
cobegin E1 (* has assignments to tick to signal termination *)
||      E2 (* has tests of tick to signal starting *)
coend
```

This introduces parallelism in program structure where there is none in the semantics. In our view, shared variables are acceptable to represent inter-process communication, but they should not be introduced where no process structure is required. Similarly, iteration (looping) is a natural programming structure and simulating it by prefixing and recursion is not acceptable.

Ochmański's co-rational expressions [14] provide syntax for Mazurkiewicz trace languages [4], which are another popular way of describing poset behaviour of 1-safe Petri nets. Again, Ochmański's co-iteration does not correspond to a natural programming language construct.

Our Approach. Whether the full class of 1-safe net behaviours can be represented in terms of programming constructs remains to be seen. In this paper we model the forking and joining transitions which are used only for hierarchical ordering of processes by *series-rational expressions* [13], which can be thought of as `while` programs with a `cobegin-coend` construct. We do not deal with the representation of communication between processes.

More precisely, we show that the series-parallel posets accepted by 1-safe nets form exactly the series-rational languages, and we define *SR-systems*, a class of 1-safe Petri nets such that the posets they accept are exactly these languages.

Other abstract ways of describing "finite-state" languages are by morphisms from the language of terms into a finite algebra, or by using a run as a model over which logical formulas can be evaluated. We use earlier work to show equivalence to this kind of algebraic recognizability and logical definability.

Thus we have a Kleene-Myhill-Nerode-Büchi description. Renaming and especially hiding are not easy operations to model in the algebraic and logical frameworks and this is a technical reason we avoid using them.

One of the nice features about Petri nets is the structural characterizations that are available for some significant subclasses. Prominent among these are S-systems, T-systems and free choice (FC) systems [11].

We characterize two subclasses of nets which fall within the ambit of sp-languages: S-systems and communication-free (CF) systems [5]. We define two subclasses of sp-languages, the right and outermost sp-languages, and show that the rsp- and osp-languages accepted by 1-safe nets can be accepted by 1-safe CF and S-systems respectively. They are also characterized in terms of algebra, logic and syntactic expressions to obtain a Kleene-Myhill-Nerode-Büchi description.

1 Preliminaries: sp-Terms and Their Runs on Nets

A (labelled) net is a tuple (P, T, F, ℓ) where P is a set of places, T a (disjoint) set of transitions, $\ell : T \to A$ a function labelling the transitions and $F \subseteq (P \times T) \cup (T \times P)$ is the flow relation.

For a place or transition x, its pre-set $F^{-1}(x)$ is conventionally denoted ${}^\bullet x$ and its post-set $F(x)$ is denoted $x^\bullet$, and their union is called the neighbourhood of x. A net is said to be unbranched if for all its places p, $|{}^\bullet p| \leq 1$ and $|p^\bullet| \leq 1$.

We will assume that F satisfies the condition that for each transition t, ${}^\bullet t$ and $t^\bullet$ are nonempty, and for each place p, either ${}^\bullet p$ or $p^\bullet$ is nonempty. A net is called acyclic if the relation F^* is antisymmetric.

A (labelled) net system is a tuple $N = (P, T, F, \ell, M_0)$, where $M_0 : P \to \mathbf{N}$ is an initial marking. The run of a net system is described by a "token game" leading from the initial marking to other markings [16]. Formally, a marking is a function $M : P \to \mathbf{N}$.

A net system is said to be 1-safe if for all markings M reachable from the initial marking and for all places p, we have $M(p) \leq 1$. Now markings can be interpreted as 0/1-vectors, or equivalently as subsets of places. We will therefore use $M \subseteq P$ instead of $M : P \to \mathbf{N}$ to describe markings of 1-safe net systems.

Our definition of a "run" of a net system is known in net theory as a "non-sequential process". To "accept" finite runs of net systems as in automata theory, we define an *accepting* 1-safe net system to be a tuple $\mathcal{N} = (N, \mathcal{F})$, where N is a 1-safe net system and $\mathcal{F} \subseteq \wp P$ is a set of final markings.

Let $\mathcal{N} = (P, T, F, \ell, M_0, \mathcal{F})$ be an accepting 1-safe net system and $O = (P', T', F', \ell')$ an unbranched, acyclic 1-safe net. O is a (terminal) process of $\mathcal{N}$ if it can be mapped onto the accepting system—formally, we require two functions $\pi : P' \to P$ and $\pi : T' \to T$ (the context will make clear which function is meant) satisfying the following properties:

- for all t in T', $\pi({}^\bullet t) = {}^\bullet \pi(t)$, $\pi(t^\bullet) = \pi(t)^\bullet$ and $\ell(\pi(t)) = \ell'(t)$ (transition neighbourhood and labelling respected);
- $\pi(\{p \in P' \mid {}^\bullet p = \emptyset\}) = M_0$ and $\pi(\{p \in P' \mid p^\bullet = \emptyset\}) \in \mathcal{F}$ (initial and final markings respected).

The derived tuple $(T', (F')^* \cap (T' \times T'), \ell' \lceil T')$ is a poset, and we will say that the net system $\mathcal{N}$ *accepts* this poset. The set of all posets $\mathcal{N}$ accepts is called $PL(\mathcal{N})$, the poset language of $\mathcal{N}$.

1.1 The sp-Runs of a Net System

We now restrict attention to the subclass of labelled N-free posets, that is, those nonempty posets which satisfy

$$\forall w, x, y, z (w \leq y,\ w \leq z,\ x \leq z,\ w \operatorname{co} x,\ y \operatorname{co} z \text{ implies } x \leq y) \qquad (1)$$

Here $a \operatorname{co} b$ says that a and b are unordered. It has been shown [10, 7] that these posets are described inductively using a set of series-parallel terms $SP(A)$ over the alphabet A, given by the syntax $u ::= a \in A \mid u_1 u_2 \mid u_1 \| u_2$, which we call *sp-terms*. (Note that there is no way of describing the empty poset.)

We use this result to inductively describe those runs of a net system which correspond to N-free posets. The $M_1[u\rangle M_2$ notation standard in net theory is used. Of these, the ones from the initial marking to a final one form $PL(N) \cap SP(A)$.

We say $M_1\,[a\rangle\,M_2$ holds if for some a-labelled transition t such that ${}^\bullet t \subseteq M_1$, $(M_1 \setminus {}^\bullet t) \cup t^\bullet = M_2$.

The term $u||v$ gives the parallel composition (disjoint union) of the posets u and v, leaving their elements unordered with respect to each other. $M_1\,[u||v\rangle\,M_2$ holds if each M_i can be split into disjoint components M_i^u and M_i^v such that $M_1^u\,[u\rangle\,M_2^u$ and $M_1^v\,[v\rangle\,M_2^v$.

The term uv stands for the poset formed by sequencing the posets u and v, that is, ordering all elements of u before those of v. We say that a marking M is *connected* if it cannot be decomposed into two markings M_1 and M_2 which can independently enable transitions. $M_1\,[uv\rangle\,M_2$ holds if there is an intermediate connected marking M such that $M_1\,[u\rangle\,M$ and $M\,[v\rangle\,M_2$.

Without the connectedness condition on intermediate markings, a run on $ab||cd$ could also be seen as a run on $(a||c)(b||d)$, and these two are distinct poset behaviours.

We have implicitly used the fact that sequencing and parallel composition are associative and that parallel composition is also commutative.

We do not know of any structural definition which will restrict nets to exactly those which have N-free behaviour.

1.2 sp-Algebras and sp-Languages

More generally, an *sp-algebra* is a set S equipped with the binary associative operations of sequential product and parallel composition, such that parallel composition is also commutative. $SP(A)$ is the free sp-algebra over generators A, built from the letters of A by these operations. In this paper, our interest will be restricted to those poset languages which can be seen as *sp-languages*, subsets of $SP(A)$ [13].

We define the width of a sp-term to be the maximum number of nested parallel operations occurring in it plus one. For instance, the term $a(b||c(a||b))$ has width three. Intuitively, width provides an upper bound on the number of processors required for a maximally parallel implementation of the poset corresponding to an sp-term. The width of an sp-language is the supremum of the widths of its terms.

We will be interested in two subclasses of $SP(A)$.

The outermost parallel sp-terms $OSP(A)$ are those where no parallel composition is nested inside a sequential product. $OSP(A)$ characterizes finite posets which are disjoint unions of chains.

The right parallel sp-terms $RSP(A)$ are those where a subterm of the form $(u_1||u_2)u_3$ is disallowed, that is, only the right multiplicand of a sequential product is allowed to be a parallel composition. $RSP(A)$ characterizes finite join-free posets, that is, those posets where there do not exist distinct elements x, y, z such that $x \leq z$, $y \leq z$ and x, y are unordered.

Clearly $A^+ \subset OSP(A) \subset RSP(A) \subset SP(A)$. If an sp-language is a subset of $RSP(A)$, we call it an rsp-language; osp-languages are similarly defined.

A zero element in an sp-algebra absorbs both operations. If it exists, it is unique and is written 0. We say an sp-algebra is *right zero* if it has a zero and for any parallel term $x_1||x_2$, right multiplying it by any x_3 yields zero, that is, $(x_1||x_2)x_3 = 0$. An sp-algebra is *outermost zero* if it has a zero and multiplying any parallel term on the left or the right yields zero.

As usual, a morphism between sp-algebras is a map preserving the two operations. An sp-language L is recognized by an sp-algebra S if there is a morphism $\phi : SP(A) \to S$ such that $L = \phi^{-1}\phi(L)$. If S is finite, we say L is recognizable.

Proposition 1 *Let L be a recognizable sp-language. Then L is an rsp-language (osp-language) if and only if it is recognized by an sp-algebra S such that S is right zero (outermost zero, respectively) and 0 is not in the image of L.*

1.3 Monadic Second-Order Logic

We now turn to a different view of labelled posets, seeing them as models of a logical language $MSO[<, A]$. The atomic formulas of this logic are $\ell(x) = a$ (for $a \in A$), $x < y$ and $x = y$. Apart from the usual first-order variables (such as x, y above) interpreted as elements of the poset under consideration, we work with monadic second-order variables, interpreted over subsets of poset elements. The formulas are closed under boolean operations, first-order and monadic second-order quantification. The definition of when the poset u satisfies the formula α ($u \models \alpha$) is standard.

Any (MSO) formula α defines the language of all the posets which satisfy it, $PL(\alpha) = \{u \mid u \models \alpha\}$. Call such a language (MSO-)definable.

For instance, the description (1) can be written as a (first-order) formula (along with a formula specifying a nonempty poset), defining the poset language $SP(A)$ of all N-free posets. Similarly, the languages $RSP(A)$ and $OSP(A)$ are definable using the formulas

$$\delta_{rsp} = \forall x, y, z(x \leq z \text{ and } y \leq z \text{ implies } x \leq y \text{ or } y \leq x)$$

$$\delta_{osp} = \delta_{rsp} \text{ and } \forall x, y, z(x \leq y \text{ and } x \leq z \text{ implies } y \leq z \text{ or } z \leq y)$$

Hence, by conjuncting a formula α with that for (say) $SP(A)$, we get the definable sp-languages. MSO-definability of sp-languages was studied by Kuske [12], who showed that the recognizable sp-languages coincide with the MSO-definable ones.

Proposition 2 *The recognizable rsp-languages (osp-languages) of bounded width equal the MSO-definable rsp-languages (osp-languages) of bounded width.*

2 Operations Corresponding to Programming Constructs

Our basic syntax will be the *series-rational expressions*, which can be seen as an abstract representation of structured programs with `cobegin-coend` statements. These expressions will be interpreted as sp-languages.

- Every $a \in A$ is a rational expression. If r_1 and r_2 are rational expressions, then so are $r_1 \cup r_2$, $r_1 r_2$, r_1^+.

- Every rational expression is a series-rational expression. If e_1 and e_2 are series-rational expressions, then so are $e_1 \cup e_2$, e_1e_2, e_1^+ and $e_1||e_2$.

The rational expressions are exactly the same as the (regular) expressions for words, except that they are interpreted over posets. Adding parallel composition (`cobegin-coend`) gives the series-rational expressions.

We again identify two subclasses of interest. An expression with parallel composition only at the outermost level is said to be *outermost series-rational*. This corresponds to one single `cobegin-coend` inside which we have a `while` program for each process.

An expression where parallel composition is only allowed on the right hand side of a sequential product is said to be *right series-rational*. (More precisely, the right series-rational expresssions are defined by the syntax below. The outermost series-rational expressions can be similarly defined.) In terms of programming languages, these are structured programs with `cobegin-coend` such that all the `coend`'s occur at the end of the program. Processes can be "forked" to make the process structure grow, but only the end of the program terminates all the processes.

$$r ::= a \mid r_1 \cup r_2 \mid r_1r_2 \mid r_1^+, \quad e ::= r \mid re_1 \mid e_1||e_2$$

Now, we associate with each expression an sp-language. $L(a)$ is the singleton set consisting of the term a, $L(e_1 \cup e_2) = L(e_1) \cup L(e_2)$, $L(e_1e_2) = L(e_1)L(e_2)$, $L(e_1^+) = L(e_1)^+$ (Kleene iteration) and $L(e_1||e_2) = L(e_1)||L(e_2)$. The operations on the right hand side are performed pointwise on sp-terms. L^+ is defined as usual inductively, to give the concatenation of L any number of times.

Finally, an sp-language over A is said to be series-rational if it is of the form $L(e)$ for some series-rational expression e over A. We similarly define the outermost and right series-rational languages. The paper [13] shows that the series-rational languages are the recognizable sp-languages of bounded width.

From the definitions, it follows that the outermost series-rational languages are subsets of $OSP(A)$ and the right series-rational languages are subsets of $RSP(A)$. Conversely, if a series-rational language is a subset of $OSP(A)/RSP(A)$, we can find an outermost/right series-rational expression generating it.

Proposition 3 *The right (outermost) series-rational languages are the recognizable rsp- (osp-)languages of bounded width.*

Putting Proposition 3 and Proposition 2 together gives us algebraic and logical characterizations for our expressions. In the rest of the paper, we tie these up with Petri nets.

3 Net Constructions

In this section, we will give constructions on nets which correspond to the expression operations above. Many of these are based on earlier work [9, 8, 20, 3, 15], but ours are the first direct constructions we have seen for net systems with final markings.

We first recall a construction which does not affect the poset language accepted by a net. The place complement of a net adds a copy P^{comp} of the set of places P of $\mathcal{N}$ in such a way that a place contains a token iff the complementary places are empty [19]. The initial marking of the new net is $(P \setminus M_0)^{comp} \cup M_0$ and the final markings are $(P \setminus M_f)^{comp} \cup M_f$ for every $M_f \in \mathcal{F}$.

We need a technical notion: the final width $fwd(u)$ of an sp-term u is the width of its last sequential component.

We call a net system $\mathcal{N} = (P, T, F, \ell, M_0, \mathcal{F})$ *behaved* if it satisfies the following properties:

- ${}^\bullet M_0 = \emptyset$; ${}^\bullet(M_0{}^\bullet) = M_0$ (initial marking a source)
- For every M_f in $\mathcal{F}$, $M_f{}^\bullet = \emptyset$; $({}^\bullet M_f)^\bullet = M_f$ (final marking a sink)
- For every M_f in $\mathcal{F}$ such that $M_0\,[u\rangle\, M_f$, $|M_f| = fwd(u)$ (final markings separated by parallel width)
- Distinct M_f^1, M_f^2 in $\mathcal{F}$ are disjoint from each other and from M_0
- For every $M_1\,[u\|v\rangle\, M_2$, $\mathcal{N}$ can be divided into disjoint parts $\mathcal{N}_u, \mathcal{N}_v$ such that $M_1\lceil\mathcal{N}_u\,[u\rangle\, M_2\lceil\mathcal{N}_u$ and $M_1\lceil\mathcal{N}_v\,[v\rangle\, M_2\lceil\mathcal{N}_v$ (parallel sub-runs disjoint).

Now we start constructing nets for expressions. The construction of a behaved net system for the expression a is trivial, we call it an *atomic* net system.

We give constructions for the other operations. Note that we use $+$ to indicate disjoint union.

3.1 Union

Let $\mathcal{N}_i = (P_i, T_i, F_i, M_0^i, \mathcal{F}^i, \ell_i), i = 1, 2$ be 1-safe net systems. Then their sum is the net system $\mathcal{N} = (P, T, F, M_0, \mathcal{F}, \ell)$ where

- $P = P_1 + P_2 + P_{new}$; $P_{new} = (M_0^1 \times M_0^2)$
- $T = T_1 + T_2 + T_{new}$; $T_{new} = (M_0^1)^\bullet \cup (M_0^2)^\bullet$
- $\ell = \ell_1 \cup \ell_2 \cup \{(t \to \ell_i(t)) \mid t \in T_{new} \cap T_i, i = 1, 2\}$
- $F = F_1 \cup F_2 \cup \{((p_1, p_2), t) \in P_{new} \times T_{new} \mid (p_1, t) \in F_1 \text{ or } (p_2, t) \in F_2\}$ $\cup \{(t, p) \in T_{new} \times (P_1 \cup P_2) \mid (t, p) \in F_1 \text{ or } (t, p) \in F_2\}$
- $M_0 = P_{new}$; $\mathcal{F} = \mathcal{F}^1 \cup \mathcal{F}^2$

The new system adds to a copy of both $\mathcal{N}_i$ a fresh set of places for the marking $M_0^1 \times M_0^2$ (which is the new initial marking, and a final marking if either M_0^i was a final marking) and a fresh copy of transitions enabled by each M_0^i. Figure 1 shows an example.

From the construction, we have for $\mathcal{N}$ that its initial marking is a source. If both the $\mathcal{N}_i$ are behaved, then the final markings of $\mathcal{N}$ are sinks, and are disjoint from each other. The parallel final width and disjoint sub-run conditions also follow from the behavedness of the $\mathcal{N}_i$.

Proposition 4 $PL(\mathcal{N}) = PL(\mathcal{N}_1) \cup PL(\mathcal{N}_2)$.

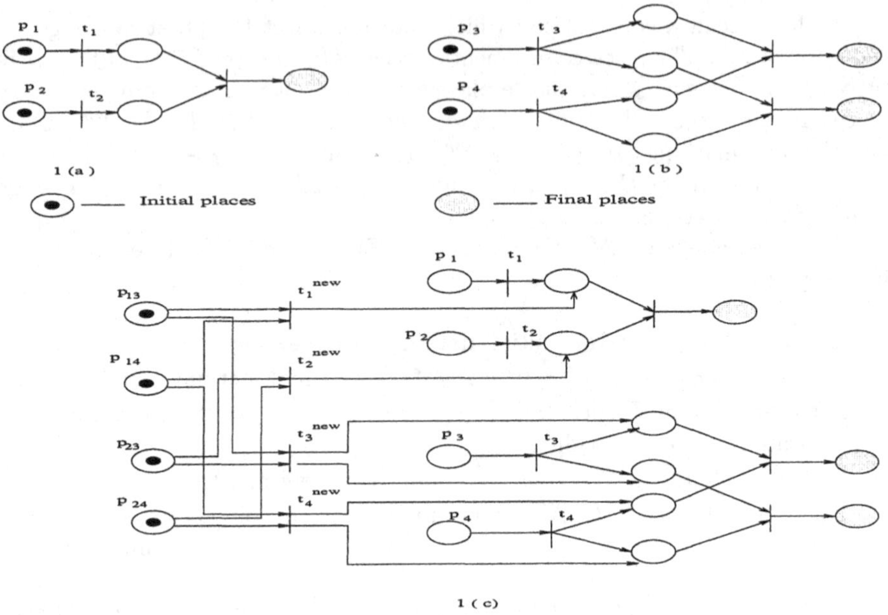

Fig. 1. $PL(1c) = PL(1a) \cup PL(1b)$

3.2 Sequencing

Let $\mathcal{N}_i = (P_i, T_i, F_i, M_0^i, \mathcal{F}^i, \ell_i), i = 1, 2$ be 1-safe net systems. Then their sequential composition is the net system $\mathcal{N} = (P, T, F, M_0, \mathcal{F}, \ell)$ where

- $P = P_1 + P_2 + P_{new}$; $P_{new} = \bigcup_{M_f^1 \in \mathcal{F}^1} (M_f^1 \times M_0^2)$
- $T = T_1 + T_2 + T_{new}$; $T_{new} = \bigcup_{M_f^1 \in \mathcal{F}^1} ({}^\bullet(M_f^1) \cup (M_0^2)^\bullet)$
- $\ell = \ell_1 \cup \ell_2 \cup \{(t \to \ell_i(t)) \mid t \in T_{new} \cap T_i, i = 1, 2\}$
- $F = F_1 \cup F_2 \cup \{(p, t) \in P_1 \times T_{new} \mid (p, t) \in F_1\}$
  $\cup \{(t, (p_1, p_2)) \in T_{new} \times P_{new} \mid (t, p_1) \in F_1\}$
  $\cup \{((p_1, p_2), t) \in P_{new} \times T_{new} \mid (p_2, t) \in F_2\}$
  $\cup \{(t, p) \in T_{new} \times P_2 \mid (t, p) \in F_2\}$
- $M_0 = M_0^1$; $\mathcal{F} = \mathcal{F}^2$

The new system uses a product of $M_f^1 \times M_0^2$ for each $M_f^1 \in \mathcal{F}^1$, making copies of transitions coming in to M_f^1 as well as leaving M_0^2. M_0^1 is the initial marking, and $\mathcal{F}^2$ the final markings. This is illustrated in Figure 2.

If both nets $\mathcal{N}_i$ are behaved, since the construction does not affect the initial marking of $\mathcal{N}_1$ or the final markings of $\mathcal{N}_2$, the source, sink and final width properties are maintained. The parallel sub-run property is also maintained by the argument presented next.

Proposition 5 *If $\mathcal{N}_1$ is place complemented and both $\mathcal{N}_i$ are behaved, $PL(\mathcal{N}) = PL(\mathcal{N}_1)PL(\mathcal{N}_2)$.*

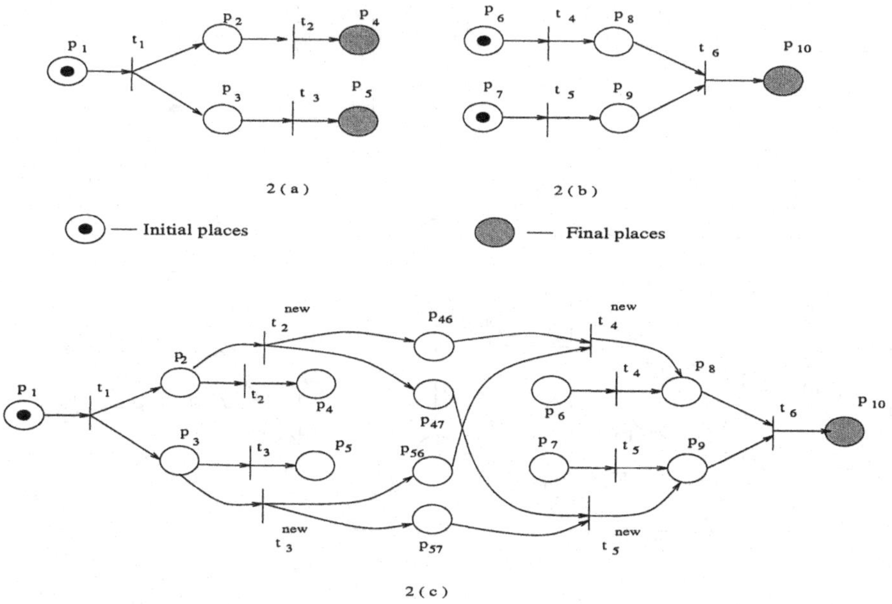

Fig. 2. $PL(2c) = PL(2a)PL(2b)$

3.3 Iteration

We follow the same idea for iteration as for sequencing. Given a 1-safe net system $\mathcal{N}_1$, take *two* copies of it, call them $\mathcal{N}_1$ and $\mathcal{N}_2$ and perform the "product" construction above, this time linking $\mathcal{F}^1$ to M_0^2 *as well as* $\mathcal{F}^2$ to M_0^1. Let M_0^1 be the initial marking, and the set of final markings is $\mathcal{F}^1 \cup \mathcal{F}^2$. Figure 3 shows an example. Here is a detailed construction.

Let $\mathcal{N}_i = (P_i, T_i, \ell_i, F_i, M_0^i, \mathcal{F}^i)$ be two copies of an accepting 1-safe net system $\mathcal{N}_1$. Then the net for its iteration is $\mathcal{N} = (P, T, \ell, F, M_0, \mathcal{F})$ where

- $P = P_1 + P_2 + P_{new}^{12} + P_{new}^{21}$;
  $P_{new}^{12} = \bigcup_{M_f^1 \in \mathcal{F}^1} (M_f^1 \times M_0^2)$; $P_{new}^{21} = \bigcup_{M_f^2 \in \mathcal{F}^2} (M_f^2 \times M_0^1)$
- $T = T_1 + T_2 + T_{new}^{12} + T_{new}^{21}$;
  $T_{new}^{12} = \bigcup_{M_f^1 \in \mathcal{F}^1} ({}^\bullet(M_f^1) \cup (M_0^2)^\bullet)$; $T_{new}^{21} = \bigcup_{M_f^2 \in \mathcal{F}^2} ({}^\bullet(M_f^2) \cup (M_0^1)^\bullet)$
- $\ell = \ell_1 \cup \ell_2 \cup \{(t \to \ell_i(t)) \mid t \in (T_{new}^{12} \cup T_{new}^{21}) \cap T_i, i = 1, 2\}$
- $F = F_1 \cup F_2 \cup F_{new}^{12} \cup F_{new}^{21}$;
  $F_{new}^{12} = \{(p, t) \in P_1 \times T_{new}^{12} \mid (p, t) \in F_1\}$
  $\cup \{(t, (p_1, p_2)) \in T_{new}^{12} \times P_{new}^{12} \mid (t, p_1) \in F_1\}$
  $\cup \{((p_1, p_2), t) \in P_{new}^{12} \times T_{new}^{12} \mid (p_2, t) \in F_2\}$
  $\cup \{(t, p) \in T_{new}^{12} \times P_2 \mid (t, p) \in F_2\}$;
  $F_{new}^{21} = \{(p, t) \in P_2 \times T_{new}^{21} \mid (p, t) \in F_2\}$
  $\cup \{(t, (p_1, p_2)) \in T_{new}^{21} \times P_{new}^{21} \mid (t, p_1) \in F_2\}$

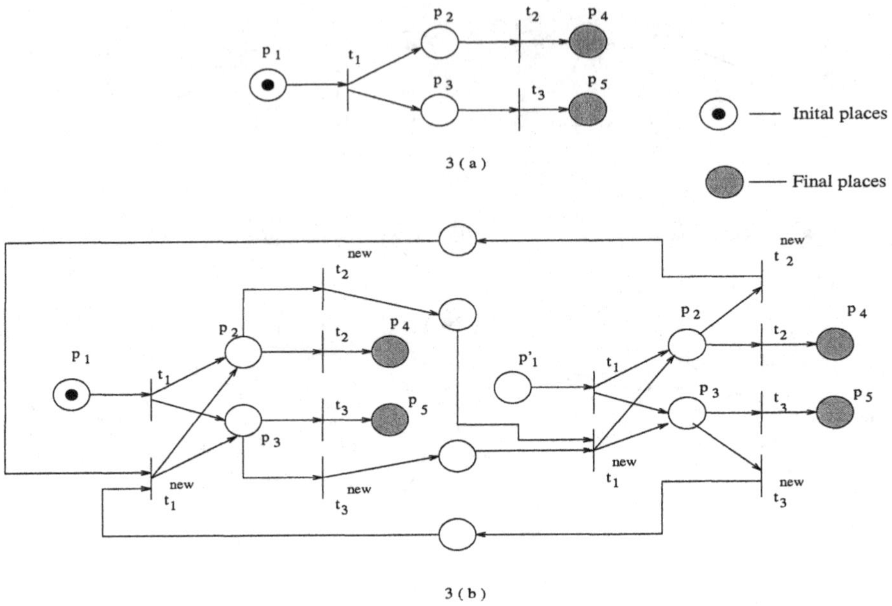

Fig. 3. $PL(3b) = PL(3a)^+$

$\cup \{((p_1, p_2), t) \in P^{21}_{new} \times T^{21}_{new} \mid (p_2, t) \in F_1\}$
$\cup \{(t, p) \in T^{21}_{new} \times P_1 \mid (t, p) \in F_1\}$
– $M_0 = M^1_0$; $\mathcal{F} = \mathcal{F}^1 \cup \mathcal{F}^2$

As for sequencing, assume that $\mathcal{N}_1$ is behaved. Using the two copies maintains the source, sink and final width properties, and the argument for parallel sub-runs follows the one used above for sequencing.

Proposition 6 *If $\mathcal{N}_1$ is place complemented and behaved, then* $PL(\mathcal{N}) = PL(\mathcal{N}_1)^+$.

3.4 Parallel Composition

The parallel composition of two 1-safe net systems $\mathcal{N}_i = (P_i, T_i, F_i, M^i_0, \mathcal{F}^i, \ell_i), i = 1, 2$ is the simple disjoint union $\mathcal{N} = (P, T, F, M_0, \mathcal{F}, \ell)$ where

– $P = P_1 + P_2$; $T = T_1 + T_2$; $\ell = \ell_1 \cup \ell_2$; $F = F_1 \cup F_2$
– $M_0 = M^1_0 \cup M^2_0$; $\mathcal{F} = \{M^1_f \cup M^2_f \mid M^1_f \in \mathcal{F}^1,\ M^2_f \in \mathcal{F}^2\}$

Clearly if both nets $\mathcal{N}_i$ are behaved, so is $\mathcal{N}$, the construction being designed to preserve the parallel sub-run and final width properties.

Proposition 7 $PL(\mathcal{N}) = PL(\mathcal{N}_1) || PL(\mathcal{N}_2)$.

3.5 Net Subclasses

Definition. *The subclass of net systems built up from the atomic systems using the constructions for union, sequencing, iteration and parallel composition is called* (1-safe) SR-systems.

Theorem 8 *Given a series-rational expression e, one can construct an SR-system $\mathcal{N}$ such that $PL(\mathcal{N}) = L(e) \subseteq SP(A)$.*

Proof. By induction, using the Proposition corresponding to each operation.

All posets accepted by an SR-system are N-free. By constructing the reachability graph of a net system and running through all four-tuples of transitions, the N-free property can be algorithmically checked (using polynomial space). We conjecture that there is a polynomial time algorithm to check that a 1-safe net system is SR.

For net systems corresponding to the outermost/right series-rational expressions, we look at some well-known subclasses of net systems. (These are, in fact, the motivation for defining these expressions.)

An *S-system* [11] is a net system where neither forking ($|t^\bullet| > 1$) nor joining ($|{}^\bullet t| > 1$) transitions are allowed. In other words, for each transition, its pre-set and post-set are both singletons. The posets in the language accepted by an S-system satisfy the property that they are disjoint unions of chains, that is, they are outermost parallel.

A *communication-free (CF) system* [5] is one where joining transitions are not allowed. The posets accepted by a CF-system are right parallel.

The table in Figure 4 summarizes the closure properties of our net subclasses. Counter-examples are also listed.

Closure under	*Sequencing*	*Iteration*	*Union*	*Parallel*
1-safe SR-systems	Yes	Yes	Yes	Yes
1-safe CF-systems	No, $(a\|\|b)c$	No, $(a\|\|b)^+$	No, $(a\|\|b) \cup c$	Yes
1-safe S-systems	No, $a(b\|\|c)$	No, $(a\|\|b)^+$	No, $(a\|\|b) \cup c$	Yes

Fig. 4. Constructions

Theorem 9 *Given a right series-rational expression e, one can construct a 1-safe CF-system $\mathcal{N}$ such that $PL(\mathcal{N}) = L(e) \subseteq RSP(A)$.*

Theorem 10 *Given an outermost series-rational expression e, one can construct a 1-safe S-system $\mathcal{N}$ such that $PL(\mathcal{N}) = L(e) \subseteq OSP(A)$.*

4 From Nets to Expressions

All the formal language machinery is now in place, and we can start the job of extracting syntax from systems. We crucially use the fact that for 1-safe systems the width of the sp-terms accepted is always bounded.

4.1 1-Safe Nets

Lemma 11 *Given a 1-safe system $\mathcal{N}$, there is a series-rational expression for $PL(\mathcal{N}) \cap SP(A)$.*

Proof. Our proof is by induction on the width of $PL(\mathcal{N}) \cap SP(A)$. We construct expressions for the following sets:

$P^k_{M \to N}$ is the set of sp-terms of width k which are runs of $\mathcal{N}$ from the marking M to the marking N, such that the term is a parallel composition (or an atomic action).

$S^k_{M \to N}$ is the set of sp-terms of width k which are runs of $\mathcal{N}$ from the marking M to the marking N, such that the term is a sequential product (or an atomic action).

We will let $L^k_{M \to N} = P^k_{M \to N} \cup S^k_{M \to N}$.

We now define the sets of parallel terms. $P^1_{M \to N}$ is the set of all a such that a transition labelled a takes M to N. For $k > 1$, we have:

$$P^k_{M \to N} = \bigcup_{\substack{j_1+j_2=k \\ M_1+M_2=M, N_1+N_2=N}} L^{j_1}_{M_1 \to N_1} || L^{j_2}_{M_2 \to N_2}.$$

The construction of $S^k_{M \to N}$ is from $P^k_{M \to N}$ and follows traditional automata-theoretic lines. We will need to work with a specified set of connected intermediate markings R. We define by induction on its size $|R|$ the set $S^{k,R}_{M \to N}$ of terms from $S^k_{M \to N}$ which only use intermediate markings from the set R. We let $L^{k,R}_{M \to N} = P^k_{M \to N} \cup S^{k,R}_{M \to N}$.

Then $S^{k,\emptyset}_{M \to N}$ is nothing but $P^k_{M \to N}$. Inductively, for $r \notin R$, we have

$$S^{k,R\cup\{r\}}_{M \to N} = S^{k,R}_{M \to N} \cup \bigcup_{\substack{j_1,j_2,j_3 \le k \\ j_1=k \text{ or } j_2=k \text{ or } j_3=k}} L^{j_1,R}_{M \to r} (L^{j_2,R}_{r \to r})^* L^{j_3,R}_{r \to N}. \quad (2)$$

This is a generalization of the usual McNaughton-Yamada expression used for word languages. The conditions on the union ensure that the width of the term added is k.

By taking the entire set of such intermediate markings, we have the desired series-rational expression.

Theorem 12 *The following classes of sp-languages are equivalent:*

(1) The series-rational languages.
(2) The poset languages accepted by 1-safe SR-systems.
(3) The sp-languages accepted by 1-safe systems.
(4) The recognizable sp-languages of bounded width.
(5) The MSO-definable sp-languages of bounded width.

Proof. (1⇒2⇒3): Theorem 8.

(3⇒1): Let K be the poset language accepted by a 1-safe system. Hence $L = K \cap SP(A)$ is an sp-language. By the lemma above, there is a series-rational expression for it.

(1⟺4): From [13], we know that the series-rational sp-languages are the recognizable sp-languages of bounded width. (The paper also gives a purely algebraic condition, expressed in terms of nilpotency of the parallel product, which corresponds to bounded width.)

(4⟺5): From [12], we know that these coincide with the MSO-definable sp-languages of bounded width.

The paper [13] also characterizes these languages as those accepted by certain "branching automata". It would be interesting to find a direct translation between these and 1-safe nets preserving the accepted sp-language. From the results of [13], we also get:

Corollary 13 *The languages accepted by 1-safe SR-systems are closed under intersection, direct and inverse morphism.*

4.2 Subclasses

Theorem 14 *The following classes of rsp-languages are equivalent, and closed under intersection.*

(1) The right series-rational languages.

(2) The poset languages accepted by 1-safe CF-systems.

(3) The rsp-languages accepted by 1-safe systems.

(4) The recognizable rsp-languages of bounded width.

(5) The MSO-definable rsp-languages of bounded width.

Proof. (1⇒2⇒3): Theorem 9.

(3⇒1): Let K be the poset language accepted by a 1-safe system. Then it accepts the rsp-language $L = K \cap RSP(A)$. Now $K \cap SP(A)$ is series-rational and $RSP(A)$ is MSO-definable, therefore series-rational by Theorem 12, so their intersection L is series-rational by Corollary 13. Since $L \subseteq RSP(A)$, the generating expression for it must be right series-rational.

(1⟺4⟺5): Proposition 3 and Proposition 2. The closure under intersection follows.

By simple modifications of the preceding arguments, we get:

Theorem 15 *The following classes of osp-languages are equivalent, and closed under intersection.*

(1) The outermost series-rational languages.

(2) The poset languages accepted by 1-safe S-systems.

(3) The osp-languages accepted by 1-safe systems.

(4) The recognizable osp-languages of bounded width.

(5) The MSO-definable osp-languages of bounded width.

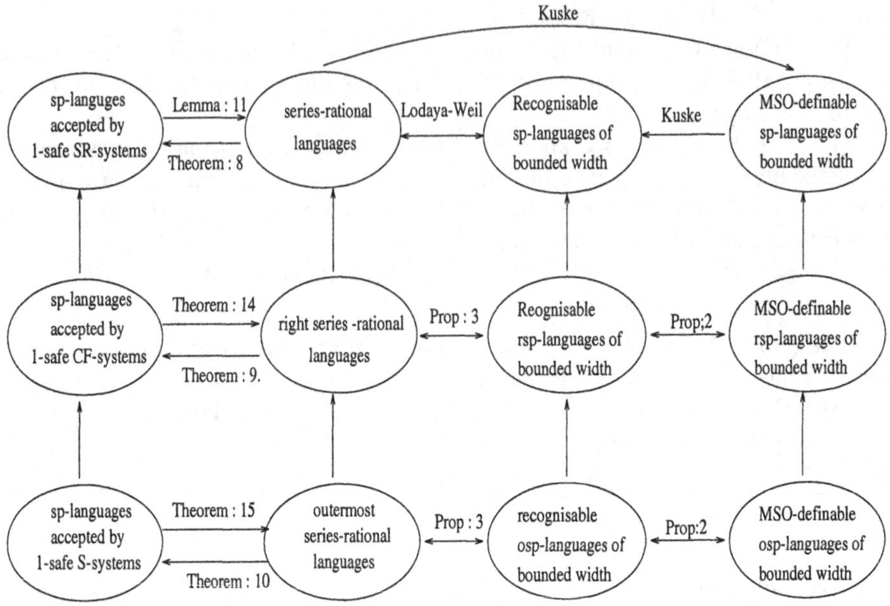

Fig. 5. Relationships

Discussion. Figure 5 summarizes the results of this paper. We believe our characterizations also work for k-safe nets, using the results of [2]. Extending the work to general (unsafe) nets is more challenging.

Petri nets are typically meant to model infinite behaviour. A theory of ω-rational expressions for N-free poset languages has been developed by Kuske [12], and a similar development can be done in our setup without too much difficulty [18].

Nets have a richer interaction structure than can be described by sp-terms. In our setup, the obvious way to move towards the full class of 1-safe Petri nets would be to include in our terms an operation corresponding to synchronization (as has been done in PBC [1].) However, carrying all the equivalences forward seems to be difficult.

References

1. E. Best, R. Devillers and M. Koutny. *Petri net algebra*, Springer (2001).
2. E. Best and H. Wimmel. Reducing k-safe Petri nets to pomset-equivalent 1-safe Petri nets, *Proc. ATPN*, Aarhus (M. Nielsen and D. Simpson, eds.), LNCS **1825** (2000) 63–82.
3. P. Degano, R. de Nicola and U. Montanari. A partial order semantics for CCS, TCS **75** (1990) 223–262.
4. V. Diekert and G. Rozenberg, eds. *The book of traces*, World Scientific (1995).
5. J. Esparza. Petri nets, commutative context-free grammars, and basic parallel processes, Fund. Inf. **30** (1997) 23–41.

6. V.K. Garg and M.T. Ragunath. Concurrent regular expressions and their relationship to Petri nets, TCS **96** (1992) 285–304.
7. J.L. Gischer. The equational theory of pomsets, TCS **61** (1988) 199–224.
8. R.J. van Glabbeek and F.W. Vaandrager. Petri net models for algebraic theories of concurrency, *Proc. PARLE*, Eindhoven (J.W. de Bakker, A.J. Nijman and P.C. Treleaven, eds.), Vol. 2, LNCS **259** (1987) 224–242.
9. U. Goltz and A. Mycroft. On representing CCS programs by finite Petri nets, *Proc. ICALP*, Antwerpen (J. Paredaens, ed.), LNCS **172** (1984) 196–208.
10. J. Grabowski. On partial languages, Fund. Inform. **IV** (1981) 427–498.
11. M.H.T. Hack. *Analysis of production schemata by Petri nets*, M.S. thesis, Dept. Elec. Engg., MIT (1972).
12. D. Kuske. Towards a language theory for infinite N-free posets, TCS **299** (2003), 347–386.
13. K. Lodaya and P. Weil. Series-parallel languages and the bounded-width property, TCS **237** (2000) 347–380.
14. E. Ochmański. Regular behaviour of concurrent systems, Bull. EATCS **27** (1985) 56–67.
15. E.-R. Olderog. *Nets, terms and formulas*, Cambridge (1991).
16. C.-A. Petri. Fundamentals of a theory of asynchronous information flow, *Proc. IFIP*, Münich (C.M. Popplewell, ed.), North-Holland (1962) 386–390.
17. V. Pratt. Modelling concurrency with partial orders, IJPP **15**(1) (1986) 33–71.
18. D. Ranganayakulu and K. Lodaya. Infinite series-parallel posets of 1-safe nets, *Proc. Algorithms & Artificial Systems*, (P. Thangavel, ed.), Allied (2003) 107–124.
19. W. Reisig. *Petri nets, an introduction*, Springer (1985).
20. D. Taubner. *Finite representations of CCS and TCSP programs by automata and Petri nets*, LNCS **369** (1989).

A Calculus for Secure Mobility

Bruno Blanchet[1] and Benjamin Aziz[2]

[1] CNRS, Département d'Informatique, École Normale Supérieure, Paris
and Max-Planck-Institut für Informatik
Bruno.Blanchet@ens.fr
[2] School of Computer Applications
Dublin City University
baziz@computing.dcu.ie

Abstract. In this paper, we introduce the crypto-loc calculus, a calculus for modelling secure mobile computations that combine the concepts of locations, cryptography, and code mobility. All these concepts exist in mobile systems, for example, Java applets run within sandboxes or downloaded under an SSL connection. We use observational equivalence of processes as a powerful means of defining security properties, and characterize observational equivalence in terms of a labelled bisimilarity relation, which makes its proof much easier.

1 Introduction

The issue of security has become central in mobile computing systems as a result of the increasing technological advances enjoyed in recent years and the appearance of new security threats associated with such advances. In process algebraic models of mobility, the modelling of the various actions that the system can perform has been captured in terms of a few important concepts. Among these are the concepts of *location*, *cryptography*, and *code mobility*. In most occasions, these concepts have been studied separately. Here, we combine the three concepts into one model with the goal of capturing the security and mobility features that already exist in platforms like Java and .NET, in a simple and elegant calculus. This combination makes it possible to analyze the security properties of cryptographic protocols also involving mobility, for instance.

Locations have significant security effects; they are name-protected areas of computation, which provide a handy isolation mechanism often useful in the modelling of concepts like firewalls and sandboxes. Communications between locations are generally restricted to either communications local to one location (ambients [12]), or communications with locations immediately inside or outside a location (boxed ambients [10]). The former implies using an opening mechanism to destroy ambient boundaries, in order to allow communication between ambients. This weakens the isolation power of locations considerably and has security drawbacks already recognized in previous work [10], so we prefer the latter choice.

The mobility of locations may be classified into *subjective* and *objective*. Subjective mobility (as in, e.g., the ambients calculus [12]) implies the presence of

V.A. Saraswat (Ed.): ASIAN 2003, LNCS 2896, pp. 188–204, 2003.

language primitives that can be used by a location as commands to directly control its movement. On the other hand, objective mobility (as in, e.g., the seal calculus [20]) dictates that locations be controlled by their context, which has primitives expressive enough to be able to send and receive locations. Furthermore, one can distinguish *weak* mobility, in which the received code always restarts its execution in the initial state, *strong* mobility, where a thread is sent along with its execution state, and *full* mobility, where a full program is sent along with its state [8]. In our model, certain kinds of data represent code. These data can be manipulated like any other piece of data: they can be sent and received (which provides *weak objective* mobility of any code, not just locations), but also manipulated by cryptographic primitives. In contrast to ordinary data, they can also be executed. This modelling of mobility corresponds to what happens in systems such as Java and .NET, and is also easier to implement than strong or full mobility.

Our representation of cryptography is borrowed from the applied pi calculus [3], in which cryptographic primitives are defined as functions satisfying an equational theory. This provides a generic treatment of primitives, which promotes a uniform understanding of the underlying theory and yields a powerful technique for specifying cryptographic systems.

As often in process calculi, some of these features can be encoded. Location-based languages can encode cryptographic operations, including symmetric and asymmetric encryption [12, 20]. (That would probably be more difficult for primitives such as xor.) Strong mobility can be encoded from weak mobility [8]. The execution of certain kinds of data can be encoded by an interpreter (such an interpreter has already been defined for the pi calculus [14]), and strong mobility could be encoded by an improved version of such an interpreter. Even if encodings exist, we choose to provide as primitives in our calculus the features that exist in Java and .NET, i.e. cryptography, sandboxes modelled by locations, and weak code mobility. It is obviously possible to encode other features in our calculus, such as strong mobility, much like one could encode them in Java.

The combination of locations, cryptography, and weak code mobility enables us to model scenarios, such as Java applets, in which code is sent on the network after a cryptographic treatment (signed applets) or inside a cryptographic protocol (applets sent over SSL, for instance). Based on the amount of trust established for an applet, it is then possible to run it inside or outside a sandbox (location). Similarly, we could also model applets that execute a cryptographic protocol, in which case the transmitted code uses cryptographic primitives. We develop a general technique based on observational equivalence to prove security properties, and use it to show some of the main properties of such examples.

Outline. In Sect. 2, we present the syntax and operational semantics of the calculus. In Sect. 3, we introduce and relate observational equivalence and labelled bisimilarity. In Sect. 4, we introduce a few examples of systems that could benefit from the calculus and discuss their security properties. In Sect. 5, we compare with related work and finally, in Sect. 6, we conclude.

2 Process Calculus

The syntax of the crypto-loc calculus is defined in Fig. 1. In this calculus, terms M, N represent passive data such as messages. These are either atomic terms, like *names* a, b, c and *variables* x, y, z, or complex terms that result from the application of functions f defined by a signature Σ. Names represent atomic data, such as keys, while variables will later be substituted by some possibly complex message. The signature Σ consists of a finite set of function symbols, with an associated arity. It is equipped with an equational theory, that is, a congruence relation on terms closed under substitutions of terms for free variables and names. We denote by $\Sigma \vdash M = N$ the equality of M and N modulo the equational theory, and we assume that there exist two different terms modulo this equational theory.

The signature Σ that we adopt in this paper mainly concentrates on the cryptographic functions, such as symmetric and asymmetric encryption/decryption, digital signatures/verification etc. For instance, shared-key cryptography can be defined by two functions **encrypt** for encryption and **decrypt** for decryption, with the equation $\mathbf{decrypt}(\mathbf{encrypt}(x, y), y) = x$. Data structures can also be encoded by including functions for tuple creation and projections. Sometimes we abbreviate tuples $(M_1, \ldots, M_n)$ as the vector $\vec{M}$. While, in this paper, our examples use only simple cryptographic primitives, the technique can also model complex cases such as xor and Diffie-Hellman key agreements [3]. The term $\mathbf{pack}(\vec{M}, \lambda\vec{x}.P)$ transforms a process P and a tuple $\vec{M}$ into data that can be treated as any other passive term. This removes the need for special input/output actions for processes. We postpone the detailed explanation of this term to after the explanation of processes.

The syntax of processes P, Q is described as follows. A null process 0 is an inactive process unable to evolve any further. The process $P \mid Q$ denotes the parallel composition of two process P and Q. A replicated process $!P$ spawns an unbounded number of copies of P. Restriction $(\nu a)P$ localizes the name a within the scope of P. A location $M[P]$ embodies the process P. The process P is said to *reside* at M. As in boxed ambients [10], an input action $M^\eta(\lambda x).P$ has three types: local-input $M^\star(\lambda x).P$, up-input $M^\uparrow(\lambda x).P$ and down-input $M^N(\lambda x).P$. A local input can only synchronize with output actions that are performed by processes local to the current location. Up-input can only receive messages from processes resident in the environment location enclosing the current location. A down-input $M^N(\lambda x).P$ can only receive messages from the sublocation N enclosed by the current location. Similarly, output actions $\overline{M}^\eta(M').P$ are divided into local-, up- and down-outputs. For instance, in the process $c[a^\uparrow(\lambda y).P] \mid \overline{a}^c(M).Q$, the down-output $\overline{a}^c(M)$ can send its message to the up-input $a^\uparrow(\lambda y)$ inside location c. The terms that represent channels in input/output actions, their η parameter, and the names of locations must reduce to names at runtime. Otherwise, the process blocks. The $\mathbf{exec}(M)$ process executes M when M is a **pack**ed process. Otherwise, it blocks. Finally, a conditional process compares two terms, M and N, and branches to either P or Q, depending on whether $\Sigma \vdash M = N$ holds true or not. As usual, we may omit an *else* clause when it consists of 0.

$M, N ::=$	terms
x, y, z	variable
a, b, c, k	name
$f(M_1, \ldots, M_n)$	function application
$\mathbf{pack}(\vec{M}, \lambda\vec{x}.P)$	processes (with $fn(P) = \emptyset, fv(P) \subseteq \{\vec{x}\}$)
$\eta ::=$	communication target
M	down
$\uparrow$	up
$\star$	local
$P, Q ::=$	processes
0	null
$P \mid Q$	parallel composition
$!P$	replication
$(\nu a)P$	restriction
$M^\eta(\lambda x).P$	input
$\overline{M}^\eta\langle M'\rangle.P$	output
$M[P]$	location
$\mathbf{exec}(M)$	execute packed process
if $M = N$ *then* P *else* Q	conditional

Fig. 1. Syntax of the process calculus

The substitution that replaces M for x is denoted by $\{M/x\}$. We extend this to tuples $\{\vec{M}/\vec{x}\}$. We denote by $P\sigma$ (resp. $M\sigma$) the application of the substitution σ to process P (resp. term M). We define *let* $x = M$ *in* P as syntactic sugar for $P\{M/x\}$. We denote by $\{\vec{x}\}$ the set of variables in the tuple $\vec{x}$. We denote by *fn* the free names and by *fv* the free variables of a process or a term, defined as usual. In $\mathbf{pack}(\vec{M}, \lambda\vec{x}.P)$, the variables $\vec{x}$ are bound. A process or a term is *closed* when it contains no free variable. It may have free names.

Let us now explain packed processes. Intuitively, in $\mathbf{pack}(\vec{M}, \lambda\vec{x}.P)$, P represents the code of the process and the tuple $\vec{M}$ represents its data. When executing such a process, the tuple $\vec{M}$ is substituted for the variables $\vec{x}$ in P, and the resulting process is executed. We include a function $\mathbf{getdata} \in \Sigma$ used (by malicious processes) to extract the data $\vec{M}$, defined by $\mathbf{getdata}(\mathbf{pack}(\vec{M}, \lambda\vec{x}.P)) = \vec{M}$.

The separation between data and code is important for security considerations, since an adversary can extract all data carried by a process. So, for example, the process:

$$\mathbf{pack}((s, k, a), \lambda(x, y, z).\overline{z}^{\uparrow}\langle\mathbf{encrypt}(x, y)\rangle)$$

reveals s, k, a when it is sent in clear over the network, whereas the process:

$$\mathbf{pack}((\mathbf{encrypt}(s, k), a), \lambda(x, z).\overline{z}^{\uparrow}\langle x\rangle)$$

reveals only $\mathbf{encrypt}(s, k)$ and a, but not s when the adversary does not have k. Then, these two processes must be represented differently, even if they perform the same actions when they are executed. The separation of code and data is enforced by the conditions $fn(P) = \emptyset$ and $fv(P) \subseteq \{\vec{x}\}$ that prevent the presence of data in P. The equational theory is such that $\Sigma \vdash \mathbf{pack}(\vec{M}, \lambda\vec{x}.P) = \mathbf{pack}(\vec{M}', \lambda\vec{x}'.P')$ if and only if $\Sigma \vdash \vec{M} = \vec{M}'$ and $P'\{\vec{x}/\vec{x}'\} \equiv P$ (with $fn(P) = fn(P') = \emptyset$, $fv(P) \subseteq \{\vec{x}\}$, and $fv(P') \subseteq \{\vec{x}'\}$), where $\equiv$ is the structural equivalence defined below.

The adversary can also observe the code of packed processes, by testing equality with processes it builds. Hence, the process:

$$c^{\eta}(\lambda x).\mathit{if}\ x = \mathbf{pack}(\mathbf{getdata}(x), \lambda\vec{y}.P)\ \mathit{then}\ \ldots\ \mathit{else}\ \ldots$$

tests whether the code of x (received on c) is structurally equivalent to P (since the equality is defined as structural equivalence for processes). We could optionally add other functions to manipulate and transform the code of packed processes, but **getdata** already gives enough power to the adversary. Indeed, the adversary can build any process, so it can rebuild the code of packed processes without having a primitive to extract it. (Note, however, that scoping constraints introduced by the restriction prevent the adversary from using private data of processes, when it does not learn them by listening to communications.)

The formal semantics of the crypto-loc calculus is given in Fig. 2. Note that all rules apply only to closed processes and that in (11), M and M' must be closed. Processes are considered equal modulo renaming of bound names and variables. Processes are prepared syntactically for communications by applying the structural equivalence relation $\equiv$, which is defined as the least equivalence satisfying the first set of rules of Fig. 2. The second set of the rules of Fig. 2 introduces the reduction relation $\rightarrow$. The first three rules (Red Local), (Red Down), and (Red Up) deal with local, downward, and upward communications with respect to the process performing the output action. Rule (Red Exec) deals with the execution of packed processes. Other rules are standard.

As an example, let us consider the following process:

$$\begin{aligned}&(\nu k)(\overline{c}^{\star}(\mathbf{pack}((d, \mathbf{encrypt}(m,k)), \lambda(x_d, x_e).x_d{}^{\uparrow}(\lambda z).\overline{x_d}^{\star}(\mathbf{decrypt}(x_e, z))))\\ &\quad \mid c^{\star}(\lambda y).b[\mathbf{exec}(y) \mid d^{\star}(\lambda x_m).0] \mid \overline{d}^{b}(k))\end{aligned}$$

This process first creates a new key k, shared between the processes that execute in parallel. The first element of the parallel composition outputs a packed process on the public channel c; the second one receives it, and executes it inside a location b. After these steps, the process becomes

$$(\nu k)(0 \mid b[d^{\uparrow}(\lambda z).\overline{d}^{\star}(\mathbf{decrypt}(\mathbf{encrypt}(m,k), z)) \mid d^{\star}(\lambda x_m).0] \mid \overline{d}^{b}(k))$$

The process that comes from the packed process waits for a message on channel d from outside location b. So it can receive the key k sent by the last element of the parallel composition. After receiving this key, it decrypts the message $\mathbf{encrypt}(m,k)$ with it, and outputs the result m on channel d locally inside location b. The message m is then received by $d^{\star}(\lambda x_m).0$.

Structural equivalence $P \equiv P'$:

$$P \mid 0 \equiv P \quad (1)$$
$$P \mid Q \equiv Q \mid P \quad (2)$$
$$(P \mid Q) \mid R \equiv P \mid (Q \mid R) \quad (3)$$
$$P \equiv Q \Rightarrow P \mid R \equiv Q \mid R \quad (4)$$
$$P \equiv Q \Rightarrow (\nu a)P \equiv (\nu a)Q \quad (5)$$
$$P \equiv Q \Rightarrow M[P] \equiv M[Q] \quad (6)$$
$$!P \equiv P \mid !P \quad (7)$$
$$(\nu a_1)(\nu a_2)P \equiv (\nu a_2)(\nu a_1)P \quad (8)$$
$$(\nu a)(P \mid Q) \equiv P \mid (\nu a)Q \text{ if } a \notin fn(P) \quad (9)$$
$$(\nu a)M[P] \equiv M[(\nu a)P] \text{ if } a \notin fn(M) \quad (10)$$
$$P\{M/x\} \equiv P\{M'/x\} \text{ if } \Sigma \vdash M = M' \quad (11)$$

Reduction $P \rightarrow P'$:

$$a^\star(\lambda y).P' \mid \overline{a}^\star(M).Q' \rightarrow P'\{M/y\} \mid Q' \quad \text{(Red Local)}$$
$$c[a^\uparrow(\lambda y).P' \mid R] \mid \overline{a}^c(M).Q' \rightarrow c[P'\{M/y\} \mid R] \mid Q' \quad \text{(Red Down)}$$
$$a^c(\lambda y).P' \mid c[\overline{a}^\uparrow(M).Q' \mid R] \rightarrow P'\{M/y\} \mid c[Q' \mid R] \quad \text{(Red Up)}$$
$$\mathbf{exec}(\mathbf{pack}(\vec{M}, \lambda\vec{x}.P)) \rightarrow P\{\vec{M}/\vec{x}\} \quad \text{(Red Exec)}$$
$$\textit{if } M = M \textit{ then } P \textit{ else } Q \rightarrow P \quad \text{(Red Then)}$$
$$\textit{if } M = N \textit{ then } P \textit{ else } Q \rightarrow Q \text{ if } \Sigma \nvdash M = N \quad \text{(Red Else)}$$
$$P \rightarrow Q \Rightarrow P \mid R \rightarrow Q \mid R \quad \text{(Red Par)}$$
$$P \rightarrow Q \Rightarrow (\nu a)P \rightarrow (\nu a)Q \quad \text{(Red Res)}$$
$$P \rightarrow Q \Rightarrow M[P] \rightarrow M[Q] \quad \text{(Red Loc)}$$
$$P' \equiv P,\, P \rightarrow Q,\, Q \equiv Q' \Rightarrow P' \rightarrow Q' \quad \text{(Red} \equiv\text{)}$$

Fig. 2. Structural equivalence and reduction relations

3 Process Equivalences

Observational equivalence is a powerful means for defining security properties of processes and for reasoning about them. In this section, we define observational equivalence and show that a labelled bisimilarity relation can be used to provide simpler proofs of observational equivalence. Thus, we extend the results proved in [3] for the applied pi calculus to locations and mobility.

Intuitively, two processes are observationally equivalent when an adversary cannot distinguish them. The adversary is formalized as any *evaluation context*, defined as follows: An evaluation context C is a context formed with the hole $\{\}$, restrictions $(\nu a)C$, parallel compositions $P \mid C$, and locations $M[C]$. Intuitively, the adversary can listen to messages sent on the network, compute its own messages, and send them. It can also insert the considered process inside locations. The application of context C to process P is denoted by $C\{P\}$. An evaluation context C *closes* P when $C\{P\}$ is closed. We say that a process P *emits on channel* a, and we write $P \Downarrow a$, when $P\,(\rightarrow \cup \equiv)^*\,(\nu b_1)\ldots(\nu b_n)(\overline{a}^\star(M).P \mid Q)$ with $a \notin \{b_1, \ldots, b_n\}$.

Definition 1. Observational equivalence $\approx$ *is the largest symmetric relation* $\mathcal{R}$ *between closed processes such that* $P \,\mathcal{R}\, Q$ *implies:*

(1) *if* $P \Downarrow a$*, then* $Q \Downarrow a$*;*
(2) *if* $P \rightarrow^* P'$ *then there exists* Q' *such that* $Q \rightarrow^* Q'$ *and* $P' \,\mathcal{R}\, Q'$*;*
(3) $C\{P\} \,\mathcal{R}\, C\{Q\}$ *for all closing evaluation contexts* C*.*

Observational equivalence can be used to define security properties of processes, by showing that the process is observationally equivalent to an ideal process representing the security specification of the system. It can also be used to define secrecy based on the notion of non-interference:

Definition 2. *A process* P preserves the secrecy *of* $fv(P)$ *if and only if for all* σ *and* σ' *substitutions of domain* $fv(P)$*,* $P\sigma \approx P\sigma'$*.*

This definition intuitively expresses that the adversary obtains no information on the value of the variables in $fv(P)$, since processes using different values for these variables are observationally equivalent, i.e. indistinguishable by the adversary. This notion of secrecy makes it possible to detect implicit flows, for instance when the adversary can test whether a secret is equal to some value it has. It is stronger than the perhaps more frequent reachability notion, saying that a value is secret when the adversary cannot reconstruct it. We refer the reader to [1] for a more detailed discussion of the definition of secrecy.

Proving observational equivalence is difficult, because we have to prove equivalence *for all* possible contexts (point (3) of the definition). We define another process equivalence, namely labelled bisimilarity, that avoids the universal quantification on contexts. We show that labelled bisimilarity equals observational equivalence. Such results are frequent in process algebras, but they are also important: they make it possible to replace a proof of observational equivalence with a much simpler proof of labelled bisimilarity.

The definition of labelled bisimilarity proceeds in several steps. First, we define the notion of *agents*. Agents represent the current state of the process as well as the current knowledge of the adversary. An agent A is of the form $(\nu\tilde{a})(\sigma, P)$, where $\tilde{a}$ is a set of names, σ is a substitution from variables to terms, and P is a process, such that $dom(\sigma) \cap (fv(P) \cup \cup_x fv(x\sigma)) = \emptyset$. In the agent $(\nu\tilde{a})(\sigma, P)$, P represents the current state of the process and σ the current knowledge of the adversary, that is, the adversary knows all terms in the image of σ, and it can designate them by using the variables in the domain of σ. The restriction $(\nu\tilde{a})$ indicates that the adversary does not have a priori knowledge of the names in $\tilde{a}$. For example, the agent $(\nu k)(\{\mathbf{encrypt}((a, b), k)/x\}, P)$ represents that the adversary has the term $M = \mathbf{encrypt}((a, b), k)$, but not the key k, so it cannot see that M is an encryption, but it can build (x, a), that is, (M, a), for instance. If it later learns k, with an agent such as $(\nu k)(\{\mathbf{encrypt}((a, b), k)/x, k/y\}, P')$, then it can decrypt M by computing $\mathbf{decrypt}(x, y)$ which is equal to (a, b) taking into account the values of x and y. We define $dom((\nu\tilde{a})(\sigma, P)) = dom(\sigma)$. An agent is closed when the image of σ and the process P do not contain free variables. A process is also an agent, by taking $\tilde{a}$ and $dom(\sigma)$ empty.

Agents are considered equal modulo renaming of bound names and variables. The structural equivalence and reduction of agents extend the ones of processes. More precisely, the structural equivalence of agents is defined as the smallest equivalence relation closed under:

$$(\nu\tilde{a})(\sigma, P) \equiv (\nu\tilde{a})(\sigma', P) \text{ if } \forall x, \Sigma \vdash x\sigma = x\sigma'$$
$$(\nu\tilde{b}, a)(\sigma, P) \equiv (\nu\tilde{b})(\sigma, (\nu a)P) \text{ if } \forall x, a \notin fn(x\sigma)$$
$$P \equiv P' \Rightarrow (\nu\tilde{b})(\sigma, P) \equiv (\nu\tilde{b})(\sigma, P')$$

The reduction of agents is defined by $A \to B$ when $A \equiv (\nu\tilde{b})(\sigma, P)$, $P \to Q$, and $(\nu\tilde{b})(\sigma, Q) \equiv B$.

The labelled operational semantics represents reductions of processes that occur in interaction with an unspecified context. It is defined by the rules of Fig. 3. The label α of the reduction indicates the nature of the interaction with this context: it can be of the form $\overline{M}^\eta(x)$ (output of a term on channel M, the term is received in variable x by the context), $M^\eta(\lambda M')$ (input of a term M' on channel M), $M''[\overline{M}^\uparrow(x)]$, or $M''[M^\uparrow(\lambda M')]$ (output and input through a location). The rules defining the labelled reduction $A \xrightarrow{\alpha} A'$ apply only when A is closed, and then A' is closed.

The rule (In) means that the process $a^\eta(\lambda x).P$ can receive a term M from the context, then it reduces to $P\{M/x\}$. The rule (Out) means that the process $\overline{a}^\eta(M).P$ can output the term M to the context, which receives it in some variable x. The reduced process is P, and the context now has knowledge of the term M, which is represented by the substitution $\{M/x\}$. The rules (Loc In) and (Loc Out) handle inputs and outputs inside a location. Only inputs and outputs to the outside of the location (using $\uparrow$: $a^\uparrow(\lambda x)$ and $\overline{a}^\uparrow(M)$) are visible to the context, so this is the only case considered in these rules. Intuitively, in these rules, $c[P]$ reduces to $c[A]$, but $c[A]$ is outside the syntax of agents, so we replace it with $c[] \circ A$ which plays the same role but yields a well-formed agent. $A \phi Q$, $(\nu a) \circ A$, and $\sigma \circ A$ are used for the same reason in the following rules. The rules (Parallel), (Restriction), and (Agent) handle reductions under evaluation contexts. In the rule (Restriction), note that when $a \in fn(\alpha)$, the context needs to know a to perform the reduction $P \xrightarrow{\alpha} A$, so it cannot perform this reduction on the process $(\nu a)P$. The rule (Agent) is complex. It can be decomposed into three steps: First, from $P \xrightarrow{\alpha} A$, we can infer $(\sigma, P) \xrightarrow{\alpha} \sigma \circ A$, provided that the domain of σ does not overlap with the domain of the substitution of A, that is, with the bound variables of α. Second, we can replace the label α with α', provided that $\Sigma \vdash \alpha\sigma = \alpha'\sigma$, that is, α and α' have the same value given the current knowledge of the adversary. Finally, we add the restriction $(\nu\tilde{a})$, in a way similar to the rule (Restriction). The rule (Struct) allows using structural equivalence to transform agents before reducing them.

We now define the *static equivalence* of agents. Two agents A and B are statically equivalent when the adversary cannot distinguish the terms given by the substitutions of these agents (without executing the processes associated with each of A and B).

$$a^\eta(\lambda x).P \xrightarrow{a^\eta(\lambda M)} P\{M/x\} \qquad (M \text{ closed}, \eta \text{ is } \star, \uparrow, \text{ or a name}) \tag{In}$$

$$\overline{a}^\eta(M).P \xrightarrow{\overline{a}^\eta(x)} \{M/x\}, P \qquad (\eta \text{ is } \star, \uparrow, \text{ or a name}) \tag{Out}$$

$$\frac{P \xrightarrow{a^\uparrow(\lambda M)} A}{c[P] \xrightarrow{c[a^\uparrow(\lambda M)]} c[] \circ A} \tag{Loc In}$$

$$\frac{P \xrightarrow{\overline{a}^\uparrow(x)} A}{c[P] \xrightarrow{c[\overline{a}^\uparrow(x)]} c[] \circ A} \tag{Loc Out}$$

$$\frac{P \xrightarrow{\alpha} A}{P \mid Q \xrightarrow{\alpha} A \phi Q} \tag{Parallel}$$

$$\frac{P \xrightarrow{\alpha} A \qquad a \notin fn(\alpha)}{(\nu a)P \xrightarrow{\alpha} (\nu a) \circ A} \tag{Restriction}$$

$$\frac{P \xrightarrow{\alpha} A \qquad bv(\alpha) \cap dom(\sigma) = \emptyset \qquad \Sigma \vdash \alpha\sigma = \alpha'\sigma \qquad \tilde{a} \cap fn(\alpha') = \emptyset}{(\nu\tilde{a})(\sigma, P) \xrightarrow{\alpha'} (\nu\tilde{a}) \circ \sigma \circ A} \tag{Agent}$$

$$\frac{A \equiv B \quad B \xrightarrow{\alpha} B' \quad B' \equiv A'}{A \xrightarrow{\alpha} A'} \tag{Struct}$$

with

$$\begin{aligned}
&(\nu\tilde{a})(\sigma, P) \phi Q = (\nu\tilde{a})(\sigma, P \mid Q\sigma) \text{ if } fn(Q) \cap \tilde{a} = \emptyset \\
&(\nu b) \circ (\nu\tilde{a})(\sigma, P) = (\nu\tilde{a}, b)(\sigma, P) \text{ if } b \notin \tilde{a} \\
&\sigma' \circ (\nu\tilde{a})(\sigma, P) = (\nu\tilde{a})(\sigma \cup \sigma'\sigma, P) \text{ if } (\nu\tilde{a})(\sigma, P) \text{ is closed,} \\
&\qquad \text{for all } x, fn(x\sigma') \cap \tilde{a} = \emptyset, \text{ and } dom(\sigma) \cap dom(\sigma') = \emptyset \\
&c[] \circ (\nu\tilde{a})(\sigma, P) = (\nu\tilde{a})(\sigma, c[P]) \text{ if } c \notin \tilde{a}
\end{aligned}$$

$$\begin{aligned}
&fv(\overline{M}^\eta(x)) = fv(M) \cup fv(\eta), fv(M^\eta(\lambda M')) = fv(M) \cup fv(\eta) \cup fv(M'), \\
&\qquad fv(M''[\alpha]) = fv(M'') \cup fv(\alpha) \text{ and similarly for the free names } fn. \\
&bv(\overline{M}^\eta(x)) = \{x\}, bv(M^\eta(\lambda M')) = \emptyset, bv(M''[\alpha]) = bv(\alpha)
\end{aligned}$$

Fig. 3. Labelled semantics

Definition 3. *We say that* $(M = N)A$ *if and only if there exist a substitution* σ, *a process* P, *and names* $\tilde{a}$ *such that* $A \equiv (\nu\tilde{a})(\sigma, P)$, $\Sigma \vdash M\sigma = N\sigma$, *and* $\tilde{a} \cap (fn(M) \cup fn(N)) = \emptyset$.

We say that $\text{isname}(M, A)$ *is true if and only if there exist a substitution* σ, *a process* P, *and names* $\tilde{a}, b$ *such that* $A \equiv (\nu\tilde{a})(\sigma, P)$, $\Sigma \vdash M\sigma = b$, *and* $\tilde{a} \cap fn(M) = \emptyset$.

Now, two agents A *and* B *are* statically equivalent *($A \approx_s B$) when* $dom(A) = dom(B)$, *and for all terms* M *and* N, $(M = N)A$ *if and only if* $(M = N)B$, *and* $\text{isname}(M, A)$ *if and only if* $\text{isname}(M, B)$.

The condition "$(M = N)A$ if and only if $(M = N)B$" takes into account that the adversary can test equality between terms. The property $\text{isname}(M, A)$

means that M is equal to a name, taking into account the values of variables given by the substitution of A. The condition "isname(M, A) if and only if isname(M, B)" models the adversary's ability to check whether M is a name, by using it as a channel: the process $M^\star(\lambda x).\overline{a}^\star(b) \mid \overline{M}^\star(b)$ emits on channel a if and only if M is equal to a name. Another possibility is to authorize communications when channels and locations are any terms instead of just names. With that semantics, the condition on isname(M, A) would be removed.

Finally, we can define the labelled bisimilarity:

Definition 4. *Labelled bisimilarity ($\approx_l$) is the largest symmetric relation $\mathcal{R}$ on closed agents such that $A \mathcal{R} B$ implies:*

(1) $A \approx_s B$;
(2) *if* $A \to A'$ *then there exists* B' *such that* $B \to^* B'$ *and* $A' \mathcal{R} B'$;
(3) *if* $A \xrightarrow{\alpha} A'$, *then there exists* B' *such that* $B \to^* \xrightarrow{\alpha} \to^* B'$ *and* $A' \mathcal{R} B'$.

Theorem 1. *Labelled bisimilarity equals observational equivalence: $P \approx_l Q$ if and only if $P \approx Q$.*

Note that, in higher-order process calculi, the characterization of observational equivalence as labelled bisimilarity is often very difficult [18], because, when the adversary receives a process, the only observation it can do is to execute that process. In our calculus, the adversary can extract data and compare the code of processes (the existence of the function **getdata** is fundamental for that, see Sect. 2), much like it can for any other piece of data. Executing the process does not give more information to the adversary than these operations. Hence, being able to send processes does not complicate the labelled bisimilarity. In contrast, the presence of locations complicates the proof of Th. 1 considerably.

4 Examples

In this section, we present three examples illustrating the features of our calculus.

4.1 Firewalls

Firewalls exist as gateways through which communications with external networks are controlled (or restricted). The concept of a firewall corresponds directly to the concept of a location. Processes within a firewall can only communicate with the external context when the firewall allows it. Such communications require a prior knowledge of the address (name) of the firewall.

A well-known property that characterizes perfectly isolating firewalls is expressed by the *perfect firewall equation* [12]:

Proposition 1. *Let P be a closed process. Then $(\nu c)c[P] \approx 0$.*

This result states that the firewall $(\nu c)c[\{\}]$ is perfectly isolating because its internal behaviour is non-observable due to the hiding effect of (νc). (This can be proved using labelled bisimilarity and noticing that $(\nu c)c[P]$ and all its reductions by the standard reduction relation do not reduce by the labelled reduction.) When P has free variables, it is easy to show, using the above proposition, that $(\nu c)c[P]$ preserves the secrecy of all its free variables, since $(\nu c)c[P\sigma] \approx 0 \approx (\nu c)c[P\sigma']$ for all closed substitutions σ and σ' of domain $fv(P)$.

In practice, a firewall often leaves some channels open for communications by extending the scope of the restriction (νc):

$$R \stackrel{\text{def}}{=} (\nu c)(c[P] \mid !a^{\star}(\lambda x).\overline{a}^{c}(x) \mid !b^{c}(\lambda x).\overline{b}^{\star}(x)) \mid Q$$

With the two replicated processes aware of the name c, messages may be forwarded over channel a from Q to P, and from P to Q over channel b. Other communications are forbidden by the firewall. Hence, for example:

Proposition 2. *Let* $P = \overline{b}^{\uparrow}(y) \mid \overline{a}^{\uparrow}(z)$. *Then* $R\{M/y\}$ *preserves the secrecy of* z, *and* $R\{M/z\}$ *does not preserve the secrecy of* y.

Indeed, y is sent to the outside of the firewall on channel b. Another form of firewalls is built by using nested locations:

Proposition 3. $c[c'[P]] \approx 0$.

Two nested locations prevent communications because communications are possible only between locations immediately inside one another. We can allow some communications by extending the scope of the location c, to include some relay processes. For example, we can model a computer as a location c with processes running inside it as locations $c_1, \ldots, c_n$ by the process:

$$c[c_1[P_1] \mid \ldots \mid c_n[P_n] \mid P]$$

The process P models the operating system. Then distinct processes can communicate with the network outside the computer and with each other only through the operating system P acting as the intermediary.

We can also model a Local Area Network (LAN) as a location c, containing several locations $c_1, \ldots, c_n$, each representing a computer, by the same process. The process P the models the routing of messages inside the LAN and the communications with the outside. (Realistically, P should simply forward all communications from a location inside the LAN to another location inside the LAN, with only some communications forwarded to the outside.)

4.2 Applets

The **pack** and **exec** primitives for packing processes and extracting them from messages allow for the modelling of applets. For example, consider the following sequence of messages exchanged between a client C and a server S:

$$C \rightarrow S : \text{"Send me your applet"}$$
$$S \rightarrow C : \{\mathbf{pack}(\vec{M}, \lambda\vec{y}.P)\}_{sk_S}$$

where digital signatures, used in the second message, require the function **sign** to sign a message, **checksign** to check it, **extract** to extract the message from a signed message, and **pk** to create a public key from its secret part. These are defined by the equations:

$$\begin{aligned} \mathbf{checksign}(\mathbf{sign}(M, sk), \mathbf{pk}(sk)) &= \mathbf{True} \\ \mathbf{checksign}(M', \mathbf{pk}(sk)) &= \mathbf{False} \quad \text{if } M' \neq \mathbf{sign}(M, sk) \text{ for all } M \\ \mathbf{extract}(\mathbf{sign}(M, sk)) &= M \end{aligned}$$

The system can then be represented by the following processes:

$$R \stackrel{\mathbf{def}}{=} (\nu sk_S) let\ pk_S = \mathbf{pk}(sk_S)\ in\ (\overline{c}^\star(pk_S) \mid C \mid S)$$

$$C \stackrel{\mathbf{def}}{=} \overline{c}^\star(\mathbf{sndapp}).c^\star(\lambda x).if\ \mathbf{checksign}(x, pk_S) = \mathbf{True}\ then\ \mathbf{exec}(\mathbf{extract}(x))$$

$$S \stackrel{\mathbf{def}}{=} !c^\star(\lambda x).if\ x = \mathbf{sndapp}\ then\ \overline{c}^\star(\mathbf{sign}(\mathbf{pack}(\vec{M}, \lambda\vec{y}.P), sk_S))$$

The process R first creates a new secret key for the server sk_S, then computes the corresponding public key pk_S, and publishes this key by $\overline{c}^\star(pk_S)$, so that the adversary can have it. Finally, it executes the client and server processes (C and S) according to the message sequence above.

The client is assured of the origin of the applet when it succeeds in verifying the signature using **checksign** (assuming the public key pk_S is validly bound to the server S at the time when **checksign** is called). It then executes the applet. Otherwise, if the applet is not signed, or it is signed with a key different from sk_S, then the client terminates.

One may arrive at the following result, which shows that the only applet that can be executed by R is $\mathbf{pack}(\vec{M}, \lambda\vec{y}.P)$:

Proposition 4. *Let R' be obtained from R by substituting "if $\mathbf{extract}(x) = \mathbf{pack}(\vec{M}, \lambda\vec{y}.P)$ then $P\{\vec{M}/\vec{y}\}$" for "$\mathbf{exec}(\mathbf{extract}(x))$" in C. Then $R \approx R'$.*

The key lemma to prove this result is to show that the only packed process that can be the parameter of **exec** is the one signed by the server.

Other protocols to obtain applets are possible. We have also modelled an example in which an applet is sent encrypted, using a simple public-key protocol. We could also model an SSL communication on which an applet is sent.

Applets that are communicated by secure means (encryption or signatures) as shown in the previous example are often trusted to a certain degree, depending on the level of trust associated with the public key of the server pk_S. However, applets received through insecure communications (non-trusted applets) are run in special *sandboxes* that limit their capabilities. For example, such applets are prevented from accessing the local file system or contacting network addresses (except the address from which the applet originated).

Consider again the client C in the signed applet example above. This time it is enhanced with a sandbox $sb[\ldots]$, within which applets not originating from the server S are run. On the other hand, trusted applets are given more privileges by running them outside $sb[\ldots]$:

$$C \stackrel{\text{def}}{=} (\overline{c}^{\star}(\mathbf{sndapp}).c^{\star}(\lambda x).\mathit{if}\ \mathbf{checksign}(x, pk_S) = \mathbf{True}\ \mathit{then}\ \mathbf{exec}(\mathbf{extract}(x))$$
$$\mathit{else}\ (\nu sb)(sb[\mathbf{exec}(\mathbf{extract}(x))] \mid P)) \quad \mid Q$$

Process P models the Java standard library. Its communications with the applet correspond to method calls and returns. The process P can communicate with the outside of the sandbox, and for instance send messages coming from the applet on the network (perhaps after examining them for security). Process Q, on the other hand, is protected from the applet by the fact that it falls outside the scope of the sandbox. Prop. 4 can be applied to the first occurrence of $\mathbf{exec}(\mathbf{extract}(x))$ in C, and the sandbox prevents direct communications between the applet and the outside world: all these communications must go through P, since one needs to know sb to communicate with the interior of the sandbox. (Obviously, we assume that P is disciplined so as not to reveal the name sb.)

4.3 Certified Email Protocol

We consider here a cryptographic protocol whose implementation relies on a Java applet: the email protocol of [5]. In this protocol, a sender S sends an email message to a receiver R, such that R has the message if and only if S has a receipt. The protocol also involves a trusted third party TTP. In a slightly simplified version, the protocol runs as follows:

Message 1. S → R: "This is a certified email.
Please read it in a Java enabled browser"
`<APPLET CODE="https://ttp.com/applet.jar"`
`PARAM=`(cleartext, em, S2TTP)`>`
Message 2. R → TTP: get `https://ttp.com/applet.jar`
Message 3. TTP → R: `applet.jar`
Message 4. R → TTP: S2TTP, "owner of RPwd wants key for h"
Message 5. TTP → R: "try k for h"
Message 6. TTP → S: **sign**("I have released the key for S2TTP to R", $\mathsf{sk}_{\mathsf{TTP}}$)

The sender S wants to send to R the message m. It creates a fresh key k, encrypts m with k, obtaining em = **encrypt**(m, k). It also computes h = **H**((cleartext, em)) and S2TTP = **pencrypt**((S, "give k to R for h"), $\mathsf{pk}_{\mathsf{TTP}}$), where **pencrypt** is public-key encryption and **H** is a one-way hash function. Then it sends to R an html email (message 1) containing a header explaining how to read the email, as well as a reference to an applet `https://ttp.com/applet.jar` taking as parameters (cleartext, em, S2TTP), where cleartext is an explanation of the contents of the certified e-mail. The reader's browser downloads the applet on a secure SSL connection (messages 2 and 3) and executes it with the indicated parameters. The applet displays cleartext to the receiver, and asks him for his password RPwd. If R decides to read the email, it enters its password RPwd and the applet sends message 4 to TTP on a secure channel built by a combination of public-key and shared-key encryption. The value of h in this message is recomputed by the applet from cleartext and em. TTP replies to R with message 5 on the same secure channel as message 4. Upon receipt of message 5, the applet decrypts em with k, and displays m. TTP also sends the receipt (message 6) to S. The delivery of messages 5 and 6 is guaranteed. We have formally modeled this protocol in our calculus, by combining the model of [2] (which omitted the applet) and a model of the applet along the same lines as the previous example. The resulting model is 229 lines long (including comments) so we do not detail it here due to the lack of space.

When one assumes that the applet behaves as expected, the protocol satisfies its security properties [2, 7]. However, when one takes into account the downloading of the applet, one finds the following attack, which was mentioned to us by the authors of the protocol: in message 1, S sends the address of an applet on its own web site. This applet behaves as expected, except that it never displays the clear message to R. Because of the security constraints on applets, the applet can contact only the web site it comes from. However, this web site will simply forward the messages to TTP. Then the protocol runs as expected, the sender gets its receipt in message 6, but the receiver never has the clear message because the applet does not display it. This contradicts the main security property of the protocol.

One can see several corrections to this problem, so that the applet can come only from TTP. The easiest one would be for the receiver to manually check the address of the applet. Since the address contains `https`, the applet is downloaded using SSL, so we have the guarantee that the obtained applet is the expected one, as mentioned in the previous example. A result similar to Prop. 4 formalizes this guarantee. Then we can use the security properties of the protocol without applet to show the security of the protocol with applet. We could also require that the applet be signed by TTP. However, browsers accept to run unsigned applets, so the receiver should have a specific piece of software that checks that. In that case, it is probably simpler not to use an applet at all: R should simply have downloaded the software that executes the protocol.

In this example, our calculus makes it possible to formally model the protocol including the applet and a combination of mobility and cryptography (the applet is sent on an SSL connection and also performs cryptographic operations itself). An attack appears in this model while it does not in usual models of protocols that cannot represent applets. Indeed, this attack relies crucially on furnishing a malicious applet to the receiver. We can also prove the correctness of corrected versions of the protocol.

5 Comparison with Other Process Calculi

Models of Cryptography. Several variants of the spi calculus [6] have been proposed for modelling cryptography. Here, we focus on the most powerful of these variants, the applied pi calculus [3]. We extend this calculus by adding locations and packed processes. There are other relatively important differences between our calculus and the applied pi calculus. We do not introduce floating substitutions and restriction on variables in the calculus, since these are useful only for the labelled bisimilarity. We prefer keeping the calculus as standard and simple as possible, even if the proof of Th. 1 requires a few more technical lemmas. We also remove the "open" rules in the labelled bisimilarity, and do not resort to a sort system to prevent channel names from being manipulated by functions. To compensate this point, our static equivalence takes into account that the adversary can test whether a term is a name by using it as a channel.

Models of Location-Based Mobility. One of the most well-known models of mobility is the ambient calculus [12]. In this calculus, locations can move according to their own will and open other ambients. It is very difficult to restrict these movements. This makes the modelling of security properties difficult. Several variants have been designed to solve this problem: the safe ambients [16], in which each movement or opening of an ambient must be authorized by a co-capability, the secure safe ambients [9], which are a variant of safe ambients with a security type system, and the boxed ambients [10] in which the opening of ambients is removed and replaced with non-local communications between ambients. We use the communication mechanism of boxed ambients, but not the ambient mobility model: we believe that objective mobility (with processes sent as messages) is closer to what happens most often in networks. In contrast, ambient calculi are probably better at modelling situations in which human beings move security devices, for example.

Boxed ambients and cryptography have already been combined in [11]. The approach differs from our work in many aspects: [11] considers only shared-key cryptography; it represents messages as moving ambients, which, we think, is less natural than considering them as sent messages; it gives a type system for proving secrecy, whereas we focus on the proof of observational equivalence.

The seal calculus [20] provides strong objective mobility: processes are sent on the network by specific input and output constructs. We focus on weak mobility, and simplify the calculus by using the ordinary input and output instructions to manipulate packed processes. In the original version [20], the seal calculus used an **open** construct, combined to a local input or output to create non-local communications. In a recent draft, G. Castagna, F. Nardelli, and J. Vitek have adopted a simpler communication mechanism similar to the one of boxed ambients, which we adopt.

The Dπ-calculus of [17] includes a notion of migration of the current location (as in ambients) but also features such as halted and running locations, that we omit from our calculus for simplicity. In the distributed π-calculus of [19], each subterm is explicitly located, instead of having locations contain a process, and communications can take place between different locations without constraints.

The Join Calculus. The previous models are all based on the pi calculus. Another process calculus that can be used for mobility is the join calculus [13]. It has the same expressive power as the pi calculus, but uses asymmetric channels with one receiver instead of symmetric channels. (One type of channel can encode the other.) It has also been extended to cryptography, similarly to the spi calculus [4]. The distributed join calculus [15] considers a tree of nested locations, with subjective mobility (but no cryptography).

6 Conclusion

In this paper, we have presented crypto-loc, a process calculus combining the concepts of cryptography, locations, and weak code mobility. We have also defined a theory of process equivalence, and showed that observational equivalence equals labelled bisimilarity. The theory was used in defining and proving security properties.

An interesting area for further research would involve extending automatic static analyses techniques that have already been developed for cryptographic protocols to this calculus. Indeed, the presence of locations, and of communication and cryptographic operations on code raises new difficulties for static analysis.

Acknowledgments

We would like to thank Cédric Fournet and Jan Vitek for very helpful comments on this work.

References

1. M. Abadi. Security Protocols and their Properties. In *Foundations of Secure Computation*, NATO Science Series, pages 39–60. IOS Press, 2000. Volume for the 20th International Summer School on Foundations of Secure Computation, held in Marktoberdorf, Germany (1999).
2. M. Abadi and B. Blanchet. Computer-Assisted Verification of a Protocol for Certified Email. In *Static Analysis, 10th International Symposium (SAS'03)*, volume 2694 of *LNCS*, pages 316–335. Springer, June 2003.
3. M. Abadi and C. Fournet. Mobile Values, New Names, and Secure Communication. In *28th ACM Symposium on Principles of Programming Languages (POPL'01)*, pages 104–115. ACM, Jan. 2001.
4. M. Abadi, C. Fournet, and G. Gonthier. Secure Implementation of Channel Abstractions. *Information and Computation*, 174(1):37–83, Apr. 2002.
5. M. Abadi, N. Glew, B. Horne, and B. Pinkas. Certified Email with a Light On-line Trusted Third Party: Design and Implementation. In *Proceedings of the Eleventh International World Wide Web Conference*, pages 387–395. ACM, May 2002.
6. M. Abadi and A. D. Gordon. A Calculus for Cryptographic Protocols: The Spi Calculus. *Information and Computation*, 148(1):1–70, Jan. 1999.
7. G. Bella, C. Longo, and L. C. Paulson. Verifying Second-Level Security Protocols. In *Theorem Proving in Higher Order Logics (TPHOLs'03)*, LNCS. Springer, Sept. 2003. To appear.
8. L. Bettini and R. D. Nicola. Translating Strong Mobility into Weak Mobility. In *Mobile Agents, 5th International Conference, MA'01*, volume 2240 of *LNCS*, pages 182–197. Springer, Dec. 2001.
9. M. Bugliesi and G. Castagna. Secure Safe Ambients. In *28th ACM Symposium on Principles of Programming Languages (POPL'01)*, pages 222–235. ACM, Jan. 2001.

10. M. Bugliesi, G. Castagna, and S. Crafa. Boxed Ambients. In *Theoretical Aspects of Computer Software, 4th International Symposium, TACS'01*, volume 2215 of *LNCS*, pages 38–63. Springer, Oct. 2001.
11. M. Bugliesi, S. Crafa, A. Prelić, and V. Sassone. Secrecy in Untrusted Networks. In *13th International Colloquium on Automata, Languages and Programming (ICALP'03)*, volume 2719 of *LNCS*, pages 969–983. Springer, July 2003.
12. L. Cardelli and A. D. Gordon. Mobile Ambients. In *Foundations of Software Science and Computation Structures, First International Conference (FoSSaCS '98)*, volume 1378 of *LNCS*, pages 140–155. Springer, 1998.
13. C. Fournet and G. Gonthier. The Reflexive Chemical Abstract Machine and the Join-Calculus. In *23rd ACM Symposium on Principles of Programming Languages (POPL'96)*, pages 372–385, Jan. 1996.
14. C. Fournet and G. Gonthier. A hierarchy of equivalences for asynchronous calculi. In *Proceedings of the 25th International Colloquium on Automata, Languages and Programming (ICALP'98)*, volume 1443 of *LNCS*, pages 844–855. Springer, July 1998.
15. C. Fournet, G. Gonthier, J.-J. Lévy, L. Maranget, and D. Rémy. A Calculus of Mobile Agents. In *7th International Conference on Concurrency Theory (CONCUR'96)*, volume 1119 of *LNCS*, pages 406–421. Springer, Aug. 1996.
16. F. Levi and D. Sangiorgi. Controlling Interference in Ambients. In *27th ACM Symposium on Principles of Programming Languages (POPL'00)*, pages 352–364. ACM, Jan. 2000.
17. J. Riely and M. Hennessy. A Typed Language for Distributed Mobile Processes. In *25th ACM Symposium on Principles of Programming Languages (POPL'98)*, pages 378–390. ACM, Jan. 1998.
18. D. Sangiorgi. *Expressing Mobility in Process Algebras: First-Order and Higher-Order Paradigms*. PhD thesis, University of Edinburgh, 1992.
19. P. Sewell. Global/Local Subtyping and Capability Inference for a Distributed π-calculus. In *Automata, Languages and Programming, 25th International Colloquium, ICALP'98*, volume 1443 of *LNCS*, pages 695–706. Springer, July 1998.
20. J. Vitek and G. Gastagna. Seal: A Framework for Secure Mobile Computations. In *Internet Programming Languages, ICCL'98 Workshop*, volume 1686 of *LNCS*, pages 47–77. Springer, May 1999.

A Calculus of Bounded Capacities*

Franco Barbanera[1], Michele Bugliesi[2],
Mariangiola Dezani-Ciancaglini[3], and Vladimiro Sassone[4]

[1] Università di Catania, Viale A.Doria 6, 95125 Catania (Italy)
barba@dmi.unict.it
[2] Università "Cà Foscari", Via Torino 155, 30170 Venezia (Italy)
michele@dsi.unive.it
[3] Università di Torino, Corso Svizzera 185, 10149 Torino (Italy)
dezani@di.unito.it
[4] University of Sussex, Falmer, Brighton BN1 9RH UK
vs@susx.ac.uk

Abstract. Resource control has attracted increasing interest in foundational research on distributed systems. This paper focuses on space control and develops an analysis of space usage in the context of an ambient-like calculus with bounded capacities and weighed processes, where migration and activation require space. A type system complements the dynamics of the calculus by providing static guarantees that the intended capacity bounds are preserved throughout the computation.

Introduction

Emerging computing paradigms, such as Global Computing and Ambient Intelligence, envision scenarios where mobile devices travel across domains and networks boundaries. Current examples include smart cards, embedded devices (e.g. in cars), mobile phones, PDAs, and the list keeps growing. The notion of third-party resource usage will raise to a central role, as roaming entities will need to borrow resources from host networks and, in turn, provide guarantees of bounded resource usage. This is the context of the present paper, which focuses on *space consumption* and *capacity bound* awareness.

Resource control, in diverse incarnations, has recently been the focus of foundational research. Topics considered include the ability to read from and to write to a channel [15], the control of the location of channel names [18], the guarantee that distributed agents will access resources only when allowed to do so [8, 14, 1, 6, 7]. Specific work on the certification of bounds on resource consumption include [9], which introduces a notion of resource type representing an abstract unit of space, and uses a linear type system to guarantee linear space consumption; [4] where quantitative bounds on time usage are enforced using a typed assembly language; and [11], which puts forward a general formulation of resource usage analysis.

* F. Barbanera is partially supported by MIUR project NAPOLI, M. Bugliesi by EU-FET project 'MyThS' IST-2001-32617, and by MIUR project MEFISTO, M. Dezani-Ciancaglini by EU-FET project DART IST-2001-33477, and by MIUR Projects COMETA and McTati, V. Sassone by EU-FET project 'MIKADO' IST-2001-32222. The funding bodies are not responsible for any use that might be made of the results presented here.

V.A. Saraswat (Ed.): ASIAN 2003, LNCS 2896, pp. 205–223, 2003.

We elect to formulate our analysis of space control in an ambient-like calculus, BoCa, because the notion of ambient mobility is a natural vehicle to address the intended application domain. Relevant references to related work in this context include [5], which presents a calculus in which resources may be moved across locations provided suitable space is available at the target location; [17], which uses typing systems to control resource usage and consumption; and [3], which uses static techniques to analyse the behaviour of finite control processes, i.e., those with bounded capabilities for ambient allocation and output creation.

BoCa relies on a physical, yet abstract, notion of "resource unit" defined in terms of a new process constructor, noted ▬ (read "*slot*"), which evolves out of the homonym notion of [5]. A slot may be interpreted as a unit of computation space to be allocated to running processes and migrating ambients. To exemplify, the configuration

$$P \mid \underbrace{\text{▬} \mid \ldots \mid \text{▬}}_{\mathsf{k}\ \text{times}}$$

represents a system which is running process P and which has k resource units available for P to spawn new subprocesses and to accept migrating agents willing to enter. In both cases, the activation of the new components is predicated to the presence of suitable resources: only processes and agents requiring cumulatively no more than k units may be activated on the system. As a consequence, process activation and agent migration involve a protocol to "negotiate" the use of resources with the enclosing, resp. receiving, context (possibly competing with other processes).

For migrating agents this is accounted for by associating each agent with a tag representing the space required for activation at the target context, as in $a^{\mathsf{k}}[\,P\,]$. A notion of well-formedness will ensure that k provides a safe estimate of the space needed by $a[\,P\,]$; namely, the number of resource units allocated to P. Correspondingly, the negotiation protocol for mobility is represented formally by the following reductions (where ▬^{k} is short for $\text{▬} \mid \ldots \mid \text{▬}$, k times):

$$a^{\mathsf{k}}[\,\mathbf{in}\, b.P \mid Q\,] \mid b[\,\text{▬}^{\mathsf{k}} \mid R\,] \searrow \text{▬}^{\mathsf{k}} \mid b[\,a^{\mathsf{k}}[\,P \mid Q\,] \mid R\,]$$

$$\text{▬}^{\mathsf{k}} \mid b[\,P \mid a^{\mathsf{k}}[\,\mathbf{out}\, b.Q \mid R\,]\,] \searrow a^{\mathsf{k}}[\,Q \mid R\,] \mid b[\,P \mid \text{▬}^{\mathsf{k}}\,]$$

In both cases, the migrating agent releases the space required for its computation at the source site and gets corresponding space at the target context. Notice that the reductions construe ▬ both as a representation of the physical space available at the locations of the system, and as a particular new kind of co-capability.

Making the weight of an ambient depend explicitly on its contents allows a clean and simple treatment of the open capability: opening does not require resources, as those needed to allocate the contents are exactly those taken by the ambient as such.

$$\mathbf{opn}\, a.P \mid a[\,\overline{\mathbf{opn}}.Q \mid R\,] \searrow P \mid Q \mid R$$

Notice that in order for these reductions to provide the intended semantics of resource negotiation, it is crucial that the redexes are well-formed. Accordingly, the dynamics of ambient mobility is inherently dependent on the assumption that all migrating agents are well-formed. As we shall discuss, this assumption is central to the definition of behavioural equivalence as well.

Resource management and consumption does not concern exclusively mobility, as *all* processes need and use space. It is natural then to expect that "spawning" (activating) processes requires resources, and that unbounded replication of processes is controlled so as to guard against processes that may consume an *infinite* amount of resources. The action of spawning a new process is made explicit in BoCa by introducing a new process construct, $\mathsf{k}\triangleright$, whose semantics is defined by the following reduction:

$$\mathsf{k}\triangleright P \mid \mathbf{-}^{\mathsf{k}} \searrow P$$

Here $\mathsf{k}\triangleright P$ is a "spawner" which launches P provided that the local context is ready to allocate enough fresh resources for the activation. The tag k represents the "activation cost" for process P, viz. its weight, while $\mathsf{k}\triangleright P$, the "frozen code" of P, weighs 0: again here the hypothesis of well-formedness of terms is critical to make sense of the spawning protocol. The adoption of an explicit spawning operator allows us to delegate to the "spawner" the responsibility of resource control in the mechanism for process replication. In particular, we restrict the replication primitive "!" to 0-weight processes only. We can then rely on the usual congruence rule that identifies $!P$ with $!P \mid P$, and use $!(\mathsf{k}\triangleright P)$ to realise a resource-aware version of replication. This results in a system which separates process *duplication* and *activation*, and so allows a fine analysis of resource consumption in computation.

BoCa is completed by two constructs that provide for dynamic allocation of resources. In our approach resources are not "created" from the void, but rather acquired dynamically – in fact, transferred – from the context, again as a result of a negotiation.

$$a^{\mathsf{k}+1}[\,\mathbf{put}.P \mid \mathbf{-} \mid Q\,] \mid b^{\mathsf{h}}[\,\mathbf{get}\,a.R \mid S\,] \searrow a^{\mathsf{k}}[\,P \mid Q\,] \mid b^{\mathsf{h}+1}[\,R \mid \mathbf{-} \mid S\,]$$
$$\mathbf{put}^{\downarrow}.P \mid \mathbf{-} \mid a^{\mathsf{k}}[\,\mathbf{get}^{\uparrow}.Q \mid R\,] \searrow P \mid a^{\mathsf{k}+1}[\,\mathbf{-} \mid Q \mid R\,]$$

Resource transfer is realised as a two-way synchronisation in which a context offers some of its resource units to any enclosed or sibling ambient that makes a corresponding request. The effect of the transfer is reflected in the tags that describe the resources allocated to the receiving ambients. We formalise slot transfers only between siblings and from father to child. As we shall see, transfers across siblings make it possible to encode a notion of private resource, while transfer from child to parent can easily be encoded in terms of the existing constructs.

The semantic theory of BoCa is supported by a labelled transition systems which gives rise to a bisimulation congruence adequate with respect to barbed congruence. Besides enabling powerful co-inductive characterizations of process equivalences, the labelled transition system yields an effective tool for contextual reasoning on process behavior. More specifically, it enables a formal representation of *open systems*, in which processes may acquire resources and space from their enclosing context. Due to the lack of space, here we only discuss the notion of barb, leaving the presentation of the transition system to the forthcoming full version of the paper. We will focus, instead, on BoCa's capacity types, a system of types that guarantees capacity bounds on computational ambients. Precisely, given lower and upper bounds for ambients capacities, the system enables us to certify statically the absence of under/over-flows, potentially arising from an uncontrolled use of dynamic space allocation capabilities.

We remark that our approach is typical of a way to couple language design with type analysis very useful in frameworks like Global Computing, where it is ultimately unrealistic to assume acquaintance with all the entities which may in the future interact with us, as it is usually done for standard type systems. The openness of the network and its very dynamic nature deny us any substantial form of global knowledge. Therefore, syntactic constructs must be introduced to support the static analysis, as e.g., our "negotiation" protocols. In our system, the possibility of dynamically checking particular space constraints is a consequence of the explicit presence of the primitive $\blacksquare$. A further reason to avoid resource control mechanisms in ambient-like calculi mainly based on static typing systems is that they tend, as perfectly illustrated in [17], to require 3-way synchronisations which, as explained in [16], make the calculus cumbersome.

Structure of the paper. In §1 we give the formal description of BoCa and its operational semantics, and we illustrate it with a few examples. The type system for the calculus is illustrated in §2. In §3 we discuss the issue of resource interference, and we extend the calculus to deal with private resources in the form of named slots.

1 The Calculus BoCa

The calculus is a conservative extension of the Ambient Calculus. We presuppose two mutually disjoint sets: $\mathcal{N}$ of names, and $\mathcal{V}$ of variables. The set $\mathcal{V}$ is ranged over by letters at the end of the alphabet, typically x, y, z, while a, b, c, d, n, m range over $\mathcal{N}$. Finally, h, k and other letters in the same font denote integers. The syntax of the calculus is defined below, with π and W types as introduced in §2.

Definition 1 (Preterms and Terms). The set of process *preterms* is defined by the following productions (where we assume $\mathsf{k} \geq 0$):

Processes $P ::= \blacksquare \mid \mathbf{0} \mid M.P \mid P|P \mid M^{\mathsf{k}}[\,P\,] \mid !P \mid (\boldsymbol{\nu} a:\pi)P \mid \mathsf{k} \triangleright P \mid (x:W)P \mid \langle M \rangle P$

Capabilities $C ::= \mathbf{in}\ M \mid \mathbf{out}\ M \mid \mathbf{opn}\ M \mid \mathbf{get}\ M \mid \mathbf{get}^{\uparrow} \mid \overline{\mathbf{opn}} \mid \mathbf{put} \mid \mathbf{put}^{\downarrow}$

Messages $M ::= nil \mid a \in \mathcal{N} \mid x \in \mathcal{V} \mid C \mid M.M$

A (well-formed) *term* P is a preterm such that $w(P) \neq \bot$, where $w : Processes \rightharpoonup \omega$ is the partial *weight* function defined as follows:

$$w(\mathbf{0}) = 0 \qquad w(\blacksquare) = 1 \qquad w(P \mid Q) = w(P) + w(Q)$$

$$w(M.P) = w((x:\chi)P) = w(\langle M \rangle P) = w((\boldsymbol{\nu} a:\pi)P) = w(P)$$

$$w(a^{\mathsf{k}}[\,P\,]) = \text{if } w(P) \text{ is } \mathsf{k} \text{ then } \mathsf{k} \text{ else } \bot$$

$$w(\mathsf{k} \triangleright P) = \text{if } w(P) \text{ is } \mathsf{k} \text{ then } 0 \text{ else } \bot$$

$$w(!P) = \text{if } w(P) \text{ is } 0 \text{ then } 0 \text{ else } \bot$$

We use the standard notational conventions for ambient calculi. We omit types when not relevant; we write $a[\,P\,]$ instead of $a^{\mathsf{k}}[\,P\,]$ when the value of k does not matter; we use $\blacksquare^{\mathsf{k}}$ as a shorthand for $\underbrace{\blacksquare \mid \ldots \mid \blacksquare}_{\mathsf{k}}$ and similarly C^{k} as a shorthand for $\underbrace{C.\ldots.C}_{\mathsf{k}}$

1.1 Reduction

The dynamics of the calculus is defined as usual in terms of structural congruence and reduction (cf. Figure 1). Unlike other calculi, however, in BoCa both relations are only defined for proper terms, a fact we will leave implicit in the rest of the presentation.

Structural Congruence: $(|, \mathbf{0})$ is a commutative monoid.

$$(\nu a)(P \mid Q) \equiv (\nu a)P \mid Q \quad (a \notin \mathrm{fn}(Q)) \qquad (\nu a)a^0[\,\mathbf{0}\,] \equiv \mathbf{0}$$
$$(\nu a)\mathbf{0} \equiv \mathbf{0} \qquad (\nu a)(\nu b)P \equiv (\nu b)(\nu a)P$$
$$!P \equiv P \mid !P \qquad a[\,(\nu b)P\,] \equiv (\nu b)a[\,P\,] \quad (a \neq b)$$

Reduction: $E ::= \{\cdot\} \mid E \mid P \mid (\nu m)E \mid m^{\mathsf{k}}[\,E\,]$ is an evaluation context

(ENTER)	$a^{\mathsf{k}}[\,\mathbf{in}\,b.P \mid Q\,] \mid b[\,\blacksquare^{\mathsf{k}} \mid R\,]$	$\searrow$	$\blacksquare^{\mathsf{k}} \mid b[\,a^{\mathsf{k}}[\,P \mid Q\,] \mid R\,]$
(EXIT)	$\blacksquare^{\mathsf{k}} \mid b[\,P \mid a^{\mathsf{k}}[\,\mathbf{out}\,b.Q \mid R\,]\,]$	$\searrow$	$a^{\mathsf{k}}[\,Q \mid R\,] \mid b[\,P \mid \blacksquare^{\mathsf{k}}\,]$
(OPEN)	$\mathbf{opn}\,a.P \mid a[\,\overline{\mathbf{opn}}.Q \mid R\,]$	$\searrow$	$P \mid Q \mid R$
(GETS)	$a^{\mathsf{k}+1}[\,\mathbf{put}.P \mid \blacksquare \mid Q\,] \mid b^{\mathsf{h}}[\,\mathbf{get}\,a.R \mid S\,]$	$\searrow$	$a^{\mathsf{k}}[\,P \mid Q\,] \mid b^{\mathsf{h}+1}[\,R \mid \blacksquare \mid S\,]$
(GETD)	$\mathbf{put}^{\downarrow}.P \mid \blacksquare \mid a^{\mathsf{k}}[\,\mathbf{get}^{\uparrow}.Q \mid R\,]$	$\searrow$	$P \mid a^{\mathsf{k}+1}[\,\blacksquare \mid Q \mid R\,]$
(SPAWN)	$\mathsf{k}\triangleright P \mid \blacksquare^{\mathsf{k}}$	$\searrow$	P
(EXCHANGE)	$(x:\chi)P \mid \langle M \rangle Q$	$\searrow$	$P\{x := M\} \mid Q$
(STRUCT)	$P \equiv P' \quad P' \searrow Q' \quad Q' \equiv Q$	$\Longrightarrow$	$P \searrow Q$
(CONTEXT)	$P \searrow Q$	$\Longrightarrow$	$E\{P\} \searrow E\{Q\}$

Fig. 1. Structural Congruence and Reduction

The reduction relation $\searrow$ is defined according to the intuitions discussed in the introduction; we denote with $\searrow_*$ the reflexive and transitive closure of $\searrow$. Structural congruence is essentially standard. The assumption of well-formedness is central to both relations. In particular, the congruence $!P \equiv P \mid !P$ only holds with P a proper term of weight 0. Thus, to duplicate arbitrary processes we need to first "freeze" them under $\mathsf{k}\triangleright$, i.e. we decompose arbitrary duplication into "template replication" and "process activation." We define $!^{\mathsf{k}} \triangleq !\mathsf{k}\triangleright$, which gives us $!^{\mathsf{k}}P \mid \blacksquare^{\mathsf{k}} \searrow !^{\mathsf{k}}P \mid P$.

A few remarks are in order on the form of the transfer capabilities. The **put** capability (among siblings) does not name the target ambient, as is the case for the dual capability **get**. We select this particular combination because it is the most liberal one for which our results hold. Of course, more stringent notions are possible, as e.g. when both partners in a synchronisation use each other's names. Adopting any of these would not change the nature of the calculus and preserve, mutatis mutandis, the validity of our results. In particular, the current choice makes it easy and natural to express interesting programming examples (cf. the memory management in §1.3), and protocols: e.g., it enables us to provide simple encoding of named (and private) resources allocated for spawning (cf. §3). Secondly, a new protocol is easily derived for transferring resources "upwards" from children to parents using the following pair of dual put and get.

$$\mathbf{get}^{\downarrow} a.P \triangleq (\nu m)(\mathbf{opn}\ m.P \mid m[\ \mathbf{get}\ a.\overline{\mathbf{opn}}\ ]), \quad \text{and} \quad \mathbf{put}^{\uparrow} \triangleq \mathbf{put}$$

Transfers affect the amount of resources allocated at different nesting levels in a system. We delegate to the type system of §2 to control that no nesting level suffers from resource over- or under-flows. The reduction semantics itself guarantees that the global amount of resources is preserved, as it can be proved by an inspection of the reduction rules.

Proposition 1 (Resource Preservation). *If $w(P) \neq \bot$, and $P \searrow_* Q$, then $w(Q) = w(P)$.*

Two remarks about the above proposition are in order. First, resource preservation is a distinctive property of *closed* systems; in open systems, instead, a process may acquire new resources from the environment, or transfer resources to the environment, by exercising the **put** and **get** capabilities. Secondly, the fact that the global weight of a process is invariant through reduction does not imply that the amount of resources available for computation also is invariant. Indeed, our notion of slot is an economical way to convey the three different concepts of a resource being *free*, *allocated*, or *wasted* , according to the context in which $\blacksquare$ occurs during the computation. Unguarded slots, as in $a[\ \blacksquare \mid P\ ]$, represent resources available for spawning or mobility at a given nesting level; guarded slots, like $M.\blacksquare$, represent allocated resources, which may potentially be released and become free; and unreachable slots, like $(\nu a)\mathbf{in}\ a.\blacksquare^{\mathsf{k}}$ or $(\nu a)a^{\mathsf{k}}[\ \blacksquare^{\mathsf{k}}\ ]$, represent wasted resources that will never be released.

Computation changes the state of resources in the expected ways: allocated resources may be freed, as in $\mathbf{opn}\ a.\blacksquare \mid a[\ P\ ] \searrow \blacksquare \mid P$; free resources may be allocated, as in $\blacksquare \mid 1 \triangleright M.\blacksquare \searrow M.\blacksquare$, or wasted as in $\mathbf{put}^{\downarrow} \mid \blacksquare \mid (\nu a)a[\ \mathbf{get}^{\uparrow}\ ] \searrow (\nu a)a[\ \blacksquare\ ]$. No further transition for wasted resource is possible: in particular, it may never become free, and re-allocated. Accordingly, while the global amount of resources is invariant through reduction, as stated in Proposition 1, the computation of a process does in general consume resources and leaves a non-increasing amount of free and allocated resources. We leave to our future work the development of a precise analysis of resource usage based on the characterization we just outlined, and focus on the behavioural semantics of the calculus instead.

1.2 Behavioural Semantics

The semantic theory of BoCa is based on *barbed congruence* [13], a standard equality relation based on reduction and a notion of observability. As usual in ambient calculi, our observation predicate, $P \downarrow_a$, indicates the possibility for process P to interact with the environment via an ambient named a. In Mobile Ambients (MA) this is defined as follows:

$$(1) \qquad P \downarrow_a \ \triangleq \ P \equiv (\nu \tilde{m})(a[\ P'\ ] \mid Q) \qquad a \notin \tilde{m}$$

Since no authorisation is required to cross a boundary, the presence of an ambient a at top level denotes a potential interaction between the process and the environment via a. In the presence of co-capabilities [12], however, the process $(\nu\tilde{m})(a[\,P\,] \mid Q)$ only represents a potential interaction if P can exercise an appropriate co-capability. The same observation applies to BoCa, as many aspects of its dynamics rely on co-capabilities: notably, mobility, opening, and transfer across ambients. Correspondingly, we have the following reasonable choices of observation (with $a \notin \{\tilde{m}\}$):

$$(2) \qquad P \downarrow_a^{opn} \;\triangleq\; P \equiv (\nu\tilde{m})(a[\,\overline{\mathbf{opn}}.P' \mid Q\,] \mid R)$$

$$(3) \qquad P \downarrow_a^{slt} \;\triangleq\; P \equiv (\nu\tilde{m})(a[\,\mathbf{\_} \mid Q\,] \mid R)$$

$$(4) \qquad P \downarrow_a^{put} \;\triangleq\; P \equiv (\nu\tilde{m})(a[\,\mathbf{put}.P' \mid \mathbf{\_} \mid Q\,] \mid R)$$

As it turns out, definitions (1)–(4) yield the same barbed congruence relation. Indeed, the presence of 0-weighted ambients makes it possible to rely on the same notion of observation as in MA, that is (1), without consequences on barbed congruences. We discuss this in further detail below.

Our notion of barbed congruence is standard, except that we require closure by well-formed contexts. Say that a relation $\mathcal{R}$ is *reduction closed* if $P\mathcal{R}Q$ and $P \searrow P'$ imply the existence of some Q' such that $Q \searrow_* Q'$ and $P'\mathcal{R}Q'$; it is *barb preserving* if $P\mathcal{R}Q$ and $P\downarrow_a$ imply $Q\Downarrow_a$, i.e. $Q\searrow_*\downarrow_a$.

Definition 2 (Barbed Congruence). Barbed bisimulation, noted $\simeq$, is the largest symmetric relation on closed processes that is reduction closed and barb preserving. Two processes P and Q are *barbed congruent*, written $P \cong Q$, if for all contexts $C[\cdot]$, preterm $C[P]$ is a term iff so is $C[Q]$, and then $C[P] \simeq C[Q]$.

Let then $\cong_i$ be the barbed congruence relation resulting from Definition 2 and from choosing the notion of observation as in (i) above (with $i \in [1..4]$).

Proposition 2 (Independence from Barbs). $\cong_i \,=\, \cong_j$ *for all* $i, j \in [1..4]$.

Since the relations differ only on the choice of barb, Proposition 2 is proved by just showing that all barbs imply each other. This can be accomplished, as usual, by exhibiting a corresponding context. For instance, to see that $\cong_3$ implies $\cong_2$ use the context $C[\cdot] = [\cdot] \mid \mathbf{opn}\; a.b^1[\,\mathbf{\_}\,]$, and note that for all P such that b is fresh in P one has $P \Downarrow_a^{opn}$ if and only if $C[P] \Downarrow_b^{slt}$.

The import of the processes' weight in the relation of behavioural equivalence is captured directly by the well-formedness requirement in Definition 2. In particular, processes of different weight are distinguished, irrespective of the their "purely" behavioral properties. To see that, note that any two processes P and Q of weight, say, k and h with $\mathsf{h} \neq \mathsf{k}$, are immediately distinguished by the context $C[\cdot] = a^{\mathsf{k}}[\,[\cdot]\,]$, as $C[P]$ is well-formed while $C[Q]$ is not.

1.3 Examples

We complete the presentation of the calculus with some encodings of systems and examples in which space usage and control is modelled.

Recovering Mobile Ambients. The Ambient Calculus [2] is straightforwardly embedded in (an untyped version of) BoCa: it suffices to insert a process $!\overline{\mathbf{opn}}$ in all ambients. The relevant clauses of the embedding are as follows:

$$[\![a[P]]\!] \triangleq a^0[\,!\overline{\mathbf{opn}} \mid [\![P]\!]\,], \quad [\![(\nu a)P]\!] \triangleq (\nu a)[\![P]\!]$$

and the remaining ones are derived similarly; clearly all resulting processes weigh 0.

Encoding Father-Son Swap. In BoCa, like in any situation where ambient weighs, this swap is possible only in case the father and child nodes have the same weight. We present it for example in the case of weight 1. Notice the use of the primitives for child to father slot exchange that we have defined in §1.

$$b^1[\,\mathbf{get}^{\downarrow}a.\mathbf{put}.\mathbf{in}\,a.\mathbf{get}^{\uparrow} \mid a^1[\,\mathbf{put}^{\uparrow}.\mathbf{out}\,b.\mathbf{get}\,b.\mathbf{put}^{\downarrow} \mid \blacksquare\,]\,] \searrow_* a^1[\,b^1[\,\blacksquare\,]\,]$$

Encoding Ambient Renaming. We can represent in BoCa a form of ambient self-renaming capability. First, define $\mathbf{spw}_a b^{\mathsf{k}}[\,P\,] \triangleq exp^0[\,\mathbf{out}\,a.\overline{\mathbf{opn}}.\mathsf{k}\triangleright b^{\mathsf{k}}[\,P\,]\,]$ and then use it to define

$$a\ \mathbf{be}^{\mathsf{k}} b.P \triangleq \mathbf{spw}_a b^{\mathsf{k}}[\,\blacksquare^{\mathsf{k}} \mid \mathbf{opn}\,a\,] \mid \mathbf{in}\,b.\overline{\mathbf{opn}}.P$$

Since $\mathbf{opn}\,exp \mid \blacksquare^{\mathsf{k}} \mid a^{\mathsf{h}}[\,\mathbf{spw}_a b^{\mathsf{k}}[\,P\,] \mid Q\,] \searrow_* b^{\mathsf{k}}[\,P\,] \mid a^{\mathsf{h}}[\,Q\,]$ where k, h are the weights of P and Q, respectively, we get

$$a^{\mathsf{k}}[\,a\ \mathbf{be}^{\mathsf{k}} b.P \mid R\,] \mid \blacksquare^{\mathsf{k}} \mid \mathbf{opn}\,exp \searrow_* b^{\mathsf{k}}[\,P \mid R\,] \mid \blacksquare^{\mathsf{k}}$$

So, an ambient needs to *borrow* space from its parent in order to rename itself. We conjecture that renaming cannot be obtained otherwise.

A Memory Module. A user can take slots from a memory module MEM_MOD using MALLOC and release them back to MEM_MOD after their use.

$$\begin{aligned} \text{MEM\_MOD} &\triangleq mem[\,\blacksquare^{256MB} \mid \overbrace{\mathbf{opn}\,m \mid \ldots \mid \mathbf{opn}\,m}^{256MB}\,] \\ \text{MALLOC} &\triangleq m[\,\mathbf{out}\,u.\mathbf{in}\,mem.\overline{\mathbf{opn}}.\mathbf{put}.\mathbf{get}\,u.\mathbf{opn}\,m\,] \\ \text{USER} &\triangleq u[\,\ldots.\text{MALLOC} \mid \ldots.\mathbf{get}\,mem\ldots\mathbf{put} \mid \ldots\,] \end{aligned}$$

2 Bounding Resources, by Typing

In this section we discuss a type system that provides static guarantees for a simple behavioural property, namely the absence of space under- and over-flows arising as a result of transfers during the computation. To deal with this satisfactorily, we need to take into account that transfer (co)capabilities can be acquired by way of exchanges. The type of a capability will hence have to express how it affects the space of the ambient in which it can be performed.

2.1 The Types

We use $\mathcal{Z}$ to denote the set of integers, and note $\mathcal{Z}^+$ and $\mathcal{Z}^-$ the sets of non-negative and non-positive integers respectively. We define the following domains:

$$\begin{array}{ll} \textit{Intervals} & \iota \in \mathfrak{I} \triangleq \{[\mathsf{n},\mathsf{N}] \mid \mathsf{n},\mathsf{N} \in \mathcal{Z}^+,\ \mathsf{n} \leq \mathsf{N}\} \\ \textit{Effects} & \varepsilon \in \mathcal{E} \triangleq \{(\mathsf{d},\mathsf{i}) \mid \mathsf{d} \in \mathcal{Z}^-,\ \mathsf{i} \in \mathcal{Z}^+\} \\ \textit{Thread Effects} & \phi \in \Phi \triangleq \mathcal{E} \to \mathcal{E} \end{array}$$

Intervals and effects are ordered in the usual way, namely: $[\mathsf{n},\mathsf{N}] \leq [\mathsf{n}',\mathsf{N}']$ when $\mathsf{n}' \leq \mathsf{n}$ and $\mathsf{N} \leq \mathsf{N}'$ and $(\mathsf{d},\mathsf{i}) \leq (\mathsf{d}',\mathsf{i}')$ when $\mathsf{d}' \leq \mathsf{d}$ and $\mathsf{i} \leq \mathsf{i}'$. It is also convenient to define the component-wise sum operator for effects: $(\mathsf{d},\mathsf{i}) + (\mathsf{d}',\mathsf{i}') = (\mathsf{d}+\mathsf{d}',\mathsf{i}+\mathsf{i}')$, and lift it to Φ pointwise: $\phi_1 + \phi_2 = \lambda\varepsilon.\phi_1(\varepsilon) + \phi_2(\varepsilon)$.

The syntax of types is defined by the following productions:

$$\begin{array}{ll} \textit{Message Types} & W ::= \mathit{Amb}\langle \iota,\varepsilon,\chi\rangle \mid \mathit{Cap}\langle \phi,\chi\rangle \\ \textit{Exchange Types} & \chi ::= \mathit{Shh} \mid W \\ \textit{Process Types} & \pi ::= \mathit{Proc}\langle \varepsilon,\chi\rangle \end{array}$$

Type $\mathit{Proc}\langle \varepsilon,\chi\rangle$ is the type of processes with ε effects and χ exchanges. Specifically, for a process P of type $\mathit{Proc}\langle (\mathsf{d},\mathsf{i}),\chi\rangle$, the effect (d,i) bounds the number of slots delivered (d) and acquired (i) by P as the cumulative result of exercising P's transfer capabilities.

Type $\mathit{Amb}\langle \iota,\varepsilon,\chi\rangle$ is the type of ambients with weight ranging in ι, and enclosing processes with ε effects and χ exchanges. As in companion type systems, values that can be exchanged include ambients and (paths of) capabilities, while the type *Shh* indicates no exchange. As for capability types, $\mathit{Cap}\langle \phi,\chi\rangle$ is the types of capabilities which, when exercised, unleash processes with χ exchanges, and compose the effect of the unleashed process with the thread effect ϕ. The functional domain of thread effects helps compute the composition of effects. In brief, thread effects accumulate the results from **gets** and **puts**, and compose these with the effects unleashed by occurrences of **opn**.

We introduce the following combinators (functions in Φ) to define the thread effects of the **put**, **get** and **open** capabilities.

$$\begin{aligned} \mathsf{Put} &= \lambda(\mathsf{d},\mathsf{i}).(\mathsf{d}-1,\mathsf{max}(0,\mathsf{i}-1)) \\ \mathsf{Get} &= \lambda(\mathsf{d},\mathsf{i}).(\mathsf{min}(0,\mathsf{d}+1),\mathsf{i}+1) \\ \mathsf{Open}(\varepsilon) &= \lambda(\mathsf{d},\mathsf{i}).(\varepsilon+(\mathsf{d},\mathsf{i})) \end{aligned}$$

The intuition is as follows. A **put** that prefixes a process P with cumulative effect (d,i), contributes to a "shift" in that effect of one unit. The effect of a **get** capability is dual. To illustrate, take $P = \mathbf{put}.\mathbf{put}.\mathbf{get}\ a$. The thread effect associated with P is computed as follows, where we use function composition in standard order (i.e. $f \circ g(x) = f(g(x))$):

$$\varepsilon \;=\; (\mathsf{Put} \circ \mathsf{Put} \circ \mathsf{Get})((0,0)) \;=\; (-2,0).$$

The intuition about an open capability is similar, but subtler, as the effect of opening an ambient is, essentially, the effect of the process unleashed by the open: in **opn** $n.P$, the process unleashed by **opn** n runs in parallel with P. As a consequence, open has an additive import in the computation of the effect. To motivate, assume that $n : Amb\langle\iota,\varepsilon,\chi\rangle$. Opening n unleashes the enclosed process in parallel to the process P. To compute the resulting effect. we may rely on the effect ε declared by n to bound the effect of the unleashed process: that effect is then is added to the effect of the continuation P. Specifically, if P has effect ε', the composite effect of **opn** $n.P$ is computed as $\mathsf{Open}(\varepsilon)(\varepsilon') = \varepsilon + \varepsilon'$.

2.2 The Typing Rules

The typing rules are collected in Figures 2 and 3, where we denote with id_Φ the identity element in the domain Φ.

The rules in Figure 2 derive judgements $\Gamma \vdash M : W$ for well-typed messages. The rules draw on the intuitions we gave earlier. Notice, in particular, that the capabilities **in**, **out** and the cocapability $\overline{\mathbf{opn}}$ have no effect, as reflected by the use id_Φ in their type. The same is true also of the the co-capability $\mathbf{put}^{\downarrow}$. In fact, by means of the superscript k in $a^{\mathsf{k}}[\,P\,]$ we can record the actual weight of the ambient (cf. reduction rule (GETD)). This implies that the weight of an ambient in which $\mathbf{put}^{\downarrow}$ is executed does not change: the ambient loses a slot, but the weight of one of its sub-ambients increases.

$$\frac{}{\Gamma, M : W \vdash M : W}\ (axiom) \qquad \frac{}{\Gamma \vdash nil : Cap\langle \mathsf{id}_\Phi, \chi\rangle}\ (nil)$$

$$\frac{\Gamma \vdash M : Amb\langle -,-,-\rangle}{\Gamma \vdash \mathbf{get}\ M : Cap\langle \mathsf{Get}, \chi\rangle}\ (\mathbf{get}\ M) \qquad \frac{}{\Gamma \vdash \mathbf{put} : Cap\langle \mathsf{Put}, \chi\rangle}\ (\mathbf{put})$$

$$\frac{}{\Gamma \vdash \mathbf{get}^{\uparrow} : Cap\langle \mathsf{Get}, \chi\rangle}\ (\mathbf{get}^{\uparrow}) \qquad \frac{}{\Gamma \vdash \mathbf{put}^{\downarrow} : Cap\langle \mathsf{id}_\Phi, \chi\rangle}\ (\mathbf{put}^{\downarrow})$$

$$\frac{\Gamma \vdash M : Amb\langle -,-,-\rangle}{\Gamma \vdash \mathbf{in}\ M : Cap\langle \mathsf{id}_\Phi, \chi\rangle}\ (\mathbf{in}\ M) \qquad \frac{\Gamma \vdash M : Amb\langle -,-,-\rangle}{\Gamma \vdash \mathbf{out}\ M : Cap\langle \mathsf{id}_\Phi, \chi\rangle}\ (\mathbf{out}\ M)$$

$$\frac{\Gamma \vdash M : Amb\langle -,\varepsilon,\chi\rangle}{\Gamma \vdash \mathbf{opn}\ M : Cap\langle \mathsf{Open}(\varepsilon), \chi\rangle}\ (\mathbf{opn}\ M) \qquad \frac{}{\Gamma \vdash \overline{\mathbf{opn}} : Cap\langle \mathsf{id}_\Phi, \chi\rangle}\ (\overline{\mathbf{opn}})$$

$$\frac{\Gamma \vdash M : Cap\langle \phi, \chi\rangle \quad \Gamma \vdash M' : Cap\langle \phi', \chi\rangle}{\Gamma \vdash M.M' : Cap\langle \phi \circ \phi', \chi\rangle}\ (path)$$

Fig. 2. Good Messages

The rules in Figure 3 derive judgements $\Gamma \vdash P : Proc\langle\varepsilon,\chi\rangle$ for well-typed processes. An inspection of the typing rules shows that any well-typed process is also well-formed (in the sense of Definition 1. We let $0_{\mathcal{E}}$ denote the null effect $(0,0)$: thus, rules (**0**) and (**▬**) simply state that the inhert process and the slot form have no effects. Rule (*prefix*) computes the effects of prefixes, by applying the thread effect of the capability to the

$$\frac{}{\Gamma \vdash \blacksquare : Proc\langle 0_{\mathcal{E}}, \chi\rangle}\ (\blacksquare) \qquad \frac{}{\Gamma \vdash \mathbf{0} : Proc\langle 0_{\mathcal{E}}, \chi\rangle}\ (\mathbf{0})$$

$$\frac{\Gamma \vdash M : Cap\langle \phi, \chi\rangle \quad \Gamma \vdash P : Proc\langle \varepsilon, \chi\rangle}{\Gamma \vdash M.P : Proc\langle \phi(\varepsilon), \chi\rangle}\ (prefix)$$

$$\frac{\Gamma \vdash P : Proc\langle \varepsilon, \chi\rangle \quad \Gamma \vdash Q : Proc\langle \varepsilon', \chi\rangle}{\Gamma \vdash P \mid Q : Proc\langle \varepsilon + \varepsilon', \chi\rangle}\ (par) \qquad \frac{\Gamma, x : W \vdash P : Proc\langle \varepsilon, W\rangle}{\Gamma \vdash (x : W)P : Proc\langle \varepsilon, W\rangle}\ (input)$$

$$\frac{\Gamma \vdash M : W \quad \Gamma \vdash P : Proc\langle \varepsilon, W\rangle}{\Gamma \vdash \langle M\rangle P : Proc\langle \varepsilon, W\rangle}\ (output) \qquad \frac{\Gamma, a : Amb\langle \iota, \varepsilon, \chi\rangle \vdash P : Proc\langle \varepsilon', \chi'\rangle}{\Gamma \vdash (\nu a : Amb\langle \iota, \varepsilon, \chi\rangle)P : Proc\langle \varepsilon', \chi'\rangle}\ (new)$$

$$\frac{\begin{array}{lll}\Gamma \vdash M : Amb\langle [\mathsf{n},\mathsf{N}], \varepsilon, \chi'\rangle & & [\max(\mathsf{k}+\mathsf{d},0), \mathsf{k}+\mathsf{i}] \leq [\mathsf{n},\mathsf{N}] \\ \Gamma \vdash P : Proc\langle (\mathsf{d},\mathsf{i}), \chi'\rangle & w(P) = \mathsf{k} & (\mathsf{d}-\mathsf{i}, \min(\mathsf{N}-\mathsf{n}, \mathsf{i}-\mathsf{d})) \leq \varepsilon\end{array}}{\Gamma \vdash M^{\mathsf{k}}[P] : Proc\langle 0_{\mathcal{E}}, \chi\rangle}\ (amb)$$

$$\frac{\Gamma \vdash P : Proc\langle 0_{\mathcal{E}}, \chi\rangle \quad w(P) = \mathsf{k}}{\Gamma \vdash \mathsf{k} \triangleright P : Proc\langle 0_{\mathcal{E}}, \chi\rangle}\ (spawn) \qquad \frac{\Gamma \vdash P : Proc\langle 0_{\mathcal{E}}, \chi\rangle \quad w(P) = 0}{\Gamma \vdash !P : Proc\langle 0_{\mathcal{E}}, \chi\rangle}\ (bang)$$

Fig. 3. Good Processes

effect of the process. Rule (*par*) adds up the effects of two parallel threads, while the constructs for input, output and restriction do not have any effect.

Rule (*amb*) governs the formation of ambient processes. The declared weight k of the ambient must reflect the weight of the enclosed process. Two further conditions ensure (*i*) that k modified by the effect (d,i) of the enclosed process lies within the interval $[\mathsf{n},\mathsf{N}]$ declared by the ambient type, and (*ii*) that effect ε declared by the ambient type is a sound approximation for the effects released by opening the ambient itself. Condition (*i*) is simply $[\max(\mathsf{k}+\mathsf{d},0), \mathsf{k}+\mathsf{i}] \leq [\mathsf{n},\mathsf{N}]$, where the use of $\max(\mathsf{k}+\mathsf{d},0)$ is justified by observing that the weight of an ambient may never grow negative as a result the enclosed process exercising **put**capabilities. To motivate condition (*ii*), first observe that opening an ambient which encloses a process with effect (d,i) may only release effects $\varepsilon \leq (\mathsf{d}-\mathsf{i}, \mathsf{i}-\mathsf{d})$. The lower bound arises in a situation in which the ambient is opened right after the enclosed process has completed its i **get** 's and is thus left with $|\mathsf{d}-\mathsf{i}|$ **put**'s unleashed in the opening context. Dually, the upper bound arises when the ambient is opened right after the enclosed process has completed its d **put**'s, and is left with $\mathsf{i}-\mathsf{d}$ **get** 's. On the other hand, we also know that the maximum increasing effect released by opening ambients with weight ranging in $[\mathsf{n},\mathsf{N}]$ is $\mathsf{N}-\mathsf{n}$. Collectively, these two observations justify the condition $(\mathsf{d}-\mathsf{i}, \min(\mathsf{N}-\mathsf{n}, \mathsf{i}-\mathsf{d})) \leq \varepsilon$ in rule (*amb*).

In rule (*spawn*), the effect of $\mathsf{k} \triangleright P$ is the same as that of the reduct P. Finally, to prevent the effects of duplicated processes to add up beyond control, with unpredictable consequences, rule (*bang*) enforces duplicated process to have null effects.

A first property of the given type system is that all typable preterms are terms.

The following result complements Proposition 1 and shows that capacity bounds on ambients are preserved during computations, while the processes' ability to shrink or expand reduces.

Theorem 1 (Subject Reduction). *Assume* $\Gamma \vdash P : Proc\langle \varepsilon, \chi \rangle$ *and* $P \searrow_* Q$. *Then* $\Gamma \vdash Q : Proc\langle \varepsilon', \chi \rangle$ *for some* $\varepsilon' \leq \varepsilon$.

It follows as a direct corollary that no ambient may be subject to under/over-flows during the computation of a process.

Theorem 2 (Absence of Under/Over-Flow). *Assume* $\Gamma \vdash P : Proc\langle \varepsilon, \chi \rangle$ *and let* $P \searrow_* Q$. *If* $a : Amb\langle [\mathsf{n}, \mathsf{N}], -, - \rangle \in \Gamma$, *then, for any subterm of* Q *of the form* $a^{\mathsf{k}}[\, R\,]$, *not in the scope of a binder for a, we have* $\mathsf{n} \leq \mathsf{k} \leq \mathsf{N}$.

2.3 Typed Examples

A Typed Memory Module. As a first illustration of the typing system at work we give a typed version of the memory module of Section 1.3. All other examples in that section are typeable too, and this can be easily verified. We start with the *malloc* ambient

$$\text{MALLOC} \triangleq m[\,\mathbf{out}\ u.\mathbf{in}\ mem.\overline{\mathbf{opn}}.\mathbf{put}.\mathbf{get}\ u.\mathbf{opn}\ m\,]$$

Since there are no exchanges, we give the typing annotation and derivation disregarding the exchange component from the types. Let P_{malloc} denote thread enclosed within the ambient m. If we let $m : Amb\langle [0,0], (-1,0) \rangle \in \Gamma$, an inspection of the typing rules for capabilities and paths shows that the following typing is derivable for any ambient type assigned to *mem*:

$$\Gamma \vdash \mathbf{out}\ u.\mathbf{in}\ mem.\overline{\mathbf{opn}}.\mathbf{put}.\mathbf{get}\ u.\mathbf{opn}\ m : Cap\langle (\mathsf{Put} \circ \mathsf{Get} \circ \lambda\varepsilon.((-1,0)+\varepsilon))(0_{\mathcal{E}}) \rangle$$

Composing the thread effects, one has: $\mathsf{Put} \circ \mathsf{Get}\,(-1,0) = (-1,0)$. From this one derives $\Gamma \vdash P_{malloc} : Proc\langle (-1,0) \rangle$, which gives $\Gamma \vdash \text{MALLOC} : Proc\langle 0_{\mathcal{E}} \rangle$. As to the memory module itself, it is a routine check to verify that the process

$$\text{MEM\_MOD} \triangleq mem[\,\blacksquare^{256MB} \mid \mathbf{opn}\ m \mid \ldots \mid \mathbf{opn}\ m\,]$$

typechecks with $m : Amb\langle [0,0], (-1,0) \rangle$, $mem : Amb\langle [0, 256MB], (-256MB, 256MB) \rangle$.

A Cab Trip. As a further example, we give a new version of the the cab trip protocol from [17], formulated in our calculus. A customer sends a request for a cab, which then arrives and takes the customer to his destination. The use of slots here enables us to model very naturally the constraint that only one passenger (or actually any fixed number of them) may occupy a cab. The typing environment contains $call : W_1$, $cab : W_1$, $trip : W_0$, $loading : W_0$, $unloading : W_0$, $bye : W_0$ where $W_1 = Amb\langle [1,1], 0_{\mathcal{E}} \rangle$, $W_0 = Amb\langle [0,0], 0_{\mathcal{E}} \rangle$.

$$
\begin{array}{ll}
\mathit{CALL}(\mathit{from},\mathit{client}) & \triangleq \\
\quad \mathit{call}^1[\,\mathbf{out}\ \mathit{client}\,.\,\mathbf{out}\ \mathit{from}\,.\,\mathbf{in}\ \mathit{cab}\,.\,\overline{\mathbf{opn}}\,.\,\mathbf{in}\ \mathit{from}\,.(\mathit{loading}^0[\,\mathbf{out}\ \mathit{cab}\,.\,\mathbf{in}\ \mathit{client}\,.\,\overline{\mathbf{opn}}\,] \mid \boldsymbol{-})\,] & \\
\mathit{TRIP}(\mathit{from},\mathit{to},\mathit{client}) & \triangleq \mathit{trip}^0[\,\mathbf{out}\ \mathit{client}\,.\,\overline{\mathbf{opn}}\,.\,\mathbf{out}\ \mathit{from}\,.\,\mathbf{in}\ \mathit{to}\,.\,\mathit{unloading}^0[\,\mathbf{in}\ \mathit{client}\,.\,\overline{\mathbf{opn}}\,]\,] \\
\mathit{CLIENT}(\mathit{from},\mathit{to}) & \triangleq (\nu c : W_1)c^1[\mathit{CALL}(\mathit{from},c) \mid \mathbf{opn}\ \mathit{loading}\,.\,\mathbf{in}\ \mathit{cab}\,.\,\mathit{TRIP}(\mathit{from},\mathit{to},c) \\
& \qquad \mid \mathbf{opn}\ \mathit{unloading}\,.\,\mathbf{out}\ \mathit{cab}\,.\,\mathit{bye}^0[\,\mathbf{out}\ c\,.\,\mathbf{in}\ \mathit{cab}\,.\,\overline{\mathbf{opn}}\,.\,\mathbf{out}\ \mathit{to}\,]] \\
\mathit{CAB} & \triangleq \mathit{cab}^1[\,\boldsymbol{-} \mid !(\mathbf{opn}\ \mathit{call}\,.\,\mathbf{opn}\ \mathit{trip}\,.\,\mathbf{opn}\ \mathit{bye})\,] \\
\mathit{SITE}(i) & \triangleq \mathit{site}_i[\,\mathit{CLIENT}(\mathit{site}_i,\mathit{site}_j) \mid \mathit{CLIENT}(\mathit{site}_i,\mathit{site}_l) \mid \cdots \mid \boldsymbol{-} \mid \boldsymbol{-} \mid \cdots\,] \\
\mathit{CITY} & \triangleq \mathit{city}[\,\mathit{CAB} \mid \mathit{CAB} \mid \cdots \mid \cdots \mid \mathit{SITE}(1) \mid \cdots \mid \mathit{SITE}(n) \mid \boldsymbol{-} \mid \boldsymbol{-} \mid \cdots\,]
\end{array}
$$

The fact that only one slot is available in *cab* together with the weight 1 of both *call* and *client* prevents the cab to receive more than one call and/or more than one client. Moreover this encoding limits also the space in each site and in the whole city.

Comparing with [17], we notice that we can deal with the cab's space satisfactorily with no need for 3-way synchronisations. Unfortunately, as already observed in [17], this encoding may lead to unwanted behaviours, since there is no way of preventing a client to enter a cab different from that called and/or the ambient bye to enter a cab different from that the client has left. We will give a safe encoding of this example in Subsection 3.2 using named slots.

3 Controlling Races for Resources

The calculus of the previous sections provides a simple, yet effective, framework for reasoning on resource usage and consumption. On the other hand, it is less effective in expressing *policies* to govern the allocation and distribution of space to distinct, possibly, competitive components. Indeed, with the current semantics it is not entirely obvious that a given resource unit can be selectively allocated to a specific agent, and protected against unintended use. To illustrate, consider the following term (and assume it well-formed):

$$a^1[\,\mathbf{in}\ b.P\,] \mid b[\,1{\rhd}Q \mid \boldsymbol{-} \mid d[\,c^1[\,\mathbf{out}\ d.R\,]\,]\,]$$

Three agents are competing for the resource unit in ambient b: ambients a and c, which would use it for their move, and the local spawner inside ambient b. While the race between a and c may be acceptable – the resource unit may be allocated by b to any migrating agent – it would also be desirable for b to reserve resources for internal use, i.e. for spawning new processes. In fact, reserving private space for spawning is possible with the current primitives, by encoding a notion of "named resource". This can be accomplished by defining:

$$\boldsymbol{-}_a^{\mathsf{k}} \triangleq a[\,\mathbf{put}^{\mathsf{k}} \mid \boldsymbol{-}^{\mathsf{k}}\,], \quad \text{and} \quad \mathsf{k}{\rhd}\,(a,P) \triangleq (\nu n)(n[\,(\mathbf{get}\ a)^{\mathsf{k}}.\mathsf{k}{\rhd}\,\overline{\mathbf{opn}}.P\,] \mid \mathbf{opn}\ n)$$

Then, assuming $w(P) = \mathsf{k}$, one has $(\nu a)(\boldsymbol{-}_a^{\mathsf{k}} \mid \mathsf{k}{\rhd}\,(a,P)) \cong P$, as desired. It is also possible to encode a form of "resource renaming", by defining:

$$\{x/y\}.P \triangleq (\nu n)(n[\,\mathbf{get}\ y.\mathbf{put}\,\overline{\mathbf{opn}}\,] \mid x[\,\mathbf{get}\ n.\mathbf{put}] \mid \mathbf{opn}\ n.P)$$

Then, a y-resource can be turned in to an x-resource: $\{x/y\}.P \mid \boldsymbol{-}_y \searrow_* P \mid \boldsymbol{-}_x$.

Encoding a similar form of named, and reserved, resources for mobility is subtler. On the one hand, it is not difficult to encode a construct for reserving a x-slot for ambients named x. For example, ambients a and b may agree on the following protocol to reserve a private slot for the move of a into b. If we want to use the space in ambient b for moving a we can write the process:

$$(\nu p,q)(p[\,\mathbf{in}\ b.\mathbf{get}\ q.1 \triangleright \overline{\mathbf{opn}}.a^1[\,\text{▬}\,]\,] \mid b[\,P \mid q[\,\text{▬} \mid \mathbf{put}\,] \mid \mathbf{opn}\ p\,])$$

On the other hand, defining a mechanism to release a named resource to the context from which it has been received is more complex, as it amounts to releasing a resource with the *same* name it was allocated to. This can be simulated loosely with the current primitives, by providing a mechanism whereby a migrating ambient releases an anonymous slot, which is then renamed by the context that is in control of it. The problem is that such a mechanism of releasing and renaming lacks the *atomicity* required to guard against unexpected races for the released resource. Indeed, we conjecture that such atomic mechanisms for named resources can not be defined in the current calculus.

3.1 The Calculus, Refined

We counter the problem by refining the calculus with named resources as primitive notions, and by tailoring the constructs for mobility, transfer and spawning accordingly. Resource units come now always with a tag, as in ▬_η, where $\eta \in \mathcal{N} + \{*\}$ is the unit name. To make the new calculus a conservative extension of the one presented in §1, we make provision for a special tag '*', to be associated with *anonymous* units: any process can be spawned on an anonymous slot, as well any ambient can be moved on it. In addition, we extend the structure of the transfer capabilities, as well as the construct for spawning and ambient as shown in the productions below, which replace the corresponding ones in §1.

Processes	$P ::= \text{▬}_\eta \mid \mathsf{k} \triangleright_\eta P \mid M[\,P\,]_\eta \mid \ldots$	as in Section 1
Capabilities	$C ::= \mathbf{get}_\eta\ M \mid \mathbf{get}^{\uparrow}{}_\eta \mid \ldots$	as in Section 1
Messages	$M ::= \ldots$	as in Section 1

Again, a (well-formed) *term* is a preterm such that in any subterm of the form $a^{\mathsf{k}}[P]$ or $\mathsf{k} \triangleright_\eta P$, P has weight k. The weight of a process can be computed by rules similar to those of Section 1. The anonymous slots ▬_* will be often denoted simply as ▬, and in general η will be omitted when equal to $*$; subscripts on ambients are omitted when irrelevant.

The dynamics of the refined calculus is again defined by means of structural congruence and reduction. Structural congruence is exactly as in Figure 1, the top-level reductions are defined in Figure 4.

The reductions for the transfer capabilities are the natural extensions of the original reductions of §1. Here, in addition to naming the target ambient, the **get** capabilities also indicate the name of the unit they request. The choice of the primitives enables natural forms of scope extrusion for the names of resources, even though resource tags may not be variables. Consider the following system:

$$S \triangleq n[\,(\nu a)(\mathbf{put}.P \mid \text{▬}_a \mid p[\,\mathbf{out}\ n.\mathbf{in}\ m.\overline{\mathbf{opn}}.\mathbf{get}_a\ n\,])\,] \mid m[\,\mathbf{opn}\ p.Q\,]$$

The reductions for ambient opening and exchanges are as in Figure 1, and the rules (ENTER) and (EXIT) have $\eta \in \{a, \star\}$ as side condition. The omitted subscripts ρ on ambients are meant to remain unchanged by the reductions.

(ENTER)	$a^{k}[\,\mathbf{in}\, b.P \mid Q\,]_{\rho} \mid b[\,\blacksquare^{k}_{\eta} \mid R\,]$	$\searrow$	$\blacksquare^{k}_{\rho} \mid b[\,a^{k}[\,P \mid Q\,]_{\eta} \mid R\,]$
(EXIT)	$\blacksquare^{k}_{\eta} \mid b[\,P \mid a^{k}[\,\mathbf{out}\, b.Q \mid R\,]_{\rho}\,]$	$\searrow$	$a^{k}[\,Q \mid R\,]_{\eta} \mid b[\,P \mid \blacksquare^{k}_{\rho}\,]$
(GETS)	$b^{h+1}[\,\mathbf{put}.P \mid \blacksquare_{\eta} \mid Q\,] \mid a^{k}[\,\mathbf{get}_{\eta}\, b.R \mid S\,]$	$\searrow$	$b^{h}[\,P \mid Q\,] \mid a^{k+1}[\,R \mid \blacksquare_{\eta} \mid S\,]$
(GETU)	$\mathbf{put}^{\downarrow}.P \mid \blacksquare_{\eta} \mid a^{k+1}[\,\mathbf{get}^{\uparrow}_{\eta}.Q \mid R\,]$	$\searrow$	$P \mid a^{k}[\,\blacksquare_{\eta} \mid Q \mid R\,]$
(SPAWN)	$\mathsf{k} \rhd_{\eta} .P \mid \blacksquare^{k}_{\eta}$	$\searrow$	P

Fig. 4. Top-level reductions with named units

Here, the private resource enclosed within ambient n is communicated to ambient m, as $S \searrow_{*} (\nu a)(n[\,P\,] \mid m[\,Q \mid \blacksquare_{a}\,])$.

The dynamics of mobility solves the problem we discussed above. To complete a move an ambient a must be granted an anonymous resource or an a-resource. The migrating ambient releases a resource under the name that it was assigned upon the move (as recorded in the tag associated with the ambient construct). Finally, the new semantics of spawning acts as expected, by associating the process to be spawned with a specific set of resources.

These definitions suggest a natural form of resource renaming (or rebinding), noted $\{{}^{\eta}/_{\rho}\}_{\mathsf{k}}$ with the following operational semantics.

$$\{{}^{\eta}/_{\rho}\}_{\mathsf{k}}.P \mid \blacksquare^{k}_{\rho} \searrow P \mid \blacksquare^{k}_{\eta}$$

Notice that this is a dangerous capability, since it allows processes to give particular names to anonymous slots, and for instance put in place possible malicious behaviours to make all public resources their own: $!\{{}^{y}/_{*}\}$. This suggests that in many situations one ought to restrict $\mathsf{k}\rhd_{\eta}$ to $\eta \in \mathcal{N}$. The inverse behaviour, that is a "communist for y spaces," is also well-formed and it is often useful (even though not commendable by everyone). Notice however that it can be harmful too: $!\{{}^{*}/_{y}\}$. We have not defined the name rebinding capability as a primitive of our calculus since it can be encoded using the new form of spawning as follows, for a fresh.

$$\{{}^{\eta}/_{\rho}\}_{\mathsf{k}}.P \triangleq (\nu a)(\mathsf{k}\rhd_{\rho} (\blacksquare^{k}_{\eta} \mid a^{0}[\,\overline{\mathbf{opn}}\,]) \mid \mathbf{opn}\, a.P)$$

Observe that the simpler encoding $\mathsf{k}\rhd_{\rho} (\blacksquare^{k}_{\eta} \mid P)$ is allowed only for processes P of weight 0.

It is easy to check that the type system of Section 2 can be used without modifications also for the calculus with named slots. For this calculus the same properties proved in Section 2 hold.

Theorem 3 (Subject Reduction and Under/Over-Flow Absence). *For the processes and reduction relation of this section, we have:*

(i) $\Gamma \vdash P : Proc\langle\varepsilon,\chi\rangle$ *and* $P \searrow_* Q$ *imply* $\Gamma \vdash Q : Proc\langle\varepsilon',\chi\rangle$ *with* $\varepsilon' \leq \varepsilon$.
(ii) If $\Gamma, a : Amb\langle[\mathsf{n},\mathsf{N}],\chi\rangle \vdash P : Proc\langle\varepsilon,\chi\rangle$, $P \searrow_* C[a^{\mathsf{k}}[R]]$, *and the showed occurrence of a is not in the scope of a binder for a, then* $\mathsf{n} \leq \mathsf{k} \leq \mathsf{N}$.

3.2 More Examples

The Cab Trip Revisited. Named slots allow us to avoid unwanted behaviours when encoding the cab trip example. The *cab* initially contains one slot named *call*, but after reaching the client's site it will contain one slot with the client private name, and lastly when the *client* goes out of the cab it leaves one slot named *bye*. The *call* exiting the *client* leaves one slot tagged *forbye*, which is reserved for spawning *bye*. The (resource) renaming in the *sites* and in the *city* allow the public reuse of resources.
Let $W_1 = Amb\langle[1,1],0_{\mathcal{F}}\rangle$, $W_0 = Amb\langle[0,0],0_{\mathcal{E}}\rangle$. As in Subsection 2.3 the typing environment contains $call : W_1, cab : W_1, trip : W_0, unloading : W_0$, but $bye : W_1$ and we do not need the ambient *loading*.

$$
\begin{aligned}
&CALL(from,client) &&\triangleq call^1[\,\mathbf{out}\ client\,.\,\mathbf{out}\ from\,.\,\mathbf{in}\ cab\,.\,\overline{\mathbf{opn}}\,.\,\mathbf{in}\ from\,.\,\blacksquare_{client}\,]_{forbye}\\
&TRIP(from,to,client) &&\triangleq trip^0[\,\mathbf{out}\ client\,.\,\overline{\mathbf{opn}}\,.\,\mathbf{out}\ from\,.\,\mathbf{in}\ to\,.\,unloading^0[\,\mathbf{in}\ client\,.\,\overline{\mathbf{opn}}\,]\,]\\
&CLIENT(from,to) &&\triangleq (\nu c : W_1)c^1[CALL(from,c)\mid \mathbf{in}\ cab\,.\,TRIP(from,to,c)\\
&&&\quad\mid \mathbf{opn}\ unloading\,.\,\mathbf{out}\ cab\,.\,1 \rhd_{forbye} bye^1[\,\mathbf{out}\ c\,.\,\mathbf{in}\ cab\,.\,\overline{\mathbf{opn}}\,.\,\mathbf{out}\ to\,.\,\blacksquare_{call}\,]_*]_{bye}\\
&CAB &&\triangleq cab^1[\,\blacksquare_{call}\mid !(\mathbf{opn}\ call\,.\,\mathbf{opn}\ trip\,.\,\mathbf{opn}\ bye)\,]_*\\
&SITE(i) &&\triangleq\\
&\quad site_i[\,CLIENT(site_i,site_j)\mid CLIENT(site_i,site_l)\mid\cdots\mid\blacksquare\mid\blacksquare\mid\cdots\mid !\{{}^*/forbye\}_1\mid !\{{}^*/bye\}_1\,]\\
&CITY &&\triangleq\\
&&&city[\,CAB\mid CAB\mid\cdots\mid SITE(1)\mid\cdots\mid SITE(n)\mid\blacksquare\mid\blacksquare\mid\cdots\mid !\{{}^*/forbye\}_1\,]
\end{aligned}
$$

A Travel Agency. We conclude the presentation with an example that shows the expressiveness of the naming mechanisms for resources in the refined calculus. We wish to model clients buying tickets from a travel agency, paying them one slot (the $\blacksquare_{fortkt}$ inside the client), and then use them to travel by plane. At most two clients may enter the travel agency, and they are served one by one. The three components of the systems are defined below.

- ▷ <u>THE AGENCY</u>: $ag^5[\,\blacksquare^2_{cl}\mid\blacksquare_{req}\mid$
  $\mathrm{desk}^1[\,\blacksquare_{req}\mid !(\mathbf{opn}\ req\,.\,1\rhd_{fortkt}.\,tkt^1[\,\mathbf{out}\ desk\,.\,\mathbf{in}\ cl\,.\,CONT\,]_{req})]\,]$
  where $CONT = (\overline{\mathbf{opn}}\,.\,\mathbf{out}\ ag\,.\,\mathbf{in}\ plane\,.\,rdy^0[\,\mathbf{out}\ cl\,]\mid\blacksquare_{getoff}\mid\mathbf{opn}\ getoff)$
- ▷ <u>THE CLIENT</u>: $\mathrm{cl}^1[\,\mathbf{in}\ ag\,.\,req^1[\,\mathbf{out}\ cl\,.\,\mathbf{in}\ desk\,.\,\overline{\mathbf{opn}}\,.\,\blacksquare_{fortkt}\,]_{tkt}\mid\mathbf{opn}\ tkt\,]_{cl}$
- ▷ <u>THE AIRCRAFT</u>: $\mathrm{plane}[\,\blacksquare^2_{cl}\mid\mathbf{opn}\ rdy^0\,.\,\mathbf{opn}\ rdy^0\,.\,ROUTE.(GETOFF\mid GETOFF)\,]$
  where $GETOFF = \mathrm{getoff}^1[\,\mathbf{in}\ \mathrm{cl}\,.\,\overline{\mathbf{opn}}\,.\,\mathbf{out}\ plane\mid\blacksquare\,]$ and *ROUTE* is the unspecified path modelling the route of the aircraft.

We assume that there exists only one sort of ticket, but it is easy to extend the example with as many kinds of ticket as possible plane routes. What makes the example interesting is the possibility of letting two clients into the agency, but serving them non-deterministically in sequence. Notice that the use of the named slots is essential for a correct implementation of the protocol. When the request goes to the desk, a slot named *tkt* is left in the client. This slot allows the ticket to enter the client. In this way we guarantee that no ticket can enter a client before its request has reached the desk.

We assume the aircraft to leave only when full. This constraint is implemented by means of the *rdy* ambient. The ambient *getoff* enables the passengers to get off once at destination; assigning weight 1 to the *getoff* ambients prevents them to get both into the same client.

4 Conclusion and Future Work

We have presented an ambient-like calculus centred around an explicit primitive representing a resource unit: the space "slot" ▬. The calculus, dubbed BoCa, features capabilities for resource control, namely pairs **get/put** to transfer spaces between sibling ambients and from parent to child, as well as the capabilities **in** a and **out** a for ambient migration, which represent an abstract mechanism of resource negotiation between travelling agent and its source and destination environments. A fundamental ingredient of the calculus is $\triangleright(\_)$, a primitive which consumes space to activate processes. The combination of such elements makes of BoCa a suitable formalism, if initial, to study the role of resource consumption, and the corresponding safety guarantees, in the dynamics of mobile systems. We have experimented with the all important notion of private resource, which has guided our formulation of a refined version of the calculus featuring named resources.

The presence of the space construct ▬ induces a notion of weight on processes, and by exercising their transfer capabilities, processes may exchange resources with their surrounding context, so making it possible to have under- and over-filled ambients. We have introduced a type system which prevents such unwanted effects and guarantees that the contents of each ambient remain within its declared capacity.

As we mentioned in the Introduction, our approach is related to the work on *Controlled Mobile Ambients* (CMA) [17] and on *Finite Control Mobile Ambients* [3]. There are, however, important difference with respect to both approaches.

In CMA the notions of process weight and capacity are entirely characterized at the typing level, and so are the mechanisms for resource control (additional control on ambient behavior is achieved by means of a three-way synchronization for mobility, but that is essentially orthogonal to the mechanisms targeted at resource control). In BoCa, instead, we characterize the notions of space and resources directly in the calculus, by means of an explicit process constructor, and associated capabilities. In particular, the primitives for transferring space, and more generally for the explicit manipulation of space and resources by means of spawning and replication appear to be original to BoCa, and suitable for the development of formal analyses of the fundamental mechanism of the usage and and consumption of resources which do not seem to be possible for CMA.

As to [3], their main goal is to isolate an expressive fragment of Mobile Ambients for which the model checking problem against the ambient logic can be made decidable. Decidability requires guarantees of finiteness which in turn raise boundedness concerns that are related to those we have investigated here. However, a more thorough comparison between the two approaches deserves to be made and we leave it to our future work.

Plans for future include further work in several directions. A finer typing discipline could be put in place to regulate the behavior of processes in the presence of primitive notions of named slots. Also, the calculus certainly needs behavioral theories and proof techniques adequate for reasoning about resource usage and consumption. Such theories and techniques could be assisted by enhanced typing systems providing static guarantees of a controlled, and bounded, use of resources, along the lines of the work by Hofmann and Jost in [10].

A further direction for future development is to consider a version of weighed ambients whose "external" weight is independent of their "internal" weight, that is the weight of their contents. This approach sees an ambient as a packaging abstraction whose weight may have a different interpretation from that of contents'. For instance, modelling a wallet the weight of its contents could represent the value of the money inside, whereas its external weight could measure the physical space it occupies. A directory's internal weight could be the cumulative size of its files, while the external weight their number.

Last, but not least, we would like to identify logics for BoCa to formulate (quantitative) resource properties and analyses; and to model general resource bounds negotiation and enforcement in the Global Computing scenario.

Acknowledgements

We gratefully acknowledge the anonymous referees for careful reading and useful suggestions.

References

1. M. Bugliesi and G. Castagna. Secure safe ambients. In *POPL'01*, pages 222–235, New York, 2001. ACM Press.
2. L. Cardelli and A. D. Gordon. Mobile ambients. *Theoretical Computer Science*, 240(1):177–213, 2000. Special Issue on Coordination, D. Le Métayer Editor.
3. W. Charatonik, A. D. Gordon, and J.-M. Talbot. Finite-control mobile ambients. In D. Le Métayer, editor, *ESOP'02*, volume 2305 of *LNCS*, pages 295–313, Berlin, 2002. Springer-Verlag.
4. K. Crary and S. Weirich. Resource bound certification. In *POPL'00*, pages 184–198, New York, 2000. ACM Press.
5. J. C. Godskesen, T. Hildebrandt, and V. Sassone. A calculus of mobile resources. In L. Brim, P. Jančar, M. Křetínský, and A. Kučera, editors, *CONCUR'02*, volume 2421 of *LNCS*, pages 272–287, Berlin, 2002. Springer-Verlag.
6. M. Hennessy, M. Merro, and J. Rathke. Towards a behavioural theory of access and mobility control in distributed system (extended abstract). In A. D. Gordon, editor, *FOSSACS'03*, volume 2620 of *LNCS*, pages 282–299, Berlin, 2003. Springer-Verlag.

7. M. Hennessy and J. Riely. Information flow vs. resource access in the asynchronous pi-calculus. *ACM Transactions on Programming Languages and Systems*, 24(5):566–591, 2002.
8. M. Hennessy and J. Riely. Resource access control in systems of mobile agents. *Information and Computation*, 173:82–120, 2002.
9. M. Hofmann. The strength of non size-increasing computation. In *POPL'02*, pages 260–269, New York, 2002. ACM Press.
10. M. Hofmann and S. Jost. Static prediction of heap space usage for first-order functional programs. In *POPL'03*, pages 185–197, New York, 2003. ACM Press.
11. A. Igarashi and N. Kobayashi. Resource usage analysis. In *POPL'02*, pages 331–342, New York, 2002. ACM Press.
12. F. Levi and D. Sangiorgi. Controlling interference in Ambients. In *POPL'00*, pages 352–364. ACM Press, New York, 2000.
13. R. Milner and D. Sangiorgi. Barbed bisimulation. In W.Kuich, editor, *ICALP'92*, volume 623 of *LNCS*, pages 685–695, Berlin, 1992. Springer-Verlag.
14. R. D. Nicola, G. Ferrari, R. Pugliese, and B. Venneri. Types for access control. *Theoretical Computer Science*, 240(1):215–254, 2000.
15. B. Pierce and D. Sangiorgi. Typing and subtyping for mobile processes. *Mathematical Structures in Computer Science*, 6(5):409–454, 1996.
16. D. Sangiorgi and A. Valente. A distributed abstract machine for safe ambients. In F. Orejas, P. Spirakis, and J. Leeuwen, editors, *ICALP'01*, volume 2076 of *LNCS*, pages 408–420, Berlin, 2001. Springer-Verlag.
17. D. Teller, P. Zimmer, and D. Hirschkoff. Using ambients to control resources. In L. Brim, P. Jančar, M. Křetínský, and A. Kučera, editors, *CONCUR'02*, volume 2421 of *LNCS*, pages 288–303, Berlin, 2002. Springer-Verlag.
18. N. Yoshida and M. Hennessy. Subtyping and locality in distributed higher order mobile processes (extended abstract). In J. C. M. Baeten and S. Mauw, editors, *CONCUR'99*, volume 1664 of *LNCS*, pages 557–573, Berlin, 1999. Springer-Verlag.

Paradigm Regained: Abstraction Mechanisms for Access Control

Mark S. Miller[1] and Jonathan S. Shapiro[2]

[1] Hewlett Packard Laboratories, Johns Hopkins University
markm@caplet.com
[2] Johns Hopkins University
shap@cs.jhu.edu

Abstract. Access control systems must be evaluated in part on how well they enable one to distribute the access rights needed for cooperation, while simultaneously limiting the propagation of rights which would create vulnerabilities. Analysis to date implicitly assumes access is controlled only by manipulating a system's protection state – the arrangement of the access graph. Because of the limitations of this analysis, capability systems have been "proven" unable to enforce some basic policies: revocation, confinement, and the *-properties (explained in the text).
In actual practice, programmers build *access abstractions* – programs that help control access, extending the kinds of access control that can be expressed. Working in Dennis and van Horn's original capability model, we show how abstractions were used in actual capability systems to enforce the above policies. These simple, often tractable programs limited the rights of arbitrarily complex, untrusted programs. When analysis includes the possibility of access abstractions, as it must, the original capability model is shown to be stronger than is commonly supposed.

1 Introduction

We live in a world of insecure computing. Viruses regularly roam our networks causing damage. By exploiting a single bug in an ordinary server or application, an attacker may compromise a whole system. Bugs tend to grow with code size, so vulnerability usually *increases* over the life of a given software system. Lacking a readily available solution, users have turned to the perpetual stopgaps of virus checkers and firewalls. These stopgaps cannot solve the problem – they provide the defender no fundamental advantage over the attacker.

In large measure, these problems are failures of access control. All widely-deployed operating systems today – including Windows, UNIX variants, Macintosh, and PalmOS – routinely allow programs to execute with excessive and largely unnecessary authority. For example, when you run Solitaire, it needs only to render into its window, receive UI events, and perhaps save a game state to a file you specify. Under the *Principle of Least Authority* (POLA – closely related to the Principle of Least Privilege [Saltzer75]), it would be limited to exactly these rights. Instead, today, it runs with all of your authority. It can scan your email for interesting tidbits and sell them on eBay to the highest bidder; all the while playing only within the rules of your

V.A. Saraswat (Ed.): ASIAN 2003, LNCS 2896, pp. 224–242, 2003.

system. Because applications are run with such excessive authority, they serve as powerful platforms from which viruses and human attackers penetrate systems and compromise data. The flaws exploited are not bugs in the usual sense. Each operating system is functioning as specified, and each specification is a valid embodiment of its access control paradigm. The flaws lie in the access control paradigm.

By *access control paradigm* we mean an access control model plus a way of thinking – a sense of what the model means, or could mean, to its practitioners, and of how its elements should be used.

For purposes of analysis, we pick a frame of reference – a boundary between a *base* system (e.g., a "kernel" or "TCB") creating the rules of permissible action, and programs running on that base, able to act only in permitted ways. In this paper, "program" refers only to programs running on the base, whose access is controlled by its rules.

Whether to enable cooperation or to limit vulnerability, we care about *authority* rather than *permissions*. Permissions determine what actions an individual program may perform on objects it can directly access. Authority describes effects a program may cause on objects it can access, either directly by permission, or indirectly by permitted interactions with other programs. To understand authority, we must reason about the interaction of program behavior and the arrangement of permissions. While Dennis and van Horn's 1966 paper, *Programming Semantics for Multiprogrammed Computations* [Dennis66] clearly suggested both the need and a basis for a unified semantic view of permissions and program behavior, we are unaware of any formal analysis pursuing this approach in the security, programming language, or operating system literature.

Over the last 30 years, the formal security literature has reasoned about bounds on authority exclusively from the evolution of state in protection graphs – the arrangement of permissions. This implicitly assumes all programs are hostile. While conservatively safe, this approach omits consideration of security enforcing programs. Like the access it controls, security policy emerges from the interaction between the behavior of programs and the underlying protection primitives. This omission has resulted in false negatives – mistaken infeasibility results – diverting attention from the possibility that an effective access control model has existed for 37 years.

In this paper, we offer a new look at the original capability model proposed by Dennis and van Horn [Dennis66] – here called *object-capabilities*. Our emphasis – which was also their emphasis – is on expressing policy by using abstraction to extend the expressiveness of object-capabilities. Using abstraction, object-capability practitioners have solved problems like revocation (withdrawing previously granted rights), overt confinement (cooperatively isolating an untrusted subsystem)[1], and the *-properties (enabling one-way communication between clearance levels). We show the logic of these solutions, using only functionality available in Dennis and van Horn's 1966 Supervisor, hereafter referred to as "DVH." In the process, we show that many policies that have been "proven" impossible are in fact straightforward.

The balance of this paper proceeds as follows. In "Terminology and Distinctions", we explain our distinction between *permission* and *authority*, adapted from Bishop and Snyder's distinction between *de jure* and *de facto* transfer. In "How Much Au-

[1] Semantic models, specifications, and correct programs deal only in *overt* causation. Since this paper examines only models, not implementations, we ignore covert and side channels. In this paper, except where noted, the "overt" qualifier should be assumed.

thority Does 'cp' Need?", we use a pair of Unix shell examples to contrast two paradigms of access control. In "The Object-Capability Paradigm", we explain the relationship between the object-capability paradigm and the object paradigm. We introduce the object-capability language ***E***, which we use to show access control abstractions. In "Confinement", we show how object- capability systems confine *programs* rather than *uncontrolled subjects*. We show how confinement enables a further pattern of abstraction, which we use to implement the *- properties.

2 Terminology and Distinctions

A *direct access right* to an *object* gives a *subject permission* to *invoke* the *behavior* of that object. Here, Alice has direct access to `/etc/passwd`, so she has permission to invoke any of its operations. She *accesses* the object, *invoking* its `read()` operation.

By *subject* we mean the finest-grain unit of computation on a given system that may be given distinct direct access rights. Depending on the system, this could be anything from: all processes run by a given user account, all processes running a given program, an individual process, all instances of a given class, or an individual instance. To encourage anthropomorphism we use human names for subjects.

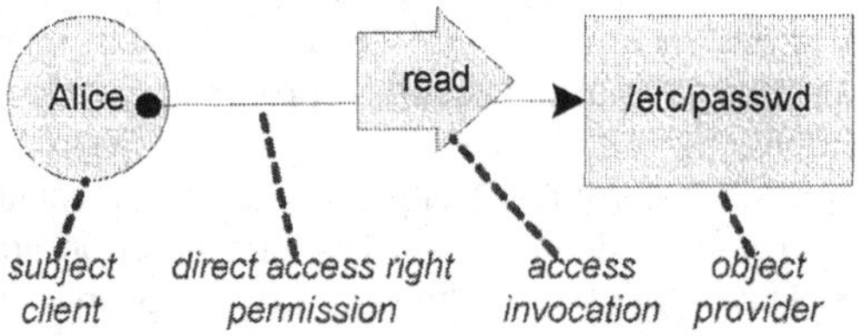

Fig. 1. *Access diagrams* depict protection state.

By *object*, we mean the finest-grain unit to which separate direct access rights may be provided, such as a file, a memory page, or another subject, depending on the system. Without loss of generality, we model restricted access to an object, such as read-only access to `/etc/passwd`, as simple access to another object whose behavior embodies the restriction, such as access to the read-only facet of `/etc/passwd` which responds only to queries.

Any discussion of access must carefully distinguish between *permission* and *authority* (adapted from Bishop and Snyder's distinction between *de jure* and *de facto* transfer [Bishop79]). Alice can directly read `/etc/passwd` by calling `read(...)` when the system's protection state says she has adequate *permission*. Bob (unshown), who does not have permission, can indirectly read `/etc/passwd` so long as Alice sends him copies of the text. When Alice and Bob arrange this relying only on the "legal" overt rules of the system, we say Alice is providing Bob with an *indirect access right* to read `/etc/passwd`, that she is acting as his proxy, and that Bob thereby has *authority* to read it. Bob's authority derives from the arrangement of permissions (Alice's read permission, Alice's permission to talk to Bob), and from the behavior of subjects and objects on permitted causal pathways (Alice's proxying behavior). The thin black arrows in our access diagrams depict permissions. We will explain the resulting authority relationships in the text.

The protection state of a system is the arrangement of permissions at some instant in time, i.e., the topology of the access graph. Whether Bob currently has permission to access `/etc/passwd` depends only on the current arrangements of permissions. Whether Bob eventually gains permission depends on this arrangement and on the state and behavior of all subjects and objects that might cause Bob to be granted permission. We cannot generally predict if Bob will gain this permission, but a conservative bound can give us a reliable "no" or "maybe".

From a given system's *update rules* – rules governing permission to alter permissions – one might be able to calculate a bound on possible future arrangements by reasoning only from the current arrangement[2]. This corresponds to Bishop and Snyder's potential *de jure* analysis, and gives us an *arrangement-only bound on permission.* With more knowledge, one can set tighter bounds. By taking the state and behavior of some subjects and objects into account, we may calculate a tighter *partially behavioral bound on permission.*

Bob's eventual authority to `/etc/passwd` depends on the arrangement of permissions, and on the state and behavior of all subjects and objects on permitted causal pathways between Bob and `/etc/passwd`. One can derive a bound on possible overt causality by reasoning only from the current arrangement of permissions. This corresponds to Bishop and Snyder's potential *de facto* analysis, and gives us an *arrangement-only bound on authority.* Likewise, by taking some state and behavior into account, we may calculate a tighter *partially behavioral bound on authority.*

Systems have many levels of abstraction. At any moment our frame of reference is a boundary between a *base* system that creates rules and the subjects hosted on that base, restricted to play by those rules. By definition, a base system manipulates only permissions. Subjects extend the expressiveness of a base system by building abstractions whose behavior further limits the authority it provides to others. Taking this behavior into account, one can calculate usefully tighter bounds on authority. As our description ascends levels of abstraction [Neumann80], the authority manipulated by the extensions of one level becomes the permissions manipulated by the primitives of the next higher base. Permission is relative to a frame of reference. Authority is invariant.

It is unclear whether Saltzer and Schroeder's *Principle of Least Privilege* is best interpreted as least permission or least authority. As we will see, there is an enormous difference between the two.

3 How Much Authority Does "cp" Need?

Consider how the following Unix shell command works:

```
$ cp foo.txt bar.txt
```

Here, your shell passes to the `cp` program the two strings `"foo.txt"` and `"bar.txt"`. By these strings, you mean particular files in your file system – your namespace of files. In order for `cp` to open the files you name, it must use your

[2] The Harrison Ruzzo Ullman paper [Harrison76] is often misunderstood to say this calculation is never decidable. HRU actually says it is possible (indeed, depressingly easy) to design a set of update rules which are undecidable. At least three protection systems have been shown to be decidably safe [Jones76, Shapiro00, Motwani00].

namespace, and it must be able to read and write any file you might name that you can read and write. Not only does `cp` operate with all your authority, it must. Given this way of using names, `cp`'s *least authority* still includes all of your authority to the file system. So long as we normally install and run applications in this manner, both security and reliability are hopeless.

By contrast, consider:

```
$ cat < foo.txt > bar.txt
```

This shell command brings about the same end effect. Although `cat` also runs with all your authority, for this example at least, it does not need to. As with function calls in any lexically scoped language (even FORTRAN), the names used to designate arguments are evaluated in the caller's namespace prior to the call (here, by opening files). The callee gets direct access to the first-class anonymous objects passed in, and designates them with parameter "names" bound in its own private name space (here, file descriptor numbers). The file descriptors are granted only to this individual process, so only this process can use these file descriptors to access these files. In this case, the two file descriptors passed in are all the authority `cat` needs to perform this request.

Today's widely deployed systems use both styles of access control. They grant permission to open a file on a per-account basis, creating the pools of authority on which viruses grow. These same systems flexibly grant access to a file descriptor on a per-process basis. Ironically, only their support of the first style is explained *as* their access control system. Object-capability systems differ from current systems more by the elimination of the first style than by the elaboration of the second.

If support for the first style were eliminated and `cat` ran with access *only* to the file descriptors passed in, it could still do its job, and we could more easily reason about our vulnerabilities to its malice or bugs. In our experience of object-capability programming, these radical reductions of authority and vulnerability mostly happen naturally.

4 The Object-Capability Paradigm

In the object model of computation [Goldberg76, Hewitt73], there is no distinction between subjects and objects. A non-primitive object, or *instance*, is a combination of code and state, where *state* is a mutable collection of *references* to objects. The *computational system* is the dynamic reference graph of objects. Objects – behaving according to their code – interact by sending messages on references. Messages carry references as arguments, thereby changing the connectivity of the reference graph.

The *object-capability* model uses the reference graph *as* the access graph, requiring that objects can interact *only* by sending messages on references. To get from objects to object- capabilities we need merely prohibit certain primitive abilities which are not part of the object model anyway, but which the object model by itself doesn't require us to prohibit – such as forged pointers, direct access to another's private state, and mutable static state [Kahn88, Rees96, Miller00]. For example, C++, with its ability to cast integers into pointers, is still within the object model but not the object-capability model. Smalltalk and Java fall outside the object-capability model because their mutable static variables enable objects to interact outside the reference graph.

Whereas the *functionality* of an object program depends only on the abilities provided by its underlying system, the *security* of an object-capability program depends on underlying inabilities as well. In a graph of mutually suspicious objects, one object's correctness depends not only on what the rules of the game say it can do, but also on what the rules say its potential adversaries cannot do.

4.1 The Object-Capability Model

The following model is an idealization of various object languages and object-capability operating systems. All its access control abilities are present in DVH (Dennis and van Horn's Supervisor) and most other object-capability systems[3]. Object-capability systems differ regarding concurrency control, storage management, equality, typing, and the primitiveness of messages, so we avoid these issues in of our model. Our model does assume reusable references, so it may not fit object-capability systems based on concurrent logic/constraint programming [Miller87, Kahn88, Roy02]. However, our examples may easily be adapted to any object-capability system despite these differences.

The static state of the reference graph is composed of the following elements.

- An object is either a *primitive* or an *instance*. Later, we explain three kinds of primitives: *data*, *devices*, and a *loader*. Data is immutable.
- An *instance* is a combination of *code* and *state*. We say it is an *instance of* the behavior described by its code. For example, we say an operating system process is an instance of its program.
- An instance's *state* is a mutable map from *indexes* to *references*.
- A *reference* provides access to an object, indivisibly combining designation of the object, the permission to access it, and the means to access it. The permission arrows on our access diagrams now depict references.
- A *capability* is a reference to non-data.
- *Code* is some form of data (such as instructions) used to describe an instance's behavior to a loader, as explained below. Code also contains literal data.
- Code describes how a *receiving instance* (or "self") reacts to an *incoming message*.
- While an instance is reacting, its *addressable references* are those in the incoming message, in the receiving instance's state, and in the literal data of the receiving instance's code. The *directly accessible objects* are those designated by addressable references.
- An *index* is some form of data used by code to indicate which addressable reference to use, or where in the receiving instance's state to store an addressable reference. Depending on the system, an index into state may be an instance variable name or offset, a virtual memory address, or a capability-list index (a c-list index, like a file descriptor number). An index into a message may be an argument position, argument keyword, or parameter name.

---

[3] Our object-capability model is essentially the untyped lambda calculus with applicativeorder local side effects and a restricted form of `eval` – the model Actors and Scheme are based on. This correspondence of objects, lambda calculus, and capabilities was noticed several times by 1973 [Goldberg76, Hewitt73, Morris73], and investigated explicitly in [Tribble95, Rees96].

Message passing and object creation dynamically change the graph's connectivity.

In the initial conditions of Figure 2, Bob and Carol are *directly accessible* to Alice. When Alice sends Bob the message "`foo(carol)`", she is both accessing Bob and permitting Bob to access Carol.

Alice can cause effects on the world outside herself only by sending messages to objects directly accessible to her (Bob), where she may include, at distinct argument indexes, references to objects directly accessible to her (Carol). We model a call-return pattern as two messages. For example, Alice gains information from Bob by causing Bob (with a query) to cause her to be informed (with a return).

Bob is affected by the world outside himself only by the arrival of messages sent by those with access to him. On arrival, the arguments of the message (Carol) become directly accessible to Bob. Within the limits set by these rules, and by what Bob may feasibly know or compute, Bob reacts to an incoming message only according to his code. All computation happens only in reaction to messages.

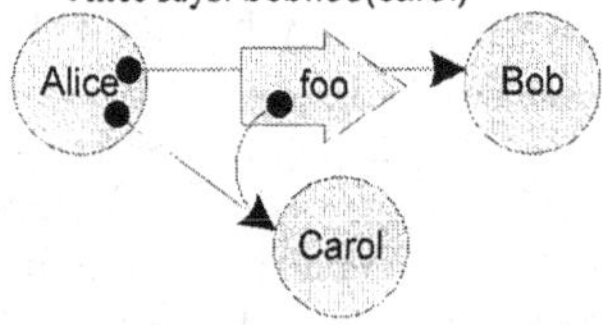

Fig. 2. Introduction by Message Passing.

Table 1. Object/Capability Corresponding Concepts.

Model Term	Capability OS Terms	Object Language Terms
instance	process, domain	instance, closure
code	non-kernel program + literal data	lambda expression, class file, method table
state	address space + c-list (capability list)	environment, instance variable frame
index	virtual memory address, c-list index	lexical name, variable offset, argument position
loader	domain creator, exec	`eval`, ClassLoader

We distinguish three kinds of primitive objects.

- *Data* objects, such as the number 3. Access to these are knowledge limited rather than permission limited. If Alice can figure out which integer she wants, whether 3 or your private key, she can have it. Data provides only information, not access. Because data is immutable, we need not distinguish between a reference to data and the data itself. (In an OS context, we model user-mode compute instructions as data operations.)
- *Devices*. For purposes of analysis we divide the world into a *computational system* containing all objects of potential interest, and an *external world*. On the boundary are primitive *devices*, causally connected to the external world by unexplained means. A non-device object can only affect the external world by sending a message to an accessible output device. A non-device object can only be affected by the external world by receiving a message from an input device that has access to it.

- A *loader* makes new instances. The creation request to a loader has two arguments: code describing the behavior of the new instance, and an index => reference map providing *all* the instance's initial state. A loader must ensure (whether by code verification or hardware protection) that the instance's behavior cannot violate the rules of our model. A loader returns the *only* reference to the new instance. (Below, use a loader to model nested lambda evaluation.)

By these rules, *only connectivity begets connectivity* – all access must derive from previous access. Two disjoint subgraphs cannot become connected as no one can introduce them. Arrangement-based analysis of bounds on permission proceeds by graph reachability arguments. Overt causation, carried only by messages, flows only along permitted pathways, so we may again use reachability arguments to reason about bounds on authority and causality. The transparency of garbage collection relies on such arguments.

The object-capability model recognizes the security properties latent in the object model. All the restrictions above are consistent with good object programming practice even when security is of no concern.

4.2 A Taste of *E*

To illustrate how the object-capability model is used to solve access control problems, we use a subset of the ***E*** language as our notation. This subset directly embodies our objectcapability model. All the functionality it provides is present in DVH. Full ***E*** extends the capability paradigm beyond the model presented above. Using a cryptographic capability protocol among mutually suspicious machines, ***E*** creates a distributed persistent reference graph, supporting decentralized access control with somewhat weaker properties than are possible within a single machine. These issues are beyond the scope of this paper. For the rest of this paper, "***E***" refers to our subset of ***E***.

In ***E***, an instance is a single-parameter closure instantiated by lambda evaluation. The single (implicit) parameter is for the incoming message. A message send applies an objectas- closure to a message-as-argument. ***E*** combines Scheme-like semantics [Kelsey98] with syntax for message sending, method dispatch, and soft type checking, explained below. Here is a simple data abstraction.

```
def pointMaker
    { to make(x :int, y :int) :any {
        ^def point {
            to getX() :int { ^x }
            to getY() :int { ^y }
            to add(otherPt) :any {
                ^pointMaker.make(x.add(otherPt.getX()),
                                 y.add(otherPt.getY()))
} } } }
```

The expressions defining `pointMaker` and `point` are object definitions – both a lambda expression and a variable definition. An object definition evaluates to a closure whose behavior is described by its body, and it defines a variable (shown in bold italics) to hold this value. The body consists of `to` clauses defining methods, and an optional `match` clause as we will see later. Because an object is always applied to a message, the message parameter is implicit, as is the dispatch on the message name to select a method. The prefix "^" acts like the return keyword of many languages. The `pointMaker` has a single method, `make`, that defines and returns a new `point`.

Method definitions (shown in bold) and variable definitions (shown in italics) can have an optional soft type declaration [Cartwright91], shown as a ":" followed by a guard expression. A guard determines which values may pass. The `any` guard used above allows any value to pass as is.

The nested definition of `point` uses `x` and `y` freely. These are its instance variables, and together form its state. The state maps from indexes `"x"` and `"y"` to the associated values from point's creation context.

Using the loader explained above, we can transform the above code to

```
def pointMaker {
     to make(x :int, y :int) :any {
       ^def point := loader.load("def point {…}",
                                 ["x" => x, "y" => y])
} }
```

Rather than a source string, a realistic loader would accept some form of separately compiled code.

The expression `["x" => x, "y" => y]` builds a map of index => reference associations. All "linking" happens only by virtue of these associations – only connectivity begets connectivity.

Applying this transformation recursively would unnest all object definitions. Nested object definitions better explain instantiation in object languages. The `loader` better explains process or domain creation in operating systems. In ***E***, we almost always use object definitions, but we use the `loader` below to achieve confinement.

4.3 Revocation: Redell's 1974 Caretaker Pattern

Capability systems modeled as unforgeable references present the other extreme, where delegation is trivial, and revocation is infeasible.

– Chander, Dean, Mitchell [Chander01]

When Alice says `bob.foo(carol)`, she gives Bob unconditional, full, and perpetual access to Carol. Given the purpose of Alice's message to Bob, such access may dangerously exceed least authority. In order to practice POLA, Alice might need to somehow restrict the rights she grants to Bob. For example, she might want to ensure she can revoke access at a later time. But in a capability system, capabilities themselves are the only representation of permission, and they provide only unconditional, full, perpetual access to the objects they designate.

What is Alice to do? She can use (a slight simplification of) Redell's Caretaker pattern for revoking access [Redell74], shown here using additional elements of ***E*** we explain below.

```
def caretakerMaker {
     to make(var target) :any {
        def caretaker {
             match [verb :String, args :any[]] {
                     E.call(target, verb, args)
        } }
        def revoker {
             to revoke() :void {
```

```
                target := null
        } }
        ^[caretaker, revoker]
} }
```

Instead of saying "`bob.foo(carol)`", Alice can instead say:

```
def [carol2, carol2Rvkr] := caretakerMaker.make(carol)
bob.foo(carol2)
```

The Caretaker `carol2` transparently forwards messages it receives to `target`'s current value. The Revoker `carol2Rvkr` changes what that current value is. Alice can later revoke the effect of her grant to Bob by saying "`carol2Rvkr.revoke()`".

Variables in ***E*** are non-assignable by default. The `var` keyword means `target` can be assigned. (`var` is the opposite of Java's `final`.) Within the scope of `target`'s definition, `make` defines two objects, `caretaker` and `revoker`, and returns them to its caller in a two element list. Alice receives this pair, defines `carol2` to be the new Caretaker, and defines `carol2Rvkr` to be the corresponding Revoker. Both objects use `target` freely, so they both share access to the same assignable `target` variable (which is therefore a separate object).

What happens when Bob invokes `carol2`, thinking he's invoking the kind of thing Carol is? An object definition contains methods and an optional `match` clause defining a matcher. If an incoming message (`x.add(3)`) doesn't match any of the methods, it is given to the matcher. The `verb` parameter is bound to the message name (`"add"`) and the `args` to the argument list (`[3]`). This allows messages to be received generically without prior knowledge of their API, much like Smalltalk's `doesNotUnderstand:` or Java's `Proxy`. Messages are sent generically using "`E.call(...)`", much like Smalltalk's `perform:`, Java's "reflection", or Scheme's `apply`.

This Caretaker[4] provides a temporal restriction of authority. Similar patterns provide other restrictions, such as *filtering facets* that let only certain messages through. Even in systems not designed to support access abstraction, many simple patterns happen naturally. Under Unix, Alice might provide a filtering facet as a process reading a socket Bob can write. The facet process would access Carol using Alice's permissions.

4.4 Analysis and Blind Spots

Given Redell's existence proof in 1974, what are we to make of subsequent arguments that revocation is infeasible in capability systems? Of those who made this impossibility claim, as far as we are aware, *none* pointed to a flaw in Redell's reasoning. The key is the difference between permission and authority analysis. ([Chander01] analyzes, in our terms, only permission.) By such an analysis, Bob was never given permission to access Carol, so there was no access to Carol to be revoked! Bob was given permission to access `carol2`, and he still has it. No permissions were revoked.

---

[4] The simple Caretaker shown here depends on Alice assuming that Carol will not provide Carol's clients with direct access to herself.

See www.erights.org/elib/capability/deadman.html for a more general treatment of revocation in ***E***.

A security officer investigating an incident needs to know who has access to a compromised object.

– Karger and Herbert [Karger84]

In their paper, Karger and Herbert propose to give a security officer a list of all subjects who are, in our terms, permitted to access Carol. This list will not include Bob's access to Carol, since this indirect access is represented only by the system's protection state taken together with the behavior of objects playing by the rules. Within their system, Alice, by restricting the authority given to Bob as she should, has inadvertently thwarted the security officer's ability to get a meaningful answer to his query.

To render a permission-only analysis useless, a threat model need not include either malice or accident; it need only include subjects following security best practices.

An arrangement-only bound on permission or authority would include the possibility of the Caretaker giving Bob direct access to Carol – precisely what the Caretaker was constructed not to do. Only by reasoning about behaviors can Alice see that the Caretaker is a "smart reference". Just as `pointMaker` extends our vocabulary of data types, raising the abstraction level at which we express solutions, so does the Caretaker extend our vocabulary for expressing access control. Alice (or her programmer) should use arrangement-only analysis for reasoning about what potential adversaries may do. But Alice also interacts with many objects, like the Caretaker, *because* she has some confidence she understands their actual behavior.

4.5 Access Abstraction

The object-capability model does not describe access control as a separate concern, to be bolted on to computation organized by other means. Rather it is a model of modular computation with no separate access control mechanisms. All its support for access control is well enough motivated by the pursuit of abstraction and modularity. Parnas' principle of *information hiding* [Parnas72] in effect says our abstractions should hand out information only on a *need to know* basis. POLA simply adds that authority should be handed out only on a *need to do* basis [Crockford97]. Modularity and security each require both of these principles.

The *object-capability paradigm*, in the air by 1967 [Wilkes79, Fabry74], and well established by 1973 [Redell74, Hewitt73, Morris73, Wulf74, Wulf81], adds the observation that the abstraction mechanisms provided by the base model are not just for procedural, data, and control abstractions, but also for *access abstractions*, such as Redell's Caretaker. (These are "communications abstractions" in [Tribble95]).

Access abstraction is pervasive in actual capability practice, including filtering facets, unprivileged transparent remote messaging systems [Donnelley76, Sansom86, Doorn96, Miller00], reference monitors [Rajunas89], transfer, escrow, and trade of exclusive rights [Miller96, Miller00], and recent patterns like the Powerbox [Wagner02, Stiegler02]. Further, every non-security-oriented abstraction that usefully encapsulates its internal state provides, in effect, restricted authority to affect that internal state, as mediated by the logic of the abstraction.

5 Confinement

... a program can create a controlled environment within which another, possibly untrustworthy program, can be run safely... call the first program a customer and the second a service. ... [the service] may leak, i.e. transmit ... the input data which the customer gives it. ... We will call the problem of constraining a service [from leaking data] the confinement problem.

– Lampson [Lampson73]

Once upon a time, in the days before wireless, you (a human customer) could buy a box containing a calculator (the service) from a manufacturer you might not trust. Although you might worry whether the calculations are correct, you can at least enter your financial data confident that the calculator cannot leak your secrets back to its manufacturer. How did the box solve the confinement problem? By letting you see that it comes with no strings attached. When the only causation to worry about would be carried by wires, the visible absence of wires emerging from the box – the isolation of the subgraph – is adequate evidence of confinement.

Here, we use this same technique to achieve confinement, substituting capabilities for wires. The presentation here is a simplification of confinement in actual object-capability systems [Hardy86, Shapiro99, Shapiro00, Wagner02, Yee03].

To solve confinement, assume that the manufacturer, Max, and customer, Cassie, have mutual access to a (`Factory`, `factoryMaker`) pair created by the following code. Assume that Cassie trusts that this pair of objects behaves according to this code.

```
{ interface Factory guards FactoryStamp {…}
  def factoryMaker {
     to make(code :String) :Factory {
       ^def factory implements FactoryStamp {
          to new(state) :any {
                ^loader.load(code, state)
  } } } }
  [Factory, factoryMaker]
}
```

The interface .. guards expression evaluates to a (*trademark guard, stamp*) pair representing a new *trademark*, similar in purpose to an interface type[5]. This syntax also defines variables to hold these objects, here named `Factory` and `FactoryStamp`. Here we use the `FactoryStamp` to mark instances of `factory`, and nothing else, as carrying this trademark. We use the `Factory` guard in soft type declarations, like "`:Factory`" above, to ensure that only objects carrying this trademark may pass. The block of code above evaluates to a (`Factory`, `factoryMaker`) pair. Only the `factoryMaker` of a pair can make objects, instances of `factory`, which will pass the `Factory` guard of that pair.

---

[5] Such trademarking can be implemented in DVH and in our model of object-capability computation [Morris73, Miller87, Tribble95, Rees96], so object-capability systems which provide trademarking primitively [Wulf81, Hardy85, Shapiro99, Yee03] are still within our model.

Max uses a `factoryMaker` to package his proprietary calculator program in a box he sends it to Cassie.

```
def calculatorFactory := factoryMaker.make("...code...")
cassie.acceptProduct(calculatorFactory)
```

In section 5.2 Cassie uses a "`:Factory`" declaration on the parameter of her `accept- Product` method to ensure that she receives only an instance of the above `factory` definition. Inspection of the factory code shows that a factory's state contains only data (here, a String) and no capabilities – no access to the world outside itself. Cassie may therefore use the factory to make as many live calculators as she wants, confident that each calculator has only that access beyond itself that Cassie authorizes. They cannot even talk to each other unless Cassie allows them to.

With lambda evaluation, a new subject's code and state both come from the same parent. To solve the confinement problem, we combine code from Max with state from Cassie to give birth to a new calculator, and we enable Cassie to verify that she is the only stateproviding parent. This state is an example of Lampson's "controlled environment". To Cassie, the calculator is a *controlled subject* – one Cassie knows is born into an environment controlled by her. By contrast, should Max introduce Cassie to an already instantiated calculation service, Cassie would not be able to tell whether it has prior connectivity. (Extending our analogy, suppose Max offers the calculation service from his web site.) The calculation service would be an *uncontrolled subject* to her.

We wish to reiterate that by "confinement", we refer to the overt subset of Lampson's problem, where the customer accepts only code ("a program") from the manufacturer and instantiates it in a controlled environment. We do not propose to confine information or authority given to uncontrolled subjects.

5.1 A Non-discretionary Model

Capabilities are normally thought to be *discretionary*, and to be unable to enforce confinement. Our confinement logic above relies on the non-discretionary nature of object-capabilities. What does it mean for an access control system to be discretionary?

> *"Our discussion ... rested on an unstated assumption: the principal that creates a file or other object in a computer system has unquestioned authority to authorize access to it by other principals. ...We may characterize this control pattern as discretionary." [emphasis in the original]*
>
> – Saltzer and Schroeder [Saltzer75]

Object-capability systems have no principals. A human user, together with his shell and "home directory" of references, participates, in effect, as just another subject. With the substitution of "subject" for "principal", we will use this classic definition of "discretionary".

By this definition, *object-capabilities are not discretionary*. In our model, in DVH, and in most actual capability system implementations, even if Alice creates Carol, Alice may still only authorize Bob to access Carol if Alice has authority to access Bob. If capabilities were discretionary, they would indeed be unable to enforce confinement. To illustrate the power of confinement, we use it below to enforce the *-properties.

5.2 The *-Properties

*Boebert made clear in [[Boebert84]] that an unmodified or classic capability system cannot enforce the *-property or solve the confinement problem.*

– Gong [Gong89]

Briefly, the *-properties taken together allow subjects with lower (such as "secret") clearance to communicate to subjects with higher (such as "top secret") clearance, but prohibit communication in the reverse direction [Bell74]. KeySafe is a concrete and realistic design for enforcing the *-properties on KeyKOS, a pure object-capability system [Rajunas89]. However, claims that capabilities cannot enforce the *-properties continue [Gong89, Kain87, Wallach97, Saraswat03], citing [Boebert84] as their support. Recently, referring to [Boebert84], Boebert writes:

The paper ... remains, no more than an offhand remark. ... The historical significance of the paper is that it prompted the writing of [[Kain87]]

– Boebert [Boebert03]

Boebert here defers to Kain and Landwehr's paper [Kain87]. Regarding object-capability systems, Kain and Landwehr's paper makes essentially the same impossibility claims, which they support only by citing and summarizing Boebert. To lay this matter to rest, we show how Cassie solves Boebert's challenge problem – how she provides a one way comm channel to subjects she doesn't trust, say Q and Bond, who she considers to have secret and top secret clearance respectively. Can Cassie prevent Boebert's attack, in which Q and Bond use the rights Cassie provides to build a reverse channel?

Completing our earlier confinement example, Cassie accepts a calculator factory from Max using this method.

```
to acceptProduct(calcFactory :Factory) :void {
    var diode :int := 0
    def diodeWriter {
      to write(val :int) :void { diode := val }
    }
    def diodeReader {
      to read() :int { ^diode }
    }
    def q  := calcFactory.new(["writeUp"  => diodeWriter, ...])
    def bond := calcFactory.new(["readDown" =>
                                     diodeReader, ...])
    ...
}
```

Cassie creates two calculators to serve as Q and Bond. She builds a data diode by defining a `diodeWriter`, a `diodeReader`, and an assignable `diode` variable they share. She gives Q and Bond access to each other only through the data diode. Applied to Cassie's arrangement, Boebert's attack starts by observing that Q can send a capability as an argument in a message to the `diodeWriter`. An arrangement-only analysis of bounds on permissions or authority supports Boebert's case – the data diode might introduce this argument to Bond. Only by examining the behavior of the data diode can we see the tighter bounds it was built to enforce. It transmits data (here, integers) in only one direction and capabilities in neither. (Q cannot even read what he just wrote!) Cassie relies on the behavior of the factory and data diode abstractions to enforce the *-properties and prevent Boebert's attack. (See [Miller03] for further detail.)

5.3 The Arena and Terms of Entry

Policies like the *-properties are generally assumed to govern a computer system as a whole, to be enforced in collaboration with a human sys-admin or security officer. In a capability system, this is a matter of *initial conditions*. If the owner of the system wishes such a policy to govern the entire system, she can run such code when the system is first generated, and when new users join. But what happens after the big bang? Let's say Alice meets Bob, who is an uncontrolled subject to her. Alice can still enforce "additive" policies on Bob, e.g., she can give him revocable access to Carol, and then revoke it. But she cannot enforce a policy on Bob that requires removing prior rights from Bob, for that would violate Bob's security!

Instead, as we see in the example above, acting as Lampson's "customer", Aliceshe sets up an *arena* – Lampson's "controlled environment" – with initial conditions she determines, governed by her rules, and over which she is the sys-admin. If her rules can be enforced on uncontrolled subjects, she can admit Bob onto her arena as a player. If her rules require the players not to have some rights, she must set *terms of entry*. "Please leave your cellphones at the door." A prospective participant (Max) provides a player (`calcFactory`) to represent his interests within the arena, where this player can pass the security check at the gate (here, `:Factory`). No rights were taken away from anyone; participation was voluntary.

The arena technique corresponds to *meta-linguistic abstraction* – an arena is a virtual machine built within a virtual machine [Abelson86, Safra86]. The resulting system can be described according to either level of abstraction – by the rules of the base level object-capability system or by the rules of the arena. The subjects built by the admitted factories are also subjects within the arena. At the base level, we would say Q has permission to send messages to `diodeWriter` and authority to send integers to Bond. At the arena level of description, we would say a data diode is a primitive part of the arena's protection state, and say Q has permission to send integers to Bond. Any base level uncontrolled subjects admitted into the arena are devices of the arena – they have mysterious connections to the arena's external world.

When the only inputs to a problem is data (here, code), any system capable of universal computation can solve any solvable problem, so questions of absolute possibility become useless for comparisons. Conventional language comparisons face the same dilemma, and language designers have learned to ask instead an engineering question: *Is this a good machine on which to build other machines?* How well did we do on Boebert's challenge? The code admitted was neither inspected nor transformed. Each arena level subject was also a base level subject. The behavior interposed by Cassie between the subjects was very thin. Mostly, we reused the security properties of the base level object-capability system to build the security properties of our new arena level machine.

5.4 Mutually Suspicious Composition

When mutually suspicious interests build a diversity of abstractions to express a diversity of co-existing policies, how do these extensions interact?

Let's say that Q builds a gizmo that might have bugs, so Q creates a Caretaker to give the gizmo revocable access to his `diodeWriter`. Q's policy relies on the behavior of his Caretaker but not necessarily on Cassie's `diodeWriter`. To Cassie,

Q's gizmo and Caretaker are part of Q's subgraph and indistinguishable from Q. Cassie's policy relies on the behavior of her `diodeWriter`, but not on Q's Caretaker. They each do a partially behavioral analysis over the same graph, each from their own subjective perspective. This scenario shows how diverse expressions of policy often compose correctly even when none of the interested parties are aware this is happening.

6 Conclusion

Just as we should not expect a base programming language to provide us all the data types we need for computation, we should not expect a base access control system to provide us all the elements we need to express our protection policies. Both issues deserve the same kind of answer: We use the base to build abstractions, extending the vocabulary we use to express our solutions. In evaluating a protection model, one must examine how well it supports the extension of its own expressiveness by abstraction and composition.

Security in computational systems emerges from the interaction between primitive protection mechanisms and the behavior of security enforcing programs. As we have shown here, such programs are able to enforce restrictions on more general, untrusted programs by building on and abstracting more primitive protection mechanisms. To our knowledge, the object-capability model is the only protection model whose semantics can be readily expressed in programming language terms: approximately, lambda calculus with local side effects. This provides the necessary common semantic framework for reasoning about permission and program behavior together. Because security-enforcing programs are often simple, the required program analysis should frequently prove tractable, *provided* they are built on effective primitives.

By recognizing that program behavior can contribute towards access control, a lost paradigm for protection – abstraction – is restored to us, and a semantic basis for extensible protection is established. Diverse interests can each build abstractions to express their policies regarding new object types, new applications, new requirements, and each other, and these policies can co-exist and interact. This extensibility is well outside the scope of traditional access graph analyses.

Analyses based on the evolution of protection state are conservative approximations. A successful verification demonstrating the enforcement of a policy using only the protection graph (as in [Shapiro00]) is robust, in the sense that it does *not* rely on the cooperative behavior of programs. Verification *failures* are *not* robust – they may indicate a failure in the protection model, but they can also result from what might be called "failures of conservatism" – failures in which the policy is enforceable but the verification model has been simplified in a way that prevents successful verification.

We have shown by example how object-capability practitioners set tight bounds on authority by building abstractions and reasoning about their behavior, using conceptual tools similar to that used by object programmers to reason about any abstraction. We have shown, using only techniques easily implementable in Dennis and van Horn's 1966 Supervisor, how actual object-capability systems have used abstraction to solve problems that analyses using only protection state have "proven" impossible for capabilities.

The object-capability paradigm, with its pervasive, fine-grained, and extensible support for the principle of least authority, enables mutually suspicious interests to cooperate more intimately while being less vulnerable to each other. When more cooperation may be practiced with less vulnerability, we may find we have a more cooperative world.

Acknowledgments

We thank Darius Bacon, Tyler Close, K. Eric Drexler, Bill Frantz, Norm Hardy, Chris Hibbert, David Hopwood, Tad Hogg, Ken Kahn, Alan Karp, Terence Kelly, Lorens Kockum, Charles Landau, Chip Morningstar, Greg Nelson, Jonathan Rees, Vijay Saraswat, Terry Stanley, Marc Stiegler, E. Dean Tribble, Bill Tulloh, Kazunori Ueda, David Wagner, Bryce Wilcox-O'Hearn, the cap-talk and e-lang discussion lists, and especially Ka-Ping Yee, our co-author on [Miller03], whose writing had substantial influence on this paper.

References

[Abelson86] H. Abelson, G. Sussman. *Structure and Interpretation of Computer Programs.* MIT Press, 1986.

[Bell74] D.E. Bell, L. LaPadula. "Secure Computer Systems" ESD-TR-83-278, Mitre Corporation, vI and II (Nov 1973), vIII (Apr 1974).

[Bishop79] M. Bishop, L. Snyder. "The Transfer of Information and Authority in a Protection System" SOSP 1979 , p. 45–54.

[Boebert84] W. E. Boebert. "On the Inability of an Unmodified Capability Machine to Enforce the *-Property" *Proceedings of 7th DoD/NBS Computer Security Conference*, September 1984, p. 291–293. http ://zesty.ca/capmyths/boebert.html

[Boebert03] (Comments on [Miller03]) http://www.eros-os.org/pipermail/cap-talk/2003-March/001133.html

[Cartwright91] R. Cartwright, M. Fagan, "Soft Typing", *Proceedings of the SIGPLAN '91 Conference on Programming Language Design and Implementation.*

[Chander01] A. Chander, D. Dean, J. C. Mitchell. "A State-Transition Model of Trust Management and Access Control" *Proceedings of the 14th Computer Security Foundations Workshop*, June 2001, p. 27–43.

[Crockford97] Douglas Crockford, personal communications, 1997.

[Dennis66] J.B. Dennis, E.C. Van Horn. "Programming Semantics for Multiprogrammed Computations" *ommunications of the ACM*, 9(3):143–155, March 1966.

[Donnelley76] J. E. Donnelley. "A Distributed Capability Computing System" *Third International Conference on Computer Communication*, Toronto, Canada, 1976.

[Doorn96] L. van Doorn, M. Abadi, M. Burrows, E. P. Wobber. "Secure Network Objects" *Proceedings of the 1996 IEEE Symposium on Security and Privacy*, p. 211–221.

[Fabry74] R. S. Fabry. "Capability-based addressing" *Communications of the ACM*, 17(7), 1974, p. 403–412.

[Goldberg76] A. Goldberg, A. Kay. *Smalltalk-72 instruction manual.* Technical Report SSL 76-6, Learning Research Group, Xerox Palo, Alto Research Center, 1976. http://www.spies.com/~ aek/pdf/xerox/alto/Smalltalk72_ Manual.pdf

[Gong89] L. Gong. "A Secure Identity-Based Capability System" *Proceedings of the 1989 IEEE Symposium on Security and Privacy*, p. 56–65.

[Hardy85] N. Hardy. "The KeyKOS Architecture" *ACM Operating Systems Review*, September 1985, p. 8–25. http://www.agorics.com/Library/KeyKos/architecture.html

[Hardy86] N. Hardy. *U.S. Patent 4,584,639: Computer Security System*,

[Harrison76] M.A. Harrison, M.L. Ruzzo, and J.D. Ullman. "Protection in operating systems" *Communications of the ACM*, 19(8) p. 461–471, 1976.

[Hewitt73] C. Hewitt, P. Bishop, R. Stieger. "A Universal Modular Actor Formalism for Artificial Intelligence" *Proceedings of the 1973 International Joint Conference on Artificial Intelligence*, p. 235–246.

[Jones76] A. K. Jones, R. J. Lipton, L. Snyder. "A Linear Time Algorithm for Deciding Security" *FOCS*, 1976, p. 33–41.

[Kahn88] K. Kahn, M. S. Miller. "Language Design and Open Systems", *Ecology of Computation*, Bernardo Huberman (ed.), Elsevier Science Publishers, North-Holland, 1988.

[Kain87] R. Y. Kain, C. E. Landwehr. "On Access Checking in Capability-Based Systems" *IEEE Symposium on Security and Privacy*, 1987.

[Karger84] P. A. Karger, A. J. Herbert. "An Augmented Capability Architecture to Support Lattice Security and Traceability of Access" *Proc. of the 1984 IEEE Symposium on Security and Privacy*, p. 2–12.

[Kelsey98] R. Kelsey, (ed.), W. Clinger, (ed.), J. Rees, (ed.), "Revised^5 Report on the Algorithmic Language Scheme"ACM Sigplan Notices, 1998.

[Lampson73] B. W. Lampson, "A Note on the Confinement Problem" *CACM on Operating Systems*, 16(10), October, 1973.

[Miller87] M. S. Miller, D. G. Bobrow, E. D. Tribble, J. Levy, "Logical Secrets" *Concurrent Prolog: Collected Papers*, E. Shapiro (ed.), MIT Press, Cambridge, MA, 1987.

[Miller96] M. S. Miller, D. Krieger, N. Hardy, C. Hibbert, E. D. Tribble. "An Automatic Auction in ATM Network Bandwidth". *Market-based Control, A Paradigm for Distributed Resource Allocation*, S. H. Clearwater (ed.), World Scientific, Palo Alto, CA, 1996.

[Miller00] M. S. Miller, C. Morningstar, B. Frantz. "Capability-based Financial Instruments" *Proceedings Financial Cryptography 2000*, Springer Verlag. http://www.erights.org/elib/capability/ode/index.html

[Miller03] M. S. Miller, K. -P. Yee, J. S. Shapiro, "Capability Myths Demolished", HP Labs Technical Report, in preparation. http://zesty.ca/capmyths/usenix.pdf

[Morris73] J. H. Morris. "Protection in Programming Languages" *CACM* 16(1) p. 15–21, 1973. http://www.erights.org/history/morris73.pdf.

[Motwani00] R. Motwani, R. Panigrahy, V. Saraswat, S. Venkatasubramanian. "On the Decidability of Accessibility Problems" AT&T Labs – Research. http://www.research.att.com/~ suresh/Papers/java.pdf

[Neumann80] P. G. Neumann, R. S. Boyer, R. J. Feiertag, K. N. Levitt, L. Robinson. *A Provably Secure Operating System: The System, Its Applications, and Proofs*, CSL-116, Computer Science Laboratory, SRI International, Inc., May 1980.

[Parnas72] D. Parnas. "On the Criteria To Be Used in Decomposing Systems into Modules" *CACM* 15(12), December 1972. http://www.acm.org/classics/may96/.

[Rajunas89] S. A. Rajunas. "The KeyKOS/KeySAFE System Design" Key Logic, Inc., SEC009-01, March, 1989.

[Redell74] D. D. Redell. *Naming and Protection in Extendible Operating Systems*. Project MAC TR-140, MIT, November 1974. (Ph. D. thesis.)

[Rees96] J. Rees, *A Security Kernel Based on the Lambda-Calculus*. MIT AI Memo No. 1564. MIT, Cambridge, MA, 1996. http://mumble.net/jar/pubs/secureos/

[Safra86] M. Safra, E. Y. Shapiro. *Meta Interpreters for Real*. Information Processing86, H. -J. Kugler (ed.), North-Holland, Amsterdam, p. 271–278, 1986.

[Saltzer75] J. H. Saltzer, M. D. Schroeder. "The Protection of Information in Computer Systems" *Proceedings of the IEEE* **63**(9), September 1975, p. 1278–1308.

[Sansom86] R. D. Sansom, D. P. Julian, R. Rashid. "Extending a Capability Based System Into a Network Environment" *Research sponsored by DOD*, 1986, p. 265–274.

[Saraswat03] V. Saraswat, R. Jagadeesan. "Static support for capability-based programming in Java" http://www.cse.psu.edu/~ saraswat/neighborhood.pdf

[Shapiro99] J. S. Shapiro, J. M. Smith, D. J. Farber. "EROS: A Fast Capability System" *Proceedings of the 17th ACM Symposium on Operating Systems Principles*, December 1999, p. 170–185.

[Shapiro00] J. S. Shapiro, S. Weber. "Verifying the EROS Confinement Mechanism" *Proceedings of the 2000 IEEE Symposium on Security and Privacy*, p. 166–176.

[Sitaker00] K. Sitaker. *Thoughts on Capability Security on the Web.* http://lists.canonical.org/pipermail/kragen - tol/2000-August/000619.html

[Stiegler02] M. Stiegler, M. Miller. "A Capability Based Client: The DarpaBrowser" http://www.combex.com/papers/darpa-report/index.html

[Tanenbaum86] A. S. Tanenbaum, S. J. Mullender, R. van Renesse. "Using Sparse Capabilities in a Distributed Operating System" *Proceedings of 6th International Conference on Distributed Computing Systems*, 1986, p. 558–563.

[Tribble95] E. D. Tribble, M. S. Miller, N. Hardy, D. Krieger, "Joule: Distributed Application Foundations", 1995. http://www.agorics.com/joule.html

[Roy02] P. Van Roy, S. Haridi, "Concepts, Techniques, and Models of Computer Programming" MIT Press, in preparation. http://www.info.ucl.ac.be/people/PVR/book.html

[Wagner02] D. Wagner, D. Tribble. *A Security Analysis of the Combex DarpaBrowser Architecture.* http://www.combex.com/papers/darpa-review/index.html

[Wallach97] D. S. Wallach, D. Balfanz, D. Dean, E. W. Felten. "Extensible Security Architectures for Java" *Proceedings of the 16th Symposium on Operating Systems Principles*, 1997, p. 116–128. http://www.cs.princeton.edu/sip/pub/sosp97.html

[Wilkes79] M. V. Wilkes, R. M. Needham. *The Cambridge CAP Computer and its Operating System.* Elsevier North Holland, 1979.

[Wulf74] William A. Wulf, Ellis S. Cohen, William M. Corwin, Anita K. Jones, Roy Levin, C. Pierson, and Fred J. Pollack. "HYDRA: The Kernel of a Multiprocessor Operating System" *Communications of the ACM*, **17**(6):337-345, 1974

[Wulf81] W. A. Wulf, R. Levin, S. P. Harbison. *HYDRA/C.mmp: An Experimental Computer System*, McGraw Hill, 1981.

[Yee03] K.-P. Yee, M. S. Miller. *Auditors: An Extensible, Dynamic Code Verification Mechanism.* http://www.erights.org/elang/kernel/auditors/index.html

The Design and Evaluation of a Middleware Library for Distribution of Language Entities

Erik Klintskog[1], Zacharias El Banna[2], Per Brand[1], and Seif Haridi[2]

[1] Swedish Institute of Computer Science,
Box 1263, SE-164 29 Kista, Sweden
http://www.sics.se/

[2] IMIT-Royal Institute of Technology,
Electrum 229 * 164 40 Kista, Sweden
http://www.it.kth.se/

Abstract. The paper presents a modular design of a distribution middleware that supports the wide variety of entities that exist in high level languages. Such entities are classified into mutables, immutables and transients. The design is factorized in order to allow multiple consistency protocols for the same entity type, and multiple coordination strategies for implementing the protocols that differ in their failure behavior. The design is implemented and evaluated. It shows a very competitive performance.

1 Introduction

We present the design and implementation of a middleware library, the DSS (Distribution SubSystem). The DSS is designed to simplify the implementation of distributed programming systems. Using the DSS we can add distributed programming facilities to programming systems/languages which are normally not distributed. We claim that the effort needed to create a distributed programming system(DPS) using the DSS to handle distribution involves much less programming effort than to explicitly program the necessary distribution support in the system itself.

Our system aims at completeness; by this we mean that different paradigms of distributed computing can easily be implemented using the DSS. By completeness we include both functional (e.g. extending objects to distributed objects with preserved semantics) as well as non-functional aspects (e.g. providing the most efficient distribution support for all patterns of use of distributed objects).

1.1 Background

Middleware support for programming language distribution – be it partial or total – can conceptually be divided into two categories: programming language dependent middleware and programming language independent middleware. Independent middleware commonly targets language interoperability and offers

V.A. Saraswat (Ed.): ASIAN 2003, LNCS 2896, pp. 243–259, 2003.

only limited distribution support, e.g. CORBA [1]. Language dependent middleware can potentially offer complete distribution support. However the design and implementation is time-consuming. In practice, the amount of actual distribution support in a distributed programming system (DPS) reflects the trade-off between desired completeness and the amount of work required to realize it.

The trade-off is, we believe, reflected in the fact that most DPSs are incomplete even as regards functional aspects, in that distribution does not preserve desirable properties of the language semantics [2–6]. Few systems are functionally complete [7–9], but none, to our knowledge, is complete as regards efficiency aspects.

1.2 Motivation

This work is motivated by the need of a language independent middleware that provides full distribution support for arbitrary high-level programming system (PS). By full support we mean that all language entities should potentially be sharable in a distributed computing environment, with preserved semantics. Distribution on the level of language entities means that threads residing in different processes can share entities as if they were residing in the same process[1].

Examples of language entities are first class data structures such as objects, primitive data types or channel abstractions. Note that we exclude unsafe data types such as C pointers. On the other hand, code can be shared (e.g. procedure values in Oz and classes in Java). Furthermore some data types will be shared with limited distribution behavior; files, for instance, could be shared as stationary objects which only allow remote access.

Sequential consistency is generally a requirement[10] to preserve the semantics of many language entities. A prototypical example is the semantics of objects in OO languages. However, this does not preclude the use of a weaker consistency model to improve the performance of a distributed application [11], but from our point-of-view this should be reflected in a different type of language entity (e.g. different type of object).

1.3 Contributions

The major contributions of this paper can be summarized as follows. Firstly, for the developer of a DPS, we provide a model of distribution support for language entities, based on the type of distribution support a given entity requires. The model is general enough to support all to us known language entities, found in almost all high-level programming languages/systems (e.g. Java, C# and Oz[12]).

Secondly, for the application developer, we provide a model of distribution that guarantees functional properties (i.e. preserving consistency) for a given distributed entity. This model also allows for fine-grained control of non-functional aspects. Assignment of entity consistency protocols can be done in runtime, based on expected pattern of use per entity instance, and not on the entity type.

[1] This means location transparency modulo failure and latency.

Thirdly, we describe a novel component-based design of entity consistency protocols. The model simplifies implementation of new protocols, increases code reuse, and enables fine-grained customization of entity consistency protocols from the DPS level.

Finally, we present the implementation and evaluation of our language independent middleware library, called the Distribution SubSystem[2] (DSS). The DSS efficiently implements the above-described contributions, as shown by our evaluation.

1.4 Paper Organization

The rest of the paper is organized as follows. In Sect. 2 the language independent entity model is described. Sect. 3 describes our novel structure of entity consistency protocols. The structure and actual implementation of our middleware is briefly discussed in Sect. 4. More attention is given to the performance of our implementation as shown in Sect. 5. The design is compared to similar systems in Sect. 6 and a conclusion is given in Sect. 7. Note that this paper focuses on the design of key concepts and evaluation of our middleware library, and not on the philosophy behind the design and practical issues such as how a PS can be coupled to the library. Those issues are explained in detail in [13].

2 An Abstract Model of Language Entities

The set of language entities found in most high-level programming languages is large. These entities are from a programming point of view semantically different, even though they might have the same name. However, from the distribution point of view, those differences can, to a large degree, be abstracted out and we are left with surprisingly few abstract entity types. The proposed model provides distribution on the level of abstract entities.

2.1 The Abstract Entity

Our shared entity model uses the notion of a *local entity instance*, acting as the local representative for a shared entity. A local entity instance is present at every process holding a reference to the shared entity. All instances are inherently equal, none is more privileged, i.e. there is no a priori centralized control. Each instance is connected to an *abstract entity instance*, coordinating operations performed by threads on the local instances.

When a local entity instance becomes shared, it may not be accessed directly anymore; operations must be directed to its abstract entity instance. All interaction with an abstract entity instance is done using *abstract operations*[3], expressing manipulations of the shared entity. An entity operation is translated

[2] Available for download at http://dss.sics.se.

[3] Analogous to the distinction between abstract and concrete language entities there are potentially many concrete operations per abstract operation.

into an abstract operation, expressing a corresponding semantic type of manipulation. The result of an abstract operation tells the calling thread how to proceed: perform the operation on the local instance, continue with the next instruction or wait for a later decision.

At any point in time a local entity instance is either *complete*, i.e. it has a representation that allows for local execution of operations, or *skeleton*, i.e. it merely acts as a proxy. The status is explicitly controlled by the abstract entity instance.

Entity types that are to be distributed must be matched with a suitable abstract entity type. The matching is based on the centralized semantics of the entity type. Different *abstract entity types* capture different functional needs and guarantee consistency according to a consistency model (e.g. sequential consistency). An abstract entity instance actually provides a single interface to a set of entity consistency protocols with the same functional properties. In order to support distribution, at least one entity consistency protocol is needed per abstract entity type. However, to efficiently capture non-functional requirements, multiple entity consistency protocols are required. A non-functional requirement might be maximum number of hops, bandwidth utilization, or resilience to failures.

2.2 Different Types of Abstract Entities

We have currently identified three meaningful abstract entity types, all guaranteeing sequential consistency.

Mutable. This type has two abstract operations. *Update* indicates that the state is to be altered while *access* means to read. The *mutable* is preferably used by language entities that allows for destructive updates, e.g. objects. Suitable protocols for this type are: remote-execution, mobile state[14], and read/write invalidation.

Immutable. The immutable state of an entity is at some point replicated to a processes referring it. It can then be accessed through *access*. This means that all entity instances eventually become complete and no synchronization is then needed. Protocols for the *immutable* are eager-, lazy- and immediate replication.

Transient. This type has two abstract operations: *access* and *bind*. *Bind* terminates the coordination of the entity, thus removing all abstract entity instances. *Access* suspends the caller until a bind operation has been performed. The *transient* is preferably used for languages entities such as logical variables in Oz[15], and futures in Multi lisp[16].

Not all language entities guarantee sequential consistency in the centralized case. Oz ports and Erlang channels are examples of such entities. Also, asynchronous remote method invocation[17] is a popular optimization in distributed object systems. To efficiently support distribution of this class of entities, we provide two abstract entity types that guarantee at most PRAM (or FIFO) [18] consistency, called *Relaxed Mutable* and *Relaxed Transient*.

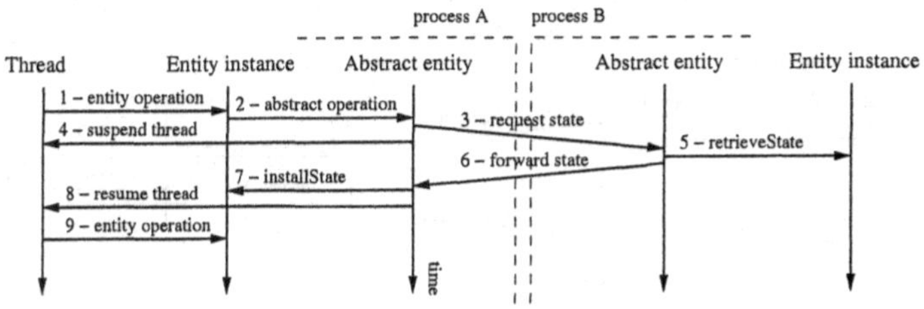

Fig. 1. Sequence diagram of the state transporting protocol, e.g. mobile state protocol.

2.3 Interacting with an Abstract Entity

A language entity interacts with its abstract entity using abstract operations. In order to resolve operations an abstract entity needs to interact with its entity instance, using four entity-instance callbacks:

retrieveState. The callback returns a state description of the entity instance, i.e. a description that can change any entity instance's status from skeleton to complete. Clearly this is only legitimate if the entity instance from which the description is retrieved is complete.

installState. Install a state description to the entity instance, making it complete.

executeOperation. The callback is given a description of a concrete entity operation to execute on the local entity instance.

resumeThread. A thread previously suspended on an abstract operation is resumed. The thread is told to either redo the operation or continue with the next instruction.

The described interaction framework[4] is complete in the sense that either a state- or an operation-transporting protocol can be used transparently. A state transporting protocol allows for local access for the entity instances by moving a state description to the executing process. In contrast, an operation transporting protocol moves an operation description to a process(es) hosting a complete instance to execute it there.

A shared object uses the mutable abstract entity. Depending on the chosen type of protocol, different events can be observed for the same abstract operation. Bellow are two examples where an object is distributed using either a state or an operation transporting protocol. The sequence diagrams show the respective events for the same method invocation on the shared entity. Note that in both cases the initiating entity instance has skeleton status.

Example: State Transporting Protocol. Fig. 1 depicts the sequence of events that occurs when a thread at process A performs a method invocation

[4] Due to space limitations the interfaces are described on a conceptual level. Concrete API descriptions and code examples can be found in [13].

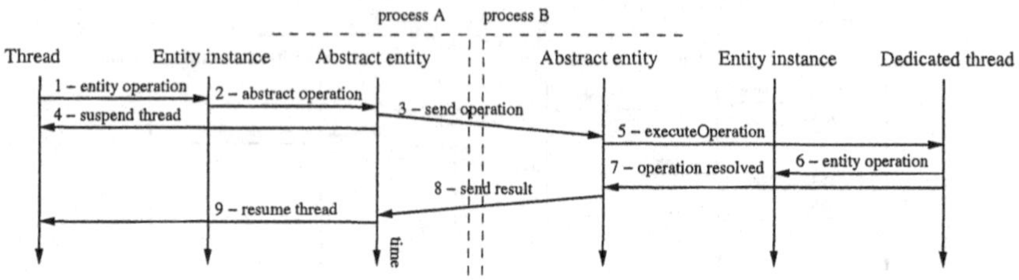

Fig. 2. Sequence diagram of the operation transporting protocol, e.g. remote execution protocol.

(1) on a shared object, whose state is located at process B. The method invocation is translated into an abstract operation and passed on (2) to the abstract entity. A request for a state description is sent[5] (3) to the abstract entity located at process B. Simultaneously the thread is told to suspend itself (4). The abstract entity at process B receives the state request (5) and uses the callback **retrieveState** to get a state description. The description is passed back (6) to the abstract entity at process A, where it is installed (7) using the **installState** callback. Finally the suspended thread is resumed (8), using **resumeThread**, and told to redo the operation (9).

Example: Operation Transporting Protocol. Fig. 2 depicts the sequence of events that occurs when a thread at process A performs a method invocation (1) on a shared object, whose state is located at process B. The method invocation is translated into an abstract operation and passed on (2) to the abstract entity. A description of the operation is sent (3) to process B. Simultaneously the thread is told to suspend itself (4). The abstract entity at process B receives (5) the operation description and uses the callback **executeOperation** to perform the operation locally. The operation is executed by a dedicated thread[6] (6) and the result is returned to the abstract entity (7). The result is passed back to the abstract entity at process B (8), that passes the result to the suspended thread and resumes it (9).

2.4 Classifying Language Entities into Abstract Entities

Assigning abstract entities to language entities can preserve the structuring imposed by the language, but is not required to. Multiple language entities can be distributed together as one abstract entity, and one language entity can be decomposed into multiple abstract entities. Note that regardless of the chosen structuring, an abstract entity must capture the semantics for the structure in the centralized case, e.g. an entity that allows for destructive updates should not use the *immutable* type.

[5] Via the coordination network, to be described later.

[6] A thread created solely for the purpose of remote execution.

For example, an array can be treated as one (composed) *mutable* entity or it can be decomposed into an *immutable* structure referring *mutable* cells. When distributed, the array structure will be replicated and the array structure in turn will refer mutable cell instances. Thus when updating an array element only one cell will be affected.

3 Coordinating Entity Instances

A *coordination proxy* is present at each process hosting a local entity instance. The coordination proxy is connected to its abstract entity (as depicted at the left of Fig. 3).

An entity consistency protocol executes over the dynamic sub-network, called the *coordination network*[7], formed by participating coordination proxies. A coordination network has a hub, called the *coordinator*. A property of the network is that proxies can always contact the coordinator, while the vice verca is not necessarily true. For the remote execution protocol, a proxy would send the operations to the coordinator, that in turn passes them to the proxy where the state is located.

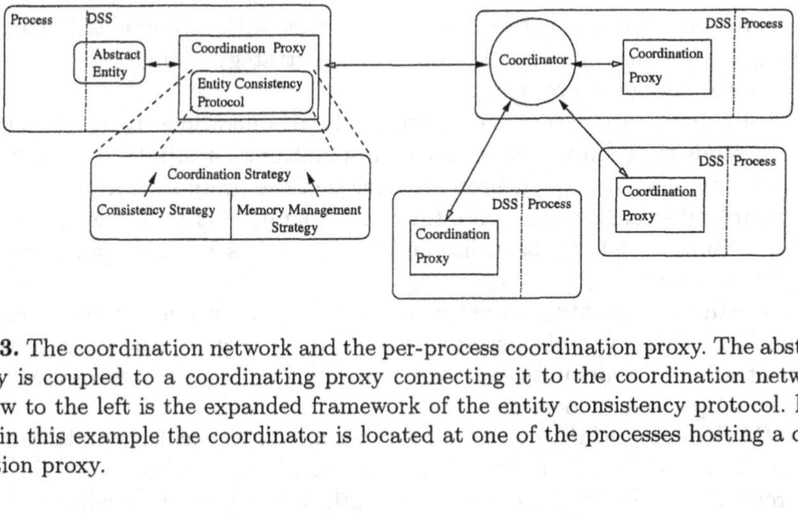

Fig. 3. The coordination network and the per-process coordination proxy. The abstract entity is coupled to a coordinating proxy connecting it to the coordination network. Bellow to the left is the expanded framework of the entity consistency protocol. Note that in this example the coordinator is located at one of the processes hosting a coordination proxy.

3.1 Three Dimensions of Entity Consistency

The entity consistency protocol is realized as a framework, as shown in the expansion of the Coordination Proxy in Fig. 3. This divides the strategy over entity consistency into three separate sub-strategies. Firstly, the *memory management strategy* detects when a shared entity is no longer needed, i.e. the number of proxies reaches one. Secondly, addressing within the coordination network is realized by a *coordination strategy*, also providing a messaging service for the

[7] To minimize this subnet, at-most-one coordination proxy is allowed per process.

other two modules. Finally the *consistency strategy* upholds the entity semantics, controlling entity instances connected to the coordination network and threads performing operations. The three strategies are implemented as three protocols running in parallel over the coordination network.

Each strategy is implemented as a module with a well-specified interface, one interface per sub-strategy type. An optimal entity consistency protocol for a particular entity and usage pattern is just a matter of composition. This potentially increases code reuse (in the form of reused sub-strategies) and simplifies development of entity consistency protocols.

Coordination Strategy. The coordination strategy defines how the messaging infrastructure and services are realized. These messaging services are then used by the consistency- and the memory management strategy. This includes defining the location and behavior of the coordinator and providing routines for inter coordination-network communication. Examples of coordination strategies are: a stationary coordinator, a mobile coordinator and replicated coordinators.

Consistency Strategy. The protocol resolves abstract operations for the abstract entity. A consistency strategy is divided into two parts: one *end-point unit*, present at each coordination proxy, and one *arbitrator*, located at the coordinator(s).

Interaction with local entity instances together with communication and addressing services, provided by the coordination strategy, simplifies implementation of a wide range of protocols:

Remote-Execution. Every end-point sends all operations to the arbitrator that sends them on to one selected end-point unit, hosting the complete local entity instance. A synchronous version of the protocol is available to the mutable abstract entity, where the write operation is acknowledged (possibly with a result). An asynchronous version exists for the relaxed mutable abstract entity.

Mobile State. The entity's state is moved between local entity instances. Regardless of the type of operation, an end-point requests the state from the arbitrator and waits until it arrives. Several consecutive writes and reads can then be performed locally.

Read/Write-Invalidation. A protocol that allows for exclusive update or concurrent access to a local state. Two versions of the protocol exist. The *eager* protocol records the readers and automatically updates them when the state has changed. The *lazy* protocol requires all readers to actively request read permission after an invalidation.

Pilgrim. A mobile state protocol inspired by the work in [19]. This protocol is optimized for the case when a small set of proxies reads and writes frequently.

Replication. This class of protocols is used by immutables. For lazy replication, the state is retrieved when an entity instance first tries to access the state. For eager replication it is requested immediately after the creation of the coordination proxy. Immediate replication transports the state with every reference to an entity, but duplicates are avoided due to the at-most-once property of coordination proxies.

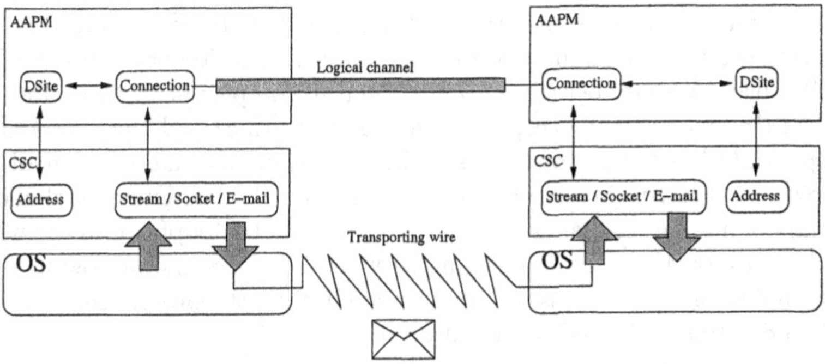

Fig. 4. The relation between a generic AAPM, a transporting CSC and the underlying communication system, e.g. the OS. The CSC is free to use whatever means desired to transport data.

Once Only. A class of protocols used to realize transient behavior, inspired in their design by [15].

Memory Management Strategy. Properly packaged distributed garbage collection algorithms [18] detect when the number of coordination proxies reaches one. When this occurs the last entity instance can be localized, hence dismantling the coordinator and freeing resources. Of course by the time when localization is achieved there may be no references left, which usually will be handed by the memory management outside the DSS.

Similar to the consistency strategy, the memory management strategy is divided into end-point units and one *detector* (located at the coordinator). The existence of an end-point at a coordination proxy guarantees that the proxy is accounted for by the detector. Using this framework the DSS implements: fractional weighted reference counting[20] , reference listing[21], time lease and persistent entities.

4 Middleware Design and Implementation

To simplify the coupling of a PS to the DSS, the DSS is internally divided in two subcomponents: the Advanced Asynchronous Protocol Machine(AAPM), and the Communication Service Component (CSC). As depicted in Fig. 4 the AAPM implements the abstract entities, protocols of the coordination network and a high level messaging service. The messaging service is based on a notion of remote processes, *DSites*, providing reliable, in order, asynchronous messaging.

The CSC is an interface for communication routines and networking tasks such as connection establishment, data transportation and failure detection for the messaging service. The purpose of the CSC is to abstract away the OS from the AAPM, as depicted in Fig. 4. The CSC is easily replaced to enable custom implementations based on application knowledge, e.g. specialized addressing schemes or failure detectors.

Our implementation of the DSS is a linkable C++ library and our CSC implementation is a fairly straight forward C++ implementation based upon TCP/IP. The DSS uses interface classes, *mediators*, for all complex data structures shared with the PS: entity references, entity states, operations and threads. Mediators are represented as C++ classes to simplify coupling. Marshaling of mediators is a cooperative activity involving both the DSS and the PS. Our model allows for late marshaling, i.e. messages are serialized when actually put onto the wire and not when inserted into the messaging service. The DSS knows how to serialize its internal data. When messages contain mediators, the programming system is asked to create a serialized representation.

5 Evaluation

In order to evaluate the performance of the DSS we have conducted three major tests. Firstly, a test that measures pure messaging speed. Secondly, a test evaluating the performance of the different consistency strategies, executed in a controlled environment. Finally, an impact evaluation of using different consistency strategies, in a real world application.

To evaluate the DSS we used four different applications/systems:

Socket-Application. A small C++ socket application which measures the raw I/O cost for messaging on our cluster.

C++DSS. A thin C++ library on top of the DSS that allows for sharing of mutable and transient data structures. This is included to measure the raw cost of abstract operations.

Mozart. Development version 1.3.0 of the distributed programming system that implements the multi-paradigm language Oz. Included to measure the difference between the tightly integrated distribution layer in Mozart compared to a pure Oz virtual machine coupled to the DSS.

Oz-DSS. Development version 1.3.0 of the Mozart system with its internal distribution support replaced by the DSS. The Oz-DSS system is far more expressive when it comes to distribution than the original Mozart system and it clearly separates the local-execution engine from the distribution subsystem.

All applications were compiled with gcc 2.95.2 using standard optimizations. The tests were conducted on a cluster of AMD ATHLON XP 1900 workstations, equipped with 512 MB of memory, interconnected by a 100Mbit LAN. The workstations run standard Red Hat Linux version 7.3 without X windows.

5.1 Messaging Performance

The test measured the time to perform 10000 sequential remote requests with one server and varying number (1-15) of simultaneously running client processes. The test was conducted with all four applications. The right diagram of Fig. 5 shows the result for the different applications running with one single client. The times are normalized to the socket application.

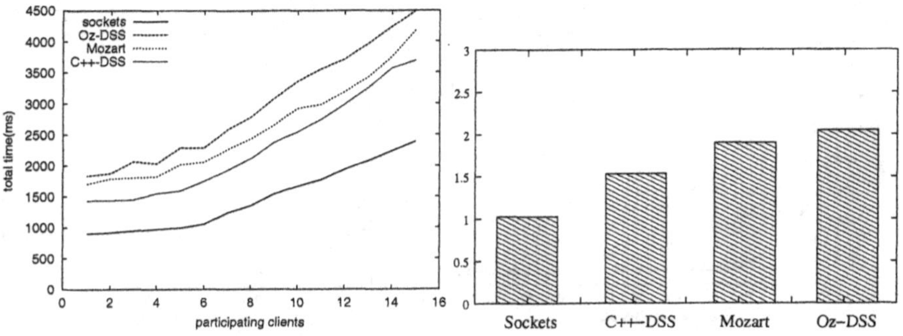

Fig. 5. The time to perform 10000 sequential remote requests for the four systems. The left graph shows the result when the number of nodes ranges from 1 to 15. The right graph show the result for one node, normalized against the socket application.

The C++-DSS application has only a 50% overhead compared to the raw socket program. This is a surprisingly small difference considering the differences in functionality. The socket program is extremely optimized for the test while the C++DSS is a generic distribution platform.

The tightly integrated distribution of Mozart gives 12% better performance over the Oz-DSS system. However, in the light of increased functionality and superior extendibility, this small difference is certainly acceptable.

The left diagram of Fig. 5 shows the total time to conduct the test when the number of clients increases. It is interesting to note that all DPSs increases the time proportionally to the socket application. This indicates, at least within the interval of 1 to 15 nodes, that the I/O capacity of the underlying operating system is the dominant factor when communicating with multiple nodes.

5.2 Protocol Evaluation

In this section, five entity consistency protocols for the mutable abstract entity are compared using the Oz-DSS. Factors like the number of participating processes, number of threads per process and the ratio between reads and writes were altered in order to show how the protocols performed under different usage patterns.

The Impact of Concurrency. Each process performed 10000 accesses to a shared state under varying degree of concurrency; i.e. one thread doing 10000 iterations, two threads doing 5000 iterations, and up to 100 threads doing 100 iterations each. The test was conducted with 12 clients, using the mobile state, pilgrim and stationary protocols. The left diagram of Fig. 6 shows the plot of the total time for all clients to conduct all iterations against the number of threads per process. Note that increased concurrency has two effects. Firstly, latency will be masked which is notable in all tests. Secondly, concurrency will also batch pending operations when threads wait for the mobile state. This is observable;

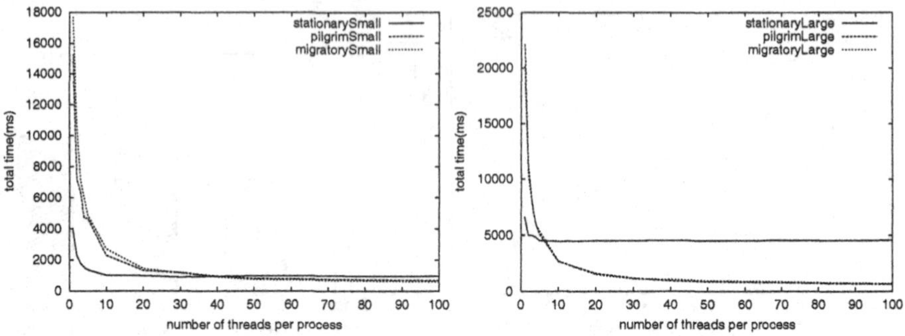

Fig. 6. The total time for 12 Oz-DSS processes to conduct 10000 accesses to a mutable state, using three different protocols, under different degree of concurrency. In the left graph the mutable state is a single integer value and in the right a list of 1000 integer values.

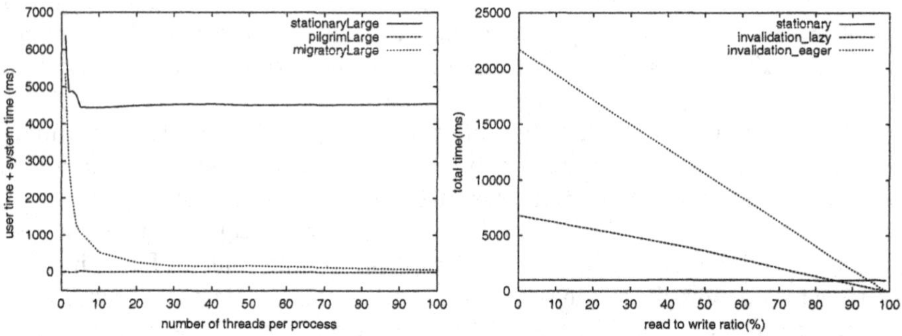

Fig. 7. Left: the total system and user time for the server process when 12 Oz-DSS processes does 10000 state accesses, using three different protocols, under different degrees of concurrency. Right: The total time for 15 Oz-DSS processes to perform sequential 10000 accesses, using three different protocols, under different read to write ratios.

the state moving protocols advance from being outperformed to outperforming the stationary protocol. When the size of the state increases, from one single integer value to a list of 1000 integer values, the cost for I/O increases, depicted in the right diagram of Fig. 6. Since the state moving protocols communicate less when the degree of concurrency is increased, they perform better than the stationary protocol.

When considering the work load of the server, measured as the sum of user and system time used by the server process, a slightly different picture emerges, (see the left diagram of Fig. 7). To start with, the pilgrim protocol does not use the server at all. This is due to the long sequences of accesses of the state. Furthermore, the stationary protocol requires almost the same amount of resources as the mobile state protocol when the number of threads is small and is quickly outperformed when concurrency is increased. This shows the strength of the state moving protocols in batching work and low utilization of the server process. It also shows their weakness: higher access time when the number of competing processes for the state grows large.

Utilizing the Read/Write Ratio. The two cache invalidation protocols, with lazy and eager updates, allows the state of a shared entity to be read in parallel, but updated at only one process at a time. This caters for substantial reduction in message traffic when the ratio of reads vs. writes is high. To validate this we conducted a test to see at which point our invalidation protocols are better than the simple stationary protocol. The test was conducted with 15 client processes, each performing 10000 sequential accesses to a shared state. The proportion of operations that were reads ranged from 0 to 99%, the resulting graph is shown in the right diagram of Fig. 7. The test shows that invalidation, with lazy updates, is overall superior to eager updating. The invalidation protocols impose a notable overhead when the access pattern has a low read to write ratio, but both protocols also improve in performance notably when the ratio gets high (above 85% for lazy and 95% for eager).

As a proof of concept, we took an already existing application developed for the Mozart platform, added the possibility to annotate the distribution behavior of single entities and tested it on our Oz-DSS system. The application, a distributed version of the snake game with self-learning actors, is interesting from a distribution point of view. Each actor, one per node(process), reads a section of a shared matrix and decides how to do a move, i.e. update an element in the matrix. The matrix is distributed on the level of single matrix elements.

The tests were conducted with the matrix elements distributed using different protocols(for mutables). The number of nodes was altered in order to show the scalability for different consistency strategies(i.e. protocol choice).

The ratio between reads to writes is high in the application. As shown in the left diagram of Fig. 8, the two invalidation protocols do very well, while both the migratory and stationary protocols simply do not scale.

5.3 Distributing a Real Application

By varying the size of the matrix, the interaction between the processes is implicitly varied. For a smaller matrix, the chance that two processes will read the same element increases, and for a larger matrix it decreases. The consequences are depicted in the right diagram of Fig. 8; the eager invalidation protocol performs better than the lazy protocol on a small matrix and vice versa. It is beneficial to distribute information on element update immediately and not wait until it is asked for, if the chance that another processes will read the element is high.

6 Related Work

We relate our work to a wide range of middleware systems, both of the language dependent and the language independent type.

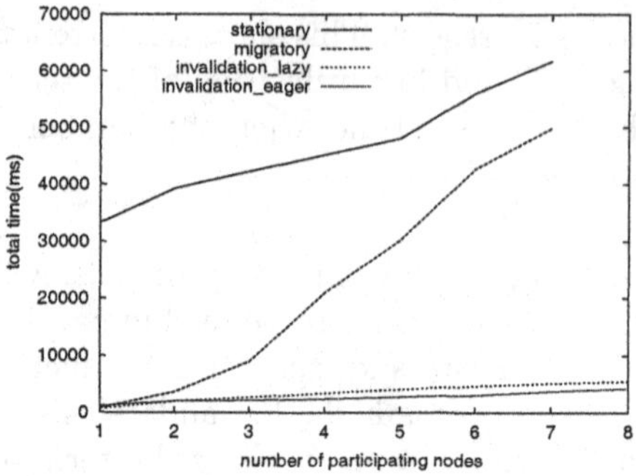

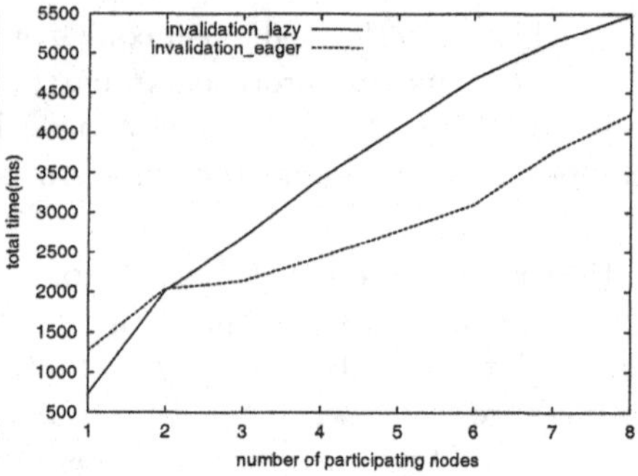

Fig. 8. Total time to run the distributed snake game for 1000 iterations, with varying number of clients. The left graph shows the result for all four protocols. The right graph shows the result for the two invalidation protocols.

CORBA [1] is an example of programming language independent middleware focusing on interoperability. CORBA requires data to be structured into objects and interaction between objects is solely achieved through method shipping. The DSS differs from CORBA in that no structuring is enforced, instead the natural structuring of the programming language can be mapped to appropriate distribution support. The DSS supports objects(mutables) in addition to many other abstract entity types with a multiplicity of entity consistency protocols, method shipping being only one choice for mutables.

InterWeave [22] is limited to distributing data on the level of abstract memory pages. Once again this is only one particular mapping to mutables and is achievable with the DSS as well. Unlike CORBA but similar to the DSS InterWeave has an open architecture for consistency protocols, called the coherence module with eligible protocols. While we have a dynamic architecture for coordination, i.e. the coordination strategy, they have chosen a static model with dedicated servers, much like the stationary coordination strategy in the DSS. Furthermore InterWeave has no support for automatic memory management.

.Net [5] offers a single entity consistency protocol for one single type of entity, objects. It is however possible to change the protocol, using the (not well-documented) interception mechanism at considerable performance cost.

JavaParty [23] and cJVM [24] are, though dedicated to just Java, two interesting systems with respect to their functionality. Using preprocessing and new library routines, JavaParty offers true transparency for Java with a proper thread distribution model and provides mobile state protocols. Similar to our model JavaParty allows for definition of entity consistency protocols in runtime for single objects. cJVM provides similar features as JavaParty but with the approach of extending the runtime system. The architecture is open for protocol addition, every object can choose from a set of consistency protocols. However, the patterns are monolithic and cannot be constructed from sub components as in our model(by composing coordination, consistency, and memory management strategies). Both systems are geared toward Java objects, and tightly integrated with the Java system.

The concept of distribution support based on a clear distinction between mutables and immutables was introduced with the Emerald[25] system. However, Emerald did not follow up on the potential strengths of this concept, allowing for a wide range of entity consistency protocols. None of the mentioned systems explore the domain of abstract entity types as we do, nor do they attempt to support all high level programming languages. Furthermore, we have found no trace in the literature exploring what we refer to as mobility for coordinators in open dynamic distributed systems.

7 Conclusion

We have presented a novel architecture for a language-independent middleware library. This library, the DSS, can be coupled to virtually all high-level programming languages thus creating powerful distributed programming systems. These distributed programming systems can then offer the programmer an extremely simple and powerful distributed programming model.

The messaging capacity of the DSS has been evaluated and compared with other systems. The evaluation shows that the implementation is both efficient and with low overhead, especially if all the functionality provided by the middleware is taken into consideration. Furthermore, we have shown that an appropriate choice of protocol is the most dominant factor when tuning a distributed application for performance.

A novel design of entity consistency protocols is presented. By separating functionality into three different parts(strategies), development of new protocols is greatly simplified. The powerful messaging framework simplifies protocol development even further. This is indicated by the few lines of C++ code required to realize the complex consistency strategies mobile-state (281 lines) and eager invalidation (219 lines).

The comparison between Mozart and Oz-DSS indicates that the benefit of tightly integrated distribution support is so small that it is not worth the effort.

We think that the abstract entity model, together with the large protocol base, should make a library based on our model, e.g. the DSS, a first choice for any programming system/language that needs distribution support.

Acknowledgments

We wish to express thanks to Joe Armstrong, Prof. Kazunori Ueda, Sameh El-Ansary, and Ali Ghodsi for invaluable help and advice.

This work is funded by the European IST-FET PEPITO project and the Swedish Vinnova PPC and VR FDC projects

References

1. OMG., December 2002. The CORBA specifications, http://www.omg.org.
2. Eli Tilevich and Yannis Smaragdakis. J-orchestra: Automatic java application partitioning. In *Proceedings of the 16th European Conference on Object-Oriented Programming*, volume 2374 of *LNCS*, pages 178–204. Springer-Verlag, 2002.

3. M. Hanus. Distributed programming in a multi-paradigm declarative language. In *Proc. of the International Conference on Principles and Practice of Declarative Programming (PPDP'99)*, pages 376–395. Springer LNCS 1702, 1999.
4. Sun Microsystems. The remote method invocation specification, dec 2002. Available from http://java.sun.com.
5. Ingo Rammer. *Advanced .NET Remoting*. APress, april 2002.
6. Jason Maassen, Thilo Kielmann, and Henri E. Bal. Efficient Replicated Method Invocation in Java. In *ACM 2000 Java Grande Conference*, pages 88–96, San Francisco, CA, June 2000.
7. S. Haridi, P-V. Roy, P. Brand, and C. Schulte. Programming languages for distributed applications. *New Generation Computing*, 16(3):223–261, 1998.
8. Christian Nester, Michael Philippsen, and Bernhard Haumacher. A more efficient RMI. In *ACM 1999 Java Grande Conference*, pages 152–159, San Francisco, June 12–14, 1999.
9. C. Wikstrom. Distributed programming in erlang. In H. Hong, editor, *First International Symposium on Parallel Symbolic Computation, PASCO'94, (Hagenberg/ Linz, Austria)*, volume 5 of *Lecture notes series in computing*, pages 284–293, Singapore; Philadelphia, PA, USA; River Edge, NJ, USA, 1994. World Scientific Publishing Co.
10. David Mosberger. Memory consistency models. *ACM SIGOPS Operating Systems Review*, 27(1):18–26, 1993.
11. Haifeng Yu and Amin Vahdat. Design and evaluation of a continuous consistency model for replicated services. In *Proceedings of the Fourth Symposium on Operating Systems Design and Implementation (OSDI)*, pages 305–318, 2000.
12. Mozart Consortium. http://www.mozart-oz.org, December 2002.
13. Per Brand Erik Klintskog, Zacharias El Banna. A generic middleware for intra-language transparent distribution. Technical Report T2003:01, Swedish Institute of Computer Science, SICS, Kista, Sweden, January 2003.
14. Peter Van Roy, Per Brand, Seif Haridi, and Raphaël Collet. A lightweight reliable object migration protocol. In *LNCS 1686*, Lecture Notes in Computer Science, vol. 1686, pages 32–46. Springer Verlag, 1999.
15. S. Haridi, P-V. Roy, P. Brand, M. Mehl, R. Scheidhauer, and G. Smolka. Efficient logic variables for distributed computing. *ACM Transactions on Programming Languages and Systems*, 21(3):569–626, 1999.
16. R-H. Halstead. Multilisp: a language for concurrent symbolic computation. In *ACM Transactions on Programming Languages and Systems (TOPLAS)*, pages 501–538, 1985.
17. K. E. Kerry Falkner, P. D. Coddington, and M. J. Oudshoorn. Implementing Asynchronous Remote Method Invocation in Java. In W. Cheng and A. S. M. Sajeev, editors, *Proceedings of 6th Annual Australasian Conference on Parallel and Real-Time Systems (PART'99), Melbourne, Australia*. Springer-Verlag, Berlin, Germany, 1999.
18. M. Raynal and A. Schiper. A suite of formal definitions for consistency criteria in distributed shared memories. In *Proceedings Int Conf on Parallel and Distributed Computing (PDCS'96)*, pages 125–130, Dijon, France, 1996. ISCA.
19. H. Guyennet, J-C. Lapayre, and M. Trehel. Distributed shared memory layer for cooperative work application. In IEEE Computer Society. Technical Committee on Computer Communications, editor, *Proceedings, 22nd annual Conference on Local Computer Networks: LCN '97: November 2–5, 1997, Minneapolis, Minnesota*, volume 22, pages 72–78, 1109 Spring Street, Suite 300, Silver Spring, MD 20910, USA, 1997. IEEE Computer Society Press.

20. P. Brand E. Klintskog, A. Neiderud and S. Haridi. Fractional weighted reference counting. In *LNCS 2150*, pages 486–490, August 2001.
21. Andrew Birrell, David Evers, Greg Nelson, Susan Owicki, and Edward Wobber. Distributed garbage collection for network objects. Technical Report 116, DEC Systems Research Center, 130 Lytton Avenue, Palo Alto, CA 94301, December 1993.
22. C. Tang, D. Chen, S. Dwarkadas, and M. Scott. Efficient distributed shared state for heterogeneous machine architectures. In *Proceedings of the 23rd International Conference on Distributed Computing Systems*, pages 412–422. IEEE Computer Society, 2003.
23. Bernhard Haumacher and Michael Philippsen. Exploiting object locality in JavaParty, a distributed computing environment for workstation clusters. In *CPC2001, 9th Workshop on Compilers for Parallel Computers*, pages 83–94. IEEE Computer Society, June 2001.
24. Yariv Aridor, Michael Factor, and Avi Teperman. cJVM: A single system image of a JVM on a cluster. In *International Conference on Parallel Processing*, pages 4–11. IEEE Computer Society, 1999.
25. Eric Jul, Henry Levy, Norman Hutchinson, and Andrew Black. Fine-grained mobility in the Emerald system. *ACM Transactions on Computer Systems*, 6(1):109–133, February 1988.

Generating Optimal Linear Temporal Logic Monitors by Coinduction

Koushik Sen, Grigore Roşu, and Gul Agha

Department of Computer Science,
University of Illinois at Urbana-Champaign
{ksen,grosu,agha}@cs.uiuc.edu

Abstract. A coinduction-based technique to generate an optimal monitor from a Linear Temporal Logic (LTL) formula is presented in this paper. Such a monitor receives a sequence of states (one at a time) from a running process, checks them against a requirements specification expressed as an LTL formula, and determines whether the formula has been violated or validated. It can also say whether the LTL formula is not monitorable any longer, i.e., that the formula can in the future neither be violated nor be validated. A Web interface for the presented algorithm adapted to extended regular expressions is available.

1 Introduction

Linear Temporal Logic (LTL) [19] is a widely used logic for specifying properties of reactive and concurrent systems. The models of LTL are infinite execution traces, reflecting the behavior of such systems as ideally always being ready to respond to requests, operating system being typical example. LTL has been mainly used to specify properties of finite-state reactive and concurrent systems, so that the full correctness of the system can be verified automatically, using model checking or theorem proving. Model checking of programs has received an increased attention from the formal methods community within the last couple of years, and several tools have emerged that directly model check source code written in Java or C [7, 26, 27]. Unfortunately, such formal verification techniques are not scalable to real-sized systems without exerting a substantial effort to abstract the system more or less manually to a model that can be analyzed.

Testing scales well, and in practice it is by far the technique most used to validate software systems. Our approach follows research which merges testing and temporal logic specification in order to achieve some of the benefits of both approaches; we avoid some of the pitfalls of ad hoc testing as well as the complexity of full-blown theorem proving and model checking. While this merger provides a scalable technique, it does result in a loss of coverage: the technique may be used to examine a single execution trace at a time, and may not be used to *prove* a system correct. Our work is based on the observation that software engineers are willing to trade coverage for scalability, so our goals is relatively

V.A. Saraswat (Ed.): ASIAN 2003, LNCS 2896, pp. 260–275, 2003.

conservative: we provide tools that use formal methods in a lightweight manner, use traditional programming languages or underlying executional engines (such as JVMs), are completely automatic, implement very efficient algorithms, and can help find *many* errors in programs.

Recent trends suggest that the software analysis community is interested in scalable techniques for software verification. Earlier work by Havelund and Roşu [10] proposed a method based on merging temporal logics and testing. The Temporal Rover tool (TR) and its successor DB Rover by Drusinsky [2] have been commercialized. These tools instrument the Java code so that it can check the satisfaction of temporal logic properties at runtime. The MaC tool by Lee et al. [14, 17] has been developed to monitor safety properties in interval past time temporal logic. In works by O'Malley et al. and Richardson et al. [20, 21], various algorithms to generate testing automata from temporal logic formulae, are described. Java PathExplorer [8] is a runtime verification environment currently under development at NASA Ames. It can analyze a single execution trace. The Java MultiPathExplorer tool [25] proposes a technique to monitor all equivalent traces that can be extracted from a given execution, thus increasing the coverage of monitoring. Giannakopoulou et al. and Havelund et al. in [4, 9] propose efficient algorithms for monitoring future time temporal logic formulae, while Havelund et al. in [11] gives a technique to synthesize efficient monitors from past time temporal formulae. Roşu et al. in [23] shows use of rewriting to perform runtime monitoring of extended regular expressions. An approach similar to this paper is used to generate optimal monitors for extended regular expressions in work by Sen et al. [24].

In this paper, we present a new technique based on the modern coalgebraic method to generate optimal monitors for LTL formulae. In fact, such monitors are the minimal deterministic finite automata required to do the monitoring. Our current work makes two major contributions. First, we give a coalgebraic formalization of LTL and show that coinduction is a viable and reasonably practical method to prove monitoring-equivalences of LTL formulae. Second, building on the coinductive technique, we present an algorithm to directly generate minimal deterministic automata from an LTL formula. Such an automaton may be used to monitor good or bad prefixes of an execution trace (this notion will be rigorously formalized in subsequent sections).

We describe the monitoring as synchronous and deterministic to obtain *minimal* good or bad prefixes. However, if the cost of such monitoring is deemed too high in some application, and one is willing to tolerate some delay in discovering violations, the same technique could be applied on the traces intermittently – in which case one would not get minimal good or bad prefixes but could either bound the delay in discovering violations, or guarantee eventual discovery. We also give lower and upper bounds on the size of such automata.

The closely related work by Geilen [3] builds monitors to detect a subclass of bad and good prefixes, which are called *informative bad and good prefixes*. Using a tableau-based technique, [3] can generate monitors of exponential size for informative prefixes. In our approach, we generate minimal monitors for detecting all kinds of bad and good prefixes. This generality comes at a price: the size of our monitors can be doubly exponential in the worst case, and this complexity cannot be avoided.

One standard way to generate an optimal monitor is to use the Büchi automata construction [16] for LTL to generate a non-deterministic finite automaton, determinize it and then to minimize it. In this method, one checks only the syntactic equivalence of LTL formulae. In the coalgebraic technique that we propose as an alternative method, we make use of the *monitoring equivalence* (defined in subsequent sections) of LTL formulae. We thus obtain the minimal automaton *in a single go* and minimize the usage of computational space. Moreover, our technique is completely based on deductive methods and can be applied to any logic or algebra for which there is a suitable behavioral specification. A related application can be found in [24] in which the minimal deterministic finite automata for extended regular expressions is generated.

2 Linear Temporal Logic and Derivatives

In order to make the paper self-contained, we briefly describe classical Linear Temporal Logic over infinite traces. We use the classical definition of Linear Temporal Logic and assume a finite set AP of atomic propositions. The syntax of LTL is as follows:

$$\begin{array}{lr} \phi ::= \text{true} \mid \text{false} \mid a \in AP \mid \neg\phi \mid \phi \wedge \phi \mid \phi \vee \phi \mid \phi \rightarrow \phi \mid \phi \equiv \phi \mid \phi \oplus \phi & \text{propositional} \\ \quad\;\; \phi \,\mathcal{U}\, \phi \mid \circ\phi \mid \Box\phi \mid \Diamond\phi & \text{temporal} \end{array}$$

The semantics of LTL is given for infinite traces. An infinite trace is an infinite sequence of program states, each state denoting the set of atomic propositions that hold at that state. The atomic propositions that hold in a given state s is given by $AP(s)$. We denote an infinite trace by ρ; $\rho(i)$ denotes the i-th state in the trace and ρ^i denotes the suffix of the trace ρ starting from the i-th state. The notion that an infinite trace ρ *satisfies* a formula ϕ is denoted by $\rho \models \phi$, and is defined inductively as follows:

$\rho \models$ true for all ρ — $\rho \not\models$ false for all ρ

$\rho \models a$ iff $a \in AP(\rho(1))$ — $\rho \models \neg\phi$ iff $\rho \not\models \phi$

$\rho \models \phi_1 \vee \phi_2$ iff $\rho \models \phi_1$ or $\rho \models \phi_2$ — $\rho \models \phi_1 \wedge \phi_2$ iff $\rho \models \phi_1$ and $\rho \models \phi_2$

$\rho \models \phi_1 \oplus \phi_2$ iff $\rho \models \phi_1$ exclusive or $\rho \models \phi_2$ — $\rho \models \phi_1 \rightarrow \phi_2$ iff $\rho \models \phi_1$ implies $\rho \models \phi_2$

$\rho \models \phi_1 \equiv \phi_2$ iff $\rho \models \phi_1$ iff $\rho \models \phi_2$ — $\rho \models \circ\phi$ iff $\rho^2 \models \phi$

$\rho \models \Box\phi$ iff $\forall j \geq 1\ \rho^j \models \phi$ — $\rho \models \Diamond\phi$ iff $\exists j \geq 1$ such that $\rho^j \models \phi$

$\rho \models \phi_1 \,\mathcal{U}\, \phi_2$ iff there exists a $j \geq 1$ such that $\rho^j \models \phi_2$ and $\forall\, 1 \leq i < j : \rho^i \models \phi_1$

The set of all infinite traces that satisfy the formula ϕ is called the language expressed by the formula ϕ and is denoted by L_ϕ. Thus, $\rho \in L_\phi$ if and only if $\rho \models \phi$. The language L_ϕ is also called the *property* expressed by the formula ϕ. We informally say that an infinite trace ρ satisfies a property ϕ iff $\rho \models \phi$.

A property in LTL can be seen as the intersection of a *safety* property and a *liveness* property [1]. A property is a liveness property if for every finite trace α there exists an infinite trace ρ such that $\alpha.\rho$ satisfies the property. A property is a safety property if for every infinite trace ρ not satisfying the property, there exists a finite prefix α such that for all infinite traces ρ', $\alpha.\rho'$ does not satisfy the property. The prefix α is called a *bad prefix* [3]. Thus, we say that a finite prefix α is a bad prefix for a property if for all infinite traces ρ, $\alpha.\rho$ does not satisfy the property. On the other hand, a *good prefix* for a property is a prefix α such that for all infinite traces ρ, $\alpha.\rho$ satisfies the property. A bad or a good prefix can also be *minimal*. We say that a bad (or a good prefix) α is minimal if α is a bad (or good) prefix and no finite prefix α' of α is bad (or good) prefix.

We use a novel coinduction-based technique to generate an optimal monitor that can detect good and bad prefixes incrementally for a given trace. The essential idea is to process, one by one, the states of a trace as these states are generated; at each step the process checks if the finite trace that we have already generated is a minimal good prefix or a minimal bad prefix. At any point, if we find that the finite trace is a minimal bad prefix, we say that the property is violated. If the finite trace is a minimal good prefix then we stop monitoring for that particular trace and say that the property holds for that trace.

At any step, we will also detect if it is not possible to monitor a formula any longer. We may stop monitoring at that point and say the trace is no longer *monitorable* and save the monitoring overhead. Otherwise, we continue by processing one more state and appending that state to the finite trace. We will see in the subsequent sections that these monitors can report a message as soon as a good or a bad prefix is encountered; therefore, the monitors are synchronous. Two more variants of the optimal monitor are also proposed; these variants can be used to efficiently monitor either bad prefixes or good prefixes (rather than both). Except in degenerate cases, such monitors have smaller sizes than the monitors that can detect both bad and good prefixes.

In order to generate the minimal monitor for an LTL formula, we will use several notions of equivalence for LTL:

Definition 1 ($\equiv$). *We say that two LTL formulae ϕ_1 and ϕ_2 are* equivalent *i.e. $\phi_1 \equiv \phi_2$ if and only if $L_{\phi_1} = L_{\phi_2}$.*

Definition 2 ($\equiv_B$). *For a finite trace α we say that $\alpha \not\models \phi$ iff α is bad prefix for ϕ i.e. for every infinite trace ρ it is the case that $\alpha.\rho \notin L_\phi$. Given two LTL formulae ϕ_1 and ϕ_2, ϕ_1 and ϕ_2 are said to be* bad prefix equivalent *i.e. $\phi_1 \equiv_B \phi_2$ if and only if for every finite trace α, $\alpha \not\models \phi_1$ iff $\alpha \not\models \phi_2$.*

Definition 3 ($\equiv_G$). *For a finite trace α we say that $\alpha \models \phi$ iff α is good prefix for ϕ i.e. for every infinite trace ρ it is that case that $\alpha.\rho \in L_\phi$. Given two LTL formulae ϕ_1 and ϕ_2, ϕ_1 and ϕ_2 are said to be* good prefix equivalent *i.e. $\phi_1 \equiv_G \phi_2$ if and only if for every finite trace α, $\alpha \models \phi_1$ iff $\alpha \models \phi_2$.*

Definition 4 ($\equiv_{GB}$). *We say that ϕ_1 and ϕ_2 are* good-bad prefix equivalent *i.e. $\phi_1 \equiv_{GB} \phi_2$ if and only if $\phi_1 \equiv_B \phi_2$ and $\phi_1 \equiv_G \phi_2$.*

Thus, for our purpose, the two non equivalent formulae $\Box\Diamond\phi$ and $\Diamond\Box\phi$ are good-bad prefix equivalent since they do not have any good or bad prefixes. Such formula are not monitorable. Note that the equivalence relation $\equiv$ is included in the equivalence relation $\equiv_{GB}$, which is in turn included in both $\equiv_G$ and $\equiv_B$. We will use the equivalences $\equiv_G$,$\equiv_B$, and $\equiv_{GB}$ to generate optimal monitors that detect good prefixes only, bad prefixes only and both bad and good prefixes respectively. We call these three equivalences *monitoring equivalences*.

2.1 Derivatives

We describe the notion of derivatives for LTL [9, 10] based on the idea of *state consumption*: an LTL formula ϕ and a state s generate another LTL formula, denoted by $\phi\{s\}$, with the property that for any finite trace α, $s\alpha \not\models \phi$ if and only if $\alpha \not\models \phi\{s\}$ and $s\alpha \models \phi$ if and only if $\alpha \models \phi\{s\}$. We define the operator $\_\{\_\}$ recursively through the following equations:

$$\begin{array}{ll}
\text{false}\ \{s\} = \text{false} & \text{true}\ \{s\} = \text{true} \\
p\{s\} = \text{if } p \in AP(s) \text{ then true else false} & (\neg\phi)\{s\} = \neg(\phi\{s\}) \\
(\phi_1 \vee \phi_2)\{s\} = \phi_1\{s\} \vee \phi_2\{s\} & (\phi_1 \wedge \phi_2)\{s\} = \phi_1\{s\} \wedge \phi_2\{s\} \\
(\phi_1 \rightarrow \phi_2)\{s\} = \phi_1\{s\} \rightarrow \phi_2\{s\} & (\phi_1 \oplus \phi_2)\{s\} = \phi_1\{s\} \oplus \phi_2\{s\} \\
(\Diamond\phi)\{s\} = \phi\{s\} \vee \Diamond\phi & (\Box\phi)\{s\} = \phi\{s\} \wedge \Box\phi \\
(\phi_1\, \mathcal{U}\, \phi_2)\{s\} = \phi_2\{s\} \vee (\phi_1\{s\} \wedge \phi_1\, \mathcal{U}\, \phi_2) &
\end{array}$$

We use the decision procedure for propositional calculus by Hsiang [13] to get a canonical form for a propositional formula. The procedure reduces a tautological formula to the constant true, a false formula to the constant false, and all other formulae to canonical forms modulo associativity and commutativity. An unusual aspect of this procedure is that the canonical forms consist of exclusive or ($\oplus$) of conjunctions. The procedure is given below using equations that are shown to be Church-Rosser and terminating modulo associativity and commutativity.

$$\begin{array}{ll}
\text{true}\ \wedge \phi = \phi & \text{false}\ \wedge \phi = \text{false} \\
\phi \wedge \phi = \phi & \text{false}\ \oplus \phi = \phi \\
\phi \oplus \phi = \text{false} & \neg\phi = \text{true}\ \oplus \phi \\
\phi_1 \wedge (\phi_2 \oplus \phi_3) = (\phi_1 \wedge \phi_2) \oplus (\phi_1 \wedge \phi_3) & \phi_1 \vee \phi_2 = (\phi_1 \wedge \phi_2) \oplus \phi_1 \oplus \phi_2 \\
\phi_1 \rightarrow \phi_2 = \text{true} \oplus \phi_1 \oplus (\phi_1 \wedge \phi_2) & \phi_1 \equiv \phi_2 = \text{true} \oplus \phi_1 \oplus \phi_2
\end{array}$$

The exclusive or operator $\oplus$ and the $\wedge$ operator are defined as commutative and associative. The equations DERIVATIVE and PROPOSITIONAL CALCULUS when regarded as rewriting rules are terminating and Church-Rosser (modulo associativity and commutativity of $\wedge$ and $\oplus$), so they can be used as a functional procedure to calculate derivatives.

In the rest of the paper, at several places we need to check if an LTL formula is equivalent to true or false. This can be done using the tableau-based proof method for LTL; the STeP tool at Stanford [18] has such an implementation.

The following result gives a way to determine if a prefix is good or bad for a formula through derivations.

Theorem 1. *a) For any LTL formula ϕ and for any finite trace $\alpha = s_1 s_2 \ldots s_n$, α is a bad prefix for ϕ if and only if $\phi\{s_1\}\{s_2\}\ldots\{s_n\} \equiv$ false. Similarly, α is a good prefix for ϕ if and only if $\phi\{s_1\}\{s_2\}\ldots\{s_n\} \equiv$ true. b) The formula $\phi\{s_1\}\{s_2\}\ldots\{s_n\}$ needs $O(2^{size(\phi)})$ space to be stored.*

Proof. b): Due to the Boolean ring equations above regarded as simplification rules, any LTL formula is kept in a canonical form, which is an exclusive disjunction of conjunctions, where conjuncts have temporal operators at top. Moreover, after a series of applications of derivatives $s_1, s_2, \ldots, s_n$, the conjuncts in the normal form $\phi\{s_1\}\{s_2\}\ldots\{s_n\}$ are subterms of the initial formula ϕ, each having a temporal operator at its top. Since there are at most $size(\phi)$ such subformulae, it follows that there are at most $2^{size(\phi)}$ possibilities to combine them in a conjunction. Therefore, one needs space $O(2^{size(\phi)})$ to store any exclusive disjunction of such conjunctions. This reasoning only applies on "idealistic" rewriting engines, which carefully optimize space needs during rewriting. □

In order to effectively generate optimal monitors, it is crucial to detect efficiently and as early as possible when two derivatives are equivalent. In the rest of the paper we use coinductive techniques to solve this problem. We define the operators $G: LTL \rightarrow \{\text{true}, \text{false}\}$ and $B: LTL \rightarrow \{\text{true}, \text{false}\}$ that return true if an LTL formula is equivalent ($\equiv$) to true or false respectively, and return false otherwise. We define an operator $GB: LTL \rightarrow \{0, 1, ?\}$ that checks if an LTL formula ϕ is equivalent to false or true and returns 0 or 1, respectively, and returns ? if the formula is not equivalent to either true or false.

3 Hidden Logic and Coinduction

We use circular coinduction, defined rigorously in the context of hidden logics and implemented in the BOBJ system [22, 5, 6], to test whether two LTL formulae are good-bad prefix equivalent. A particularly appealing aspect of circular coinduction in the framework of LTL formula is that it not only shows that two LTL formulae are good-bad prefix equivalent, but also generates a larger set of good-bad prefix equivalent LTL formulae which will all be used in order to generate the target monitor. Readers familiar with circular coinduction may assume the result in Theorem 4 and read Section 4 concurrently.

Hidden logic is a natural extension of algebraic specification which benefits of a series of generalizations in order to capture various natural notions of behavioral equivalence found in the literature. It distinguishes *visible* sorts for data from *hidden* sorts for states, with states *behaviorally equivalent* if and only if they are indistinguishable under a formally given set of experiments. In order to keep the presentation simple and self-contained, we define a simplified version of hidden logic together with its associated circular coinduction proof rule which is nevertheless general enough to support the definition of LTL formulae and prove that they are behaviorally good and/or bad prefix equivalent.

3.1 Algebraic Preliminaries

We assume that the reader is familiar with basic equational logic and algebra but recall a few notions in order to just make our notational conventions precise. An S-sorted signature Σ is a set of sorts/types S together with operational symbols on those, and a Σ-algebra A is a collection of sets $\{A_s \mid s \in S\}$ and a collection of functions appropriately defined on those sets, one for each operational symbol. Given an S-sorted signature Σ and an S-indexed set of variables Z, let $T_\Sigma(Z)$ denote the Σ-term algebra over variables in Z. If $V \subseteq S$ then $\Sigma\restriction_V$ is a V-sorted signature consisting of all those operations in Σ with sorts entirely in V. We may let $\sigma(X)$ denote the term $\sigma(x_1, ..., x_n)$ when the number of arguments of σ

and their order and sorts are not important. If only one argument is important, then to simplify writing we place it at the beginning; for example, $\sigma(t, X)$ is a term having σ as root with no important variables as arguments except one, in this case t. If t is a Σ-term of sort s' over a special variable $*$ of sort s and A is a Σ-algebra, then $A_t : A_s \to A_{s'}$ is the usual interpretation of t in A.

3.2 Behavioral Equivalence, Satisfaction and Specification

Given disjoint sets V, H called *visible* and *hidden sorts*, a *hidden* (V, H)*-signature*, say Σ, is a many sorted $(V \cup H)$-signature. A *hidden subsignature of* Σ is a hidden (V, H)-signature Γ with $\Gamma \subseteq \Sigma$ and $\Gamma\restriction_V = \Sigma\restriction_V$. The *data signature* is $\Sigma\restriction_V$. An operation of visible result not in $\Sigma\restriction_V$ is called an *attribute*, and a hidden sorted operation is called a *method.*

Unless otherwise stated, the rest of this section assumes fixed a hidden signature Σ with a fixed subsignature Γ. Informally, Σ-algebras are universes of possible states of a system, i.e., "black boxes," for which one is only concerned with behavior under experiments with operations in Γ, where an experiment is an observation of a system attribute after perturbation.

A Γ*-context for sort* $s \in V \cup H$ is a term in $T_\Gamma(\{* : s\})$ with one occurrence of $*$. A Γ-context of visible result sort is called a Γ*-experiment.* If c is a context for sort h and $t \in T_{\Sigma,h}$ then $c[t]$ denotes the term obtained from c by substituting t for $*$; we may also write $c[*]$ for the context itself.

Given a hidden Σ-algebra A with a hidden subsignature Γ, for sorts $s \in (V \cup H)$, we define Γ*-behavioral equivalence of* $a, a' \in A_s$ by $a \equiv_\Sigma^\Gamma a'$ iff $A_c(a) = A_c(a')$ for all Γ-experiments c; we may write $\equiv$ instead of $\equiv_\Sigma^\Gamma$ when Σ and Γ can be inferred from context. We require that all operations in Σ are compatible with $\equiv_\Sigma^\Gamma$. Note that behavioral equivalence is the identity on visible sorts, since the trivial contexts $* : v$ are experiments for all $v \in V$. A major result in hidden logics, underlying the foundations of coinduction, is that Γ-behavioral equivalence is the largest equivalence which is identity on visible sorts and which is compatible with the operations in Γ.

Behavioral satisfaction of equations can now be naturally defined in terms of behavioral equivalence. A hidden Σ-algebra A Γ*-behaviorally satisfies* a Σ-equation $(\forall X)\ t = t'$, say e, iff for each $\theta : X \to A$, $\theta(t) \equiv_\Sigma^\Gamma \theta(t')$; in this case we write $A \models_\Sigma^\Gamma e$. If E is a set of Σ-equations we then write $A \models_\Sigma^\Gamma E$ when A Γ-behaviorally satisfies each Σ-equation in E. We may omit Σ and/or Γ from $\models_\Sigma^\Gamma$ when they are clear.

A *behavioral* Σ*-specification* is a triple (Σ, Γ, E) where Σ is a hidden signature, Γ is a hidden subsignature of Σ, and E is a set of Σ-sentences equations. Non-data Γ-operations (i.e., in $\Gamma - \Sigma\restriction_V$) are called *behavioral.* A Σ-algebra A *behaviorally satisfies* a behavioral specification $\mathcal{B} = (\Sigma, \Gamma, E)$ iff $A \models_\Sigma^\Gamma E$, in which case we write $A \models \mathcal{B}$; also $\mathcal{B} \models e$ iff $A \models \mathcal{B}$ implies $A \models_\Sigma^\Gamma e$.

LTL can be very naturally defined as a behavioral specification. The enormous benefit of doing so is that the behavioral inference, including most importantly coinduction, provide a *decision procedure* for good-bad prefix equivalence.

Example 1. A behavioral specification of LTL defines a set of two visible sorts $V = \{Triple,\ State\}$, one hidden sort $H = \{Ltl\}$, one behavioral attribute $GB : Ltl \to Triple$ (defined as an operator in Subsection 2.1) and one behavioral method, the derivative, $\_\{\_\} : Ltl \times State \to Ltl$, together with all the other operations in Section 2 defining LTL, including the states in S which are defined as visible constants of sort *State*, and all the equations in Subsection 2.1. The sort *Triple* consists of three constants 0, 1, and ?. We call this the *LTL behavioral specification* and we use $\mathcal{B}_{LTL/GB}$ to denote it.

Since the only behavioral operators are the test for equivalence to true and false and the derivative, it follows that the experiments have exactly the form $GB(*\{s_1\}\{s_2\}...\{s_n\})$, for any states s_1, s_2, ..., s_n. In other words, an experiment consists of a series of derivations followed by an application of the operator GB, and therefore two LTL formulae are *behavioral equivalent* if and only if they cannot be distinguished by such experiments. Such behavioral equivalence is exactly same as good-bad prefix equivalence. In the specification of $\mathcal{B}_{LTL/GB}$ if we replace the attribute *GB* by *B* (or *G*), as defined in Subsection 2.1, the behavioral equivalence becomes same as bad prefix (or good prefix) equivalence. We denote such specifications by $\mathcal{B}_{LTL/B}$ (or $\mathcal{B}_{LTL/G}$). Notice that the above reasoning applies within *any algebra* satisfying the presented behavioral specification. The one we are interested in is, of course, the *free* one, whose set carriers contain exactly the LTL formulae as presented in Section 2, and the operations have the obvious interpretations. We informally call it the *LTL algebra*.
Letting $\equiv_b$ denote the behavioral equivalence relation generated on the LTL algebra, then Theorem 1 immediately yields the following important result.

Theorem 2. *If ϕ_1 and ϕ_2 are two LTL formulae then $\phi_1 \equiv_b \phi_2$ in $\mathcal{B}_{LTL/GB}$ iff ϕ_1 and ϕ_2 are good-bad prefix equivalent. Similarly, $\phi_1 \equiv_b \phi_2$ in $\mathcal{B}_{LTL/B}$ (or $\mathcal{B}_{LTL/G}$) if and only if ϕ_1 and ϕ_2 are bad prefix (or good prefix) equivalent.*

This theorem allows us to prove good-bad prefix equivalence (or bad prefix or good prefix equivalence) of LTL formulae by making use of behavioral inference in the LTL behavioral specification $\mathcal{B}_{LTL/GB}$ (or $\mathcal{B}_{LTL/B}$ or $\mathcal{B}_{LTL/G}$) including (especially) circular coinduction. The next section shows how circular coinduction works and how it can be used to show LTL formulae good-bad prefix equivalent (or bad prefix equivalent or good prefix equivalent). From now onwards we will refer $\mathcal{B}_{LTL/GB}$ simply by $\mathcal{B}$.

3.3 Circular Coinduction as an Inference Rule

In the simplified version of hidden logics defined above, the usual equational inference rules, i.e., reflexivity, symmetry, transitivity, substitution and congruence [22] are all sound for behavioral satisfaction. However, equational reasoning can derive only a very limited amount of interesting behavioral equalities. For that reason, *circular coinduction* has been developed as a very powerful automated technique to show behavioral equivalence. We let $\Vdash$ denote the relation being defined by the equational rules plus circular coinduction, for deduction from a specification to an equation.

Before formally defining circular coinduction, we give the reader some intuitions by duality to structural induction. The reader who is only interested in using the presented procedure or who is not familiar with structural induction, can skip this paragraph. Inductive proofs show equality of terms $t(x), t'(x)$ over a given variable x (seen as a constant) by showing $t(\sigma(x))$ equals $t'(\sigma(x))$ for all σ in a basis, while circular coinduction shows terms t, t' behaviorally equivalent by showing equivalence of $\delta(t)$ and $\delta(t')$ for all behavioral operations δ. Coinduction applies behavioral operations at the top, while structural induction applies generator/constructor operations at the bottom. Both induction and circular coinduction assume some "frozen" instances of t, t' equal when checking the inductive/coinductive step: for induction, the terms are frozen at the bottom by replacing the induction variable by a constant, so that no other terms can be placed beneath the induction variable, while for coinduction, the terms are frozen at the top, so that they cannot be used as subterms of other terms (with some important but subtle exceptions which are not needed here; see [6]).

Freezing terms at the top is elegantly handled by a simple trick. Suppose every specification has a special visible sort b, and for each (hidden or visible) sort s in the specification, a special operation $[\_] : s \rightarrow b$. No equations are assumed for these operations and no user defined sentence can refer to them; they are there for technical reasons. Thus, with just the equational inference rules, for any behavioral specification $\mathcal{B}$ and any equation $(\forall X)\ t = t'$, it is necessarily the case that $\mathcal{B} \Vdash (\forall X)\ t = t'$ iff $\mathcal{B} \Vdash (\forall X)\ [t] = [t']$. The rule below preserves this property. Let the sort of t, t' be hidden; then
Circular Coinduction:

$$\frac{\mathcal{B} \cup \{(\forall X)\ [t] = [t']\} \Vdash (\forall X, W)\ [\delta(t, W)] = [\delta(t', W)], \text{for all appropriate } \delta \in \Gamma}{\mathcal{B} \Vdash (\forall X)\ t = t'}$$

We call the equation $(\forall X)\ [t] = [t']$ added to $\mathcal{B}$ a **circularity**; it could just as well have been called a coinduction hypothesis or a co-hypothesis, but we find the first name more intuitive because from a coalgebraic point of view, coinduction is all about finding circularities.

Theorem 3. *The usual equational inference rules together with* Circular Coinduction *are sound. That means that if* $\mathcal{B} \Vdash (\forall X)\ t = t'$ *and* $sort(t, t') \neq b$*, or if* $\mathcal{B} \Vdash (\forall X)\ [t] = [t']$*, then* $\mathcal{B} \models (\forall X)\ t = t'$.

Circular coinductive rewriting[5, 6] iteratively rewrites proof tasks to their normal forms followed by an one step coinduction if needed. Since the rules in $\mathcal{B}_{LTL/GB}$, $\mathcal{B}_{LTL/B}$, and $\mathcal{B}_{LTL/G}$ are ground Church-Rosser and terminating, this provides us with a decision procedure for good-bad prefix equivalence, bad prefix equivalence, and good prefix equivalence of LTL formulae respectively.

Theorem 4. *If* ϕ_1 *and* ϕ_2 *are two LTL formulae, then* $\phi_1 \equiv_{GB} \phi_2$ *if and only if* $\mathcal{B}_{LTL/GB} \Vdash \phi_1 = \phi_2$*. Similarly, if* ϕ_1 *and* ϕ_2 *are two LTL formulae, then* $\phi_1 \equiv_B \phi_2$ *(or* $\phi_1 \equiv_G \phi_2$*) if and only if* $\mathcal{B}_{LTL/B} \Vdash \phi_1 = \phi_2$ *(or* $\mathcal{B}_{LTL/G} \Vdash \phi_1 = \phi_2$*). Moreover,* circular coinductive rewriting *provides us with a decision procedure for good-bad prefix equivalence, bad prefix equivalence, and good prefix equivalence of LTL formulae.*

Proof. By soundness of behavioral reasoning (Theorem 3), one implication follows immediately via Theorem 2. For the other implication, assume that ϕ_1 and ϕ_2 are good-bad prefix equivalent (or good prefix or bad prefix equivalent, respectively) and that the equality $\phi_1 = \phi_2$ is not derivable from $\mathcal{B}_{LTL/GB}$ (or $\mathcal{B}_{LTL/G}$ or $\mathcal{B}_{LTL/B}$, respectively). By Theorem 1, the number of formulae into which any LTL formula can be derived via a sequence of events is finite, which means that the total number of equalities $\phi'_1 = \phi'_2$ that can be derived via the circular coinduction rule is also finite. That implies that the only reason for which the equality $\phi_1 = \phi_2$ *cannot* be proved by circular coinduction is because it is in fact *disproved* by some experiment, which implies the existence of some events a_1, ..., a_n such that $GB(\phi_1\{a_1\}\cdots\{a_n\}) \neq GB(\phi_2\{a_1\}\cdots\{a_n\})$ (or the equivalent ones for B or G). However, this is obviously a contradiction because if ϕ_1 and ϕ_2 are good-bad (or good or bad) prefix equivalent that so are $\phi_1\{a_1\}\cdots\{a_n\}$ and $\phi_2\{a_1\}\cdots\{a_n\}$, and *GB* (or *G* or *B*) preserve this equivalence.

4 Generating Optimal Monitors by Coinduction

We now show how one can use the set of circularities generated by applying the circular coinduction rules in order to generate, from any LTL formula, an optimal monitor that can detect both good and bad prefixes. The optimal monitor thus generated will be a minimal deterministic finite automaton containing two final states true and false. We call such a monitor *GB-automaton*. We conclude the section by modifying the algorithm to generate smaller monitors that can detect either bad or good prefixes. We call such monitors *B-automaton* and *G-automaton* respectively. The main idea behind the algorithm is to associate states in GB-automaton to LTL formulae obtained by deriving the initial LTL formula; when a new LTL formula is generated, it is tested for good-bad prefix equivalence with all the other already generated LTL formulae by using the coinductive procedure presented in the previous section. A crucial observation which significantly reduces the complexity of our procedure is that once a good-bad prefix equivalence is proved by circular coinductive rewriting, the entire set of circularities accumulated represent good-bad prefix equivalent LTL formulae. These can be used to quickly infer the other good-bad prefix equivalences, without having to generate the same circularities over and over again.

Since BOBJ does not (yet) provide any mechanism to return the set of circularities accumulated after proving a given behavioral equivalence, we were unable to use BOBJ to implement our optimal monitor generator. Instead, we have implemented our own version of coinductive rewriting engine for LTL formulae, which is described below.

We are given an initial LTL formula ϕ_0 over atomic propositions P. Then $\sigma = 2^P$ is the set of possible states that can appear in an execution trace; note that σ will be the set of alphabets in the GB-automaton. Now, from ϕ_0 we want to generate a GB-automaton $D = (S, \sigma, \delta, s_0, \{\text{true}, \text{false}\})$, where S is the set of states of the GB-automaton, $\delta : S \times \sigma \to S$ is the transition function, s_0 is the initial state of the GB-automaton, and $\{\text{true}, \text{false}\} \subseteq S$ is the set of final states of the DFA. The coinductive rewriting engine explicitly accumulates the proven circularities in a set. The set is initialized to an empty set at the beginning of the algorithm. It is updated with the accumulated circularities whenever we prove good-bad prefix equivalence of two LTL formulae in the algorithm. The algorithm maintains the set of states S in the form of non good-bad prefix equivalent LTL formulae. At the beginning of the algorithm S is initialized with two elements, the constant formulae true and false. Then, we check if the initial LTL formula ϕ_0 is equivalent to true or false. If ϕ_0 is equivalent to true or false, we set s_0 to true or false respectively and return D as the GB-automaton. Otherwise, we set s_0 to ϕ_0, add ϕ_0 to the set S, and invoke the procedure **dfs** (see Fig 1) on ϕ_0.

The procedure **dfs** generates the derivatives of a given formula ϕ for all $x \in \sigma$ one by one. A derivative $\phi_x = \phi\{x\}$ is added to the set S, if the set does not contain any LTL formula good-bad prefix equivalent to the derivative ϕ_x. We then extend the transition function by setting $\delta(\phi, x) = \phi_x$ and recursively invoke **dfs** on ϕ_x. On the other hand, if an LTL formula ϕ' equivalent to the derivative already exists in the set S, we extend the transition function by setting $\delta(\phi, x) = \phi'$. To check if an LTL formula, good-bad prefix equivalent to the derivative ϕ_x, already exists in the set S, we sequentially go through all the elements of the set S and try to prove its good-bad prefix equivalence with ϕ_x. In testing the equivalence we first add the set of circularities to the initial $\mathcal{B}_{LTL/GB}$. Then we invoke the coinductive procedure. If for some LTL formula $\phi' \in S$, we are able to prove that $\phi' \equiv_{GB} \phi_x$ i.e $\mathcal{B}_{LTL/GB} \cup Eq_{\text{all}} \cup Eq_{\text{new}} \Vdash \phi' = \phi_x$, then we add the new equivalences Eq_{new}, created by the coinductive procedure, to the set of circularities. Thus we reuse the already proven good-bad prefix equivalences in future proofs.

$S \leftarrow \{\text{true}, \text{false}\}$
dfs(ϕ)
begin
  foreach $x \in \sigma$ **do**
    $\phi_x \leftarrow \phi\{x\}$;
    if $\exists \phi' \in S$ such that $\mathcal{B}_{LTL/GB} \cup Eq_{\text{all}} \cup Eq_{\text{new}} \Vdash \phi' = \phi_x$ **then**
      $\delta(\phi, x) = \phi'$; $Eq_{\text{all}} \leftarrow Eq_{\text{all}} \cup Eq_{\text{new}}$
    else $S \leftarrow S \cup \{\phi_x\}$; $\delta(\phi, x) = \phi_x$; **dfs**(ϕ_x); **fi**
  endfor
end

Fig. 1. LTL to optimal monitor generation algorithm

The GB-automaton generated by the procedure **dfs** may now contain some states which are non-final and from which the GB-automaton can never reach a final state. We remove these redundant states by doing a breadth first search in backward direction from the final states. This can be done in time linear in the size of the GB-automaton. If the resultant GB-automaton contains the initial state s_0 then we say that the LTL formula is monitorable. That is for the LTL formula to be monitorable there must be path from the initial state to a final state i.e.

to true or false state. Note that the GB-automaton may now contain non-final states from which there may be no transition for some $x \in \sigma$. Also note that no transitions are possible from the final states.

The correctness of the algorithm is given by the following theorem.

Theorem 5. *If D is the GB-automaton generated for a given LTL formula ϕ by the above algorithm then*

1) $\mathcal{L}(D)$ is the language of good and bad prefixes of ϕ,
2) D is the minimal deterministic finite automaton accepting the good and bad prefixes of ϕ.

Proof. 1) Suppose $s_1 s_2 \ldots s_n$ be a good or bad prefix of ϕ. Then by Theorem 1, $GB(\phi\{s_1\}\{s_2\}\ldots\{s_n\}) \in \{0,1\}$. Let $\phi_i = \phi\{s_1\}\{s_2\}\ldots\{s_i\}$; then $\phi_{i+1} = \phi_i\{a_{i+1}\}$. To prove that $s_1 s_2 \ldots s_n \in \mathcal{L}(D)$, we use induction to show that for each $1 \leq i \leq n$, $\phi_i \equiv_{GB} \delta(\phi, s_1 s_2 \ldots s_i)$. For the base case if $\phi_1 \equiv_{GB} \phi\{s_1\}$ then **dfs** extends the transition function by setting $\delta(\phi, s_1) = \phi$. Therefore, $\phi_1 \equiv_{GB} \phi = \delta(\phi, s_1)$. If $\phi_1 \not\equiv_{GB} \phi$ then **dfs** extends δ by setting $\delta(\phi, s_1) = \phi_1$. So $\phi_1 \equiv_{GB} \delta(\phi, s_1)$ holds in this case also. For the induction step let us assume that $\phi_i \equiv_{GB} \phi' = \delta(\phi, s_1 s_2 \ldots s_i)$. If $\delta(\phi', s_{i+1}) = \phi''$ then from the **dfs** procedure we can see that $\phi'' \equiv_{GB} \phi'\{s_{i+1}\}$. However, $\phi_i\{s_{i+1}\} \equiv_{GB} \phi'\{s_{i+1}\}$, since $\phi_i \equiv_{GB} \phi'$ by induction hypothesis. So $\phi_{i+1} \equiv_{GB} \phi'' = \delta(\phi', s_{i+1}) = \delta(\phi, s_1 s_2 \ldots s_{i+1})$. Also notice $GB(\phi_n \equiv_{GB} \delta(\phi, s_1 s_2 \ldots s_n)) \in \{0,1\}$; this implies that $\delta(\phi, s_1 s_2 \ldots s_n)$ is a final state and hence $s_1 s_2 \ldots s_n \in \mathcal{L}(D)$.

Now suppose $s_1 s_2 \ldots s_n \in \mathcal{L}(D)$. The proof that $s_1 s_2 \ldots s_n$ is a good or bad prefix of ϕ goes in a similar way by showing that $\phi_i \equiv_{GB} \delta(\phi, s_1 s_2 \ldots s_i)$.
2) If the automaton D is not minimal then there exists at least two states p and q in D such that p and q are equivalent [12] i.e. $\forall w \in \sigma^* : \delta(p, w) \in F$ if and only if $\delta(q, w) \in F$, where F is the set of final states. This means, if ϕ_1 and ϕ_2 are the LTL formulae associated with p and q respectively in **dfs** then $\phi_1 \equiv_{GB} \phi_2$. But **dfs** ensures that no two LTL formulae representing the states of the automaton are good-bad prefix equivalent. So we get a contradiction. □

The GB-automaton thus generated can be used as a monitor for the given LTL formula. If at any point of monitoring we reach the state true in the GB-automaton we say that the monitored finite trace satisfies the LTL formula. If we reach the state false we say that the monitored trace violates the LTL formula. If we get stuck at some state i.e. we cannot take a transition, we say that the monitored trace is not monitorable. Otherwise we continue monitoring by consuming another state of the trace.

In the above procedure if we use the specification $\mathcal{B}_{LTL/B}$ (or $\mathcal{B}_{LTL/G}$) instead of $\mathcal{B}_{LTL/GB}$ and consider false (or true) as the only final state, we get a B-automaton (or G-automaton). These automata can detect either bad or good prefixes. Since the final state is either false or true the procedure to remove redundant states will result in smaller automata compared to the corresponding GB-automaton.

We have an implementation of the algorithm adapted to extended regular expressions which is available for evaluation on the internet via a CGI server reachable from `http://fsl.cs.uiuc.edu/rv/`.

5 Time and Space Complexity

Any possible derivative of an LTL formula ϕ, in its normal form, is an *exclusive or* of *conjunctions* of temporal subformulae (subformulae having temporal operators at the top) in ϕ. The number of such temporal subformulae is $O(m)$, where m is the size of ϕ. Hence, by counting argument, the number of possible conjuncts is $O(2^m)$. The number of possible exclusive ors of these conjuncts is then $O(2^{2^m})$. Therefore, the number of possible distinct derivatives of ϕ is $O(2^{2^m})$. Since the number states of the GB-automaton accepting good and bad prefixes of ϕ cannot be greater than the number of derivatives, 2^{2^m} is an upper bound on the number of possible states of the GB-automaton. Hence, the size of the GB-automaton is $O(2^{2^m})$. Thus we get the following lemma:

Lemma 1. *The size of the minimal GB-automaton accepting the good and bad prefixes of any LTL formula of size m is $O(2^{2^m})$.*

For the lower bound on the size of the automata we consider the language

$$L_k = \{\sigma\#w\#\sigma'\$w \mid w \in \{0,1\}^k \text{ and } \sigma, \sigma' \in \{0,1,\#\}^*\}.$$

This language was previously used in several works [15, 16, 23] to prove lower bounds. The language can be expressed by the LTL formula [16] of size $O(k^2)$:

$$\phi_k = [(\neg\$)\mathcal{U}(\$\mathcal{U}\circ\Box(\neg\$))] \wedge \Diamond[\# \wedge \circ^{n+1}\# \wedge \bigwedge_{i=1}^{n}((\circ^i 0 \wedge \Box(\$ \rightarrow \circ^i 0)) \vee (\circ^i 1 \wedge \Box(\$ \rightarrow \circ^i 1)))].$$

For this LTL formula the following result holds.

Lemma 2. *Any GB-automaton accepting good and bad prefixes of ϕ_k will have size $\Omega(2^{2^k})$.*

Proof: In order to prove the lower bound, the following equivalence relation on strings over $(0+1+\#)^*$ is useful. For a string $\sigma \in (0+1+\#)^*$, define $S(\sigma) = \{w \in (0+1)^k \mid \exists\lambda_1, \lambda_2.\ \lambda_1\#w\#\lambda_2 = \sigma\}$. We will say that $\sigma_1 \equiv_k \sigma_2$ iff $S(\sigma_1) = S(\sigma_2)$. Now observe that the number of equivalence classes of $\equiv_k$ is 2^{2^k}; this is because for any $S \subseteq (0+1)^k$, there is a σ such that $S(\sigma) = S$.

We will prove this lower bound by contradiction. Suppose A is a GB-automaton that has a number of states less than 2^{2^k} for the LTL formula ϕ_k. Since the number of equivalence classes of $\equiv_k$ is 2^{2^k}, by pigeon hole principle, there must be two strings $\sigma_1 \not\equiv_k \sigma_2$ such that the state of A after reading $\sigma_1\$$ is the same as the state after reading $\sigma_2\$$. In other words, A will reach the same state after reading inputs of the form $\sigma_1\$w$ and $\sigma_2\$w$. Now since $\sigma_1 \not\equiv_k \sigma_2$, it follows that $(S(\sigma_1) \setminus S(\sigma_2) \cup (S(\sigma_2) \setminus S(\sigma_1)) \neq \emptyset$. Take $w \in (S(\sigma_1) \setminus S(\sigma_2) \cup (S(\sigma_2) \setminus S(\sigma_1))$. Then clearly, exactly one out of $\sigma_1\$w$ and $\sigma_2\$w$ is in L_k, and so A gives the wrong answer on one of these inputs. Therefore, A is not a correct GB-automaton. □

Combining the above two results we get the following theorem.

Theorem 6. *The size of the minimal GB-automaton accepting the good and bad prefixes of any LTL formula of size* m *is* $O(2^{2^m})$ *and* $\Omega(2^{2^{\sqrt{m}}})$.

The space and time complexity of the algorithm is given by the following:

Theorem 7. *The LTL to optimal monitor generation algorithm requires* $2^{O(2^m)}$ *space and* $c2^{O(2^m)}$ *time for some constant* c.

Proof: The number of distinct derivatives of an LTL formula of size m can be $O(2^{2^m})$. Each such derivative can be encoded in space $O(2^m)$. So the number of circularities that are generated in the algorithm can consume $O(2^{2^m}2^m2^m)$ space. The space required by the algorithm is thus $2^{O(2^m)}$. □

The number of iterations that the algorithm makes is less than the number of distinct derivatives. In each iteration the algorithm generates a set of circularities that can be at most $2^{O(2^m)}$. So the total time taken by the algorithm is $c2^{O(2^m)}$ for some constant c.

6 Conclusion and Future Work

In this paper we give a behavioral specification for LTL, which has the appealing property that two LTL formulae are *equivalent with respect to monitoring* if and only if they are indistinguishable under carefully chosen experiments. To our knowledge, this is the first coalgebraic formalization of LTL. The major benefit of this formalization is that one can use *coinduction* to prove LTL formulae monitoring-equivalent, which can further be used to generate optimal LTL monitors on a single go. As future work we want to apply our coinductive techniques to generate monitors for other logics.

Acknowledgements

The work is supported in part by the Defense Advanced Research Projects Agency (the DARPA IPTO TASK Program, contract number F30602-00-2-0586, the DARPA IXO NEST Program, contract number F33615-01-C-1907), the ONR Grant N00014-02-1-0715, the Motorola Grant MOTOROLA RPS #23 ANT, and the joint NSF/NASA grant CCR-0234524. We would like to thank Klaus Havelund and Predrag Tosic for reading a previous version of this paper and giving us valuable feedback and Howard Barringer for very helpful discussions, valuable feedback on the paper and pointers to references.

References

1. B. Alpern and F. B. Schneider. Defining liveness. *Information Processing Letters*, 21(4), 1985.
2. D. Drusinsky. The Temporal Rover and the ATG Rover. In *SPIN Model Checking and Software Verification*, volume 1885 of *LNCS*. Springer, 2000.

3. M. Geilen. On the construction of monitors for temporal logic properties. In *ENTCS*, volume 55. Elsevier, 2001.
4. D. Giannakopoulou and K. Havelund. Automata-Based Verification of Temporal Properties on Running Programs. In *Proceedings, International Conference on Automated Software Engineering (ASE'01)*. IEEE, 2001. Coronado Island, California.
5. J. Goguen, K. Lin, and G. Roşu. Circular coinductive rewriting. In *Proceedings, International Conference on Automated Software Engineering (ASE'00)*. IEEE, 2000. (Grenoble, France).
6. J. Goguen, K. Lin, and G. Rosu. Conditional circular coinductive rewriting with case analysis. In *Recent Trends in Algebraic Development Techniques (WADT'02)*, LNCS, Frauenchiemsee, Germany, September 2002. Springer.
7. K. Havelund and T. Pressburger. Model Checking Java Programs using Java PathFinder. *International Journal on Software Tools for Technology Transfer*, 2(4), Apr. 2000.
8. K. Havelund and G. Roşu. Java PathExplorer – A Runtime Verification Tool. In *The 6th International Symposium on Artificial Intelligence, Robotics and Automation in Space: A New Space Odyssey*, Montreal, Canada, June 18 - 21, 2001.
9. K. Havelund and G. Roşu. Monitoring Programs using Rewriting. In *Proceedings, International Conference on Automated Software Engineering (ASE'01)*. IEEE, 2001. Coronado Island, California.
10. K. Havelund and G. Roşu. *Runtime Verification 2002*, volume 70(4) of *ENTCS*. Elsevier, 2002. Proceedings of a *Computer Aided Verification (CAV'02)* satellite workshop.
11. K. Havelund and G. Roşu. Synthesizing monitors for safety properties. In *Tools and Algorithms for Construction and Analysis of Systems (TACAS'02)*, volume 2280 of *LNCS*. Springer, 2002.
12. J. E. Hopcroft and J. D. Ullman. *Introduction to Automata Theory, Languages and Computation*. Addison Wesley, 1979.
13. J. Hsiang. Refutational theorem proving using term rewriting systems. *Artificial Intelligence*, 25, 1985.
14. M. Kim, S. Kannan, I. Lee, and O. Sokolsky. Java-MaC: a Run-time Assurance Tool for Java. In *Proceedings of Runtime Verification (RV'01)*, volume 55 of *ENTCS*. Elsevier, 2001.
15. O. Kupferman and M. Y. Vardi. Freedom, Weakness, and Determinism: From linear-time to branching-time. In *Proceedings of the IEEE Symposium on Logic in Computer Science (LICS'98)*, 1998.
16. O. Kupferman and M. Y. Vardi. Model Checking of Safety Properties. In *Proceedings of the Conference on Computer-Aided Verification (CAV'99)*, 1999.
17. I. Lee, S. Kannan, M. Kim, O. Sokolsky, and M. Viswanathan. Runtime Assurance Based on Formal Specifications. In *Proceedings of the International Conference on Parallel and Distributed Processing Techniques and Applications*, 1999.
18. Z. Manna, N. Bjørner, and A. B. et al. An update on STeP: Deductive-algorithmic verification of reactive systems. In *Tool Support for System Specification, Development and Verification*, LNCS. Springer, 1998.
19. Z. Manna and A. Pnueli. *Temporal verification of reactive systems: Safety*. Springer-Verlag N.Y., Inc., 1995.
20. T. O'Malley, D. Richardson, and L. Dillon. Efficient Specification-Based Oracles for Critical Systems. In *Proceedings of the California Software Symposium*, 1996.
21. D. J. Richardson, S. L. Aha, and T. O. O'Malley. Specification-Based Test Oracles for Reactive Systems. In *Proceedings of the Fourteenth International Conference on Software Engineering (ICSE'92)*, 1992.

22. G. Roşu. *Hidden Logic.* PhD thesis, University of California at San Diego, 2000.
23. G. Roşu and M. Viswanathan. Testing extended regular language membership incrementally by rewriting. In *Rewriting Techniques and Applications (RTA'03)*, LNCS. Springer, 2003.
24. K. Sen and G. Roşu. Generating Optimal Monitors for Extended Regular Expressions. In *Proceedings of Runtime Verification (RV'03) (To appear)*, volume 89(2) of *ENTCS*. Elsevier, 2003.
25. K. Sen, G. Roşu, and G. Agha. Runtime Safety Analysis of Multithreaded Programs. In *ACM SIGSOFT Conference on the Foundations of Software Engineering / European Software Engineering Conference (FSE / ESEC '03)*, Helsinki, Finland, 2003.
26. S. D. Stoller. Model-Checking Multi-threaded Distributed Java Programs. In *SPIN Model Checking and Software Verification*, volume 1885 of *LNCS*. Springer, 2000.
27. W. Visser, K. Havelund, G. Brat, and S. Park. Model Checking Programs. In *Proceedings, The 15th IEEE International Conference on Automated Software Engineering (ASE'00)*. IEEE CS Press, Sept. 2000.

Probabilistic Timed Simulation Verification and Its Application to Stepwise Refinement of Real-Time Systems

Satoshi Yamane

Dept. of Information Engineering, Kanazawa University
Kanazawa City, Japan, ZIP/CODE 920-8667
syamane@is.t.kanazawa-u.ac.jp
Tel: +81.76.234.4856, Fax: +81.76.234.4900

Abstract. Today, timed automaton is the standard tool for specifying and verifying real-time systems. On the other hand, recently, probabilistic timed automata have been developed in order to express the relative likelihood of the system exhibiting certain behavior. In this paper, we develop the verification method of timed simulation relation of probabilistic timed automata, and apply this method to stepwise refinement developments of real-time systems. This kind of simularity is a valuable theoretical tool to prove soundness of refinements.

1 Introduction

Today, timed automaton [1] is the standard tool for specifying and verifying real-time systems by model-checking methods [2, 3]. On the other hand, in order to express the relative likelihood of the system exhibiting certain behavior, M. Kwiatkowska has developed probabilistic timed automata and their model-checking method [4]. In this paper, we develop timed simulation relations of probabilistic timed automata and its automatic verification method. This kind of simularity is a valuable theoretical tool to prove soundness of refinements. There have been several refinement verification methods of timed automata as follows:

1. As timed language containment is undecidable [1], K. Cerans has showed timed bisimulation is decidable in 1992 [5].
2. S. Tasiran and his colleagues have developed a compositional safety timed simulation verification method in 1996 [6].
3. S. Yamane has developed both $\forall$- and $\exists$-timed simulation verification methods in 1998 [7].

On the other hand, there have been several refinement verification methods of probabilistic timed systems as follows:

1. H.A. Hansson has developed both model-checking methods and bisimulation verification methods of discrete time probabilistic systems in 1991 [8].
2. R. Segala has developed the model of probabilistic timed automata, which is a dense time model, but is used in the context of manual simulation and bisimulation verification techniques in 1995 [9].

V.A. Saraswat (Ed.): ASIAN 2003, LNCS 2896, pp. 276–290, 2003.

3. A notable contribution to the area of the verification of probabilistic systems operating in dense time was offered by Alur, Courcoubetis and Dill [10, 11], who provided a model checking technique for a variant of Generalized Semi-Markov Processes against timed properties in 1991.

To the best of our knowledge, timed simulation verification methods of probabilistic timed automata have never been developed before now (but we have published a preliminary version of some simple timed simulation verification of probabilistic timed automata [12]). In this paper, we develop timed simulation verification methods of probabilistic timed automata with discrete probability distributions, and apply our proposed methods to stepwise refinement development of real-time systems.

The paper is organized as follows: In section 2, we introduce some preliminary concepts and notations. In section 3, we define probabilistic timed automata. In section 4, we define a timed simulation relation of probabilistic timed automata. In section 5, we propose verification method of a timed simulation relation. In section 6, we apply our proposed methods to stepwise refinement development of real-time systems. Finally, in section 7, we present conclusions.

2 Preliminaries

In this section, we introduce some preliminary concepts and notations.

First, we define discrete probability distributions as follows:

Definition 1 (Discrete probability distribution)
We denote the set of discrete probability distributions over a finite set S by $\mu(S)$. Therefore, each $p \in \mu(S)$ is a function $p : S \to [0,1]$ such that $\sum_{s \in S} p(s) = 1$. ■

Next we define Markov decision processes as follows:

Definition 2 (Markov decision processes)
A Markov decision process is denoted by $(Q, Steps)$, where Q is a set of states, and $Steps : Q \to 2^{\mu(Q)}$ is a function assigning a set of probability distributions to each state. Our intuition is that the Markov decision process traverses the state space by making transitions determined by Steps; that is, in the state $q \in Q$, a transition is made by first nondeterministically selecting a probability distribution $p \in Steps(q)$, and then performing a probabilistic choice according to p as to which move to. If the state selected by q is $q\prime$, then we denote such a transition by $q \xrightarrow{p} q\prime$.

Occasionally we will require an additional event in the definition of Steps, so that, for some set Σ, $Steps : Q \to 2^{\Sigma \times \mu(Q)}$ is now a function assigning a pair (σ, p), comprising of an event and a probability distribution, to each state (a transition is now denoted by $q \xrightarrow{\sigma, p} q\prime$). ■

Next we define clocks and clock valuations as follows:

Definition 3 (Clocks and clock valuations)
A clock is a real-valued variable which increases at the same rate as real-time. Let $\chi = \{x_1, \ldots, x_n\}$ be a set of clocks. A valuation of χ is a vector $\mathbf{a}$ of length

n in $\mathbf{R}^n$, which, intuitively, assigns a real value $\mathbf{a}_i$ to each variable $x_i \in \chi$. We denote the set of all clock valuations of χ by $\mathbf{R}^\chi$ or $\mathbf{R}^n$. A valuation can also be regarded as defining a point in $\mathbf{R}^n$-space. We write $\mathbf{0}$ for the valuation which assigns 0 to each variable $x \in \chi$, and $\mathbf{a} + \delta$ to represent the valuation which assigns $\mathbf{a}_i + \delta$ to each variable $x_i \in \chi$, for the valuation $\mathbf{a} \in \mathbf{R}^n$ and the real value $\delta \in \mathbf{R}^n$.

Next we define reset operation on valuations as follows: Let $X \subseteq \chi$ be a subset of variables, $\mathbf{a} \in \mathbf{R}^n$ be a valuation. Then $\mathbf{a}[X := 0]$ is the set of valuations such that $\mathbf{a}_{i'} \in \mathbf{a}[X := 0]$ if and only if, for all $x_i \in X$, we have $\mathbf{a}_{i'} = 0$ and for all other $x_i \in \chi \setminus X$, we have $\mathbf{a}_{i'} = \mathbf{a}_i$. ■

Next we define clock constraints as follows:

Definition 4 (Clock constraints)
A constraint over χ is an expression of the form $x_i \sim c$ or $x_i - x_j \sim c$, where $1 \le i \neq j \le n$, $\sim \in \{<, \le, \ge, >\}$, $c \in \mathbf{N} \cup \{\infty\}$, $x_0 = 0$. ■

Next we define zones as follows:

Definition 5 (Zones)
A zone of χ, written ζ, is a convex subset of the valuation space $\mathbf{R}^n$ described by a conjunction of constraints. Formally, a zone ζ is the set of valuations which satisfy the conjunction of $n \cdot (n+1)$ constraints given by:

$$\bigwedge_{0 \le i \neq j \le n} x_i - x_j \sim c_{ij}$$

Let $\mathbf{Z}_\chi$ be the set of all zones of χ. We denote by $c_{max}(\zeta)$ the largest constant used in the description of a zone.

For any zones $\zeta \in \mathbf{Z}_\chi$, and $X \subseteq \chi$ a set of clocks, let $\zeta[X := 0] = \{\mathbf{a}[X := 0] | \mathbf{a} \in \zeta\}$.

We write $\mathbf{a} \models \mathbf{Z}_\chi$ if the valuation $\mathbf{a}$ satisfies the set of all zones $\mathbf{Z}_\chi$. ■

3 Probabilistic Timed Automata

In this section, we introduce probabilistic timed automata as a modelling framework for real-time systems with probability [4].

3.1 Syntax and Semantics of Probabilistic Timed Automata

First we define syntax of probabilistic timed automata. We extend timed automata with discrete probability distributions over edges, so that the choice of the next location of the automaton is now probabilistic, in addition to nondeterministic, in nature.

Definition 6 (Syntax of probabilistic timed automata)
A probabilistic timed automaton is a tuple $\mathbf{G} = (S, \Sigma, \overline{s}, \chi, inv, prob, < \tau_s >_{s \in S})$ which contains:

1. *a finite set S of nodes,*
2. *a finite set Σ of events,*
3. *a start node $\overline{s} \in S$,*
4. *a finite set χ of clocks,*
5. *a function $inv : S \to \mathbf{Z}_\chi$ assigning to each node an invariant condition,*
6. *a function $prob : S \to 2^{\Sigma \times 2^\chi \times \mu(S \times \mathbf{R}^n)}$ assigning to each node both a set of discrete probability distributions on $S \times \mathbf{R}^n$ and $\Sigma \times 2^\chi$,*
7. *a family of functions $< \tau_s >_{s \in S}$ where, for any $s \in S$, $\tau_s : prob(s) \to \mathbf{Z}_\chi$ assigns to each $(\sigma, \lambda, p) \in prob(s)$ an enabling condition, where $\sigma \in \Sigma$, $p \in \mu(S \times \mathbf{R}^n)$, λ gives the clocks to be reset with this function.* ∎

Next we informally define semantics of probabilistic timed automata. A state of a probabilistic timed automaton $\mathbf{G} = (S, \Sigma, \overline{s}, \chi, inv, prob, < \tau_s >_{s \in S})$ is a pair $< s, \mathbf{a} > \in S \times \mathbf{R}^n$, where $s \in S$ is a node, and $\mathbf{a} \in \mathbf{R}^n$ is a clock valuation such that $\mathbf{a} \in inv(s)$. The set of $< s, \mathbf{a} >$ is denoted by $\mathbf{\Pi}$. The distributions available for nondeterministic choice in a state s can be categorised as corresponding either to time transitions or probabilistic discrete transitions:

1. A time transition of duration $\delta \in \mathbf{R}^n$ is possible if the clock values obtained by adding δ to each of the current values satisfy the invariant condition associated with the current node. More formally, if $< s, \mathbf{a} >$ is the current state of the system, then a time transition of duration $\delta \in \mathbf{R}^n$ to the state $< s, \mathbf{a} + \delta >$ is possible if $\mathbf{a} + \delta \in inv(s)$.
2. A probabilistic discrete transition corresponding to the distribution p is possible if and only if p belongs to the set of distributions associated with the current node, and the current clock values satisfy the enabling condition of p. That is, if $< s, \mathbf{a} >$ is the current state of the system, then a probabilistic transition corresponding to the distribution p can be performed if $(\sigma, \lambda, p) \in prob(s)$ and $\mathbf{a} \in \tau_s((\sigma, \lambda, p))$.

Paths in a probabilistic timed automaton based on the above semantics arise by resolving both the nondeterministic and probabilistic choices. A path of the probabilistic timed automaton $\mathbf{G} = (S, \Sigma, \overline{s}, \chi, inv, prob, < \tau_s >_{s \in S})$ is a non-empty finite or infinite sequence:

$$\omega = < s_0, \mathbf{0} > \stackrel{\delta_0}{\longrightarrow} < s_0, \mathbf{0} + \delta_0 > \stackrel{\sigma_0,\lambda_0,p_0,\tau_{s_0}(p_0)}{\longrightarrow} < s_1, \mathbf{0} + \delta_0[\lambda_0 := 0] > \stackrel{\delta_1}{\longrightarrow}$$

$$< s_1, \mathbf{0} + \delta_0[\lambda_0 := 0] + \delta_1 > \stackrel{\sigma_1,\lambda_1,p_1,\tau_{s_1}(p_1)}{\longrightarrow}$$

$$< s_2, \mathbf{0} + (\delta_0[\lambda_0 := 0] + \delta_1)[\lambda_1 := 0] > \stackrel{\delta_2}{\longrightarrow}$$

$$< s_2, \mathbf{0} + (\delta_0[\lambda_0 := 0] + \delta_1)[\lambda_1 := 0] + \delta_2 > \stackrel{\sigma_2,\lambda_2,p_2,\tau_{s_2}(p_2)}{\longrightarrow} \ldots\ldots$$

where $s_i \in S$, $(\sigma_i, \lambda_i, p_i) \in prob(s_i)$, $\sigma_i \in \Sigma$, $\delta_i \in \mathbf{R}^n$ for all $i \geq 0$, $\overline{s} = s_0$. $\lambda_i \subseteq \chi$ gives the set of clocks to be reset.

We can also write ω as follows:

$$\omega = < s_0, \mathbf{0} > \stackrel{\delta_0,\sigma_0,\lambda_0,p_0,\tau_{s_0}(p_0)}{\longrightarrow} < s_1, \mathbf{0} + \delta_0[\lambda_0 := 0] > \stackrel{\delta_1,\sigma_1,\lambda_1,p_1,\tau_{s_1}(p_1)}{\longrightarrow}$$

$$< s_2, \mathbf{0} + (\delta_0[\lambda_0 := 0] + \delta_1)[\lambda_1 := 0] > \stackrel{\delta_2,\sigma_2,\lambda_2,p_2,\tau_{s_2}(p_2)}{\longrightarrow} \ldots\ldots$$

We can also write ω as follows:

$$\omega = < s_0, \mathbf{a}^0 > \stackrel{\delta_0,\sigma_0,\lambda_0,p_0,\tau_{s_0}(p_0)}{\longrightarrow} < s_1, \mathbf{a}^1 > \stackrel{\delta_1,\sigma_1,\lambda_1,p_1,\tau_{s_1}(p_1)}{\longrightarrow}$$

$$< s_2, \mathbf{a}^2 > \stackrel{\delta_2,\sigma_2,\lambda_2,p_2,\tau_{s_2}(p_2)}{\longrightarrow} \ldots\ldots$$

where $\mathbf{a}^0 = \mathbf{0}$, $\mathbf{a}^1 = \mathbf{0} + \delta_0[\lambda_0 := 0]$, $\mathbf{a}^2 = \mathbf{0} + (\delta_0[\lambda_0 := 0] + \delta_1)[\lambda_1 := 0]$.

3.2 Parallel Composition of Probabilistic Timed Automata

Next we define parallel composition of probabilistic timed automata. The key operator to build complex real-time systems from simpler ones is parallel composition.

Definition 7 (Parallel composition of probabilistic timed automata) *Given* $\mathbf{G_1} = (S_1, \Sigma_1, \overline{s}_1, \chi_1, inv_1, prob_1, < \tau_{s_1} >_{s_1 \in S_1})$ *and* $\mathbf{G_2} = (S_2, \Sigma_2, \overline{s}_2, \chi_2, inv_2, prob_2, < \tau_{s_2} >_{s_2 \in S_2})$ *, parallel composition of* $\mathbf{G_1}$ *and* $\mathbf{G_2}$ *is denoted by* $\mathbf{G_1} \parallel \mathbf{G_2}$*. We assume that* χ_1 *and* χ_2 *are disjoint.* $\mathbf{G} = (S, \Sigma, \overline{s}, \chi, inv, prob, < \tau_s >_{s \in S})$ *consists of the followings:*

1. $S = S_1 \times S_2$
2. $\Sigma = \Sigma_1 \cup \Sigma_2$
3. $\overline{s} = (\overline{s}_1, \overline{s}_2)$
4. $\chi = \chi_1 \cup \chi_2$
5. $inv((s_1, s_2)) = inv_1(s_1) \wedge inv_2(s_2)$*, where for any* $s_1 \in S_1$ *and* $s_2 \in S_2$
6. *Both* $prob : S \rightarrow 2^{\Sigma \times 2^{\chi} \times \mu(S \times \mathbf{R}^n)}$ *and a family of functions* $< \tau_{(s_1,s_2)} >_{(s_1,s_2) \in S_1 \times S_2}$ *are defined as follows:*
   (a) *if* $a \in \Sigma_1$ *and* $a \in \Sigma_2$*:*
   $(a, \lambda_1, p_1) \in prob_1(s_1)$ *exists if* $a \in \Sigma_1$*, and* $(a, \lambda_2, p_2) \in prob_2(s_2)$ *exists if* $a \in \Sigma_2$*. We can define* $(a, \lambda_1 \cup \lambda_2, p_1 \otimes p_2) \in prob((s_1, s_2))$*, where* $s_1 \in S_1$*,* $s_2 \in S_2$*. Here we can define* $p_1 \otimes p_2$ *by* $p_1(s_1) \times p_2(s_2)$*.*
   Moreover, we can define $\tau_{(s_1,s_2)} : prob((s_1, s_2)) \rightarrow \mathbf{Z}_\chi$ *assigning an enabling condition to each* $(a, \lambda_1 \cup \lambda_2, p_1 \otimes p_2) \in prob((s_1, s_2))$*, where* $\mathbf{Z}_\chi = \mathbf{Z}_{\chi_1} \times \mathbf{Z}_{\chi_2}$*.*
   (b) *if* $a \in \Sigma_1$ *and* $b \in \Sigma_2 (a \neq b)$*:*
   $(a, \lambda_1, p_1) \in prob_1(s_1)$ *exists if* $a \in \Sigma_1$*, and* $(b, \lambda_2, p_2) \in prob_2(s_2)$ *if* $b \in \Sigma_2$*. We can define* $(a, \lambda_1, p_1) \in prob((s_1, s_2))$ *and, we can define* $(b, \lambda_2, p_2) \in prob((s_1, s_2))$*, where* $s_1 \in S_1$*,* $s_2 \in S_2$*.*
   Moreover, we can define $\tau_{(s_1,s_2)} : prob((s_1, s_2)) \rightarrow \mathbf{Z}_{\chi_1}$ *assigning an enabling condition to each* $(a, \lambda_1, p_1) \in prob((s_1, s_2))$*, and we can define* $\tau_{(s_1,s_2)} : prob((s_1, s_2)) \rightarrow \mathbf{Z}_{\chi_2}$ *assigning an enabling condition to each* $(b, \lambda_2, p_2) \in prob((s_1, s_2))$ ■

4 A Timed Simulation Relation

In this section, we define a timed simulation relation between two probabilistic timed automata.

First, we define a simulation relation between two probabilistic distributions borrowed from the reference [13].

Definition 8 (A simulation relation between probability distributions) *Let $(p_0, p_1) \in R$ be a relation between two probability distributions p_0, p_1. Formally, $(p_0, p_1) \in R$ if there is a function $w : Q_0 \times Q_1 \rightarrow [0, 1]$ such that*

1. *if $w(q_0, q_1) > 0$ then $(q_0, q_1) \in R$, where $q_0 \in Q_0$ and $q_1 \in Q_1$.*
2. *for each $q_0 \in Q_0$, $\sum_{q_1 \in Q_1} w(q_0, q_1) = p_0(q_0)$.*
3. *for each $q_1 \in Q_1$, $\sum_{q_0 \in Q_0} w(q_0, q_1) = p_1(q_1)$.*

where Q_0 and Q_1 are finite sets. The function w is called a weight function. ■

Next, we define a timed simulation relation by combining both a Segala's simulation relation between probability distributions [13] and a Tasiran's timed simulation relation [6] as follows:

Definition 9 (A timed simulation relation) *Given two probabilistic timed automata $\mathbf{G_1} = (S_1, \Sigma_1, \overline{s}_1, \chi_1, inv_1, prob_1, < \tau_{s_1} >_{s_1 \in S_1})$ and $\mathbf{G_2} = (S_2, \Sigma_2, \overline{s}_2, \chi_2, inv_2, prob_2, < \tau_{s_2} >_{s_2 \in S_2})$, a timed simulation relation from $\mathbf{G_1}$ to $\mathbf{G_2}$ is a binary relation $R \subseteq \mathbf{\Pi}_1 \times \mathbf{\Pi}_2$, denoted by $\mathbf{G_1} \preceq \mathbf{G_2}$, if the following three conditions are satisfied, where $\mathbf{\Pi}_1$ is a set of $< s_1, \mathbf{a} >$ and $\mathbf{\Pi}_2$ is a set of $< s_2, \mathbf{b} >$, $s_1 \in S_1$, $\mathbf{a} : \chi_1 \rightarrow \mathbf{R}^{\chi_1}$, $s_2 \in S_2$, $\mathbf{b} : \chi_2 \rightarrow \mathbf{R}^{\chi_2}$:*

1. *A timed simulation condition:*
   for every $(< s_1, \mathbf{a} >, < s_2, \mathbf{b} >) \in R$, and for every δ, σ, λ_1 and $\tau_{s_1}(p_1)$, if
   $$< s_1, \mathbf{a} > \overset{\delta, \sigma, \lambda_1, \tau_{s_1}(p_1)}{\longrightarrow} < s_1\prime, \mathbf{a}\prime >$$
   then there exists $< s_2\prime, \mathbf{b}\prime >$ such that
   $$< s_2, \mathbf{b} > \overset{\delta, \sigma, \lambda_2, \tau_{s_2}(p_2)}{\longrightarrow} < s_2\prime, \mathbf{b}\prime >$$
   and $(< s_1\prime, \mathbf{a}\prime >, < s_2\prime, \mathbf{b}\prime >) \in R$, where $\mathbf{a} + \delta \models \tau_{s_1}(p_1)$ and $\mathbf{b} + \delta \models \tau_{s_2}(p_2)$, $(\sigma, \lambda_1, p_1) \in prob(s_1)$ and $(\sigma, \lambda_2, p_2) \in prob(s_2)$, $\mathbf{a}\prime = (\mathbf{a} + \delta)[\lambda_1 := 0]$ and $\mathbf{b}\prime = (\mathbf{b} + \delta)[\lambda_2 := 0]$.
2. *A probability distribution simulation condition:*
   for every $(< s_1, \mathbf{a} >, < s_2, \mathbf{b} >) \in R$ and every transition
   $$< s_1, \mathbf{a} > \overset{\delta, \sigma, \lambda_1, p_1, \tau_{s_1}(p_1)}{\longrightarrow} < s_1\prime, \mathbf{a}\prime >$$
   of $\mathbf{G_1}$, there exists a transition
   $$< s_2, \mathbf{b} > \overset{\delta, \sigma, \lambda_2, p_2, \tau_{s_2}(p_2)}{\longrightarrow} < s_2\prime, \mathbf{b}\prime >$$
   of $\mathbf{G_2}$ such that $(p_1, p_2) \in R$.
3. *An initial condition:*
   for every $< \overline{s}_1, \mathbf{0} >$, there exists an initial state $< \overline{s}_2, \mathbf{0} >$ with $(< \overline{s}_1, \mathbf{0} >, < \overline{s}_2, \mathbf{0} >) \in R$. ■

5 Verification Method of a Timed Simulation Relation

In this section, we propose automatic verification method of a timed simulation relation of probabilistic timed automata. We achieve this by converting this verification to a finite check on the finitely many equivalence classes of an equivalence relation.

5.1 Equivalence of Clock Valuations

We first define an equivalence relation on the space of clock valuations in order to define region graphs in the next subsection.

Definition 10 (Agreement with integral parts of clock valuations) *For any $t \in \mathbf{R}$, $\lfloor t \rfloor$ denotes the integral part of t. Then, for any $t, t\prime \in \mathbf{R}$, t and $t\prime$ agree on their integral parts if and only if:*

1. $\lfloor t \rfloor = \lfloor t\prime \rfloor$
2. *both t and $t\prime$ are integers or neither is an integer.* ■

Definition 11 (Clock equivalence) *The valuations $\mathbf{a}, \mathbf{b} \in \mathbf{R}^{\chi}$ are clock equivalence, denoted by $\mathbf{a} \cong \mathbf{b}$, if and only if they satisfy the following conditions:*

1. *$\forall x_i \in \chi$, either $\mathbf{a}_i$ and $\mathbf{b}_i$ agree on their integral parts, or both $\mathbf{a}_i > c$ and $\mathbf{b}_i > c$, and*
2. *$\forall x_i, x_j \in \chi$, either $\mathbf{a}_i - \mathbf{a}_j$ and $\mathbf{b}_i - \mathbf{b}_j$ agree on their integral parts, or both $\mathbf{a}_i - \mathbf{a}_j > c$ and $\mathbf{b}_i - \mathbf{b}_j > c$.*

where $c = c_{max}(\mathbf{G})$. $c_{max}(\mathbf{G})$ denotes the largest constant appearing in probabilistic timed automaton $\mathbf{G}$. ■

Let $[\mathbf{a}]$ denote the equivalence class of $\cong$ to which $\mathbf{a}$ belongs. We refer to elements such as $< s, [\mathbf{a}] >$ as regions.

5.2 Region Graph

We construct a region graph based on regions. We define a region graph [4] which captures both the probabilistic transitions and the movement to new regions due to the passage of time, which takes the form of a Markov decision process.

First we define successor class and successor region in order to construct a region graph.

Definition 12 (Successor class and successor region) *Let α and β be distinct equivalence classes of $\mathbf{R}^{\chi}$. We define successor class as follows:*

> *The equivalence class β is said to be the successor of α if and only if, for each $\mathbf{a} \in \alpha$, there exists a positive $t \in \mathbf{R}^n$ such that $\mathbf{a} + t \in \beta$ and $\mathbf{a} + t\prime \in \alpha \cup \beta$ for all $t\prime \leq t$.*

The successor relation can be extended to regions in the following way:
$< s\prime, \beta >$ *is the successor region of* $< s, \alpha >$ *if* $s\prime = s$ *and* $\beta = succ(\alpha)$. ■

Next we define region graph of probabilistic timed automaton as Markov decision process.

Definition 13 (Region graph)
The region graph $\mathbf{R}(\mathbf{G})$ *is defined to be the Markov decision process* $(V^*, Steps^*)$ *corresponding to probabilistic timed automaton* $\mathbf{G} = (S, \Sigma, \overline{s}, \chi, inv, prob, < \tau_s >_{s \in S})$, *where* V^* *is the set of regions,* $Steps^* : V^* \rightarrow 2^{\mu(\Sigma\prime \times V^*)}$. $Steps^* : V^* \rightarrow 2^{\mu(\Sigma\prime \times V^*)}$ *includes two types of transitions, where* $\Sigma\prime = \Sigma \cup \{succ\}$. *For each region* $< s, \alpha > \in V^*$:

1. **Passage of Time:**
if the invariant condition $inv(s)$ *is satisfied by* $succ(\alpha)$, *then* $p^{s,\alpha}_{succ} \in Steps^* (< s, \alpha >)$, *where for any* $< s\prime, \beta > \in V^*$:

$$p^{s,\alpha}_{succ} < s\prime, \beta > = \begin{cases} 1 & if \quad < s\prime, \beta > = < s, succ(\alpha) > \\ 0 & otherwise. \end{cases}$$

We denote $< s, \alpha > \stackrel{succ}{\longrightarrow} < s\prime, \beta >$ *if* $< s\prime, \beta > = < s, succ(\alpha) >$.
2. **Discrete Transitions:**
$p^{s,\alpha} \in Steps^*(< s, \alpha >)$ *if there exists* $(\sigma, X, p) \in prob(s)$ *and* α *satisfies* $\tau_s(p)$ *such that for any* $\sigma \in \Sigma$ *and equivalence class* β:

$$p^{s,\alpha} < s\prime, \beta > = \sum_{X \subseteq \chi \quad and \quad \alpha[X:=0]=\beta} p(s\prime, X).$$

where for any $s\prime \in S$ *and* $X \subseteq \chi$, *the probability will make a state transition node* $s\prime$, *and reset all the clocks in* X *to* 0, *given by* $p(s\prime, X)$.
We denote this by $< s, \alpha > \stackrel{\sigma, p^{s,\alpha}}{\longrightarrow} < s\prime, \beta >$. ■

5.3 A Region Simulation Relation

We first define a region simulation relation on region graph, secondly check a timed simulation by reducing the problem to a finite check on the equivalence classes of a relation defined on region graphs.

Given two probabilistic timed automata $\mathbf{G_1} = (S_1, \Sigma, \overline{s}_1, \chi_1, inv_1, prob_1, < \tau_{s_1} >_{s_1 \in S_1})$ and $\mathbf{G_2} = (S_2, \Sigma, \overline{s}_2, \chi_2, inv_2, prob_2, < \tau_{s_2} >_{s_2 \in S_2})$, we define parallel composition $\mathbf{G_1} \parallel \mathbf{G_2}$ of $\mathbf{G_1}$ and $\mathbf{G_2}$ as $\mathbf{G} = (S, \Sigma, \overline{s}, \chi, inv, prob, < \tau_s >_{s \in S})$. We can also define $\mathbf{R}(\mathbf{G_1} \parallel \mathbf{G_2})$.

First, we require some preliminary definitions such as $\mathbf{R}(< \mathbf{s_1}, \mathbf{a} >, < \mathbf{s_2}, \mathbf{b} >)$ and $\mathbf{R_{G_1 \parallel G_2}}$.

Definition 14 ($\mathbf{R}(< \mathbf{s_1}, \mathbf{a} >, < \mathbf{s_2}, \mathbf{b} >)$ and $\mathbf{R_{G_1 \parallel G_2}}$)
We define $\mathbf{R}(< \mathbf{s_1}, \mathbf{a} >, < \mathbf{s_2}, \mathbf{b} >)$ *and* $\mathbf{R_{G_1 \parallel G_2}}$ *as follows:*

1. *With* $\mathbf{R}(<\mathbf{s_1},\mathbf{a}>,<\mathbf{s_2},\mathbf{b}>)$, *we denote the equivalence class that the state* $(<s_1,\mathbf{a}>,<s_2,\mathbf{b}>)\in\mathbf{\Pi_{G_1\|G_2}}$ *belongs to.*
2. *Let* $\mathbf{R_{G_1\|G_2}}$ *be the set of equivalence classes of* $\cong$ *on* $\mathbf{G_1}\parallel\mathbf{G_2}$. ■

Definition 15 (A region simulation relation)
A subset of equivalence classes $\eta\subseteq\mathbf{R_{G_1\|G_2}}$ *is a region simulation relation from* $\mathbf{G_1}$ *to* $\mathbf{G_2}$ *iff for each* $\mathbf{R}(<\mathbf{s_1},\mathbf{a}>,<\mathbf{s_2},\mathbf{b}>)\in\eta$, *the following three conditions are satisfied:*

1. *for every* δ, σ, λ_1 *and* $\tau_{s_1}(p_1)$, *if*

$$<s_1,\mathbf{a}>\stackrel{\delta,\sigma,\lambda_1,\tau_{s_1}(p_1)}{\longrightarrow}<s_1\prime,\mathbf{a}\prime>$$

then $<s_2,\mathbf{b}>\stackrel{\delta,\sigma,\lambda_2,\tau_{s_2}(p_2)}{\longrightarrow}<s_2\prime,\mathbf{b}\prime>$ *for some* $<s_2\prime,\mathbf{b}\prime>$ *such that* $\mathbf{R}(<\mathbf{s_1}\prime,\mathbf{a}\prime>,<\mathbf{s_2}\prime,\mathbf{b}\prime>)\in\eta$, *where* $\mathbf{a}+\delta\models\tau_{s_1}(p_1)$ *and* $\mathbf{b}+\delta\models\tau_{s_2}(p_2)$, $(\sigma,\lambda_1,p_1)\in prob(s_1)$ *and* $(\sigma,\lambda_2,p_2)\in prob(s_2)$, $\mathbf{a}\prime=(\mathbf{a}+\delta)[\lambda_1:=0]$ *and* $\mathbf{b}\prime=(\mathbf{b}+\delta)[\lambda_2:=0]$.
2. $\mathbf{R}(<\mathbf{s_1},\mathbf{a}>,<\mathbf{s_2},\mathbf{b}>)\in\eta$ *and every transition*

$$<s_1,\mathbf{a}>\stackrel{\delta,\sigma,\lambda_1,p_1,\tau_{s_1}(p_1)}{\longrightarrow}<s_1\prime,\mathbf{a}\prime>$$

of $\mathbf{G_1}$, *there exists a transition*

$$<s_2,\mathbf{b}>\stackrel{\delta,\sigma,\lambda_2,p_2,\tau_{s_2}(p_2)}{\longrightarrow}<s_2\prime,\mathbf{b}\prime>$$

of $\mathbf{G_2}$ *such that* $(p_1,p_2)\in\eta$ *and* $\mathbf{R}(<\mathbf{s_1}\prime,\mathbf{a}\prime>,<\mathbf{s_2}\prime,\mathbf{b}\prime>)\in\eta$.
3. *If* $\mathbf{G_1}$ *can wait for* δ *in* $<s_1,\mathbf{a}>$, *then* $\mathbf{G_2}$ *can wait for* δ *in* $<s_2,\mathbf{b}>$. ■

From the following theorem, there is an algorithm which, given two probabilistic timed automata $\mathbf{G_1}$ and $\mathbf{G_2}$, decides whether $\mathbf{G_2}$ simulates $\mathbf{G_1}$ or not.

Theorem 1 (Timed simulation and region simulation)
Given $\eta\subseteq\mathbf{R_{G_1\|G_2}}$, *let* $\mathbf{R}_\eta=\{(<s_1,\mathbf{a}>,<s_2,\mathbf{b}>)|\mathbf{R}(<s_1,\mathbf{a}>,<s_2,\mathbf{b}>)\in\eta\}$. $\mathbf{R}_\eta$ *is a timed simulation relation from* $\mathbf{G_1}$ *to* $\mathbf{G_2}$ *denoted by* $\mathbf{G_1}\preceq\mathbf{G_2}$ *iff* η *is a region simulation relation from* $\mathbf{G_1}$ *to* $\mathbf{G_2}$.

Proof 1 *We simply show outlines of proof of the above theorem as follows:*

1. η *is a region simulation relation if* $\mathbf{R}_\eta$ *is a timed simulation relation:*
Assume that $\mathbf{R}_\eta$ *is a timed simulation relation from* $\mathbf{G_1}$ *to* $\mathbf{G_2}$.
Let $(<s_1,\mathbf{a}>,<s_2,\mathbf{b}>)\in\mathbf{R}_\eta$, $(\sigma,\lambda_1,p)\in prob((s_1,s_2))$ *and* $\tau_{(s_1,s_2)}(p)$ *be such that* $<s_1,\mathbf{a}>\stackrel{\delta,\sigma,\lambda_1,p,\tau_{(s_1,s_2)}(p)}{\longrightarrow}<s_1\prime,\mathbf{a}\prime>$. *As* $\mathbf{R}_\eta$ *is a timed simulation relation, some* $<s_2\prime,\mathbf{b}\prime>$ *exists such as* $<s_2,\mathbf{b}>\stackrel{\delta,\sigma,\lambda_2,p,\tau_{(s_1,s_2)}(p)}{\longrightarrow}<s_2\prime,\mathbf{b}\prime>$.
This $<s_2\prime,\mathbf{b}\prime>$ *satisfying conditions of a region simulation relation.*
From the above, η *is a region simulation relation.*

2. $\mathbf{R}_\eta$ *is a timed simulation relation if* η *is a region simulation relation:* *Assume that* η *is a region simulation relation. Let* $(< s_1, \mathbf{a} >, < s_2, \mathbf{b} >) \in \mathbf{R}_\eta$ *and let* $< s_1, \mathbf{a} > \stackrel{\delta,\sigma,\lambda_1,p_1,\tau_{s_1}(p_1)}{\longrightarrow} < s_1\prime, \mathbf{a}\prime >$ *for some* δ, σ, λ_1, p_1 *and* $\tau_{s_1}(p_1)$. *We need to show that there exists* $< s_2\prime, \mathbf{b}\prime >$ *such that* $< s_2, \mathbf{b} > \stackrel{\delta,\sigma,\lambda_2,p_2,\tau_{s_2}(p_2)}{\longrightarrow} < s_2\prime, \mathbf{b}\prime >$ *and* $(< s_1\prime, \mathbf{a}\prime >, < s_2\prime, \mathbf{b}\prime >) \in \mathbf{R}_\eta$.
   By the fact that η *is a region simulation relation,* $< s_2, \mathbf{b} > \stackrel{\delta,\sigma,\lambda,p,\tau_{s_2}(p)}{\longrightarrow} < s_2\prime, \mathbf{b}\prime >$ *for some* $< s_2\prime, \mathbf{b}\prime >$ *such that* $\mathbf{R}(< \mathbf{s_1}\prime, \mathbf{b}\prime >, < \mathbf{s_2}\prime, \mathbf{b}\prime >) \in \eta$, *where* $(p_1, p) \in \eta$, *and if* $\mathbf{G_1}$ *can wait for* δ *in* $< s_1, \mathbf{a} >$ *then* $\mathbf{G_2}$ *can wait for* δ *in* $< s_2, \mathbf{b} >$.
   We claim that $< s_2, \mathbf{b} > \stackrel{\delta,\sigma,\lambda_2,p_2,\tau_{s_2}(p_2)}{\longrightarrow} < s_2\prime, \mathbf{b}\prime >$ *which will imply the desired result. Here, we define* $p_2 = p$, $\mathbf{a} + \delta \models \tau_{s_1}(p_1)$, $\mathbf{b} + \delta \models \tau_{s_2}(p_2)$, $(\sigma, \lambda_1, p_1) \in prob(s_1)$, $(\sigma, \lambda_2, p_2) \in prob(s_2)$, $\mathbf{a}\prime = (\mathbf{a} + \delta)[\lambda_1 := 0]$, $\mathbf{b}\prime = (\mathbf{b} + \delta)[\lambda_2 := 0]$. *Moreover, for every* $< \overline{s}_1, \mathbf{0} >$, *there exists an initial state* $< \overline{s}_2, \mathbf{0} >$ *with* $(< \overline{s}_1, \mathbf{0} >, < \overline{s}_2, \mathbf{0} >) \in \mathbf{R}_\eta$.
   From the above result, we can show $(< s_1\prime, \mathbf{a}\prime >, < s_2\prime, \mathbf{b}\prime >) \in \mathbf{R}_\eta$.
   From the above, $\mathbf{R}_\eta$ *is a timed simulation relation.* ■

Thus, the problem of checking whether a probabilistic timed automaton $\mathbf{G_1}$ timed-simulates another probabilistic timed automaton $\mathbf{G_2}$ can be reduced to computing the region simulation relation over the equivalence classes $\mathbf{R}_{\mathbf{G_1}\|\mathbf{G_2}}$. For this purpose, any of the existing algorithms for computing simulation [14] can be adopted to obtain an algorithm.

6 Application of Our Method to Stepwise Refinement Development

In general, we develop real-time systems with discrete probability distributions by stepwisely refining them. That is, we refine abstract specification into concrete specification. In this case, proving both trace distribution inclusion and timed trace inclusion are difficult [1, 13]. However, from our proposed method in this paper, if we can show that each move of a probabilistic timed automaton $\mathbf{G_1}$ can be simulated by a probabilistic timed automaton $\mathbf{G_2}$, then we can conclude that each timed trace distribution of $\mathbf{G_1}$ is also a timed trace distribution of $\mathbf{G_2}$. This idea is known as the simulation method [15] and constitutes a very useful technique for the analysis of real-time and distributed systems [6, 9].

Therefore, in this section, we apply our proposed method to stepwise development of real-time systems. Moreover, we consider internal behaviors and propose timed weak simulation such as process algebra [15]. We propose stepwise refinement using timed weak simulation as follows:

1. First, we refine abstract specification into concrete specification by adding internal behaviors.
2. Secondly, we consider concrete specification should be weakly simulated by abstract specification. That is, concrete specification should be designed such that concrete specification is contained in abstract specification.

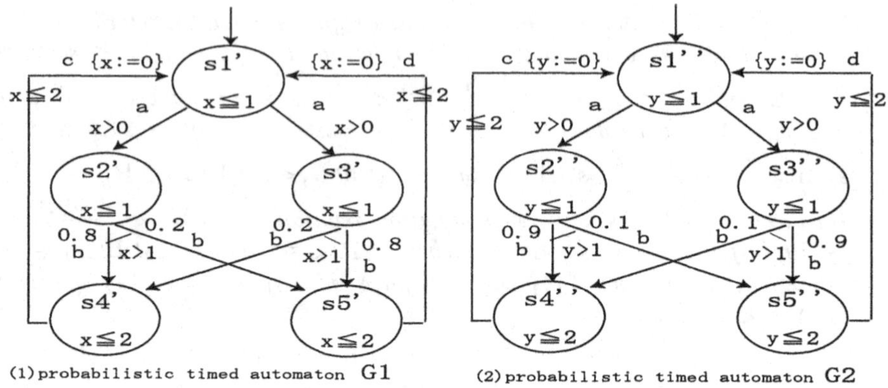

Fig. 1. A probabilistic timed simulation relation

3. Consider Figure 1. According to previous timed simulation relation, there does not exist a timed simulation relation from $\mathbf{G_1}$ to $\mathbf{G_2}$. But $\mathbf{G_1}$ moves from $s2\prime$ and $s3\prime$ to $s4\prime$ with probability 1.0, and moves from $s2\prime$ and $s3\prime$ to $s5\prime$ with probability 1.0. On the other hand, $\mathbf{G_2}$ moves from $s2\prime\prime$ and $s3\prime\prime$ to $s4\prime\prime$ with probability 1.0, and moves from $s2\prime\prime$ and $s3\prime\prime$ to $s5\prime\prime$ with probability 1.0. If we consider practical problems, it is better that there exists a probabilistic timed simulation relation from $\mathbf{G_1}$ to $\mathbf{G_2}$ by extending a timed simulation relation.

From these results, we propose a probabilistic timed simulation relation, and apply this relation to stepwise refinement development of real-time systems.

6.1 A Probabilistic Timed Weak Simulation Relation

We stepwisely refine abstract specification into concrete specification using a probabilistic timed weak simulation relation. We consider both a combined transition and an internal event *int*. Intuitionally, there exists a probabilistic timed weak simulation relation from $\mathbf{G_1}$ to $\mathbf{G_2}$ in Figure 2, where $\mathbf{G_1}$ is concrete specification, $\mathbf{G_2}$ is abstract specification.

First we define both a combined transition and an internal transition in order to show that $\mathbf{G_1}$ is simulated by $\mathbf{G_2}$.

Definition 16 (A combined transition)
Let $< s, \mathbf{a} >$ *be a state of a probabilistic timed automaton* $\mathbf{G}$. *We say that* $< s, \mathbf{a} > \sum_j \overset{\delta,\sigma,\lambda,p_j,\tau_s(p_j)}{\longrightarrow}{}_C < s_j, \mathbf{a}^j >$ *is a combined transition of* $< s, \mathbf{a} >$ *if* μ *is a convex combination of the set*

$$C = \{\mu_i | < s, \mathbf{a} > \overset{\delta,\sigma,\lambda,p_j,\tau_s(p_j)}{\longrightarrow} < s\prime, \mathbf{a}\prime > \textit{ and } p_j \in \mu_i(< s\prime, \mathbf{a}\prime >)\}$$

of distributions, that is, for each μ_i, *there is a nonnegative real number* w_i *such that* $\sum_i \mu_i = 1$ *and* $\mu = \sum_{\mu_i \in C} w_i * \mu_i$. ■

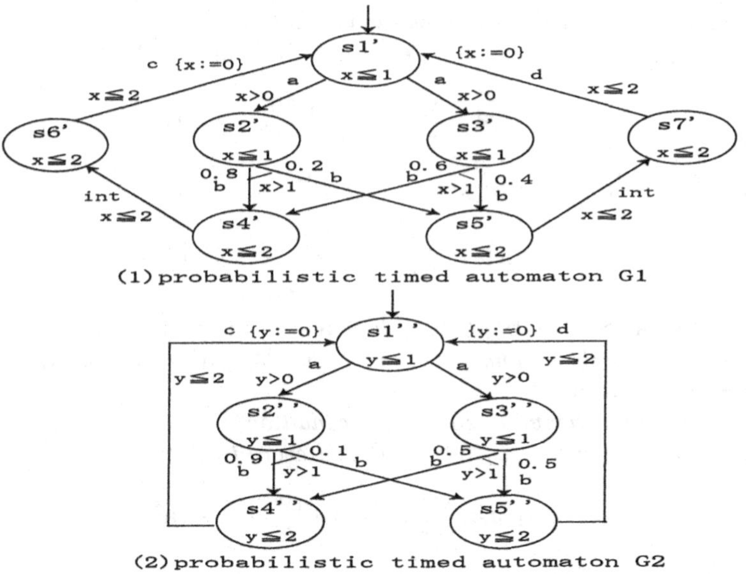

Fig. 2. A probabilistic timed weak simulation relation

Definition 17 (An internal transition)
There exists a transition $< s_1, \mathbf{a}_1 > \overset{\delta,\sigma,\lambda,p,\tau_{s_1}(p)}{\Longrightarrow} < s_n, \mathbf{a}_n >$ *if the following transition occurs:*

$$< s_1, \mathbf{a}_1 > \overset{\delta_1,int,\lambda_1,p_1,\tau_{s_1}(p_1)}{\longrightarrow} < s_2, \mathbf{a}_2 > \overset{\delta_2,int,\lambda_2,p_2,\tau_{s_2}(p_2)}{\longrightarrow} \ldots$$

$$\ldots \overset{\delta_j,\sigma,\lambda_j,p_j,\tau_{s_j}(p_j)}{\longrightarrow} < s_{j+1}, \mathbf{a}_{j+1} > \overset{\delta_{j+1},int,\lambda_{j+1},p_{j+1},\tau_{s_{j+1}}(p_{j+1})}{\longrightarrow} \ldots$$

$$\ldots \overset{\delta_{n-1},int,\lambda_{n-1},p_{n-1},\tau_{s_{n-1}}(p_{n-1})}{\longrightarrow} < s_n, \mathbf{a}_n >$$

where $\delta = \delta_1 + \ldots + \delta_{n-1}$, $p = p_1 \otimes \ldots \otimes p_{n-1}$, $\lambda = \lambda_1 \cup \ldots \lambda_{n-1}$. ■

Finally we define a probabilistic timed weak simulation relation.

Definition 18 (A probabilistic timed weak simulation relation)
Given two probabilistic timed automata $\mathbf{G_1} = (S_1, \Sigma_1, \overline{s}_1, \chi_1, inv_1, prob_1, < \tau_{s_1} >_{s_1 \in S_1})$ *and* $\mathbf{G_2} = (S_2, \Sigma_2, \overline{s}_2, \chi_2, inv_2, prob_2, < \tau_{s_2} >_{s_2 \in S_2})$, *a probabilistic timed weak simulation relation from* $\mathbf{G_1}$ *to* $\mathbf{G_2}$ *is a binary relation* $R \subseteq \Omega_1 \times \Omega_2$, *denoted by* $\mathbf{G_1} \preceq \mathbf{G_2}$, *if the following conditions(both a timed simulation condition and an initial condition) are satisfied:*

where Ω_1 *is a set of* $< s_1, \mathbf{a} >$ *and* Ω_2 *is a set of* $< s_2, \mathbf{b} >$, $s_1 \in S_1$, $\mathbf{a} : \chi_1 \rightarrow \mathbf{R}^{\chi_1}$, $s_2 \in S_2$, $\mathbf{b} : \chi_2 \rightarrow \mathbf{R}^{\chi_2}$, $\mathbf{G_1}$ *is concrete specification,* $\mathbf{G_2}$ *is abstract specification,* Σ_1 *and* Σ_2 *contain int.*

1. *A probabilistic timed weak simulation condition:*
for every $(< s_1, \mathbf{a} >, < s_2, \mathbf{b} >) \in R$, *and for every* δ,σ,λ_1,$\tau_{s_1}(p_j)$, *if*
$$< s_1, \mathbf{a} > \sum_j \overset{\delta,\sigma,\lambda_1,\tau_{s_1}(p_j)}{\Longrightarrow} {}_C < s_j, \mathbf{a}^j >$$
then there exists $< s_2\prime, \mathbf{b}\prime >$ *such that*
$$< s_2, \mathbf{b} > \sum_k \overset{\delta,\sigma,\lambda_2,\tau_{s_2}(p_k)}{\longrightarrow} {}_C < s_k, \mathbf{b}^k >$$
and $(< s_j, \mathbf{a}^j >, < s_k, \mathbf{b}^k >) \in R$, *where* $\mathbf{a} + \delta \models \tau_{s_1}(p_j)$ *and* $\mathbf{b} + \delta \models \tau_{s_2}(p_k)$, $(\sigma, \lambda_1, p_j) \in prob(s_1)$ *and* $(\sigma, \lambda_2, p_k) \in prob(s_2)$, $\mathbf{a}^j = (\mathbf{a} + \delta)[\lambda_1 := 0]$ *and* $\mathbf{b}^k = (\mathbf{b} + \delta)[\lambda_2 := 0]$.
2. *A probability distrinution simulation condition:*
for every $(< s_1, \mathbf{a} >, < s_2, \mathbf{b} >) \in R$ *and every transition*
$$< s_1, \mathbf{a} > \sum_j \overset{\delta,\sigma,\lambda_1,p_j,\tau_{s_1}(p_j)}{\Longrightarrow} {}_C < s_j, \mathbf{a}^j >$$
of $\mathbf{G_1}$, *there exists a transition*
$$< s_2, \mathbf{b} > \sum_k \overset{\delta,\sigma,\lambda_2,p_k,\tau_{s_2}(p_k)}{\longrightarrow} {}_C < s_k, \mathbf{b}^k >$$
of $\mathbf{G_2}$ *such that* $(p_j, p_k) \in R$ *and* $(< s_j, \mathbf{a}^j >, < s_k, \mathbf{b}^k >) \in R$.
3. *An initial condition:*
for every $< \overline{s}_1, \mathbf{0} >$, *there exists an initial state* $< \overline{s}_2, \mathbf{0} >$ *with* $(< \overline{s}_1, \mathbf{0} >, < \overline{s}_2, \mathbf{0} >) \in R$. ∎

6.2 Example of Stepwise Refinement

In this section, we show simple example of real-time systems. We use Ethernet CSMA/CD protocol [16] consisting of senders and receivers. Here we will specify a concrete sender and an abstract sender, and verify whether there exists a probabilistic timed weak simulation relation from concrete specification to abstract specification.

In Figure 3(1)(abstract specification), abstract specification moves from $s1 \to s2$ in order to send data. If abstract specification moves from $s2 \to s4$ (that is, if we start data send), it moves from $s4 \to s6$ (during data send), and finally it moves from $s6 \to s1$. If it moves from $s5 \to s7$(if lines are busy), it moves from $s5 \to s7$ (that is, we try to send data again). In abstract specification, it nondeterministically moves from $s1 \to s2$ or from $s1 \to s3$. Moreover, it probabilistically moves from $s2 \to s4$ or from $s2 \to s5$.

In Figure 3(2)(concrete specification), we refine abstract specification by adding an internal behavior such that it moves from $s6\prime \to s7\prime$, and by adding another internal behavior such that it moves from $s8\prime \to s9\prime$.

There exists a probabilistic timed weak simulation relation from concrete specification to abstract specification clearly.

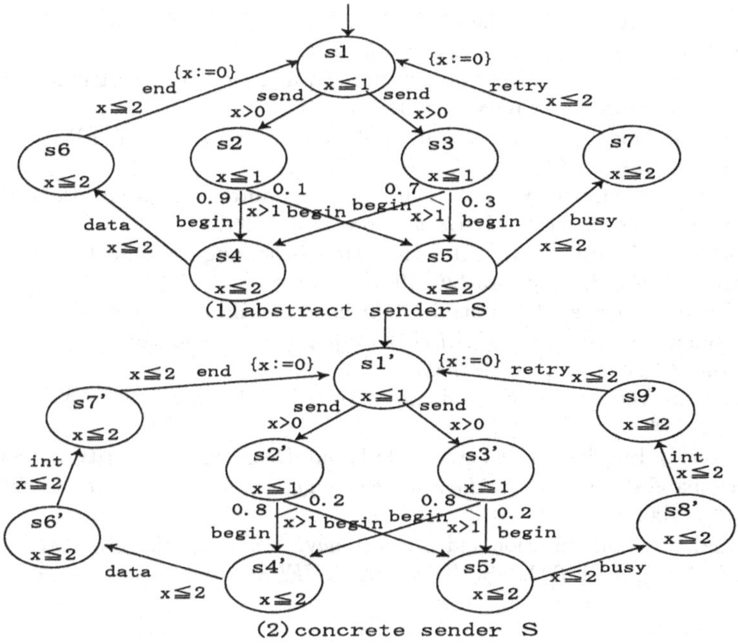

Fig. 3. Example of stepwise refinement

7 Conclusion

In this paper, we define a timed simulation relation between probabilistic timed automata, and define the automatic verification method. Moreover, we define a probabilistic timed weak simulation relation, and apply it to stepwise refinement of real-time systems. We are now working for both implementing an effective verification system and applying our proposed methods to real problems.

References

1. R. Alur, D.L. Dill. A theory of timed automata. *Theoretical Computer Science*, Vol. 126, pp.183-235, 1994.
2. R. Alur, C. Courcoubetis, D.L. Dill. Model-Checking in Dense Real-Time. *Information and Computation*, Vol. 104, pp. 2-34, 1993.
3. T. A. Henzinger, X. Nicollin, J. Sifakis, S. Yovine. Symbolic model checking for real-time systems. *Information and Computation*, Vol. 111, pp. 193-244, 1994.
4. M. Kwiatkowska, G. Norman, R. Segala, J. Sproston. Automatic verication of real-time systems with discrete probability distributions. *Theoretical Computer Science*, 282(1), pp. 101-150, 2002.
5. K. Cerans. Decidability of Bisimulation Equivalences for Processes with Parallel Timers. *LNCS 663*, pp.302-315, 1992.
6. S. Tasiran, R. Alur, R.P. Kurshan, R.K. Brayton. Verifying abstractions of timed systems. *LNCS 1119*, pp.546-562, 1996.

7. S. Yamane. A Practical Hierarchical Design by Timed Simulation Relations for Real-Time Systems. *LNCS 1641*, pp.151-167, 1998.
8. H.A. Hansson. Time and Probability in Formal Design of Distributed Systems. *PhD thesis*, Uppsala University, 1991
9. R. Segala. Modeling and Verification of Randomized Distributed Real-Time Systems. *PhD thesis*, MIT, 1995.
10. R. Alur, C. Courcoubetis, D.L. Dill. Verifying automata specifications of probabilistic real-time systems. *LNCS 600*, pp. 28-44, 1991.
11. R. Alur, C. Courcoubetis, D.L. Dill. Model-checking for probabilistic real-time systems. *LNCS 510*, pp. 115-136, 1991.
12. S. Yamane. Formal Probabilistic Refinement Verification Method of Embedded Real-Time Systems. *Proc.of IEEE Workshop on Software Technologies for Future Embedded Systems*, pp.79-82, 2003.
13. R. Segala. Verification of Randomized Distributed Algorithms. *LNCS 2090*, pp. 232-260, 2001.
14. C. Baier, B. Engelen, M. Majster-Cederbaum. Deciding Bisimilarity and Similarity for Probabilistic Processes. *Journal of Computer and System Sciences*, 60(1) , pp 187-231, 2000.
15. R. Milner. Communication and Concurrency. *Prentice Hall*, New York, 1989.
16. IEEE. ANSI/IEEE 802.3,ISO/DIS 8802/3. *IEEE computer society*, 1985.

Model Checking Probabilistic Distributed Systems

Benedikt Bollig[1] and Martin Leucker[2,*]

[1] Lehrstuhl für Informatik II, RWTH Aachen, Germany
bollig@informatik.rwth-aachen.de
[2] IT department, Uppsala University, Sweden
Martin.Leucker@it.uu.se

Abstract. Protocols for distributed systems make often use of random transitions to achieve a common goal. A popular example are randomized leader election protocols. We introduce *probabilistic product automata* (PPA) as a natural model for this kind of systems. To reason about these systems, we propose to use a product version of linear temporal logic ($LTL^{\otimes}$). The main result of the paper is a model-checking procedure for PPA and $LTL^{\otimes}$. With its help, it is possible to check qualitative properties of distributed systems automatically.

1 Introduction

Randomization techniques have been employed to solve numerous problems of computing both sequentially and in parallel. Examples of probabilistic algorithms that are asymptotically better than their deterministic counterparts in solving various fundamental problems abound. It has also been shown that they allow solutions of problems which cannot be solved deterministically [LR81]. They have the advantages of simplicity and better performance both in theory and often in practice. Prominent examples for distributed randomized algorithms are randomized leader election protocols [BGJ99]. An overview of the domain of randomized algorithms is given in [PRRR01].

As for any kind of hardware or software system, it is important to develop formal methods and tools for verifying their correctness, thus also for probabilistic programs. *Model checking*, introduced independently in [CES83] and [QS82], turned out to be one fruitful approach to automatically verify systems (see [CW96] for an overview of model checking in practice). In the model-checking approach, usually a finite system $\mathcal{M}$, often an abstraction of a real system, and a property, usually expressed as a temporal-logic formula φ or as an automaton describing the computations that adhere to the property, are given. The *model-checking procedure* decides whether the set or tree formed of all *computations* of $\mathcal{M}$ *satisfies* φ, or, in other words, whether the given system satisfies the required property. Temporal logics used for expressing requirements are usually linear temporal logics (LTL) (as initially proposed by Pnueli in [Pnu77]) or branching-time logics like computation-tree logics CTL and CTL*.

* This author is supported by the European Research Training Network "Games".

V.A. Saraswat (Ed.): ASIAN 2003, LNCS 2896, pp. 291–304, 2003.

In the probabilistic setting, one is no longer interested in *all* but only *almost all* computations. Thus, (sets or paths of trees of) computations with zero probability are ignored when deciding whether a given property is satisfied.

Temporal logics for probabilistic programs were initially studied in [LS82]and [HS84]. [Var85]introduced the notion of *Concurrent Probabilistic Programs* (CPPs) and provided a procedure for checking their LTL properties.

In this paper, we introduce *Probabilistic Product Automata* (PPA) as a model for *distributed* probabilistic systems. Roughly, a PPA is a parallel product of CPPs. They are enriched, however, with *actions* to synchronize the concurrent execution. In the non-randomized setting, product automata have proven to be a reasonable model for distributed systems. To support their analysis, a product version of linear temporal logic ($LTL^{\otimes}$) has been defined. It allows the definition of properties for each process, i.e., each single automaton or CPP of the overall system. The properties for each process are then combined by means of Boolean connectives to a single formula. Model-checking procedures for $LTL^{\otimes}$ and product automata have been studied in [Thi95]. We show in this paper, how $LTL^{\otimes}$ properties of PPA can be checked automatically.

Our method follows the automata-theoretic approach: Given a PPA $\mathcal{A}$, we can construct a single concurrent probabilistic program $\mathcal{M}$ with the same probabilistic behavior. For a property φ expressed as an $LTL^{\otimes}$ formula, we consider its negation $\neg\varphi$ and construct a (non-randomized) product automaton $\mathcal{A}_{\neg\varphi}$ that captures the behavior violating φ. This automaton is transformed into a deterministic Streett automaton $\mathcal{B}_{\neg\varphi}$. The common behavior of $\mathcal{M}$ and $\mathcal{B}_{\neg\varphi}$ represents the behavior of the underlying system that does not satisfy our property. If the behavior is empty in a probabistic sense, φ is satisfied by $\mathcal{A}$.

We define a kind of intersection of $\mathcal{M}$ and $\mathcal{B}_{\neg\varphi}$ and provide simple graph algorithms that answer the question whether $\mathcal{M}$ and $\mathcal{B}_{\neg\varphi}$ have a common behavior, in the probabilistic sense mentioned above. Our procedure is quadratic in the size of $\mathcal{M}$ (which grows exponentially with the number of parallel CPPs) and double exponential in size of φ.

Often, distributed systems are modelled as a single nondeterministic one. While our model-checking procedure makes use of this idea, our approach starting with a distributed system has several advantages. Firstly, it is more direct to model a distributed protocol as a PPA rather than as a single system. Secondly, it is more direct to formulate properties of the distributed system on a "per process basis" as done in $LTL^{\otimes}$ rather than for a system capturing the interleaved behavior. Thirdly, performance benefits can be expected in practice, since our procedure works *on-the-fly*: The main question to answer is whether the intersection of $\mathcal{M}$ and $\mathcal{B}_{\neg\varphi}$ has empty behavior. If a single behavior is found, the model checking procedure can stop and provide this counter example. Since the combined system can be checked in a top-down manner, often only a part of this system has to be constructed. This implies that only a part of $\mathcal{M}$ and a part of $\mathcal{B}_{\neg\varphi}$ has to be constructed. Since $\mathcal{M}$ and $\mathcal{B}_{\neg\varphi}$ are (double) exponentially larger than the underlying structures $\mathcal{A}$ and φ, this has a considerable effect in practice.

This paper is organized as follows. In the next section, we introduce the necessary concepts and notation of words, graphs, and automata. Section 3 presents our model for distributed probabilistic systems, probabilistic product automata. LTL$^{\otimes}$ is defined in Section 4. The main contribution of the paper, the model checking algorithm for PPA and LTL$^{\otimes}$ is explained in Section 5. We sum up our approach and mention directions for future work in the last section.

2 Preliminaries

Given an alphabet Σ, Σ^* denotes the set of *finite* and Σ^ω the set of *infinite words* over Σ, respectively. Furthermore, let $\Sigma^\infty = \Sigma^* \cup \Sigma^\omega$ be the set of *words*. For a word $\sigma = a_1 a_2 \ldots \in \Sigma^\omega$ and a natural $i \geq 1$, let σ^i denote $a_i a_{i+1} \ldots$, the ith suffix of σ, and let $\sigma(i)$ denote a_i, the ith letter of σ. Furthermore, take $\mathit{inf}(\sigma)$ as the *infinity set* of σ, i.e., the set of letters that occur infinitely often in σ. For a word $\sigma = a_1 \ldots a_n \in \Sigma^*$ and a natural $i \in \{1, \ldots, n+1\}$, we accordingly define σ^i to be the word σ' with $a_1 \ldots a_{i-1}\sigma' = \sigma$ (thus, σ^{n+1} is the empty word ε) and, if $i \leq n$, $\sigma(i)$ to be a_i.

Given a word σ and an alphabet Σ, let $\sigma \downharpoonright \Sigma$ denote the word we get by erasing from σ the letters that are not contained in Σ.

Given a (directed) graph G with nodes V and edges E, we call a node $v \in V$ (a set $D \subseteq V$ of nodes) *reachable* from $v' \in V$ if there is a path from v' to v (to a node contained in D). A *strongly connected component* (SCC) of G is a maximal set D of nodes such that every two nodes contained in D are reachable from each other. A SCC is called *bottom* if there is no edge leading out of it. We define G to be *strongly connected* if V forms a SCC. Furthermore, G is called *nontrivial* if it contains at least one edge. A set $D \subseteq V$ is said to be *nontrivial* if $G[D]$, the subgraph of G *induced* by D, is nontrivial. The *size* of G, denoted by $|G|$, is defined to be $|V| + |E|$.

Let Σ be an alphabet. An *extended Streett automaton* over Σ is a tuple $\mathcal{A} = (S, S_0, \delta, F, \mathcal{G})$ where S is its nonempty finite set of *states*, $S_0 \subseteq S$ is the set of *initial states*, $\delta : S \times \Sigma \to 2^S$ is its *transition function*, $F \subseteq S$ is its set of *final states*, and $\mathcal{G}$ is a subset of $(2^S)^2$. A *run* of $\mathcal{A}$ on a word $\sigma = a_1 a_2 \ldots \in \Sigma^\omega$ (on a word $\sigma = a_1 \ldots a_n \in \Sigma^*$) is a sequence of states $\rho = s_0 s_1 s_2 \ldots \in S^\omega$ (a sequence of states $\rho = s_0 s_1 \ldots s_n \in S^*$) such that $s_0 \in S_0$ and, for each natural i (for each $i \in \{0, 1, \ldots, |\rho| - 1\}$), $s_{i+1} \in \delta(s_i, a_{i+1})$. We call ρ *accepting* if either σ is finite and $s_{|\sigma|} \in F$ or σ is infinite and, for all pairs $(U, V) \in \mathcal{G}$, $\mathit{inf}(\rho) \cap U \neq \emptyset$ implies $\mathit{inf}(\rho) \cap V \neq \emptyset$. The *language* of $\mathcal{A}$, denoted by $L(\mathcal{A})$, is the set $\{\sigma \in \Sigma^\infty \mid$ there is an accepting run of $\mathcal{A}$ on $\sigma\}$. $\mathcal{A}$ is called *deterministic* if both $|S_0| = 1$ and $|\delta(s, a)| = 1$ for all $s \in S$, $a \in \Sigma$. Furthermore, the *size* $|\mathcal{A}|$ of $\mathcal{A}$ is defined to be the size of its (transition) graph. An extended Büchi automaton over Σ is just an extended Streett automaton, but it employs an acceptance component $\mathcal{F} \subseteq S$ instead of $\mathcal{G}$. A run over an infinite word is henceforth accepting if it visits at least one state from $\mathcal{F}$ infinitely often.

Given an extended Büchi automaton $\mathcal{A}$ over an alphabet Σ, there is a deterministic extended Streett automaton $\mathcal{B}$ over Σ such that $L(\mathcal{B}) = L(\mathcal{A})$ [GTW02].

3 Probabilistic Product Automata

Before we present our model for distributed concurrent probabilistic programs, we define the notion of its building blocks, the concurrent probabilistic programs. Let us describe the systems we want to study intuitively first. Figure 1 shows two concurrent probabilistic programs. The system starts in a *nondeterministic* state, shown as a circle, and selects nondeterministically a randomizing state, represented as a box. The transitions are labelled by actions which will later be used to synchronize the parallel execution of several concurrent probabilistic programs. In a randomizing state, the system chooses a nondeterministic successor state according to the probabilities of the outgoing arcs. Let us be more precise:

Definition 1 (Concurrent Probabilistic Program). *A* concurrent probabilistic program *(CPP) over an alphabet Σ is a tuple $\mathcal{M} = (Q, N, R, \Delta, P, Q^{in})$ where*

- *N and R are disjoint nonempty finite sets of* nondeterministic *and* randomizing states, *respectively, and $Q = N \cup R$ is the set of* states,
- *$\Delta \subseteq N \times \Sigma \times R$ is the set of* transitions,
- *$P : R \times N \to [0,1]$ is the* transition probability distribution[1] *such that, for each $q \in R$, $\sum_{q' \in N} P(q,q') = 1$, and*
- *$Q^{in} \subseteq Q$ is the set of* initial states.

A nondeterministic state $q \in N$ is called *enabled* in $\mathcal{M}$, if has outgoing transitions, i.e. if there is a $q' \in R$ and an $a \in \Sigma$ such that $(q, a, q') \in \Delta$. The set of enabled states of $\mathcal{M}$ is denoted by $N^{en}_{\mathcal{M}}$.

Sequences of transitions of a CPP involve actions as well as random choices. To be able to handle both kinds of transitions in the same manner, we use the symbol $\mathfrak{p}$ to denote a random move and set $\Sigma_{\mathfrak{p}} := \Sigma \uplus \{\mathfrak{p}\}$. To study the probabilistic behavior of a CPP, we consider its possible random executions, when fixing the nondeterministic choices by means of a scheduler. Given a partial execution of the system, i.e., a sequence of states and actions (including $\mathfrak{p}$), ending in an enabled nondeterministic state, a scheduler tells us which action and successor state to choose: A *scheduler* of a CPP $\mathcal{M} = (Q, N, R, \Delta, P, Q^{in})$ over Σ is a mapping $u : (Q\Sigma_{\mathfrak{p}})^* N^{en}_{\mathcal{M}} \to \Sigma \times R$ such that, for each $x \in (Q\Sigma_{\mathfrak{p}})^*$ and $q \in N^{en}_{\mathcal{M}}$, $u(xq) = (a, q')$ implies $(q, a, q') \in \Delta$.

For the rest of the paper, we fix a natural $K \geq 1$, the set $Proc = \{1, \ldots, K\}$ of *processes*, and a *distributed alphabet* $\tilde{\Sigma} = (\Sigma_1, \ldots, \Sigma_K)$, a tuple of (not necessarily disjoint) alphabets Σ_i. We use $\bigcup_i \Sigma_i$ as a shorthand for $\bigcup_{i \in Proc} \Sigma_i$. For $a \in \bigcup_i \Sigma_i$, let $loc(a) := \{i \in Proc \mid a \in \Sigma_i\}$ be the set of processes that the action a participates in.

We are now ready to define our model for distributed concurrent probabilistic programs:

[1] We usually write $P(q, q')$ instead of $P((q, q'))$.

Definition 2 (Probabilistic Product Automaton). *A* probabilistic product automaton *(PPA) over $\tilde{\Sigma}$ is a structure $\mathcal{A} = ((\mathcal{A}_i)_{i\in Proc}, S^{in})$ such that*

- *for each $i \in Proc$, $\mathcal{A}_i$ is a CPP $(Q_i, N_i, R_i, \Delta_i, P_i)$ (without set of initial states) over Σ_i and*
- *$S^{in} \subseteq \prod_{i\in Proc} Q_i$ is the set of* global initial states.

The two CPPs shown in Figure 1 form together a PPA over $(\{a,b\},\{b,c\})$ when setting the initial state of the system to (p_0, q_0). Note that the probability distributions P_i are reflected by transition arcs in case of nonzero transition probabilities, respectively.

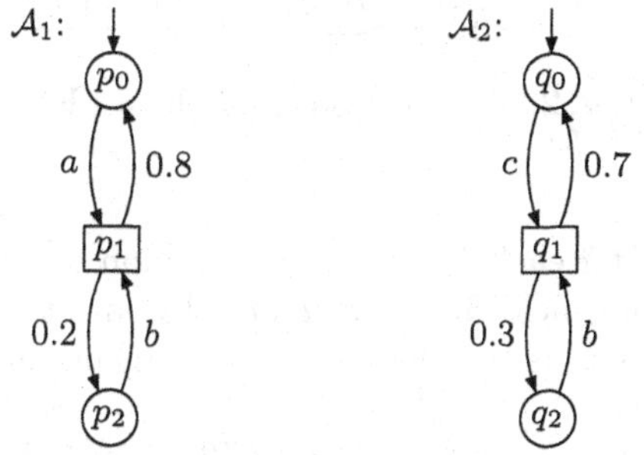

Fig. 1. A probabilistic product automaton

A PPA $\mathcal{A} = ((\mathcal{A}_i)_{i\in Proc}, S^{in})$, $\mathcal{A}_i = (Q_i, N_i, R_i, \Delta_i, P_i)$, determines the CPP $\mathcal{M}_{\mathcal{A}} = (Q_{\mathcal{A}}, N_{\mathcal{A}}, R_{\mathcal{A}}, \Delta_{\mathcal{A}}, P_{\mathcal{A}}, Q^{in}_{\mathcal{A}})$ over $\bigcup_i \Sigma_i$ where

- $Q_{\mathcal{A}} = \prod_{i\in Proc} Q_i$
  (in the following, for $\overline{q} = (q_1, \ldots, q_K) \in Q_{\mathcal{A}}$ and $i \in Proc$, let $\overline{q}[i]$ denote q_i)
- $N_{\mathcal{A}} = \prod_{i\in Proc} N_i$,
- $R_{\mathcal{A}} = Q_{\mathcal{A}} \setminus N_{\mathcal{A}}$,
- $(\overline{q}, a, \overline{q}') \in \Delta_{\mathcal{A}}$ if
  - $(\overline{q}[i], a, \overline{q}'[i]) \in \Delta_i$ for all $i \in loc(a)$ and
  - $\overline{q}[i] = \overline{q}'[i]$ for all $i \notin loc(a)$,
- $Q^{in}_{\mathcal{A}} = S^{in}$, and
- $P(\overline{q}, \overline{q}') = \begin{cases} \prod_{i\in Proc,\ \overline{q}[i]\in R_i} P_i(\overline{q}[i], \overline{q}'[i]) & \text{if, for each } i \in Proc, \\ & \overline{q}[i] \in N_i \text{ implies } \overline{q}[i] = \overline{q}'[i] \\ 0 & \text{otherwise} \end{cases}$

It is easy to verify that $\mathcal{M}_{\mathcal{A}}$ is indeed a CPP.

The PPA from Figure 1 induces the CPP given by Figure 2.

Let us now recall the probabilistic setting needed to reason about probabilistic programs.

A nonempty set of possible outcomes of an experiment of chance is called *sample space*. Let Ω be a sample space. A set $\mathfrak{B} \subseteq 2^{\Omega}$ is called *Borel field* over Ω

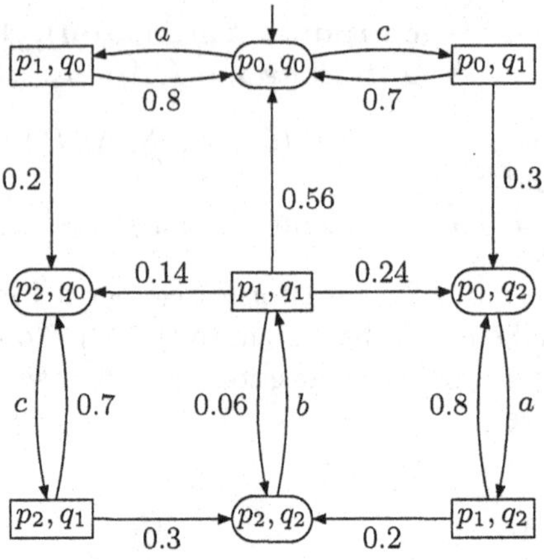

Fig. 2. The CPP generated by a PPA

if it contains Ω, $\Omega \setminus E$ for each $E \in \mathfrak{B}$, and the union of any countable sequence of sets from $\mathfrak{B}$. A Borel field $\mathfrak{B}$ is *generated* by an at most countable set $\mathcal{E}$, denoted by $\mathfrak{B} = \langle \mathcal{E} \rangle$, if $\mathfrak{B}$ is the closure of $\mathcal{E}$'s elements under complement and countable union.

A *probability space* is a triple $\mathcal{PS} = (\Omega, \mathfrak{B}, \mu)$ where Ω is a sample space, $\mathfrak{B}$ is a Borel field over Ω, and μ is a mapping $\mathfrak{B} \to [0, 1]$ such that $\mu(\Omega) = 1$ and $\mu(\bigcup_{i=1}^{\infty} E_i) = \sum_{i=1}^{\infty} \mu(E_i)$ for any sequence $E_1, E_2, \ldots$ of pairwise disjoint sets from $\mathfrak{B}$. We call μ a *probability measure.* An event $E \in \mathfrak{B}$ is said to occur *almost surely* if $\mu(E) = 1$.

A scheduler u of a CPP $\mathcal{M} = (Q, N, R, \Delta, P, Q^{in})$ over an alphabet Σ induces a probability space $\mathcal{PS}_{\mathcal{M},u} = (\Omega_{\mathcal{M},u}, \mathfrak{B}_{\mathcal{M},u}, \mu_{\mathcal{M},u})$ as follows:

- the sample space consists all infinite and maximal finite sequences of states and actions (including $\mathfrak{p}$) that respect the transition relation and can be stepwise taken with non-zero probability. Furthermore, the nondeterministic transitions must follow the scheduler. We only consider a finite sequence when it ends in a state with no outgoing transitions: Let $\Omega_{\mathcal{M},u} = \{q_1 a_1 q_2 a_2 \ldots \in (Q\Sigma_{\mathfrak{p}})^{\omega} \mid q_1 \in Q^{in}$ and, for all $i \geq 1$, ($q_i \in R$ and $q_{i+1} \in N$ and $a_i = \mathfrak{p}$ and $P(q_i, q_{i+1}) > 0$) or ($q_i \in N_{\mathcal{M}}^{en}$ and $a_i \in \Sigma$ and $u(q_1 a_1 \ldots q_i) = (a_i, q_{i+1})$)$\} \cup \{q_1 a_1 \ldots q_{n-1} a_{n-1} q_n \in (Q\Sigma_{\mathfrak{p}})^*(N \setminus N_{\mathcal{M}}^{en}) \mid q_1 \in Q^{in}$ and, for all $i \in \{1, \ldots, n-1\}$, ($q_i \in R$ and $q_{i+1} \in N$ and $a_i = \mathfrak{p}$ and $P(q_i, q_{i+1}) > 0$) or ($q_i \in N_{\mathcal{M}}^{en}$ and $u(q_1 a_1 \ldots q_i) = (a_i, q_{i+1})$)$\}$ be the set of *trajectories* of $\mathcal{M}$ wrt. u,
- $\mathfrak{B}_{\mathcal{M},u} = \langle \{\mathcal{C}_{\mathcal{M},u}(x) \mid x \in (Q\Sigma_{\mathfrak{p}})^* N\} \rangle$ where $\mathcal{C}_{\mathcal{M},u}(x) = \{x' \in \Omega_{\mathcal{M},u} \mid x$ is a prefix of $x'\}$ is the *basic cylinder set* of x wrt. $\mathcal{M}$ and u, and
- $\mu_{\mathcal{M},u}$ is uniquely given by $\mu_{\mathcal{M},u}(\Omega_{\mathcal{M},u}) = 1$ and, for $n \geq 1$,

$$\mu_{\mathcal{M},u}(\mathcal{C}_{\mathcal{M},u}(q_1 a_1 \ldots q_{n-1} a_{n-1} q_n)) = P'(q_1, q_2) \cdot \ldots \cdot P'(q_{n-1}, q_n)$$

where

$$P'(q_i, q_{i+1}) = \begin{cases} P(q_i, q_{i+1}) & \text{if } q_i \in R \\ 1 & \text{if } q_i \in N \end{cases}$$

4 Product LTL

In this section, we recall the definition of a product version of linear temporal logic, denoted by $\mathrm{LTL}^{\otimes}$, as defined in [MD97]. It is based on Pnueli's LTL. However, since we deal with action-based systems, we provide an action-based version of the logic as well. Furthermore, we extend the definition in a straightforward manner to deal with finite and infinite sequences.

Let Σ be an alphabet. The set $\mathrm{LTL}(\Sigma)$ of Linear Temporal Logic (LTL) formulas over Σ is given by the following grammar:

$$\varphi ::= \mathrm{tt} \mid \neg\varphi \mid \varphi_1 \vee \varphi_2 \mid \langle a\rangle\varphi \ (a \in \Sigma) \mid \varphi\mathcal{U}\psi$$

An $\mathrm{LTL}(\Sigma)$ formula is inductively interpreted over $\sigma \in \Sigma^{\infty}$ as follows:

- $\sigma \models_{\Sigma} \mathrm{tt}$
- $\sigma \models_{\Sigma} \neg\varphi$ if $\sigma \not\models_{\Sigma} \varphi$
- $\sigma \models_{\Sigma} \varphi \vee \psi$ if $\sigma \models_{\Sigma} \varphi$ or $\sigma \models_{\Sigma} \psi$
- $\sigma \models_{\Sigma} \langle a\rangle\varphi$ if $\sigma \neq \varepsilon$, $\sigma(1) = a$, and $\sigma^2 \models_{\Sigma} \varphi$
- $\sigma \models_{\Sigma} \varphi\mathcal{U}\psi$ if there is an $i \geq 0$ such that $\sigma^i \models_{\Sigma} \psi$ and, for each $j \in \{1, \ldots, i-1\}$, $\sigma^j \models_{\Sigma} \varphi$

The language of a formula $\varphi \in \mathrm{LTL}(\Sigma)$, denoted by $L(\varphi)$, is defined to be the set $\{\sigma \in \Sigma^{\infty} \mid \sigma \models_{\Sigma} \varphi\}$. Note that one can construct an extended Büchi automaton over Σ such that $L(\mathcal{B}) = L(\varphi)$ [VW86].

Product LTL formulas are Boolean combinations of LTL formulas, each formulated for a single process. More specifically, the set $\mathrm{LTL}^{\otimes}(\tilde{\Sigma})$ of Product Linear Temporal Logic ($\mathrm{LTL}^{\otimes}$) formulas over $\tilde{\Sigma}$ is given as:

$$\varphi ::= [\psi_i]_i \ (\psi_i \in \mathrm{LTL}(\Sigma_i)) \mid \varphi_1 \vee \varphi_2 \mid \varphi_1 \wedge \varphi_2$$

An $\mathrm{LTL}^{\otimes}(\tilde{\Sigma})$ formula is inductively interpreted over $\sigma \in (\bigcup_i \Sigma_i)^{\infty}$ as follows:

- $\sigma \models_{\otimes} [\psi_i]_i$ if $\sigma \lfloor \Sigma_i \models_{\Sigma_i} \psi_i$
- $\sigma \models_{\otimes} \varphi \vee \psi$ if $\sigma \models_{\otimes} \varphi$ or $\sigma \models_{\otimes} \psi$
- $\sigma \models_{\otimes} \varphi \wedge \psi$ if $\sigma \models_{\otimes} \varphi$ and $\sigma \models_{\otimes} \psi$

Thus, given a system, we restrict the run to the actions "interesting" for the process i and take the usual semantics of the LTL formula.

Note that we did not introduce negation on the outer $\mathrm{LTL}^{\otimes}$ level since it can be "pushed inwards" to each single $\mathrm{LTL}(\Sigma_i)$ formula.

One might be tempted to understand an $\mathrm{LTL}^{\otimes}$ formula as an LTL formula over the alphabet $\Sigma = \bigcup_i \Sigma_i$ (abstracting away $[]_i$). But it is easy to see that this yields a different semantics.

The language of a formula $\varphi \in \mathrm{LTL}^{\otimes}(\tilde{\Sigma})$, denoted by $L(\varphi)$, is defined to be the set $\{\sigma \in (\bigcup_i \Sigma_i)^{\infty} \mid \sigma \models_{\otimes} \varphi\}$. According to the LTL case, we can construct a PPA $\mathcal{A}$ over $\tilde{\Sigma}$ such that $L(\mathcal{A}) = L(\varphi)$ and, from $\mathcal{A}$, build an extended Büchi automaton $\mathcal{B}$ over $\bigcup_i \Sigma_i$ with $L(\mathcal{B}) = L(\mathcal{A}) = L(\varphi)$ [MD97].

5 Probabilistic Model Checking

In this section, we clarify the notion when a PPA satisfies an LTL$^{\otimes}$ formula in a probabilistic sense. Furthermore, we provide an algorithm answering this question.

5.1 Satisfaction

For checking whether a PPA satisfies a formula, we first define the set of sequences following a given scheduler and satisfying a given formula or being accepted by an automaton (let Σ be an alphabet):

1. For a CPP $\mathcal{M}$ over Σ, a scheduler u of $\mathcal{M}$, and a formula $\varphi \in \mathrm{LTL}(\Sigma)$, let $L_{\mathcal{M},u}(\varphi) := \{x \in \Omega_{\mathcal{M},u} \mid x \downharpoonleft \Sigma \models_\Sigma \varphi\}$.
2. For a PPA $\mathcal{A}$ over $\tilde{\Sigma}$, a scheduler u of $\mathcal{M}_\mathcal{A}$, and a formula $\varphi \in \mathrm{LTL}^{\otimes}(\tilde{\Sigma})$, let $L_{\mathcal{A},u}(\varphi) := \{x \in \Omega_{\mathcal{M}_\mathcal{A},u} \mid x \downharpoonleft (\bigcup_i \Sigma_i) \models_\otimes \varphi\}$.
3. For a CPP $\mathcal{M}$ over Σ, a scheduler u of $\mathcal{M}$, and an extended Streett (Büchi) automaton $\mathcal{B}$ over Σ, let $L_{\mathcal{M},u}(\mathcal{B}) := \{x \in \Omega_{\mathcal{M},u} \mid x \downharpoonleft \Sigma \in L(\mathcal{B})\}$.

We can show, using a simple induction, that these sets are measurable:

Proposition 1. *Let Σ be an alphabet.*

1. *Given a CPP $\mathcal{M}$ over Σ and a formula $\varphi \in \mathrm{LTL}(\Sigma)$, we have $L_{\mathcal{M},u}(\varphi) \in \mathfrak{B}_{\mathcal{M},u}$ for each scheduler u of $\mathcal{M}$.*
2. *Given a PPA $\mathcal{A}$ over $\tilde{\Sigma}$ and a formula $\varphi \in \mathrm{LTL}^{\otimes}(\tilde{\Sigma})$, it holds $L_{\mathcal{A},u}(\varphi) \in \mathfrak{B}_{\mathcal{M}_\mathcal{A},u}$ for each scheduler u of $\mathcal{M}_\mathcal{A}$.*
3. *Given a CPP $\mathcal{M}$ over Σ and an extended Streett (Büchi) automaton $\mathcal{B}$ over Σ, we have $L_{\mathcal{M},u}(\mathcal{B}) \in \mathfrak{B}_{\mathcal{M},u}$ for each scheduler u of $\mathcal{M}$.*

We can now define the satisfaction relation for CPPs and LTL, PPA and LTL$^{\otimes}$, as well as CPPs and Streett automata.

Definition 3. *Let Σ be an alphabet.*

1. *A CPP $\mathcal{M}$ over Σ is said to* satisfy *a formula $\varphi \in \mathrm{LTL}(\Sigma)$ if, for all schedulers u of $\mathcal{M}$, $\mu_{\mathcal{M},u}(L_{\mathcal{M},u}(\varphi)) = 1$.*
2. *A PPA $\mathcal{A}$ over $\tilde{\Sigma}$ is said to* satisfy *a formula $\varphi \in \mathrm{LTL}^{\otimes}(\tilde{\Sigma})$ if, for all schedulers u of $\mathcal{M}_\mathcal{A}$, $\mu_{\mathcal{M}_\mathcal{A},u}(L_{\mathcal{A},u}(\varphi)) = 1$.*
3. *Given a CPP $\mathcal{M}$ over Σ and an extended Streett (Büchi) automaton $\mathcal{B}$ over Σ, $\mathcal{M}$ is said to* satisfy *$\mathcal{B}$ if, for all schedulers u of $\mathcal{M}$, $\mu_{\mathcal{M},u}(L_{\mathcal{M},u}(\mathcal{B}))=1$.*

For example, the formula $[\Diamond\langle a\rangle\langle b\rangle\mathrm{tt}]_1 \wedge [\Diamond\langle c\rangle\langle b\rangle\mathrm{tt}]_2 \in \mathrm{LTL}^{\otimes}((\{a,b\},\{b,c\}))$ is satisfied by the PPA from Figure 1.

A logic that specifies properties of a product system should not differentiate between different linearizations of its parallel execution, a well-known requirement in the domain of Mazurkiewicz traces [Leu02]. Let us check that this is the case for our notion of satisfaction of PPA and LTL$^{\otimes}$.

For two words $\sigma, \sigma' \in (\bigcup_i \Sigma_i)^*$, we say that they are *equivalent* (with respect to $\tilde{\Sigma}$) and write $\sigma \sim \sigma'$ if $\sigma \downharpoonright \Sigma_i = \sigma' \downharpoonright \Sigma_i$ for all $i \in Proc$. In other words, two words are equivalent if they only differ in the ordering of independent actions. We say that two actions are *independent* if they are not member of a single Σ_i for one $i \in Proc$.

As already a simple product automaton, a PPA is robust with respect to the order in which independent actions are executed. To illustrate this, let us consider the PPA from Figure 1. Both components can independently execute the independent actions a and c whereupon a random move follows, respectively. Such independence is reflected in the global system (cf. Figure 2): Starting from the initial state (p_0, q_0), constituting ac as the order in which a and c are executed spans the same probability space wrt. all the possible nondeterministic successor states (p_0, q_0), (p_0, q_2), (p_2, q_0), and (p_2, q_2) as constituting ca.

5.2 The Algorithm

Model checking PPA against LTL$^\otimes$ formulas is the problem whether a given LTL$^\otimes$ formula is satisfied by a given PPA. As we will show in this subsection, we can reduce this problem to the question whether the language defined by a scheduler for a Streett automaton has positive measure with respect to a given CPP. Therefore, we study this problem first:

Let Σ be an alphabet, $\mathcal{M} = (Q, N, R, \Delta, P, Q^{in})$ be a CPP over Σ, and $\mathcal{B} = (S, S_0, \delta, F, \mathcal{G})$ be an extended Streett automaton over Σ. The *product* of $\mathcal{M}$ and $\mathcal{B}$, the CPP $\mathcal{M}_{\mathcal{M},\mathcal{B}} = (Q_{\mathcal{M},\mathcal{B}}, N_{\mathcal{M},\mathcal{B}}, R_{\mathcal{M},\mathcal{B}}, \Delta_{\mathcal{M},\mathcal{B}}, P_{\mathcal{M},\mathcal{B}}, Q^{in}_{\mathcal{M},\mathcal{B}}, F_{\mathcal{M},\mathcal{B}}, \mathcal{G}_{\mathcal{M},\mathcal{B}})$ (with acceptance condition) over Σ, is given as follows:

- $Q_{\mathcal{M},\mathcal{B}} = Q \times S$
- $N_{\mathcal{M},\mathcal{B}} = N \times S$
- $R_{\mathcal{M},\mathcal{B}} = R \times S$
- $((q,s), a, (q',s')) \in \Delta_{\mathcal{M},\mathcal{B}}$ if $(q,a,q') \in \Delta$ and $s' \in \delta(s,a)$
- $P_{\mathcal{M},\mathcal{B}}((q,s),(q',s')) = \begin{cases} P(q,q') & \text{if } s = s' \\ 0 & \text{if } s \neq s' \end{cases}$
- $Q^{in}_{\mathcal{M},\mathcal{B}} = Q^{in} \times S_0$
- $F_{\mathcal{M},\mathcal{B}} = (N \setminus N^{en}_{\mathcal{M}}) \times F$
- $\mathcal{G}_{\mathcal{M},\mathcal{B}} = \{((Q \times U), (Q \times V)) \mid (U,V) \in \mathcal{G}\}$

We want to mark some SCCs of $\mathcal{M}_{\mathcal{M},\mathcal{B}}$ to be good in some sense and call a set D of its states *accepting* if, for all pairs $(U,V) \in \mathcal{G}_{\mathcal{M},\mathcal{B}}$, $(q,s) \in D$ with $s \in U$ implies $(q',s') \in D$ for some q' and $s' \in V$. Otherwise, D is called *rejecting*. We say that a state (r,f) of a rejecting set D is *rejecting* if there is a pair $(U,V) \in \mathcal{G}$ such that $f \in U$ and D contains no state (q,s) with $s \in V$.

Theorem 1. *For a CPP $\mathcal{M} = (Q, N, R, \Delta, P, Q^{in})$ over an alphabet Σ and a deterministic extended Streett automaton $\mathcal{B} = (S, \{s_0\}, \delta, F, \mathcal{G})$ over Σ, there is a scheduler u of $\mathcal{M}$ with $\mu_{\mathcal{M},u}(L_{\mathcal{M},u}(\mathcal{B})) > 0$ iff*

- *there is a path in (the graph of) $\mathcal{M}_{\mathcal{M},\mathcal{B}}$ from an initial state to a final state from $F_{\mathcal{M},\mathcal{B}}$ or*

- *there is a set D of states of $\mathcal{M}_{\mathcal{M},\mathcal{B}}$ satisfying the following:*
  (1) $\mathcal{M}_{\mathcal{M},\mathcal{B}}[D]$ is nontrivial and strongly connected,
  (2) D is accepting and reachable from a state of $Q^{in} \times \{s_0\}$, and
  (3) for all transitions $((q,s),(q',s')) \in \Delta_{\mathcal{M},\mathcal{B}}$ with $(q,s) \in D$ and $(q',s') \notin D$, (q,s) is nondeterministic, i.e., it holds $(q,s) \in N_{\mathcal{M},\mathcal{B}}$ (or, equivalently, $q \in N$).

Proof. ($\Leftarrow$) Suppose there is a path $\beta \in (Q_{\mathcal{M},\mathcal{B}})^*$ through $\mathcal{M}_{\mathcal{M},\mathcal{B}}$ from an initial state to a state (q,s) of $F_{\mathcal{M},\mathcal{B}}$. It is easy to see that then a corresponding scheduler (simply following the path) forces $\mathcal{M}_{\mathcal{M},\mathcal{B}}$ to visit (q,s) with nonzero probability. Otherwise, fix a path $\beta \in (Q_{\mathcal{M},\mathcal{B}})^*$ through $\mathcal{M}_{\mathcal{M},\mathcal{B}}$ from an initial state to a state of D. Let β' be the projection of β onto the first component. The scheduler u of $\mathcal{M}'$ satisfying $\mu_{\mathcal{M},u}(L_{\mathcal{M},u}(\mathcal{B})) > 0$ follows β' taking $\mathcal{M}_{\mathcal{M},\mathcal{B}}$ from the initial state to D and, henceforth, forces the trajectory both to stay within D and to almost surely visit each state of D infinitely often. This can be accomplished by, for a given nondeterministic state (q,s), alternately choosing the transitions $(q,s) \xrightarrow{a} (q',s')$ of $\mathcal{M}_{\mathcal{M},\mathcal{B}}$ with $(q',s') \in D$ (recall that the history of a trajectory is at the scheduler's disposal.) Clearly, $\mu_{\mathcal{M},u}(\mathcal{C}_{\mathcal{M},u}(\beta'))$ is nonzero. Given $\mathcal{C}_{\mathcal{M},u}(\beta')$, the conditional probability that $\mathcal{M}$, wrt. u, follows a trajectory that visits each state of D infinitely often is one. As such a trajectory is contained in $L_{\mathcal{M},u}(\mathcal{B})$, we conclude $\mu_{\mathcal{M},u}(L_{\mathcal{M},u}(\mathcal{B})) > 0$.

($\Rightarrow$) Note that a trajectory x of $\mathcal{M}$ wrt. u unambiguously defines a path $\widetilde{x}$ through $\mathcal{M}_{\mathcal{M},\mathcal{B}}$ starting from an initial state. This is due to the fact that $\mathcal{B}$ is deterministic. Let $\mathcal{D}$ contain the subsets D of states of $\mathcal{M}_{\mathcal{M},\mathcal{B}}$ such that $\mathcal{M}_{\mathcal{M},\mathcal{B}}[D]$ is strongly connected. Furthermore, for $D \in \mathcal{D}$, let $E(D) := \{x \in \Omega_{\mathcal{M},u} \mid \mathit{inf}(\widetilde{x}) = D\}$. Now suppose that $\mu_{\mathcal{M},u}(L_{\mathcal{M},u}(\mathcal{B})) > 0$ for a scheduler u of $\mathcal{M}$. If u leads $\mathcal{M}_{\mathcal{M},\mathcal{B}}$ from an initial state into a final state from $F_{\mathcal{M},\mathcal{B}}$, we are done. Otherwise, as

$$L_{\mathcal{M},u}(\mathcal{B}) = \bigcup_{D \in \mathcal{D} \text{ is accepting}} E(D),$$

we can find an accepting set $D \in \mathcal{D}$ that satisfies $\mu_{\mathcal{M},u}(E(D)) > 0$. (Otherwise, the probability of the countable union $L_{\mathcal{M},u}(\mathcal{B})$ of events would be zero.) As D is the infinity set of at least one infinite path through $\mathcal{M}_{\mathcal{M},\mathcal{B}}$ starting from an initial state, it forms a nontrivial (strongly connected) subgraph of $\mathcal{M}_{\mathcal{M},\mathcal{B}}$, satisfying condition (1). Now suppose there is a transition $(q,s) \xrightarrow{\mathfrak{p}} (q',s')$ of $\mathcal{M}_{\mathcal{M},\mathcal{B}}$ with $(q,s) \in D$, $(q',s') \notin D$, and $q \in R$. As, for every trajectory $x \in E(D)$, $\widetilde{x}$ visits (q,s) infinitely often (and each time the probability to exit D is nonzero), it will almost surely leave D infinitely often so that we have $\mu_{\mathcal{M},u}(E(D)) = 0$ contradicting our assumption. It follows that D also satisfies condition (3) from Proposition 1, which concludes our proof. □

Note that, in the above proof, we explicitly make use of the fact that a trajectory of $\mathcal{M}$ determines exactly one corresponding run of $\mathcal{M}_{\mathcal{M},\mathcal{B}}$ starting from an initial state (recall that $\mathcal{B}$ is deterministic).

Table 1. Model checking $\mathrm{LTL}^{\otimes}$ specifications of PPA

Given a PPA $\mathcal{A}$ over $\tilde{\Sigma}$ and a formula $\varphi \in \mathrm{LTL}^{\otimes}(\tilde{\Sigma})$.
Goal: Decide whether, for all schedulers u of $\mathcal{M}_{\mathcal{A}}$, it holds $\mu_{\mathcal{M}_{\mathcal{A}},u}(L_{\mathcal{A},u}(\varphi)) = 1$.
Solution:

1. From $\mathcal{A}$, we construct the CPP $\mathcal{M}_{\mathcal{A}}$, and from φ, we construct the deterministic extended Streett automaton $\mathcal{B}_{\neg\varphi}$ with $L(\mathcal{B}_{\neg\varphi}) = L(\neg\varphi)$.
2. Compute (the graph of) $\mathcal{M}_{\mathcal{M}_{\mathcal{A}},\mathcal{B}_{\neg\varphi}}$, remove those states that are not reachable from an initial state of $\mathcal{M}_{\mathcal{M}_{\mathcal{A}},\mathcal{B}_{\neg\varphi}}$, and let G denote the resulting graph.
3. Repeat
   (a) Determine the sets $\mathcal{AC}$ of nontrivial and accepting and $\mathcal{RC}$ of nontrivial and rejecting SCCs of G, respectively.
   (b) For each $C \in \mathcal{RC}$, remove the transitions going out from rejecting states.
   (c) For each $C \in \mathcal{AC}$, do the following:
      i. Find the set H of states $(\overline{q}, s) \in C$ with randomizing $\overline{q}$ from where there is a transition leaving C.
      ii. If H is the empty set, then return "No". Otherwise, remove the states of H and corresponding transitions from G.

   until $\mathcal{AC} \cup \mathcal{RC} = \emptyset$.
4. Test whether a scheduler can force $\mathcal{M}_{\mathcal{M}_{\mathcal{A}},\mathcal{B}_{\neg\varphi}}$ from an initial state into a final state with probability greater than 0, i.e., whether there is a path from an initial state of $\mathcal{M}_{\mathcal{M}_{\mathcal{A}},\mathcal{B}_{\neg\varphi}}$ to a state in $F_{\mathcal{M}_{\mathcal{A}},\mathcal{B}_{\neg\varphi}}$. If this is the case, return "No". Otherwise, return "Yes".

Based on Theorem 1, we now provide an algorithm that solves the model-checking problem for PPA, i.e., it decides for a given PPA $\mathcal{A}$ over $\tilde{\Sigma}$ and a formula $\varphi \in \mathrm{LTL}^{\otimes}(\tilde{\Sigma})$ whether, for all schedulers u of $\mathcal{M}_{\mathcal{A}}$, $\mu_{\mathcal{M}_{\mathcal{A}},u}(L_{\mathcal{A},u}(\varphi)) = 1$ (namely iff there is no scheduler u of $\mathcal{M}_{\mathcal{A}}$ such that $\mu_{\mathcal{M}_{\mathcal{A}},u}(L_{\mathcal{A},u}(\neg\varphi)) > 0$). The algorithm is shown in Table 1. In the first step, the given PPA is transformed into a CPP. The given formula is negated and translated into a product automaton accepting the models of the formula. This step is described in [MD97] and is omitted here. It is straightforward to translate a product automaton into an extended Büchi automaton, which again can be translated into a deterministic extended Streett automaton [GTW02]. In the second step, we combine the obtained CPP and Streett automaton into a single system. The characterization provided in Theorem 1 is used in items 3 and 4 to answer the model checking question. Obviously, the algorithm terminates. Furthermore, it returns the answer "No" iff there is a scheduler u of $\mathcal{M}_{\mathcal{A}}$ such that $\mu_{\mathcal{M}_{\mathcal{A}},u}(L_{\mathcal{M}_{\mathcal{A}},u}(\mathcal{B}_{\neg\varphi})) > 0$.

To simplify our presentation, we described the algorithm in a stepwise manner. It is clear that steps 1 and 2 can be done on demand by steps 3 and 4. Thus, we can get an on-the-fly procedure.

Furthermore, the algorithm can easily be adapted to answer the model-checking problem for LTL or Büchi-automata specifications. Only step 1 has to be adjusted to produce a Streett automaton for a given LTL or Büchi automaton.

Let us discuss the complexity of our algorithm. Starting from a Büchi automaton $\mathcal{B}$ with n states, construct an equivalent deterministic extended Streett automaton $\mathcal{B}'$ with $2^{O(n \log n)}$ states and $O(n)$ pairs in the acceptance component. Say our CPP $\mathcal{M}$ has m states. The number of states of $\mathcal{M}_{\mathcal{M},\mathcal{B}'}$ is not greater than $m \cdot 2^{O(n \log n)}$. Thus, steps (a), (b), and (c) are repeated at most $m \cdot 2^{O(n \log n)}$-times, respectively. Determining the SCCs of G can be done in time linear in the size of $\mathcal{M}_{\mathcal{M},\mathcal{B}'}$. Overall, the algorithm (modified for CPPs and Büchi automata) runs in time $O(m^3 \cdot 2^{O(n \log n)})$, i.e., it is quadratic in $|\mathcal{M}|$ and exponential in $|\mathcal{B}|$.

Proposition 2. *Given a CPP $\mathcal{M}$ and a Büchi automaton $\mathcal{B}$, it can be decided in time $O(|\mathcal{M}|^2 \cdot 2^{O(|\mathcal{B}|)})$ whether $\mu_{\mathcal{M},u}(L_{\mathcal{M},u}(\mathcal{B})) > 0$ for some scheduler u of $\mathcal{M}$.*

Translating an LTL$^{\otimes}$ formula into a product automaton is of exponential complexity with respect to the length of the formula. The product automaton gives rise to a Büchi automaton of same order[2]. Thus, translating an LTL$^{\otimes}$ formula into a deterministic extended Streett automaton is of double exponential complexity. Together with Proposition 2, we get

Theorem 2. *Given a PPA $\mathcal{A}$ and an* LTL$^{\otimes}$ *formula φ, checking whether $\mathcal{A}$ satisfies φ can be done in time polynomial in the size of $\mathcal{A}$ and double exponential in the size of φ.*

6 Conclusion and Future Work

In this paper, we presented probabilistic product automata (PPA) as a model for distributed probabilistic programs. It is based on the well-known model of product automata, but extended by random transitions. Thus, a probabilistic product automaton is a product of probabilistic systems that run in parallel and synchronize by common actions. Every probabilistic system is able to do labelled nondeterministic and as well as randomized transitions.

For the product version of linear temporal logic LTL$^{\otimes}$, originally defined for product automata, we extended the notion of satisfaction to the probabilistic setting. Intuitively, we say that a PPA satisfies an LTL$^{\otimes}$ formula, if for every scheduler (that fixes the nondeterministic choices of the system) almost all runs satisfy the given formula.

The main contribution of the paper is a procedure that automatically answers the question whether a given PPA satisfies a given LTL$^{\otimes}$ formula. This problem is also known as the *model-checking problem*.

[2] Note that a Büchi automaton corresponding to a product automaton grows exponentially in the number of components. Fixing the number of components, however, it grows polynomially with respect to the size of the components.

Our procedure is automata-based and can be implemented *on-the-fly*, which often provides good run-time behavior in practice, despite high worst-case complexity.

Additionally, we get a procedure for checking automata specifications and LTL specifications of PPA.

It would be interesting to extend our work to the setting of fair executions of the product system and, more specifically, while we check satisfaction for all schedulers, to see whether the restriction to fair schedulers gives different results.

Furthermore, it would be interesting to see whether techniques as used in [CY95] can improve our procedure to get single exponential complexity with respect to the length of the formula.

References

[BGJ99] J. Beauquier, M. Gradinariu, and C. Johnen. Randomized self-stabilizing and space optimal leader election under arbitrary scheduler on rings. Technical Report 99-1225, Université Paris Sud, 1999.

[CES83] E. M. Clarke, E. A. Emerson, and A. P. Sistla. Automatic verification of finite state concurrent systems using temporal logic specifications: A practical approach. In *Conference Record of the Tenth Annual ACM Symposium on Principles of Programming Languages*, pages 117–126, Austin, Texas, January 24–26, 1983. ACM SIGACT-SIGPLAN.

[CW96] Edmund M. Clarke and Jeanette M. Wing. Formal methods: State of the art and future directions. *ACM Computing Surveys*, 28(4):626–643, December 1996.

[CY95] Costas Courcoubetis and Mihalis Yannakakis. The complexity of probabilistic verification. *Journal of the ACM*, 42(4):857–907, July 1995.

[GTW02] Erich Grädel, Wolfgang Thomas, and Thomas Wilke, editors. *Automata, Logics and Infinite Games*, volume 2500 of *Lecture Notes in Computer Science*. Springer, 2002.

[HS84] S. Hart and M. Sharir. Probabilistic temporal logics for finite and bounded models. In *ACM Symposium on Theory of Computing (STOC '84)*, pages 1–13, Baltimore, USA, April 1984. ACM Press.

[Leu02] Martin Leucker. *Logics for Mazurkiewicz traces*. PhD thesis, Lehrstuhl für Informatik II, RWTH Aachen, 2002.

[LR81] D. Lehman and M. O. Rabin. On the advantage of free choice: A fully symmetric and fully distributed solution to the dining philosophers problem. In *Proceedings of 10th ACM Symposium of Principles of Programming Languages*, pages 133–138, Williamsburg, 1981.

[LS82] Daniel Lehmann and Saharon Shelah. Reasoning with time and chance. *Information and Control*, 53(3):165–198, June 1982.

[MD97] P. Madhusudan and Deepak D'Souza. On-the-fly verification of Product-LTL. In *Proocedings of the National Seminar on Theoretical Computer Science*, Madras, June 1997.

[Pnu77] Amir Pnueli. The temporal logic of programs. In *Proceedings of the 18th IEEE Symposium on the Foundations of Computer Science (FOCS-77)*, pages 46–57, Providence, Rhode Island, October 31–November 2 1977. IEEE Computer Society Press.

[PRRR01] P. Pardalos, S. Rajasekaran, J. Reif, and J. Rolim, editors. *Handbook on Randomized Computing*. Kluwer Academic Publishers, Dordrecht, The Netherlands, June 2001.

[QS82] J.P. Queille and J. Sifakis. Specification and verification of concurrent systems in CESAR. In *Proceedings of the Fifth International Symposium in Programming*, volume 137 of *Lecture Notes in Computer Science*, pages 337–351, New York, 1982. Springer.

[Thi95] P. S. Thiagarajan. PTL over product state spaces. Technical Report TCS-95-4, School of Mathematics, SPIC Science Foundation, 1995.

[Var85] Moshe Y. Vardi. Automatic verification of probabilistic concurrent finite-state programs. In *26th Annual Symposium on Foundations of Computer Science*, pages 327–338, Portland, Oregon, 21–23 October 1985. IEEE.

[VW86] M. Y. Vardi and P. Wolper. An automata-theoretic approach to automatic program verification. In *Symposium on Logic in Computer Science (LICS'86)*, pages 332–345, Washington, D.C., USA, June 1986. IEEE Computer Society Press.

Author Index

Lecture Notes in Computer Science

For information about Vols. 1–2828
please contact your bookseller or Springer-Verlag

Vol. 2629: A.E. Abdallah, P. Ryan, S. Schneider (Eds.), Formal Aspects of Security. Proceedings, 2002. X, 239 pages. 2003.

Vol. 2760: R. Dingledine (Ed.), Privacy Enhancing Technologies. Proceedings, 2003. VIII, 223 pages. 2003.

Vol. 2829: A. Cappelli, F. Turini (Eds.), AI*IA 2003: Advances in Artificial Intelligence. Proceedings, 2003. XIV, 552 pages. 2003. (Subseries LNAI).

Vol. 2830: F. Pfenning, Y. Smaragdakis (Eds.), Generative Programming and Component Engineering. Proceedings, 2003. IX, 397 pages. 2003.

Vol. 2831: M. Schillo, M. Klusch, J. Müller, H. Tianfield (Eds.), Multiagent System Technologies. Proceedings, 2003. X, 229 pages. 2003. (Subseries LNAI).

Vol. 2832: G. Di Battista, U. Zwick (Eds.), Algorithms – ESA 2003. Proceedings, 2003. XIV, 790 pages. 2003.

Vol. 2833: F. Rossi (Ed.), Principles and Practice of Constraint Programming – CP 2003. Proceedings, 2003. XIX, 1005 pages. 2003.

Vol. 2834: X. Zhou, S. Jähnichen, M. Xu, J. Cao (Eds.), Advanced Parallel Processing Technologies. Proceedings, 2003. XIV, 679 pages. 2003.

Vol. 2835: T. Horváth, A. Yamamoto (Eds.), Inductive Logic Programming. Proceedings, 2003. X, 401 pages. 2003. (Subseries LNAI).

Vol. 2836: S. Qing, D. Gollmann, J. Zhou (Eds.), Information and Communications Security. Proceedings, 2003. XI, 416 pages. 2003.

Vol. 2837: N. Lavrač, D. Gamberger, H. Blockeel, L. Todorovski (Eds.), Machine Learning: ECML 2003. Proceedings, 2003. XVI, 504 pages. 2003. (Subseries LNAI).

Vol. 2838: N. Lavrač, D. Gamberger, L. Todorovski, H. Blockeel (Eds.), Knowledge Discovery in Databases: PKDD 2003. Proceedings, 2003. XVI, 508 pages. 2003. (Subseries LNAI).

Vol. 2839: A. Marshall, N. Agoulmine (Eds.), Management of Multimedia Networks and Services. Proceedings, 2003. XIV, 532 pages. 2003.

Vol. 2840: J. Dongarra, D. Laforenza, S. Orlando (Eds.), Recent Advances in Parallel Virtual Machine and Message Passing Interface. Proceedings, 2003. XVIII, 693 pages. 2003.

Vol. 2841: C. Blundo, C. Laneve (Eds.), Theoretical Computer Science. Proceedings, 2003. XI, 397 pages. 2003.

Vol. 2842: R. Gavaldà, K.P. Jantke, E. Takimoto (Eds.), Algorithmic Learning Theory. Proceedings, 2003. XI, 313 pages. 2003. (Subseries LNAI).

Vol. 2843: G. Grieser, Y. Tanaka, A. Yamamoto (Eds.), Discovery Science. Proceedings, 2003. XII, 504 pages. 2003. (Subseries LNAI).

Vol. 2844: J.A. Jorge, N.J. Nunes, J.F. e Cunha (Eds.), Interactive Systems. Proceedings, 2003. XIII, 429 pages. 2003.

Vol. 2846: J. Zhou, M. Yung, Y. Han (Eds.), Applied Cryptography and Network Security. Proceedings, 2003. XI, 436 pages. 2003.

Vol. 2847: R. de Lemos, T.S. Weber, J.B. Camargo Jr. (Eds.), Dependable Computing. Proceedings, 2003. XIV, 371 pages. 2003.

Vol. 2848: F.E. Fich (Ed.), Distributed Computing. Proceedings, 2003. X, 367 pages. 2003.

Vol. 2849: N. García, J.M. Martínez, L. Salgado (Eds.), Visual Content Processing and Representation. Proceedings, 2003. XII, 352 pages. 2003.

Vol. 2850: M.Y. Vardi, A. Voronkov (Eds.), Logic for Programming, Artificial Intelligence, and Reasoning. Proceedings, 2003. XIII, 437 pages. 2003. (Subseries LNAI)

Vol. 2851: C. Boyd, W. Mao (Eds.), Information Security. Proceedings, 2003. XI, 443 pages. 2003.

Vol. 2852: F.S. de Boer, M.M. Bonsangue, S. Graf, W.-P. de Roever (Eds.), Formal Methods for Components and Objects. Proceedings, 2003. VIII, 509 pages. 2003.

Vol. 2853: M. Jeckle, L.-J. Zhang (Eds.), Web Services – ICWS-Europe 2003. Proceedings, 2003. VIII, 227 pages. 2003.

Vol. 2854: J. Hoffmann, Utilizing Problem Structure in Planning. XIII, 251 pages. 2003. (Subseries LNAI)

Vol. 2855: R. Alur, I. Lee (Eds.), Embedded Software. Proceedings, 2003. X, 373 pages. 2003.

Vol. 2856: M. Smirnov, E. Biersack, C. Blondia, O. Bonaventure, O. Casals, G. Karlsson, George Pavlou, B. Quoitin, J. Roberts, I. Stavrakakis, B. Stiller, P. Trimintzios, P. Van Mieghem (Eds.), Quality of Future Internet Services. IX, 293 pages. 2003.

Vol. 2857: M.A. Nascimento, E.S. de Moura, A.L. Oliveira (Eds.), String Processing and Information Retrieval. Proceedings, 2003. XI, 379 pages. 2003.

Vol. 2858: A. Veidenbaum, K. Joe, H. Amano, H. Aiso (Eds.), High Performance Computing. Proceedings, 2003. XV, 566 pages. 2003.

Vol. 2859: B. Apolloni, M. Marinaro, R. Tagliaferri (Eds.), Neural Nets. Proceedings, 2003. X, 376 pages. 2003.

Vol. 2860: D. Geist, E. Tronci (Eds.), Correct Hardware Design and Verification Methods. Proceedings, 2003. XII, 426 pages. 2003.

Vol. 2861: C. Bliek, C. Jermann, A. Neumaier (Eds.), Global Optimization and Constraint Satisfaction. Proceedings, 2002. XII, 239 pages. 2003.

Vol. 2862: D. Feitelson, L. Rudolph, U. Schwiegelshohn (Eds.), Job Scheduling Strategies for Parallel Processing. Proceedings, 2003. VII, 269 pages. 2003.

Vol. 2863: P. Stevens, J. Whittle, G. Booch (Eds.), «UML» 2003 – The Unified Modeling Language. Proceedings, 2003. XIV, 415 pages. 2003.

Vol. 2864: A.K. Dey, A. Schmidt, J.F. McCarthy (Eds.), UbiComp 2003: Ubiquitous Computing. Proceedings, 2003. XVII, 368 pages. 2003.

Vol. 2865: S. Pierre, M. Barbeau, E. Kranakis (Eds.), Ad-Hoc, Mobile, and Wireless Networks. Proceedings, 2003. X, 293 pages. 2003.

Vol. 2867: M. Brunner, A. Keller (Eds.), Self-Managing Distributed Systems. Proceedings, 2003. XIII, 274 pages. 2003.

Vol. 2868: P. Perner, R. Brause, H.-G. Holzhütter (Eds.), Medical Data Analysis. Proceedings, 2003. VIII, 127 pages. 2003.

Vol. 2869: A. Yazici, C. Şener (Eds.), Computer and Information Sciences – ISCIS 2003. Proceedings, 2003. XIX, 1110 pages. 2003.

Vol. 2870: D. Fensel, K. Sycara, J. Mylopoulos (Eds.), The Semantic Web - ISWC 2003. Proceedings, 2003. XV, 931 pages. 2003.

Vol. 2871: N. Zhong, Z.W. Raś, S. Tsumoto, E. Suzuki (Eds.), Foundations of Intelligent Systems. Proceedings, 2003. XV, 697 pages. 2003. (Subseries LNAI)

Vol. 2873: J. Lawry, J. Shanahan, A. Ralescu (Eds.), Modelling with Words. XIII, 229 pages. 2003. (Subseries LNAI)

Vol. 2874: C. Priami (Ed.), Global Computing. Proceedings, 2003. XIX, 255 pages. 2003.

Vol. 2875: E. Aarts, R. Collier, E. van Loenen, B. de Ruyter (Eds.), Ambient Intelligence. Proceedings, 2003. XI, 432 pages. 2003.

Vol. 2876: M. Schroeder, G. Wagner (Eds.), Rules and Rule Markup Languages for the Semantic Web. Proceedings, 2003. VII, 173 pages. 2003.

Vol. 2877: T. Böhme, G. Heyer, H. Unger (Eds.), Innovative Internet Community Systems. Proceedings, 2003. VIII, 263 pages. 2003.

Vol. 2878: R.E. Ellis, T.M. Peters (Eds.), Medical Image Computing and Computer-Assisted Intervention - MICCAI 2003. Part I. Proceedings, 2003. XXXIII, 819 pages. 2003.

Vol. 2879: R.E. Ellis, T.M. Peters (Eds.), Medical Image Computing and Computer-Assisted Intervention - MICCAI 2003. Part II. Proceedings, 2003. XXXIV, 1003 pages. 2003.

Vol. 2880: H.L. Bodlaender (Ed.), Graph-Theoretic Concepts in Computer Science. Proceedings, 2003. XI, 386 pages. 2003.

Vol. 2881: E. Horlait, T. Magedanz, R.H. Glitho (Eds.), Mobile Agents for Telecommunication Applications. Proceedings, 2003. IX, 297 pages. 2003.

Vol. 2882: D. Veit, Matchmaking in Electronic Markets. XV, 180 pages. 2003. (Subseries LNAI)

Vol. 2883: J. Schaeffer, M. Müller, Y. Björnsson (Eds.), Computers and Games. Proceedings, 2002. XI, 431 pages. 2003.

Vol. 2884: E. Najm, U. Nestmann, P. Stevens (Eds.), Formal Methods for Open Object-Based Distributed Systems. Proceedings, 2003. X, 293 pages. 2003.

Vol. 2885: J.S. Dong, J. Woodcock (Eds.), Formal Methods and Software Engineering. Proceedings, 2003. XI, 683 pages. 2003.

Vol. 2886: I. Nyström, G. Sanniti di Baja, S. Svensson (Eds.), Discrete Geometry for Computer Imagery. Proceedings, 2003. XII, 556 pages. 2003.

Vol. 2887: T. Johansson (Ed.), Fast Software Encryption. Proceedings, 2003. IX, 397 pages. 2003.

Vol. 2888: R. Meersman, Zahir Tari, D.C. Schmidt et al. (Eds.), On The Move to Meaningful Internet Systems 2003: CoopIS, DOA, and ODBASE. Proceedings, 2003. XXI, 1546 pages. 2003.

Vol. 2889: Robert Meersman, Zahir Tari et al. (Eds.), On The Move to Meaningful Internet Systems 2003: OTM 2003 Workshops. Proceedings, 2003. XXI, 1096 pages. 2003.

Vol. 2891: J. Lee, M. Barley (Eds.), Intelligent Agents and Multi-Agent Systems. Proceedings, 2003. X, 215 pages. 2003. (Subseries LNAI)

Vol. 2892: F. Dau, The Logic System of Concept Graphs with Negation. XI, 213 pages. 2003. (Subseries LNAI)

Vol. 2893: J.-B. Stefani, I. Demeure, D. Hagimont (Eds.), Distributed Applications and Interoperable Systems. Proceedings, 2003. XIII, 311 pages. 2003.

Vol. 2894: C.S. Laih (Ed.), Advances in Cryptology - ASIACRYPT 2003. Proceedings, 2003. XIII, 543 pages. 2003.

Vol. 2895: A. Ohori (Ed.), Programming Languages and Systems. Proceedings, 2003. XIII, 427 pages. 2003.

Vol. 2896: V.A. Saraswat (Ed.), Advances in Computing Science – ASIAN 2003. Proceedings, 2003. VIII, 305 pages. 2003.

Vol. 2897: O. Balet, G. Subsol, P. Torguet (Eds.), Virtual Storytelling. Proceedings, 2003. XI, 240 pages. 2003.

Vol. 2898: K.G. Paterson (Ed.), Cryptography and Coding. Proceedings, 2003. IX, 385 pages. 2003.

Vol. 2899: G. Ventre, R. Canonico (Eds.), Interactive Multimedia on Next Generation Networks. Proceedings, 2003. XIV, 420 pages. 2003.

Vol. 2901: F. Bry, N. Henze, J. Małuszyński (Eds.), Principles and Practice of Semantic Web Reasoning. Proceedings, 2003. X, 209 pages. 2003.

Vol. 2902: F. Moura Pires, S. Abreu (Eds.), Progress in Artificial Intelligence. Proceedings, 2003. XV, 504 pages. 2003. (Subseries LNAI).

Vol. 2903: T.D. Gedeon, L.C.C. Fung (Eds.), AI 2003: Advances in Artificial Intelligence. Proceedings, 2003. XVI, 1075 pages. 2003. (Subseries LNAI).

Vol. 2904: T. Johansson, S. Maitra (Eds.), Progress in Cryptology – INDOCRYPT 2003. Proceedings, 2003. XI, 431 pages. 2003.

Vol. 2905: A. Sanfeliu, J. Ruiz-Shulcloper (Eds.), Progress in Pattern Recognition, Speech and Image Analysis. Proceedings, 2003. XVII, 693 pages. 2003.

Vol. 2910: M.E. Orlowska, S. Weerawarana, M.P. Papazoglou, J. Yang (Eds.), Service-Oriented Computing – ICSOC 2003. Proceedings, 2003. XIV, 576 pages. 2003.

Vol. 2911: T.M.T. Sembok, H.B. Zaman, H. Chen, S.R. Urs, S.H.Myaeng (Eds.), Digital Libraries: Technology and Management of Indigenous Knowledge for Global Access. Proceedings, 2003. XX, 703 pages. 2003.

Vol. 2913: T.M. Pinkston, V.K. Prasanna (Eds.), High Performance Computing – HiPC 2003. Proceedings, 2003. XX, 512 pages. 2003.

Vol. 2914: P.K. Pandya, J. Radhakrishnan (Eds.), FST TCS 2003: Foundations of Software Technology and Theoretical Computer Science. Proceedings, 2003. XIII, 446 pages. 2003.

Vol. 2916: C. Palamidessi (Ed.), Logic Programming. Proceedings, 2003. XII, 520 pages. 2003.